D1612224

FIFTH EDITION

PROJECT MANAGEMENT
A Managerial Approach

Jack R. Meredith

Broyhill Distinguished Scholar and Chair in Operations
Babcock Graduate School of Management
Wake Forest University

Samuel J. Mantel, Jr.

Joseph S. Stern Professor Emeritus of Operations Management
University of Cincinnati

John Wiley & Sons, Inc.

To Avery and Mitchell,
from "papajack."
J. R. M.

To the new members of the cast, in the order of their appearance:
Natalie, Rachel, Rivkah, Tyler, Kyle, Ryan,
Alison, Alexandra, Caroline, and Preston, with love.
S. J. M., Jr.

ACQUISITIONS EDITOR   Beth Lang Golub
ASSISTANT EDITOR   Lorraina Raccuia
MARKETING MANAGER   Gitti Lindner
SENIOR PRODUCTION EDITOR   Norine M. Pigliucci
SENIOR DESIGNER   Kevin Murphy
PHOTO EDITOR   Lisa Gee
PRODUCTION MANAGEMENT SERVICES   Ingrao Associates
COVER PHOTO   VCL/Spencer Rowell/Getty Images

This book was set in 10.5/12 Times by Pine Tree Composition and printed and bound by Donnelley Craw-fordsville.
The cover was printed by Lehigh Press, Inc.

This book is printed on acid-free paper.∞

Library of Congress Cataloging-in-Publication Data
Meredith, Jack R.
    Project management : a managerial approach / Jack R. Meredith, Samuel J. Mantel, Jr.—
5th ed.
      p. cm.
    Includes index.
    ISBN 0-471-07323-7 (cloth : alk. paper)
      1. Project management.   I. Mantel, Samuel J. II. Title.

 HD69.P75 M47 2002
658.4'04—dc21

                                                                      2002032391

ISBN 0-471-07323-7
WIE ISBN: 0-471-42907-4

Printed in the United States of America

10 9 8 7 6 5 4 3 2

Preface

APPROACH

The use of projects and project management continues to grow in our society and its organizations. We are able to achieve goals through project organization that could be achieved only with the greatest of difficulty if organized in traditional ways. Though project management has existed since before the days of the great pyramids, it has enjoyed a surge of popularity beginning in the 1960s. A project put U.S. astronaut Neil Armstrong on the moon. A project named "Desert Storm" freed the nation of Kuwait. An annual project brings us Girl Scout cookies as a sign that winter is just about finished. The use of project management to accomplish the many and diverse aims of society's varied organizations continues to grow.

Businesses regularly use project management to accomplish unique outcomes with limited resources under critical time constraints. In the service sector of the economy, the use of project management to achieve an organization's goals is even more common. Advertising campaigns, voter registration drives, political campaigns, a family's annual summer vacation, and even management seminars on the subject of project management are organized as projects. A relatively new growth area in the use of project management is the use of projects as a way of accomplishing organizational reorganization and change. Indeed, there is a rapid increase in the number of firms that use projects as the preferred way of accomplishing almost everything they undertake. Not even the most optimistic prognosticators foresaw the explosive growth that has occurred in the field.

As the field has grown, so has its literature. There are "cookbooks" that describe in detail the specific steps required to carry out a project, but they do not address the *whys* nor do they usually discuss how and why the parts fit together. Another type of book focuses on scheduling networks. These are quite helpful for scheduling, but scheduling is only one of the serious problems a project manager must face. There are books, seemingly dozens of them, that "talk about" project management—but only occasionally about how to manage a project. There are books on earned value calculations, cost estimating, team building, purchasing, project management software, leadership, planning

IT projects, and similar specialized or subspecialized subjects. These are valuable for experienced project managers who can profit from an advanced education in specific areas of knowledge, but one cannot learn to manage projects from these specialized sources. There are also handbooks—collections of articles written mainly by academics and consultants on selected topics of interest to project managers. Handbooks do not, nor do they pretend to, offer broad coverage of the things project managers need to know. Once the project manager has been educated on the basics of project management, these handbooks often represent valuable collections of relevant readings.

Unfortunately, project management seems to be reentering a stage that we thought had passed—arguments within the profession (and among those who teach it) about what we *really* need to know to manage projects. Must we know "how to manage people" or "how to use computers and do quantitative methods"? Lately we have been receiving email from teachers such as the one who urged us to drop "all the math" and pay more attention to conflict resolution, and another who suggested that we cut back on the "touchy-feely stuff and stick with the important things like scheduling and budgeting." We believe that insight into human behavior, knowledge of organizational issues, and skill with certain quantitative methods are all necessary (though not necessarily sufficient) for successful project management. This book reflects that belief.

It addresses project management from a *management* perspective rather than a cookbook, special area treatise, or collection of loosely associated articles. Such a book should address the basic nature of managing all types of projects—public, business, engineering, information systems, and so on—as well as the specific techniques and insights required to carry out this unique way of getting things done. It should deal with the problems of selecting projects, initiating them, and operating and controlling them. It should discuss the demands made on the project manager and the nature of the manager's interaction with the rest of the parent organization. The book should cover the difficult problems associated with conducting a project using people and organizations that represent different cultures and may be separated by considerable distances. Finally, it should even cover the issues arising when the decision is made to terminate a project.

This managerial perspective is the view we have taken here. As we noted earlier, we are occasionally advised to "cut the BS," apparently a reference to any aspect of project management that is not mathematical, technical, or governed by strict rules of procedure. The argument is that "management is just common sense." It is quite possible that such a statement is true, but if so, the word "common" is used in the sense of "common carrier"—something available to everyone. Sadly, everyone does not seem to have managerial common sense. If everyone did, there would be no market for Scott Adam's *Dilbert*—selected illustrations of which are reproduced here where appropriate.

The book is primarily intended for use as a college textbook for teaching project management at the advanced undergraduate or master's level. The book is also intended for current and prospective project managers who wish to share our insights and ideas about the field. We have drawn freely on our personal experiences working with project managers and on the experience of friends and colleagues who have spent much of their working lives serving as project managers in what they like to call the "real world." Thus, in contrast to the books described earlier *about* project management, this book teaches students how to *do* project management.

As well as being a text that is equally appropriate for classes on the management of service, product, or engineering projects, we have found that information systems (IS) students in our classes find the material particularly helpful for managing their IS projects. Thus, we have included some coverage of material concerning information systems and how IS projects differ from and are similar to regular business projects.

ORGANIZATION AND CONTENT

Given this managerial perspective, we have arranged the book to use the *project life cycle* as the primary organizational guideline. We have found it to be a comfortable framework for the reader. Following an introductory chapter that comments on the role and importance of projects in our society and discusses project management as a potential career for aspiring managers, the book covers the major events and issues arising during the management of projects in the order in which they usually occur in the life of a project. *Part I, Project Initiation* describes how projects are selected for implementation. It also covers the role of the project manager, the various ways that projects can be organized, and the special requirements for managing a cross-cultural project. This is followed by a description of the project planning process and some tools used in project planning. Part I concludes with a topic of major importance to the project manager: negotiation.

Project budgeting, scheduling, resource allocation, monitoring/information systems, and controlling are then discussed in *Part II, Project Implementation*. Finally, *Part III, Project Termination* concludes the discussion with a description of project auditing and termination. The book ends with an epilogue that comments on our ideas about the state of the field and notes three fundamental problems that must be solved if project management is to progress beyond its current state of sophistication.

We have relegated the discussion of two important aspects of projects that usually occur very early in the project life cycle—creativity/idea generation and technological forecasting—to the book's website. Although few project managers engage in either of these tasks (typically being appointed to project leadership after these activities have taken place), we believe that a knowledge of these subjects will make the project manager more effective.

Any way chosen to organize knowledge carries with it an implication of neatness and order that rarely occurs in reality. We are quite aware that projects almost never proceed in an orderly, linear way through the stages and events we describe here. The need to deal with change and uncertainty is a constant task for the project manager. We have tried to reflect this in repeated references to the organizational, interpersonal, economic, and technical glitches that create crises in the life cycle of every project, and thus in the life of every project manager.

Finally, although we use a life-cycle approach to organization, the chapters include material concerning the major areas of the *Project Management Body of Knowledge* (PMBOK) as defined by the Project Management Institute. (See Bibliography for Chapter 1.) Anyone wishing to prepare thoroughly in some of these areas may have to go beyond the information covered in this text.

PEDAGOGY

Because this book is primarily a textbook, we have included numerous pedagogical aids to foster this purpose. As in earlier editions, *short summaries* appear at the end of the text of each chapter, followed by *glossaries* defining key terms and concepts introduced in the chapter. End-of-chapter materials also include *review questions* and *problems* revisiting the materials covered in the chapter. The answers (though not the detailed solutions) to the even-numbered problems are on the book's Web site. There are also sets of conceptual *discussion questions* intended to broaden the students' perspectives and to force them to think beyond the chapter materials to its implications. Finally, there are questions covering the Project Management in Practice application examples located throughout the chapters.

As in the past, we include *incidents for discussion,* which are brief "caselettes" oriented primarily toward the specific subjects covered in the chapter, but sometimes allow use of materials and concepts covered in earlier chapters. And at the end of each chapter we offer a *reading* and/or a *case*, with questions concerning the reading and/or case at the end. In the fourth edition, we removed many of the "major" cases from the book and inserted them in the Instructor's Manual and on the book's Web site. Teachers let us know, in no uncertain terms, that these larger cases belonged in the book. We returned some of them to the book and added a number of newer cases as well. Of course, many of the older cases are still available in the Instructor's Manual and on the website. They are laid out to facilitate copying, should the instructor wish to use them for class handouts and discussion.

We have made some assumptions about student and professional readers in writing this text. First, we assume that all readers have taken an elementary course in management or have had equivalent experience. The reader with a background in management theory or practice will note that many of the principles of good project management are also principles of good general administrative management. Project management and administrative management are not entirely distinct. Further, we assume that readers are familiar with the fundamental principles of accounting, behavioral science, finance, and statistics as would be a typical manager. Because the assumption concerning statistics is not always met, we include Appendix A on the Web site (http://www.wiley.com/college/project@MGT).This appendix on probability and statistics serves as an initial tutorial or as a refresher for rusty knowledge.

WHAT'S NEW

In this fifth edition, we have made quite a few substantial changes, First, in line with the trend in industry, we have taken a more strategic perspective of project management. Chapter 2 is now oriented toward using project selection as a major tool for achieving the strategic objectives of the organization through what is called the Project Portfolio Process.

In addition, Chapter 8 (Scheduling) has been completely rewritten. Since all of the easily available and inexpensive software uses activity-on-node (AON) notation, we have given it prominence in Chapter 8. We continue, however, to teach both AOA and AON and use whichever is most pedagogically helpful whenever networks are required. For example, we prefer AON for scheduling because network construction is simpler. On the other hand, we adopt AOA for teaching how projects are crashed (Chapter 9) because AOA networks illustrate crashing more clearly.

Coverage of earned value analysis has been extended once again in Chapter 10 (Monitoring). In addition, a lengthy example has been added illustrating the calculation of earned value during the execution of a project. Substantial discussion of the Project Management Office has been added to Chapter 4 (Project Organization) with additional references to the Project Office appearing throughout the text.

We have also greatly expanded the coverage of risk management. The added emphasis on risk management is accompanied by a student version of Crystal Ball® 2000, an Excel® add-in, that comes with the book. This software makes simulation reasonably straightforward and not particularly complicated. Discussions of risk management are scattered throughout the entire text, sometimes amounting to a few words and sometimes to whole sections of a chapter. The use of simulation as a technique for risk analysis is demonstrated in several ways in different chapters. (Because relatively few students are familiar with simulation software, step-by-step instruction is included in the text.)

Microsoft Project® has become the dominant application software in the field, outselling its closest competitor about 4 to 1. As with the last edition, a free 120-day trial version of Microsoft Project Professional 2002® is included on a CD in every copy of the book. Our coverage of software tends, therefore, to be centered on Microsoft Project® (and on Crystal Ball®), but includes a brief discussion of the many "add-ons" that are now available to supplement Microsoft Project® and its competitors. Because the various versions of Microsoft Project® are quite similar in the way that they perform most of the basic tasks of project management, we generally do not differentiate between the versions, referring to any and all simply as Microsoft Project (MSP). We have also added some exercises to the end-of-chapter material that can utilize computer software. Similar materials are also available on the website.

In the past, we grouped the Microsoft Project® and Excel® printouts in one chapter. This worked fine for those early, simple versions of project management software. However, as software capabilities expanded, it became necessary to illustrate them in the same chapters where those capabilities were described. For example, when trying to understand a work breakdown structure, it is helpful to see the computer printout and to observe the assignment of WBS numbers as one develops the project plan. MSP and Excel® printouts therefore now appear where they are relevant to the material being covered.

There is, of course, the danger that human nature, operating in its normal discreet mode, will shift the task of learning project management to that of learning project management software. Projects have often failed because the project manager started managing the software instead of the project. Instructors need to be aware of the problem and must caution students not to fall into this trap.

SUPPLEMENTS

The *Instructor's Resource Guide* on the CD-ROM provides additional assistance to the project management instructor. In addition to the answers/solutions to the problems, questions, readings, and cases, this edition includes teaching tips, a test bank, a computerized test bank, and Power Point slides. The books' accompanying Web site (http://www.wiley.com/college/project@MGT) contains, given the password, the following valuable resources for the instructor: an electronic version of the Instructor's

Resource Guide. In addition, the student Web site contains Web quizzes, and Appendix A: Probability and Statistics and Appendix B: Answers to the Even-Numbered Problems, a glossary, and additional cases, topics, and incidents for discussion.

ACKNOWLEDGMENTS

We owe a debt of gratitude to all those who have helped us with this book. First, we thank the managers and students who helped us solidify our ideas about proper methods for managing projects and proper ways of teaching the subject. Second, we thank the project teams and leaders in all of our project management classes. We are especially grateful to Margaret Sutton and Scott Shafer whose creative ideas, extensive skills with software, and ability to sniff out inconsistencies saved us countless hours of fumbling and potential embarrassment. Last, but never least, we thank Suzanne Ingrao, editor nonpareil.

Special thanks are due those who have significantly influenced our thinking about project management or supplied materials to help us write this book: Jeffrey Camm, James Evans, Martin Levy, John McKinney and William Meyers, all of the University of Cincinnati; Larry Crowley, Auburn University; Jeffrey Pinto, Pennsylvania State University of Erie; Robert Riley, consultant; Gerhard Rosegger, Case Western Reserve University; and the Staff of the Project Management Institute. We owe a massive debt of gratitude to the reviewers for previous editions: Nicholas Aquilano, University of Arizona; Bud Baker, Wright State University; Robert J. Berger, University of Maryland; Maj. Mark D. Camdle, Air Force Institute of Technology; Howard Chamberlin, Texas A&M University; Desmond Cook, Ohio State University; Edward Davis, University of Virginia; Kwasi Amoako-Gyampah, University of North Carolina, Greensboro; Richard E. Gunther, California State University, Northridge; Jane E. Humble, Arizona State University; Richard H. Irving, York University; Ted Klastorin, University of Washington; Bill Leban, Keller Graduate School of Management; Barin Nag, Towson University; John E. Nicolay, Jr., University of Minnesota; David L. Overbye, Keller Graduate School of Management; David J. Robb, University of Calgary; Arthur C. Rogers, City University, Washington; John Shanfi, DeVry Institute of Technology, Irving, Texas; Richard V. Sheng, DeVry Institute of Technology, San Marino, California; Joyce T. Shirazi, University of Maryland University College; Herbert Spirer, University of Connecticut; Jerome Weist, University of Utah; Burton Dean, San Jose State University; Samuel Taylor, University of Wyoming; William G. Wells, Jr., The George Washington University; and James Willman, University of Bridgeport.

For this edition, we thank these reviewers: Michael H. Ensby, Clarkson University; David L. Keeney, Stevens Institute of Technology; Abe Meilich, Walden University; Jaindeep Motwani, Grand Valley State University.

Jack Meredith
Broyhill Distinguished Scholar
  and Chair in Operations
Babcock Graduate School of Management
Wake Forest University, P.O. Box 7659
Winston-Salem, NC 27109
jack.meredith@mba.wfu.edu
www.mba.wfu.edu

Samuel J. Mantel, Jr.,
Joseph S. Stern Professor Emeritus of Operations
  Management
University of Cincinnati
608 Flagstaff Drive
Cincinnati, OH 45215
mantelsj@uc.edu

Contents

CHAPTER 3   The Project Manager   **118**

CHAPTER 4   Project Organization   **185**

CHAPTER 5   Project Planning   **239**

CHAPTER 6   Conflict and Negotiation   **295**

PROJECT IMPLEMENTATION

CHAPTER 7   Budgeting and Cost Estimation   **333**

CHAPTER 8   Scheduling   379

CHAPTER 9   Resource Allocation   443

CHAPTER 10   Monitoring and Information Systems   505

Please visit http://www.wiley.com/college/project@mgt for Appendix A: Probability and Statistics and Appendix B: Answers to the Even-Numbered Problems.

CHAPTER

1

Projects in Contemporary Organizations

The past several decades have been marked by rapid growth in the use of project management as a means by which organizations achieve their objectives. Project management provides an organization with powerful tools that improve its ability to plan, implement, and control its activities as well as the ways in which it utilizes its people and resources.

It is popular to ask, "Why can't they run government the way I run my business?" In the case of project management, however, business and other organizations learned from government, not the other way around. A lion's share of the credit for the development of the techniques and practices of project management belongs to the military, which faced a series of major tasks that simply were not achievable by traditional organizations operating in traditional ways. The United States Navy's Polaris program, NASA's Apollo space program, and more recently, the space shuttle and the development of "smart" bombs and missiles are a few of the many instances of the application of these specially developed management approaches to extraordinarily complex projects. Following such examples, nonmilitary government sectors, private industry, public service agencies, and volunteer organizations have all used project management to increase their effectiveness. Almost all firms in the computer software business routinely develop their output as projects or groups of projects.

Project management has emerged because the characteristics of our contemporary society demand the development of new methods of management. Of the many forces involved, three are paramount: (1) the exponential expansion of human knowledge; (2) the growing demand for a broad range of complex, sophisticated, customized goods and services; and (3) the evolution of worldwide competitive markets for the production and consumption of goods and services. All three forces combine to mandate the use of teams to solve problems that used to be solvable by individuals. These three forces combine to increase greatly the complexity of goods and services

1

produced plus the complexity of the processes used to produce them. This, in turn, leads to the need for more sophisticated systems to control both outcomes and processes.

Forces Fostering Project Management

First, the expansion of knowledge allows an increasing number of academic disciplines to be used in solving problems associated with the development, production, and distribution of goods and services. Second, satisfying the continuing demand for more complex and customized products and services depends on our ability to make product design an integrated and inherent part of our production and distribution systems. Third, worldwide markets force us to include cultural and environmental differences in our managerial decisions about what, where, when, and how to produce and distribute output. The requisite knowledge does not reside in any one individual, no matter how well educated or knowledgable. Thus, under these conditions, teams are used for making decisions and taking action. This calls for a high level of coordination and cooperation between groups of people not particularly used to such interaction. Largely geared to the mass production of simpler goods, traditional organizational structures and management systems are simply not adequate to the task. Project management is.

The organizational response to the forces noted above cannot take the form of an instantaneous transformation from the old to the new. To be successful, the transition must be systematic, but it tends to be slow and tortuous for most enterprises. Accomplishing organizational change is a natural application of project management, and many firms have set up projects to implement their goals for strategic and tactical change.

Another important societal force is the intense competition among institutions, both profit and not-for-profit, fostered by our economic system. This puts extreme pressure on organizations to make their complex, customized outputs available as quickly as possible. "Time-to-market" is critical. Responses must come faster, decisions must be made sooner, and results must occur more quickly. Imagine the communications problems alone. Information and knowledge are growing explosively, but the time permissible to locate and use the appropriate knowledge is decreasing.

In addition, these forces operate in a society that assumes that technology can do anything. The fact is, this assumption is reasonably true, within the bounds of nature's fundamental laws. The problem lies not in this assumption so much as in a concomitant assumption that allows society to ignore both the economic and noneconomic costs associated with technological progress until some dramatic event focuses our attention on the costs (e.g., the Chernobyl nuclear accident, the *Exxon Valdez* oil spill, or the possibility of global warming). At times, our faith in technology is disturbed by difficulties and threats arising from its careless implementation, as in the case of industrial waste, but on the whole we seem remarkably tolerant of technological change. For a case in point, consider California farm workers who waited more than 20 years to challenge a University of California research program devoted to the development of labor-saving farm machinery (Sun, 1984). The acceptance of technological advancement is so strong it took more than two decades to muster the legal attack. Consider also the easy acceptance of communication by e-mail and shopping on the Internet.

Finally, the projects we undertake are large and getting larger. The modern advertising company, for example, advances from blanket print ads to regionally focused television ads to personally focused Internet ads. As each new capability extends our grasp, it serves as the base for new demands that force us to extend our reach even farther. Projects increase in size and complexity because the more we can do, the more we try to do.

The projects that command the most public attention tend to be large, complex, multidisciplinary endeavors. Often, such endeavors are both similar to and different from previous projects with which we may be more or less familiar. Similarities with the past provide a base from which to start, but the differences imbue every project with considerable risk. The complexities and multidisciplinary aspects of projects require that many parts be put together so that the prime objectives—performance, time (or schedule), and cost—are met.

Three Project Objectives

While multimillion dollar, five-year projects capture public attention, the overwhelming majority of all projects are comparatively small—though nonetheless important to doer and user alike. They involve outcomes, or deliverables, such as a new basketball floor for a professional basketball team, a new insurance policy to protect against a specific casualty loss, a new Web site, a new casing for a four-wheel drive minivan transmission, a new industrial floor cleanser, the installation of a new method for peer-review of patient care in a hospital, even the development of new software to help manage projects. The list could be extended almost without limit. These undertakings have much in common with their larger counterparts. They are complex, multidisciplinary, and have the same general objectives—performance (or *scope*), time, and cost.

There is a tendency to think of a project solely in terms of its outcome—that is, its performance. But the time at which the outcome is available is itself a part of the outcome, as is the cost entailed in achieving the outcome. The completion of a building on time and on budget is quite a different outcome from the completion of the same physical structure a year late or 20 percent over budget, or both.

Indeed, even the concept of performance or scope is more complex than is apparent. Much has been written in recent years arguing that, in addition to time, cost, and specifications, there is a fourth dimension to be considered. This fourth dimension is the expectations of the client (see Darnell, 1997), which sometimes tend to increase as the project progresses, known as "scope creep" (see Chapter 11). However, we feel strongly that the expectations of the client are not an additional target, *but an inherent part of the project specifications*. To consider the client's desires as different from the project specifications is to court conflict between client and project team, each of whom has unique ideas about the deliverables' nature. Also, to separate client desires from project specifications creates conflict because client and team rarely act in concert. The client specifies a desired outcome. *Then* the project team designs and implements the project. *Then* the client views the result of the team's ideas. Given the creative juices of human beings, there is little chance of unchanged specifications during the process. The project manager never wins when such a conflict arises. To be acceptable to the client, a building must meet the client's expectations as well as those of the builder, which may require more than slavish conformity to the builder's blueprints. There are quality, safety, esthetic, and environmental dimensions to performance that cannot be overlooked if the project is to meet its goals. The expectations of client and project team should be integrated throughout the entire project.

In a more basic sense, the project manager, the project team, senior management, the client, and anyone else with a stake in the project, is interested in making a success of the project. The problem is that not all parties-at-interest have the same idea of what constitutes success. In a thoughtful piece of research that we will consider in more detail in Chapter 12, Shenhar, Levy, and Dvir (1997) have concluded that project success has four dimensions: project efficiency, impact on the customer, the business impact on the organization, and opening new opportunities for the future. We agree with their assessment, but again argue that all of these elements of success must be contained in the "specifications" of the project. The specifications of the project are no more and no less than the set of objectives the project is meant to deliver to all its stakeholders.

The prime objectives of project management are shown in Figure 1-1, with the specified project objectives on the axes. This illustration implies that there is some "function" (not shown in the figure) that relates them, one to another—and so there is! Although the functions vary from project to project, and from time to time for a given project, we will be constantly referring to these relationships, or trade-offs, throughout this book. The primary task of the project manager is to manage these trade-offs.

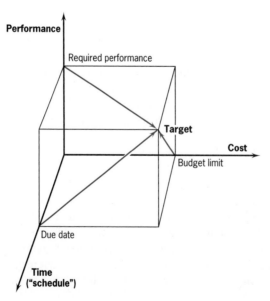

Figure 1-1   Project targets—performance, cost, time.

The Project Manager

While managing the trade-offs, the project manager (PM) is expected to integrate all aspects of the project, ensure that the proper knowledge and resources are available when and where needed, and above all, ensure that the expected results are produced in a timely, cost-effective manner.

The complexity of the problems faced by the PM, taken together with the rapid growth in the number of project-oriented organizations, has contributed to the professionalization of project management. The Project Management Institute (PMI) was established in 1969. By 1990, the PMI had 7,500 members. Five years later, it had grown to over 17,000, and by the end of 2001 it had exploded to 86,000 (see Figure 1-2). This exponential growth is indicative of the rapid growth in the use of projects, but also reflects the importance of the PMI as a force in the development of project management as a profession. Its mission is to foster the growth of project management as well as "building professionalism" in the field. The *Project Management Journal* and *PM Network* magazines were founded by the PMI to communicate ideas about project management, as well as solutions for commonly encountered problems. Another PMI objective is to codify the areas of learning required for competent project management. This project management body of knowledge, PMBOK, is meant to serve as the fundamental basis for education for project managers (Project Management Institute, 2001). The profession has flourished, with the result that many colleges and universities offer training in project management and some offer specialized degree programs in the area.

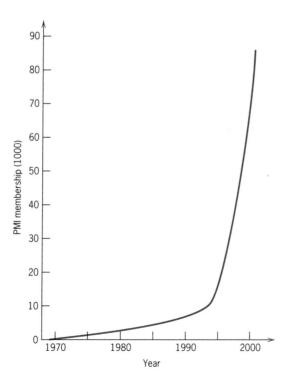

Figure 1-2 Project Management Institute growth history.

Clearly, rapid growth in the number of project managers and of the PMI membership were the result, not the cause, of tremendous growth in the number of projects being carried out. The software industry alone has been responsible for a significant percent of the growth. Another major source of growth has been the need to control project activity in large organizations. As the number of nonroutine activities increases in an organization, there is an increased need in senior management to understand and control the system. Project management, with its schedules, budgets, due dates, risk assessments, statements of expected outcomes, and people who take responsibility, is a way to meet this need. These forces have combined and led to the creation of a project-organized firm. Much more will be said about project-oriented organizations in Chapter 4.

As we note in the coming chapters, the project manager's job is not without problems. There is the ever-present frustration of being responsible for outcomes while lacking full authority to command the requisite resources or personnel. There are the constant problems of dealing with the parties involved in any project—senior management, client, project team, and public—all of whom seem to speak different languages and have different objectives. There are the ceaseless organizational and technical "fires to be fought." There are vendors who cannot seem to keep "lightning-strike-me-dead" promises about delivery dates. This list of troubles only scratches the surface.

Difficult as the job may be, most project managers take a considerable amount of pleasure and job satisfaction from their occupation. The challenges are many and the risks significant, but so are the rewards of success. Project managers usually enjoy organizational visibility, considerable variety in their day-to-day duties, and often have the prestige associated with work on the enterprise's high-priority objectives. The profession, however, is not one for the timid. Risk and conflict avoiders do not make happy project managers. Those who can stomach the risks and enjoy practicing the arts of conflict resolution, however, can take substantial monetary and psychological rewards from their work.

Recent Changes in Managing Organizations

In the almost two decades since the first edition of this book was published, the process of managing organizations has been impacted by three revolutionary changes. First, we have seen an accelerating replacement of traditional, hierarchical management by consensual management. Second, we are currently witnessing the adoption of the "systems approach" (sometimes called "systems engineering") to deal with organizational or technological problems because it is abundantly clear that when we act on one part of an organization or system, we are certain to affect other parts. Third, we have seen organizations establishing projects as the preferred way to accomplish their goals. Examples vary from the hundreds of projects required to accomplish the "globalization" of a multibillion dollar household products firm to the incremental tailoring of products and services for individual customers. We elaborate on this tie between the organization's goals and the projects it selects for implementation in the following chapter. And as we will note in Chapter 4 and elsewhere, there has been a rapid and sustained growth in the number of organizations that use projects to accomplish almost all of the nonroutine tasks they undertake. While all three of these phenomena have been known for many years, it is comparatively recent that they have been widely recognized and practiced.

In his fascinating book, *Rescuing Prometheus* (Hughes, 1998), technology historian Thomas Hughes examines four large-scale projects that required the use of a nontraditional management style, a nontraditional organizational design, and a nontraditional approach to problem solving in order to achieve their objectives. These huge projects—Semiautomatic Ground Environment (SAGE) air defense system, the Atlas Intercontinental Ballistic Missile, the Boston Central Artery/Tunnel, and the Department of Defense Advanced Research Projects Agency's Internet (ARPANET)—were all characterized by extraordinarily diverse knowledge and information input requirements.* The size and technological complexity of these projects required input from a large number of autonomous organizations—governmental, industrial, and academic—that usually did not work cooperatively with other organizations, were sometimes competitors, and could be philosophical and/or political opponents. Further, any actions taken to deal with parts of the total project often had disturbing impacts on many other parts of the system.

Obviously, these projects were not the first, complex, large-scale projects carried out in this country or elsewhere. For example, the Manhatten Project—devoted to the development of the atomic bomb—was such a project. The Manhatten Project, however, was the sole and full-time work for a large majority of the individuals and organizations working on it. The organizations contributing to the projects Hughes describes were, for the most part, working on many other tasks. For example, Massachusetts Institute of Technology (MIT), the Pentagon, IBM, Bell Labs (now Lucent Technologies), RAND Corporation, the Massachusetts Department of Highways, and a great many other organizations were all highly involved in one or more of these projects while still carrying on their usual work. The use of multiple organizations (both within and outside of the sponsoring firm) as contributors to a project is no longer remarkable. Transdisciplinary projects are more the rule than the exception.

These revolutions and modifications in the style of management and organization of projects will be reflected throughout this book. For example, we have come to believe that the use of a traditional, hierarchical management style rather than a consensual style to manage multiorganizational projects is a major generator of conflict between members of the project team. We have long felt, and are now certain, that staffing multidisciplinary projects with individuals whose primary focus is on a specific discipline rather than on the problem(s) embodied in the project will also lead to high levels of interpersonal conflict between project team members. In Chapter 4 we will discuss some issues involved in the widespread use of projects to accomplish organizational change. As in the first edition, we adopt a systems approach to dealing with the problems of managing projects.

---

*Hughes's term for this is "transdisciplinary" (across disciplines), which is rather more accurate than the usual "interdisciplinary" (between discliplines).

This book identifies the specific tasks facing PMs. We investigate the nature of the projects for which the PM is responsible, the skills that must be used to manage projects, and the means by which the manager can bring the project to a successful conclusion in terms of the three primary criteria: performance, time, and cost. Before delving into the details of this analysis, however, we clarify the nature of a project and determine how it differs from the other activities that are conducted in organizations. We also note a few of the major advantages, disadvantages, strengths, and limitations of project management. At this end of this chapter, we describe the approach followed throughout the rest of the book.

1.1   THE DEFINITION OF A "PROJECT"

The PMI has defined a project as "A temporary endeavor undertaken to create a unique product or service" (Project Management Institute, 2001, p. 167). There is a rich variety of projects to be found in our society. Although some may argue that the construction of the Tower of Babel or the Egyptian pyramids were some of the first "projects," it is probable that cavemen formed a project to gather the raw material for mammoth stew. It is certainly true that the construction of Boulder Dam and Edison's invention of the light bulb were projects by any sensible definition. Modern project management, however, is usually said to have begun with the Manhattan Project. In its early days, project management was used mainly for very large, complex research and development (R & D) projects like the development of the Atlas Intercontinental Ballistic Missile and similar military weapon systems. Massive construction programs were also organized as projects—the construction of dams, ships, refineries, and freeways, among others.

As the techniques of project management were developed, mostly by the military, the use of project organization began to spread. Private construction firms found that project organization was helpful on smaller projects, such as the building of a warehouse or an apartment complex. Automotive companies used project organization to develop new automobile models. Both General Electric and Pratt & Whitney used project organization to develop new jet aircraft engines for airlines, as well as the Air Force. Project management has even been used to develop new models of shoes and ships (though possibly not sealing wax). More recently, the use of project management by international organizations, and especially organizations producing services rather than products, has grown rapidly. Advertising campaigns, global mergers, and capital acquisitions are often handled as projects, and the methods have spread to the nonprofit sector. Teas, weddings, scout-o-ramas, fund drives, election campaigns, parties, and recitals have all made use of project management. Most striking has been the widespread adoption of project management techniques for the development of computer software.

In discussions of project management, it is sometimes useful to make a distinction between terms such as *project, program, task,* and *work packages.* The military, source of most of these terms, generally uses the term *program* to refer to an exceptionally large, long-range objective that is broken down into a set of projects. These projects are divided further into *tasks,* which are, in turn, split into *work packages* that are themselves composed of *work units.* But exceptions to this hierarchical nomenclature abound. The Manhattan Project was a huge "program," but a "task force" was created to investigate the many potential futures of a large steel company.

In the broadest sense, a project is a specific, finite task to be accomplished. Whether large- or small-scale or whether long- or short-run is not particularly relevant. What is relevant is that the project be seen as a unit. There are, however, some attributes that characterize projects.

Purpose

A project is usually a one-time activity with a well-defined set of desired end results. It can be divided into subtasks that must be accomplished in order to achieve the project goals. The project is complex enough that the subtasks require careful coordination and control in terms of timing, precedence, cost, and performance. Often, the project itself must be coordinated with other projects being carried out by the same parent organization.

Life Cycle

Like organic entities, projects have life cycles. From a slow beginning they progress to a buildup of size, then peak, begin a decline, and finally must be terminated. (Also like organic entities, they often resist termination.) Some projects end by being phased into the normal, ongoing operations of the parent organization. The life cycle is discussed further in Section 1.3 where an important exception to the usual description of the growth curve is mentioned.

Interdependencies

Projects often interact with other projects being carried out simultaneously by their parent organization; but projects always interact with the parent organization's standard, ongoing operations. Although the functional departments of an organization (marketing, finance, manufacturing, and the like) interact with one another in regular, patterned ways, the patterns of interaction between projects and these departments tend to be changeable. Marketing may be involved at the beginning and end of a project, but not in the middle. Manufacturing may have major involvement throughout. Finance is often involved at the beginning and accounting (the controller) at the end, as well as at periodic reporting times. The PM must keep all these interactions clear and maintain the appropriate interrelationships with all external groups.

Uniqueness

Every project has some elements that are unique. No two construction or R & D projects are precisely alike. Though it is clear that construction projects are usually more routine than R & D projects, some degree of customization is a characteristic of projects. In addition to the presence of risk, as noted earlier, this characteristic means that projects, by their nature, cannot be completely reduced to routine. The PM's importance is emphasized because, as a devotee of *management by exception,* the PM will find there are a great many exceptions to manage by.

Conflict

More than most managers, the PM lives in a world characterized by conflict. Projects compete with functional departments for resources and personnel. More serious, with the growing proliferation of projects, is the project-versus-project conflict for resources within multiproject organizations. The members of the project team are in almost constant conflict for the project's resources and for leadership roles in solving project problems.

The four parties-at-interest or "stakeholders" (client, parent organization, project team, and the public) in any project even define success and failure in different ways (see Chapters 12 and 13). The client wants changes, and the parent organization wants profits, which may be reduced if those changes are made. Individuals working on projects are often responsible to two bosses at the same time; these bosses may have different priorities and objectives. Project management is no place for the timid.

If the characteristics listed above define a project, it is appropriate to ask if there are nonprojects. There are. The use of a manufacturing line to produce a flow of standard products is a nonproject. The production of weekly employment reports, the preparation of school lunches, the delivery of mail, the flight of Delta-1288 from Dallas to Dulles, checking your e-mail, all are nonprojects. While one might argue that each of these activities is, to some degree, unique, it is not their uniqueness that characterizes them. They are all *routine*. They are tasks that are performed over and over again. This is not true of projects. Each project is a one-time event. Even the construction of a section of interstate highway is a project. No two miles are alike and constructing them demands constant adaptation to the differences in terrain and substructure of the earth on which the roadbed is to be laid. Projects cannot be managed adequately by the managerial routines used for routine work.

Project Management in Practice
The Olympic Torch Relay Project

Getting the Olympic Flame, known as the Olympic Torch Relay, to the Salt Lake City, Utah, USA 2002 Olympic Games promised to be no simple matter. Generally, the Torch Relay has gotten longer and more complex with every Olympic event. This complexity is driven by the realization of host-country citizens that it is a rare opportunity to have the Olympic torch pass through your hometown and the corresponding goal of the Olympic Committee to touch as many lives as possible in a positive way.

Planning for the 1996 Atlanta Olympic Torch Relay took two years, cost over $20 million, and involved an 84 day, 42 state campaign using 10,000 runners to carry the torch for 15,000 miles! Accompanying the runners was a 40-vehicle caravan carrying security officers, media personnel, medical personnel, computers, telecommunications gear, clothing, food, and spare lanterns with extra flames in case the original torch went out. The caravan included: 50 cellular telephones; 60 pagers; 120 radios; 30 cars; 10 motorcycles; and clothing for 10,000 runners, 10,000 volunteers, as well as 2,500 escort runners.

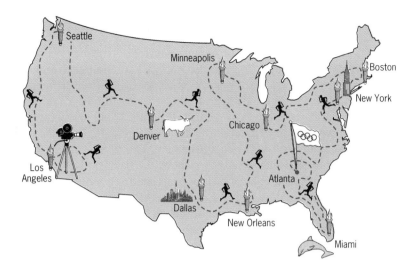

However, the torch relay is also a major marketing campaign, primarily for the relay's sponsors. Thus, accompanying the Atlanta-bound caravan were trucks hawking Olympic memorabilia: t-shirts, sweatshirts, baseball caps, tickets to the soccer matches, and on and on. In addition to retail commercialism, a number of companies were piggybacking on the torch relay to further their own commercial interests: IBM, Motorola, Bell-South, Texaco, BMW, Lee, Coca-Cola, and so on. All in all, a very successful relay!

Source: G. Ruffenach, "Getting the Olympic Flame to Atlanta Won't be a Simple Cross-Country Run," *The Wall Street Journal,* February 26, 1996.

1.2 WHY PROJECT MANAGEMENT?

The basic purpose for initiating a project is to accomplish specific goals. The reason for organizing the task as a project is to focus the responsibility and authority for the attainment of the goals on an individual or small group.

In spite of the fact that the PM often lacks authority at a level consistent with his or her responsibility, the manager is expected to coordinate and integrate all activities needed to reach the project's goals. In particular, the project form of organization allows the manager to be responsive to: (1) the client and the environment, (2) identify and correct problems at an early date, (3) make timely decisions about trade-offs between conflicting project goals, and (4) ensure that managers of the separate tasks that comprise the project do not optimize the performance of their individual tasks at the expense of the total project—that is, that they do not suboptimize.

Actual experience with project management indicates that the majority of organizations using it experience better control and better customer relations (Davis, 1974), and probably an increase in their project's return on investment (Ibbs and Kwak, 1997). A significant proportion of users also report shorter development times, lower costs, higher quality and reliability, and higher profit margins. Other reported advantages include a sharper orientation toward results, better interdepartmental coordination, and higher worker morale.

On the negative side, most organizations report that project management results in greater organizational complexity. Many also report that project organization increases the likelihood that organizational policy will be violated—not a surprising outcome, considering the degree of autonomy required for the PM. A few firms reported higher costs, more management difficulties, and low personnel utilization.

As we will see in Chapter 4, the disadvantages of project management stem from exactly the same sources as its advantages. The disadvantages seem to be the price one pays for the advantages. On the whole, the balance weighs in favor of project organization if the work to be done is appropriate for a project.

The tremendous diversity of uses to which project management can be put has had an interesting, and generally unfortunate, side-effect. While we assert that all projects are to some extent unique, there is an almost universal tendency for those working on some specific types of projects to argue, "Software (or construction, or R & D, or marketing, or machine maintenance, or . . .) projects are different and you can't expect us to schedule (or budget, or organize, or manage, or . . .) in the same way that other kinds of projects do." Disagreement with such pleas for special treatment is central to the philosophy of this book. The fundamental similarities between all sorts of projects, be they long or short, product- or service-oriented, parts of all-encompassing programs or stand-alone, are far more pervasive than are their differences.

There are real limitations on project management. For example, the mere creation of a project may be an admission that the parent organization and its managers cannot accomplish the desired outcomes through the functional organization. Further, conflict seems to be a necessary side-effect. As we noted, the PM often lacks authority that is consistent with the assigned level of responsibility. Therefore, the PM must depend on the goodwill of managers in the parent organization for some of the necessary resources. Of course, if the goodwill is not forthcoming, the PM may ask senior officials in the parent organization for their assistance. But to use such power often reflects poorly on the skills of the PM and, while it may get cooperation in the instance at hand, it may backfire in the long run.

We return to the subject of the advantages, disadvantages, and limitations of the project form of organization later. For the moment, it is sufficient to point out that project management is difficult even when everything goes well. When things go badly, PMs have been known to turn gray overnight and take to hard drink! The trouble is that project organization is the only feasible way to accomplish certain goals. It is literally not possible to design and build a major weapon system, for example, in a timely and economically acceptable manner, except by project organization. The stronger the emphasis on achievement of results in an organization, the more likely it will be to adopt some form of project management. The stake or risks in using project management may be high, but no more so than in any other form of management. And for projects, it is less so. Tough as it may be, it is all we have—and it works!

All in all, the life of a PM is exciting, rewarding, at times frustrating, and tends to be at the center of things in most organizations. Project management is now being recognized as a "career path" in a growing number of firms, particularly those conducting projects with lives extending more than a year or two. In such organizations, PMs may have to function for several years, and it is important to provide promotion potential for them. It is also common for large firms to put their more promising young managers through a "tour of duty" during which they manage one or more projects (or parts of projects). This serves as a good test of the aspiring manager's ability to coordinate and manage complex tasks and to achieve results in a politically challenging environment where negotiation skills are required.

1.3 THE PROJECT LIFE CYCLE

Most projects go through similar stages on the path from origin to completion. We define these stages, shown in Figure 1-3, as the project's *life cycle*. The project is born (its start-up phase) and a manager is selected, the project team and initial resources are assembled, and the work program is organized. Then work gets under way and momentum quickly builds. Progress is made. This continues until the end is in sight. But completing the final tasks seems to take an inordinate amount of time, partly because there are often a number of parts that must come together and partly because team members "drag their feet" for various reasons and avoid the final steps.

The pattern of slow-rapid-slow progress toward the project goal is common. Anyone who has watched the construction of a home or building has observed this phenomenon. For the most part, it is a result of the changing levels of resources used during the successive stages of the life cycle. Figure 1-4 shows project effort, usually in

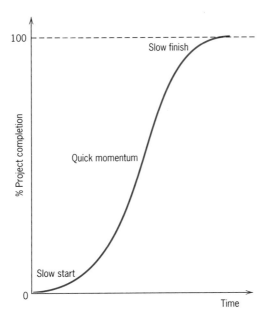

Figure 1-3 The project life cycle.

terms of person-hours or resources expended per unit of time (or number of people working on the project) plotted against time, where time is broken up into the several phases of project life. Minimal effort is required at the beginning, when the project concept is being developed and subjected to project selection processes. (Later, we will argue that increasing effort in the early stages of the life cycle will improve the chance of project success.)

If this hurdle is passed, activity increases as planning is completed and the real work of the project gets underway. This rises to a peak and then begins to taper off as the project nears completion, finally ceasing when evaluation is complete and the project is terminated. While this rise and fall of effort always occurs, there is no particular pattern that seems to typify all projects, nor any reason for the slowdown at the end of the project to resemble the buildup at its beginning. Some projects end without being dragged out, as is shown in Figure 1-4. Others, however, may be like T. S. Eliot's world, and end "not with a bang but a whimper," gradually slowing down until one is almost surprised to discover that project activity has ceased. In some cases, the effort may never fall to zero because the project team, or at least a cadre group, may be maintained for the next appropriate project that comes along. The new project will then rise, phoenix-like, from the ashes of the old.

The everpresent goals of meeting performance, time, and cost are the major considerations throughout the project's life cycle. It was generally thought that performance took precedence early in the project's life cycle. This is the time when planners focus on finding the specific methods required to meet the project's performance goals. We refer to these methods as the project's *technology* because they require the application of a science or art.

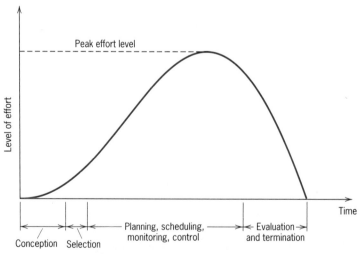

Figure 1-4 Time distribution of project effort.

When the major "how" problems are solved, project workers sometimes become preoccupied with improving performance, often beyond the levels required by the original specifications. This search for better performance delays the schedule and pushes up the costs.

At the same time that the technology of the project is defined, the project schedule is designed and project costs are estimated. Just as it was thought that performance took precedence over schedule and cost early in the life cycle, cost was thought to be of prime importance during the periods of high activity, and then schedule became paramount during the final stages, when the client demanded delivery. This conventional wisdom turns out to be untrue. Recent research indicates that performance and schedule are more important than cost during *all* stages. The reality of time-cost-performance trade-offs will be discussed in greater detail in Chapter 3.

Figure 1-3 presents the conventional view of the project life cycle. There are, however, many projects that have a life cycle quite different from the S-shaped Figure 1-3, conventional wisdom to the contrary. Remember that Figure 1-3 shows "percent project completion" as a function of "time." The life-cycle function is essentially unchanged if, for the horizontal axis, we use "resources" instead. In effect, the life cycle shows what an economist might call "return on input," that is, the amount of project completion resulting from inputs of time or resources. While the S-shaped return curve reflects reality on many projects, it is seriously misleading for others.

To understand the difference, let us consider baking a cake. Once the ingredients are mixed, we are instructed to bake the cake in a 350° (F) oven for 35 minutes. At what point in the baking process do we have "cake?" Experienced bakers know that the mixture changes from "goop" (a technical term well known to bakers and cooks) to "cake" quite rapidly in the last few minutes of the baking process. The life cycle of this process looks like the curve shown in Figure 1-5. A number of actual projects have a similar life cycle, for example, some computer software projects, or chemistry and chemical engineering projects. In general, this life cycle often exists for projects in which the output is composed or constructed of several *subunits* (or subroutines)

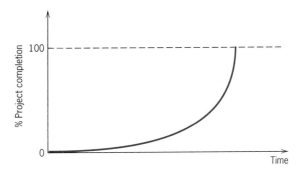

Figure 1-5 Another possible project life cycle.

that have little use in and of themselves, but are quite useful when put together. This life-cycle curve would also be typical for projects where a chemical-type reaction occurs that rapidly transforms the output from useless to useful—from goop to cake. Another example is the preparation of the manuscript for the current edition of this book. A great deal of information must be collected, a great deal of rewriting must be done and new materials gathered, but there is no visible result until everything is assembled.

Figure 1-3 shows that, as the project nears completion, continued inputs of time or resources result in successively smaller increments of completion—diminishing marginal returns. Figure 1-5 shows the opposite. As these projects near completion, additional inputs result in successively larger increments of completion—increasing marginal returns, obviously bounded at 100 percent completion. In Chapter 7, we will see that the distinction between these types of life cycles plays a critical role in developing budgets and schedules for projects. It is not necessary for the PM to estimate the precise shape of the life-cycle curve, but the PM must know which type of project life cycle applies to the project at hand.

There is another comparison between the two types of project life cycles that is instructive. For the S-shaped life cycle in Figure 1-3, percentage of project completion is closely correlated with cost, or the use of resources. In fact, this is the basis for the use of "earned value," a technique for monitoring project progress that we will describe in more detail in Chapter 10. However, for the exponential progress curve in Figure 1-5, the expenditure of resources has little correlation with progress, at least in terms of final benefit. Thus, the meaning of the term "progress" toward the project goal, or equivalently, percent of project completion, should be interpreted in terms of benefits received, not resources expended. In fact, the resource expenditures for the project illustrated in Figure 1-5 *may be substantially greater* earlier in the project duration than those for the project in Figure 1-3.

Risk During the Life Cycle

It would be a great source of comfort if one could predict with certainty, at the start of a project, how the performance, time, and cost goals would be met. In a few cases, routine construction projects, for instance, we can generate reasonably accurate predictions, but often we cannot. There may be considerable uncertainty about our ability to meet project goals. The crosshatched portion of Figure 1-6 illustrates that uncertainty.

Figure 1-6 shows the uncertainty as seen at the beginning of the project. Figure 1-7 shows how the uncertainty decreases as the project moves toward completion. From project start time, t_0, the band of uncertainty grows until it is quite wide by the estimated end of the project. As the project actually develops, the degree of uncertainty about the final outcome is reduced. (See the estimate made at t_1, for example.) A later forecast, made at t_2, reduces the uncertainty further. It is common to make new forecasts about project performance, time, and cost either at fixed intervals in the life of the project or when specific technological milestones are reached. In any event, the more progress made on the project, the less uncertainty there is about achieving the final goal.

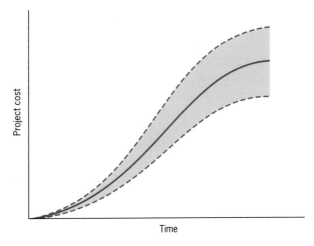

Figure 1-6 Estimate of project cost: estimate made at project start.

Note that the focus in Figures 1-6 and 1-7 is on the uncertainty associated with project cost—precisely, the uncertainty of project cost at specific points in time. Without significantly altering the shapes of the curves, we could exchange titles on the axes. The figures would then show the uncertainty associated with estimates of the project schedule, given specific levels of expenditure. The relationship between time and cost (and performance) is emphasized throughout this book. Dealing with the uncertainty surrounding this relationship is a major responsibility of the PM.

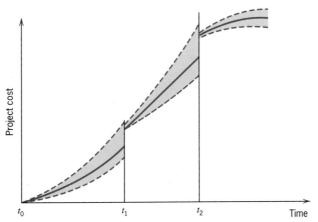

Figure 1-7 Estimates of project cost: estimates made at time t_0, t_1, and t_2.

Project Management in Practice
Demolishing San Francisco's Bridges Safely

The Central Freeway Viaduct in downtown San Francisco suffered major structural damage during the 1989 Loma Prieta earthquake and recently had to be safely demolished. The task was complicated because the bilevel, multispan bridge passed within six feet of heavily populated buildings, ran in the vicinity of both overhead and underground utilities (gas, water, electric, and sewer lines), and crossed both commercial and residential areas with strict vibration and sound level restrictions. Thus, managing the demolition while ensuring the safety of both the on-going population and existing facilities was a major challenge.

The primary tools for conducting such a delicate, but dangerous operation were detailed planning and thorough communications with all related parties. An extensive Demolition Plan was required and included:

—a Code of Safe Practice describing personal protective equipment for the workers, as well as a maintenance plan for the equipment;

—a demolition sequence plan (sequence of work, staging, equipment location, restraints, safety structures, traffic control)

—a dust control plan

—work-hour schedule

—noise-level monitoring

—load determinations and structural analyses.

Most of the demolition was accomplished using a breaker on the upper deck of the bridge and a pulverizer on the lower deck. First the roadway slab was demolished, then the girders were pulverized and all the debris pushed down to the ground. Then the cap, columns, and restrainers

were demolished. This process continued along the length of the bridge until the entire distance was demolished. Constant monitoring was conducted for noise, vibration, safety, and procedures throughout the project. Continuous communication was made with utility companies and others concerned with a particular segment being demolished. In this fashion, the entire viaduct was demolished with no major accidents or injuries.

Source: O. Y. Abudayyeh, "Safety Issues in Bridge Demolition Projects: A Case Study," *PM Network,* January 1997, pp. 43–45.

1.4   THE STRUCTURE OF THIS TEXT

This book, a project in itself, has been organized to follow the life cycle of all projects. It begins with the creative idea that launches most projects and ends with termination of the project. This approach is consistent with our belief that it is helpful to understand the entire process of project management in order to understand and manage its parts. In addition, although this book is intended primarily for the student who wants to study project management, we feel it can also be of value to the prospective or acting PM, and to senior managers who initiate projects and select, work with, or manage PMs. Therefore, our interests often go beyond the issues of primary concern to beginning students.

Most actual projects will not be of the size and complexity addressed in many of our discussions. Though our intent was not to confine our remarks only to large engineering-oriented projects, these are typically the most complex and place the greatest demands on project management. Smaller, simpler projects may therefore not require the depth of tools and techniques we will present, but the student or manager should be aware that such tools exist.

Project management actually begins with the initial concept for the project. We feel that this aspect of project management is so important, yet so universally ignored in books on project management, that we included two appendices covering this area in previous editions of this book. In one appendix we discussed *creativity* and *idea generation.* In another, we described some of the techniques of *technological forecasting.* While our notion about the importance of these subjects is unchanged, the location of the two appendices has been moved from the end of this work to the Internet. The complete text of both appendices now appears in *http://www.wiley.com/college/projectmgt/* (along with other items noted in the preface to this edition). We realize that these topics may be of more direct interest to the senior manager than the PM. Though a PM may prefer to skip this material, since what is past is past, we believe that history holds lessons for the future. Wise PMs will wish to know the reasons for, and the history behind, the initiation of their project.

In years past, there were arguments between those who insisted that project management was primarily a quantitative science and those who maintained that it was a behavioral science. It has become clear that one cannot adequately manage a project without depending heavily on both mathematics and the science of human behavior. To contend that mathematics is exact and that behavioral science is "mushy" is to ignore the high level of subjectivity in most of the numeric estimates made about the times, costs, and risks associated with projects. On the other hand, to assert that "people don't really use that stuff" (mathematical models) is to substitute wishful thinking for reality. For nonmathematicians, we have computers to help with the requisite arithmetic. For the nonbehaviorists, there is no help except hard work and an accepting attitude toward the subject.

Before undertaking any journey, it is useful to know what roads are to be traveled. While each individual chapter begins with a more detailed account of its contents, what follows is a brief description of chapter contents along with their organization into three general areas: project initiation, project implementation, and project termination. Following this introductory chapter, the material in Part I focuses on *project initiation* beginning with strategic management through judicious selection of the organization's projects. Chapter 2 describes strategic project management through an eight-step procedure called the "project portfolio process." It then details the problems of evaluating and selecting projects, including descriptions of the major models used to select projects for funding in government, as well as in industry. In addition, this chapter also covers some of the technical details of proposals. Chapter 3, "The Project Manager," concerns the PM's roles, responsibilities, and some personal characteristics a project manager should possess. It also discusses the problems a PM faces when operating in a multicultural environment. Next, Chapter 4 concentrates on establishing the project organization. Different organizational forms are described, as well as their respective advantages and disadvantages. The staffing of the project team is also discussed. Chapter 5 deals with project planning and presents tools useful in organizing and staffing the various project tasks. It also contains a short discussion of phase-gate management systems and other ways of dealing with the problems raised when multidisciplinary teams work on complex projects. Concluding Part I of the book, Chapter 6 covers a subject of critical importance to the PM that is almost universally ignored in project management texts, the art of negotiating for resources. The chapter also includes some major sources of interpersonal conflict among members of the project team.

In Part II we consider *project implementation.* This section of the text discusses the essentials of ongoing project management. Because of its importance, budgeting is addressed first in Chapter 7. Scheduling, a crucial aspect of project planning, is then described in Chapter 8, along with the most common scheduling models such as the Program Evaluation and Review Technique (PERT), the Critical Path Method (CPM), and precedence diagramming. Resource allocation is covered in Chapter 9. For single projects, we discuss how the resource allocation problem concerns resource *leveling* to minimize the cost of the resources; but for multiple projects, we learn that the issue is how to allocate limited resources among several projects in order to achieve the objectives of each.

Chapter 10 examines the information requirements of a project and the need for monitoring critical activities. Included in this chapter is a description of some common Project Management Information Systems (PMIS). In general, it is not possible to manage adequately any but the smallest of projects without the use of a computerized PMIS. There are many such systems available and several are briefly discussed, but in this book all examples using PMIS will use *Microsoft Project Professional 2002*® (as well as *Excel*® and other software made to interact easily with *Microsoft*

Project® and *Excel*®), by far the most popular project management software. While Microsoft has been a driving force in the development of project management software, there is a wide variety of PMIS available. We must add that to use any project management software wisely, the user must understand the principles of project management. Concluding Part II, the implementation phase, Chapter 11 describes the control process in project management. This chapter covers standards for comparison and tools to aid the manager in maintaining control.

The final section of the book, Part III, concerns *project termination.* Chapter 12 deals with methods for both ongoing and terminal evaluations of a project, as well as identifying factors associated with project success and failure. Chapter 13 describes the different forms of project termination, such as outright shutdown, integration into the regular organization, or extension into a new project. Each of these forms presents unique problems for the PM to solve.

The subject of *risk management* and its component parts, *risk management planning, risk identification, risk assessment, risk quantification, risk response development,* and *risk monitoring and control* (Project Management Institute, 2001), is given extensive coverage throughout this book. We considered the addition of a chapter specifically devoted to the management of risk, but the fact that risk and uncertainty are inherent in all aspects of project life led us to incorporate discussions of risk management when they were relevant to the problem at hand.

Determination of the sources and nature of risks that might affect a project is risk identification and, in our opinion, should be the subject of an ongoing analysis carried out by the project council, the Project Management Office, and the project team itself. Risk identification, therefore, should be embedded as a part of any project and we deal with the subject in Chapter 4 when we discuss project organization.

Risk analysis, a term we use to cover both risk quantification and risk response planning, is devoted to estimating the specific impacts that various uncertainties may have on project outcomes. The techniques used to estimate and describe uncertain outcomes vary with the particular problem at hand. Determination of the impact of risks on the project selection process, for example, is significantly different from a study of the impact of risks on project budgets or schedules. Each will be considered in its appropriate place. The use of Decisioneering's Crystal Ball® 2000 (enclosed with this volume) will greatly simplify the mathematical difficulties often associated with risk analysis.

With this introduction, let us begin our study, a project in itself, and, we hope, an interesting and pleasant one.

■ SUMMARY

This chapter introduced the subject of project management and discussed its importance in our society. It defined what we mean by a "project," discussed the need for project management, and described the project life cycle. The final section explained the structure of this text and gave an overview of the material to be described in coming chapters.

The following specific points were made in the chapter.

- The Project Management Institute (PMI) was founded in 1969 to foster the growth and professionalism of project management.

- Project management is now being recognized as a valuable "career path" in many organizations, as well as a way to gain valuable experience within the organization.

- Project management, initiated by the military, provides managers with powerful planning and control tools.

- The three primary forces behind project management are (1) the growing demand for complex, customized goods and services; (2) the exponential expansion of human knowledge; and (3) the global production-consumption environment.

- The three prime objectives of project management are to meet specified performance within cost and on schedule.

- Our terminology follows in this order: program, project, task, work package, work unit.

- Projects are characterized by a singleness of purpose, a definite life cycle, complex interdependencies, some or all unique elements, and an environment of conflict.

- Project management, though not problem-free, is the best way to accomplish certain goals.

- Projects often start slowly, build up speed while using considerable resources, and then slow down as completion nears.

- This text is organized along the project life cycle concept, starting with project initiation in Chapters 2 to 6, where selection of the project and project manager occurs and project organization and planning begin. Project implementation, Chapters 7 to 11, is concerned with budgeting, scheduling, resource allocation, and activity monitoring and control. Project termination, concerning final evaluation and completion, is covered in Chapters 12 and 13.

GLOSSARY

Deliverables   The desired outcomes or results of a project.

Interdependencies   Relations between organizational functions where one function or task is dependent on others.

Life Cycle   A standard concept of a product or project wherein it goes through a start-up phase, a building phase, a maturing phase, and a termination phase.

Parties-at-Interest   Individuals or groups with a special interest in a project, usually the project team, client, senior management, and specific public interest groups.

Program   Often not distinguished from a project, but frequently meant to encompass a group of similar projects oriented toward a specific goal.

Project Management   The means, techniques, and concepts used to run a project and achieve its objectives.

Risk   The chance that outcomes will not turn out as planned.

Stakeholder   see "Parties-at-interest."

Suboptimize   Doing the best within a function or area but at a cost to the larger whole.

Task   A subset of work elements in a project.

Technology   The means for accomplishing difficult tasks.

Trade-off   Taking less on one measure, such as performance, in order to do better on another, such as schedule or cost.

Uncertainty   Having only partial information about the situation or outcomes.

Work Package   A subelement of a task that needs to be accomplished in order to achieve the objectives of the task.

QUESTIONS

Material Review Questions

1. Name and briefly describe the societal forces that have contributed to the need for project management.

2. Describe the life cycle of a project in terms of (1) the degree of project completion; (2) required effort.

3. Describe the limitations of project management.

4. List the five main characteristics of a project and briefly describe the important features of each.

5. Name and briefly describe the three primary goals of a project.

6. Discuss the advantages and disadvantages of project management.

7. How do projects, programs, tasks, and work packages differ?

8. How would you define a project?

9. What are some of the interdependencies related to a project?

10. What are some sources of conflict the project manager must deal with?

Class Discussion Questions

11. Give several examples of projects found in our society, avoiding those already discussed in the chapter.

12. Describe some situations in which project management would probably not be effective.

13. How does the rate-of-project-progress chart (Fig. 1-3) help a manager make decisions?

14. Expound on the adage, "Projects proceed smoothly until 90 percent complete, and then remain at 90 percent forever."

15. Discuss the duties and responsibilities of the project manager. How critical is the project manager to the success of the project?

16. Would you like to be a project manager? Why, or why not?

17. Discuss why there are trade-offs among the three prime objectives of project management.

18. Why is the life cycle curve often "S" shaped?

19. How might project management be used when doing a major schoolwork assignment?

20. Why is there such a pronounced bend in the curve of Figure 1-2?

Questions for Project Management in Practice

The Olympic Torch Relay Project

21. Is the torch relay another part of the Olympics themselves, perhaps a sub-project?

22. Given the geography of Australia, with most of the populace living on the edges of the continent and few in the interior, what path for the torch relay would make sense?

23. Is the life cycle for this project S-shaped or shaped like the right half of a U?

Demolishing San Francisco's Bridges Safely

24. What was the main consideration in this demolition project?

25. How would a demolition project differ from a more common construction project? Consider performance, schedule, and budget.

26. Would the life cycle for this project be S-shaped or the right half of a U shape? A freeway construction project?

INCIDENTS FOR DISCUSSION

T.T.S Candle Company

Ciera Miller, president of T.T.S. Candle Company, has just completed a two-day seminar on project management and is anxious to use the new techniques on a recurring problem faced by her company. About 60 percent of T.T.S.'s gross revenues result from the pre-Christmas sale of the firm's major product, XMAS-PAK. XMAS-PAK consists of twelve candles, all of one color and size. There are six different colors available in three different lengths. XMAS-PAK was introduced eight years ago, and sales have been increasing by approximately 20 percent per year.

Because of the seasonal nature of the product, all orders unfilled on December 16 are lost. Ms. Miller estimated that XMAS-PAK sales would have been about 10 percent higher last year were it not for lost orders. It was a frustrating problem because the loss was not due to a shortage of capacity. Sales forecasts were not very accurate, and her manufacturing managers had strict instructions to minimize investment in finished goods inventories. Miller was sure that project management could somehow help solve the problem without appreciably increasing inventories.

On her return from the seminar, she assigned Sam Joseph, marketing manager, and Garrett Knight, vice-president of manufacturing, as project managers for this problem. She reviewed the problem with them and gave them eight years of historical sales data, broken down by line item and geographical region. These were the data that she herself had used during her initial investigation. The project objective was to reduce lost sales to 0.5 percent within five years.

Question: Discuss Ms. Miller's approach to the problem and list the pros and cons.

Maladroit Cosmetics Company

The plant manager of the Maladroit Cosmetics Company must replace several of his filling machines that have become obsolete. He is about to take delivery of six machines at a total cost of $4 million. These machines must be installed and fully tested in time to be used on a new production line scheduled to begin operation in six months. Because this project is important, the plant manager would like to devote as much time as possible to the job, but he is currently handling several other projects. He thinks he has three basic choices: (1) he can handle the project informally out of his office; (2) he can assign the project to a member of his staff; or (3) the company that manufactures the machines can handle the installation project for a fee close to what the installation would cost Maladroit.

Questions: Which of the three choices do you recommend, and why? If the project was one small machine at a total cost of $4,000, would your answer be different? Discuss the relative importance of the capital investment required versus the role of the investment in machinery.

 BIBLIOGRAPHY

ARCHIBALD, R. D. *Managing High Technology Programs and Projects.* New York: Wiley, 1992.

BENNINGSON, L. A. "The Strategy of Running Temporary Projects." *Innovation,* September 1971.

CLELAND, D. I. *Project Management Handbook: Proceedings of the Third International Symposium.* New York: Van Nostrand Reinhold, 1988.

CLELAND, D. I. *Project Management Techniques Handbook—Advanced.* Centerville, VA: Management Control Institute, 1990.

DARNELL, R. "The Emerging Role of the Project Manager." *PM Network,* July 1997.

DAVIS, E. W. "CPM Use in Top 400 Construction Firms." *Journal of the Construction Division,* American Society of Civil Engineers, 1974.

DAVIS, E. W. *Project Management: Techniques, Applications, and Managerial Issues,* 2nd ed. Norcross, GA: AIIE Monograph, 1983.

DEAN, B. V. *Project Management: Methods and Studies.* New York: Elsevier, 1985.

GOODMAN, L. J. *Project Planning and Management: An Integrated System for Improving Productivity.* New York: Van Nostrand Reinhold, 1987.

GRAHAM, R. J. *Project Management: Combining Technical and Behavioral Approaches for Effective Implementation.* New York: Van Nostrand Reinhold, 1985.

GROD, M. C., ET AL. *Project Management in Progress.* New York: Elsevier, 1986.

HARRISON, F. L. *Advanced Project Management,* 2nd ed. Halstead Press, New York, 1985.

HOCKNEY, J. W., AND K. K. HUMPHREYS. *Control and Management of Capital Projects,* 2nd ed. New York: McGraw-Hill, 1991.

HUGHES, T. P. *Rescuing Prometheus.* New York, Pantheon, 1998.

IBBS, C. W., AND Y-H KWAK. "Measuring Project Management's Return on Investiment." *PM Network,* Nov. 1997.

KERZNER, H. *Project Management: A Systems Approach to Planning, Scheduling, and Controlling,* 6th ed. New York: Wiley, 1998.

LOCK, D. *Project Management,* 4th ed. Hants, England: Gower Publications, 1988.

LOCK, D., ed. *Project Management Handbook.* Hants, England: Gower Publications, 1987.

Project Management Institute. *A Guide to the Project Management Body of Knowledge.* Newtown Square, PA: Project Management Institute, 2001.

ROMAN, D. D. *Managing Projects: A Systems Approach.* New York: Elsevier, 1986.

ROSENAU, M. D., Jr. *Successful Project Management,* 2nd ed. New York: Van Nostrand Reinhold, 1991.

SHENHAR, A. J., O. LEVY, AND D. DVIR. "Mapping the Dimensions of Project Success." *Project Management Journal,* June 1997.

SILVERMAN, M. *Project Management: A Short Course for Professionals,* 2nd ed. New York: Wiley, 1988.

SPIRER, H. F. "The Basic Principles of Project Management." *Operations Management Review,* Fall 1982.

STEWART, J. M. "Making Project Management Work." *Business Horizons,* Fall 1965.

SUN, M. "Weighing the Social Costs of Innovation." *Science,* March 30, 1984.

 The following reading describes the common occurrence of someone suddenly being appointed a project manager and finding he or she has been inadequately trained for the task. Based on the authors' own experiences and interviews with dozens of senior project managers, they distill twelve guidelines for new project managers. The guidelines run the gamut from project initiation, through planning, to execution and close-out. Some are technical, some are uncommon sense, and many are philosophical, and sometimes political. But they are sage advice, not only for the novice but for the experienced project manager as well.

R E A D I N G

LESSONS FOR AN ACCIDENTAL PROFESSION

J. K. Pinto and O. P. Kharbanda: Lessons for an Accidental Profession.
Reprinted with permission from *Business Horizons,* March–April 1995.

Projects and project management are the wave of the future in global business. Increasingly technically complex products and processes, vastly shortened time-to-market windows, and the need for cross-functional expertise make project management an important and powerful tool in the hands of organizations that understand its use. But the expanded use of such techniques is not always being met by a concomitant increase in the pool of competent project managers. Unfortunately, and perhaps ironically, it is the very popularity of project management that presents many organizations with their most severe challenges. They often belatedly discover that they simply do not have sufficient numbers of the sorts of competent project managers who are often the key driving force behind successful product or service development. Senior managers in many companies readily acknowledge the ad hoc manner in which most project managers acquire their skills, but they are unsure how to better develop and provide for a supply of well-trained project leaders for the future.

In this article, we seek to offer a unique perspective on this neglected species. Though much has been written on how to improve the process of project management, less is known about the sorts of skills and challenges that specifically characterize project managers. What we do know tends to offer a portrait of successful project managers as strong leaders, possessing a variety of problem-solving, communication, motivational, visionary and team-building skills. Authors such as Posner (1987), Einsiedel (1987), and Petterson (1991) are correct. Project managers are a special breed. Managing projects is a unique challenge that requires a strategy and methodology all its own. Perhaps most important, it requires people willing to function as leaders in every sense of the term. They must not only chart the appropriate course, but provide the means, the support, and the confidence for their teams to attain these goals. Effective project managers often operate less as directive and autocratic decision makers than as facilitators, team members, and cheerleaders. In effect, the characteristics we look for in project managers are varied and difficult to pin down. Our goal is to offer some guidelines for an accidental profession, based on our own experiences and interviews with a number of senior project managers—most of whom had to learn their own lessons the hard way.

"Accidental" Project Managers.   Project managers occupy a unique and often precarious position within many firms. Possessing little formal authority and forced to operate outside the traditional organizational hierarchy, they quickly and often belatedly learn the real limits of their power. It has been said that an effective project manager is the kingpin, but not the king. They are the bosses, it is true, but often in a loosely de-

fined way. Indeed, in most firms they may lack the authority to conduct performance appraisals and offer incentives and rewards to their subordinates. As a result, their management styles must be those of persuasion and influence, rather than coercion and command.

Because of these and other limitations on the flexibility and power of project managers, project management has rightly been termed the "accidental profession" by more than one writer. There are two primary reasons for this sobriquet. First, few formal or systematic programs exist for selecting and training project managers, even within firms that specialize in project management work. This results at best in ad hoc training that may or may not teach these people the skills they need to succeed. Most project managers fall into their responsibilities by happenstance rather than by calculation. Second, as Frame (1987) cogently observed, few individuals grow up with the dream of one day becoming a project manager. It is neither a well-defined nor a well-understood career path within most modern organizations. Generally, the role is thrust upon people, rather than being sought.

Consider the typical experiences of project managers within many corporations. Novice managers, new to the company and its culture, are given a project to complete with the directive to operate within a set of narrowly defined constraints. These constraints most commonly include a specified time frame for completion, a budget, and a set of performance characteristics. Those who are able to quickly master the nature of their myriad duties succeed; those who do not generally fail. This "fly or die" mentality goes far toward creating an attitude of fear among potential project managers. Generation after generation of them learn their duties the hard way, often after having either failed completely or stumbled along from one crisis to another. The predictable result is wasteful: failed projects; managers battling entrenched bureaucracy and powerful factions; money, market opportunities, and other resources irretrievably lost to the company.

The amazing part of this scenario is that it is repeated again and again in company after company. Rather than treating project management as the unique and valuable discipline it is, necessitating formal training and selection policies, many companies continue to repeat their past mistakes. This almost leads one to believe they implicitly view experience and failure as the best teacher.

We need to shed light on the wide range of demands, opportunities, travails, challenges, and vexations that are part of becoming a better project manager. Many of the problems these individuals struggle with every day are far more managerial or behavioral in nature than technical. Such behavioral challenges are frequently vexing, and though they can sometimes seem inconsequential, they have a tremendous impact on the successful implementation of projects. For example, it does not take long for many project managers to discover exactly how far their personal power and status will take them in interacting with the rest of the organization. Hence, an understanding of influence tactics and political behavior is absolutely essential. Unfortunately, novice project managers are rarely clued into this important bit of information until it is too late—until, perhaps, they have appealed through formal channels for extra resources and been denied.

Consider the following examples:

- A long-distance telephone company whose CEO became so enamored of the concept of high-profile project teams—or "skunkworks," as they have come to be called—that he assigned that title to the few most highly visible, strategically important projects. Quickly, both senior and middle managers in departments across the organization came to realize that the only way to get their pet projects the resources necessary to succeed was to redesignate all new projects as "skunkworks." At last report, there were more than 75 high-profile skunkworks projects whose managers report directly to the CEO. The company now has severe difficulties in making research allocation decisions among its projects and routinely underfunds some vital projects while overfunding other, less important ones.

- A large computer hardware manufacturer has been dominated by the members of the hardware engineering department to such an extent that practically all new product ideas originate internally, within the department. By the time marketing personnel (sneeringly called "order takers" by the engineering department) are brought on board, they are presented with a fait accompli: a finished product they are instructed to sell. Marketing managers are now so cynical about new projects that they usually do not even bother sending a representative to new product development team meetings.

- A medium-sized manufacturing firm made it a policy to reward and punish project managers on the basis of their ability to bring projects in on time and under budget. These project managers were never held to any requirement that the project be accepted by its clients or become commercially successful. They quickly learned that their rewards were simply tied to satisfying the cost accountants, so they began to cut corners and make decisions that seriously undermined product quality.

- Projects in one division of a large, multinational corporation are routinely assigned to new managers who often have less than one year of experience with the company. Given a project scheduling software package and the telephone number of a senior project manger to be used "only in emergencies," they are instructed to form their project teams and begin the development process without any formal training or channels of communication to important clients and functional groups. Not surprisingly, senior managers at this company estimate that fewer than 30 percent of new product development efforts are profitable. Most take so long to develop, or incur such high cost overruns, that they are either abandoned before scheduled introduction or never live up to their potential in the marketplace.

This ad hoc approach to project management—coupled, as it frequently is, with an on-the-job training philosophy—is pervasive. It is also pernicious. Under the best of circumstances, project managers are called upon to lead, coordinate, plan, and control a diverse and complex set of processes and people in the pursuit of achieving project objectives. To hamper them with inadequate training and unrealistic expectations is to unnecessarily penalize them before they can begin to operate with any degree of confidence or effectiveness. The successful management of projects is simultaneously a human and technical challenge, requiring a far-sighted, strategic outlook coupled with the flexibility to react to conflicts and trouble areas as they arise on a daily basis. The project managers who are ultimately successful at their profession must learn to deal with and anticipate the constraints on their project team and personal freedom of action while consistently keeping their eyes on the ultimate prize.

From Whence Comes the Challenge?   One of the most intriguing and challenging aspects of project management lies in the relationship of project teams to the rest of the parent organization. With the exception of companies that are set up with matrix or project structures, most firms using project management techniques employ some form of standard functional structure. When project teams are added to an organization, the structural rules change dramatically. The vast majority of personnel who serve on project teams do so while maintaining links back to their functional departments. In fact, they typically split their time between the project and their functional duties.

The temporary nature of projects, combined with the very real limitations on power and discretion most project managers face, constitutes the core challenge of managing projects effectively. Clearly the very issues that characterize projects as distinct from functional work also illustrate the added complexity and difficulties they create for project managers. For example, within a functional department it is common to find people with more homogenous backgrounds. This means that the finance department is staffed with finance people, the marketing department is made up of marketers, and so on. On the other hand, most projects are constructed from special, cross-functional teams composed of representatives from each of the relevant functional departments, who bring their own attitudes, time frames, learning, past experiences, and biases to the team. Creating a cohesive and potent team out of this level of heterogeneity presents a challenge for even the most seasoned and skilled of project managers.

But what is the ultimate objective? What determines a successful project and how does it differ from projects we may rightfully consider to have failed? Any seasoned project manager will usually tell you that a successful project is one that has come in on time, has remained under budget, and performs as expected (that is, it conforms to specifications). Recently, though, there has been a reassessment of this traditional model for project success. The old triple constraint is rapidly being replaced by a new model, invoking a fourth hurdle for project success: client satisfaction. This means that a project is only successful if it satisfies the needs of its intended user. As a result, client satisfaction places a new and important constraint on project managers. No wonder, then, that there is a growing interest in the project manager's role within the corporation.

1. **Understand** the context of project management.
2. **Recognize** project team conflict as progress.
3. **Understand** who the stakeholders are and what they want.
4. **Accept** and use the political nature of organizations.
5. **Lead** from the front.
6. **Understand** what "success" means.
7. **Build** and maintain a cohesive team.
8. **Enthusiasm** and despair are both infectious.
9. **One look** forward is worth two looks back.
10. **Remember** what you are trying to do.
11. **Use time** carefully or it will use you.
12. **Above all,** plan, plan, plan.

Figure 1   Twelve points to remember.

The Vital Dozen For Project Managers

Over the last several years, we have conducted interviews with dozens of senior project managers in which we asked them a simple question: "What information were you never given as a novice project manager that, in retrospect, could have made your job easier?" From the data gathered in these interviews, we have synthesized some of the more salient issues, outlined in Figure 1 and detailed below, that managers need to keep in mind when undertaking a project implementation effort. While not intended to appear in any particular order, these 12 rules offer a useful way to understand the challenge project managers face and some ways to address these concerns.

1. Understand the context of project management.

Much of the difficulty in becoming an effective project manager lies in understanding the particular challenges project management presents in most coporations. Projects are a unique form of organizational work, playing an important role within many public and private organizations today. They act as mechanisms for the effective introduction of new products and services. They offer a level of intraorganizational efficiency that all companies seek but few find. But they also force managers to operate in a temporary environment outside the traditional functional lines of authority, relying upon influence and other informal methods of power. In essence, it is not simply the management of a project per se that presents such a unique challenge; it is also the atmosphere within which the manager operates that adds an extra dimension of difficulty. Projects exist outside the established hierarchy. They threaten, rather than support, the status quo because they represent change. So it is important for project managers to walk into their assigned role with their eyes wide open to the monumental nature of the tasks they are likely to face.

2. Recognize project team conflict as progress.

One of the common responses of project managers to team conflict is panic. This reaction is understandable in that project managers perceive—usually correctly—that their reputation and careers are on the line if the project fails. Consequently, any evidence they interpret as damaging to the prospects of project success, such as team conflict, represents a very real source of anxiety. In reality, however, these interpersonal tensions are a natural result of putting individuals from diverse backgrounds together and requiring them to coordinate their activities. Conflict, as evidenced by the stages of group development is more often a sign of healthy maturation in the group.

The result of differentiation among functional departments demonstrates that conflict under these circumstances is not only possible but unavoidable. One of the worst mistakes a project manager can make when conflicts emerge is to immediately force them below the surface without first analyzing the nature of the conflict. Although many interpersonal conflicts are based on personality differences, others are of a professional nature and should be addressed head-on.

Once a project manager has analyzed the nature of the conflict among team members, a variety of conflict handling approaches may be warranted, including avoidance, defusion, or problem-solving. On the other hand, whatever approach is selected should not be the result of a knee-jerk reaction to suppress conflict. In our experience, we have found many examples that show that even though a conflict is pushed below the surface, it will continue to fester if left unaddressed. The resulting eruption, which will inevitably occur later in the project development cycle, will have a far stronger effect than would the original conflict if it had been handled initially.

3. Understand who the stakeholders are and what they want.

Project management is a balancing act. It requires managers to juggle the various and often conflicting demands of a numbers of powerful project stakeholders. One of the best tools a project manager can use is to develop a realistic assessment early in the project identifying the principal stakeholders and their agendas. In some projects, particularly those with important external clients or constituent groups, the number of stakeholders may be quite large, particularly when "intervenor" groups are included. Intervenors, according to Cleland (1983), may included any external group that can drastically affect the potential for project success, such as environmental activists in a nuclear plant construction project. Project managers who acknowledge the impact of stakeholders and work to minimize their effect by fostering good relations with them are often more successful than those who operate in a reactive mode, continually surprised by unexpected demands from groups that were not initially considered.

As a final point about stakeholders, it is important for a project manager's morale to remember that it is essentially impossible to please all the stakeholders all the time. The conflicting nature of their demands suggests that when one group is happy, another is probably upset. Project managers need to forget the idea of maximizing everyone's happiness and concentrate instead on maintaining satisfactory relations that allow them to do their job with a minimum of external interference.

4. Accept the political nature of organizations and use it to your advantage.

Like it or not, we exist in a politicized world. Unfortunately, our corporations are no different. Important decisions involving resources are made through bargaining and deal-making. So project managers who wish to succeed must learn to use the political system to their advantage. This involves becoming adept at negotiation as well as using influence tactics to further the goals of the project.

At the same time, it is importat to remember that any project representing possible organizational change is threatening, often because of its potential to reshuffle the power relationships among the key units and actors. Playing the political system acknowledges this reality. Successful project managers are those who can use their personal reputations, power, and influence to ensure cordial relations with important stakeholders and secure the resources necessary to smooth the client's adoption of the project.

Pursuing a middle ground of political sensibility is the key to project implementation success. There are two alternative and equally inappropriate approaches to navigating a firm's political waters: becoming overly political and predatory—we call these people "sharks"—and refusing to engage in politics to any degree—the politically "naive." Political sharks and the politically naive are at equal disadvantage in managing their projects: sharks because they pursue predatory and self-interested tactics that arouse distrust, and the naive because they insist on remaining above the fray, even at the cost of failing to attain and keep necessary resources for their projects.

Figure 2 illustrates some of the philosophical differences among the three types of political actors. The process of developing and applying appropriate political tactics means using politics as it can most effectively be used: as a basis for negotiation and bargaining. "Politically sensible" implies being politically sensitive to the concerns (real or imagined) of powerful stakeholder groups. Legitimate or not, their concerns over a new project are real and must be addressed. Politically sensible managers understand that initiating any sort of organizational disruption or change by developing a new project is bound to reshuffle the distribution of power within the firm. That effect is likely to make many departments and managers very nervous as they begin to wonder how the future power relationships will be rearranged.

Appropriate political tactics and behavior include making alliances with powerful members of other stakeholder departments, networking, negotiating mutually acceptable solutions to seemingly insoluble problems, and recognizing that most organizational activities are predicated on the give-and-take of negotiation and compromise. It is through these uses of political behavior that managers of project implementation efforts put themselves in the position to most effectively influence the successful introduction of their systems.

5. Lead from the front; the view is better.

One message that comes through loud and clear is that project management is a "leader intensive" undertaking. Strong, effective leaders can go a long way toward helping a project succeed even in the face of a number of external or unforeseen problems. Conversely, a poor, inflexible leader can often ruin the chances of many important projects ever succeeding. Leaders are the focal point of their projects. They serve as a rallying point for the team and are usually the major source of information and communication for external stakeholders. Because their role is so central and so vital, it is important to recognize and cultivate the attributes project "leaders" must work to develop.

The essence of leadership lies in our ability to use it flexibly. This means that not all subordinates or situations merit the same response. Under some circumstances an autocratic approach is appropriate; other situations will be far better served by adopting a consensual style. Effective project leaders seem to understand this idea intuitively. Their approach must be

Characteristics	Naive	Sensible	Sharks
Underlying Attitude	Politics is unpleasant	Politics is necessary	Politics is an opportunity
Intent	Avoid at all costs	Further departmental goals	Self-serving and predatory
Techniques	Tell it like it is	Network; expand connections; use system to give and receive favors	Manipulate; use fraud and deceit when necessary
Favorite Tactics	None—the truth will win out	Negotiate, bargain	Bully; misuse information; cultivate and use "friends" and other contacts

Figure 2   Characteristics of political behaviors.

tailored to the situation; it is self-defeating to attempt to tailor the situation to a preferred approach. The worst leaders are those who are unaware of or indifferent to the freedom they have to vary their leadership styles. And they see any situation in which they must involve subordinates as inherently threatening to their authority. As a result, they usually operate under what is called the "Mushroom" Principle of Management." That is, they treat their subordinates the same way the would raise a crop of mushrooms—by keeping them in the dark and feeding them a steady diet of manure.

Flexible leadership behavior consists of a realistic assessment of personal strengths and weaknesses. It goes without saying that no one person, including the project manager, possesses all necessary information, knowledge, or expertise to perform the project tasks on his own. Rather, successful project managers usually acknowledge their limitations and work through subordinates' strengths. In serving as a facilitator, one of the essential abilities of an exceptional project manager is knowing where to go to seek the right help and how to ask the right questions. Obviously, the act of effective questioning is easier said than done. However, bear in mind that questioning is not interrogation. Good questions challenge subordinates without putting them on the spot; they encourage definite answers rather than vague responses, and they discourage guessing. The leader's job is to probe, to require subordinates to consider all angles and options, and to support them in making reasoned decisions. Direct involvement is a key component of a leader's ability to perform these tasks.

6. Understand what "success" means.

Successful project implementation is no longer subject to the traditional "triple constraint." That is, the days when projects were evaluated solely on adherence to budget, schedule, and performance criteria are past. In modern business, with its increased emphasis on customer satisfaction, we have to retrain project managers to expand their criteria for project success to include a fourth item: client use and satisfaction. What this suggests is that project "success" is a far more comprehensive word than some managers may have initially thought. The implication for rewards is also important. Within some organizations that regularly implement projects, it is common practice to reward the implementation manager when, in reality, only half the job

has been accomplished. In other words, giving managers promotions and commendations before the project has been successfully transferred to clients, is being used, and is affecting organizational effectiveness is seriously jumping the gun.

Any project is only as good as it is used. In the final analysis, nothing else matters if a system is not productively employed. Consequently, every effort must be bent toward ensuring that the system fits in with client needs, that their concerns and opinions are solicited and listened to, and that they have final sign-off approval on the transferred project. In other words, the intended user of the project is the major determinant of its success. Traditionally, the bulk of the team's efforts are centered internally, mainly on their own concerns: budgets, timetables, and so forth. Certainly, these aspects of the project implementation process are necessary, but they should not be confused with the ultimate determinant of success: the client.

7. Build and maintain a cohesive team.

Many projects are implemented through the use of cross-functional teams. Developing and maintaining cordial team relations and fostering a healthy intergroup atmosphere often seems like a full-time job for most project managers. However, the resultant payoff from a cohesive project team cannot be overestimated. When a team is charged to work toward project development and implementation, the healthier the atmosphere within that team, the greater the likelihood the team will perform effectively. The project manager's job is to do whatever is necessary to build and maintain the health (cohesion) of the team. Sometimes that support can be accomplished by periodically checking with team members to determine their attitudes and satisfaction with the process. Other times the project manager may have to resort to less conventional methods, such as throwing parties or organizing field trips. To effectively intervene and support a team, project managers play a variety of roles—motivator, coach, cheerleader, peacemaker, conflict resolver. All these duties are appropriate for creating and maintaining an effective team.

8. Enthusiasm and despair are both infectious.

One of the more interesting aspects of project leaders is that they often function like miniaturized billboards, projecting an image and attitude that signals the current status of the project and its likelihood for success. The team takes its cue from the attitudes and emotions the manager exhibits. So one of the most important roles of the leader is that of motivator and encourager. The worst project managers are those who play their cards close to their chests, revealing little or nothing about the status of the project (again, the "Mushroom Manager"). Team members want and deserve to be kept abreast of what is happening. It is important to remember that the success or failure of the project affects the team as well as the manager. Rather than allowing the rumor mill to churn our disinformation, team leaders need to function as honest sources of information. When team members come to the project manager for advice or project updates, it is important to be honest. If the manager does not know the answer to the questions, he should tell them that. Truth in all forms is recognizable, and most project team members are much more appreciative of honesty than of eyewash.

9. One look forward is worth two looks back.

A recent series of commercials from a large computer manufacturer had as their slogan the dictum that the company never stop asking "What if?." Asking "What if?" questions is another way of saying we should never become comfortable with the status of the project under development. One large-scale study found that the leading determinant of project failure was the absence of any troubleshooting mechanisms—that is, no one was asking the "What if?" questions. Projecting a skeptical eye toward the future may seem gloomy to some managers. But in our opinion, it makes good sense. We cannot control the future but we can actively control our response to it.

A good example of the failure to apply this philosophy is evidenced by the progress of the "Chunnel" intended to link Great Britain with France. Although now in full operation, it was not ready for substantial traffic until some 15 months later than originally scheduled. As a result, chunnel traffic missed the major summer vacation season with a concomitant loss in revenue. At the same time, the final cost (£15 billion) is likely to be six times the original estimate of £2.3 billion (O'Connor 1993). It is instructive to take note of a recent statement by one of the project's somewhat harassed directors who, when pressed to state when the Chunnel

would be ready, replied, "Now it will be ready when it's ready and not before!" Clearly, the failure to apply adequate contingency planning has led to the predictable result: a belief that the project will simply end when it ends.

10 Remember what you are trying to do.

Do not lose sight of the purpose behind the project. Sometimes it is easy to get bogged down in the minutiae of the development process, fighting fires on a daily basis and dealing with thousands of immediate concerns. The danger is that in doing so, project managers may fail to maintain a view of what the end product is supposed to be. This point reemphasizes the need to keep the mission in the forefront—and not just the project manager, but the team as well. The goal of the implementation serves as a large banner the leader can wave as needed to keep attitudes and motives focused in the right direction. Sometimes a superordinate goal can serve as a rallying point. Whatever technique project managers use, it is important that they understand the importance of keeping the mission in focus for all team members. A simple way to discover whether team members understand the project is to intermittently ask for their assessment of its status. They should know how their contributions fit into the overall installation plan. Are they aware of the specific contributions of other team members? If no, more attention needs to be paid to reestablishing a community sense of mission.

11. Use time carefully or it will use you.

Time is a precious commodity. Yet when we talk to project managers, it seems that no matter how hard they work to budget it, they never have enough. They need to make a realistic assessment of the "time killers" in their daily schedule: How are they spending their time and what are they doing profitably or unprofitably? We have found that the simple practice of keeping a daily time log for a short time can be an eye-opening experience. Many project managers discover that they spend far too much of their time in unproductive ways: project team meetings without agendas that grind on and on, unexpected telephone calls in the middle of planning sessions, quick "chats" with other managers that end up taking hours, and so forth. Efficient time management—one of the keys to successful project development—starts with project managers. When they actively plan their days and stick to a time budget, they usually find they are operating efficiently. On the other hand, when they take each problem as it comes and function in an ad hoc, reactive mode, they are likely to remain prisoners of their own schedules.

A sure recipe for finding the time and resources needed to get everything done without spending an inordinate amount of time on the job or construction site is provided by Gosselin (1993). The author lists six practical suggestions to help project managers control their tasks and projects without feelings constantly behind schedule:

- Create a realistic time estimate without overextending yourself.
- Be absolutely clear about what the boss or client requires.
- Provide for contingencies (schedule slippage, loss of key team member).
- Revise original time estimate and provide a set of options as required.
- Be clear about factors that are fixed (specifications, resources, and so on).
- Learn to say "Yes, and . . ." rather than "No, but. . . ." Negotiation is the key.

12. Above all, plan, plan, plan.

The essence of efficient project management is to take the time to get it as right as possible the first time. "It" includes the schedule, the team composition, the project specifications, and the budget. There is a truism that those who fail to plan are planning to fail. One of the practical difficulties with planning is that so many of us distinguish it from other aspects of the project development, such as doing the work. Top managers are often particularly guilty of this offense as they wait impatiently for the project manager to begin doing the work.

Of course, too much planning is guaranteed to elicit repeated and pointed questions from top management and other stakeholders as they seek to discover the reason why "nothing is being done." Experienced project managers, though, know that it is vital not to rush this stage by reacting too quickly to top management inquiries. The planning stage must be managed carefully to allow the project manager and team the time necessary to formulate appropriate and workable plans that will form the basis for the development process. Dividing up the tasks and starting the "work" of the project too quickly is often ultimately wasteful. Steps that were poorly done are often steps that must be redone.

A complete and full investigation of any proposed project does take significant time and effort. However, bear in mind that overly elaborate or intricate planning can be detrimental to a project; by the time an opportunity is fully investigated, it may no longer exist. Time and again we have emphasized the importance of planning, but is also apparent that there comes a limit, both to the extent and the time frame of the planning cycle. A survey among entrepreneurs, for example, revealed that only 28 percent of them drew up a full-scale plan (Sweet 1994). A lesson here for project managers is that, like entrepreneurs, they must plan, but they must also be smart enough to recognize mistakes and change their strategy accordingly. As is noted in an old military slogan, "No plan ever survives its first contact with the enemy."

Project Managers in the Twenty-First Century

In our research and consulting experiences, we constantly interact with project managers, some with many years of experience, who express their frustration with their organizations because of the lack of detailed explication of their assigned tasks and responsibilities. Year after year, manager after manager, companies continue to make the same mistakes in "training" their project managers, usually through an almost ritualized baptism of fire. Project managers deserve better. According to Rodney Turner (1993), editor of the *International Journal of Project Management*:

> Through the 90's and into the 21st century, project-based management will sweep aside traditional functional line management and (almost) all organizations will adopt flat, flexible organizational structures in place of the old bureaucratic hierarchies. . . . [N]ew organizational structures are replacing the old. . . . [M]anagers will use project-based management as a vehicle for introducing strategic planning and for winning and maintaining competitive advantage.

Turner presents quite a rosy future, one that is predicated on organizations recognizing the changes they are currently undergoing and are likely to continue to see in the years ahead. In this challenging environment, project management is emerging as a technique that can provide the competitive edge necessary to succeed, given the right manager.

At the same time, there seems to have been a sea change in recent years regarding the image of project managers. The old view of the project manager as essentially that of a decision maker, expert, boss, and director seems to be giving way to a newer ideal: that of a leader, coach, and facilitator. Lest the reader assume these duties are any easier, we would assert that anyone who has attempted to perform these roles knows from personal experience just how difficult they can be. As part of this metamorphosis, says Clarke (1993), the new breed of project manager must be a natural salesperson who can establish harmonious customer (client) relations and develop trusting relationships with stakeholders. In addition to some of the obvious keys to project managers' success—personal commitment, energy, and enthusiasm—it appears that, most of all, successful project managers must manifest an obvious desire to see others succeed.

For successful project managers, there will always be a dynamic tension between the twin demands of technical training and an understanding of human resource needs. It must be clearly understood, however, that in assessing the relative importance of each challenge, the focus must clearly be on managing the human side of the process. As research and practice consistently demonstrate, project management is primarily a challenge in managing people. This point was recently brought to light in an excellent review of a book on managing the "human side" of projects (Horner 1993):

> There must be many project managers like me who come from a technological background, and who suffered an education which left them singularly ill-prepared to manage people.

Leading researchers and scholars perceive the twenty-first century as the upcoming age of project management. The globablization of markets, the merging of many European economies, the enhanced expenditures of money on capital improvement both in the United States and abroad, the rapidly opening borders of Eastern European and Pacific Rim countries, with their goals of rapid infrastructure expansion—all of this offers an eloquent argument for the enhanced popularity of project management as a technique for improving the efficiency and effectiveness of organizational operations. With so much at stake, it is vital that we immediately begin to address some of the deficiencies in our project management theory and practice.

Project management techniques are well known. But until we are able to take further steps toward formalizing training by teaching the necessary skill set, the problems with efficiently developing, implementing, and gaining client acceptance for these projects are likely to continue growing. There is currently a true window of opportunity in the field of project management. Too often in the past, project managers have been forced to learn their skills the hard way, through practical experience coupled with all the problems of trial and error. Certainly, experience is a valuable component of learning to become an effective project manager, but it is by no means the best.

What conclusions are to be drawn here? If nothing else, it is certain that we have painted a portrait of project management as a complex, time-consuming, often exasperating process. At the same time, it is equally clear that successful project managers are a breed apart. to answer the various calls they continually receive, balance the conflicting demands of a diverse set of stakeholders, navigate tricky corporate political waters, understand the fundamental process of subordinate motivation, develop and constantly refine their leadership skills, and engage in the thousands of pieces of detailed minutiae while keeping their eyes fixed firmly on project goals requires individuals with special skills and personalities. Given the nature of their duties, is it any wonder successful project managers are in such short supply and, once identified, so valued by their organizations?

There is good news, however. Many of these skills, though difficult to master, can be learned. Project management is a challenge, not a mystery. Indeed, it is our special purpose to demystify much of the human side of project management, starting with the role played by the linchpin in the process: the project manager. The problem in the past has been too few sources for either seasoned or novice project managers to turn to in attempting to better understand the nature of their unique challenge and methods for performing more effectively. Too many organizations pay far too little attention to the process of selecting, training, and encouraging those people charged to run project teams. The predictable result is to continually compound the mistake of creating wave after wave of accidental project managers, forcing them to learn through trial and error with minimal guidance in how to perform their roles.

Managing project is a challenge that requires a strategy and methodology all its own. Perhaps most important, it requires a project manager willing to function as a leader in every sense of the term. We have addressed a wide range of challenges, both contextual and personal, that form the basis under which projects are managed in today's organizations. It is hoped that readers will find something of themselves as well as something of use contained in these pages.

References

B. N. BAKER, P. C. MURPHY, and D. FISHER, "Factors Affecting Project Success," in D. I. Cleland and W. R. King, eds., *Project Management Handbook* (New York: Van Nostrand Reinhold, 1983): 778–801.

K. CLARKE, "Survival Skills for a New Breed," *Management Today,* December 1993, p. 5.

D. I. CLELAND, "Project Stakeholder Management," in D. I. Cleland and W. R. King, eds., *Project Management Handbook* (New York:Van Nostrand Reinhold, 1983): 275–301.

J. C. DAVIS, "The Accidental Profession," *Project Management Journal, 15,* 3 (1984): 6.

A. A. EINSIEDEL, "Profile of Effective Project Managers," *Project Management Journal, 18,* 5 (1987): 51–56.

J. DAVIDSON FRAME, *Managing Projects in Organizations* (San Francisco: Jossey-Bass, 1987).

T. GOSSELIN, "What to Do with Last-Minute Jobs," *World Executive Digest,* December 1993, p. 70.

R. J. GRAHAM, "A Survival Guide for the Accidental Project Manager," *Proceedings of the Annual Project Management Institute Symposium* (Drexel Hill, PA: Project Management Institue, 1992), pp. 355–361.

M. HORNER, "Review of 'Managing People for Project Success,'" *International Journal of Project Management, 11* (1993): 125–126.

P. R. LAWRENCE and J. W. LORSCH, "Differentiation and Integration in Complex Organizations," *Administrative Science Quarterly, 11,* (1967):1–47.

M. NICHOLS, "Does New Age Business Have a Message for Managers?" *Harvard Business Review,* March–April 1994, pp. 52–60.

L. O'CONNOR, "Tunnelling Under the Channel," *Mechanical Engineering,* December 1993, pp. 60–66.

N. PETTERSEN, "What Do We Know About the Effective Project Manager?" *International Journal of Project Management, 9* (1991): 99–104.

J. K. PINTO and O. P. KHARBANDA, *Successful Project Managers: Leading Your Team to Success* (New York: Van Nostrand Reinhold, 1995).

J. K. PINTO and D. P. SLEVIN, "Critical Factors in Successful Project Implementation," *IEEE Transactions on Engineering Management,* EM-34, 1987, pp. 22–27.

B. Z. POSNER, "What it Takes to be a Good Project Manager," *Project Management Journal, 18,* 1 (1987): 51–54.

W. A. RANDOLPH and B. Z. POSNER, "What Every Manager Needs to Know about Project Management," *Sloan Management Review, 29,* 4 (1988): 65–73.

P. SWEET, "A Planner's Best Friend," *Accountancy, 113* (1994): 56–58.

H. J. THAMHAIN, "Developing Project Management Skills, " *Project Management Journal, 22,* 3 (1991): 39–53.

R. TURNER, "Editorial," *International Journal of Project Management, 11* (1993): 195.

Questions

1. What are the reasons the author advances for project management to be considered an "accidental profession?" The twelve guidelines are presented in no particular order. Order them by level of importance and explain your reasoning.

2. Where would you place yourself in Figure 2?

3. A few of the guidelines are related to the need to understand the reason for the project in the first place. Which guidelines would you place in this category? Why is this so crucial?

4. Why, in lesson 9, is always thinking about "what if" so important?

5. Lesson 12 warns about not planning enough, but also about spending too much time planning. How do you draw the line?

2

Strategic Management and Project Selection

More and more, the accomplishment of important tasks and goals in organizations today is being achieved through the use of projects. The phrases we hear and read about daily at our work and in conversations with our colleagues, such as "management by projects" and "project management maturity," reflect this increasing trend in our society. The almost explosively rapid adoption of such a powerful tool as project management to help organizations achieve their goals and objectives is certainly awesome. As noted by one set of scholars (Clelland and King, 1983, p. 155), however, it is also undoubtedly true with the rapid adoption of this new managerial approach that:

- there are many projects that fall outside the organization's stated mission;
- there are many projects being conducted that are completely unrelated to the strategy and goals of the organization; and
- there are many projects with funding levels that are excessive relative to their expected benefits.

In addition to the growth in the number of organizations adopting project management, there is also an accelerating growth in the number of multiple, simultaneously ongoing, and often interrelated projects in organizations—particularly construction, consulting, auditing, systems development, maintenance, and matrixed organizations. Thus, the issue naturally arises as to how one manages all these projects. Are they all really projects? (It has been suggested that perhaps up to 80 percent of all "projects" are not actually projects at all, since they do not include the three project requirements for objectives, budget, and due date.) Should we be undertaking all of them? Of those we should implement, what should be their priorities?

It is not unusual these days for organizations to be wrestling with hundreds of new projects. With so many ongoing projects it becomes difficult for smaller projects to get adequate support, or even the attention of senior management. Three particularly common problems in organizations trying to manage multiple projects are:

1. Delays in one project delay other projects because of common resource needs or technological dependencies.
2. The inefficient use of corporate resources results in peaks and valleys of resource utilization.
3. Bottlenecks in resource availability or lack of required technological inputs result in project delays that depend on those scarce resources or technology.

As might be expected, the report card on organizational success with management by projects is not stellar. For example, one research study (Thomas, Delisle, Jugdev, and Buckle, 2001) has found that 30 percent of all projects are canceled midstream, and over half of completed projects came in up to 190 percent over budget and 220 percent late. This same study found that the primary motivation of organizations to improve and expand their project management processes was due to major troubled or failed projects, new upcoming mega-projects, or to meet competition or maintain their market share. Those firms that "bought" project management skills from consultants tended to see it as a "commodity." These firms also commonly relied on outsourcing difficult activities, or even entire projects. Those who developed the skills internally, however, saw project management as offering a proprietary competitive advantage. The latter firms also moved toward recognizing project management as a viable career path in their organization, leading to senior management positions.

A major recent development among those choosing to develop project management expertise in house, particularly those interested in using projects to accomplish organizational goals and strategies, is the initiation of a Project Management Office (PMO), described in detail in Chapter 4. This office strives to develop multi-project management expertise throughout the organization and evaluate the interrelationships both between projects (e.g., such as resource and skill requirements) and between projects and the organization's goals. It is expected that the PMO will promote those projects that capitalize on the organization's strengths, offer a competitive advantage, and mutually support each other, while avoiding those with resource or technology needs in areas where the organization is weaker.

The challenges thus facing the contemporary organization are how to tie their projects more closely to the organization's goals and strategy, how to handle the growing number of ongoing projects, and how to make these projects more successful. The latter two of these objectives concern "project management maturity"—the development of project and multi-project management expertise. Following a discussion of project management maturity, we launch into a major aspect of multi-project management: selecting projects for implementation and handling the uncertainty, or risk, involved.

Given that the organization has an appropriate mission statement and strategy, projects must be selected that are consistent with the strategic goals of the organization. *Project selection* is the process of evaluating individual projects or groups of projects and then choosing to implement some set of them so that the objectives of the parent organization will be achieved. Because one's initial notions of precisely how most projects will be carried out, what resources will be required, and how long it will take to complete the project are uncertain, we will introduce risk analysis into the selection process. Following this, we illustrate the process of strategically selecting the best set of projects, called the Project Portfolio Process, for implementation. Last, the chapter closes with a short discussion of *project proposals.*

Before proceeding, a final comment is pertinent. It is not common to discuss project selection, the construction of a project portfolio, and similar matters in any detail in elementary texts on project management. The project manager typically has little or no say in the project funding decision, nor is he or she usually asked for input concerning the development of organizational strategy. Why then discuss these matters? The answer is simple, yet persuasive. The project manager who does not understand what a given project is expected to contribute to the parent organization lacks the critical information needed to manage the project in order to maximize that contribution.

2.1 PROJECT MANAGEMENT MATURITY

As organizations have employed more and more projects for accomplishing their objectives (often referred to as "managing organizations by projects"), it has become natural for senior managers—as well as scholars—to wonder if the organization's project managers have a mastery of the skills required to manage projects competently. In the last few years, a number of different ways to measure this—referred to as "project management maturity" (Fincher and Levin, 1997)—have been suggested, such as basing the evaluation on PMI's *PMBOK Guide* (Lubianiker, 2000; see also *www.pmi .org/opm3/*) or the ISO 9001 standards (contact the American Society for Quality).

A number of consulting firms, as well as scholars, have devised formal maturity measures, many of which are based on Carnegie Mellon University's "Capability Maturity Model" for software development (*www.sei.cmu.edu/cmm/se-cmm.html*). One of these measures, named PM$^{3®}$, was described by R. Remy (1997). In this system, the final project management "maturity" of an organization is assessed as being at one of five levels: ad-hoc (disorganized, accidental successes and failures); abbreviated (some processes exist, inconsistent management, unpredictable results); organized (standardized processes, more predictable results); managed (controlled and measured processes, results more in line with plans); and adaptive (continuous improvement in processes, success is normal, performance keeps improving).

Since then, another maturity model, also based on Carnegie-Mellon's capability maturity model, has been devised and applied to 38 organizations in four different industries (Ibbs and Kwak, 2000). This model consists of 148 questions divided into six processes/life-cycle phases (initiating, planning, executing, controlling, closing, and project-driven organization environment), and eight PMBOK knowledge areas (scope, time, cost, quality, human resources, communication, risk, and procurement). The model assesses an organization's project management maturity in terms of essentially the same five stages as just described but called: ad-hoc, planned, managed, integrated, and sustained.

Regardless of model form, it appears that most organizations do not score very well in terms of maturity. On one form, about three-quarters are no higher than level 2 (planned) and fewer than 6 percent are above level 3 (managed). On another scale, the average of the 38 organizations was only slightly over 3, though individual firms ranged between 1.8 and 4.6 on the five-point scale.

Next we detail the project selection process, discussing the various types of selection models commonly used, the database needed for selection, and the management of risk.

Project Management in Practice
Implementing Strategy through Projects at Blue Cross/Blue Shield

Since strategic plans are usually developed at the executive level, implementation by middle level managers is often a problem due to poor understanding of the organization's capabilities and top management's expectations. However, bottom-up development of departmental goals and future plans invariably lacks the vision of the overall market and competitive environment. At Blue Cross/Blue Shield (BC/BS) of Louisiana, this problem was avoided by closely tying project management tools to the organizational strategy. The resulting system provided a set of checks and balances for both BC/BS executives and project managers.

Overseeing the system is a newly created Corporate Project Administration Group (CPAG) that helps senior management translate their strategic goals and objectives into project management performance, budget, and schedule targets. These may include new product development, upgrading information systems, or implementing facility automation systems. CPAG also works with the project teams to develop their plans, monitoring activities, and reports so they dovetail with the strategic intentions.

The primary benefits of the system have been that it allows:

- senior management to select any corporate initiative and determine its status;
- PMs to report progress in a relevant, systematic, timely manner;
- all officers, directors, and managers to view the corporate initiatives in terms of the overall strategic plan; and
- senior management to plan, track, and adjust strategy through use of financial project data captured by the system.

Source: P. Diab, "Strategic Planning + Project Management = Competitive Advantage," *PM Network,* July 1998, pp. 25–28.

2.2 PROJECT SELECTION AND CRITERIA OF CHOICE

Project selection is the process of evaluating individual projects or groups of projects, and then choosing to implement some set of them so that the objectives of the parent organization will be achieved. This same systematic process can be applied to any area of the organization's business in which choices must be made between competing alternatives. For example, a manufacturing firm can use evaluation/selection techniques to choose which machine to adopt in a part-fabrication process; a TV station can select which of several syndicated comedy shows to rerun in its 7:30 P.M. weekday time-slot; a construction firm can select the best subset of a large group of potential projects on which to bid; or a hospital can find the best mix of psychiatric, orthopedic, obstetric, and other beds for a new wing. Each project will have different costs, benefits, and risks. Rarely are these known with certainty. In the face of such differences, the selection of one project out of a set is a difficult task. Choosing a number of different projects, a *portfolio,* is even more complex.

In the following sections, we discuss several techniques that can be used to help senior managers select projects. Project selection is only one of many decisions associated with project management. To deal with all of these problems, we use *decision-aiding models.* We need such models because they abstract the relevant issues about a problem from the plethora of detail in which the problem is embedded. Realists cannot solve problems, only idealists can do that. Reality is far too complex to deal with in its entirety. An "idealist" is needed to strip away almost all the reality from a problem, leaving only the aspects of the "real" situation with which he or she wishes to deal. This process of carving away the unwanted reality from the bones of a problem is called *modeling the problem.* The idealized version of the problem that results is called a *model.*

The model represents the problem's *structure,* its form. Every problem has a form, though often we may not understand a problem well enough to describe its structure. We will use many models in this book—graphs, analogies, diagrams, as well as *flow graph* and *network* models to help solve scheduling problems, and *symbolic* (mathematical) models for a number of purposes.

Models may be quite simple to understand, or they may be extremely complex. In general, introducing more reality into a model tends to make the model more difficult to manipulate. If the input data for a model are not known precisely, we often use probabilistic information; that is, the model is said to be *stochastic* rather than *deterministic.* Again, in general, stochastic models are more difficult to manipulate. [Readers who are not familiar with the fundamentals of decision making might find a book such as *The New Science of Management Decisions* (Simon, 1977) or *Quantitative Business Modeling* (Meredith, Shafer, and Turban, 2002) useful.]

We live in the midst of what has been called the "knowledge explosion." We frequently hear comments such as "90 percent of all we know about physics has been discovered since Albert Einstein published his original work on special relativity"; and "80 percent of what we know about the human body has been discovered in the past 50 years." In addition, evidence is cited to show that knowledge is growing exponentially. Such statements emphasize the importance of the *management of change.* To survive, firms must develop strategies for assessing and reassessing the use of their resources. Every allocation of resources is an investment in the future. Because of the complex nature of most strategies, many of these investments are in projects.

To cite one of many possible examples, special visual effects accomplished through computer animation are common in the movies and television shows we watch daily. A few years ago they were unknown. When the capability was in its idea stage, computer companies as well as the firms producing movies and TV shows faced the decision whether or not to invest in the development of these techniques. Obviously valuable as the idea seems today, the choice was not quite so clear a decade ago when an entertainment company compared investment in computer animation to alternative investments in a new star, a new rock group, or a new theme park.

The proper choice of investment projects is crucial to the long-run survival of every firm. Daily we witness the results of both good and bad investment choices. In our daily newspapers we read of Cisco System's decision to purchase firms that have developed valuable communication network software rather than to develop its own software. We read of Procter and Gamble's decision to invest heavily in marketing its products on the Internet; British Airways' decision to purchase passenger planes from Airbus instead of from its traditional supplier, Boeing; or problems faced by school systems when they update student computer labs—should they invest in Windows®-based systems or stick with their traditional choice, Apple®. But can such important choices be made rationally? Once made, do they ever change, and if so, how? These questions reflect the need for effective selection models.

Within the limits of their capabilities, such models can be used to increase profits, select investments for limited capital resources, or improve the competitive position of the organization. They can be used for ongoing evaluation as well as initial selection, and thus are a key to the allocation and reallocation of the organization's scarce resources.

When a firm chooses a project selection model, the following criteria, based on Souder (1973), are most important.

1. *Realism* The model should reflect the reality of the manager's decision situation, including the multiple objectives of both the firm and its managers. Without a common measurement system, direct comparison of different projects is impossible. For example, Project A may strengthen a firm's market share by extending its facilities, and Project B might improve its competitive position by strengthening its technical staff. Other things being equal, which is better? The model should take into account the realities of the firm's limitations on facilities, capital, personnel, and so forth. The model should also include factors that reflect project risks, including the technical risks of performance, cost, and time as well as the market risks of customer rejection and other implementation risks.

2. *Capability* The model should be sophisticated enough to deal with multiple time periods, simulate various situations both internal and external to the project (e.g., strikes, interest rate changes), and optimize the decision. An optimizing model will make the comparisons that management deems important, consider major risks and constraints on the projects, and then select the best overall project or set of projects.

3. *Flexibility* The model should give valid results within the range of conditions that the firm might experience. It should have the ability to be easily modified, or to be self-adjusting in response to changes in the firm's environment; for example, tax laws change, new technological advancements alter risk levels, and, above all, the organization's goals change.

4. *Ease of use* The model should be reasonably convenient, not take a long time to execute, and be easy to use and understand. It should not require special interpretation, data that are difficult to acquire, excessive personnel, or unavailable equipment. The model's variables should also relate one-to-one with those real-world parameters the managers believe significant to the project. Finally, it should be easy to simulate the expected outcomes associated with investments in different project portfolios.

5. *Cost* Data-gathering and modeling costs should be low relative to the cost of the project and must surely be less than the potential benefits of the project. All costs should be considered, including the costs of data management and of running the model.

We would add a sixth criterion:

6. *Easy computerization* It must be easy and convenient to gather and store the information in a computer database, and to manipulate data in the model through use of a widely available, standard computer package such as Excel®, Lotus 1-2-3®, Quattro Pro®, and like programs. The same ease and convenience should apply to transferring the information to any standard decision support system.

In what follows, we first examine fundamental types of project selection models and the characteristics that make any model more or less acceptable. Next we consider the limitations, strengths, and weaknesses of project selection models, including some suggestions of factors to consider when making a decision about which, if any, of the project selection models to use. We then discuss the problem of selecting projects when high levels of uncertainty about outcomes, costs, schedules, or technology are present, as well as some ways of managing the risks associated with the uncertainties. Finally, we comment on some special aspects of the information base required for project selection. Then we turn our attention to the selection of a set of projects to help the organization achieve its goals and illustrate this with a technique called the *Project Portfolio Process*. We finish the chapter with a discussion of project proposals.

2.3   THE NATURE OF PROJECT SELECTION MODELS

There are two basic types of project selection models, *numeric* and *nonnumeric*. Both are widely used. Many organizations use both at the same time, or they use models that are combinations of the two. Nonnumeric models, as the name implies, do not use numbers as inputs. Numeric models do, but the criteria being measured may be either objective or subjective. It is important to remember that the *qualities* of a project may be represented by numbers, and that *subjective* measures are not necessarily less useful or reliable than so-called *objective* measures. (We will discuss these matters in more detail in Section 2.6.)

Before examining specific kinds of models within the two basic types, let us consider just what we wish the model to do for us, never forgetting two critically important, but often overlooked, facts.

- Models do not make decisions—people do. The manager, not the model, bears responsibility for the decision. The manager may "delegate" the task of making the decision to a model, but the responsibility cannot be abdicated.

- All models, however sophisticated, are only partial representations of the reality they are meant to reflect. Reality is far too complex for us to capture more than a small fraction of it in any model. Therefore, no model can yield an optimal decision except within its own, possibly inadequate, framework.

We seek a model to assist us in making project selection decisions. This model should possess the characteristics discussed previously and, above all, it must evaluate potential projects by the degree to which they will meet the firm's objectives. To construct a selection/evaluation model, therefore, it is necessary to develop a list of the firm's objectives.

A list of objectives should be generated by the organization's top management. It is a direct expression of organizational philosophy and policy. The list should go beyond the typical clichés about "survival" and "maximizing profits," which are certainly real goals but are just as certainly not the only goals of the firm. Other objectives might include maintenance of share of specific markets, development of an improved image with specific clients or competitors, expansion into a new line of business, decrease in sensitivity to business cycles, maintenance of employment for specific categories of workers, and maintenance of system loading at or above some percent of capacity, just to mention a few.

A model of some sort is implied by any conscious decision. The choice between two or more alternative courses of action requires reference to some objective(s), and the choice is thus made in accord with some, possibly subjective, "model."

Since the development of computers and the establishment of operations research as an academic subject in the mid-1950s, the use of formal, numeric models to assist in decision making has expanded. Many of these models use financial metrics such as profits and/or cash flow to measure the "correctness" of a managerial decision. Project selection decisions are no exception, being based primarily on the degree to which the financial goals of the organization are met. As we will see later, this stress on financial goals, largely to the exclusion of other criteria, raises some serious problems for the firm, irrespective of whether the firm is for-profit or not-for-profit.

When the list of objectives has been developed, an additional refinement is recommended. The elements in the list should be *weighted*. Each item is added to the list because it represents a contribution to the success of the organization, but each item does not make an equal contribution. The weights reflect different degrees of contribution each element makes in accomplishing a set of goals.

Once the list of goals has been developed, one more task remains. The probable contribution of each project to each of the goals must be estimated. A project is selected or rejected because it is predicted to have certain outcomes if implemented. These outcomes are expected to contribute to goal achievement. If the estimated level of goal achievement is sufficiently large, the project is selected. If not, it is rejected. The relationship between the project's expected results and the organization's goals must be understood. In general, the kinds of information required to evaluate a project can be listed under production, marketing, financial, personnel, administrative, and other such categories.

Table 2-1 is a list of factors that contribute, positively or negatively, to these categories. In order to give focus to this list, we assume that the projects in question involve the possible substitution of a new production process for an existing one. The list is meant to be illustrative. It certainly is not exhaustive.

Some factors in this list have a one-time impact and some recur. Some are difficult to estimate and may be subject to considerable error. For these, it is helpful to identify a *range of uncertainty*. In addition, the factors may occur at different times. And some factors may have *thresholds*, critical values above or below which we might wish to reject the project. We will deal in more detail with these issues later in this chapter.

Table 2–1. Project Evaluation Factors

Production Factors
1. Time until ready to install
2. Length of disruption during installation
3. Learning curve—time until operating as desired
4. Effects on waste and rejects
5. Energy requirements
6. Facility and other equipment requirements
7. Safety of process
8. Other applications of technology
9. Change in cost to produce a unit output
10. Change in raw material usage
11. Availability of raw materials
12. Required development time and cost
13. Impact on current suppliers
14. Change in quality of output

Marketing Factors
1. Size of potential market for output
2. Probable market share of output
3. Time until market share is acquired
4. Impact on current product line
5. Consumer acceptance
6. Impact on consumer safety
7. Estimated life of output
8. Spin-off project possibilities

Financial Factors
1. Profitability, net present value of the investment
2. Impact on cash flows

3. Payout period
4. Cash requirements
5. Time until break-even
6. Size of investment required
7. Impact on seasonal and cyclical fluctuations

Personnel Factors
1. Training requirements
2. Labor skill requirements
3. Availability of required labor skills
4. Level of resistance from current work force
5. Change in size of labor force
6. Inter- and intra-group communication requirements
7. Impact on working conditions

Administrative and Miscellaneous Factors
1. Meet government safety standards
2. Meet government environmental standards
3. Impact on information system
4. Reaction of stockholders and securities markets
5. Patent and trade secret protection
6. Impact on image with customers, suppliers, and competitors
7. Degree to which we understand new technology
8. Managerial capacity to direct and control new process

Clearly, no single project decision need include all these factors. Moreover, not only is the list incomplete, also it contains redundant items. Perhaps more important, the factors are not at the same level of generality: *profitability* and *impact on organizational image* both affect the overall organization, but *impact on working conditions* is more oriented to the production system. Nor are all elements of equal importance. *Change in production cost* is usually considered more important than *impact on current suppliers.* Shortly, we will consider the problem of generating an acceptable list of factors and measuring their relative importance. At that time we will discuss the creation of a Decision Support System (DSS) for project evaluation and selection. The same subject will arise once more in Chapters 12 and 13 when we consider project auditing, evaluation, and termination.

Although the process of evaluating a potential project is time-consuming and difficult, its importance cannot be overstated. A major consulting firm has argued (Booz, Allen, and Hamilton, 1966) that the primary cause for the failure of R & D projects is insufficient care in evaluating the proposal before the expenditure of funds. What is true for R & D projects also appears to be true for other kinds of projects, and it is clear that product development projects are more successful if they incorporate user needs and satisfaction in the design process (Matzler and Hinterhuber, 1998). Careful analysis of a potential project is a *sine qua non* for profitability in the construction business. There are many horror stories (Meredith, 1981) about firms that undertook projects for the installation of a computer information system without sufficient analysis of the time, cost, and disruption involved.

Later in this chapter we will consider the problem of conducting an evaluation under conditions of uncertainty about the outcomes associated with a project. Before dealing with this problem, however, it helps to examine several different evaluation/ selection models and consider their strengths and weaknesses. Recall that the problem of choosing the project selection model itself will also be discussed later.

2.4   TYPES OF PROJECT SELECTION MODELS

Of the two basic types of selection models (numeric and nonnumeric), nonnumeric models are older and simpler and have only a few subtypes to consider. We examine them first.

Nonnumeric Models

The Sacred Cow   In this case the project is suggested by a senior and powerful official in the organization. Often the project is initiated with a simple comment such as, "If you have a chance, why don't you look into . . . ," and there follows an undeveloped idea for a new product, for the development of a new market, for the design and adoption of a global data base and information system, or for some other project requiring an investment of the firm's resources. The immediate result of this bland statement is the creation of a "project" to investigate whatever the boss has suggested. The project is "sacred" in the sense that it will be maintained until successfully concluded, or until the boss, personally, recognizes the idea as a failure and terminates it.

The Operating Necessity   If a flood is threatening the plant, a project to build a protective dike does not require much formal evaluation, is an example of this scenario. XYZ Steel Corporation has used this criterion (and the following criterion also) in evaluating potential projects. If the project is required in order to keep the system operating, the primary question becomes: Is the system worth saving at the estimated cost of the project? If the answer is yes, project costs will be examined to make sure they are kept as low as is consistent with project success, but the project will be funded.

The Competitive Necessity   Using this criterion, XYZ Steel undertook a major plant rebuilding project in the late 1960s in its steel-bar-manufacturing facilities near Chicago. It had become apparent to XYZ's management that the company's bar mill needed modernization if the firm was to maintain its competitive position in the Chicago market area. Although the planning process for the project was quite sophisticated, the decision to undertake the project was based on a desire to maintain the company's competitive position in that market.

In a similar manner, many business schools are restructuring their undergraduate and MBA programs to stay competitive with the more forward-looking schools. In large part, this action is driven by declining numbers of tuition-paying students and the stronger competition to attract them.

Investment in an *operating necessity* project takes precedence over a *competitive necessity* project, but both types of projects may bypass the more careful numeric analysis used for projects deemed to be less urgent or less important to the survival of the firm.

The Product Line Extension   In this case, a project to develop and distribute new products would be judged on the degree to which it fits the firm's existing product line, fills a gap, strengthens a weak link, or extends the line in a new, desirable direction. Sometimes careful calculations of profitability are not required. Decision makers can act on their beliefs about what will be the likely impact on the total system performance if the new product is added to the line.

Comparative Benefit Model   For this situation, assume that an organization has many projects to consider, perhaps several dozen. Senior management would like to select a subset of the projects that would most benefit the firm, but the projects do not seem to be easily comparable. For example, some projects concern potential new products, some concern changes in production methods, others concern computerization of certain records, and still others cover a variety of subjects not easily categorized (e.g., a proposal to create a daycare center for employees with small children). The organization has no formal method of selecting projects, but members of the Selection Committee think that some projects will benefit the firm more than others, even if they have no precise way to define or measure "benefit."

The concept of comparative benefits, if not a formal model, is widely adopted for selection decisions on all sorts of projects. Most United Way organizations use the concept to make decisions about which of several social programs to fund. Senior management of the funding organization then examines all projects with positive recommendations and attempts to construct a portfolio that best fits the organization's aims and its budget.

Of the several techniques for ordering projects, the Q-Sort (Helin and Souder, 1974) is one of the most straightforward. First, the projects are divided into three groups—*good, fair,* and *poor*—according to their relative merits. If any group has more than eight members, it is subdivided into two categories, such as *fair-plus* and *fair-minus.* When all categories have eight or fewer members, the projects within each category are ordered from best to worst. Again, the order is determined on the basis of relative merit. The rater may use specific criteria to rank each project, or may simply use general overall judgment. (See Figure 2-1 for an example of a Q-Sort.)

The process described may be carried out by one person who is responsible for evaluation and selection, or it may be performed by a committee charged with the responsibility. If a committee handles the task, the individual rankings can be developed anonymously, and the set of anonymous rankings can be examined by the committee itself for consensus. It is common for such rankings to differ somewhat from rater to rater, but they do not often vary strikingly because the individuals chosen for such committees rarely differ widely on what they feel to be appropriate for the parent organization. Projects can then be selected in the order of preference, though they are usually evaluated financially before final selection.

There are other, similar nonnumeric models for accepting or rejecting projects. Although it is easy to dismiss such models as unscientific, they should not be discounted casually. These models are clearly goal-oriented and directly reflect the pri-

Steps	Results at Each Step
1. For each participant in the exercise, assemble a deck of cards, with the name and description of one project on each card.	
2. Instruct each participant to divide the deck into two piles, one representing a high priority, the other a low-priority level. (The piles need not be equal.)	
3. Instruct each participant to select cards from each pile to form a third pile representing the medium-priority level.	
4. Instruct each participant to select cards from the high-level pile to yield another pile representing the very high level of priority; select cards from the low-level pile representing the very low level of priority.	
5. Finally, instruct each participant to survey the selections and shift any cards that seem out of place until the classifications are satisfactory.	

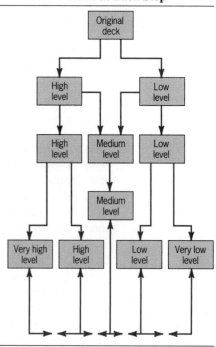

Figure 2-1   The Q-sort method. *Source: Souder 1983.*

mary concerns of the organization. The sacred cow model, in particular, has an added feature; sacred cow projects are visibly supported by "the powers that be." Full support by top management is certainly an important contributor to project success (Meredith, 1981). Without such support, the probability of project success is sharply lowered.

Numeric Models: Profit/Profitability

As noted earlier, a large majority of all firms using project evaluation and selection models use profitability as the sole measure of acceptability. We will consider these models first, and then discuss models that surpass the profit test for acceptance.

Payback Period The payback period for a project is the initial fixed investment in the project divided by the estimated annual net cash inflows from the project. The ratio of these quantities is the number of years required for the project to repay its initial fixed investment. For example, assume a project costs $100,000 to implement and has annual net cash inflows of $25,000. Then

$$\text{Payback period} = \$100,000/\$25,000 = 4 \text{ years}$$

This method assumes that the cash inflows will persist at least long enough to pay back the investment, and it ignores any cash inflows beyond the payback period. The method also serves as an (inadequate) proxy for risk. The faster the investment is recovered, the less the risk to which the firm is exposed.

Average Rate of Return Often mistaken as the reciprocal of the payback period, the average rate of return is the ratio of the average annual profit (either before or after taxes) to the initial or average investment in the project. Because average annual profits are usually not equivalent to net cash inflows, the average rate of return does not usually equal the reciprocal of the payback period. Assume, in the example just given, that the average annual profits are $15,000:

$$\text{Average rate of return} = \$15,000/\$100,000 = 0.15$$

Neither of these evaluation methods is recommended for project selection, though payback period is widely used and does have a legitimate value for cash budgeting decisions. The major advantage of these models is their simplicity, but neither takes into account the time-value of money. Unless interest rates are extremely low and the rate of inflation is nil, the failure to reduce future cash flows or profits to their present value will result in serious evaluation errors.

Discounted Cash Flow Also referred to as the net present value method, the discounted cash flow method determines the net present value of all cash flows by discounting them by the required rate of return (also known as the *hurdle rate, cutoff rate,* and similar terms) as follows:

$$\text{NPV (project)} = A_0 + \sum_{t=1}^{n} \frac{F_t}{(1+k)^t}$$

where

F_t = the net cash flow in period t,

k = the required rate of return, and

A_0 = initial cash investment (because this is an outflow, it will be negative).

To include the impact of inflation (or deflation) where p_t is the predicted rate of inflation during period t, we have

$$\text{NPV (project)} = A_0 + \sum_{t=1}^{n} \frac{F_t}{(1+k+p_t)^t}$$

Early in the life of a project, net cash flow is likely to be negative, the major outflow being the initial investment in the project, A_0. If the project is successful, however, cash flows will become positive. The project is *acceptable* if the sum of the net present values of all estimated cash flows over the life of the project is positive. A simple example will suffice. Using our $100,000 investment with a net cash inflow of $25,000 per year for a period of eight years, a required rate of return of 15 percent, and an inflation rate of 3 percent per year, we have

$$\text{NVP (project)} = -\$100,000 + \sum_{t=1}^{8} \frac{\$25,000}{(1+0.15+0.03)^t}$$

$$= \$1939$$

Because the present value of the inflows is greater than the present value of the outflow—that is, the net present value is positive—the project is deemed acceptable.

PsychoCeramic Sciences, Inc.

PsychoCeramic Sciences, Inc. (PSI), a large producer of cracked pots and other cracked items, is considering the installation of a new marketing software package that will, it is hoped, allow more accurate sales information concerning the inventory, sales, and deliveries of its pots as well as its vases designed to hold artificial flowers.

The information systems (IS) department has submitted a project proposal that estimates the investment requirements as follows: an initial investment of $125,000 to be paid up-front to the Pottery Software Corporation; an additional investment of $100,000 to modify and install the software; and another $90,000 to integrate the new software into the overall information system. Delivery and installation is estimated to take one year; integrating the entire system should require an additional year. Thereafter, the IS department predicts that scheduled software updates will require further expenditures of about $15,000 every second year, beginning in the fourth year. They will not, however, update the software in the last year of its expected useful life.

The project schedule calls for benefits to begin in the third year, and to be up-to-speed by the end of that year. Projected additional profits resulting from better and more timely sales information are estimated to be $50,000 in the first year of operation and are expected to peak at $120,000 in the second year of operation, and then to follow the gradually declining pattern shown in the table at the end of this box.

Project life is expected to be 10 years from project inception, at which time the proposed system will be obsolete for this division and will have to be replaced. It is estimated, however, that the software can be sold to a smaller division of PSI and will thus have a salvage value of $35,000.

PSI has a 12 percent hurdle rate for capital investments and expects the rate of inflation to be about 3 percent over the life of the project. Assuming that the initial expenditure occurs at the beginning of the year and that all other receipts and expenditures occur as lump sums at the end of the year, we can prepare the Net Present Value analysis for the project as shown in the table below.

The Net Present Value of the project is positive and, thus, the project can be accepted. (The project would have been rejected if the hurdle rate were 14 percent.)

Just for the intellectual exercise, note that the total inflow for the project is $759,000, or $75,900 per year on average for the 10 year project. The required investment is $315,000 (ignoring the biennial overhaul charges). Assuming 10 year, straight line depreciation or $31,500 per year, the payback period would be:

$$PB = \frac{\$315,000}{\$75,900 + 31,500} = 2.9 \text{ years}$$

A project with this payback period would probably be considered quite desirable.

Year A	Inflow B	Outflow C	Net Flow $D = (B - C)$	Discount Factor $1/(1 + k + p)^t$	Net Present Value D (Disc. Fact.)
1996*	$ 0	$125,000	$-125,000	1.0000	$-125,000
1996	0	100,000	-100,000	0.8696	-86,960
1997	0	90,000	-90,000	0.7561	-68,049
1998	50,000	0	50,000	0.6575	32,875
1999	120,000	15,000	105,000	0.5718	60,039
2000	115,000	0	115,000	0.4972	57,178
2001	105,000	15,000	90,000	0.4323	38,907
2002	97,000	0	97,000	0.3759	36,462
2003	90,000	15,000	75,000	0.3269	24,518
2004	82,000	0	82,000	0.2843	23,313
2005	65,000	0	65,000	0.2472	16,068
2005	35,000		35,000	0.2472	8,652
Total	$759,000	$360,000	$ 399,000		$ 18,003

*$t = 0$ at the beginning of 1996

Internal Rate of Return   If we have a set of expected cash inflows and cash outflows, the internal rate of return is the discount rate that equates the present values of the two sets of flows. If A_t is an expected cash outflow in the period t and R_t is the expected inflow for the period t, the internal rate of return is the value of k that satisfies the following equation (note that the A_0 will be positive in this formulation of the problem):

$$A_0 + A_1/(1 + k) + A_2/(1 + k)^2 + \cdots + A_n/(1 + k)^n = R_1/(1 + k) + R_2/(1 + k)^2 + \ldots + R_n/(1 + k)^n$$

The value of k is found by trial and error.

Profitability Index   Also known as the benefit–cost ratio, the profitability index is the net present value of all future expected cash flows divided by the initial cash investment. (Some firms do not discount the cash flows in making this calculation.) If this ratio is greater than 1.0, the project may be accepted.

Other Profitability Models   There are a great many variations of the models just described. These variations fall into three general categories: (1) those that subdivide net cash flow into the elements that comprise the net flow; (2) those that include specific terms to introduce risk (or uncertainty, which is treated as risk) into the evaluation; and (3) those that extend the analysis to consider effects that the project might have on other projects or activities in the organization.

Several comments are in order about all the profit-profitability numeric models. First, let us consider their advantages:

1. The undiscounted models are simple to use and understand.
2. All use readily available accounting data to determine the cash flows.
3. Model output is in terms familiar to business decision makers.
4. With a few exceptions, model output is on an "absolute" profit/profitability scale and allows "absolute" go/no-go decisions.
5. Some profit models account for project risk.

The disadvantages of these models are the following:

1. These models ignore all nonmonetary factors except risk.
2. Models that do not include discounting ignore the timing of the cash flows and the time–value of money.
3. Models that reduce cash flows to their present value are strongly biased toward the short run.
4. Payback-type models ignore cash flows beyond the payback period.
5. The internal rate of return model can result in multiple solutions.
6. All are sensitive to errors in the input data for the early years of the project.
7. All discounting models are nonlinear, and the effects of changes (or errors) in the variables or parameters are generally not obvious to most decision makers.
8. All these models depend for input on a determination of cash flows, but it is not clear exactly how the concept of cash flow is properly defined for the purpose of evaluating projects.

A complete discussion of profit/profitability models can be found in any standard work on financial management—see Moyer (1998) or Ross, Westerfield, and Jordan (1995), for example. In general, the net present value models are preferred to the internal rate of return models. Despite wide use, financial models rarely include nonfinancial outcomes in their benefits and costs. In a discussion of the financial value of adopting project management (that is, selecting as a project the use of project management) in a firm, Githens (1998) notes that traditional financial models "simply cannot capture the complexity and value-added of today's process-oriented firm.

In our experience, the payback period model, occasionally using discounted cash flows, is one of the most commonly used models for evaluating projects and other investment opportunities. Managers generally feel that insistence on short payout periods tends to minimize the risks associated with the passage of time. While this is certainly logical, we prefer evaluation methods that discount cash flows and deal with uncertainty more directly by considering specific risks. Using the payout period as a cash-budgeting tool aside, *its only virtue is simplicity,* a dubious virtue at best.

Project Management in Practice
Project Selection for Spent Nuclear Fuel Cleanup

In 1994, Westinghouse Hanford Co., on contract to the Department of Energy's Hanford Nuclear Fuel Site, reorganized for "projectization" to help Hanford with facility shutdown, decommissioning, and site cleanup. The major project in this overall task was the site cleanup of 2,100 metric tons of degraded spent nuclear fuel slugs submerged beneath 16 feet of water (as a radiation shield) in two rectangular, 25 foot deep, half-football field–sized basins. Of the over 105,000 slugs, about 6,000 were severely damaged or corroded and leaking radiation into the basin water. The 40-year old basins, located only 400 yards from Washington State's pristine Columbia River, had an original 20-year design life and were in very poor condition, experiencing major leaks in the late 1970s and again in 1993. Operating and attempting to maintain these "accidents waiting to happen" cost $100,000 a day.

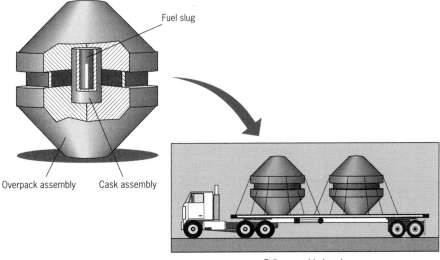

Fuel slug

Overpack assembly   Cask assembly

Fully assembled cask
and transporting vehicle

Fuel slug packaging system developed to transport and store fuel capsules.

To address this problem, Westinghouse Hanford went to the site's stakeholders—the media, activists, regulators, oversight groups, three Indian tribes, government leaders, Congress, and Hanford employees—to determine acceptable options for dealing with this immense problem. It required five months of public discussion for the stakeholders to understand the issues and regain their trust in Hanford. Another two months were required to develop four project options as follows:

1. Better encapsulate the fuel and leave it in the basins.

2. Place the fuel in wet storage elsewhere at Hanford.

3. Place the fuel in dry storage at Hanford.

4. Ship the fuel overseas for reprocessing.

Following three months of evaluation, the third option was selected and an environmental impact statement (EIS) begun, which required eleven more months to complete (yet half the normal EIS completion time). The project is now underway and is expected to be complete by December 1999, three years ahead of the original schedule and thereby saving taxpayers $350 million. Also, the cost of maintaining the fuel is expected to drop to only $3,000 per day.

Source: J.C. Fulton, "Complex Problem . . . Simple Concepts . . . Transformed Organization," *PM Network,* July 1996, pp. 15–21.

Numeric Models: Scoring

In an attempt to overcome some of the disadvantages of profitability models, particularly their focus on a single decision criterion, a number of evaluation/selection models that use multiple criteria to evaluate a project have been developed. Such models vary widely in their complexity and information requirements. The examples discussed illustrate some of the different types of numeric scoring models.

Unweighted 0–1 Factor Model   A set of relevant factors is selected by management and then usually listed in a preprinted form. One or more raters score the project on each factor, depending on whether or not it qualifies for an individual criterion. The raters are chosen by senior managers, for the most part from the rolls of senior management. The criteria for choice are (1) a clear understanding of organizational goals and (2) a good knowledge of the firm's potential project *portfolio.* Figure 2-2 shows an example of the rating sheet for an unweighted, 0–1 factor model.

The columns of Figure 2-2 are summed and those projects with a sufficient number of qualifying factors may be selected. The main advantage of such a model is that it uses several criteria in the decision process. The major disadvantages are that it assumes all criteria are of equal importance and it allows for no gradation of the degree to which a specific project meets the various criteria.

Unweighted Factor Scoring Model   The second disadvantage of the 0–1 factor model can be dealt with by constructing a simple linear measure of the degree to which the project being evaluated meets each of the criteria contained in the list. The x marks in Figure 2-2 would be replaced by numbers. Often a five-point scale is used, where 5 is very good, 4 is good, 3 is fair, 2 is poor, 1 is very poor. (Three-, seven-, and

Project _____

Rater _____ Date _____

	Qualifies	**Does Not Qualify**
No increase in energy requirements	x	
Potential market size, dollars	x	
Potential market share, percent	x	
No new facility required	x	
No new technical expertise required		x
No decrease in quality of final product	x	
Ability to manage project with current personnel		x
No requirement for reorganization	x	
Impact on work force safety	x	
Impact on environmental standards	x	
Profitability		
Rate of return more than 15% after tax	x	
Estimated annual profits more than $250,000	x	
Time to break-even less than 3 years	x	
Need for external consultants		x
Consistency with current line of business		x
Inpact on company image		
With customers	x	
With our industry		x
Totals	12	5

Figure 2-2   Sample project evaluation form.

10-point scales are also common.) The second column of Figure 2-2 would not be needed. The column of scores is summed, and those projects with a total score exceeding some critical value are selected. A variant of this selection process might choose the highest-scoring projects (still assuming they are all above some critical score) until the estimated costs of the set of projects equaled the resource limit. However, the criticism that the criteria are all assumed to be of equal importance still holds.

The use of a discrete numeric scale to represent the degree to which a criterion is satisfied is widely accepted. To construct such measures for project evaluation, we proceed in the following manner. Select a criterion, say, "estimated annual profits in dollars." For this criterion, determine five ranges of performance so that a typical project, chosen at random, would have a roughly equal chance of being in any one of the five performance ranges. (Another way of describing this condition is: Take a large number of projects that were selected for support in the past, regardless of whether they were actually successful or not, and create five levels of predicted performance so that about one-fifth of the projects fall into each level.) This procedure will usually create unequal ranges, which may offend our sense of symmetry but need not concern us otherwise. It ensures that each criterion performance measure utilizes the full scale of possible values, a desirable characteristic for performance measures.

Consider the following two simple examples. Using the criterion just mentioned, "estimated annual profits in dollars," we might construct the following scale:

Score	Performance Level
5	Above $1,100,000
4	$750,001 to $1,100,000
3	$500,001 to $750,000
2	$200,000 to $500,000
1	Less than $200,000

As suggested, these ranges might have been chosen so that about 20 percent of the projects considered for funding would fall into each of the five ranges.

The criterion "no decrease in quality of the final product" would have to be re-stated to be scored on a five-point scale, perhaps as follows:

Score	Performance Level
	The quality of the final product is:
5	significantly and visibly improved
4	significantly improved, but not visible to buyer
3	not significantly changed
2	significantly lowered, but not visible to buyer
1	significantly and visibly lowered

This scale is an example of scoring cells that represent opinion rather than objective (even if "estimated") fact, as was the case in the profit scale.

Weighted Factor Scoring Model   When numeric weights reflecting the relative importance of each individual factor are added, we have a weighted factor scoring model. In general, it takes the form

$$S_i = \sum_{j=1}^{n} s_{ij} w_j$$

where

S_i = the total score of the ith project,

s_{ij} = the score of the ith project on the jth criterion, and

w_j = the weight of the jth criterion.

The weights, w_j, may be generated by any technique that is acceptable to the organization's policy makers. There are several techniques available to generate such numbers, but the most effective and most widely used is the Delphi technique. The Delphi technique was developed by Brown and Dalkey of the RAND Corporation during the 1950s and 1960s (Dalkey, 1969). It is a technique for developing numeric values that are equivalent to subjective, verbal measures of relative value. The method of successive comparisons (or pairwise comparisons) may also be used for the same purpose (Khorramshahgol, Azani, and Gousty 1988).

Another popular and quite similar approach is the Analytic Hierarchy Process, developed by Saaty (1990). For an extensive example involving finance, sales, and purchasing, see pages 306–316 of Turban and Meredith (1994). This example also illustrates the use of Expert Choice®, a software package to facilitate the application of the Analytic Hierarchy Process.

When numeric weights have been generated, it is helpful (but not necessary) to scale the weights so that

$$0 \leq w_j \leq 1 \qquad j = 1, 2, 3, \ldots, n$$

$$\sum_{j=1}^{n} w_j = 1$$

The weight of each criterion can be interpreted as the "percent of the total weight accorded to that particular criterion."

A special caveat is in order. It is quite possible with this type of model to include a large number of criteria. It is not particularly difficult to develop scoring scales and weights, and the ease of gathering and processing the required information makes it tempting to include marginally relevant criteria along with the obviously important items. Resist this temptation! After the important factors have been weighted, there usually is little residual weight to be distributed among the remaining elements. The result is that the evaluation is simply insensitive to major differences in the scores on trivial criteria. A good rule of thumb is to discard elements with weights less than 0.02 or 0.03. (If elements are discarded, and if you wish $Sw_j = 1$, the weights must be rescaled to 1.0.) As with any linear model, the user should be aware that the elements in the model are assumed to be independent. This presents no particular problems for these scoring models because they are used to make estimates in a "steady–state" system, and we are not concerned with transitions between states.

It is useful to note that if one uses a weighted scoring model to aid in project selection, the model can also serve as an aid to project *improvement*. For any given criterion, the difference between the criterion's score and the highest possible score on that criterion, multiplied by the weight of the criterion, is a measure of the potential improvement in the project score that would result were the project's performance on that criterion sufficiently improved. It may be that such improvement is not feasible, or is more costly than the improvement warrants. On the other hand, such an analysis of each project yields a valuable statement of the comparative benefits of project improvements. Viewing a project in this way is a type of sensitivity analysis. We examine the degree to which a project's score is sensitive to attempts to improve it—usually by adding resources. We will use sensitivity analysis several times in this book. It is a powerful managerial technique.

It is not particularly difficult to computerize a weighted scoring model by creating a template on Excel® or one of the other standard computer spreadsheets. In Chapter 13 we discuss an example of a computerized scoring model used for the project termination decision. The model is, in fact, a project selection model. The logic of using a "selection" model for the termination decision is straightforward: Given the time and resources required to take a project from its current state to completion, should we make the investment? A "Yes" answer to that question "selects" for funding the partially completed project from the set of all partially finished and not-yet-started projects.

Gettin' Wheels

Rather than using an example in which actual projects are selected for funding with a weighted factor scoring model (hereafter "scoring model") that would require tediously long descriptions of the projects, we can demonstrate the use of the model in a simple, common problem that many readers will have faced—the choice of an automobile for purchase. This problem is nicely suited to use of the scoring model because the purchaser is trying to satisfy multiple objectives in making the purchase and is typically faced with several different cars from which to choose.

Our model must have the following elements:

1. A set of criteria on which to judge the value of any alternative;

2. A numeric estimate of the relative importance (i.e., the "weight") of each criterion in the set; and

3. Scales by which to measure or score the performance or contribution–to–value of each alternative on each criterion.

The criteria weights and measures of performance must be numeric in form, but this does not mean that they must be either "objective" or "quantitative." (If you find this confusing, look ahead in this chapter and read the subsection entitled "Measurements" in Section 2.6.) Criteria weights, obviously, are subjective by their nature, being an expression of what the decision maker thinks is important. The development of performance scales is more easily dealt with in the context of our example, and we will develop them shortly.

Assume that we have chosen the criteria and weights shown in Table A to be used in our eval-

Table A. Criteria and Weights for Automobile Purchase

Appearance	4	(.10)
Braking	3	(.07)
Comfort	7	(.17)
Cost, operating	5	(.12)
Cost, original	10	(.24)
Handling	7	(.17)
Reliability	5	(.12)
Total	41	.99

uations.* The weights represent the relative importance of the criteria measured on a 10-point scale. The numbers in parentheses show the proportion of the total weight carried by each criterion. (They add to only .99 due to rounding.) Raw weights work just as well for decision making as their percentage counterparts, but the latter are usually preferred because they are a constant reminder to the decision maker of the impact of each of the criteria.

Prior to consideration of performance standards and sources of information for the criteria we have chosen, we must ask, "Are there any characteristics that must be present (or absent) in a candidate automobile for it to be acceptable?" Assume, for this example, that to be acceptable, an alternative must not be green, must have air conditioning, must be able to carry at least four adults, must have at least 10 cubic feet of luggage space, and must be priced less

---

*The criteria and weights were picked arbitrarily for this example. Because this is typically an individual or family decision, techniques like Delphi or successive comparisons are not required.

Table B. Automobile Selection Criteria, Measures and Data Sources

Appearance	Subjective judgment, personal
Braking	Distance in feet, 60–0 mph, automotive magazine[a]
Comfort	Subjective judgment, 30 min. road test
Cost, operating	Annual insurance cost plus fuel cost[b]
Cost, original	Dealer cost, auto-cost service[c]
Handling	Average speed through standard slalom, automotive magazine[a]
Reliability	Score on *Consumer Reports,* "Frequency-of-Repair" data (average of 2 previous years)

[a]Many automotive periodicals conduct standardized performance tests of new cars.

[b]Annual fuel cost is calculated as (17,500 mi/DOE ave. mpg) × $1.25/gal.

[c]There are several sources for dealer-cost data (e.g., AAA, which provides a stable database on which to estimate the price of each alternative).

than $34,000. If an alternative violates any of these conditions, it is immediately rejected.

For each criterion, we need some way of measuring the estimated performance of each alternative. In this case, we might adopt the measures shown in Table B. Our purpose is to transform a measure of the degree to which an alternative meets a criterion into a score, the s_{ij}, that is a general measure of the utility or value of the alternative with respect to that criterion. Note that this requires us to define the criterion precisely, as well as to specify a source for the information.

Figure A shows the scores for each criterion transformed to a 5-point scale, which will suffice for our ratings.

Using the performance scores shown in Figure A, we can evaluate the cars we have identified as our alternatives: the Leviathan 8, the Nuevo-Econ, the Maxivan, the Sporticar 100, and the Ritzy 300. Each car is scored on each criterion according to the categories shown in Figure A. Then each score is multiplied by the criterion weight and the result is entered into the appropriate box in Figure B. Last, the results for each alternative are summed to represent the weighted score.

According to this set of measures, we prefer the Ritzy 300, but while it is a clear winner over the Leviathan 8 and the Maxivan, and scores about 8 percent better than the Sporticar, it rates only about 0.13 points or 4 percent above the NuevoEcon. Note that if we overrated the Ritzy by one point on comfort or handling, or if we underrated the NuevoEcon by one point on either of these criteria, the result would have been reversed. (We assume that the original cost data are accurate.) With the scores this close, we might want to evaluate these two cars by additional criteria (e.g., ease of carrying children, status, safety features like dual airbags or ABS) prior to making a firm decision.

All in all, if the decision maker has well delineated objectives, and can determine how specific kinds of performance contribute to those criteria,

Criteria	Scores				
	1	**2**	**3**	**4**	**5**
Appearance	Ugh	Poor	Adequate	Good	WOW
Braking	>165	165–150	150–140	140–130	<130
Comfort	Bad	Poor	Adequate	Good	Excellent
Cost, operating*	>$2.5	$2.1–2.5	$1.9–2.1	$1.6–1.9	<$1.6
Cost, original*	>$32.5	$26–32.5	$21–26	$17–21	<$17
Handling	<45	45–49.5	49.5–55	55–59	>59
Reliability	Worst	Poor	Adequate	Good	Excellent

*Cost data in $1000s

Figure A Performance measures and equivalent scores for selection of an automobile.

and finally, can measure those kinds of performance for each of the alternative courses of action, then the scoring model is a powerful and flexible tool. To the extent that criteria are not carefully defined, perfor- mance is not well linked to the criteria, and is carelessly or wrongly measured, the scoring model rests on a faulty foundation and is merely a convenient path to error.

	Criteria and Weights							
Alternatives	*Appearance* (0.10)	*Braking* (0.07)	*Comfort* (0.17)	*Cost, operating* (0.12)	*Cost, original* (0.24)	*Handling* (0.17)	*Reliability* (0.12)	$\Sigma s_{ij}w_j$
Leviathan 8	3×0.1 = 0.30	1×0.07 = 0.07	4×0.17 = 0.68	2×0.12 = 0.24	1×0.24 = 0.24	2×0.17 = 0.34	3×0.12 = 0.36	2.23
NuevoEcon	3×0.1 = 0.30	3×0.07 = .21	2×0.17 = 0.34	5×0.12 = 0.60	4×0.24 = 0.96	2×0.17 = 0.34	4×0.12 = 0.48	3.23
Maxivan	2×0.1 = 0.20	1×0.07 = 0.07	4×0.17 = 0.68	4×0.12 = 0.48	3×0.24 = 0.72	1×0.17 = 0.17	3×0.12 = 0.36	2.68
Sporticar 100	5×0.1 = 0.50	4×0.07 = 0.28	3×0.17 = 0.51	2×0.12 = 0.24	2×0.24 = 0.48	5×0.17 = 0.85	2×0.12 = 0.24	3.10
Ritzy 300	4×0.1 = 0.40	5×0.07 = 0.35	5×0.17 = 0.85	2×0.12 = 0.24	1×0.24 = 0.24	4×0.17 = 0.68	5×0.12 = 0.60	3.36

Figure B   Scores for alternative cars on selection criteria.

Constrained Weighted Factor Scoring Model   The temptation to include marginal criteria can be partially overcome by allowing additional criteria to enter the model as constraints rather than weighted factors. These constraints represent project characteristics that must be present or absent in order for the project to be acceptable. In our example concerning a product, we might have specified that we would not undertake any project that would significantly lower the quality of the final product (visible to the buyer or not).

We would amend the weighted scoring model to take the form:

$$S_i = \sum_{j=1}^{n} s_{ij}w_j \prod_{k=1}^{v} c_{ik}$$

where $c_{ik} = 1$ if the ith project satisfies the kth constraint, and 0 if it does not. Other elements in the model are as defined earlier.

Although this model is analytically tidy, in practice we would not bother to evaluate projects that are so unsuitable in some ways that we would not consider supporting them regardless of their expected performance against other criteria. For example, except under extraordinary circumstances, Procter & Gamble would not consider a project to add a new consumer product or product line:

- that cannot be marketed nationally;
- that cannot be distributed through mass outlets (grocery stores, drugstores);
- that will not generate gross revenues in excess of $—million;

- for which Procter & Gamble's potential market share is not at least 50 percent; and

- that does not utilize Procter & Gamble's scientific expertise, manufacturing expertise, advertising expertise, or packaging and distribution expertise.

Again, a caveat is in order. Exercise care when adopting constraints. It may seem obvious that we should not consider a project if it has no reasonable assurance of long-run profitability. Such a constraint, however, can force us to overlook a project that, though unprofitable itself, might have a strong, positive impact on the profitability of other potential projects.

Other Scoring Models Goal programming is a variation of the general linear programming method that can optimize an objective function with multiple objectives. A detailed discussion of goal programming is beyond the scope of this book. The interested reader should consult any modern text on management science, for example, Meredith, Shafer, and Turban (2002). As was the case with profitability models, scoring models have their own characteristic advantages and disadvantages. The advantages are:

1. These models allow multiple criteria to be used for evaluation and decision making, including profit/profitability models and both tangible and intangible criteria.
2. They are structurally simple and therefore easy to understand and use.
3. They are a direct reflection of managerial policy.
4. They are easily altered to accommodate changes in the environment or managerial policy.
5. Weighted scoring models allow for the fact that some criteria are more important than others.
6. These models allow easy sensitivity analysis. The trade-offs between the several criteria are readily observable.

The disadvantages are the following:

1. The output of a scoring model is strictly a relative measure. Project scores do not represent the value or "utility" associated with a project and thus do not directly indicate whether or not the project should be supported.
2. In general, scoring models are linear in form and the elements of such models are assumed to be independent.
3. The ease of use of these models is conducive to the inclusion of a large number of criteria, most of which have such small weights that they have little impact on the total project score.
4. Unweighted scoring models assume all criteria are of equal importance, which is almost certainly contrary to fact.
5. To the extent that profit/profitability is included as an element in the scoring model, this element has the advantages and disadvantages noted earlier for the profitability models themselves.

An interesting alternative to scoring models is an iterative rating process developed by Raz (1997). His method starts with a set of attributes that can be used to rank potential projects. He then removes all attributes that do not differentiate between the alternatives and all projects that are dominated by others. If a choice can then be made, it is made. If not, the process is repeated. In another paper, Pascale, et al. compare a weighted scoring model with an unweighted scoring model for the evaluation of innovations. They conclude that the former works well with incremental change, and the latter works better when the innovation is a "new idea" (Pascale, Carland, and Carland, 1997). They also investigate the impact of the evaluation methods on idea generation.

Choosing a Project Selection Model

Selecting the type of model to aid the evaluation/selection process depends on the philosophy and wishes of management. Liberatore and Titus (1983) conducted a survey of 40 high-level staff persons from 29 *Fortune 500* firms. Eighty percent of their respondents report the use of one or more financial models for R & D project decision making. Although their sample is small and nonrandom, their findings are quite consistent with the present authors' experience. None of the respondent firms used mathematical programming techniques for project selection or resource allocation.

We strongly favor weighted scoring models for three fundamental reasons. First, they allow the multiple objectives of all organizations to be reflected in the important decision about which projects will be supported and which will be rejected. Second, scoring models are easily adapted to changes in managerial philosophy or changes in the environment. Third, they do not suffer from the bias toward the short run that is inherent in profitability models that discount future cash flows. This is not a prejudice against discounting and most certainly does not argue against the inclusion of profits/profitability as an important factor in selection, but rather *it is an argument against the exclusion of nonfinancial factors* that may require a longer-run view of the costs and benefits of a project. For a powerful statement of this point, see Hayes and Abernathy (1980).

It is also interesting to note that Liberatore and Titus (1983, p. 969) found that firms with a significant amount of contract research funded from outside the organization used scoring models for project screening much more frequently than firms with negligible levels of outside funding. It was also found that firms with significant levels of outside funding were much less likely to use a payback period.

The structure of a weighted scoring model is quite straightforward. Its virtues are many. Nonetheless, the actual use of scoring models is not as easy as it might seem. Decision makers are forced to make difficult choices and they are not always comfortable doing so. They are forced to reduce often vague feelings to quite specific words or numbers. Multiattribute, multiperson decision making is not simple. [For an interesting discussion of this process, see Irving and Conrath (1988).]

Project Management in Practice
Selecting a Composting Project at Larry's Markets

In 1991, Larry's Markets of Seattle, Washington, adopted a comprehensive environmental program that included recycling, waste reduction, energy conservation, water management, environmental landscaping, environmental product evaluation, community project support, and other environmental initiatives. One of the possible initiatives was a project to recover all of the produce and floral department's by-products through a regular, daily process of composting. Not only did this project promise to reduce the company's impact on the local natural environment but also appeared to offer potential cost savings.

A 1991 waste audit revealed that the company's five stores produced 3000 tons of waste by-products consisting of garbage, cardboard, food waste, plastics, glass, and so on. Of this, over 700 tons, most of which were produced by the produce and floral departments, were estimated to be compostable. Due to its high local visibility and potential cost savings, this project was selected for implementation with a goal of completion by late 1993.

In 1991, before composting, fully 69 percent of Larry's Markets by-product stream was going to landfill. When full-scale composting began in 1992 with 350 tons composted, this figure dropped to 47 percent. Continuing their efforts, in 1993 Larry's Markets composted almost 700 tons which further reduced the landfill percentage to 36, exceeding the county's 1995 goal of 50 percent and the state's 2000 goal of 40 percent. The project also saved the company over $20,000 a year in garbage fees, gave the employees and customers a sense of pride, and fostered community goodwill as represented by numerous letters, customer comments, and local government and environmental group awards.

Source: B. Rogers, "Food Waste Composting at Larry's Markets," *PM Network,* February 1995, pp. 32–33.

2.5 ANALYSIS UNDER UNCERTAINTY— THE MANAGEMENT OF RISK

During the past several years, increasing attention has been paid to the subject of managing some of the risks inherent in most projects. The subject first appeared in PMI's 1987 edition of *A Guide to the Project Management Body of Knowledge* (Project Management Institute, 2001). For the most part, risk has been interpreted as being unsure about project task durations and/or costs, but uncertainty plagues all aspects of the work on projects and is present in all stages of project life cycles. In this section, we will consider uncertainty as it affects the selection process. The impact of imperfect knowledge on the way a project is organized and on its budget and schedule will be discussed in the chapters devoted to those subjects.

Before proceeding, it is useful to discuss briefly the distinction between two words, "risk," and "uncertainty." The outcome of any decision depends on two things:

(1) what the decision maker does; and (2) what nature does—"nature" being the set of exogenous factors that interact with the decision maker's course of action to produce an outcome. If the decision maker knows the probability of each and every state of nature and thus of each and every outcome, she can find the *expected value* of each alternative course of action she has. The expected value of an action is the sum of the values of each outcome associated with the action times the probability that it will occur. She can select the course of action associated with the best of these expected outcomes. This is decision making under conditions of *risk*.

If the decision maker's information is not so complete and she does not know and cannot collect sufficient data to determine the probability of occurrence for some states of nature, she cannot find the expected value for each of her alternative actions. This is decision making under conditions of *uncertainty*. There is no way to solve problems under uncertainty without altering the nature of the problem. One can estimate, guess, or call "Psychic Friend" to assume some probability for each known state of nature and then deal with the problem as if it were one of risk. If the decision maker elects to ignore all states of nature except the one she thinks most likely, she then assumes there is one and only one possible outcome—which is decision making under conditions of *certainty*. Finally, the decision maker could assume that an opponent controls the state of nature and try to use *game theory* to solve her problem of decision making under conditions of *conflict*.

In the real world of project management, it has been common to deal with estimates of task durations, costs, etc. as if the information were known with certainty. On occasion, project task workers inflated times and costs and deflated specifications on the grounds that the boss would arbitrarily cut the project budget and duration and add to the specifications, thereby treating the problem as a decision under conflict with the boss as an opponent.

In fact, a great majority of all decisions made in the course of managing a project are actually made under conditions of uncertainty. In general, we will adopt the view that it is usually best to act as if decisions were made under conditions of risk. This will force us to make some estimates about the probability of various outcomes. If we use appropriate methods for doing this, we can apply what knowledge we have to solving project decision problems. We will not always be correct, but we will be doing the best we can. Such estimates are called "subjective probabilities," and are dealt with in most elementary courses on probability and statistics. While such probabilities are no more than guesses, they can be processed just as empirically determined probabilities are. Schuyler (1995) presents a brief, basic description of the use of subjective probability in decision-making problems. In the world of project management, a best guess is always better than no information at all. Now we can examine some of the effects of uncertainty on project selection.

At times an organization may wish to evaluate a project about which there is little information. R & D projects sometimes fall into this general class. But even in the comparative mysteries of R & D activities, the level of uncertainty about the outcomes of R & D is not beyond analysis. As we noted earlier, there is actually not much uncertainty about whether a product, process, or service can be developed, but there can be considerable uncertainty about *when* it will be developed and at *what* cost.

As they are with R & D projects, time and cost are also often uncertain in other types of projects. When the organization undertakes projects in which it has little or no recent experience—for example, the installation of a computer network, investment in an unfamiliar business, engaging in international trade, and a myriad of other projects common enough to organizations, in general, but uncommon to any single organization—there are three distinct areas of uncertainty. First, there is uncertainty about the timing of the project and the cash flows it is expected to generate. Second, though not as common as generally believed, there may be uncertainty about the direct outcomes of the project—that is, what it will accomplish. Third, there is uncertainty about the side effects of the project—its unforeseen consequences.

Typically, we try to reduce such uncertainty by the preparation of *pro forma* documents. *Pro forma* profit and loss statements and break-even charts are examples of such documents. The results, however, are not very satisfactory unless the amount of uncertainty is reflected in the data that go into the documents. When relationships between inputs and outputs in the projects are complex, Monte Carlo simulation (Evans and Olson, 1998; Law and Kelton, 1990; Meredith, Shafer, and Turban, 2002) can handle such uncertainty by exposing the many possible consequences of embarking on a project. *Risk analysis* is a method based on such a procedure. With the great availability of microcomputers and user-friendly software (e.g., CrystalBall®), these procedures are becoming very common.

Risk Analysis and Simulation

As we noted in Chapter 1, risk analysis techniques will be introduced when they are relevant to a problem at hand. The information associated with project selection is characterized by uncertainty and is thus appropriate for the application of risk analysis. Before proceeding to demonstrate analytic techniques, however, it is helpful to understand the underlying nature of risk analysis.

The duration of project activities, the amounts of various resources that will be required to complete a project, the estimates made of the value of accomplishing a project, all these and many other aspects of a project are uncertain. There is little a project manager can do to eliminate the uncertainty. Decisions must be made in the face of the ambiguity that results from uncertain information. Risk analysis does not remove the ambiguity, it simply describes the uncertainties in a way that provides the decision maker with a useful insight into their nature.

To apply risk analysis, one must make assumptions about the probability distributions that characterize key parameters and variables associated with a decision and then use these to estimate the *risk profiles* or probability distributions of the outcomes of the decision. This can be done analytically or by Monte Carlo simulation. When the decisions involve several input variables or parameters, simulation is highly preferable to the tedious calculations required by analytic methods. The simulation software (in our case Crystal Ball®, an Excel® Add-In) allows the decision to be represented by a mathematical model and then selects samples from the assumed distributions for each input. The software then plugs these inputs into the model and finds the outcome(s) of the decision.

This process is repeated many times and the statistical distribution of the outcomes is then displayed. The object of this process is to show the decision maker the distribution of the outcomes. This risk profile is used to assess the value of the decision along with other factors that might be relevant such as strategic concerns, socio/political factors, and impact on market share. Following a few comments about the nature of the input data and assumptions as in the case of R & D projects, we illustrate the use of Crystal Ball® (CB) to aid in the project selection decision.

General Simulation Analysis

Simulation combined with sensitivity analysis is also useful for evaluating R & D projects while they are still in the conceptual stage. Using the net present value approach, for example, we would support an R & D project if the net present value of the cash flows (including the initial cash investment) is positive and represents the best available alternative use of the funds. When these flows are estimated for purposes of analysis, it is well to avoid the *full-cost* philosophy that is usually adopted. The full-cost approach to estimating cash flows necessitates the inclusion of arbitrarily determined overheads in the calculation—overheads which, by definition, are not affected by change in product or process and, thus, are not relevant to the decision. The only relevant costs are those that will be changed by the implementation of the new process or product.

The determination of such costs is not simple. If the concept being considered involves a new process, it is necessary to go to the detailed *route sheet,* or *operations sequence sheet,* describing the operation in which the new process would be used. Proceeding systematically through the operating sequence step-by-step, one asks whether the present time and cost required for this step are likely to be altered if the new process concept is installed. If, and only if, the answer is yes, three estimates (optimistic, most likely, and pessimistic) are made of the size of the expected change. These individual estimated changes in production cost and time, together with upstream- or downstream-time and cost changes that might also result (e.g., a production method change on a part might also alter the cost of inspecting the final product), are used to generate the required cash flow information—presuming that the time savings have been properly costed. This estimation process will be explained in detail in Chapter 8.

The analysis gives a picture of the proposed change in terms of the costs and times that will be affected. The uncertainty associated with each individual element of the process is included. Simulation runs will then indicate the likelihood of achieving various levels of savings. Note also that investigation of the simulation model will expose the major sources of uncertainty in the final cost distributions.

Those without considerable experience in simulation should use this tool with caution. Simulation software is indifferent to assumptions-contrary-to-fact, and cares not a wit that the experimenter specifies a statistical distribution that implies a universe that never was nor ever will be. In such cases, the results of the simulation— often taken by the unwary as an estimate of reality—are apt to mislead.

PsychoCeramic Sciences Revisited

There is great value in performing risk analysis in order to confront the uncertainties in project selection. Reconsider the PsychoCeramic Sciences example we solved in the section devoted to finding the discounted cash flows associated with a project.

Setting this problem up on Excel® is straightforward and the earlier solution is shown here in Table 2-2 for convenience. We found that the project cleared the barrier of a 12 percent hurdle rate for acceptance. The net cash flow over the project's life is just under $400,000, and discounted at the hurdle rate plus 3 percent annual inflation, the net present value of the cash flow is about $18,000. The rate of inflation is shown in a separate column because it is another uncertain variable that should be included in the risk analysis.

Now let us assume that the expenditures in this example are fixed by contract with an outside vendor. Thus, there is no uncertainty about the outflows, but there is, of course, uncertainty about the inflows. Assume that the estimated inflows are as shown in Table 2-3 and include a most likely estimate, a minimum (pessimistic) estimate, and a maximum (optimistic) estimate. (In Chapters 7, "Budgeting and Cost Estimation" and 8, "Scheduling", we will deal in more detail with the methods and meaning of making such estimates.) Both the beta and the triangular statistical distributions are well suited for modeling variables with these three parameters, but fitting a beta distribution is complicated and not particularly intuitive. Therefore, we will

Table 2-2   Single-Point Estimate of the Cash Flows for PsychoCeramic Sciences Inc.

	A	B	C	D	E	F	G
1					**Discount**	**Net Present**	
2	**Year**	**Inflow**	**Outflow**	**Net Flow**	**Factor**	**Value**	**Inflation**
3	**A**	**B**	**C**	**D = (B - C)**	**$1/(1 + K + p)^t$**	**D × (Disc. Factor)**	**Rate**
4	1996*	$0	$125,000	-$125,000	1.0000	-$125,000	0.03
5	1996	0	100,000	-$100,000	0.8696	-$86,957	0.03
6	1997	0	90,000	-$90,000	0.7561	-$68,053	0.03
7	1998	50,000	0	$50,000	0.6575	$32,876	0.03
8	1999	120,000	15,000	$105,000	0.5718	$60,034	0.03
9	2000	115,000	0	$115,000	0.4972	$57,175	0.03
10	2001	105,000	15,000	$90,000	0.4323	$38,909	0.03
11	2002	97,000	0	$97,000	0.3759	$36,466	0.03
12	2003	90,000	15,000	$75,000	0.3269	$24,518	0.03
13	2004	82,000	0	$82,000	0.2843	$23,310	0.03
14	2005	65,000	0	$65,000	0.2472	$16,067	0.03
15	2005	35,000		$35,000	0.2472	$8,651	0.03
16							
17	Total	$759,000	$360,000	$399,000		$17,997	
18							
19		*t = 0 at the beginning of 1996					
20							
21	**Formulae**						
22	Cell D4		= (B4-C4) copy to D5:D15				
23	Cell E4		= 1/(1 + .12 + G4)^0				
24	Cell E5		= 1/(1 + .12 + G5)^1				
25	Cell E6		= 1/(1 + .12 + G6)^0(A6-1995) copy to E7:E15				
26	Cell F4		= D4*E4 copy to F5:F15				
27	Cell B17		Sum(B4:B15) copy to C17, D17, F17				

Table 2-3   Pessimistic, Most Likely, and Optimistic Estimates of the Cash Flows for PsychoCeramic Sciences Inc.

Year	Minimum Inflow	Most Likely Inflow	Maximum Inflow
1998	$35,000	$50,000	$60,000
1999	95,000	120,000	136,000
2000	100,000	115,000	125,000
2001	88,000	105,000	116,000
2002	80,000	97,000	108,000
2003	75,000	90,000	100,000
2004	67,000	82,000	91,000
2005	51,000	65,000	73,000
2005	30,000	35,000	38,000
Total	$656,200	$759,000	$1,415,200

assume that the triangular distribution will give us a reasonably good fit for the inflow variables.

The hurdle rate of return is fixed by the firm, so the only remaining variable is the rate of inflation that is included in finding the discount factor. We have assumed a 3 percent rate with a normal distribution, plus or minus 1 percent (i.e., 1 percent represents three standard deviations).

It is important to remember that other approaches in which only the most likely estimate of each variable is used are equivalent to an assumption of certainty. The major benefit of simulation is that it allows all possible values for each variable to be considered. Just as the distribution of possible values for a variable is a better reflection of reality (as the estimator sees reality) than a single "most likely" value, the distribution of outcomes developed by simulation is a better forecast of uncertain future reality than a forecast of any single outcome can be. As any security analyst knows, a forecast of corporate quarterly earnings of $0.50–0.58 per share is far more likely to be accurate than a forecast of $0.54 per share. In general, precise forecasts will be precisely wrong.

Using CB to run a Monte Carlo simulation requires us to define two types of cells in the Excel® spreadsheet. The cells that contain variables or parameters are defined as *assumption cells*. For the PsychoCeramic Sciences case, these are the cells in Table 2-2, columns B and G, the inflows and the rate of inflation, respectively. The cells that contain outcomes of the model are called *forecast cells,* cell F17 in Table 2-2. Each forecast cell typically contains a formula that is dependent on one or more of the assumption cells. Simulations may have many assumption and forecast cells, but they must have at least one of each.

To illustrate the process of defining an assumption cell, consider cell B7, the cash inflow estimate for 1998. We can see from Table 2-3 that the minimum expected cash inflow is $35,000, the most likely cash flow is $50,000, and the maximum is $60,000. Also remember that we decided to model all these flows with a triangular distribution.

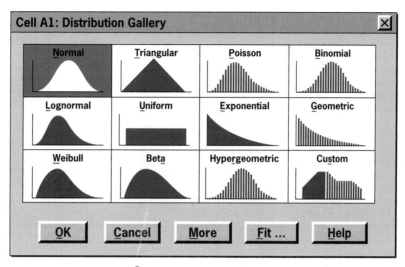

Figure 2-3 Crystal Ball® 2000's Distribution Gallery.

Once one has entered the original information in Table 2-2, the process of defining the assumption cells and entering the pessimistic and optimistic data is straightforward and involves six steps:*

1. Click on cell **B7** to identify it as the relevant assumption cell.
2. Select the menu option **Cell** at the top of the screen.
3. From the dropdown menu that appears, select **Define Assumption**. CB's Distribution Gallery is now displayed as shown in Figure 2-3.
4. CB allows you to choose from a wide variety of probability distributions. Double-click on the **Triangular** box to select it.
5. CB's Triangular Distributon dialog box is displayed as in Figure 2-4. In the Assumption Name textbox at the top of the dialog box enter a descriptive label, e.g., *Cash Inflow-1998*. Then, enter the pessimistic, most likely, and optimistic costs of $35,000, $50,000, and $60,000 in the Min, Likeliest, and Max boxes, respectively.
6. Click on the **OK** button. When you do this step, note that the inflow in cell B7 changes from the most likely entry to the *mean* of the triangular distribution which is (Min + Likeliest + Max) / 3.

Now repeat steps 1–6 for the remaining cash flow assumption cells (cells B8:B15). Remember that the proper information to be entered is found in Table 2-3.

When finished with the cash flow cells, repeat the six-step procedure for assump-

---

*It is generally helpful for the reader to work the problem as we explain it. If Crystal Ball® has been installed on your computer but is not running, select **Tools,** and then **Add-Ins** from Excel®'s menu. Next, click on the **CB** checkbox and select **OK.** If the CB Add-In has not been installed on your computer, consult your Excel® manual and the CD-ROM that accompanies this book to install it.

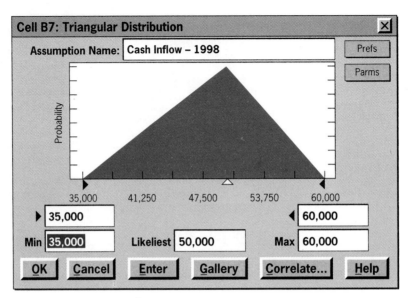

Figure 2-4   Crystal Ball® 2000 dialog box for model inputs assuming the triangular distribution.

tion cells G4:G15. For this assumption select the **Normal** distribution and the entry for each cell in the series will be identical. We decided earlier to use a 3 percent inflation rate, plus or minus 1 percent. Recall that the normal distribution is "bell-shaped" and that the mean of the distribution is its center point. Also recall that the mean, plus or minus three standard deviations includes 99+ percent of the data. The normal distribution dialog box, Figure 2-5, calls for the distribution's mean and its standard deviation. The mean will be 0.03 (3 percent) for all cells. The standard deviation will be .0033 (one third of 1 percent) for all cells. (Note that Figure 2-5 displays only the first two decimal places of the standard deviation. (The actual standard deviation of .0033 is used by the program.) As you enter this data you will note that the distribution will show a mean of 3 percent and a range from 2 percent to 4 percent.

Note that there are two cash flows for the year 1996, but one of those occurs at the beginning of the year and the other at the end of the year. The entry at the beginning of the year is not discounted so there is no logical reason for an entry in G-4. CB seems to like one, however, so go ahead and enter it. In the **Assumption Name:** textbox for the G4 entry type *Inflation rate—1995*. Each of the following entries should be labeled with its appropriate year. The year 2005 raises a similar problem with two cash flows, but these both occur at the end of the year. When you constructed the spreadsheet, you probably copied cell E6 to the range E7:E15. If the inflation rate is fixed at 3 percent, that raises no problem, but when we make the inflation rate a random variable that would allow G14 and G15, inflation for 2005, to be different. The fix is simple. First, click on **E15.** Then press the key **F2.** This shows the formula for E15 in its cell and it should appear as follows: =1/(1+0.12+G15)^(A15-1995). Move your cursor next to the "5" in "G15." Delete the "5" and change it to

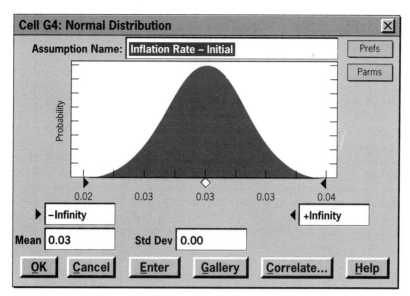

Figure 2-5   Crystal Ball® 2000 dialog box for model inputs assuming the normal distribution.

"4." You may now delete the entry in cell G15; the same inflation rate will now be used for both 2005 calculations.*

Now we consider the forecast or outcome cell. In this example we wish to find the net present value of the cash flows we have estimated. The process of defining a forecast cell involves five steps.

1. Click on the cell **F17** to identify it as containing an outcome that interests us.
2. Select the menu option **Cell** at the top of the screen.
3. From the dropdown menu that appears, select **Define Forecast...**
4. CB's Define Forecast dialog box is now displayed as shown in Figure 2-6. In the Forecast Name: textbox, enter a descriptive name such as *Net Present Value of Project*. Then enter a descriptive label such as *Dollars* in the Units: textbox.
5. Click **OK.** There is only one Forecast cell in this example, but there may be several. Use the same five steps for each.

When you have completed all entries, what was Table 2-2 is now changed and appears as Table 2-4.

We are now ready to simulate. CB randomly selects a value for each assumption cell based on the probability distributions we specified and then calculates the net

---

*You may wonder why we spend time with this kind of detail. The reason is simple. Once you have dealt with this kind of problem, and it is common in such analyses, you won't make this mistake in the real world where having such errors called to your attention may be quite painful.

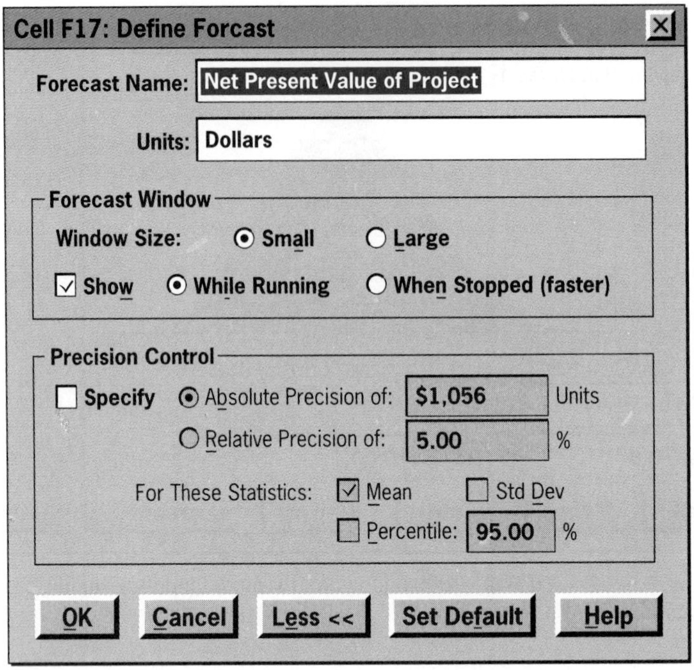

Cell F17: Define Forcast   ☒

Forecast Name: | Net Present Value of Project |

Units: | Dollars |

Forecast Window

Window Size: ⊙ **Small**   ○ **Large**

☑ Show   ⊙ While Running   ○ When Stopped (faster)

Precision Control

☐ Specify   ⊙ Absolute Precision of: | **$1,056** | Units

○ Relative Precision of: | 5.00 | %

For These Statistics: ☑ Mean   ☐ Std Dev

☐ Percentile: | 95.00 | %

OK   **Cancel**   **Less <<**   **Set Default**   **Help**

Figure 2-6   Crystal Ball® 2000 dialog box for the model forecast or outcome.

Table 2-4   Three-Point Estimates of Cash Flows and Inflation Rate for PsychoCeramic Sciences, Inc. All Assumptions and Forecast Cells Defined.

	A	B	C	D	E	F	G
1					Discount	Net Present	
2	Year	Inflow	Outflow	Net Flow	Factor	Value	Inflation
3	A	B	C	D = (B – C)	$1/(1 + K + p)^t$	D × (Disc. Factor)	Rate
4	1996*	$0	$125,000	–$125,000	1.0000	–$125,000	0.03
5	1996	0	100,000	–100,000	0.8696	–$86,957	0.03
6	1997	0	90,000	–$90,000	0.7561	–$68,053	0.03
7	1998	48,333	0	$48,333	0.6575	$31,780	0.03
8	1999	117,000	15,000	$102,000	0.5718	$58,319	0.03
9	2000	113,333	0	$113,333	0.4972	$56,347	0.03
10	2001	103,000	15,000	$88,00	0.4323	$38,045	0.03
11	2002	95,000	0	$95,000	0.3759	$35,714	0.03
12	2003	88,333	15,000	$73,333	0.3269	$23,973	0.03
13	2004	80,000	0	$80,000	0.2843	$22,741	0.03
14	2005	63,000	0	$63,000	0.2472	$15,573	0.03
15	2005	34,333		$34,333	0.2472	$8,487	
16							
17	Total	$742,333	$360,000	$382,333		$10,968	
18		*t = 0 at the beginning of 1996					

present value of the cell values selected. By repeating this process many times we can get a sense of the distribution of possible outcomes.

To simulate the model you have constructed 1,000 times, select the **Run** menu item from the toolbar at the top of the page. In the dropdown box that appears, select **Run Preferences**. In the Run Preferences dialog box that appears enter **1,000** in the Ma<u>x</u>imum Number of Trials textbox and then click **OK.** To perform the simulation, select the **Run** menu item again and then **Run** from the dropdown menu. CB summarizes the results of the simulation in the form of a frequency chart that changes as the simulations are executed. See the results of one such run in Figure 2-7.

CB provides considerable information about the forecast cell in addition to the frequency chart including percentile information, summary statistics, a cumulative chart, and a reverse cumulative chart. For example, to see the summary statistics for a forecast cell, select **<u>V</u>iew** from the toolbar and then select **Statistics** from the dropdown menu that appears. The Statistics view for the frequency chart (Figure 2-7) is illustrated in Figure 2-8.

Figure 2-8 contains some interesting information. Both the mean and median outcomes from the simulation are nicely positive and thus well above the hurdle rate of 12 percent There are, however, several negative outcomes and those are below the hurdle rate. What is the likelihood that this project will achieve an outcome at or above the hurdle rate? With CB, the answer is easy. Using the display shown in Figure 2-9, erase *–Infinity* from the box in the lower left corner. Type *$0* (or *$1*) in that box and press **Enter.** Figure 2-7 now changes as shown in Figure 2–9. The boxes at the bottom of Figure 2–9 show that given our estimates and assumptions of the cash flows and the rate of inflation, there is a .90+ probability that the project will yield an outcome at or above the 12 percent hurdle rate.

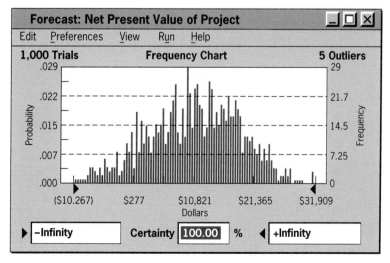

Figure 2-7   Frequency chart of the simulation output for net present value of PsychoCeramic Sciences project.

Forecast: Net Present Value of Project	

Edit   Preferences   View   Run   Help

Cell F17   **Statistics**

Statistic	Value
Trials	1,000
Mean	$10,965
Median	$11,296
Mode	—
Standard Deviation	$8,066
Variance	$65,052,849
Skewness	−0.21
Kurtosis	2.71
Coeff. of Variability	0.74
Range Minimum	($15,656)
Range Maximum	$31,909
Range Width	$47,566
Mean Std. Error	$255.05

Figure 2-8   Summary statistics of the simulation output for net present value of PsychoCeramic Sciences project.

Even in this simple example the power of including uncertainty in project selection should be obvious. Because a manager is always uncertain about the amount of uncertainty, it is also possible to examine various levels of uncertainty quite easily using CB. We could, for instance, alter the degree to which the inflow estimates are uncertain by expanding or contracting the degree to which optimistic and pessimistic estimates vary around the most likely estimate. We could increase or decrease the level of

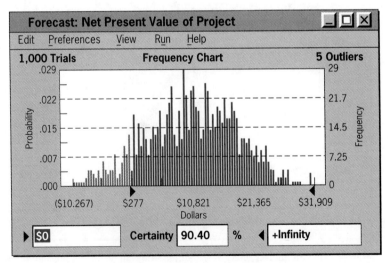

Figure 2-9   Calculating the probability that the net present value of the PsychoCeramic Sciences project is equal to or greater than the firm's hurdle rate.

inflation. Simulation runs made with these changes provide us with the ability to examine just how sensitive the outcomes (forecasts) are to possible errors in the input data. This allows us to focus on the important risks and to ignore those that have little effect on our decisions.

Window-of-Opportunity Analysis   In the early stages of new product development, one may know little more than the fact that the potential product seems technically feasible. That one can achieve a new technology does not necessarily imply that the new technology is worth implementing, or economically profitable. Fundamentally, the decision to invest in the development of a new process or product depends on an estimate of cash flows and other benefits expected to result if the innovation is successful—a difficult problem at best. The traditional approach has been to implement the technology in question (or a pilot version of it) and then test it to see if it qualifies as useful and economic. This is often a wasteful process because it assumes the innovation will be successful—a condition not always met in practice.

Given some idea for a new product or process, we can invert this traditional approach by attempting to determine the cost and performance specifications that must be met by the new technology before any R & D is undertaken. (This is called the *window-of-opportunity* for the innovation.) The method for conducting such an analysis is straightforward. Given a potential production process, for example, the current production process is analyzed in detail and any element of that process that might be affected by the innovation is noted. Baseline data on the current process is collected (e.g., its cycle time, its cost) and the effect of the innovation is estimated relative to (usually some fraction or multiple of) the baseline system. Having thus estimated the economic impact of the innovation, the decision of whether or not to undertake the development project is much simpler. For an example of such an approach see Evans and Mantel (1985) and Mantel, Evans, and Tipnis (1985).

2.6   COMMENTS ON THE INFORMATION BASE FOR SELECTION

Our bias in favor of weighted scoring models is quite clear and weighted scoring models can be simulated because both the scores and the weights are usually estimates. But irrespective of which model is chosen for project selection, a data base must be created and maintained to furnish input data for the model. Directions for the actual construction of the data base go beyond the scope of this book, but some comments about the task are in order.

The use of any project selection model assumes that the decision-making procedure takes place in a reasonably rational organizational environment. Such is not always the case. In some organizations, project selection seems to be the result of a political process, and sometimes involves questionable ethics, complete with winners and losers (Baker and Menon, 1995). In others, the organization is so rigid in its approach to decision making that it attempts to reduce all decisions to an algorithmic proceeding in which predetermined programs make choices so that humans have minimal involvement—and responsibility. Here too, Saaty's (1990) Analytic Hierarchy

Process can lend rationality to a sometimes irrational process. In an interesting paper, Huber (1981) examines the impact that the organizational environment has on the design of decision support systems.

The remainder of this section deals with three special problems affecting the data used in project selection models.

Accounting Data

Whether managers are familiar with accounting systems or not, they can find it useful to reflect on the methods and assumptions used in the preparation of accounting data. Among the most crucial are the following:

1. Accountants live in a linear world. With few exceptions, cost and revenue data are assumed to vary linearly with associated changes in inputs and outputs.

2. The accounting system often provides cost-revenue information that is derived from standard cost analyses and equally standardized assumptions regarding revenues. These standards may or may not be accurate representations of the cost-revenue structure of the physical system they purport to represent.

3. As noted in the previous section, the data furnished by the accounting system may or may not include overhead costs. In most cases, the decision maker is concerned solely with cost-revenue elements that will be changed as a result of the project under consideration. Incremental analysis is called for, and great care must be exercised when using pro forma data in decision problems. Remember that the assignment of overhead cost is always arbitrary. The accounting system is the richest source of information in the organization, and it should be used—but with great care and understanding.

Measurements

It is common for those who oppose a project, for whatever reason, to complain that information supporting the project is "subjective." This epithet appears to mean that the data are biased and therefore untrustworthy.

To use the scoring methods discussed or to practice risk management in project selection, we need to *represent* though not necessarily *collect* expected project performance for each criterion in numeric form. If a performance characteristic cannot be measured directly as a number, it may be useful to characterize performance verbally and then, through a word/number equivalency scale, use the numeric equivalents of verbal characterizations as model inputs.

Subjective versus Objective   The distinction between subjective and objective is generally misunderstood. All too often the word *objective* is held to be synonymous with *fact* and *subjective* is taken to be a synonym for *opinion*—where fact = true and opinion = false. The distinction in measurement theory is quite different, referring to the location of the standard for measurement. A measurement taken by reference to an external standard is said to be "objective." Reference to a standard that is internal to the system is said to be "subjective." A yardstick, incorrectly divided into 100 divisions and labeled "meter," would be an objective but inaccurate measure. The eye of an experienced judge is a subjective measure that may be quite accurate.

Quantitative versus Qualitative   The distinction between quantitative and qualitative is also misunderstood. It is not the same as numeric and nonnumeric. Both quantity and quality may be measured numerically. The number of words on this page is a quantity. The color of a red rose is a quality, but it is also a wavelength that can be measured numerically, in terms of microns. The true distinction is that one may apply the law of addition to quantities but not to qualities (van Gigch, 1978). Water, for example, has a volumetric measure and a density measure. The former is quantitative and the latter qualitative. Two one-gallon containers of water poured into one larger container give us two gallons, but the density of the water, before and after joining the two gallons, is still the same: 1.0.

Reliable versus Unreliable   A data source is said to be reliable if repetitions of a measurement produce results that vary from one another by less than a prespecified amount. The distinction is important when we consider the use of statistical data in our selection models.

Valid versus Invalid   Validity measures the extent to which a piece of information actually means what we believe it to mean. A measure may be reliable but not valid. Consider our mismarked 36-inch yardstick pretending to be a meter. It performs consistently, so it is reliable. It does not, however, match up accurately with other meter rules, so it would not be judged valid.

To be satisfactory when used in the previous project selection models, the measures may be either subjective or objective, quantitative or qualitative, but they must be numeric, reliable, and valid. Avoiding information merely because it is subjective or qualitative is an error and weakens decisions. On the other hand, including information of questionable reliability or validity in selection models, even though it may be numeric, is dangerous. It is doubly dangerous if decision makers are comfortable dealing with the selection model but are unaware of the doubtful character of some input data. A condition a colleague has referred to as GIGO—garbage in, *gospel out*—may prevail.

Uncertain Information

In the section on weighted scoring models, we noted some useful methods for finding the numeric weights and criteria scores when they take the form of verbal descriptors rather than numbers. These same methods are also useful when estimating the inputs for risk analysis models. Indeed, one of the first applications of the Delphi method (Dalkey, 1969) was technological forecasting—forecasting the time period in which some specific technological capability would be available. These methods are commonly used when a group must develop a consensus concerning such items as the importance of a technological change, an estimate of cash flows, a forecast of some economic variable, and similar uncertain future conditions or events.

In Chapter 4 we will deal with the problem of organizing the activity of risk analysis and making such estimates as are required for dealing with uncertainty, either through simulation or by analytic methods. Next, we exemplify the project selection process described previously by detailing an eight-step process that holds promise for improving an organization's project management maturity and at the same time ties the projects more closely to the organization's goals.

2.7   PROJECT PORTFOLIO PROCESS (PPP)

Important inputs to this process are the organization's goals and strategies, and we assume here that the organization has already identified its mission, goals, and strategies—by using some formal analytic method such as SWOT analysis (strengths, weaknesses, opportunities, threats), and that these are well known throughout the organization. If this is not the case, then any attempt to tie the organization's projects to its goals is folly and the PPP will have little value.

If the goals and strategies have been well articulated, however, then the PPP can serve many purposes:

- To identify proposed projects that are not really projects and should be handled through other processes
- To prioritize the list of available projects
- To intentionally limit the number of overall projects being managed so the important projects get the resources and attention they need
- To identify projects that best fit the organization's goals and strategy
- To identify projects that support multiple organizational goals and cross-reinforce other important projects
- To eliminate projects that incur excessive risk and/or cost
- To eliminate projects that bypassed a formal selection process and may not provide benefits corresponding to their risks and/or costs
- To keep from overloading the organization's resource availability
- To balance the resources with the needs
- To balance short-, medium-, and long-term returns

The PPP attempts to link the organization's projects directly to the goals and strategy of the organization. This occurs not only in the project's initiation and planning phases, but also throughout the life cycle of the projects as they are managed and eventually brought to completion. Thus, the PPP is also a means for monitoring and controlling the organization's strategic projects. On occasion this will mean shutting down projects prior to their completion because their risks have become excessive, their costs have escalated out of line with their expected benefits, another (or a new) project does a better job of supporting the goals, or any variety of similar reasons. It should be noted that a significant portion of the administration of this process could be managed by the Project Management Office, a concept to be discussed in Chapter 4.

The steps in this process generally follow those described in Longman, Sandahl, and Speir (1999) and Englund and Graham (2000).

Step 1: Establish a Project Council

The main purpose of the project council is to establish and articulate a strategic direction for those projects spanning internal or external boundaries of the organization, such as cross-departmental or joint venture. Thus, senior managers must play a major role in this council. Without the commitment of senior management, the PPP will be incapable of achieving its main objectives. The council will also be responsible for allocating funds to those projects that support the organization's goals and controlling the allocation of resources and skills to the projects.

In addition to senior management, others who should be members of the project council are:

- the project managers of major projects;
- the head of the Project Management Office, if one exists;
- particularly relevant general managers;
- those who can identify key opportunities and risks facing the organization; and
- anyone who can derail the progress of the PPP later on in the process.

Step 2: Identify Project Categories and Criteria

In this step, various project categories are identified so the mix of projects funded by the organization will be spread appropriately across those areas making major contributions to the organization's goals. In addition, within each category criteria are established to discriminate between very good and even better projects. The criteria are also weighted to reflect their relative importance. Identifying separate categories not only facilitates achievement of multiple organizational goals (e.g., long term, short term, internal, external, tactical, strategic) but also keeps projects from competing with each other on inappropriate categories.

The first task in this step is to list the goals of each existing and proposed project—what is the mission, or purpose of this project. Relating these to the organization's goals and strategies should allow the council to identify a variety of categories that are important to achieving the organization's goals. Some of these were noted above but another way to position some of the projects (particularly product/service development projects) is in terms of their extent of product and process changes.

Wheelwright and Clark (1992) have developed a matrix called the *aggregate project plan* illustrating these changes, as shown in Figure 2-10. Based on the extent of product change and process change, they identified four separate categories of projects:

1. **Derivative projects.** These are projects with objectives or deliverables that are only incrementally different in both product and process from existing offerings. They are often meant to replace current offerings or add an extension to current offerings (lower priced version, upscale version).

2. **Platform projects.** The planned outputs of these projects represent major departures from existing offerings in terms of either the product/service itself or the process used to make and deliver it, or both. As such, they become "platforms" for the next generation of organizational offerings, such as a new model of automobile or a new type of insurance plan. They thus form the basis for follow-on derivative projects that attempt to extend the platform in various dimensions.

3. **Breakthrough projects.** Breakthrough projects typically involve a newer technology than platform projects. It may be a "disruptive" technology that is known to

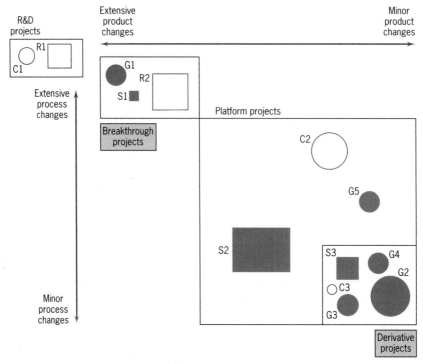

Figure 2-10   An example aggregate project plan.

the industry or something proprietary that the organization has been developing over time. Examples here include the use of fiber-optic cables for data transmission, cash-balance pension plans, and hybrid gasoline-electric automobiles.

4. **R&D projects.** These projects are "blue-sky," visionary endeavors oriented toward using newly developed technologies, or existing technologies in a new manner. They may also be for acquiring new knowledge, or developing new technologies themselves.

The size of the projects plotted on the array indicates the size/resource needs of the project and the shape may indicate another aspect of the project, e.g., internal/external, long/medium/short term, or whatever aspect needs to be shown. The numbers indicate the order, or time frame, in which the projects are to be (or were) implemented, separated by category, if desired.

The aggregate project plan can be used for many purposes:

- To view the mix of projects within each illustrated aspect (shape)
- To analyze and adjust the mix of projects within each category or aspect
- To assess the resource demands on the organization, indicated by the size, timing, and number of projects shown
- To identify and adjust the gaps in the categories, aspects, sizes, and timing of the projects

- To identify potential career paths for developing project managers, such as team member of a derivative project, then team member of a platform project, manager of a derivative project, member of a breakthrough project, and so on

Next, the council must develop separate criteria and cost ranges for each category that determine those projects that will support the organizational strategy and goals. Example criteria might include alignment with the organization's goals/strategy, riskiness of the project, financial return, probability of success, likelihood of achieving a breakthrough in a critical offering, appeal to a large (or new) market, impact on customer satisfaction, contribution to employee development, knowledge acquisition, and availability of staff/resources.

Scales also need to be determined for each criterion to measure how different projects score on each of them. The scales on which these criteria are measured must be challenging so that the scores separate the best projects from those that are merely good. The scales should also serve as an initial screen, to start the process of winnowing out the weakest projects. Thus, they should include limits on their extremes, such as minimum rate of return (if a financial criterion is appropriate), maximum probability of technical failure given proposed budget and schedule, or minimum acceptable potential market share.

Finally, the council needs to set an importance weighting for the various criteria in each category. Note that even if the same criteria apply to multiple categories, their weights might be different. For example, if a firm needs to develop high-level, skilled project managers for their strategic projects, employee development might be more important for breakthrough projects but less important for derivative projects. Also, the weights might change depending on the life cycle stage of the project. For example, early in a project's life, strategic considerations are often most important while in the midpoint of a project, tactical considerations might be more important.

The model we have described above is a "weighted, factor scoring model," as described earlier. As noted then, there are some standard, well-known tools to help develop the weights, scales, and criteria such as the Delphi method (Dalkey, 1969), the analytic hierarchy process (AHP), (Saaty, 1980), a simplified version of AHP by Frame (1997), and even software such as *Expert Choice*®. For more complex situations, with large numbers of projects and or large councils, the more sophisticated approaches are often more helpful, particularly if used with software that automatically calculates the scores and ranks the projects.

Step 3: Collect Project Data

For each existing and proposed project, assemble the data appropriate to that category's criteria. Be sure to update the data for ongoing projects and not just use the data from the previous evaluation. For cost data, use "activity based costs" (see Section 7.1) rather than incremental costs. Challenge and try to verify all data; get other people involved in validating the data, perhaps even customers (e.g., market benefit). Include the timing, both date and duration, for expected benefits and resource needs. Use the project plan, a schedule of project activities, past experience, expert opinion, whatever is available to get a good estimate of this data. Then document any assumptions made so that they can be checked in the future as the project progresses. If the project is new, you may want to fund only enough work on the project to verify the assumptions or determine the window-of-opportunity for the proposed product or process, holding off full funding until later. Similarly, identify any projects that can be deferred to a later time period, those that must precede or follow other projects, those that support other projects or should be done in conjunction with them, those that can be outsourced, and other such special aspects of the projects.

Next, use the criteria score limits to screen out the weaker projects: Have costs on existing projects escalated beyond the project's expected benefits? Has the benefit of a project lessened because the organization's goals have changed? Does a competitor's new entry obviate the advantages of a project? Does a new (or old) project dominate an existing or proposed project in terms of its benefits, furtherance of organizational goals, reduced costs? Also, screen *in* any projects that do not require deliberation, such as projects mandated by regulations or laws, projects that are operating or competitive necessities, projects required for environmental or personnel reasons, and so on. The fewer projects that need to be compared and analyzed, the easier the work of the council.

Step 4: Assess Resource Availability

Next, assess the availability of both internal and external resources, by type, department, and timing. Note that labor availability should be estimated conservatively, leaving time for vacations, personal needs, illness, holidays, and most important, regular functional (nonproject) work. After allowing for all of these things that limit labor availability, add a bit more, perhaps 10 percent, to allow for the well-known fact that human beings need occasional short breaks to rest or meet other human needs. Timing is particularly important, since project resource needs by type typically vary up to 100 percent over the life cycle of projects. Needing a normally plentiful resource at the same moment it is fully utilized elsewhere may doom an otherwise promising project. Eventually, the council will be trying to balance aggregate project resource needs over future periods with resource availabilities so timing is as important as the amount of maximum demand and availability. This is the major subject of Chapter 9.

Step 5: Reduce the Project and Criteria Set

In this step, multiple screens are employed to try to narrow down the number of competing projects. As noted earlier, the first screen is each project's support of the organization's goals. Other possible screens might be criteria such as:

- Whether the required competence exists in the organization
- Whether there is a market for the offering
- How profitable the offering is likely to be
- How risky the project is
- If there is a potential partner to help with the project
- If the right resources are available at the right times

- If the project is a good technological/knowledge fit with the organization
- If the project uses the organizations strengths, or depends on its weaknesses
- If the project is synergistic with other important projects
- If the project is dominated by another existing or proposed project
- If the project has slipped in its desirability since the last evaluation

One way to evaluate the dominance of some projects over others, and at the same time eliminate nondifferentiating criteria, is by comparing the coefficients of variation of each of the criteria across the projects. This technique allows an analyst to maximize the variation within the project set across relevant criteria, eliminating similar projects that are dominated, and identifying criteria that, at least in this evaluation round, do not differentiate among the projects. See Raz (1997) for an example of this approach.

The result of this step may involve canceling some ongoing projects or replacing them with new, more promising projects. Beware, however, of the tendency to look more favorably upon new, untested concepts than on current projects experiencing the natural problems and hurdles of any promising project.

Step 6: Prioritize the Projects within Categories

Apply the scores and criterion weights to rank the projects within each category. It is acceptable to hold some hard-to-measure criteria out for subjective evaluation, such as riskiness, or development of new knowledge. Subjective evaluations can be translated from verbal to numeric terms easily by the Delphi or other methods and used in the weighted factor scoring model. It must be remembered that such criteria as riskiness are usually composite measures of a set of "risks" in different areas. The same is true of criteria like "development of new knowledge."

When checking the results of this step, however, reconsider the projects in terms of their benefits first and their resource costs second. The former are commonly more difficult to assess and a reconsideration based on more familiarity with the project profiling process and other project evaluations may suggest interchanging the priority of neighboring projects. This could be especially critical around the project cutoff point. Because the projects competing around the cutoff point are typically quite close in benefit/cost scores there are usually no serious consequences resulting from "errors." This is, however, an excellent problem on which to use *sensitivity analysis*.

It is also possible at this time for the council to summarize the "returns" from the projects to the organization. However, this should be done by category, not for each project individually since different projects are offering different packages of benefits that are not comparable. For example, R&D projects will not have the expected monetary return of derivative projects; yet it would be foolish to eliminate them simply because they do not measure up on this (irrelevant, for this category) criterion.

Step 7: Select the Projects to be Funded and Held in Reserve

The first task in this step is an important one: determining the mix of projects across the various categories (and aspects, if used) and time periods. Next, be sure to leave some percent (often 10–15 percent) of the organization's resource capacity free for new opportunities, crises in existing projects, errors in estimates, and so on. Then allocate the categorized projects in rank order to the categories according to the mix desired. It is usually a good practice to include some speculative projects in each category to allow future options, knowledge improvement, additional experience in new areas, and such.

Overall, the focus should be on committing to fewer projects but with sufficient funding to allow project completion. Document why late projects were delayed and why some, if any, were defunded. One special type of delayed project mentioned earlier is sometimes called an "out-plan" project (in contrast to the selected "in-plan" projects) (Englund and Graham, 2000). Out-plan projects are those that appear promising but are awaiting further investigation before a final decision is made about their funding, which could occur in the next PPP cycle or sooner, if they warrant the use of some of the 10–15 percent funding holdout.

The result of this step (and most of the project portfolio process) is illustrated in the Plan of Record shown in Figure 2-11. Here, the mix across categories is listed, the priorities and resource needs of each project are given, the timing (schedule) of each project over the PPP cycle (6 months assumed here) is shown (to match resource availability), the out-plan projects, if any, are shown, and the total resource needs and availabilities are listed.

Step 8: Implement the Process

The first task in this final step is to make the results of the PPP widely known, including the documented reasons for project cancellations, deferrals, and non-selection as was mentioned earlier. Top management must now make their commitment to this project portfolio process totally clear by supporting the process and the results. This may require a PPP champion near the top of the organization. As project proposers come to understand the workings and importance of the PPP, their proposals will more closely fit the profile of the kinds of projects the organization wishes to fund. As this happens, it is important to note that the council will have to concern itself with the reliability and accuracy of proposals competing for limited funds.

Senior management must fully fund the selected projects. It is not appropriate for senior management to undermine PPP and the council as well as strategically important projects by playing a game of arbitrarily cutting X percent from project budgets. The council needs to be wary of interpersonal or interdepartmental competition entering the scene at this point also. In some organizations, individuals with their own particular agenda will ignore committees and processes (they may be heard to argue that committees never affect anything anyway) until implementation time rolls around, and then they attempt to exercise their political power to undermine the results of others' long labors. If this does occur, it is indicative of serious organizational problems and the PPP process will fail until the problems are corrected.

Of course, the process will need to be repeated on a regular basis. The council should determine how often this should be, and to some extent it depends on the speed of change in the industry the organization is in. For some industries, quarterly analysis may be best while in slow-moving industries, yearly may be fine.

Category	Priority	Project	Resources	May	June	July	Aug	Sept	Oct
Derivative									
50% of mix	1	R	500						
	2	K	800						
	3	M	300						
Total			1600						
Available			(1800)						
External									
20% of mix	1	S	500						
	2	V	150						
	out-plan	LT							
Total			650						
Available			(720)						
Strategic									
30% of mix	1	A	600						
	2	W	370						
	0ut-plan	SB							
Total			970						
Available			(1080)						
Aggregate Total			3220						
Unspent			380						
10% reserve			400						
Total Available			4000						

Figure 2–11   Plan of Record

Finally, the process should be flexible and improved continuously. Instinct may suggest ways that the process may be altered to better match the competitive environment, or to reflect more closely the organization's goals. The process should be changed when it is found appropriate to do so, including categories, criteria, steps, the order of tasks, and so on.

2.8   PROJECT PROPOSALS

Now that project selection methods have been discussed, it is appropriate to consider what documentation is needed to evaluate a project that is being considered. The set of documents submitted for evaluation is called the *project proposal,* whether it is brief (a page or two) or extensive, and regardless of the formality with which it is presented. Several issues face firms preparing proposals, particularly firms in the aerospace, construction, defense, and consulting industries. These are:

1. Which projects should be bid on?
2. How should the proposal-preparation process be organized and staffed?
3. How much should be spent on preparing proposals for bids?
4. How should the bid prices be set? What is the bidding strategy? Is it ethical?

Generally, these decisions are made on the basis of their overall expected values, perhaps as reflected in a scoring model. In-house proposals submitted by a firm's personnel to that firm's top management do not usually require the extensive treatment given to proposals submitted to outside clients or agencies such as the Department of Defense. For the Department of Defense, a proposal must be precisely structured to meet the requirements contained in the official Request for Proposal (RFP) or Request for Quotation (RFQ)—more specifically, in the Technical Proposal Requirements (TPR) that is part of the RFP or RFQ.

The construction and preparation of a proposal to be submitted to the government or other outside funder is beyond the scope of this book. Fortunately, the subject has been well treated by Knutson (1996a, 1996b, and 1996c) in a three-part paper that begins with a discussion of the decision whether or not to seek some particular business. The series then covers the composition of a team to write the proposal and Knutson's view of how to structure, price, and submit the proposal. The interested reader is also referred to Rosenau (1991). Finally, it should be noted that customs, practices, rules, and laws concerning proposals vary from nation to nation (e.g., see Jergeas and Cooke, 1997).

All proposals should begin with a short summary statement (an "Executive Summary") covering the fundamental nature of the proposal in *minimally technical language,* as well as the general benefits that are expected. All proposals should be accompanied by a "cover letter." Roman (1986, pp. 67–68] emphasizes that the cover letter is a key marketing document and is worthy of careful attention. In addition to the Executive Summary and the cover letter, every proposal should deal with four distinct issues: (1) the nature of the technical problem and how it is to be approached; (2) the plan for implementing the project once it has been accepted; (3) the plan for logistic support and administration of the project; and (4) a description of the group proposing to do the work, plus its past experience in similar work.

The precise way in which the contents of a proposal are organized usually follows the directions found in the TPR or RFP, the stated requirements of a specific potential funder, the traditional form used by the organization issuing the proposal, or, occasionally, the whim of the writer. As is the case with most products, the highest probability of acceptance will occur when the proposal meets the expectations of the "buyer," as to form and contents. At times there is a tendency to feel that "nontechnical" projects (by which is usually meant projects that are not concerned with the physical sciences or a physical product) are somehow exempt from the need to describe how the problem will be approached and how the project will be implemented—including details such as milestones, schedules, and budgets. To deal with nontechnical projects casually is folly and casts considerable doubt on the proposer's ability to deliver on promises. (It is all too common for projects concerned with the development of art, music, drama, and computer software, among other "nontechnical" areas, to be quite vague as to deliverables, deadlines, and costs.) On the other hand, when the proposal is aimed at another division or department of the same parent organization, the technical requirements of the proposal may be greatly relaxed, but the technical approach and implementation plan are still required—even if their form is quite informal.

The Technical Approach

The proposal begins with a general description of the problem to be addressed or project to be undertaken. If the problem is complex, the major subsystems of the problem or project are noted, together with the organization's approach to each. The presentation is in sufficient detail that a knowledgeable reader can understand what the proposer intends to do. The general method of resolving critical problems is outlined. If there are several subsystems, the proposed methods for interfacing them are covered.

In addition, any special client requirements are listed along with proposed ways of meeting them. All test and inspection procedures to assure performance, quality, reliability, and compliance with specifications are noted.

The Implementation Plan

The implementation plan for the project contains estimates of the time required, the cost, and the materials used. Each major subsystem of the project is listed along with estimates of its cost. These costs are aggregated for the whole project, and totals are shown for each cost category. Hours of work and quantities of material used are shown (along with the wage rates and unit material costs). A list of all equipment costs is added, as is a list of all overhead and administrative costs.

Depending on the wishes of the parent organization and the needs of the project, time charts, Program Evaluation and Review Technique (PERT)/Critical Path Method (CPM), or Gantt charts are given for each subsystem and for the system as a whole. (See Chapter 8 for more about PERT/CPM and Gantt charts.) Personnel, equipment, and resource usages are estimated on a period-by-period basis in order to ensure that resource constraints are not violated. Major milestones are indicated on the time charts. Contingency plans are specifically noted. For any facility that might be critical, load charts are prepared to make sure that the facility will be available when needed.

The Plan for Logistic Support and Administration

The proposal includes a description of the ability of the proposer to supply the routine facilities, equipment, and skills needed during any project. Having the means to furnish artist's renderings, special signs, meeting rooms, stenographic assistance, reproduction of oversized documents, computer graphics, word processing, video teleconferencing, and many other occasionally required capabilities provides a "touch of class." Indeed, their unavailability can be irritating. Attention to detail in all aspects of project planning increases the probability of success for the project—and impresses the potential funder.

It is important that the proposal contain a section explaining how the project will be administered. Of particular interest will be an explanation of how control over sub-contractors will be administered, including an explanation of how proper subcontractor performance is to be insured and evaluated. The nature and timing of all progress reports, budgetary reports, audits, and evaluations are covered, together with a description of the final documentation to be prepared for users of the proposed deliverables. Termination procedures are described, clearly indicating the disposition of project personnel, materials, and equipment at project end.

A critical issue, often overlooked, that should be addressed in the administrative section of the proposal is a reasonably detailed description of how *change orders* will be handled and how their costs will be estimated. Change orders are a significant source of friction (and lawsuits) between the organization doing the project and the client. The client rarely understands the chaos that can be created in a project by the introduction of a seemingly simple change. To make matters worse, the group proposing the project seems to have a penchant for misleading the potential client about the ease with which "minor" changes can be adopted during the process of implementing the project. Control of change orders is covered in Chapter 11.

Past Experience

All proposals are strengthened by including a section that describes the past experience of the proposing group. It contains a list of key project personnel together with their titles and qualifications. For outside clients, a full résumé for each principal should be attached to the proposal.When preparing this and the other sections of a proposal, the proposing group should remember that the basic purpose of the document is to convince a potential funder that the group and the project are worthy of support. The proposal should be written accordingly.

Project Management in Practice
The Military Mobile Communications System—a Procurement Innovation

In 1981, the U.S. military was using a hodge-podge of communication equipment that largely didn't intercommunicate. Different services used different vendors, each with their own protocol, and equipment for voice communication was completely different than that for data, facsimile, or e-mail. James Ambrose, then Under-secretary of the Army, thus initiated a $4.2 billion project to completely revamp the entire

Army communications system, the largest communications program ever placed by the Army. His conception of the need included six unique acquisition guidelines that led to an extremely successful project:

1. The contractor is responsible for all aspects of systems acquisition, production, integration, fielding, training, logistics, and maintenance.

2. The contractor will satisfy 19 required design and functional features and as many of 82 desired features as possible.

3. The contractor will provide only fully developed, working equipment; there is to be virtually no engineering development.

4. Delivery of the system will start after 22 months and be completed 60 months after basic operations.

5. The contractor will buy every piece of equipment needed for each system, even if that equipment is already in use.

6. The contract is firm fixed price with the contractor accepting all cost risks.

In 1985, GTE won the bidding with a proposal $3 billion lower than the next competitor's. GTE has developed and refined their program management capabilities over a period of 35 years. A project team was assembled consisting of 32 sub-

contractors and 700 vendors to supply over 8,000 mobile radios, 1,400 telephone switching centers, and 25,000 telephones. This system can send and receive calls, electronic mail, data, and facsimiles to mobile units without interruption over an area of 37,500 square kilometers, even while the connective elements of the system are on the move.

The system interconnects with the existing U.S. Army communications equipment, as well as that of the other military services, NATO, and commercial satellite and landline telephone networks around the world. The system was tested in late 1985 for 10 slushy days during winter in eastern France. Mobile units crossed fields and roads, reconnecting between coverage areas, while switching centers jumped from location to location, simulating a regular Army corps during combat.

The final system met the requirement of 19 necessary features and 69 of the 82 desired features. The project also met the strict delivery deadlines and realized $21.7 million in cost savings as well. In 1991, the system was very successfully employed in the Persian Gulf for Operation Desert Shield/Storm. During the war period, the system operated for two straight weeks with only 45 minutes of downtime. It also was able to be set up and taken down in just the 30 minutes specified (completed in five minutes in one instance). It truly achieved the goal of "Ef-

fective communications from the foxhole to the theater commander to the President." This outstanding performance has been honored in four separate U.S. Army awards, including the Department of Defense (DoD) Value Engineering Contractor of the Year Award.

Source: A. A. Dettbarn, et al., "Excellence in Cost, Schedule, and Quality Performance," *PM Network,* January 1992.

SUMMARY

This chapter initiated our discussion of the project management process by describing procedures for strategically evaluating and selecting projects. We first described the strategic objective of using projects to help achieve the organization's goals and strategy, and a project portfolio process to help achieve this. We then outlined some criteria for project selection models and then discussed the general nature of these models. The chapter then described the types of models in use and their advantages and disadvantages. Considering the degree of uncertainty associated with many projects, a section was devoted to evaluating the impact of risk and uncertainty. Concluding the discussion, some general comments were made about data requirements and the use of these models. The final section discussed the documentation of the evaluation/selection process via project proposals.

The following specific points were made in this chapter:

- The role of projects in achieving the organization's goals and strategy is critical.

- The eight-step project portfolio process is an effective way to select and manage projects that are tied to the organization's goals.

- Primary model selection criteria are realism, capability, flexibility, ease of use, and cost.

- Preparatory steps in using a model include: (1) identifying the firm's objectives; (2) weighting them relative to each other; and (3) determining the probable impacts of the project on the firm's competitive abilities.

- Project selection models can generally be classified as either numeric or nonnumeric; numeric models are further subdivided into profitability and scoring categories.

- Nonnumeric models include: (1) the sacred cow; (2) the operating necessity; (3) the competitive necessity; and (4) comparative benefit.

- Profitability models include standard forms such as: (1) payback period; (2) average rate of return; (3) discounted cash flow; (4) internal rate of return; and (5) profitability index.

- Project management maturity measurement is a way of assessing an organization's ability to conduct projects successfully.

- Scoring models—the authors' preference—include: (1) the unweighted 0–1 factor model; (2) the unweighted factor scoring model; (3) the weighted factor scoring model; and (4) the constrained weighted factor scoring model.

- For handling uncertainty: (1) pro forma documents; (2) risk analysis; (3) and simulation with sensitivity analyses are all helpful.

- Special care should be taken with the data used in project selection models. Of concern are data taken from an accounting data base, how data are measured and conceived, and the effect of technological shock.

- Project proposals generally consist of a number of sections: (1) the technical approach; (2) the implementation plan; (3) the plan for logistic support and administration; and (4) past experience.

In the next chapter we consider the selection of the appropriate manager for a project and what characteristics are most helpful for such a position. We also address the issue of the project manager's special role, and the demands and responsibilities of this critical position.

GLOSSARY

Decision Support System A computer package and data base to aid managers in making decisions. It may include simulation programs, mathematical programming routines, and decision rules.

Delphi A formalized method of group decision making that facilitates drawing on the knowledge of experts in the group.

Deterministic Predetermined, with no possibility of an alternate outcome. Compare with stochastic.

Expert System A computer package that captures the knowledge of recognized experts in an area and can make inferences about a problem based on decision rules and data input to the package.

Maturity The sophistication and experience of an organization in managing multiple projects.

Model A way of looking at reality, usually for the purpose of abstracting and simplifying it, to make it understandable in a particular context.

Network A group of items connected by some common mechanism.

Portfolio A group or set of projects with varying characteristics.

Pro forma Projected or anticipated, usually applied to financial data such as balance sheets and income statements.

Programming An algorithmic methodology for solving a particular type of complex problem, usually conducted on a computer.

Project portfolio process An eight-step procedure for selecting, implementing, and reviewing projects that will help an organization achieve its strategic goals.

Risk analysis A procedure that uses a distribution of input factors and probabilities and returns a range of outcomes and their probabilities.

Sensitivity analysis Investigation of the effect on the outcome of changing some parameters or data in the procedure or model.

Simulation A technique for emulating a process, usually conducted a considerable number of times to understand the process better and measure its outcomes under different policies.

Stochastic Probabilistic, or not deterministic.

QUESTIONS

Material Review Questions

1. What are the four parts of a technical proposal?

2. By what criteria do you think managers judge selection models? What criteria *should* they use?

3. Contrast the competitive necessity model with the operating necessity model. What are the advantages and disadvantages of each?

4. What is a sacred cow? Give some examples.

5. Give an example of a Q-Sort process for project selection.

6. What are some of the limitations of project selection models?

7. What is the distinction between a qualitative and a quantitative measure?

8. How does the discounted cash flow method answer some of the criticisms of the payback period and average rate of return methods?

9. What are some advantages and disadvantages of the profit/profitability numeric models?

10. How is sensitivity analysis used in project selection?

11. Contrast risk with uncertainty. Describe the window-of-opportunity approach.

12. Describe the eight-step project portfolio process.

13. What does the term "maturity" mean?

14. How does a risk analysis operate? How does a manager interpret the results?

Class Discussion Questions

15. Which of the many purposes of the project portfolio process are most important to a firm with a low project management maturity? Which to a firm with high maturity?

16. What varieties of information can the portfolio diagram of Figure 2-1 show?

17. What is the real difference between profitability and scoring models? Describe a model that could fit both categories.

18. Can risk analysis be used for nonproject business decision making? Explain how.

19. Discuss how the following project selection models are used in real-world applications.
   (a) Capital investment with discounted cash flow.
   (b) Simulation models.

20. Why do you think managers underutilize project selection models?

21. Would uncertainty models be classified as profitability models, scoring models, or some other type of model?

22. Contrast validity with reliability. What aspects, if any, are the same?

23. Contrast subjective and objective measures. Give examples of the proper use of each type of measure when evaluating competing projects.

24. Can a measure be reliable, yet invalid? Explain.

25. What are some possible extensions of project evaluation models for the future?

26. Are there certain types of projects that are better suited for nonnumeric selection methods as opposed to numeric ones?

27. Identify some of the ethical issues that can arise in a bid response to an RFP.

28. Interpret the columns of data in Table 2-4. Does the $10,968 value mean that the project is expected to return only this amount of discounted money?

29. How would you find the probability in Figure 2-9 of an NPV of over $20,000?

30. Reconsider Table 2-3 to explain why the simulated outcome in Table 2-4 is only about half as much as the value originally obtained in Table 2-1. Does the spread of the data in Table 2-3 appear realistic?

Questions for Project Management in Practice

Implementing Strategy through Projects at Blue Cross/Blue Shield

31. Is the new project management approach to implementing strategy bottom-up or top-down?

32. What is the role of projects and their management in this new process? That is, wouldn't a functional approach have worked just as well?

33. What other benefits might you expect from a system such as this?

Project Selection for Spent Nuclear Fuel Cleanup

34. Why did it take five months to explain the problem to the stakeholders?

35. Why do you think the stakeholders no longer trusted the authorities?

36. What might have been the problems with options 1, 2, and 4?

37. How is option 3 a solution?

Selecting a Composting Project at Larry's Markets

38. Why do you think this particular project was selected?

39. If 69 percent of their waste byproducts were going to landfill in 1991, where were the rest going?

40. Of the numeric models, which would probably be most appropriate for selection among these types of projects?

The Military Mobile Communications System

41. What was apparently different about this acquisition project than previous ones?

42. Was the $3 billion lower proposal a significant portion of the total project cost?

43. What does Guideline #3 indicate about how previous contracting was done?

PROBLEMS

1. Two new Internet site projects are proposed to a young start-up company. Project A will cost $250,000 to implement and is expected to have annual net cash flows of $75,000. Project B will cost $150,000 to implement and should generate annual net cash flows of $52,000. The company is very concerned about their cash flow. Using the payback period, which project is better, from a cash flow standpoint?

2. Sean, a new graduate at a telecommunications firm, faces the following problem his first day at the firm: What is the average rate of return for a project that costs $200,000 to implement and has an average annual profit of $30,000?

3. A four-year financial project has net cash flows of $20,000; $25,000; $30,000 and $50,000 in the next four years. It will cost $75,000 to implement the project. If the required rate of return is 0.2, conduct a discounted cash flow calculation to determine the NPV.

4. What would happen to the NPV of the above project if the inflation rate was expected to be 4 percent in each of the next four years?

5. Calculate the profitability index for Problem 3. For Problem 4.

6. Use a weighted score model to choose between three methods (A, B, C) of financing the acquisition of a major competitor. The relative weights for each criterion are shown in the following table as are the scores for each location on each criterion. A score of 1 represents unfavorable, 2 satisfactory, and 3 favorable.

		Method		
Category	*Weight*	*A*	*B*	*C*
Consulting costs	20	1	2	3
Acquisition time	20	2	3	1
Disruption	10	2	1	3
Cultural differences	10	3	3	2
Skill redundancies	10	2	1	1
Implementation risks	25	1	2	3
Infrastructure	10	2	2	2

7. Develop a spreadsheet for Problem 6.
   a. What would your recommendation be if the weight for the implementation risks went down to 10 and the weight of cultural differences went up to 25?
   b. Suppose instead that method A received a score of 3 for implementation risks. Would your recommendation change under these circumstances?
   c. The vice president of finance has looked at your original scoring model and feels that tax considerations should be included in the model with a weight of 15. In addition, the VP has scored the methods on tax considerations as follows: method A received a score of 3, method B received a score of 2, and method C received a score of 1. How would this additional information affect your recommendation?

8. Nina is trying to decide in which of four shopping centers to locate her new boutique. Some locations attract to a higher class of clientele than others, some are in an indoor mall, some have a much greater customer traffic volume than others, and, of course, rent varies considerably from one location to another. Because of the nature of her store, she has decided that the class of clientele is the most important consideration, the higher the better. Following this, however, she must pay attention to her expenses and rent is a major item, probably 90 percent as important as clientele. An indoor, temperature-controlled mall is a big help, however, for stores such as hers where 70 percent of sales are from passersby slowly strolling and window shopping. Thus, she rates this as about 95 percent as important as rent. Last, a higher traffic volume of shoppers means more potential sales; she thus rates this factor as 80 percent as important as rent.
   As an aid in visualizing her location alternatives, she has constructed the following table. A "good" is scored as 3, "fair" as 2, and "poor" as 1. Use a weighted score model to help Nina come to a decision.

	Location			
	1	**2**	**3**	**4**
Class of clientele	Fair	Good	Poor	Good
Rent	Good	Fair	Poor	Good
Indoor mall	Good	Poor	Good	Poor
Traffic volume	Good	Fair	Good	Poor

9. Referring to Problem 8, develop a spreadsheet to help Nina select a location for her boutique. Suppose Nina is able to negotiate a lower rent at location 3 and thus raise its ranking to "good." How does this affect the overall rankings of the four locations?

10. A dot-com startup has decided to upgrade its server computers. It is also contemplating a shift from its Unix-based platform to a Windows-based platform. Three major cost items will be affected whichever platform they choose: hardware costs, software conversion costs, and employee training costs. The firm's technical group has studied the matter and has made the following estimates for the cost changes.

Using Crystal Ball® and assuming that the costs may all be represented by triangular distributions, simulate the problem 1000 times. Given the information resulting from the simulation, discuss the decision problem.

	A	B	C	D	E	F	G	H
1		Windows Platform				Unix Platform		
2		**Low**	**Likeliest**	**High**		**Low**	**Likeliest**	**High**
3	Hardware cost	$100,000	$125,000	$200,000		$80,000	$110,000	$210,000
4	Software conversion cost	$275,000	$300,000	$500,000		$250,000	$300,000	$525,000
5	Employee training cost	$9,000	$10,000	$15,000		$8,000	$10,000	$17,500
6								
7	Likeliest Total Project Cost		$435,000				$420,000	

INCIDENTS FOR DISCUSSION

Multiplex Company

Multiplex Company is in its third year of using a rather complex and comprehensive financial planning process. Shannon Chase, CEO of Multiplex, is very pleased with the output of the planning process. *Pro-forma* cash flow statements in particular are logical, organized, and pertinent to the firm's business strategy. However, implementation of the plans leaves something to be desired. Shannon is convinced that her departmental managers do a poor job of estimating the costs of resources and time required to complete the projects associated with the plan.

This fiscal year, eleven new strategic projects were identified. There were six major types of projects: new products, modifications of existing products, research and development, new applications studies, manufacturing process improvements, and reorganization of the sales department. Each project is sponsored by one of the functional department managers, who is required to prepare a simple financial analysis and a Gantt chart (see Chapter 8, Section 8.3) showing the aggregate time required to finish a project. This sponsor usually, but not always, winds up being assigned as the PM.

Tomorrow is the final day of the current year's strategic planning session. Ms. Chase plans to make a strong pitch to her managers to prioritize the projects to ensure that those most important to the company get done. In the past, it seemed as though all the projects lagged behind when resource problems arose. In the future, she wants a consensus from the managers about which projects will go on the back burner and which will proceed on schedule when problems are encountered.

Questions: Ms. Chase is not sure how to go about ranking the projects. Will the managers be able to achieve consensus? Should they use the financial analysis done by the project sponsor? Perhaps the planning group could use their collective experience to rank the projects subjectively. What method would you recommend to Ms. Chase? Support your recommendation.

L & M Power

In the next two years, a large municipal gas company must begin constructing new gas storage facilities to accommodate the Federal Energy Regulatory Commission's Order 636 deregulating the gas industry. The vice-president in charge of the new project believes there are two options. One option is an underground deep storage facility (UDSF) and the other is a liquified natural gas facility (LNGF). The vice-president has developed a project selection model and will use it in presenting the project to the president. For the models she has gathered the following information:

	Initial Cost	Operating Cost/ Cu.Ft.	Expected Life	Salvage Value
UDSF	$10,000,000	$0.004	20 years	10%
LNGF	25,000,000	0.002	15	5

Since the vice-president's background is in finance, she believes the best model to use is a financial one, net present value analysis.

Questions: Would you use this model? Why or why not? Base your answer on the five criteria developed by Souder and evaluate this model in terms of the criteria.

BIBLIOGRAPHY

ARCHIBALD, R. D. *Managing High Technology Programs and Projects.* New York: Wiley, 1992.

BAKER, B., and R. MENON. "Politics and Project Performance: The Fourth Dimension of Project Management." *PM Network,* November 1995.

BEALE, P., and M. FREEMAN. "Successful Project Execution: A Model," *Project Management Journal,* December 1991.

BOOZ, ALLAN, AND HAMILTON, INC. *Management of New Products.* New York: Booz, Allen, and Hamilton, Inc., 1966.

CHURCHMAN, C. W., R. L. ACKOFF, and E. L. ARNOFF. *Introduction to Operations Research.* New York: Wiley, 1957.

CLELLAND, D. I., AND W. R. KING. *Project Management Handbook.* New York: Van Nostrand-Reinhold, 1983.

DALKEY, N. C. *The Delphi Method: An Experimental Study of Group Opinion* (RM-5888-PR). Santa Monica, CA: The RAND Corporation, June 1969.

ENGLUND, R. L., AND R. J. GRAHAM. "From Experience: Linking Projects to Strategy," *Journal of Product Innovation Management,* Vol. 16, No. 1, 1999.

EVANS, J. R., and S. J. MANTEL, JR. "A New Approach to the Evaluation of Process Innovations." *Technovation,* October 1985.

EVANS, J. R., AND D. L. OLSON. *Introduction to Simulation and Risk Analysis.* Upper Saddle River, NJ: Prentice-Hall, 1998.

FINCHER, A., AND G. LEVIN. "Project Management Maturity Model," *Proceedings of the 28th Annual PMI Symposium,* Newtown Square, PA: PMI, 1997.

FRAME, J. D. *The New Project Management: Tools for an Age of Rapid Change, Corporate Reengineering, and other Business Realities,* San Francisco: Jossey-Bass, 1997.

GARCIA, A., and W. COWDREY. "Information Systems: A Long Way from Wall-Carvings to CRTs." *Industrial Engineering,* April 1978.

GITHENS, G. "Financial Models, Right Questions, Good Decision." *PM Network,* July 1998.

HAYES, R., and W. J. ABERNATHY. "Managing Our Way to Economic Decline." *Harvard Business Review,* July–August 1980.

HELIN, A. F., and W. E. SOUDER. "Experimental Test of a Q-Sort Procedure for Prioritizing R & D Projects." *IEEE Transactions on Engineering Management,* November 1974.

HERTZ, D. B., and H. THOMAS. *Risk Analysis and Its Applications.* New York: Wiley, 1983.

HUBER, G. P. "The Nature of Organizational Decision Making and the Design of Decision Support Systems," *MIS Quarterly,* June 1981.

IBBS, C. W., AND Y.H. KWAK. "Assessing Project Management Maturity," *Project Management Journal,* March 2000.

IRVING, R. H., and D. W. CONRATH. "The Social Context of Multiperson, Multiattribute Decision-making," *IEEE Transactions on Systems, Man, and Cybernetics,* May–June 1988.

JERGEAS, G. F., and V. G. COOKE. "Law of Tender Applied to Request for Proposal Process." *Project Management Journal,* December 1997.

KHORRAMSHAHGOL, R., H. AZANI, and Y. GOUSTY. "An Integrated Approach to Project Evaluation and Selection," *IEEE Transactions on Engineering Management,* November 1988.

KNUTSON, J. "Proposal Management: Analyzing Business Opportunities." *PM Network,* January, 1996a.

KNUTSON, J. "Proposal Management: Generating Winning Proposals, Part 1." *PM Network,* February 1996b.

KNUTSON, J. "Proposal Management: Generating Winning Proposals, Part 2." *PM Network,* March 1996c.

LAW, A. M., and W. KELTON. *Simulation Modeling and Analysis,* 2nd ed. New York: McGraw-Hill, 1990.

LIBERATORE, M. J., and G. J. TITUS. "The Practice of Management Science in R & D Project Management." *Management Science,* August 1983.

LONGMAN, A., D. SANDAHL, AND W. SPEIR. "Preventing Project Proliferation," *PM Network,* July 1999.

LUBIANIKER, S. "Opening the Book on the Open Maturity Model," *PM Network,* March 2000.

MANN, G. A. "VERT: A Risk Analysis Tool for Program Management." *Defense Management,* May–June 1979.

MANTEL, S. J., JR., J. R. EVANS, and V. A. TIPNIS. "Decision Analysis for New Process Technology," in B. V. Dean, ed., *Project Management: Methods and Studies.* Amsterdam: North-Holland, 1985.

MATZLER, K., and H. H. HINTERHUBER. "How to make product development projects more successful by integrating Kano's model of customer satisfaction into quality function deployment." *Technovation,* January 1998.

MEREDITH, J. "The Implementation of Computer Based Systems." *Journal of Operations Management,* October 1981.

MEREDITH, J., S. M. SHAFER, AND E. TURBAN. *Quantitative Business Modeling,* Cincinnati: South-Western, 2002.

MOYER, R. C., J. R. MCGUIGAN, and W. J. KRETLOW. *Contemporary Financial Management,* 7th ed., Cincinnati: South-Western, 1998.

PASCALE, S., CARLAND, J. W., and J. C. CARLAND. "A Comparative Analysis of Two Concept Evaluation Methods for New Product Development Projects." *Project Management Journal,* December 1997.

PROJECT MANAGEMENT INSTITUTE. *A Guide to the Project Management Body of Knowledge.* Newtown Square, PA: Project Management Institute, 2001.

RAZ, T. "An Iterative Screening Methodology for Selecting Project Alternatives." *Project Management Journal,* December 1997.

REMY, R. "Adding Focus to Improvement Efforts with PM³," *PM Network,* July 1997.

ROMAN, D. D. *Managing Projects: A Systems Approach.* New York: Elsevier, 1986.

ROSENAU, M. D., JR. *Successful Project Management,* 2nd ed. New York: Van Nostrand Reinhold, 1991.

ROSS, S. A., R. W. WESTERFIELD, and B. D. JORDAN. *Fundamentals of Corporate Finance,* 3rd ed., Homewood, IL: Irwin, 1995.

SAATY, T. S. *Decision for Leaders: The Analytic Hierarchy Process.* Pittsburgh: University of Pittsburgh, 1990.

SCHMIDT, R. L. "A Model for R & D Project Selection with Combined Benefit, Outcome and Resource Interactions," *IEEE Transactions on Engineering Management,* November 1993.

SCHUYLER, J. R. "Decision Analysis in Projects: Judgments and Biases." *PM Network,* January 1995.

SIMON, H. *The New Science of Management Decisions,* rev. ed. Englewood Cliffs, NJ: Prentice Hall, 1977.

SOUDER, W. E. "Utility and Perceived Acceptability of R & D Project Selection Models." *Management Science,* August 1973.

SOUDER, W. E. "Project Evaluation and Selection," in D. I. Cleland, and W. R. King, eds., *Project Manage-*

ment Handbook. New York: Van Nostrand Reinhold, 1983.

THOMAS, J., C.L. DELISLE, K. JUGDEV, AND P. BUCKLE. "Mission Possible: Selling Project Management to Senior Executives," *PM Network,* January 2001.

TOWNSEND, H. W. R., and G. E. WHITEHOUSE. "We Used Risk Analysis to Move Our Computer." *Industrial Engineering,* May 1977.

TURBAN, E., and J. R. MEREDITH. *Fundamentals of Management Science,* 6th ed. Homewood, IL: Irwin, 1994.

VAN GIGCH, J. P. *Applied General Systems Theory,* 2nd ed. New York: Harper & Row, 1978.

WHEELWRIGHT, S. C., AND K. B. CLARK. "Creating Project Plans to Focus Product Development," *Harvard Business Review,* March–April 1992.

The following case concerns a European firm trying to choose between almost a dozen capital investment projects being championed by different executives in the firm. However, there are many more projects available for funding than there are funds available to implement them, so the set must be narrowed down to the most valuable and important to the firm. Financial, strategic, and other data are given concerning the projects in order to facilitate the analysis needed to make a final investment recommendation to the Board of Directors.

C A S E

PAN-EUROPA FOODS S.A.*
C. Opitz and R. F. Bruner

In early January 1993, the senior-management committee of Pan-Europa Foods was to meet to draw up the firm's capital budget for the new year. Up for consideration were 11 major projects that totaled over (European Currency Unit) ECU208 million. Unfortunately, the board of directors had imposed a spending limit of only ECU80 million; even so, investment at that rate would represent a major increase in the firm's asset base of ECU656 million. Thus the challenge for the senior managers of Pan-Europa was to allocate funds among a range of compelling projects: new-product introduction, acquisition, market expansion, efficiency improvements, preventive maintenance, safety, and pollution control.

The Company

Pan-Europa Foods, headquartered in Brussels, Belgium, was a multinational producer of high-quality ice cream, yogurt, bottled water, and fruit juices. Its products were sold throughout Scandinavia, Britain, Belgium, the Netherlands, Luxembourg, western Germany, and northern France. (See Exhibit 1 for a map of the company's marketing region.)

The company was founded in 1924 by Theo Verdin, a Belgian farmer, as an offshoot of his dairy business. Through keen attention to product development, and shrewd marketing, the business grew steadily over the years. The company went public in 1979 and by 1993 was listed for trading on the London, Frankfurt, and Brussels exchanges. In 1992, Pan-Europa had sales of almost ECU1.1 billion.

Ice cream accounted for 60 percent of the com-

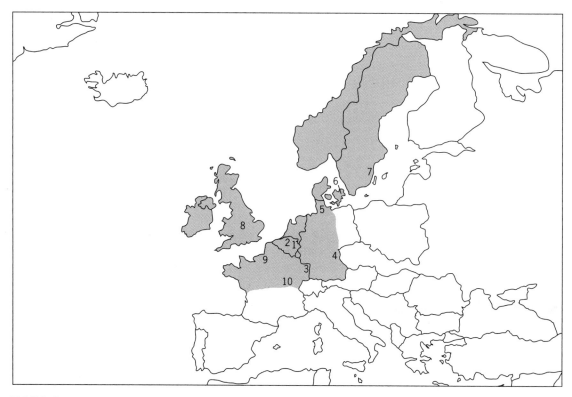

Exhibit 1   Pan-Europa Foods S. A. Nations where Pan-Europa Competed

Note: The shaded area in this map reveals the principal distribution region of Pan-Europa's products. Important facilities are indicated by the following figures:

1. Headquarters, Brussels, Belgium
2. Plant, Antwerp, Belgium
3. Plant, Strasbourg, France
4. Plant, Nuremberg, Germany
5. Plant, Hamburg, Germany

6. Plant, Copenhagen, Denmark
7. Plant, Svald, Sweden
8. Plant, Nelly-on-Mersey, England
9. Plant, Caen, France
10. Plant, Melun, France

pany's revenues; yogurt, which was introduced in 1982, contributed about 20 percent. The remaining 20 percent of sales was divided equally between bottled water and fruit juices. Pan-Europa's flagship brand name was "Rolly," which was represented by a fat, dancing bear in farmers' clothing. Ice cream, the company's leading product, had a loyal base of customers who sought out its high butterfat content, large chunks of chocolate, fruit, nuts, and wide range of original flavors.

Pan-Europa sales had been static since 1990 (see Exhibit 2), which management attributed to low pop-

ulation growth in northern Europe and market saturation in some areas. Outside observers, however, faulted recent failures in new-product introductions. Most members of management wanted to expand the company's market presence and introduce more new products to boost sales. These managers hoped that increased market presence and sales would improve the company's market value. Pan-Europa's stock was currently at eight times earnings, just below book value. This price/earnings ratio was below the trading multiples of comparable companies, but it gave little value to the company's brands.

Exhibit 2 Summary of Financial Results
(all values in ECU millions except
per-share amounts)

	Fiscal Year Ending December 31		
	1990	1991	1992
Gross sales	1,076	1,072	1,074
Net income	51	49	37
Earnings per share	0.75	0.72	0.54
Dividends	20	20	20
Total assets	477	580	656
Shareholders' equity (book value)	182	206	235
Shareholders' equity (market value)	453	400	229

Resource Allocation

The capital budget at Pan-Europa was prepared annually by a committee of senior managers who then presented it for approval by the board of directors. The committee consisted of five managing directors, the *président directeur-général* (PDG), and the finance director. Typically, the PDG solicited investment proposals from the managing directors. The proposals included a brief project description, a financial analysis, and a discussion of strategic or other qualitative considerations.

As a matter of policy, investment proposals at Pan-Europa were subjected to two financial tests, payback and internal rate of return (IRR). The tests, or hurdles, had been established in 1991 by the management committee and varied according to the type of project:

Type of Project	Minimum Acceptable IRR	Maximum Acceptable Payback Years
1. New product or new markets	12%	6 years
2. Product or market extension	10%	5 years
3. Efficiency improvements	8%	4 years
4. Safety or environmental	No test	No test

In January 1993, the estimated weighted-average cost of capital (WACC) for Pan-Europa was 10.5 percent. In describing the capital-budgeting process, the finance director, Trudi Lauf, said, "We use the sliding scale of IRR tests as a way of recognizing differences in risk among the various types of projects. Where the company takes more risk, we should earn more return. The payback test signals that we are not prepared to wait for long to achieve that return."

Ownership and the Sentiment of Creditors and Investors

Pan-Europa's 12-member board of directors included three members of the Verdin family, four members of management, and five outside directors who were prominent managers or public figures in northern Europe. Members of the Verdin family combined owned 20 percent of Pan-Europa's shares outstanding, and company executives owned 10 percent of the shares. Venus Asset Management, a mutual-fund management company in London, held 12 percent. Banque du Bruges et des Pays Bas held 9 percent and had one representative on the board of directors. The remaining 49 percent of the firm's shares were widely held. The firm's shares traded in London, Brussels, and Frankfurt.

At a debt-to-equity ratio of 125 percent, Pan-Europa was leveraged much more highly than its peers in the European consumer-foods industry. Management had relied on debt financing significantly in the past few years to sustain the firm's capital spending and dividends during a period of price wars initiated by Pan-Europa. Now, with the price wars finished, Pan-Europa's bankers (led by Banque du Bruges) strongly urged an aggressive program of debt reduction. In any event, they were not prepared to finance increases in leverage beyond the current level. The president of Banque du Bruges had remarked at a recent board meeting,

> Restoring some strength to the right-hand side of the balance sheet should now be a first priority. Any expansion of assets should be financed from the cash flow after debt amortization until the debt ratio returns to a more

prudent level. If there are crucial investments that cannot be funded this way, then we should cut the dividend!

At a price-to-earnings ratio of eight times, shares of Pan-Europa common stock were priced below the average multiples of peer companies and the average multiples of all companies on the exchanges where Pan-Europa was traded. This was attributable to the recent price wars, which had suppressed the company's profitability, and to the well-known recent failure of the company to seize significant market share with a new product line of flavored mineral water. Since January 1992, all of the major securities houses had been issuing "sell" recommendations to investors in Pan-Europa shares. Venus Asset Management in London had quietly accumulated shares during this period, however, in the expectation of a turnaround in the firm's performance. At the most recent board meeting, the senior managing director of Venus gave a presentation in which he said,

> Cutting the dividend is unthinkable, as it would signal a lack of faith in your own future. Selling new shares of stock at this depressed price level is also unthinkable, as it would impose unacceptable dilution on your current shareholders. Your equity investors expect an improvement in performance. If that improvement is not forthcoming, or worse, if investors' hopes are dashed, your shares might fall into the hands of raiders like Carlo de Benedetti or the Flick brothers.[1]

At the conclusion of the most recent meeting of the directors, the board voted unanimously to limit capital spending in 1993 to ECU80 million.

Members of the Senior Management Committee

The capital budget would be prepared by seven senior managers of Pan-Europa. For consideration,

[1]De Benedetti of Milan and the Flick brothers of Munich were leaders of prominent hostile-takeover attempts in recent years.

each project had to be sponsored by one of the managers present. Usually the decision process included a period of discussion followed by a vote on two to four alternative capital budgets. The various executives were well known to each other:

Wilhelmina Verdin (Belgian), PDG, age 57. Granddaughter of the founder and spokesperson on the board of directors for the Verdin family's interests. Worked for the company her entire career, with significant experience in brand management. Elected "European Marketer of the Year" in 1982 for successfully introducing low-fat yogurt and ice cream, the first major roll-out of this type of product. Eager to position the company for long-term growth but cautious in the wake of recent difficulties.

Trudi Lauf (Swiss), finance director, age 51. Hired from Nestlé in 1982 to modernize financial controls and systems. Had been a vocal proponent of reducing leverage on the balance sheet. Also had voiced the concerns and frustrations of stockholders.

Heinz Klink (German), managing director for Distribution, age 49. Oversaw the transportation, warehousing, and order-fulfillment activities in the company. Spoilage, transport costs, stockouts, and control systems were perennial challenges.

Maarten Leyden (Dutch), managing director for Production and Purchasing, age 59. Managed production operations at the company's 14 plants. Engineer by training. Tough negotiator, especially with unions and suppliers. A fanatic about production-cost control. Had voiced doubts about the sincerity of creditors' and investors' commitment to the firm.

Marco Ponti (Italian), managing director for Sales, age 45. Oversaw the field sales force of 250 representatives and planned changes in geographical sales coverage. The most vocal proponent of rapid expansion on the senior-management committee. Saw several opportunities for ways to improve geographical positioning. Hired from Unilever in 1985 to revitalize the sales organization, which he successfully accomplished.

Fabienne Morin (French), managing director for Marketing, age 41. Responsible for marketing research, new-product development, advertising, and, in general, brand management. The primary advocate of the recent price war, which, although financially difficult, realized solid gains in market share. Perceived a "window of opportunity" for product and market expansion and tended to support growth-oriented projects.

Nigel Humbolt (British), managing director for Strategic Planning, age 47. Hired two years previously from a well-known consulting firm to set up a strategic-planning staff for Pan-Europa. Known for asking difficult and challenging questions about Pan-Europa's core business, its maturity, and profitability. Supported initiatives aimed at growth and market share. Had presented the most aggressive proposals in 1992, none of which were accepted. Becoming frustrated with what he perceived to be his lack of influence in the organization.

The Expenditure Proposals

The forthcoming meeting would entertain the following proposals:

Project	Expenditure (ECU millions)	Sponsoring Manager
1. Replacement and expansion of the truck fleet	22	Klink, Distribution
2. A new plant	30	Leyden, Production
3. Expansion of a plant	10	Leyden, Production
4. Development and introduction of new artificially sweetened yogurt and ice cream	15	Morin, Marketing
5. Plant automation and conveyor systems	14	Leyden, Production
6. Effluent water treatment at four plants	4	Leyden, Production
7. Market expansion eastward	20	Ponti, Sales
8. Market expansion southward	20	Ponti, Sales
9. Development and roll-out of snack foods	18	Morin, Marketing
10. Networked, computer-based inventory-control system for warehouses and field representatives	15	Klink, Distribution
11. Acquisition of a leading schnapps brand and associated facilities	40	Humbolt, Strategic Planning

1. *Replacement and expansion of the truck fleet.* Heinz Klink proposed to purchase 100 new refrigerated tractor-trailer trucks, 50 each in 1993 and 1994. By doing so, the company could sell 60 old, fully depreciated trucks over the two years for a total of ECU1.2 million. The purchase would expand the fleet by 40 trucks within two years. Each of the new trailers would be larger than the old trailers and afford a 15 percent increase in cubic meters of goods hauled on each trip. The new tractors would also be more fuel and maintenance efficient. The increase in number of trucks would permit more flexible scheduling and more efficient routing and servicing of the fleet than at present and would cut delivery times and, therefore, possibly inventories. It would also allow more frequent deliveries to the company's major markets, which would reduce the loss of sales caused by stock-outs. Finally, expanding the fleet would support geographical expansion over the long term.

As shown in Exhibit 3, the total net investment in trucks of ECU20 million and the increase in working capital to support added maintenance, fuel, payroll, and inventories of ECU2 million was expected to yield total cost savings and added sales potential of ECU7.7 million over the next seven years. The resulting IRR was estimated to be 7.8 percent,

Exhibit 3 Free Cash Flows and Analysis of Proposed Projects[1] (all values in ECU millions)

Project	1 Expand Truck Fleet (note 3)	2 New Plant	3 Expanded Plant	4 Artificial Sweetener	5 Automation and Conveyer Systems	7 Eastward Expansion (note 5)	8 Southward Expansion (note 5)	9 Snack Foods	10 Inventory-Control System	11 Strategic Acquisition (note 6)
Investment										
Property	20.00	25.00	10.00	15.00	14.00	20.00	20.00	15.00	15.00	30.00
Working Capital	2.00	5.00						3.00		10.00
Year	**EXPECTED FREE CASH FLOWS** (note 4)									
0	(11.40)	(30.00)	(10.00)	(5.00)	(14.00)	(20.00)	(20.00)	(18.00)	(12.00)	(15.00)
1	(7.90)	2.00	1.25	(5.00)	2.75	3.50	3.00	3.00	5.50	(20.00)
2	3.00	5.00	1.50	(5.00)	2.75	4.00	3.50	4.00	5.50	5.00
3	3.50	5.50	1.75	3.00	2.75	4.50	4.00	4.50	5.00	9.00
4	4.00	6.00	2.00	3.00	2.75	5.00	4.50	5.00		11.00
5	4.50	6.25	2.25	4.00	2.75	5.50	5.00	5.00		13.00
6	5.00	6.50	2.50	4.50	2.75	6.00	5.50	5.00		15.00
7	7.00	6.75	1.50	5.00	2.75	6.50	6.00	5.00		17.00
8		5.00	1.50	5.50		7.00	6.50	5.00		19.00
9		5.25	1.50	6.00		7.50	7.00	5.00		21.00
10		5.50	1.50	6.50		8.00	7.50	5.00		59.00
Undiscounted Sum	7.70	23.75	7.25	22.50	5.25	37.50	32.50	28.50	4.00	134.00
Payback (years)	6	6	6	7	6	5	6	5	3	5
Maximum Payback Accepted	4	5	5	6	4	6	6	6	4	6
IRR	7.8%	11.3%	11.2%	17.3%	8.7%	21.4%	18.8%	20.5%	16.2%	28.7%
Minimum Accepted ROR	8.0%	10.0%	10.0%	12.0%	8.0%	12.0%	12.0%	12.0%	8.0%	12.0%
Spread	-0.2%	1.3%	1.2%	5.3%	0.7%	9.4%	6.8%	8.5%	8.2%	16.7%
NPV at Corp. WACC (10.6%)	-1.92	0.99	0.28	5.21	-0.87	11.99	9.00	8.95	1.16	47.97
NPV at Minimum ROR	-0.13	1.87	0.55	3.88	0.32	9.90	7.08	7.31	1.78	41.43
Equivalent Annuity (note 2)	-0.02	0.30	0.09	0.69	0.06	1.75	1.25	1.29	0.69	7.33

[1]The effluent treatment program is not included in this exhibit.

[2]The equivalent annuity of a project is that level annual payment over 10 years that yields a net present value equal to the NPV at the minimum required rate of return for that project. Annuity corrects for differences in duration among various projects. For instance, project 5 lasts only 7 years and has an NPV of 0.32 million; a 10-year stream of annual cash flows of 0.06 million, discounted at 8.0 percent (the required rate of return) also yields an NPV of 0.32 million. In ranking projects on the basis of equivalent annuity, bigger annuities create more investor wealth than smaller annuities.

[3]This reflects ECU11 million spent both initially and at the end of year 1.

[4]Free cash flow = incremental profit or cost savings after taxes + depreciation − investment in fixed assets and working capital.

[5]Franchisees would gradually take over the burden of carrying receivables and inventory.

[6]ECU15 million would be spent in the first year, 20 million in the second, and 5 million in the third.

marginally below the minimum 8 percent required return on efficiency projects. Some of the managers wondered if this project would be more properly classified as "efficiency" than "expansion."

2. *A new plant.* Maarten Leyden noted that Pan-Europa's yogurt and ice-cream sales in the southeastern region of the company's market were about to exceed the capacity of its Melun, France, manufacturing and packaging plant. At present, some of the demand was being met by shipments from the company's newest, most efficient facility, located in Strasbourg, France. Shipping costs over that distance were high, however, and some sales were undoubtedly being lost when the marketing effort could not be supported by delivery. Leyden proposed that a new manufacturing and packaging plant be built in Dijon, France, just at the current southern edge of Pan-Europa's marketing region, to take the burden off the Melun and Strasbourg plants.

The cost of this plant would be ECU25 million and would entail ECU5 million for working capital. The ECU14 million worth of equipment would be amortized over seven years, and the plant over ten years. Through an increase in sales and depreciation, and the decrease in delivery costs, the plant was expected to yield after-tax cash flows totaling ECU23.75 million and an IRR of 11.3 percent over the next ten years. This project would be classified as a market extension.

3. *Expansion of a plant.* In addition to the need for greater production capacity in Pan-Europa's southeastern region, its Nuremberg, Germany, plant had reached full capacity. This situation made the scheduling of routine equipment maintenance difficult, which, in turn, created production-scheduling and deadline problems. This plant was one of two highly automated facilities that produced Pan-Europa's entire line of bottled water, mineral water, and fruit juices. The Nuremberg plant supplied central and western Europe. (The other plant, near Copenhagen, Denmark, supplied Pan-Europa's northern European markets.)

The Nurmeberg plant's capacity could be expanded by 20 percent for ECU10 million. The equipment (ECU7 million) would be depreciated over seven years, and the plant over ten years. The increased capacity was expected to result in additional production of up to ECU1.5 million per year, yielding an IRR of 11.2 percent. This project would be classified as a market extension.

4. *Development and introduction of new artificially sweetened yogurt and ice cream.* Fabienne Morin noted that recent developments in the synthesis of artificial sweeteners were showing promise of significant cost savings to food and beverage producers as well as stimulating growing demand for low-calorie products. The challenge was to create the right flavor to complement or enhance the other ingredients. For ice-cream manufacturers, the difficulty lay in creating a balance that would result in the same flavor as was obtained when using natural sweeteners; artificial sweeteners might, of course, create a superior taste.

ECU15 million would be needed to commercialize a yogurt line that had received promising results in laboratory tests. This cost included acquiring specialized production facilities, working capital, and the cost of the initial product introduction. The overall IRR was estimated to be 17.3 percent.

Morin stressed that the proposal, although highly uncertain in terms of actual results, could be viewed as a means of protecting present market share, because other high-quality ice-cream producers carrying out the same research might introduce these products; if the Rolly brand did not carry an artificially sweetened line and its competitors did, the Rolly brand might suffer. Morin also noted the parallels between innovating with artificial sweeteners and the company's past success in introducing low-fat products. This project would be classed in the new-product category of investments.

5. *Plant automation and conveyor systems.* Maarten Leyden also requested ECU14 million to increase automation of the production lines at six of the company's older plants. The result would be improved throughput speed and reduced accidents, spillage, and production tie-ups. The last two plants the company had built included conveyer systems that eliminated the need for any heavy lifting by employees. The systems reduced the chance of injury to employees; at the six older plants, the company had sustained an average of 75 missed worker-days per year per plant in the last two years because of muscle injuries sustained in heavy lifting. At an average hourly wage of ECU14.00 per hour, over ECU150,000 per year was thus lost, and the possibility always existed of more serious injuries and lawsuits. Overall cost savings and depreciation totaling ECU2.75 million per year for the project were expected to yield an IRR of 8.7 percent. This project would be classed in the efficiency category.

6. *Effluent water treatment at four plants.* Pan-Europa preprocessed a variety of fresh fruits at its Melun and Strasbourg plants. One of the first stages of processing involved cleaning the fruit to remove dirt and pesticides. The dirty water was simply sent down the drain and into the Seine or Rhine rivers. Recent European Community directives called for any waste water containing even slight traces of poisonous chemicals to be treated at the sources and gave companies four years to comply. As an environmentally oriented project, this proposal fell outside the normal financial tests of project attractiveness. Leyden noted, however, that the water-treatment equipment could be purchased today for ECU4 million; he speculated that the same equipment would cost ECU10 million in four years when immediate conversion became mandatory. In the intervening time, the company would run the risks that European Community regulators would shorten the compliance time or that the company's pollution record would become public and impair the image of the company in the eyes of the consumer. This project would be classed in the environmental category.

7. and **8.** *Market expansions eastward and southward.* Marco Ponti recommended that the company expand its market eastward to include eastern Germany, Poland, Czechoslovakia, and Austria and/or southward to include southern France, Switzerland, Italy, and Spain. He believed the time was right to expand sales of ice cream, and perhaps yogurt, geographically. In theory, the company could sustain expansions in both directions simultaneously, but practically, Ponti doubted that the sales and distribu-

tion organizations could sustain both expansions at once.

Each alternative geographical expansion had its benefits and risks. If the company expanded eastward, it could reach a large population with a great appetite for frozen dairy products, but it would also face more competition from local and regional ice-cream manufacturers. Moreover, consumers in eastern Germany, Poland, and Czechoslovakia did not have the purchasing power that consumers did to the south. The eastward expansion would have to be supplied from plants in Nuremberg, Strasbourg, and Hamburg.

Looking southward, the tables were turned: more purchasing power and less competition but also a smaller consumer appetite for ice cream and yogurt. A southward expansion would require building consumer demand for premium-quality yogurt and ice cream. If neither of the plant proposals (i.e., proposals 2 and 3) were accepted, then the southward expansion would need to be supplied from plants in Melun, Strasbourg, and Rouen.

The initial cost of either proposal was ECU20 million of working capital. The bulk of this project's costs was expected to involve the financing of distributorships, but over the ten-year forecast period, the distributors would gradually take over the burden of carrying receivables and inventory. Both expansion proposals assumed the rental of suitable warehouse and distribution facilities. The after-tax cash flows were expected to total ECU37.5 million for eastward expansion and ECU32.5 million for southward expansion.

Marco Ponti pointed out that eastward expansion meant a higher possible IRR but that moving southward was a less risky proposition. The projected IRRs were 21.4 percent and 18.8 percent for eastern and southern expansion, respectively. These projects would be classed in the new market category.

9. *Development and roll-out of snack foods.* Fabienne Morin suggested that the company use the excess capacity at its Antwerp spice- and nut-processing facility to produce a line of dried fruits to be test-marketed in Belgium, Britain, and the Netherlands. She noted the strength of the Rolly brand in those countries and the success of other food and beverage companies that had expanded into snack-food production. She argued that Pan-Europa's reputation for wholesome, quality products would be enhanced by a line of dried fruits and that name association with the new product would probably even lead to increased sales of the company's other products among health-conscious consumers.

Equipment and working-capital investments were expected to total ECU15 million and ECU3 million, respectively, for this project. The equipment would be depreciated over seven years. Assuming the test market was successful, cash flows from the project would be able to support further plant expansions in other strategic locations. The IRR was expected to be 20.5 percent, well above the required return of 12 percent for new-product projects.

10. *Networked, computer-based inventory-control system for warehouses and field representatives.* Heniz Klink had pressed for three years unsuccessfully for a state-of-the-art computer-based inventory-control system that would link field sales representatives, distributors, drivers, warehouses, and even possibly retailers. The benefits of such a system would be shortening delays in ordering and order processing, better control of inventory, reduction of spoilage, and faster recognition of changes in demand at the customer level. Klink was reluctant to quantify these benefits, because they could range between modest and quite large amounts. This year, for the first time, he presented a cash-flow forecast, however, that reflected an initial outlay of ECU12 million for the system, followed by ECU3 million in the next year for ancillary equipment. The inflows reflected depreciation tax shields, tax credits, cost reductions in warehousing, and reduced inventory. He forecasted these benefits to last for only three years. Even so, the project's IRR was estimated to be 16.2 percent. This project would be classed in the efficiency category of proposals.

11. *Acquisition of a leading schnapps brand and associated facilities.* Nigel Humbolt had advocated making diversifying acquisitions in an effort to move beyond the company's mature core business but doing so in a way that exploited the company's skills in brand management. He had explored six possible related industries, in the general field of consumer packaged goods, and determined that cordials and liqueurs offered unusual opportunities for real growth and, at the same time, market protection through branding. He had identified four small producers of well-established brands of liqueurs as acquisition candidates. Following exploratory talks with each, he had determined that only one company could be purchased in the near future, namely, the leading private European manufacturer of schnapps, located in Munich.

The proposal was expensive: ECU15 million to buy the company and ECU25 million to renovate the company's facilities completely while simultaneously expanding distribution to new geographical markets.[2] The expected returns were high: after-tax cash flows were projected to be ECU134 million, yielding an IRR of 28.7 percent. This project would be classed in the new-product category of proposals.

Conclusion

Each member of the management committee was expected to come to the meeting prepared to present and defend a proposal for the allocation of Pan-Europa's capital budget of ECU80 million. Exhibit 3 summarizes the various projects in terms of their free cash flows and the investment-performance criteria.

---

[2]Exhibit 3 shows negative cash flows amounting to only ECU35 million. The difference between this amount and the ECU40 million requested is a positive operating cash flow of ECU5 million in year 1 expected from the normal course of business.

QUESTIONS

1. Using NPV, conduct a straight financial analysis of the investment alternatives and rank the projects.

2. What aspects of the projects might invalidate the ranking you just derived?

3. Reconsider the projects in terms of:
   - are any "must do" projects of the non-numeric type?
   - what elements of the projects might imply greater or lesser riskiness?
   - might there be any synergies between the projects?
   - do any of the projects have nonquantitative benefits or costs that should be considered in an evaluation?

4. Considering all the above, what screens/factors might you suggest to narrow down the set of most desirable projects? What criteria would you use to evaluate the projects on these various factors? Do any of the projects fail to pass these screens due to their extreme values on some of the factors?

5. Divide the projects into the four Project Profile Process categories of incremental, platform, breakthrough, and R&D. Draw an aggregate project plan and array the projects on the chart.

6. Based on all the above, which projects should the management committee recommend to the Board of Directors?

The following reading describes the approach Hewlett-Packard uses to select and monitor its projects for relevance to the firm's strategic goals. The article describes the behavioral aspects of the process as well as many of the technical tools, such as the aggregate project plan, the plan of record, and the software aids they employed. In addition, the authors give tips and identify pitfalls in the process so anyone else implementing their approach will know what problems to watch out for.

R E A D I N G

FROM EXPERIENCE: LINKING PROJECTS TO STRATEGY
R. L. Englund and R. J. Graham

Growth in organizations typically results from successful projects that generate new products, services, or procedures. Managers are increasingly concerned about getting better results from the projects under way in their organizaitons and in getting better cross-organizational cooperation. One of the most vocal complaints of project managers is that projects appear almost randomly. The projects seem unlinked to a coherent strtategy, and people are unaware of the total number and scope of projects. As a result, people feel they are working at cross-purposes, on too many unneeded projects, and on too many projects generally. Selecting projects for their strategic emphasis helps resolve such feelings and is a corner anchor in putting together the pieces of a puzzle that create an environment for successful projects [6].

This article covers a series of steps for linking projects to strategy. These steps constitute a process that can be applied to any endeavor. Included throughout

Reprinted from *Journal of Product Innovation Management*, Vol. 16, No. 1, pp. 58–69, 1999. Copyright ©1999 with permission from Elsevier Science Publishers.

are suggestions for action as well as guidelines to navigate many pitfalls along the path. Process tools help illustrate ways to prioritize projects. The lessons learned are from consulting with many firms over a long time period and from personal experiences in applying the lessons within Hewlett-Packard Company (HP), a $40 billion plus company where two thirds of its revenue derives from products introduced within the past 2 years.

The Importance of Upper Management Teamwork

Developing cooperation across an organization requires that upper managers take a systems approach to projects. That means they look at projects as a system of interrelated activities that combine to achieve a common goal. The common goal is to fulfill the overall strategy of the organization. Usually all projects draw from one resource pool, so they interrelate as they share the same resources. Thus, the system of projects is itself a project, with the smaller projects being the activities that lead to the larger project (organizational) goal.

Any lack of upper management teamwork reverberates throughout the organization. If upper managers do not model desired behaviors, there is little hope that the rest of the organization can do it for them. Any lack of upper management cooperation will surely be reflected in the behavior of project teams, and there is little chance that project managers alone can resolve the problems that arise.

A council concept is one mechanism used at HP to establish a strategic direction for projects spanning or-

ganizational boundaries. A council may be permanent or temporary, assembled to solve strategic issues. As a result, a council typically will involve upper managers. Usually its role is to set directions, manage multiple projects or a set of projects, and aid in cross-organizational issue resolution. Several of these council-like activities become evident through the examples in this article.

Employing a comprehensive and systematic approach illustrates the vast and important influence of upper management teamwork on project success. Increasingly evident are companies who initiate portfolio selection committees. We suggest that organizations begin by developing councils to work with project managers and to implement strategy. These councils exercise leadership by articulating a vision, discussing it with the project managers, asking them their concerns about and needs for implementing the strategy, listening carefully to them, and showing them respect so they become engaged in the process. In this way, upper managers and project managers develop the joint vision that is so necessary for implementation of strategy.

Process for Project Selection and Prioritization

Once the upper management team is established, they can follow a process to select sets of projects that achieve organizational goals. They are then ideally positioned to implement consistent priorities across all departments. Figure 1 represents a mental model of a way to structure this process. Outputs from the four steps interrelate in a true systems approach. This model comes from experience in researching and applying a

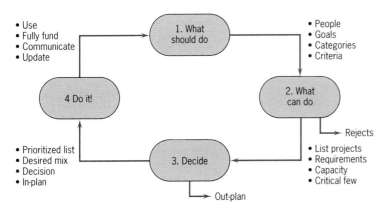

Figure 1 A systematic approach to selecting projects.

thorough approach to all the issues encountered in a complex organization. It is both simple in concept and complex in richness. The authors use the model both as an educational tool and to facilitate management teams through the process.

What the Organization Should Do and How to Know When You Are Doing It.   First, identify who is leading the process and who should be on the management team. More time spent here putting together a "mission impossible" team pays dividends later by getting up-front involvement of the people who will be affected by the decisions that will be made. Take care not to overlook any key-but-not-so-visible players who later may speak up and jeopardize the plan. This team may consist solely of upper managers or may include project managers, a general manager, and possibly a customer. Include representation of those who can best address the key opportunities and risks facing the organization. Ideally they control the resources and are empowered to make decisions on all projects. The leader needs to get explicit commitment from all these people to participate actively in the process and to use the resulting plan when making related decisions. Be aware that behavioral issues become super urgent. This process hits close to home and may have a severe impact on projects that people care personally about. Uncertainty and doubt are created if management does not tread carefully and pay attention to people concerns.

The team begins by listing all projects proposed and under way in the organization. Many times this step is a revelation in itself. A usual reaction is, "I didn't realize we had so many projects going on." The intent is to survey the field of work and begin the organizing effort, so avoid going into detailed discussion about specific projects at this point.

The team clarifies or develops the goals expected from projects. Be careful not to get constrained through considering only current capabilities. Many teams get sidetracked by statements such as "We don't know how to do that," effectively curtailing discussion on whether the organization ought to pursue the goal and develop or acquire the capability. Rather, the discussions at this stage center around organizational purpose, vision, and mission. This is a crucial step that determines if the rest of the project selection process can be successful. In the authors' experience, those organizations with clear, convincing, and compelling visions about what they should be doing move ahead rapidly.

Any lack of understanding or commitment to the vision by a member of the team leads to frustration, wheel spinning, and eventual disintegration of the whole process. This pattern is so prevalent that clarity of the goal or strategy is applied as a filter before agreeing to facilitate teams through the process.

Organize the projects into categories that will later make it easier to facilitate a decision-making process. Wheelwright and Clark [14] suggest using grids where the axes are the extent of product change and the extent of process change. Some organizations use market segments. The benefit to this effort is that seeing all projects and possible projects on a continuum allows checking for completeness, gaps, opportunities, and compliance with strategy. This might also be a good time to encourage "out-of-the-box" thinking about new ways to organize the work. Use creative discussion sessions to capture ideas about core competences, competitive advantage, and the like to determine a set of categories most effective for the organization. For example, the categories might be:

Evolutionary or derivative—sustaining, incremental, enhancing.
Platform—next generation, highly leveraged; and
Revolutionary or breakthrough—new core product, process, or business.

The actual products in Figure 2 were introduced to the market over time in alphabetical order and positioning shown. Although the figure represents a retrospective view, it illustrates a successful strategy of sequencing projects and products. There is a balanced mix of breakthrough products, such as A, followed by enhancements, B through E, before moving on to new platforms, F through H, and eventually developing a new architecture and product family with L. At the time, this strategy was improvisational [1]; it now represents a learning opportunity for planning new portfolios. No one area of the grid is overpopulated, and where large projects exist there are not too many of them.

Another reason to organize projects into these "strategic buckets" is to better realize what business(es) the organization is in. Almost every group the authors work with get caught in the "tyranny of the OR" instead of embracing the "genius of the AND" [2]. In trying to do too many projects and facing the need to make tradeoffs among them, the decision becomes *this* OR *that*. In reality, most organizations need a balanced portfolio that creates complete solutions for their cus-

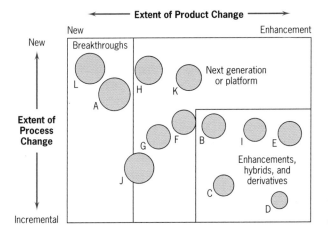

Figure 2 Bubble diagram of a product grid for one HP division. Size of bubble = size of project.

tomers. They need to do *this* AND *that*. The way to achieve this goal is to set limits on the size of each category and then focus efforts on selecting the best set of projects within each category. The collective set of categories becomes the desired mix, a way of framing the work of the organization. The ideal percentage that constitutes the size of each category can be determined from the collective wisdom of the team or perhaps through experimentation. The organization can learn the right mix over time but only if it makes a concerted effort to do so.

Within each category, determine criteria that can assess the "goodness"—quality or best fit—of choices for the plan. A criterion is a standard on which a comparative judgment or decision may be based. Because the types of projects and the objectives within categories may be quite different, develop unique criteria for each category or have a core set of criteria that can be modified. Many teams never get to the point of developing or clarifying criteria, and they usually want to discuss projects before agreeing on criteria; reversing the order is much more effective.

Several works on research and development project selection [8, 9, 12] provide a robust set of criteria for consideration. Examples include strategic positioning, probability of success, market size, and availability of staff. Most important is to identify the criteria that are of greatest significance to the organization; fewer are better. However, teams usually need to brainstorm many criteria before focusing on the few.

The role of each criterion is to help compare projects, not specify them. Select criteria that can measurably compare how projects support the organizational

strategy. For example, one criterion may be degree of impact on HP business as interpreted by a general manager. On a scaling model from 1 to 10, small impact scores a 2, strong a 6, critical to the success of one business an 8, and critical to the success of multiple businesses a 10. Most likely all proposed projects meet meaningful specifications and provide value to the organization. The task is to develop tough criteria to select the best of the best.

Some organizations use narratives to describe how each project contributes to the vision; others use numerical scores on whether one project is equal, moderate, or strongly better than another. It is also helpful to set thresholds or limits for projects that will be considered for the plan. These help to screen out projects so that later prioritization efforts can focus on fewer projects.

Writing a thorough description of each criterion helps ensure understanding of the intent and expectations of data that must be supplied to fulfill it. One team of three or four people at HP spent 5 days working only on the criteria they were to use for decision-making. And this was only the beginning; they next involved customers in the same discussion before reaching consensus and beginning to evaluate choices. An "Aha" occurred when people found they were wrong to assume that everyone meant the same thing by terms such as packaging; some used wider definitions than others did, and the misunderstanding only surfaced through group discussion. Asked if the selection process ever failed the team, its leader replied, "If the results didn't make sense, it was usually because the criteria weren't well defined." Unfortunately, most teams do not exhibit the same patience and discipline that allowed this team to be successful.

Before moving to the next step, the team should establish relative importance among criteria. Assign a weighting factor for each criterion. All criteria are important but some more so than others. The example in Figure 3 is the result of one team's brainstorming session that ultimately led to selecting four criteria. Breakout groups subsequently defined each criterion with subcriteria. They also devised scoring methods to apply the criteria. Collectively they then determined the respective weighting or importance of each criterion (see the Process Tools section for how they did this). Unlike threshold criteria that "gate" whether a project is go or no-go, all projects have to satisfy selection criteria to some extent. Weighting of criteria is the technique that can optimize and determine the best of the best. Another "Aha" that helped teams get through the hurdle to develop effective criteria is when they realized the task at this point is "weighting, not gating."

It is the authors' experience that criteria, while universally desired, are usually lacking or not formalized. One benefit of effective criteria is the shaping effect it has on behavior in the organization. When people know how projects will be scored, they tend to shape proposals in positive ways to meet the criteria better. A pitfall is when people play games to establish criteria that support personal agendas. Then it is up to the leader to identify and question these tactics. Remind people to support the greater good of the organization. Significant effort could be devoted to the behavioral aspects that become relevant when deciding upon criteria; suffice to say, be warned that this is a touchy area to approach with sensitivity and persuasiveness.

What the Organization Can Do.   The next step for the team is to gather data on all projects. Use similar factors when describing each project in order to ease the evaluation process. Engage people in extensive analysis and debate to get agreement on the major characteristics for each project. This is a time to ask basic questions about product and project types and how they contribute to a diversified set of projects. Reexamine customer needs, future trends, commercial opportunities, and new markets. The person consolidating the data should challenge assertions about benefits and costs instead of accepting assumptions that may have been put together casually. It is important for each member of the team to assess the quality of the data, looking closely at sources and the techniques for gathering the data. When putting cost figures together, consider using activity-based costing models instead of traditional models based on parts, direct labor, and overhead. Activity-based costing includes the commu-

Customer Satisfaction (28%) • Improves service levels • Results in more consistent and accurate information/transactions • Helps ensure services are delivered as promised & expected	**Employee Satisfaction (7%)** • Improves employee knowledge • Increases employee efficiency or effectiveness • Improves work/life balance • Positive impact to employee survey • Helps balance workload
Business Value (46%) • Achieves results that are critical for a specific window of opportunity • Minimizes risk for implementation and ongoing sustainability • Improves integration and relationships with partners • Provides a positive ROI in < 2 yrs • Aligns with business goals	**Process Effectiveness (19%)** • Enables employees to do things right the first time • Increases the use of technology for service delivery • Reduces manual work and non-value added activities • Increases employee self-sufficiency

Figure 3   Sample criteria and weighting, plus subcriteria, developed by one HP team.

nications, relationship building, and indirect labor costs that usually are required to make a project successful.

The team needs to constantly apply screening criteria to reduce the number of projects that will be analyzed in detail. Identify existing projects that can be canceled, downscaled, or reconceived because their resource consumption exceeds initial expectations, costs of materials are higher than expected, or a competitive entry to the market changed the rules of the game. The screening process helps eliminate projects that require extensive resources but are not justified by current business strategies; maybe the projects were conceived based on old paradigms about the business. The team can save discussion time by identifying must-do projects or ones that require simple go/no-go decisions, such as legal, personnel, or environmental projects. These fall right through the screens and into the allocation process. Determine if some projects can be postponed until others are complete or until new resources or funding become available. Can project deliverables be obtained from a supplier or subcontractor rather than internally? Involve customers in discussions. The team constantly tests project proposals for alignment with organizational goals.

It is not necessary to constrain the process by using the same criteria across all categories of projects. In fact, some teams found that different criteria for each category of projects was more effective. Also, consider adjusting the weighting of criteria as projects move through their life cycles. Kumar et al. [7] documented research showing that the most significant variable for initial screening of projects is the extent to which "project objectives fit the organization's global corporate philosophy and strategy." Other factors, such as available science and technology, become significant later during the commercial evaluation stage. A big "Aha" experienced by some teams when confronted with this data is that they usually did it the other way around. That explains why they got into trouble—by focusing on technology or financial factors before determining the link to strategic goals.

Cooper (and others before him) report that top-performing companies do not use financial methods for portfolio planning. Rather, they use strategic portfolio management methods where strategy decides project selection [3]. This lesson is still a hotly debated one, especially for those who cling to net present value as the single most important criterion. The difficulty lies in relying upon forecast numbers that are inherently fictitious. The authors' experience is that teams get much better results tapping their collective wisdom about the merits of each project based upon tangible assessments against strategic goals. Using computed financial numbers more often leads to arguments about computation methods and reliability of the data, resulting in unproductive team dynamics.

The next part of gathering data is to estimate the time and resources required for each potential and existing project. Get the data from past projects, statistical projections, or simulations. The HP Project Management Initiative particularly stresses in its organizational initiatives to get accurate bottom-up project data from work breakdown structures and schedules. Reconcile this data with top-down project goals. Document assumptions so that resource requirements can be revisited if there are changes to the basis for an assumption. For new or unknown projects, make a best estimate, focussing first on the investigation phase with the intent to fund only enough work to determine feasibility. The team can revisit the estimates when more information becomes available. Constantly improve estimation accuracy over time by tracking actuals with estimated task durations.

Next, the team identifies the resource capacity both within and outside the organization that will be available to do projects. Balance project with nonproject work by using realistic numbers for resource availability, taking into account other projects, vacations, meetings, personal appointments, and other interruptions. Tip: a wise planner consumes no more than about 50% of a person's available time.

One assessment about the quality of projects in a portfolio is to look at the rejects. In a story attributed to HP founder Bill Hewlett, he once established a single metric for how he would evaluate a portfolio manager's performance. He asked to see only the rejects. He reasoned that if the rejects looked good, then the projects that were accepted must be excellent.

All the actions in this step of the process are intended to screen many possible projects to find the critical few. The team may take a path through multiple screens or take multiple passes through screens with different criteria to come up with a short list of viable projects. Figure 4 represents one scenario where Screen 1 is a coarse screen that checks for impact on the strategic goal. Subsequent screens apply other criteria when more data are available. Any number of screens may be applied, up to the number n, until the team is satisfied that the remaining projects

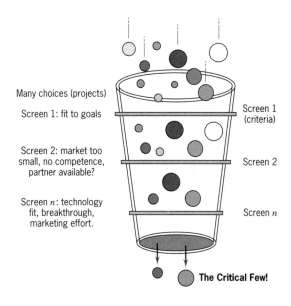

Many choices (projects)

Screen 1: fit to goals

Screen 1
(criteria)

Screen 2: market too
small, no competence,
partner available?

Screen 2

Screen *n*: technology
fit, breakthrough,
marketing effort.

Screen *n*

The Critical Few!

Figure 4   Application of criteria screens during a funneling process eliminates the *trivial many* projects from the *critical few* that the organization can realistically complete.

relate to compelling business needs. These steps actually save time because the next section on analysis can get quite extensive if all possible projects go through it.

It usually is necessary to go through several validation cycles before finishing the next step: the upper management team proposes project objectives, project teams provide preliminary estimates based on scope, schedule, and resources back to management, management is not happy with this response and makes adjustments, and so on. This exercise in due diligence is a healthy negotiation process that results in more realistic projects getting through the funnel.

Analyze and Decide on Projects.   The next step is to compare estimated resource requirements with available resources. A spreadsheet is useful to depict allocation of resources according to project priority.

Part of the analysis is qualitative: Consider the opportunity costs of committing to short-term, opportunistic, or poorly conceived projects that take resources away from future prospects that may be a better fit strategically. Also, avoid selecting "glamorous" new ideas over addressing the tough issues from ongoing projects. Some people lack the stamina to deal with the details of implementation and so are ready to jump to a new solution at the slightest glimmer of hope from the latest technology. This is a recipe for disaster. Also, be careful to balance the important

projects rather than giving in to urgent, but not so important, demands.

Documenting all the findings and supportive data using a common set of descriptive factors makes it easier to compare similar factors across projects. Use a "project charter" form or a template where all information about each project, its sponsors, and key characteristics is recorded.

The team can now prioritize the remaining projects. Focus on project benefits before costs; that way the merits of each project get full consideration. Later include costs to determine the greatest value for the money. Compute overall return from the set of projects, not from individual projects, because some projects may have greater strategic than monetary value. Requiring each and every project to promise a high financial return actually diminishes cooperation across an organization. Also, optimize return over time and continuity or uniformity of revenue from the projects. Some future projects must be funded early to ensure a revenue stream when current projects taper off.

Using previously agreed-upon criteria and weighting factors, the team compares each project with every other one within a category. Repeat the process for each criterion. See the discussion and example later in this article about using an analytical hierarchy process (AHP) to facilitate this step. Consider using software to compute results—an ordered list of projects within each category. A pitfall to avoid that engenders fear among the team is showing one list that prioritizes all projects from top to bottom. People get concerned when their project is on the line. It is not fair to compare internal development projects with high grossing products; keep them separated and within their respective categories.

Finally, the team is ready to decide which projects to pursue. Be prepared to do fewer projects and to commit complete resources required by projects that are selected. Decide on a mix of projects consistent with business strategy, such as 50% platform projects, 20% derivative projects, 10% breakthrough projects, and 10% partnerships. Note that these total only 90%; taking some lessons from financial portfolio management, diversify the set of projects by investing in some speculative projects. The team may not be sure which markets or technologies will grow, so buy an "option" and make a small investment to investigate the possibilities. Include experimental projects. It is also important to leave a small percent of development capacity uncommitted to take advantage of unexpected opportunities and to deal with crises when they arise.

Wheelwright and Clark [14] cite an organization that reduced the number of its development projects from 30 to 11: "The changes led to some impressive gains . . . as commercial development productivity improved by a factor of three. Fewer products meant more actual work got done, and more work meant more products." Addressing an internal project management conference, an HP Executive Vice President emphasized the need to focus on doing fewer projects, especially those that are large and complex: "We have to be very selective. You can manage cross-organizational complex programs if you don't have very many. If you have a lot of them with our culture, it just won't work. First of all, we need to pick those opportunities very, very selectively. We need to then manage them aggressively across the company. That means have joint teams work together, strong project management and leadership, constant reviews, a framework, a vision, a strong owner—all those things that make a program and project successful." Subsequently, a number of organizations sought help from the HP Project Management Initiative to systematically reduce 120 projects down to 30. Another organization went from 50 projects down to 17. It appears counter-intuitive, but by prioritizing and more carefully selecting projects, organizations actually get more projects completed.

Figure 5 illustrates a document that captures the output of this process. Record projects that are fully funded in an aggregate project plan (*in-plan*). In a separate section or another document, list projects for future consideration (*out-plan*); also capture and communicate reasons for delaying or not funding projects. The *plan of record* (POR) is both a process and a tool used by some organizations at HP to keep track of the total list of projects. It lists all projects under way or under consideration by the entity. If a project is funded and has resources assigned, it has achieved *in-plan* status. Projects below the cutoff line of available resources or that have not yet achieved priority status are on the *out-plan*. The figure also categorizes the projects and specifies the desired mix.

Project managers at HP describe one benefit of the POR process as identifying gaps between required and actual resources. For flexible changes, the process gets all people into the communications loop. If people want to add something, the management team has to decide what should be deleted. The process helps two divisions that work together agree on one prioritized list instead of two. They utilize direct electronic connections for bottom-up entry of projects and resources by all project managers into a centralized administration point.

Implement the Plan. No job is complete until it is acted upon. The team needs to "evangelize" all others in the organization to use the aggregate project plan or POR to guide people who plan work, make decisions, and execute projects. Although it may be countercultural to do so, do not starve committed projects of the resources they need. The team or the responsible upper managers need to enforce the plan by fully staffing committed projects; that now becomes possible because fewer projects are happening simultaneously. Also, use the plan to identify opportunities for leverage across projects or for process reengineering. Match people skills to project categories to tap their strengths and areas for contribution.

The team or a program management office needs to maintain the plan in a central place, such as a project office or online. Make it known to, and accessible by, all people in the organization doing projects, subject to confidentiality requirements. All the work to this point may go for naught if the process, the steps, and the results are not widely communicated.

The same people who develop the plan are also the ones who can best update it periodically, perhaps quarterly or as changes occur. Use tools such as an online shared database to gather data directly from project

ID	Strategic Category	Priority	Project	Head Ct	Timeline (Feb–Sep)
1	**Platform (Mix = 40%)**				
2	In Plan	1	Proj F	2	
3		2	Proj G	2	
4		3	Proj H	4	
5		4	Proj J	5	
6		5	Proj K	3	
7	Out Plan		Next Step		
8					
9	**Enhance (Mix = 20%)**				
10	In Plan	1	Proj B	2	
11		2	Proj C	1	
12		3	Proj D	1	
13		4	Proj E	2	
14		5	Proj I	1	
15	Out Plan		Fat City		
16					
17	**R & D (Mix = 30%)**				
18	In Plan	1	Proj A	7	
19		2	Proj L	5	
20					
21					
22					
23	Out Plan		Blue Sky		
24					
25	**Infrastructure (Mix = 10%)**				
26	In Plan	1	Bus. Plan	1	
27		2	Portfolio	1	
28		3	Update plan	1	
29					
30					
31	Out Plan		Corner Office		

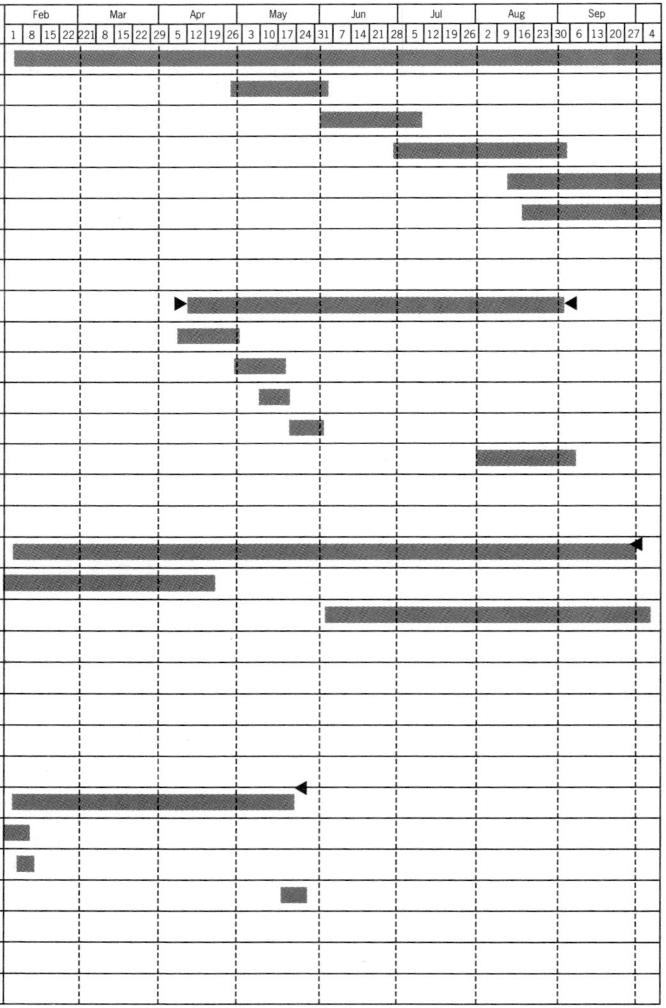

Timeline axis months: Feb | Mar | Apr | May | Jun | Jul | Aug | Sep

Figure 5 An example plan of record showing the mix of projects in priority order and the time line for each project.

managers about resources needed for each project. This system can be used both to gather data when developing the plan and to update it. View the plan as a "living document" that accurately reflects current realities.

The challenge for HP and many companies is to "master both adaptive innovation and consistent execution . . . again and again and again . . . in the context of relentless change . . . Staying on top means remaining poised on the edges of chaos and time . . . These edges are places of adaptive behavior. They are also unstable. This instability means that managers have to work at staying on the edge" [1]. The advice is clear: the plan is indispensable as a strategic guideline, but don't fall in love with it! Be prepared to adapt it and to communicate the changes.

Process Tools

One tool that can assist in the decision-making process is the AHP [10]. Because of the interactions among many factors affecting a complex decision, it is essential to identify the important factors and the degree that they affect each other before a clear decision can be made. The AHP helps structure a complex situation, identify its criteria and other intangible or concrete factors, measure the interactions among them in a simple way, and synthesize all the information to obtain priorities. The priorities then can be used in a benefit-to-cost determination to decide which projects to select. The AHP organizes feelings and intuition alongside logic in a structured approach to decision-making— helpful in complex situations where it is difficult to comprehend multiple variables together. An individual or team focuses on one criterion at a time and applies it step by step across alternatives. A number of sites across HP find value in using AHP.

In another example, a team got together to choose among a set of services they will offer to customers. More choices were available than the organization had capacity to support. After defining organizational strategy or product goals, the first task was to identify which criteria to enter into the decision-making process. After give-and-take discussion, they decided that the criteria were customer satisfaction, business value, process effectiveness, and employee satisfaction.

Next, the criteria were ranked according to priority by making pairwise comparisons between them. Which is the more desirable criterion and by how much, customer satisfaction or business value? Process effectiveness or employee satisfaction? Business value or

process effectiveness? These questions were asked about all possible pairs.

Each potential project or service then was scored underneath each criterion, and decisions were made about which projects to include in the portfolio, based upon existing resources. This team went on to create a POR similar to Figure 5.

A detailed explanation for computing the priority scores and the final rank ordering list can be quite complex, involving eigenvalues and eigenvectors, so it is much easier to get a software package (Expert Choice [4]) that does the computations. As an alternative, a spreadsheet could be constructed to normalize the numbers.

This process appears complex and analytical but is easy when the software handles the computations, and the management team concentrates on the comparisons. It is thorough in guiding the team to consider all criteria, both emotional and logical, and to apply them to all projects. One team rejected the process as too analytical, so be aware that it does not work for everyone.

The key benefit in doing this process is the improved quality of dialogue that occurs among the management team members. In facilitating a number of teams at HP through this process, each one achieved far more progress than they thought possible. People admit that they become addicted to the AHP process. They immediately buy the software. The systematic approach is feasible whether selecting products for a product line, projects that comprise a portfolio, or the best supplier or candidate for a job. In reality, the discussions are more valuable than the analysis. The process in this case provides the discipline that makes the dialogue happen.

Frame [5] offers an alternative "poor man's hierarchy." He puts selection criteria along the side as well as across the top of a grid. If the criterion on the side is preferred to the one on the top, put a 1 in the cell. If the criterion on top is preferred, put a 0 in the cell. Diagonals are blanked out where criteria would be compared to themselves. Below the diagonal, put the opposite value from corresponding cells above the diagonal. Then add up the numbers across the rows to get total scores, which provide a rank order. One team at HP modified this process to replace the 1s and 0s with an actual count of how 18 people voted in each pairwise comparison of alternatives. Again, they added up the rows and normalized the results for a priority order and weighted ranking (Figure 6).

This simplified hierarchy is especially helpful for

	Business	Customer	Technology	Employee		Total Votes	%
Business	***	16	16	18	=	50	46
Customer	2	***	13	15	=	30	28
Technology	2	5	***	14	=	21	19
Employee	0	3	4	***	=	7	7

Figure 6   A simplified hierarchy used by one HP team to weight criteria.

weighting criteria. It can be used for prioritizing projects when applied to one criterion at a time. It becomes bulky and less useful when applied to multiple projects over multiple criteria.

Barriers to Implementation

Now for a reality check. The model depicted in this article is thorough, and it integrates objective and subjective data. When all is said and done, however, people may throw out the results and make a different decision. Sometimes the reason is a hunch, an instinct, or simply a desire to try something different. Sometimes people have a pet project and use the process to justify its existence, or a hidden agenda may be at play—perhaps the need to maneuver among colleagues, trading projects for favors. Politics at this stage cannot be ignored, nor are they likely to disappear. It is imperative for leaders to become skilled in the political process. Any attempt at leading change in how an organization links projects to strategy is bound to meet resistance. The concept receives almost unanimous intellectual support. Implementing it into the heart and soul of all people in the organization is another story. It goes against the cultural norms in many organizations and conjures up all kinds of resistance if the values it espouses are not the norm in that organization. The path is full of pitfalls, especially if information is presented carelessly or perceived as final when it is work in process.

Some people resist because the process is too analytical. Some want decision-making to be purely interactive, intuitive, or the purview of a few people. A complete process cannot be forced upon people if the organization has more immediate concerns or unre-

solved issues. Resistance occurs when there is no strategy, the strategy is unclear, or people are uncomfortable with the strategy. Work on the process may come to a standstill when people realize how much work is involved to fully link projects to strategy. If the pain is not great enough with the status quo, people are not going to be ready to change.

And if people sense that the leader does not authentically believe in the elements, such as the goals, the process, or the tools, they are hesitant to follow with any enthusiasm. When the leader lacks integrity and exhibits incongruity between words and actions, people may go through the motions but do not exert an effort that achieves meaningful results.

Enablers for Effective Implementation

It is possible to lead people through this change process if the leader asks many questions, listens to the concerns of all people involved, and seeks to build support so that people feel they have an active role in developing the process [9]. A flexible process works better than a rigid one. Cultivate "champions" who have the credibility and fortitude to carry the process across the organization. Believe that change is possible.

When the effort appears too massive, one approach is to go after the low-hanging fruit. Start with one of the more pressing issues and use the general concepts of this model to address it. Still have a vision for what the organization ultimately can achieve but understand that patience and pacing are necessary to get there. Consider also that this process is hierarchical—it can be applied singularly or collectively, up or down the organization.

For people who get frustrated when all linkages are not present, the authors urge teams and individuals to "just do it." Small changes in initial conditions have enormous consequences. Eventually successes or small wins are noticed. The practices start to permeate an organization. This can happen in the middle, move up, and then over to other organizations. Incidentally, a corporate group like HP's Project Management Initiative helps facilitate this transformation. We do this by acting as a conduit for success stories and best practices.

Over the long run, we believe that organizations that follow a process similar to the one described increase their odds for greater success. This happens because teams of people following a systematic process and using convincing data to support their arguments more often produce better results than individuals. Their projects have more visibility, and the quality of dialogue and decision-making improve. The power of using criteria that are tightly linked with strategy and known by everyone in the organization is the mitigating effect it has to guide behavior in constructive ways. Having a process means it can be replicated and improved over time until it is optimized. It also means other people can learn the process and coach others, thereby creating a learning organization.

Questions

1. Why are successful projects so important to Hewlett-Packard?

2. How far should an evaluation team go in trying to quantify project contributions to the firm's mission or goals? What is the role of financial selection criteria in HP's project selection process?

3. Considerable attention is paid to the measures HP uses to evaluate its projects. Is the aim of carefully defining these measures to simplify the project selection process or something else?

4. What do the aggregate project plan and the plan of record illustrate to upper management?

5. When should out-plan projects be reconsidered for inclusion?

6. What was your impression of the the impact that HP's project selection process had on the number of projects underway? How do you expect HP would score on project management maturity?

7. How did the new project selection process handle non-numeric type projects? Risk? How did this new process alter new project proposals at HP?

References

1. BROWN, S. L., AND EISENHARDT, K. M. *Competing on the Edge: Strategy as Structured Chaos.* Boston: Harvard Business School Press, 1998.

2. COLLINS, J. C. AND PORRAS, J. I. *Built to Last: Successful Habits of Visionary Companies.* New York: HarperCollins, 1994.

3. COOPER, R. G., EDGETT, S. J. AND KLEINSCHMIDT, E. J. *Portfolio Management for New Products.* Reading, MA: Addison-Wesley, 1998.

4. "Expert Choice," Pittsburgh, PA: Expert Choice Inc. (see *www.expertchoice.com*).

5. FRAME, J. D. *The New Project Management: Tools for an Age of Rapid Change, Corporate Reengineering, and Other Business Realities.* San Francisco: Jossey-Bass Publishers, 1994.

6. GRAHAM, ROBERT J. AND ENGLUND, RANDALL L. *Creating an Environment for Successful Projects: The Quest to Manage Project Management.* San Francisco: Jossey-Bass Publishers, 1997.

7. KUMAR, V., et al. To terminate or not an ongoing R&D project: A managerial dilemma. *IEEE Transactions on Engineering Management* 279 (1996).

8. MARTINO, J. *R&D Project Selection.* New York: Wiley, 1995.

9. O'TOOLE, J. *Leading Change: Overcoming the Ideology of Comfort and the Tyranny of Custom.* San Francisco: Jossey-Bass Publishers, 1995.

10. SAATY, T. L. *Decision Making for Leaders.* Pittsburgh, PA: RWS, 1990.

11. STACEY, R. D. *Managing the Unknowable: Strategic Boundaries Between Order and Chaos in Organizations.* San Francisco: Jossey-Bass Publishers, 1992, p. 62.

12. TURTLE, Q. C. *Implementing Concurrent Project Management.* Englewood Cliffs, NJ: Prentice Hall, 1994.

13. WESTNEY, R. E. *Computerized Management of Multiple Small Projects.* New York: Dekker, 1992.

14. WHEELWRIGHT, STEPHEN and CLARK, KIM. Creating project plans to focus product development. *Harvard Business Review* March–April (1992).

CHAPTER

3

The Project Manager

In the last chapter, we described how projects are evaluated and selected for development. Before more progress can be made, a project manager (PM) must be appointed. This person will take responsibility for planning, implementing, and completing the project, beginning with the job of getting things started. Actually, the way to get things started is to hold a meeting. We will delay discussion of the initial project meeting, however, until Chapter 5 because it is the first step in the process of planning the project.

The PM can be chosen and installed as soon as the project is selected for funding or at any earlier point that seems desirable to senior management. If the PM is appointed prior to project selection or if the PM originated the project, several of the usual start-up tasks are simplified. On occasion, a PM is chosen late in the project life cycle, usually to replace another PM who is leaving the project for other work. For example, a large agricultural products firm regularly uses a senior scientist as PM until the project's technical problems are solved and the product has been tested. Then it replaces the scientist with a middle manager from the marketing side of the firm as marketing becomes the focal point of the project. (The transition is difficult and, according to firm spokespeople, the results are sometimes unsatisfactory.)

Usually, a senior manager briefs the PM on the project so that the PM can understand where it fits in the general scheme of things in the parent organization, and its priority relative to other projects in the system and to the routine work of the organization. The PM's first set of tasks is typically to prepare a preliminary budget and schedule, to help select people to serve on the project team, to get to know the client, to make sure that the proper facilities are available, to ensure that any supplies required early in the project life are available when needed, and to take care of the routine details necessary to get the project moving.

As people are added to the project, plans and schedules are refined. The details of managing the project through its entire life cycle are spelled out, even to the point of planning for project termination when the work is finally completed.

Mechanisms are developed to facilitate communication between the PM and top management, the functional areas, and the client. As plans develop still further, the PM holds meetings and briefings to ensure that all those who will affect or be affected by the project are prepared in advance for the demands they will have to meet as the project is implemented.

In this chapter we discuss the unique nature of project management and some of the ways project management differs from *functional* management. Our emphasis is on the role and responsibilities of the PM. We concentrate on the demands placed on the PM, particularly on those unique to project management. For example, consider the differences in the challenges faced by the project manager who must add a security/privacy segment in a software program and those faced by the PM who must design and implement a global database for an international chemical firm. We then identify the skills required by the project manager and link them to the nature of the task faced by the PM.

It is best to describe the PM's job relative to some assumptions about the nature of projects and the organization within which the project must function. We assume that the parent firm is functionally organized and is conducting many projects simultaneously with its ongoing, routine operations. We also assume a fairly large firm, a project that has some technical components, with an output to be delivered to an "arms-length" customer. Clearly, not all, and possibly even not most, projects operate under these circumstances, but these are the most demanding and we address the most difficult problems a PM might have to face. Smaller, simpler projects may not require the tools we will present here, but the PM for these projects should be aware that such tools exist. The term *technical components* as we apply it includes more than hardware. Any firm with a well-defined methodology of carrying out its mission has a technical component, as we use the phrase. For example, a systems analysis and functional requirements are among the technical components in most information systems projects, as is the due diligence document in a security offering.

Thus far, we have had in mind a PM with reasonably normal skills, and operating under reasonably normal circumstances. In the last three sections of this chapter, we will discuss a major complication for project managers—managing a project being carried out in a *multicultural,* environment. We emphasize the word multicultural, a word that is not synonymous with (but includes) projects whose member organizations and geographical locations may transcend national boundaries. In fact, it is not the differences in national boundaries that matter; it is differences in *cultures*. Moreover, it is not merely the differences in cultures that matter, it is also differences between the *environments* within which the projects are conducted—economic, political, legal, and sociotechnical environments. Multicultural projects present major challenges for the PM. They also have the potential for yielding great satisfaction and, one hopes, great rewards. In the interest of clarity, we will delay a discussion of these problems until Section 3.4.

In this chapter, two conditions receive special attention. Both have a profound effect on the outcome of the project, and neither is under the complete control of the

PM—though the PM can greatly influence both by dealing with the conditions early in the project life. The first of these concerns the degree to which the project has the support of top management. If that support is strong and reasonably unqualified, the project has a much better chance of success (Pinto and Slevin, 1989; Zimmerer and Yasin, 1998).

The second condition concerns the general orientation of the project team members. If they are highly oriented toward their individual, functional disciplines, as opposed to the project itself, project success is threatened. If, on the other hand, they tend to be oriented toward the project (that is, problem-oriented rather than discipline-oriented), the likelihood of success is much greater. As Thomas Hughes (1998) writes about the SAGE and Atlas projects,

> Teams of engineers, technicians, and scientists polarized around problems rather than disciplines. As a result, new discipline-transcending organizational forms . . . presided over system-building projects rather than discipline-bound departments. The transdisciplinary team approach is still considered front-edge management almost half a century later.

3.1   PROJECT MANAGEMENT AND THE PROJECT MANAGER

The Functional Manager versus the Project Manager

The best way to explain the unique role of the PM is to contrast it with that of a functional manager in charge of one of a firm's functional departments such as marketing, engineering, or finance (see Figure 3-1). Such department heads are usually specialists in the areas they manage. Being specialists, they are analytically oriented and they know something of the details of each operation for which they are responsible. When a technically difficult task is required of their departments, they know how to analyze and attack it. As functional managers, they are administratively responsible for deciding how something will be done, who will do it, and what resources will be devoted to accomplish the task.

A PM generally starts his or her career as a specialist in some field who is blithely informed by a senior manager that he/she is being promoted to the position of Project Manager on the Whizbang Project. The PM must now metamorphose from technical caterpillar into generalist butterfly. (For an excellent set of instructions for the transformation see Matson (1998).) The PM, new or experienced, must oversee many functional areas, each with its own specialists (see Figure 3-2). Therefore, what

Figure 3-1   Functional management organization chart: marketing department of an insurance company.

Figure 3-2   Project management organization showing typical responsibilities of a project manager.

is required is an ability to put many pieces of a task together to form a coherent whole—that is, the project manager must be more skilled at synthesis, whereas the functional manager must be more skilled at analysis. The functional manager uses the *analytic approach* and the PM uses the *systems approach.*

The phrase "systems approach" requires a short digression describing briefly what is meant by those words. A system can be defined as a set of interrelated components that accepts inputs and produces outputs in a purposeful manner. This simple statement is a bit more complicated than it appears. First, the word "purposeful" restricts our attention to systems that involve humans in some way. Machines are not purposeful, people are. Second, the notion of "inputs" and "outputs" implies some boundary across which the system's inputs arrive and outputs depart. This boundary differentiates the system from its "environment." Third, the nature of the interrelationships between the components defines the "structure" of the system.

The analytic method focuses on breaking the components of a system into smaller and smaller elements. We are not saying that this is wrong, it is merely inadequate for understanding a complex system. Regardless of the dissector's skill or the degree to which, say, a frog is dissected, the dissection allows only a partial understanding of the total animal "frog." The systems approach maintains that to understand a component, we must understand the system of which the component is a part. And to understand the system, we must understand the environment (or larger system) of which it is a part. At the beginning of his excellent book on the systems approach, John van Gigch (1978) quotes Blaise Pascal: "I find as impossible to know the parts without knowing the whole, as to know the whole without specifically knowing the parts."

Adoption of the systems approach is crucial for the project manager. One cannot understand and, thus, cannot manage a project without understanding the organizational program of which the project is a part, and the organization in which the program exists, as well as the environment of the organization. Consider, if you will, the problem of managing a project devoted to the development of software that will create and maintain a database, and to undertake this task without knowing anything about the decision support system in which the database will be used, or the operating system of the computers that will contain the DSS, or the purposes for which the information in the database will be used, and so forth. The literature on the systems approach is extensive, but Boulding (1956), Churchman (1979), van Gigch (1978), and Sir Stafford Beer's works (see, e.g., Beer, 1985), are classics in the field.

Our comparison between the PM and the functional manager reveals another crucial difference between the two. The functional manager is a direct, technical supervisor. The project manager is a facilitator and generalist. These simple statements, while true, are misleading. Both require specialized technical knowledge. The functional manager's knowledge must be in the technology of the process being managed. The PM must be competent in the science of project management (Sahlin, 1998; Zimmerer and Yasin, 1998), but this is not sufficient. The PM must also have technical competence in some aspects of the work being performed on the project. It appears, however, that there is considerable disagreement between researchers on the issue of how much technical knowledge is required. For a review of much of the relevant research on this problem, see Grant, Baumgardener, and Stone (1997). None of this lessens the importance of the PM's role as facilitator. In our opinion, there is strong evidence that the PM must be both generalist/facilitator and have a reasonably high level of technical competence in the science of the project. We will revisit the issue below when we discuss the need for the PM to have technical credibility.

Three major questions face the PM in this task of synthesis: What needs to be done, when must it be done (if the project is not to be late), and how are the resources required to do the job to be obtained. In spite of the fact that the PM is responsible for the project, and depending on how the project is organized, the functional managers will probably make some of the fundamental and critical project decisions. For example, they usually select the people who will actually do the work required to carry out the project. They may also develop the technological design detailing how the project will be accomplished. And they frequently influence the precise deployment of the project's resources. Once again, depending on how the project is organized, the functional managers have little or no direct responsibility for the results. As presented later (and in Chapter 4, "Project Organization"), this separation of powers between functional and project managers, which may aid in the successful completion of the project, is also a source of considerable "discomfort" for both.

Note here that the PM is responsible for organizing, staffing, budgeting, directing, planning, and controlling the project. In other words, the PM "manages" it, but the functional managers may affect the choice of technology to be used by the project and the specific individuals who will do the work. (It is not uncommon, however, for the PM to negotiate with functional managers about the assignment of special individuals to carry out certain project work.) Arguments about the logic or illogic of such an arrangement will fall on deaf ears. The PM cannot allow the functional manager to usurp control of the project. If this happens, work on the project is likely to become secondary to the work of the functional group and the project will suffer. But the functional manager cannot allow the PM to take over authority for technical decisions in the functional area or to control the assignment of functional area personnel.

At times, a senior manager (often the PM's immediate superior) will, in effect, take over the PM's job by exercising extremely close supervision over every action the PM takes, or will actually tell the PM precisely what to do. All of the powers normally delegated to the PM are withdrawn and the PM's boss runs the project. This condition is known as *micromanagement*. It stamps out any creativity or initiative from the PM or project workers, frustrates almost everyone connected with the project, and generally ensures mediocre performance, if not failure. The senior rationalizes the need for control with such statements as: "After all, the project is my responsibility," or "You must understand how important this project is to the firm," or "Superboss expects me to keep my eye on everything that goes on around here." Such nonsense sounds logical until subjected to analysis. The first comment denies the virtue of delegation. The second assumes that everyone except the speaker is stupid. The third is a paean to "self-importance." To be frank, we do not know how to cure or prevent micromanagement. It is practiced by individuals who have so little trust in their co-workers that they must control everything. Micromanagers are rarely likable enough for anyone to try to help them. Our considered advice to PMs who are micromanaged is to request a transfer.

At the other end of the spectrum, the relationship between the PM, the functional managers, the project team, and the PM's superior may be characterized as "collegial," and the organization may be populated by talented people. In such organizations conflict is minimized, cooperation is the norm, no one is terribly concerned with who gets the credit, and the likelihood of success is high. We will have more to say later in this chapter and in other chapters about building and maintaining teams. Effective teams tend to operate in a collegial mode. It is worth noting, however, that collegiality without talent leads to failure—even if the project team smiles a lot while failing.

Project Responsibilities

The PM's responsibilities are broad and fall primarily into three separate areas: responsibility to the parent organization, responsibility to the project and the client, and responsibility to the members of the project team. Responsibilities to the firm itself include proper conservation of resources, timely and accurate project communications, and the careful, competent management of the project. Many formal aspects of the communications role will be covered in Chapter 10 when the Project Management Information System is discussed, but one matter must be emphasized here. It is very important to keep senior management of the parent organization fully informed about the project's status, cost, timing, and prospects. Senior managers should be warned about likely future problems. The PM should note the chances of running over budget or being late, as well as methods available to reduce the likelihood of these dread events. Reports must be accurate and timely if the PM is to maintain credibility, protect the parent firm from high risk, and allow senior management to intercede where needed. ***Above all, the PM must never allow senior management to be surprised!***

The PM's responsibility to the project and client is met by ensuring that the integrity of the project is preserved in spite of the conflicting demands made by the many parties who have legitimate interests in the project. The manager must deal with the engineering department when it resists a change advised by marketing, which is responding to a suggestion that emanated from the client. In the meantime, contract administration says the client has no right to request changes without the submission of a formal Request for Change order. Manufacturing says that the argument is irrelevant because marketing's suggestion cannot be incorporated into the project without a complete redesign.

The PM is in the middle of this turmoil. The PM must sort out understanding from misunderstanding, soothe ruffled feathers, balance petty rivalries, and cater to the demands of the client. One must, of course, remember that none of these strenuous activities relieves the PM of the responsibility of keeping the project on time, within budget, and up to specifications.

In Chapter 4 it will become evident that it is very common for the PM to have no direct subordinates in spite of the fact that several, perhaps many, people "work for him/her" on the project. These people form what we have been referring to as the "project team." In spite of the strange circumstance where people are said to work for someone who is not their boss, the PM's relationship to the team may be considerably closer than one might expect, particularly when individuals are assigned to spend much or all of their time working on the project.

The project manager's responsibilities to members of the project team are dictated by the finite nature of the project itself and the specialized nature of the team. Because the project is, by definition, a temporary entity and must come to an end, the PM must be concerned with the future of the people who serve on the team. If the PM does not get involved in helping project workers with the transition back to their functional homes or to new projects, then as the project nears completion, project workers will pay more and more attention to protecting their own future careers and less to completing the project on time. These matters are discussed in more detail in Chapter 13, "Project Termination."

Some years ago, it was suggested that highly educated researchers required a "special type" of managing. In one large, research-oriented firm, when a scientist came up with a promising idea, the scientist was appointed project manager. Senior management in the firm decided that the scientist/PM should not be bothered with the mundane details of managing schedules and budgets. As a result, all such information was kept away from him or her and an outside person, with no formal connection to the project and little or no knowledge of the substance of the project maintained all cost and time data. This type of arrangement became known as "tweed coat management." The notion is based on two interesting assumptions; first that all research scientists wear tweed jackets (presumably with leather patches on the elbows), and second that the higher the level of formal education, the lower the level of "street smarts." To the best of our knowledge, there is no evidence supporting these odd assumptions. Like most people, scientists seem to respond positively to a caring, supportive managerial style. They also seem to be able to keep such records as are required by a reasonable senior management.

PM Career Paths

Many firms have a wide variety of types and sizes of projects in progress simultaneously. Of these, it is typical to find that most are not large enough or sufficiently complex to require a full-time manager. Quite a few project managers are in charge of several projects simultaneously. For example, it is not unusual to find that when a medium or large firm undertakes a program to computerize written records, several hundred projects result. In order to ensure consistency and easy intergroup transfer of data, the program is commonly managed by the division or department housing the computer software group rather than being spread out in the units developing or using particular records. The entire process is apt to take several years.

At the same time that the computerization program is going on, the firm may be planning and building a new factory (three years), undertaking several dozen R & D projects (one to seven years), improving the landscape surrounding its factory in Mussent Point (two months), considering the acquisition of another firm (six months), upgrading the equipment in its thiotimolene plant (two years), buying art works produced by artists in each city in which the firm operates for display in corporate offices (one year), planning the annual stockholders' meeting (three months), and doing a large number of other things, many of which are organized as projects.

Who manages these projects? Where does the company find people competent to manage such a wide variety of projects? In Chapter 1, we referred to the professionalization and rapid growth of project management, to PMBOK (the project management body of knowledge), as well as to the development of college and university-level courses and degree programs available in the field. Although the percentage of PMs who are academically trained is increasing, many of the current group of project managers have no college-level training in the field. By far, the largest group got their training in one or more of three ways: on-the-job, project management seminars and workshops lasting from one-half day to two weeks, or active participation in the programs of the local chapters attached to the Project Management Institute. A rapidly growing number of private consulting firms offer instruction in project management as well as programs preparing individuals for the PMI's examination for certification as Project Management Professionals (PMPs).

The great number of fairly small, short-term projects being carried out, when managed by an experienced PM, serve a purpose beyond the output of the projects themselves. They provide an excellent training ground for new project managers who frequently begin their preparation with involvement in some major aspect of a small project. A number of firms, Procter & Gamble for one, often take management trainees and give them some project-management responsibility; for instance, the guidance of a new cosmetic through test procedures to ensure that it is not toxic to users. Such experience serves to teach trainees many things, not the least of which are the importance of an organized plan for reaching an objective, of "follow-through," of negotiation with one's co-workers, and of sensitivity to the political realities of organizational life. The skills and experiences gained from managing a project, even a small one, are a scaled-down version of what it is like to run a full-sized organization. Thus, projects provide an excellent growth environment for future executives and for developing managerial skills.

One final note on this subject. If we have made the process of project management seem orderly and rational, we apologize. If any single descriptor could be used to characterize project management, the adjective would be "messy." In an excellent article that should be read by anyone interested in understanding the reality of management, Kotter (1982) has shown that general managers are less organized, less formal, and less structured than college students are led to believe. The same is undoubtedly true of project managers. This fundamental lack of organization and structure makes it all the more important that PMs implement good planning and organizational skills where possible, or the chaos becomes unmanageable.

The career path of a PM often starts with participation in small projects, and later in larger projects, until the person is given command over small and then larger projects. For example, the path could be tooling manager for small Project U, project engineer for larger Project V, manufacturing manager for large Project W, deputy project manager for large Project X, project manager for small Project Y, and project manager for large Project Z.

The actual establishment of multiple career paths to the top of organizations is more talked about than acted on. Wishful thinking aside, with a very few notable exceptions,* we know of no *specific* career paths that can take project managers to CEO positions. In a great many firms, however, experience as a PM is seen as a mandatory or desirable step on the way up the corporate ladder. The logic of such a view is obvious. The capability of a PM to meet the demands of senior management positions is clearly evidenced by the PM's ability to achieve the project's goals without the need for de jure authority while operating in an environment typified by uncertainty, if not chaos.

---

* For example, Eli Lilly and Co., the pharmaceutical firm, finds that projects involving new drugs often last 8–12 years. No PM would be willing to manage a project that long without the opportunity for promotion. Lilly, therefore, has established a career path for their PMs that potentially leads to the top of the firm. They already had career paths progressing through "administration" or "R & D" to the top and have clearly demonstrated the reality of both paths.

Project Management in Practice
The Project Management Career Path at AT&T

1889   1900   1939   1964   1969   1984

In 1988, as a result of the deregulation of the phone industry, AT&T announced that it was going to split itself into 19 separate Strategic Business Units. One of these, Business Communications Systems (BCS), is primarily focused on the customer PBX market. Following divestiture,

the executives at BCS realized that the old ways of doing business would not be competitive in the new, open market they now faced and decided to reengineer their whole process of providing PBXs to the market. They decided that organizing by project management would give them better control over their business and bring a competitive advantage to BCS. Thus, they set the goal of becoming the leader in project management in the industry.

AT&T had previously used project managers in many of its activities but in a significantly different way. For instance, it was more a project coordination responsibility that could be successfully completed through achieving the activities on a task list. However, the position was of low status and seen as only a temporary activity serving to carry someone on to a better functional position. Thus, the reward for doing a good job was to move into a functional position and get out of project management.

BCS realized it would have to change the whole nature of the project management role, and the entire structure of the organization as well, if it were to be successful in this strategy. They needed to develop professional project managers, plus a support system to maintain their abilities and careers in project management. The managerial mentality of two or three years on a project and then moving on to a functional job had to be changed to an attitude of professional pride in project management and staying in the field for the remainder of their careers. Equally important, the organizational mentality of admiring heroic rescues of projects in trouble had to be replaced with admiration for doing a competent job from the beginning and time after time. The challenge was to survive during the years it would take to evolve into a professional project management organization.

The reorganization for project management was a major project in itself, including the areas of candidate selection, education and training, compensation, career development, organizational restructuring, and methods development. In terms of organizational structure, a National Project Management (NPM) organization was created at the corporate level reporting to the service operating vice-president. Reporting to the director of NPM were three project directors spread across the United States, a systems support organization, and a methods and support staff. Program managers, project managers, and their subordinates reported to the project directors. This structure provided an integrated, self-contained project management group.

The project management career path now consists of:

- Trainee: a six-month position to learn about project management.
- Cost Analysis/Schedule Engineer: a 6–18 month team position reporting to a project manager.
- Site Manager: a 6–12 month position responsible for a large site and reporting to a program manager.
- Small Project Manager: sole responsibility for a $1M to $3M revenue project.
- Project Manager: responsible for $3M to $25M projects.
- Program Manager: responsible for multiyear projects and programs over $25M.

Candidates for the project manager career track are selected from BCS's Leadership Continuity Plan, a program to identify the people with the most potential to progress to middle and senior management levels of responsibility, as well as from career people within the organization. Particular skills sought are interpersonal leadership skills; oral and written communication skills; a presidential, big-picture perspective; political sensitivity; delegating, problem-solver orientation; optimistic, can-do attitude; planner mentality; kaizen (continuous improvement) spirit; and administrative, in-charge credibility.

BCS's Project Management organization now includes a staff in Denver and groups of project managers in Los Angeles, San Francisco, Atlanta, Chicago, Washington D.C., and New York City. These groups now manage over $500 million in projects, ranging in size from $1M to $92M. The project management approach is deemed the most capable in the field, setting the pace for AT&T's competitors.

Source: D. Ono, "Implementing Project Management in AT&T's Business Communications System," *PM Network,* October 1990.

3.2   SPECIAL DEMANDS ON THE PROJECT MANAGER

A number of demands are unique to the management of projects, and the success of the PM depends to a large extent on how capably they are handled. These special demands can be categorized under the following headings.

Acquiring Adequate Resources

It was noted earlier that the resources initially budgeted for a project are frequently insufficient to the task. In part, this is due to the natural optimism of the project proposers about how much can be accomplished with relatively few resources. Sometimes, it is caused by purposeful understatement of resource requirements to ensure that a project is accepted for funding. At times it is caused by the great uncertainty associated with a project. Many details of resource purchase and usage are deferred until the project manager knows specifically what resources will be required and when. For instance, there is no point in purchasing a centrifuge now if in nine months we will know exactly what type of centrifuge will be most useful.

The good PM knows there are resource trade-offs that need to be taken into consideration. A skilled machinist can make do with unsophisticated machinery to construct needed parts, but a beginning machinist cannot. Subcontracting can make up for an inadequate number of computer programmers, but subcontractors will have to be carefully instructed in the needs of the contractor, which is costly and may cause delays. Crises occur that require special resources not usually provided to the project manager. All these problems produce glitches in the otherwise smooth progress of the project. To deal with these glitches, the PM must scramble, elicit aid, work late, wheedle, threaten, or do whatever seems necessary to keep the project on schedule. On occasion, the additional required resources simply alter the project's cost-benefit ratio to the point that the project is no longer cost-effective. Obviously, the PM attempts to avoid these situations, but some of what happens is beyond the PM's control. This issue will be dealt with in detail in Chapter 13.

The problems of time and budget are aggravated in the presence of a phenomenon that has been long suspected but only proved in the mid-1980s (Gagnon, 1982; Gagnon and Mantel, 1987). The individual who has the responsibility for performing and completing a task sometimes overestimates the time and cost required. That individual's immediate supervisor often discounts the worker's pessimism but, in so doing, may underestimate the time and cost. Moving up the management hierarchy, each successive level frequently lowers the time and cost estimates again, becoming more optimistic about the ability of those working for them to do with less—or, perhaps, more forgetful about what things were like when they worked at such jobs. The authors have informally observed—and listened to complaints about—such doings in a variety of organizations. We suspect they reflect the superior's natural tendency to provide challenging work for subordinates and the desire to have it completed efficiently. The mere recognition of this phenomenon does not prevent it. Complaints to upper-level managers are usually met with a hearty laugh, a pat on the back, and a verbal comment such as, "I know you can do it. You're my best project manager, and you can. . . ."

Another issue may complicate the problem of resource acquisition for the PM. Project and functional managers alike perceive the availability of resources to be strictly limited and thus a strict "win-lose" proposition. Under these conditions, the "winners" may be those managers who have solid political connections with top management. Often, there are times in the life of any project when success or survival may depend on the PM's "friendship" with a champion high in the parent organization (Pinto and Slevin, 1989).

In an interesting book, Pinto (1996) makes clear the importance for the PM of understanding and cultivating "appropriate" political tactics. Occasionally, research on project management concludes that politics is unimportant or a hindrance to success for project managers. Our experience leads us to suspect that such research findings are suspect, possibly because of bias in the test instrument or possibly because the test subjects are inexperienced. "Politics" should be viewed as the mechanism by which the people in organizations make decisions. Those mechanisms may be used "appropriately" or "inappropriately," to use Pinto's terms. To use the political system for personal gain is inappropriate. To shun the political system simply because it might be used inappropriately is unwise. More will be said about this important subject in Chapter 6.

Acquiring and Motivating Personnel

A major problem for the PM is the fact that most of the people needed for a project must be "borrowed." With few exceptions, they are borrowed from the functional departments. The PM must negotiate with the functional department managers for the desired personnel, and then, if successful, negotiate with the people themselves to convince them to take on these challenging temporary project assignments.

Most functional managers cooperate when the PM comes seeking good people for the project, but the cooperative spirit has its limits. The PM will be asking for the services of the two types of people most needed and prized by the functional manager: first, individuals with scarce but necessary skills and, second, top producers. Both the PM and functional manager are fully aware that the PM does not want a "has-been," a "never-was," or a "never-will-be." Perceptions about the capabilities of individuals may differ, but the PM is usually trying to borrow precisely those people the functional manager would most like to keep.

A second issue may reduce the willingness of the functional manager to cooperate with the PM's quest for quality people. At times, the functional manager may perceive the project as more glamorous than his or her function and hence a potent source of managerial glory. The functional manager may thus be a bit jealous or suspicious of the PM, a person who may have little interest in the routine work of the functional area even if it is the bread and butter of the organization.

On its surface, the task of motivating good people to join the project does not appear to be difficult, because the kind of people who are most desired as members of a project team are those naturally attracted by the challenge and variety inherent in project work. Indeed, it would not be difficult except for the fact that the functional manager is trying to keep the same people that the PM is trying to attract. The subordinate who is being seduced to leave the steady life of the functional area for the glamour of a project can be gently reminded that the functional manager retains control of personnel evaluation, salary, and promotion for those people lent out to projects. (A few exceptions to these general rules will be discussed in Chapter 4.) There may even be comments about how easy it is to lose favor or be forgotten when one is "out of sight."

Unless the PM can hire outsiders with proven ability, it is not easy to gather competent people; but having gathered them, they must be motivated to work. Because the functional manager controls pay and promotion, the PM cannot promise much beyond the challenge of the work itself. Fortunately, as Herzberg (1968) has argued, that is often sufficient (also see Pinto and Slevin, 1989). Many of the project personnel are professionals and experts in their respective specialties. Given this, and the voluntary nature of their commitment to the project, there is the assumption that they must be managed "delicately."

It has long been assumed that in order to ensure creativity, professionals require minimal supervision, maximum freedom, and little control. As a matter of fact, William Souder (1974) has shown that the output of R & D laboratories is actually not correlated with the level of freedom in the lab. This finding is significant. The most likely explanation is that individual scientists have unique requirements for freedom and control. Some want considerable direction in their work, whereas others find that a lack of freedom inhibits creativity. Those who need freedom thus tend to work in organizations where they are allowed considerable latitude, and those who desire direction gravitate to organizations that provide it.

Motivation problems are often less severe for routine, repeated projects such as those in construction and maintenance, or for projects carried out as the sole activity of an organization (even if it is part of a larger organization). In such cases, the PM probably has considerable de facto influence over salary and promotion. Frequently, the cadre of these projects see themselves as engaged in similar projects for the long term. If the project is perceived as temporary, risky, and important, about all the PM can offer people is the chance to work on a challenging, high-visibility assignment, to be "needed," and to operate in a supportive climate. For most, this is sufficient incentive to join the project.

A story has it that when asked "How do you motivate astronauts?" a representative of NASA responded, "We don't motivate them, but, boy, are we careful about whom we select." The issue of motivating people to join and work creatively for a project is closely related to the kind of people who are invited to join. The most effective team members have some common characteristics. A list of the most important of these follows, but only the first is typically considered during the usual selection process.

1. *High-quality technical skills*   Team members must be able to solve most of the technical problems of a project without recourse to outside assistance. Even if the relevant functional department has furnished technical specialists to the project, the exact way technology is applied usually requires adaptation by the project team. In addition, a great many minor technical difficulties occur, always at inconvenient times, and need to be handled rapidly. In such cases, project schedules will suffer if these difficulties must be referred back to the functional departments where they will have to stand in line for a solution along with (or behind) the department's own problems.

2. *Political sensitivity*   It is obvious that the PM requires political skills of a high order. Although it is less obvious, senior project members also need to be politi-

cally skilled and sensitive to organizational politics. As we have noted several times, project success is dependent on support from senior management in the parent organization. This support depends on the preservation of a delicate balance of power between projects and functional units, and between the projects themselves. The balance can be upset by individuals who are politically inept.

3. *Strong problem orientation* Research conducted by Pill (1971), more than 25 years before Hughes's (1998) work, has shown that the chances for successful completion of a multidisciplinary project are greatly increased if project team members are *problem-oriented* rather than *discipline-oriented.* Pill indicates that problem-oriented people tend to learn and adopt whatever problem-solving techniques appear helpful, but discipline-oriented individuals tend to view the problem through the eyes of their discipline, ignoring aspects of the problem that do not lie within the narrow confines of their educational expertise. This is, of course, consistent with our insistence earlier in this chapter that the PM should adopt a systems approach to project management.

4. *Strong goal orientation* Projects do not provide a comfortable work environment for individuals whose focus is on activity rather than on results. Work flow is rarely even, and for the professionals a 60-hour week is common, as are periods when there seems to be little to do. "Clock watchers" will not be successful team members.

5. *High self-esteem* As we noted earlier, a prime law for projects (and one that applies equally well to the entire organization) is: *Never surprise the boss.* Projects can rapidly get into deep trouble if team members hide their failures, or even a significant risk of failure, from the PM. Individuals on the team should have sufficient self-esteem that they are not threatened by acknowledgment of their own errors, or by pointing out possible problems caused by the work of others. Egos must be strong enough that all can freely share credit and blame. We trust that the PM is aware that "shooting the messenger who brings bad news" will immediately stop the flow of any negative information from below—though negative surprises from above will probably be more frequent.

Dealing with Obstacles

> "What I need is a list of specific unknown problems that we will encounter."*
>
> Anonymous manager

---

*In mid-1988, the author received this and several other "Management Quotes" in an e-mail communication. They were reported to be entries in a magazine contest and supposedly came from "real-life managers." They have been set in a distinctive type so they will be easy to recognize. We list other such quotes in the same typeface, but without credit and without repeating this footnote.

One characteristic of any project is its uniqueness, and this characteristic means that the PM will have to face and overcome a series of crises. From the beginning of the project to its termination, crises appear without warning. The better the planning, the fewer the crises, but no amount of planning can take account of the myriad of changes that can and do occur in the project's environment. The successful PM is a fire fighter by avocation.

At the inception of the project, the "fires" tend to be associated with resources. The technical plans to accomplish the project have been translated into a budget and schedule and forwarded up the managerial hierarchy or sent to the client for approval. In an earlier section we noted that some of the budget and schedule is pared away at each successive step up the hierarchy. Each time this happens, the budget and schedule cuts must be translated into changes in the technical plans. Test procedures may be shortened, suppliers' lead times may be cut. The required cost and schedule adjustments are made, a nip here and a tuck there. To the people affected, these may well be crises. As we will note in Chapter 7, an obvious cure for these crises is to "pad" the budget when it is originally submitted. This is a bad idea and generally creates more serious problems than it solves.

The PM learns by experience; the wise PM learns from the experiences of others. Every project on which the PM has worked, whether as the project manager or not, is a source of learning. The war stories and horror tales of other PMs are vicarious experiences to be integrated with direct personal experience into a body of lore that will provide early-warning signals of trouble on the way. The lore will also serve as a bank of pretested remedies for trouble already at hand.

To be useful, experience must be generalized and organized. Managing a project is much like managing a business. Business firms often develop special routines for dealing with various types of fires. Expediters, order entry clerks, purchasing agents, dispatchers, shippers, and similar individuals keep the physical work of the system moving along from order to shipment. Human resource departments help put out "people fires" just as engineering helps deal with "mechanical fires." Fire fighting, to be optimally effective, should be organized so that fires are detected and recognized as early as possible. This allows the fires to be assigned to project team members who specialize in dealing with specific types of fires. Although this procedure does not eliminate crises, it does reduce the pain of dealing with them.

As the project nears completion, obstacles tend to be clustered around two issues: first, last-minute schedule and technical changes, and second, a series of problems that have as their source the uncertainty surrounding what happens to members of the project team when the project is completed. These two types of problems are very different from one another, as well as from the problems that faced the PM earlier in the life cycle of the project. The way to deal with last-minute schedule and technical changes is "the best you can." Beyond knowing that such changes will occur and will be disruptive to the project, there is little the PM can do except be prepared to "scramble."

Coping with the uncertainty surrounding what happens at the end of a project is a different matter. The issue will be covered at greater length in Chapter 13, but it deserves mention here because it is certainly an obstacle that the PM must overcome. The key to solving such problems is communication. The PM must make open communications between the PM and team members first priority. The notion of "open communications" requires that emotions, feelings, worries, and anxieties be communicated, as well as factual messages.

Making Project Goal Trade-offs

The PM must make trade-offs between the project goals of cost, time, and performance. The PM must also make trade-offs between project progress and process—that is, between the technical and managerial functions. The first set of trade-offs is required by the need to preserve some balance between the project time, cost, and performance goals. Conventional wisdom had it that the precise nature of the trade-offs varied depending on the stage of the project life cycle. At the beginning of the life cycle, when the project is being planned, performance was felt to be the most important of the goals, with cost and schedule sacrificed to the technical requirements of the project. Following the design phase, the project builds momentum, grows, and operates at peak levels. Because it accumulates costs at the maximum rate during this period, cost was felt to take precedence over performance and schedule. Finally, as the project nears completion, schedule becomes the high-priority goal, and cost (and perhaps performance) suffers. Research (Kalu 1993) has shown that these assumptions, sensible as they seem, are not true.

During the design or formation stage of the project life cycle, there is no significant difference in the importance project managers place on the three goals. It appears that the logic of this finding is based on the assumption that the project must be designed to meet all the client-set goals. If compromises must be made, each of the objectives is vulnerable. At times, however, a higher level of technical performance may be possible that, in the client's eyes, merits some softening of the cost or schedule goals. For example, a computer software project required that an information system be able to answer queries within 3 seconds 95 percent of the time. The firm designed such a system by ensuring that it would respond within 1.5 seconds 50 percent of the time. By meeting this additional standard, more stringent than that imposed by the client, it was able to meet the specified standard.

Schedule is the dominant goal during the buildup stage, being significantly more important than performance, which is in turn significantly more important than cost. Kloppenborg (1990, p. 127) conjectures that this is so because scheduling commitments are made during the buildup stage. Scheduling and performance are approximately tied for primacy during the main stage of the life cycle when both are significantly more important than cost, though the importance of cost increases somewhat between the buildup and main stages. During the final stage, phaseout, performance is significantly more important than schedule, which is significantly more important than cost. Table 3-1 shows the relative importance of each objective for each stage of the project life cycle.

The second set of trade-offs concerns sacrificing smoothness of running the project team for technical progress. Near the end of the project it may be necessary to insist that various team members work on aspects of the project for which they are not well trained or which they do not enjoy, such as copying or collating the final report. The PM can get a fairly good reading on team morale by paying attention to the

Table 3-1. Relative Importance of Project Objectives during Different Stages of the Project Life Cycle

Life Cycle Stage	Cost	Schedule	Performance
Formation	1	1	1
Buildup	3	1	2
Main	3	1	1
Phaseout	3	2	1

Note: 1 = most important.

Source: Kloppenborg and Mantel, 1990, p. 78.

response to such requests. This is, of course, another reason why the PM should select team members who have a strong problem orientation. Discipline-oriented people want to stick to the tasks for which they have been prepared and to which they have been assigned. Problem-oriented people have little hesitation in helping to do whatever is necessary to bring the project in on time, to "spec," and within budget.

The PM also has responsibility for other types of trade-offs, ones rarely discussed in the literature of project management. If the PM directs more than one project, he or she must make trade-offs between the several projects. As noted earlier, it is critical to avoid the appearance of favoritism in such cases. Thus, we strongly recommend that when a project manager is directing two or more projects, care should be taken to ensure that the life cycles of the projects are sufficiently different that the projects will not demand the same constrained resources at the same time, thereby avoiding forced choices between projects.

In addition to the trade-offs between the goals of a project, and in addition to trade-offs between projects, the PM will also be involved in making choices that require balancing the goals of the project with the goals of the firm. Such choices are common. Indeed, the necessity for such choices is inherent in the nature of project management. The PM's enthusiasm about a project—a prime requirement for successful project management—can easily lead him or her to: (1) overstate the benefits of a project, (2) understate the probable costs of project completion, (3) ignore technical difficulties in achieving the required level of performance, and (4) make trade-off decisions that are clearly biased in favor of the project and antithetical to the goals of the parent organization. Similarly, this enthusiasm can lead the PM to take risks not justified by the likely outcomes.

Finally, the PM must make trade-off decisions between the project, the firm, and his or her own career goals. Depending on the PM's attitudes toward risk, career considerations might lead the PM to take inappropriate risks or avoid appropriate ones.

Failure and the Risk and Fear of Failure

In Chapter 13, we will consider some research on characteristics that seem to be associated with project success or failure, but sometimes it is difficult to distinguish between project failure, partial failure, and success. Indeed, what appears to be a failure at one point in the life of a project may look like success at another. If we divide all projects into two general categories according to the degree to which the project is understood, we find some interesting differences in the nature and timing of perceived difficulties in carrying out a project. These perceptions have a considerable effect on the PM.

Assume that Type 1 projects are generally well-understood, routine construction projects. Type 2 projects are at the opposite pole; they are not well understood, and there may be considerable uncertainty about specifically what must be done. When they are begun, Type 1 projects appear simple. As they progress, however, the natural flow of events will introduce problems. Mother Nature seems habitually hostile. The later in the life cycle of the project these problems appear, the more difficult it is to keep the project on its time and cost schedule. Contingency allowances for the time and cost to overcome such problems are often built into the budgets and schedules for type 1 projects. But unless the project has considerable slack in both budget and schedule, an unlikely condition, little can be done about the problems that occur late in the project life cycle. As everyone from engineers to interior decorators knows, change orders are always received after the final design is set in concrete. And yet, Type 1 projects rarely fail because they are late or over budget, though they commonly are both. They fail because they are not organized to handle unexpected crises and deviations from plan and/or do not have the appropriate technical expertise to do so (Pinto and Slevin, 1989).

Type 2 projects exhibit a different set of problems. There are many difficulties early in the life of the project, most of which are so-called planning problems. By and large, these problems result from a failure to define the mission carefully and, at times, from a failure to get the client's acceptance on the project mission. Failure to define the mission leads to subsequent problems (e.g., failure to develop a proper schedule/plan, failure to have the proper personnel available to handle the technical problems that will arise, as well as failure to handle the crises that occur somewhat later in the project's life cycle) (Pinto and Mantel, 1990). These failures often appear to result from the inability to solve the project's technical problems. In fact, they result from a failure to define project requirements and specifications well enough to deal with the technical glitches that always occur. (See Chapter 12 for a further discussion of this subject.)

Perhaps more serious are the psychic consequences of such technical snags. The occurrence and solution of technical problems tend to cause waves of pessimism and optimism to sweep over the project staff. There is little doubt that these swings of mood have a destructive effect on performance. The PM must cope with these alternating periods of elation and despair, and the task is not simple. Performance will be strongest when project team members are "turned on," but not so much that they blandly assume that "everything will turn out all right in the end," no matter what. Despair is even worse because the project is permeated with an attitude that says, "Why try when we are destined to fail?"

Maintaining a balanced, positive outlook among team members is a delicate job. Setting budgets and schedules with sufficient slack to allow for Murphy's law, but not sufficient to arouse suspicion in cost and time-conscious senior management, is also a delicate job. But who said the PM's job would be easy?

Breadth of Communication

As is the case with any manager, most of the PM's time is spent communicating with the many groups interested in the project (Mintzberg, 1973). Running a project requires constant selling, reselling, and explaining the project to outsiders, top management, functional departments, clients, and a number of other such parties-at-interest to the project, as well as to members of the project team itself. The PM is the project's liaison with the outside world, but the manager must also be available for problem solving in the lab, for crises in the field, for threatening or cajoling subcontractors, and for reducing interpersonal conflict between project team members. And all these demands may occur within the span of one day—a typical day, cynics would say.

To some extent, every manager must deal with these special demands; but for a PM such demands are far more frequent and critical. As if this were not enough, there are also certain fundamental issues that the manager must understand and deal with so that the demands noted can be handled successfully. First, the PM must know *why* the project exists; that is, the PM must fully understand the project's intent. The PM must have a clear definition of how *success* or *failure* is to be determined. When making trade-offs, it is easy to get off the track and strive to meet goals that were really never intended by top management.

Second, any PM with extensive experience has managed projects that failed. As is true in every area of business we know, competent managers are rarely ruined by a single failure, but repeated failure is usually interpreted as a sign of incompetence. On occasion a PM is asked to take over an ongoing project that appears to be heading for failure. Whether or not the PM will be able to decline such a doubtful honor depends on a great many things unique to each situation: the PM's relationship with the program manager, the degree of organizational desperation about the project, the PM's seniority and track record in dealing with projects like the one in question, and other matters, not excluding the PM's ability to be engaged elsewhere when the "opportunity" arises. Managing successful projects is difficult enough that the PM is, in general, well advised not to volunteer for undertakings with a high probability of failure.

Third, it is critical to have the support of top management (Pinto and Slevin, 1989). If support is weak, the future of the project is clouded with uncertainty, and if it is a R&D project, it is more likely to be terminated (Green, 1995). Suppose, for example, that the marketing vice-president is not fully in support of the basic project concept. Even after all the engineering and manufacturing work has been completed, sales may not go all out to push the product. In such a case, only the chief executive officer (CEO) can force the issue, and it is very risky for a PM to seek the CEO's assistance to override a lukewarm vice-president. If the VP acquiesces and the product fails (and what are the chances for success in such a case?), the project manager looks like a fool. If the CEO does not force the issue, then the VP has won and the project manager may be out of a job. As noted earlier, political sensitivity and acumen are mandatory attributes for the project manager. The job description for a PM should include the "construction and maintenance of alliances with the leaders of functional areas."

Fourth, the PM should build and maintain a solid information network. It is critical to know what is happening both inside and outside the project. The PM must be aware of customer complaints and department head criticism, who is favorably inclined toward the project, when vendors are planning to change prices, or if a strike is looming in a supplier industry. Inadequate information can blind the PM to an incipient crisis just as excessive information can desensitize the PM to early warnings of trouble.

Finally, the PM must be flexible in as many ways, with as many people, and about as many activities as possible throughout the entire life of the project. The PM's primary mode of operation is to trade off resources and criteria accomplishment against one another. Every decision the PM makes limits the scope of future decisions, but failure to decide can stop the project in its tracks. Even here, we have a trade-off. In the end, regardless of the pressures, the PM needs the support of the non-involved middle and upper-middle management.

Negotiation

In order to meet the demands of the job of project manager—acquiring adequate resources, acquiring and motivating personnel, dealing with obstacles, making project goal trade-offs, handling failure and the fear of failure, and maintaining the appropriate patterns of communication—the project manager must be a highly skilled negotiator. There is almost no aspect of the PM's job that does not depend directly on this skill. We have noted the need for negotiation at several points in the previous pages, and we will note the need again and again in the pages that follow. The subject is so important, Chapter 6 is devoted to a discussion of the matter.

Project Management in Practice
The Wreckmaster at a New York Subway Accident

At 12:16 A.M., Wednesday August 28, 1991, a 10-car subway train on the Lexington Line beneath New York City jumped the track and crashed in the subway tunnel. Damage was massive—five cars were derailed, one was cut in half, another bent in two, possibly 150 persons injured, four dead. The train ripped out steel-girder support columns used to hold up the tunnel ceiling, as well as the street above which immediately sunk a half inch. Two tracks and a third rail had been ripped out and two signal sets, two stitches, and an air compressor room destroyed.

When such an emergency occurs, the New York City Transit Authority (NYCTA) immediately appoints a project master, called a "Wreckmaster," to oversee the handling of the disaster rescue and repair activities, and make sure that operations are returned to a safe condition as soon as possible. In this case, the goal was to have the subway back to normal operation by Tuesday morning rush hour, September 3, after the three-day holiday weekend. Such disasters are handled in eight phases:

Phase 1: Respond to injury—Get people out of danger, provide needed medical care, remove bodies and ensure that no victims remain in the debris.

Phase 2: Secure the area—Simultaneously with phase 1, eliminate other threats to life and property be disconnecting power, providing emergency lighting and ven-tilation, stopping other trains from entering the area, keeping nonrelevant pedestrian and vehicular traffic out.

Phase 3: Initiate command facilities—Concurrent with phases 1 and 2, set up and activate command and coordination structure for all emergency activities.

Phase 4: Remove debris—Collect and remove the elements and debris of the accident which would hinder rescue, clean-up, or repair.

Phase 5: Remove damaged equipment—Use cranes, cutting torches, and other equipment to remove the large, major equipment.

Phase 6: Facility repair—Repair the facilities as quickly as possible for continuing and normal use.

A worker looks at the wreckage of a subway car in the 135th Street Station in New York early Friday, July, 4, 1997, following a Thursday night derailment. Fifteen people were injured, two seriously, when the express train in Harlem derailed, leaving the unoccupied last car crushed and severed in half, according to police. (AP Photo/Emile Wamsteker)

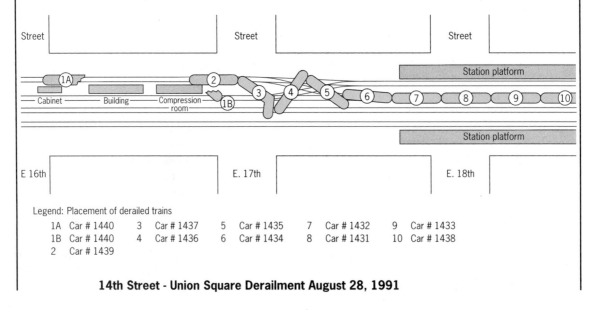

14th Street - Union Square Derailment August 28, 1991

Phase 7: Test—Make certain that all facilities are fully operational and safe by testing under the watchful eye of engineering, operations, and safety.

Phase 8: Clean-up—Clean the premises to the best possible state to permit normal operations.

The crash was heard at NYCTA's Union Square District 4 and about 40 transit police officers ran to assist passengers at the smoke-filled scene. Soon, officers from District 2, the Fire Department, and the Office of Emergency Management joined them. The Fire Department brought fans to help clear the smoke and steel cable to rope the wreckage to the support pillars so they could reach people still in the train cars without the roof caving in on them. Buses were dispatched to transport people to hospitals and the Red Cross provided food and drink for the injured. Some rescuers fainted from heat exhaustion as the temperature climbed over 110 degrees in the tunnel and two dozen police and fire workers were treated for injuries and smoke inhalation. Transit police officer Emanuel Bowser was riding the train when it crashed but helped people get off for more than four hours after the crash even though he had a broken arm and fingers himself.

After learning about the crash, NYCTA appointed Larry Gamache, general superintendent of track operations, as Wreckmaster. Larry set up team captains to coordinate activities throughout each phase of the disaster operations. A command center was established at a nearby subway station to direct and coordinate the operations. Gamache formulated a mental flow chart of how work needed to proceed. Each task had to be analyzed to determine what tasks had to precede it and what tasks could be conducted concurrently with it. Gamache also initiated regular meetings for all involved parties. This kept everyone informed of what progress had been made and provided them with estimates of future progress so activities could be coordinated and sequenced.

The plan was to remove the wreckage as quickly as possible from one track to allow worktrains to reach the disaster site, bringing needed materials to the site and removing debris. Since work had to continue throughout the Labor Day weekend on 12-hour shifts, facilities for the workers—food, drink, toilets—also had to be provided. Diesel trains pulled out the five cars that didn't derail, but getting out the other five was a special problem. A new Hoersh hydraulic jacking system was brought in from another district that could lift a 44-ton car, move it sideways, and set it back down on the tracks. Using these jacks reduced by half the labor required to rerail the cars, thereby significantly expediting the recovery. As work progressed through the long weekend, it became apparent that the disaster recovery plan would meet its Tuesday morning completion goal and, in fact, trains began running again by late evening on Monday.

Lawrence Gamache, Wreckmaster

Larry Gamache started at NYCTA 24 years ago as a trackworker and progressed through many managerial positions on his way to general superintendent, track operations. His experience over those years clearly qualified him for the responsibility of this assignment, particularly his involvement as field supervisor of several earlier derailments.

He was also highly involved in a three-year subway reconstruction project that required extensive coordination and negotiation with other city agencies, communities, and political leaders, all the while battling inclement weather and difficult conditions-yet, the project was completed ahead of time and well under budget. This experience, too, was valuable in coordinating the activities of the many groups involved in the disaster recovery.

Source: S. Nacco, "PM in Crisis Management at NYCTA: Recovering from a Major Subway Accident," *PM Network,* February 1992.

3.3   SELECTING THE PROJECT MANAGER

Selection of the project manager is one of the two or three most important decisions concerning the project. In this section, we note a few of the many skills the PM should possess in order to have a reasonable chance of success.

The following is a list of some of the most popular attributes, skills, and qualities that have been sought when selecting project managers:

- A strong technical background
- A hard-nosed manager
- A mature individual
- Someone who is currently available
- Someone on good terms with senior executives
- A person who can keep the project team happy
- One who has worked in several different departments
- A person who can walk on (or part) the waters

These reasons for choosing a PM are not so much wrong as they are "not right." They miss the key criterion. Above all, the best PM is the one who can get the job done! As any senior manager knows, hard workers are easy to find. What is rare is the individual whose focus is on the completion of a difficult job. Of all the characteristics desirable in a PM, this *drive to complete the task* is the most important.

If we consider the earlier sections of this chapter, we can conclude that there are four major categories of skills that are required of the PM and serve as the key criteria for selection, given that the candidate has a powerful bias toward task completion. Moreover, it is not sufficient for the PM simply to possess these skills; they must also be perceived by others. The fact and the perception are equally important.

Credibility

The PM needs two kinds of credibility. First is *technical credibility*. The PM must be perceived by the client, senior executives, the functional departments, and the project team as possessing sufficient technical knowledge to direct the project. A PM with reasonable technical competence seems to be associated with project success and is seen by project team members to be a "positive" leadership characteristic (Ford and McLaughlin, 1992; Zimmerer and Yasin, 1998). (We remind the reader that "technical credibility" includes technical knowledge in such arcane fields as accounting, law, psychology, anthropology, religion, history, playwriting, Greek, and a host of other nonhard sciences.) The PM does not need to have a high level of expertise, know more than any individual team members (or all of them), or be able to stand toe-to-toe and intellectually slug it out with experts in the various functional areas. Quite simply, the PM has to have a reasonable understanding of the base technologies on which the project rests, must be able to explain project technology to senior management, and must be able to interpret the technical needs and wants of the client (and senior management) to the project team. Similarly, the PM must be able to hear the problems of the project team and understand them sufficiently to address them, possibly by communicating them to upper management.

Second, the PM must be *administratively credible*. The PM has several key administrative responsibilities that must be performed with apparently effortless skill. One of these responsibilities is to the client and senior management—to keep the project on schedule and within cost and to make sure that project reports are accurate and timely. This can place the PM in an ethically awkward situation sometimes. Another responsibility is to the project team—to make sure that material, equipment, and labor are available when needed. Still another responsibility is to represent the interests of all parties to the project (team, management, functional departments, and client) to one another. The PM is truly the "person in the middle." Finally, the PM is responsible for making the tough trade-off decisions for the project, and must be perceived as a person who has the mature judgment and courage to do so consistently.

Sensitivity

The preceding pages contain many references to the PM's need for political sensitivity. There is no point in belaboring the issue further. In addition to a good, working set of political antennae, the PM needs to sense interpersonal conflict on the project team or between team members and outsiders. Successful PMs are not conflict avoiders. Quite the opposite, they sense conflict early, then confront and deal with it before the conflict escalates into interdepartmental and intradepartmental warfare.

The PM must keep project team members "cool." This is not easy. As with any group of humans, rivalries, jealousies, friendships, and hostilities are sure to exist. The PM must persuade people to cooperate irrespective of personal feelings, to set aside personal likes and dislikes, and to focus on achieving project goals.

Finally, the PM needs a sensitive set of technical sensors. It is common, unfortunately, for otherwise competent and honest team members to try to hide their failures. Individuals who cannot work under stress would be well advised to avoid project organizations. In the pressure-cooker life of the project, failure is particularly threatening. Remember that we staffed the team with people who are task-oriented. Team members with this orientation may not be able to tolerate their own failures (though they are rarely as intolerant of failure in others), and will hide failure rather than admit to it. The PM must be able to sense when things are being "swept under the rug" and are not progressing properly.

Leadership and Management Style

Leadership has been defined (Tannenbaum and Massarick, 1957) as "interpersonal influence, exercised in situations and directed through the communication process, toward the attainment of a specified goal or goals." Much has been written about how interpersonal influence is generated and the impact of leadership characteristics on team performance. Examples are Jiang, Klein, and Margulis (1998); Scott and Bruce (1998); Whitten (1996); and Zimmerer and Yasin (1998).

To all the skills and attributes we have mentioned, add enthusiasm, optimism, energy, tenacity, courage, and personal maturity. It is difficult to explain leadership. We tend to recognize it after the fact, rather than before. We define it anecdotally by saying that this person or that one acted like a leader. The PM must capitalize on people's strengths, cover their weaknesses, know when to take over and when to "give the team its head," know when to punish and when to reward, know when to communicate and when to remain silent. Above all, the PM must know how to get others to share commitment to the project. In a word, the PM must be a leader. (Note: Slevin and Pinto (1991) is an excellent article on leadership for the project manager.)

Another aspect of leadership that is important in a project manager is a strong sense of ethics. There is a considerable amount of attention to this topic in the news media these days, both good and bad. For instance, the unauthorized invasion of a private telephone system by a *Cincinnati Enquirer* reporter while pursuing a story about alleged improper labor practices at Chiquita Brands International, Inc. raises serious ethical issues, as does the tobacco industry's longstanding public denial of the effects of smoking on human health. Nixon (1987) has identified some ethical missteps that are relatively common in business:

- "wired" bids and contracts (the winner has been predetermined)
- "buy-in" (bidding low with the intent of cutting corners or forcing subsequent contract changes)
- kickbacks
- "covering" for team members (group cohesiveness)
- taking "shortcuts" (to meet deadlines or budgets)
- using marginal (substandard) materials
- compromising on safety
- violating standards
- consultant (e.g., auditors) loyalties (to employer or to client or to public)

A project manager, particularly in the public sector, may easily become embroiled in the ethics concerning such issues as pollution, public safety, industrial plant locations, the use of public lands, and so on. A code of ethics for project managers was created at the PMI 1982 symposium on Project Management (Ireland, Pike, and Schrock, 1982), updated and approved in 1989, and again in 1995. The current version of the code is shown in Table 3-2. The issue is receiving an increasing amount of attention. A humorous column on the subject published several years ago in the PMI's magazine *PM Network* (Phillips, 1995) elicited several irate letters from readers who seemed unsure about whether or not to take the article seriously (cf. "From Our Readers," *PM Network,* January 1996).

An "ethics audit" has also been recommended for nonprofit organizations (Schaefer and Zaller, 1998), and we would recommend a similar audit for any firm. The extent of this subject is far beyond what we can cover here, but, fortunately, there

Table 3-2.   Code of Ethics for the Project Management Profession*

PREAMBLE: Project Management Professionals, in the pursuit of the profession, affect the quality of life for all people in our society. Therefore, it is vital that Project Management Professionals conduct their work in an ethical manner to earn and maintain the confidence of team members, colleagues, employees, employers, clients, and the public.

ARTICLE I: Project Management Professionals shall maintain high standards of personal and professional conduct and:

a. Accept responsibility for their actions.
b. Undertake projects and accept responsibility only if qualified by training or experience, or after full disclosure to their employers or clients of pertinent qualifications.
c. Maintain their professional skills at the state of art and recognize the importance of continued personal development and education.
d. Advance the integrity and prestige of the profession by practicing in a dignified manner.
e. Support this code and encourage colleagues and co-workers to act in accordance with this code.
f. Support the professional society by actively participating and encouraging colleagues and co-workers to participate.
g. Obey the laws of the country in which work is being performed.

ARTICLE II: Project Management Professionals shall, in their work:

a. Provide necessary project leadership to promote maximum productivity while striving to minimize cost.
b. Apply state of the art project management tools and techniques to ensure quality, cost and time objectives, as set forth in the project plan, are met.
c. Treat fairly all project team members, colleagues and co-workers, regardless of race, religion, sex, age or national origin.
d. Protect project team members from physical and mental harm.
e. Provide suitable working conditions and opportunities for project team members.
f. Seek, accept and offer honest criticism of work, and properly credit the contribution of others.
g. Assist project team members, colleagues and co-workers in their professional development.

ARTICLE III: Project Managment Professionals shall, in their relations with their employers and clients:

a. Act as faithful agents or trustees for their employers and clients in professional business matters.
b. Keep information on the business affairs or technical processes of an employer or client in confidence while employed, and later, until such information is properly released.
c. Inform their employers, clients, professional societies or public agencies of which they are members or to which they may make any presentations, of any circumstances that could lead to a conflict of interest.
d. Neither give nor accept, directly or indirectly, any gift, payment or service of more than nominal value to or from those having business relationships with their employers or clients.
e. Be honest and realistic in reporting project quality, cost and time.

ARTICLE IV: Project Management Professionals shall, in fulfilling their responsibilities to the community:

a. Project the safety, health and welfare of the public and speak out against abuses in these areas affecting the public interest.
b. Seek and extend public knowledge and appreciation of the project management profession and its achievements.

* *Source:* Project Management Institute.

are a number of excellent books on the topic (Barry, 1979; Blanchard and Peale, 1988; Pastin, 1986). A concise bibliography on business ethics in included in Robb (1996).

While a great deal has been written about the leadership attributes required or desirable in a project manager, comparatively little has been written about the proper management style for a PM. It has generally been assumed, and we are as guilty as most other writers, that whatever style is good for general managers is also good for project managers. A somewhat informal brand of "participative management" is generally preferred. Of course, each profession (information technology, construction, medicine, research and development in any area of science, ad infinitum) that uses project management is quite certain that its problems are significantly different and more difficult. They argue, therefore, that they require less managerial control.

Shenhar (1998) classifies projects across two dimensions and concludes that management style should be adapted to certain differences in the type of project. His dimensions are: (1) the level of technological uncertainty; and (2) the level of system complexity. As the uncertainty increases from "low tech" to "medium tech" to "high tech" to "very high tech," the appropriate management style progresses from "firm, rigid, and formal" to "moderately firm" to "moderately flexible" to "highly flexible." As the system complexity increases from "assembly" to "system" to "array," the style progresses from "in-house informal" to "formal main/subcontractor relationship" to "remote and highly formal." There are also significant differences in some managerial practices, e.g., the use of project management tools, across the uncertainty and complexity dimensions.

Ability to Handle Stress

Throughout this chapter and elsewhere in this book, we have noted that the life of the project manager is rarely serene. While we know of no scientific research on the issue, casual observation leads us to believe that the basic environment surrounding projects is not fundamentally different from the environment existing in the parent organization within which the projects are being conducted. Life in some organizations is quite hectic and projects in those firms and agencies tend to be equally hectic.

There are a great many factors in life that cause stress and project managers are as subject to them as other humans. There do, however, appear to be four major causes of stress often associated with the management of projects. First, some PMs never develop a reasonably consistent set of procedures and techniques with which to manage their work. Second, many simply have "too much on their plates." Third, some have a high need to achieve that is consistently frustrated. Fourth, the parent organization is in the throes of major change.

This book is primarily devoted to helping the PM deal with the first cause of stress. As for the second cause, we would remind the PM to include him/herself as a "resource" when planning a project. Almost all project management software packages will signal the planner when a project plan calls for a resource to be used beyond its capacity (see Chapters 9 and 10). Such signals, at least, provide PMs

Source: DILBERT reprinted by permission of United Feature Syndicate, Inc.

with some evidence with which to discuss the work load with the appropriate senior manager.

Concerning the third cause of stress, Slevin (1989) points out that stress results when the demands made on an individual are greater than the person's ability to cope with them, particularly when the person has a high need for achievement. It is axiomatic that senior managers give the toughest projects to their best project managers. It is the toughest projects that are most apt to be beset with unsolvable problems. The cure for such stress is obvious, except to the senior managers who continue the practice.

Finally, in this era of restructuring and downsizing, stress from worry about one's future is a common condition in modern organizations. Dealing with and reducing these stresses as well as the stress resulting from everyday life is beyond the scope of this book as well as the expertise of its authors. Fortunately, any bookstore will have entire sections devoted to the subject of stress and its relief. We refer the reader to such works.

3.4 PROBLEMS OF CULTURAL DIFFERENCES

In this and the following two sections, we raise a number of issues that plague certain projects. Sometimes these projects require cooperation by individuals and groups from different countries. Sometimes they require cooperation by individuals or groups in one country, but from different industries or even from different divisions of the same firm. It is not, however, the geographical or organizations differences that matter, it is the differences in *cultures*. Moreover, it is not merely the differences in culture than matter, it is also differences in the *environments* within which projects are conducted, as we mentioned at the start of this chapter, the economic, political, legal, and sociotechnical environments.

We will discuss particulars next, but we must emphasize that the differences in culture and environment are not confined to so-called "international" projects, which should be evident. Different industries have different cultures and environments, as do firms from different regions of a given country, as do different firms from the same geographical area, as do different divisions of a given firm. While the impacts of these dissimilarities are greatest and most visible in the case of international projects, they exist to some extent any time different organizations (including different parts of one organization) are asked to work together on a project.

Inferentially, if a project manager must cope with multiple cultures and different environments, it follows that more than one organization is involved in the project. This fact alone complicates matters. Throughout this book we stress that the PM must manage and reduce conflict between the parties-at-interest or stakeholders in a project: the project team, client, senior management, and the public. One has only to read Hughes (1998, pp. 197 ff.) on the subject of the Boston Central Artery/Tunnel, a chapter aptly titled "Coping with Complexity," to get a good feel for the issues. If the parties-at-interest represent different nations, industries, and firms, the conflicts and problems besetting the project are greater by an order of magnitude. In particular, the conceptually simple issue of maintaining communications between the various parties becomes, in reality, almost impossibly complex.

The term "culture" refers to the entire way of life for a group of people. It encompasses every aspect of living and has four elements that are common to all cultures: technology, institutions, language, and arts (*The World Book*, 1997).

The *technology* of a culture includes such things as the tools used by people, the material things they produce and use, the way they prepare food, their skills, and their attitudes toward work. It embraces all aspects of their material lives.

The *institutions* of a culture make up the structure of the society. This category contains the organization of the government, the nature of the family, the way in which religion is organized as well as the content of religious doctrine, the division of labor, the kind of economic system adopted, the system of education, and the way in which voluntary associations are formed and maintained.

Language is another ingredient of all cultures. The language of a culture is always unique because it is developed in ways that meet the express needs of the culture of which it is a part. The translation of one culture's language into another's is rarely precise. Words carry connotative meanings as well as denotative meanings. The English word "apple" may denote a fruit, but it also connotes health ("keeps the doctor away"), bribery ("for the teacher"), New York city, a color, a computer, a dance (late 1930s), favoritism ("of my eye"), as well as several other things.

Finally, the *arts* or aesthetic values of a culture are as important to communication as the culture's language. If communication is the glue that binds a culture together, art is the most efficient means of communicating. Aesthetic values dictate what is found beautiful and satisfying. If a society can be said to have "style," it is from the culture's aesthetic values that style has its source.

Culture and the Project

A nation's culture affects projects in many ways. One of the most obvious ways is in how people of different cultures regard time. In the United States and several other

Western industrialized nations, time is highly valued as a resource (Smith and Haar, 1993). We say, "Time is money." It isn't, of course, but the expression is one way of expressing impatience with delay and lateness. Latin Americans, on the other hand, hold quite different views of time. The pace of life differs from one culture to another, just as do the values that people place on family or success. The PM conducting a construction project in South America will learn that to be half-an-hour late to a project meeting is to be "on time." In Japan, lateness causes loss of face. In some cultures, the quality of the work is seen to be considerably more important than on-time delivery. The great value placed on time in the United States and the American's distaste for tardiness leads to a common perception that American managers are "impatient."

The fundamental philosophy of staffing projects varies greatly in different cultures. In Latin America, for example, the *compadre* system leads a manager to give preference to relatives and friends when hiring.* North Americans feel that such practices are a major source of inefficiency in Latin American firms. In fact, there appears to be scant evidence that this is so. One private study of several firms in the North American and Latin American chemical industries indicates that the differences in management practices between North American and Latin American chemical firms were, in general, significantly less than the differences between the North American chemical firms and North American clothing manufacturers.

A view almost uniformly held by non-Americans is that American managers understand everything about technology and nothing about people (e.g., Smith and Haar, 1993). This view apparently originates in the American's desire to "get down to business," while many foreign cultures—certainly Asian, Middle Eastern, Latin American, and southern European—value "getting to know you" as a precursor to the trust required to have satisfying business relationships. In many cultures, the manager is expected to take a personal interest in his or her subordinates' lives, to pay calls on them, to take an interest in the successes of family members, and to hold a caring attitude. This flies in the face of the usual (bad) advice given to an American manager to "Keep your nose out of your employees' personal affairs." On the other hand, it is clear that American project managers are being urged to value cultural diversity in ways that are often not shared by their foreign cohorts. The following article appeared in *The Wall Street Journal.***

Multiculturism Stalls at the National Divide

Valuing diversity is a uniquely American idea that may not travel well.

Asked by AT&T to study race and gender issues in overseas work places, New York consultants Cornelius Grove and Willa Hallowell found "the values that give impetus to diversity issues here don't necessarily exist abroad," says Mr. Grove.

Based on interviews with AT&T managers and executives, the two report that other societies view ethnic differences as an appropriate basis for assign-

---

*We are quite aware that the *compadre* system is a system of networks of extended family members, and is far more complex than is implied in this simple example.

**Reprinted by permission of *The Wall Street Journal* © 1994 Dow Jones & Company. Inc. All Rights Reserved Worldwide.

ing workplace roles. In Mexico, for example, an American manager shouldn't expect to find indigenous Indians in management positions, which are controlled by European descendants. In Japan, it took an AT&T manager months to get Japanese managers to talk to key East Indian employees, Ms. Hallowell says.

In the newsletter *Cultural Diversity at Work,* the consultants advise American managers abroad to value equality without judging cultural norms. (Wynter, 1994)

Without attesting to the accuracy or fairness of its portrayal of Japanese culture and politics, we would strongly recommend that American project managers read Michael Chrichton's (1992) mystery thriller, *Rising Sun.* This book is a rich source of examples of the subtle and not-so-subtle ways in which cultures collide. It is an excellent illustration of the impact that a nation's culture, its technology, language, institutions, and aesthetic values have on human behavior and communications.

Microcultures and the Project

For some years, management theorists have been writing about "corporate culture." We call these "microcultures" to differentiate them from the broader national or regional cultures about which we have been writing. It is just as true, though less obvious, to observe that microcultures vary from industry to industry and from firm to firm just as cultures do from nation to nation. Sales techniques perfectly permissible in one industry, the wholesale automobile industry, for instance, would cause outrage and lawsuits in the business-machine industry. Promises have very different meanings in different areas of business. No one takes seriously the "promised" date of completion of a software application project, any more than a finish-date promise made by a home-remodeling contractor, or, for that matter, an author's promise made to a publisher for the delivery of a manuscript on or before the deadline.

The impact of interindustry, interfirm, and intrafirm microcultural diversity on the project manager is significant. Perhaps more than any other type of manager, the PM is dependent on commitments made by people, both inside and outside the parent organization, who owe little allegiance to the project, have little cause for loyalty to the PM, and over whom the PM has little or no de jure authority. Hence, the PM must know whose promises can be relied upon and whose cannot.

The PM cannot even count on a simple acceptance of accountability (Dodson, 1998), or of the concepts of empowerment or a customer-oriented view of quality (de Macedo-Soares and Lucas, 1995). In a major study of fifty transnational projects, Hauptman and Hirji (1996) found that the accomplishment of product development teams depended on the skill with which they handled two-way communication and problem solving, plus their willingness to deal with ambiguous and uncertain information. The team's ability to deal with cultural differences in these areas was critical to success. On the positive side, Levinson and Asahi (1995) spell out several steps that allow "interorganizational learning" for groups that form international alliances (see also, Fedor and Werther 1996).

Project Management in Practice
Success at Energo by Integrating Two Diverse Cultures

A major project involving some hundreds of millions of dollars was stymied due to the cultural differences between the owner/client, a state-run Middle East developer, and the contractor, a state-run European international designer and builder of industrial and construction projects. As can be imagined, the difference in the cultures is extreme and includes religions, the role of women in society, the difference in power between managers and workers, and the style of management itself. These differences were exacerbated by the conditions surrounding the project: an isolated desert, poor communication, extremely harsh living/working conditions, and a highly unstable legal/political environment (taxes, regulations, restrictions, even client reorganizations) that was changing daily.

The client and contractor came to realize that the two separate organizational systems created an interface, or boundary, between them that was almost impenetrable. They thus decided to try to integrate the two systems into one unified system (see Exhibit 1). This was done methodically, with a plan being drawn up, environmental impacts recognized, restructuring of the overall organization, designing the integration, and then implementing the design.

As perhaps expected, neither side's personnel were able to give up their perspective to see the larger picture. The project managers kept working on this issue, however, watched for problems, did a lot of management-by-walking-around, and gradually, the integration began to occur, gathering speed as it went. At project termination, when all costs and engineering changes were hammered out for final payment by tough external bargaining agents (rather than by principled negotiation, typically), no agreement could be reached. Instead, the project managers were brought back and allowed to terminate the project in their own fashion. They simply continued the integration process they had used earlier and quietly phased out the successful project.

THE PROJECT STYLE CHARACTERISTICS		Actions
Physical Appearance:	Counterparts working together (teamwork) ◄———	Tour the site with counterpart project manager daily
	Project-related pictures, charts, and schedules on office walls	Make your office look like a "war room"
Myths and Stories:	We are one team with two sides	Whenever possible, let the counterparts have a joint office
	Both cultures are interesting	
	Both sides' interests should be satisfied	
	We trust young managers	
	Get the job done ◄———	Organize group visits to local historical sites
	Separate yourself from the position and stick to the problem	
	Both project managers are good, and committed to the project	

Cermonies:	Gather ideas and information from all over the project organization Frequent meetings at all levels ◄—— Frequent social gatherings and festivities	From time to time, attend lower level joint project meetings Celebrate each key event completion
Management Style:	Plan, organize and control with your counterparts Make decisions ◄—— No finger pointing for wrong decisions, learn the lesson Quickly execute the decision If you need help, don't hesitate to refer to your boss	Ask counterparts for joint report on an issue Recognize high-performance managers monthly

Exhibit 1 Examples of Integrative Actions.

Source: D.Z. Milosevic, "Case Study: Integrating the Owner's and the Contractor's Project Organization," *Project Management Journal,* December 1990.

3.5 IMPACT OF INSTITUTIONAL ENVIRONMENTS

In general systems theory, the *environment* of a system is defined as everything outside the system that receives system outputs from it or delivers inputs to it. A culture's institutions are a part of the environment for every project.

Socioeconomic Environment

Of all the nations in which a project manager might find him- or herself, the need to interact with governments and representatives of governments is probably lower in the United States than almost anywhere else. This is true regardless of whether the government controls industry or industry controls the government in the country involved. On international projects, therefore, the PM (or the PM's senior management) can expect to deal with bureaucracy at several different levels (i.e., local, regional, and national government functionaries).

Popular movies and television to the contrary, the intentions of foreign governments and their officials are rarely evil. Foreign governments are usually devoted to ensuring that local citizens are well-treated by invading companies, that national treasures are not disturbed, that employment for their nationals is maximized, that some profits are reinvested in the host country, that safety regulations are not violated, and that other unintended exploitations are prevented. At times, rules and regulations may result from ancient traditions—no consumption of alcoholic beverages in Islamic nations, no consumption of pork products in Israel, and avoiding the "A-OK" hand-sign in several South American countries, though the latter is not a rule or regulation.

The job description of any PM should include responsibility for acquiring a working knowledge of the culture of any country in which he or she is to conduct a project. As far as possible, the project should be conducted in such a way that host-country norms are honored. To do so, however, will often raise problems for management of the parent firm. An unwelcome truth is that the cultures of many countries will not offer a female PM the same level of respect shown a male PM. Thus, senior management is faced with the awkward choice of violating its own policy against sex discrimination or markedly increasing the risk of project failure. The same problem may also exist with the use of a Jewish PM in an Arab country, or an Armenian PM in Turkey.

Legal Environment

The United States is, by far, the most litigious society on this planet. This does not mean that there are fewer disagreements in other societies, but rather that there is less recourse to courts of law, and, therefore, more recourse to negotiation as a means of resolving conflict. Martin (1993) examines the nature of the negotiation process in an international setting. He notes the impact that different cultures have on the process of negotiation, with special attention paid to the society's institutional structure and patterns of communication. He concludes that the failure to understand the culture of a nation in which negotiations are taking place puts the ignorant party at a severe disadvantage. The same conclusion is obviously true for microcultures.

Many authors have noted, as we have above, that trust plays an important role in business relationships (Gogal and Ireland, 1988, for example). The impact of trust on project management, with its dependence on the ability and willingness of others to meet commitments, is clear. The importance of trust is also demonstrated by the critical role played by the *compadre* system in Latin America. Use of a general agreement with the extended family, as trusted suppliers to a project for example, is a substitute for the detailed and highly explicit contracts usually required for dealing with "arms-length" suppliers in the United States.

Finally, it is sometimes forgotten that each nation's laws are a product of its history. Law results from the attempt to reduce conflict by a regularized process. Because the conflicts in a country are, in part, a reflection of its unique culture, it follows that the laws of a nation will also be unique. For instance, in the United States there is a strong tradition condemning conspiracies to restrain trade that is effectuated through regulatory law, but law is constantly changing. In recent years, certain types of collaboration between competitors have grown rapidly, even in the United States (Rosegger and Mantel, 1990). In the United States, SEMATECH is a consortium of semiconductor manufacturers conducting joint research projects in the field; and the Automotive Composites Consortium is a collaborative group formed of Chrysler, Ford, and General Motors to study the use of plastic-processing technologies in automobile manufacture. These are merely two of many collaborative efforts allowed by the National Cooperative Research Act passed in 1984. European nations have also backed research consortia, for example, between 1961 and 1983, Japan had more than 60 research consortia, some with more than 40 members (Lynn and McKeown, 1988).

The move to collaborative projects has also been transnational. Airbus Industrie, the British-French-German-Spanish venture, operating with financial support from its several governments, has achieved outstanding success in commercial aircraft development and production. Other examples are CFM International composed of GE (USA) and Snecma (France), and International Aero Engines composed of Pratt & Whitney (USA), Rolls Royce (UK), Japan Aero Engines, MTU (Germany), and Fiat (Italy).

International projects exist in such great numbers because there is some resource required by the project that is not readily available in the host nation. Most commonly, that resource is technological knowledge.* Many firms invited into projects for their proprietary knowledge found, after the project was completed, that their knowledge was no longer proprietary. The world of information technology is replete with cases in which "ownership" of software developed through the joint efforts of two or more firms is strongly disputed. In the United States, such cases are usually settled in the courts. When two or more countries are involved, solution of the problem is not so simple. Patent laws differ from nation to nation, as do national attitudes about the sanctity of patents.

The project manager and senior management must, if proprietary knowledge is valuable, make adequate provision for its protection. How to accomplish that is idiosyncratic to the case at hand. The North American Free Trade Agreement (NAFTA) affords protection of the intellectual property rights of firms to the three signers of the agreement, the United States, Canada, and Mexico. All areas of technology are patentable under NAFTA, and it is the first international agreement to include protection for trade secrets in addition to copyrights and patents (Chopra, 1993).

The upshot of all this is that business laws, and laws that affect businesses, vary widely from nation to nation. For the project manager, there is no substitute for qualified legal assistance.

The Business Cycle as an Environment

The project manager must be aware of the general level of business conditions in the nation hosting the project. While it is common for business cycles in economically developed countries generally to rise and fall together, they rarely match precisely. The depth of the cycle will be greater in one nation than another. The cycle will start or end in one country before it does in another. Occasionally, a cycle downturn may skip a country entirely. Therefore, local perceptions about the level of prosperity or recession will differ from region to region. These different perceptions will be reflected in positive or negative attitudes toward investment, and employment. The risks associated with a project will differ from country to country. Even notions about the proper timeframe for a project will be affected.

In times of relatively high unemployment, most nations will erect institutional barriers in order to slow or prevent projects that might negatively affect their balances of trade. These barriers may take the form of mandated delays, failure to approve investments, unwillingness to allow repatriation of earnings, "inability" to locate neces-

---

*Entry into a heretofore closed foreign market is another common reason for initiating international projects. This was certainly a major factor in the formation of both CFM International and International Aero Engines.

sary scarce resources (human and/or capital), severe "foot-dragging" on the part of local officials to grant required "permissions," lack of needed capital equipment, and a great many other forms. Almost all of the above affected a large construction project in a Middle Eastern nation. The creativity of bureaucrats (and we do *not* use that term in a pejorative sense) can be boundless when attempting to impede a project they see as undesirable or untimely.

When questioned about the U.S. trade deficit with Japan, Robert Solow is reported to have responded that a deficit with any one nation was not important. He noted that he consistently ran a "trade deficit" with his barber—and presumably with his plumber and local grocer. While the Noble laureate economist is undoubtedly correct about his barber et al., it should be noted that he runs large positive trade balances with his employer, MIT, and with his consulting clients. Further, while Professor Solow's barber and grocer are unlikely customers for his services, Japan is clearly a potential customer for many goods and services produced in the United States. We would not for a moment argue with the notion of "comparative advantage," but that economic concept assumes reasonable freedom for goods and services to cross national boundaries in both directions. That does not appear to be the case with the importation of foreign goods into Japan. Aho (1993) presents an interesting discussion of the American-Japanese trade conflict.

Most nations handle such problems in very much the same way that private firms do. They practice commercial reciprocity. It is illegal, in the United States, to restrain trade by specifying reciprocity, but a great many firms manage to buy some required inputs from those customers that are able to supply them. Project managers can earn valuable goodwill by purchasing goods and services from vendors in the host country, and by employing qualified nationals. Indeed, in some cases the hiring of nationals is a condition placed on the project by the host organization. Above all, PMs must be sensitive to economic problems in the host country and be willing to adapt, as far as possible, to local commercial customs.

Technological Environment

Though the state of a nation's technology is not really an "institutional" environment, it is appropriate to mention the issue at this juncture. The ability to complete a project with success is often dependent on the PM's ability to plan the project in such a way as to be compatible with the technology available in the host nation. This point is made in Graham and Minghe (1988) as well as in the following incident.

Operations research pioneer, Russell Ackoff, tells the story of being invited to India as a consultant to the government and being taken on a sight-seeing "inspection" tour in the nearby countryside. He observed several men dipping pails into a water-filled irrigation ditch on one side of the road and carrying the water across the road to a dry ditch on the other side. He then explained to his host, a government official, that if a pipe were installed under the road to connect the two sides, a simple gate could accomplish the water transfer. The gate could be operated by one person, thereby saving labor cost. The official listened politely and then asked, "And how will the men we replace support their families?"

The technology used by any nation is largely a function of the relative cost (supply) of the factors of production—always modified by relevant tradition, policy, and law.

In the next chapter, we will discuss "virtual" projects, which are transfunctional and/or geographically dispersed. Multicultural projects are "virtual" by definition. In recent years, communication problems have been greatly eased for virtual projects through email, the Internet, conference calls, and videoconferencing (Dodson, 1998). While overused email may be a curse for project managers, it is also a blessing when frequent communication with other organizations is required. Of course, these technologies do not relieve the PM from the demands of cultural sensitivity. Though it is not electronic, the technology of negotiation is critical for the PM with a multicultural project. Dodson writes:

> Project management is ultimately expectation management. Effective management of expectations requires negotiation skills that eclipse more quantitative, "metrical" skills. Projects are only as successful as the degree to which the project manager is an effective negotiator. . . .
>
> For at least three-quarters of the world's population, relationship comes above all else: above time, above budget, above specification. The savvy project manager knows this and knows that he or she will always be balancing, for instance, the needs of the Japanese for meeting deadlines against the Latin American tendency toward a more relaxed approach to dealing with others. (Dodson, 1998)

We will have much more to say about negotiation in Chapter 6.

Project Management in Practice
Project Management in Brazil during Unstable Times

The government of Rio de Janiero, needing a permanent facility for their annual festival, embarked on a unique project. They decided to build a combined school and carnival stadium to house the crowds that come to see the annual Lent parades and festivities for four days every March, just before Lent. The stadium had to seat 70,000 Samba fans, with the whole facility accommodating 200,000 overall for rock concerts and similar events. The rest of the year the structure would operate as a school for 4000 students. Since the annual cost of facilities for the festival was $10 million a year and the project would only cost $15 million, it would pay for itself very quickly. The project had to be done by the following Lent, only four and a half months later.

The challenges of completing such a mammoth task in such a short time were severely exacerbated by the project environment of political uncertainty, rampant inflation, governmental bureaucracy, and local contractor politics. However, the extreme public pressure and strong desire by the project participants to complete the project on time led to a successful project completed not only on time but to high-quality standards and within budget. Moreover, the short time span actually contributed to success in some ways, as described in the problems below.

Political Uncertainty

The project began under a new governor of Brazil who wanted to show results in a short time. In general, new governments often make drastic changes in the economy-freezing assets, freezing prices, changing tax rates, changing the banking system, revaluing the currency (or even replacing it)—to correct the mistakes of previous administrations, set the economy straight, and fend off impending problems. Also, the priority of federal programs can often change abruptly because of domestic problems or dwindling funds. The result of such uncertainty is often a "wait and see" attitude in the entire economy, depressing all transactions and projects.

Rampant Inflation

A particularly difficult aspect of economic uncertainty is in judging the "reasonableness" for what things should cost when the inflation spirals upward. Some system is needed to be able to check against price fixing by suppliers and contractors, as well as for simply knowing what items should cost. Thus, sophisticated indexing systems are used to help provide a cost index, but these are imperfect, particularly for individual items that may not have inflated at the same rate as most

other goods. Another complication is knowing when a payment is coming. At the inflation rate of 25 percent per month during this period, even a week's delay in payment by the government can turn a profitable project into a major loss. Thus, another invoice is commonly sent for "escalation" between the time the first invoice was submitted and the time of payment by the customer. This invoice, of course, is also subject to inflation if payment is not forthcoming by the expected time!

Governmental Bureaucracy

Governmental laws on bidding for public projects are extensive and place a heavy bureaucratic burden on all personnel. In addition, bureaucratic delays and forms, licenses, and other such procedural matters can delay and drive up the costs of any project indefinitely. In the case of this project, special simplified bidding and purchasing procedures were established by special government concession, and bureaucratic barriers were circumvented by access to the highest state and local officials for expediting on a case-by-case basis.

Brazil shuts down for four days for the Carnival.

Local Contractor Politics

Even local politics with the contractors added problems in that they refused to participate, stating that the project deadline was impossible. Thus, two out-of-state contractors were engaged to conduct the project, after which the local contractors reconsidered and thus obtained contracts for about 30 percent of the project work.

Source: P. C. Dinsmore and J. O. Brizola, "PM Under Rampant Inflation," *PM Network,* December 1993.

Carnival parade in the new stadium in Rio de Janiero.

3.6 MULTICULTURAL COMMUNICATIONS AND MANAGERIAL BEHAVIOR

The importance of language cannot be overstated. Almost every writer on the subject of managing international projects, or of managing any business in another country, advises the manager to learn the language of the host nation. It is usually not necessary (though it is always helpful) for a project manager to be fluent in the language of the host nation. When precise communication is required, a skilled translator can be used. It is, however, usually pleasing to the citizens of the host nation when visiting PMs speak their language, even haltingly.

Language is a complex composite of words, signs, symbols, movements and positions of the body, pictures, sounds, equations, and objects—the things with which we communicate with one another. The ways in which we use the elements of communication, the ways in which we send and receive messages are integral parts of the communication. The media are a part of the message, to paraphrase Marshall McLuhan's famous statement. Even the source and destination of the message may alter its meaning. Identical words may carry quite different meanings depending on the context within which the words are spoken or on who delivers the words to whom. (Consider the words, "I'll give you a ring" spoken by a young man to a young lady at the end of a date.)

Because the communication cannot be separated from the communicator, the managerial and personal behaviors of the project manager are discussed along with the more commonly mentioned aspects of the communication process.

Structure and Style of Communications

Some years ago the American steel industry supported a training program for young engineers educated in India. The program was one of several responses from the United States to the Soviet Union's gift of steel production plants and equipment to India. Based on the (accurate) assumption that American management and production methods in the steel business were significantly better than the USSR's, a project was developed to train the engineers on operations by having them work as first-line supervisors in steel mills in Cleveland and Pittsburgh. At the same time, they attended universities in those cities for academic training in relevant American business practices and techniques. Several problems arose.

All the engineers were reasonably fluent in written and spoken English so they received training in the in-plant communications methods employed by American steel companies. It was several months later before an American academic (who had not been involved in planning the program) pointed out that only 17 percent of the workers in an Indian steel mill could read. This obviated much of the elaborate communication system the engineers were being trained to use, most of which depended heavily on written memoranda and instructions. It is appropriate to wonder why the Indian engineers did not make this fact known to those teaching the communications courses. The reason is, in Asiatic nations, teachers (and senior officials in general) are held in very high regard. It would be impolite, almost unthinkable, to question or correct them.

Cultural differences caused another problem. In the United States, it is common to train supervisors in the steel industry (and also in other industries) by giving them some "hands-on" experience in production methods. The young Indians felt that it was beneath them to pick up and use a shovel while working on the blast furnace floor. To convince the engineers to continue in this aspect of their training, without resentment, required an on-site demonstration by a very senior American executive.

These types of multicultural problems are ubiquitous on international projects. In the United States, delegation is a preferred managerial style. When authority is diffused, information moves to the manager from the delegatees. Workers report to supervisors who, in turn, report to middle and senior managers. In cultures where authority is highly centralized, it becomes the project manager's responsibility to seek out information (Smith and Haar, 1993). At several different points in this book, we have urged the PM never to let the boss be surprised. This is a fundamental tenet of our approach to project management. The manager of an international project *cannot count on being voluntarily informed* of problems and potential problems by his or her subordinates.

The Gogal and Ireland study (1988) and the small-sample survey of Graham and Minghe (1988) both examine project management as it currently exists in China. They did not examine multicultural projects, but studied projects conducted by Chinese managers and workers in China. They are, nonetheless, instructive. It is clear that management in China is authoritarian, and that the need to negotiate—largely with the state—is just as, if not more, important than it is in the projects of any other culture. The role of negotiation will not decrease for multicultural projects involving China. It will be extended.

Managerial and Personal Behavior

We have already noted the difference in the bottom-up flow of information in American projects and the top-down flow in countries where the management style is authoritarian. There are other cross-cultural differences that create problems for a project manager whose experience is restricted to the United States. In a fascinating paper, Grinbergs and Rubenstein (1993) compare the managerial characteristics of Swiss and American managers/engineers of the same general age, education, and salary levels, all of whom were working on software projects.

Several of these comparisons illustrate culturally based differences in managerial and interpersonal style. The study revealed that Swiss managers were "much more formal" with each other than Americans. This demonstrates the interaction of interpersonal style and language. Many languages have both formal and informal modes of addressing other people (e.g., the formal German "*Sie*" and French "*vous*" compared to the informal "*du*" and "*tu*." If an American in Germany uses "du" to a German counterpart, it will certainly be understood, but it may also carry overtones of rudeness.

Because we have emphasized planning so strongly throughout this book, we find the differences in the Swiss and American approaches to planning of special interest.

The U.S. respondents did not consider thorough planning and a long-term strategy as absolute prerequisites for beginning a project. . . . Though promptness is highly valued in both countries, long-term strategy is considered much more important in the Swiss company. (Grinbergs and Rubenstein, 1993, p. 24)

In addition to these areas, the Swiss and Americans differed in a number of other ways of import to the PM. The Swiss showed a stronger work ethic, were more resistant to change, were more risk averse, more accepting of bureaucracy, and more focused on quality. The Americans were more collegial, more willing to experiment and innovate, had a shorter time horizon, and communicated more openly.

When conducting a project in an Asian nation, an American PM must exercise considerable care while criticizing the work of indigenous subordinates. Loss of face is a serious problem in Oriental cultures. In communist states such as China, the pseudoegalitarianism* may make criticism completely unacceptable (cf. Gogal and Ireland 1988 and elsewhere).

In a society with highly structured social classes, it is also difficult to practice participative management. There is, apparently, a built-in assumption that the more educated, higher-class manager's authority will be denigrated by using a participative style. (It is interesting to note that one does not have to leave the United States in order to see this culturally based trait in action. In many U.S. firms, management is quite authoritarian and the social gulf between manager and worker is as wide as in much more class-conscious nations.) The more structured a country's social system, the less direct managerial communication tends to be. In North America, it is common for senior managers to interact with first-line supervisors, and even with blue- and white-collar workers. Communication flows easily across functional lines. In most other areas of the world, the communication will be more indirect, and will tend to follow the lines of authority established on the organizational chart.

Dinsmore and Codas (1993) list five factors that they contend require special consideration by the PM heading a multicultural project. We have already noted some of these factors (e.g., the importance of language and culture, the need to deal with the politics and politicians in the host nation, the fact that the PM may have to use indigenous staff members, the possibility of input supply and technology problems, and the need to obey local laws and customs). In addition, they note two other matters that may cause serious problems for the PM. First, there are additional risk factors such as kidnapping, disease, and faulty medical care. Of course, in many countries, project workers will face less risk from crime than in the United States as well as easier access to medical care. Second, Dinsmore and Codas (1993, p. 458) point out that the PM may have to provide for the physical and psychological needs of people who are transferred to the host nation and must live in a "strange land with different customs and way of life." They refer to this as the "expatriate way of life."

The PM is warned, however, not to go too far in accommodating to foreign cultures. "Going native" is not helpful. An Austrian economist of our acquaintance remarked, "American managers who come over here and wear lederhosen and funny hats are laughable. No one takes them seriously."

---

*We refer to this egalitarianism as "pseudo" because the actual managment style is highly authoritarian. Recall George Orwell's *Animal Farm* in which it was noted that all animals were equal, *but some were more equal than others.*

Final Comments on Multicultural Projects

The project manager is ill-advised to take on an international project without adequate preparation in the culture and language of the host nation. Lack of preparation is apt to cause cultural shock which results in frustration, usually followed by withdrawal. It is a no-win situation. If there are no resources inside the organization to prepare those moving into a different culture, outside consultants with appropriate knowledge and teaching skills are needed. (Note: a current employee of the firm who happens to be of the right nationality is not a suitable resource for the training.) Lessons in the foreign language are mandatory, even if the language training does not extend to technical language.* In most cases, the willingness to speak in the hostnation's tongue on social occasions and for routine business—if not for technical discussions—will be appreciated by the hosts and earn goodwill from the indigenous members of the project team.

Finally, research has shown the importance of the psychosocial aspect of service on project teams. "In practical terms, this finding suggests that it is important for project team members to enjoy working with other team members, and to perceive the project as a valuable way to spend their time." (Pinto and Pinto, 1991, p. 17) This is doubly important for multicultural projects, particularly for expatriate team members. They are away from home and depend, for the most part, on their national cohorts to meet psychosocial needs. Given this cultural isolation, the project becomes a critical source of both psychological and social payoffs, and the PM, with a strong tendency to focus only on task outcomes, must make sure that these other needs are met.

Because all people invariably seem to view the values of other cultures in terms of their own, the process of understanding and working comfortably in another culture requires great effort. But it seems to us that most Americans underestimate their own abilities to manage international projects with skill and sensitivity. Americans seem to feel that being able to speak more than one language, as citizens of many other countries do, implies acceptance and sensitivity to another culture. It takes no more than a quick glance at the Balkans or the Middle East to know that the implication is untrue. If a PM from Toronto can manage a project in Quebec, if a PM from Boston can manage a project in Albuquerque, it is probable that an American Southern Baptist can function in Israel or a Tex-Mex from Corpus Christi can be effective in Berlin. Multicultural management does take effort, but it is do-able.

 **SUMMARY**

This chapter addressed the subject of the PM. The PM's role in the organization and responsibilities to both the organization and the project team were discussed first. Common PM career paths were also described. Next,

the unique demands typically placed on project managers were detailed and the task of selecting the PM was addressed. Last, the issue of culture and its effect on project communication and success was discussed.

---

*It is interesting to note that English comes closest of any language to being the universal tongue for science, technology, and business. The underlying reason for this is probably the preeminence of American higher education in these fields. This generalization does not, however, apply to China—and possibly not to Paris.

The following specific points were made in the chapter.

Two factors crucial to the success of the project are its support by top management and the existence of a problem orientation, rather than discipline orientation, within the team members.

Compared to a functional manager, a PM is a generalist rather than a specialist, a synthesizer rather than an analyst, and a facilitator rather than a supervisor.

The PM has responsibilities to the parent organization, the project itself, and the project team. The unique demands on a PM concern seven areas:

- Acquiring adequate physical resources
- Acquiring and motivating personnel
- Dealing with obstacles
- Making goal trade-offs
- Maintaining a balanced outlook in the team
- Communicating with all parties
- Negotiating

The most common characteristics of effective project team members are:

- High-quality technical skills
- Political sensitivity
- Strong problem orientation
- High self-esteem

To handle the variety of project demands effectively, the PM must understand the basic goals of the project, have the support of top management, build and maintain a solid information network, and remain flexible about as many project aspects as possible.

The best person to select as PM is the one who will get the job done.

Valuable skills for the PM are technical and administrative credibility, political sensitivity, and an ability to get others to commit to the project, a skill otherwise known as leadership.

Some important points concerning the impact of culture on project management are:

- Cultural elements refer to the way of life for any group of people and include technology, institutions, language, and art.
- The project environment includes economic, political, legal, and sociotechnical aspects.
- Examples of problematic cultural issues include the group's perception of time and the manner of staffing projects.
- Language is a particularly critical aspect of culture for the project.

In the next chapter we move to the first task of the PM, organizing the project. We deal there not only with various organizational forms, such as functional, project, and matrix, but also with the organization of the project office. This task includes setting up the project team and managing the human element of the project.

GLOSSARY

Analytic Approach   Breaking problems into their constituent parts to understand the parts better and thereby solve the problem.

Benefit-Cost   A ratio to evaluate a proposed course of action.

Champion   A person who spearheads an idea or action and "sells" it throughout the organization.

Contingency Plan   An alternative for action if the expected result fails to materialize.

Culture   The way of life of any group of people.

Discipline   An area of expertise.

Environment   Everything outside the system that delivers inputs or receives outputs from the system.

Facilitator   A person who helps people overcome problems, either with technical issues or with other people.

Functional   One of the standard organization disciplines such as finance, marketing, accounting, or operations.

Microculture   The "corporate culture" within the organization, or even project

Systems Approach   A wide-ranging, synthesizing method for addressing problems that considers multiple and interacting relationships. Commonly contrasted with the analytic approach.

Technological   Having to do with the methods and techniques for doing something.

Trade-Off   Allowing one aspect to get worse in return for another aspect getting better.

Tweed Coat Management   The concept that highly educated people such as engineers require a special type of management.

QUESTIONS

Material Review Questions

1. How does the project act as a stepping-stone for the project manager's career?

2. Name the categories of skills that should be considered in the selection of a project manager.

3. Discuss the PM's responsibilities toward the project team members.

4. What are the major differences between functional managers and project managers?

5. What are some of the essential characteristics of effective project team members?

6. What is the most important characteristic of a project manager?

7. What project goals are most important during the project life cycle stages?

8. Why must project management team members have good technical skills?

9. Describe each of the four elements of culture.

10. Identify some important types of project environments.

11. Contrast culture, microculture, and multiculture.

12. In what ways is language crucial in project management?

13. Identify the five multicultural factors requiring special consideration.

Class Discussion Questions

14. Can you think of several ways to assure "breadth of communication" in a project? Do you think "socialization" off the job helps or hinders?

15. Contrast the prime law for projects, "Never surprise the boss," with the corporate adage "Bad news never travels up."

16. How does a project manager, in some cases, work like a politician?

17. What are some of the conflicts that are bound to occur between parties that have legitimate interests in the project?

18. Project managers must be generalists rather than specialists. Yet, team members need to have more specialized, technical skills. Can a generalist manage a team of specialists effectively?

19. Why do you think cost drops in importance as an objective right after the formation stage?

20. Why is it more difficult to keep the project on its

time and cost schedules the later the project gets in its life cycle?

21. Suppose you have a talented scientist temporarily working for you on a client contract who is due to be transferred back to her regular job. Although you could do without her efforts at this point of the contract, you happen to know that she will be laid off for lack of work at her regular job and her personal financial situation is dire. You feel it is important that her talent be kept on the company payroll, although keeping her on the contract will increase expenses unnecessarily. Is the transfer decision a business decision or an ethical one? Why? If the decision were yours to make, what would you decide?

22. Contrast cultural differences with environmental differences. Isn't the culture part of the environment?

23. How is communications through art different than through language?

24. What should a firm do when an accepted practice in a foreign country is illegal in its own country?

25. If employing people to use pails to move water

Questions for Project Management in Practice

The Project Management Career Path at AT&T

26. How difficult is it to change a culture where project management is perceived as of low status and something to get out of to one where project management is respected? How would you approach such a task?

27. What was the problem with the mentality of admiring heroic rescues of projects in trouble?

28. Compare the skills sought for project managers among BCS's Leadership Continuity Plan with those listed in the chapter.

The Wreckmaster at a New York Subway Accident

29. In what phase of the disaster plan does providing for alternate services probably occur? In what phase does bringing new equipment and supplies occur?

30. How much preplanning could be done for wrecks

helps the economy, why not use spoons instead and thus hire even more people? How should the official have been answered?

such as these in terms of disaster teams, command center locations, task sequencing, and so on?

31. What experience credentials does NYCTA look for in appointing wreckmasters?

Success at Energo by Integrating Two Diverse Cultures

32. What was the key to solving this dilemma?

33. How did the two PMs implement their strategy?

34. What actions in Exhibit 1 might have been key to making this project a success?

Project Management in Brazil During Unstable Times

35. What key background factors led to making this project a success?

36. How does "escalation" work? Is escalation allowed in the escalation?

37. How were bureaucracy and local contractor politics avoided?

 INCIDENTS FOR DISCUSSION

Smithson Company

Keith Smithson is the CEO of the Smithson Company, a privately owned, medium-size computer services company. The company is 20 years old and, until recently, had experienced rapid growth. Mr. Smithson believes that the company's recent problems are closely related to the depressed Asian economy.

Brianna Smatters was hired as the director of corporate planning at Smithson six months ago. After reviewing the performance and financial statements of Smithson for the last few years, Ms. Smatters has come to the conclusion that the economic conditions are not the real problem, but rather exacerbate the real problems. She believes that in this Internet era, Smithson Company's services are becoming obsolete but the department heads have not been able to effectively cooperate in reacting to information technology threats and opportunities. She believes that the strong functional organization impedes the kinds of action required to remedy the situation. Accordingly, she has recommended that Mr.

Smithson create a new position, manager of special operations, to promote and use project management techniques. The new manager would handle several critical projects in the role of project manager.

Mr. Smithson is cool to the idea. He believes that his functional departments are managed by capable professional people. Why can't these high-level managers work together more efficiently? Perhaps a good approach would be for him to give the group some direction (what to do, when to do it, who should do it) and then put the functional manager most closely related to the problems in charge of the group. He assumes that the little push from him (Smithson) as just described would be enough to "get the project rolling."

Questions: After this explanation Ms. Smatters is more convinced than ever that a separate, nonfunctional project manager is required. Is she right? If you were Smatters, how would you sell Mr. Smithson on the idea? If a new position is created, what other changes should be made?

Ohio Hospital

A 500-bed hospital in Ohio is in the planning and design stage of adding a new ambulatory service building and is scheduled to begin construction in two months. The engineering department is normally responsible for assigning a project manager for all projects within the hospital. Currently, the engineering department has no one with experience in the construction of an entire building. As a result, the hospital administrator is considering using the architectural firm that is currently designing the building to do the project management as well. The engineering division head believes his senior project engineer can handle the job for three reasons: she has a good technical background, she pays meticulous attention to detail, and she is currently available.

Questions: If you were the hospital administrator, what would your choice be? Why? What additional information would you try to obtain before making a decision? Would someone with experience in building construction be an even better choice?

International Microcircuits, Inc.

Megan Bedding, vice-president of sales for International Microcircuits, Inc. (IM), was delighted when IM was one of the few firms invited to enter a bid to supply a large industrial customer with their major product in a small foreign country. However, her top salesperson for that region had just called and informed her of certain "expectations" of doing business in the country:

1. Local materials representing at least 50 percent of the product's value must be purchased in reciprocity.

2. The local politicians will expect continual significant donations to their party.

3. Industrial customers normally receive a 40 percent "rebate" (kickback) when they purchase goods from suppliers such as IM. (IM's profit margin is only 20 percent.)

With this new information, Megan was unsure about changing or proceeding with the bid. If it was withdrawn, a lot of effort would be wasted as well as a chance to get a foothold in the international market. But if she proceeded, how could these expectations be met in a legal and ethical way?

Question: Devise a solution that addresses Megan's concerns.

▌ BIBLIOGRAPHY

AHO, C. M. "America and the Pacific Century: Trade Conflict or Cooperation?" *IEEE Engineering Management Review,* Winter 1993.

ARCHIBALD, R. D. *Managing High Technology Programs and Projects.* New York: Wiley, 1992.

ATKINS, W. "Selecting a Project Manager." *Journal of Systems Management,* October 1980.

BARRY, V. *Moral Issues in Business.* Belmont, CA: Wadsworth, 1979.

BEER, S. *Diagnosing The System for Organizations.* New York: Wiley, 1985.

BLANCHARD, K., and N. V. PEALE. *The Power of Ethical Management.* New York: Morrow, 1988.

BOBROWSKI, P. M., and P. KUMAR. "Learning Project Management Outside the Classroom: The Internship." *Project Management Journal,* March 1992.

BOULDING, K. E. "General Systems Theory—The Skeleton of Science." *Management Science,* Vol. 2, No. 3, April 1956.

CHOPRA, K. J. "NAFTA: Implications for Project Management." *PM Network,* November 1993.

CHRICHTON, M. *Rising Sun.* New York: Knopf, 1992.

CHURCHMAN, C. W., *The Systems Approach, rev. ed.* New York: Delta, 1979.

COOKE-DAVIES, T. "Return of the Project Managers." *Management Today,* May 1990.

DE MACEDO-SOARES, T. D. L.v. A., and D. C. LUCAS. "Empowerment and total quality: comparing research findings in the USA and Brazil." *Technovation,* October 1995.

DINSMORE, P.C., and M.M.B. CODAS. "Challenges in Managing International Projects." In P. C. Dinsmore, ed., *The AMA Handbook of Project Management.* New York: AMACOM, 1993.

DODSON, W. R. "Virtually International." *PM Network,* April 1998.

FEDOR, K. J., and W. B. WERTHER, JR. "The Fourth Dimension: Creating Culturally Responsive International Alliances." *IEEE Engineering Management Review,* Fall 1997, as reprinted from *Organizational Dynamics,* Autumn 1996.

FORD, R. C., and F. S. MCLAUGHLIN. "Successful Project Teams: a Study of MIS Managers." *IEEE Transactions on Engineering Management,* November 1992.

GADDIS, P. O. "The Project Manager." *Harvard Business Review,* May–June 1959.

GAGNON, R. J. *An Exploratory Analysis of the Relevant Cost Structure of Internal and External Engineering Consulting,* Ph.D. dissertation. Cincinnati: University of Cincinnati, 1982.

GAGNON, R. J., and S. J. MANTEL, JR. "Strategies and Performance Improvement for Computer-Assisted Design." *IEEE Transactions on Engineer-ing Management,* November 1987.

GEMMILL, G. R., and H. J. THAMHAIN. "Influence Styles of Project Managers: Some Project Performance Correlates." *Academy of Management Journal,* June 1974.

GOGAL, H. C., and L. R. IRELAND. "Project Management: Meeting China's Challenge." *Project Management Journal,* February 1988.

GRAHAM, R. G., and S. MINGHE. "An Empirical Analysis of Project Management in a Selected Area in the People's Republic of China." *Project Management Journal,* June 1988.

GRANT, K. P., C. R. BAUMGARDENER, and G. S. STONE. "The Perceived Importance of Technical Competence to Project Managers in the Defense Acquisition Community." *IEEE Transactions on Engineering Management,* February 1997.

GRINBERGS, A., and A. H. RUBENSTEIN. "Software Engineering Management: A Comparison of Methods in Switzerland and the United States." *IEEE Transactions on Engineering Management,* February 1993.

GREEN, S. G. "Top Management Support of R&D Projects: A Strategic Leadership Perspective." *IEEE Transactions on Engineering Management,* August 1995.

HAMBURGER, D. H. "The Project Manager: Risk Taker and Contingency Planner." *Project Management Journal,* June and December 1990.

HAUPTMAN, O., and K. K. HIRJI. "The Influence of Process Concurrency on Project Outcomes in Product Development: An Empirical Study of Cross-Functional Teams." *IEEE Transactions on Engineering Management,* May 1996.

HERZBERG, F. H. "One More Time: How Do You Motivate Employees?" *Harvard Business Review,* January–February 1968.

HUGHES, T. P. *Rescuing Prometheus.* New York, Pantheon, 1998.

IRELAND, L. R., W. J. PIKE, and J. L. SCHROCK. "Ethics for Project Managers." *Proceedings of the 1982 PMI Seminar/Symposium on Project Management,* Toronto, Ontario, Canada.

JIANG, J. J., G. KLEIN, and S. MARGULIS. "Important Behavioral Skills for IS Project Managers: The Judgments of Experienced IS Professionals." *Project Management Journal,* March 1998.

KALU, T. C. U. "A Framework for the Management of Projects in Complex Organizations." *IEEE Transactions on Engineering Management,* May 1993.

KLOPPENBORG, T J., and S. J. MANTEL, Jr. "Trade-offs on Projects: They May Not Be What You Think." *Project Management Journal,* March 1990.

KOTTER, J. P. "What Effective General Managers Really Do." *Harvard Business Review,* November–December 1982

LEVINSON, N. S., and M. ASAHI. "Cross-National Alliances and Interorganizational Learning." *IEEE Engineering Management Review,* Fall 1997, as re-printed from *Organizational Dynamics,* Autumn, 1995.

LYNN, L. H., and T. J. MCKEOWN. *Organizing Business: Trade Associations in America and Japan.* Washington, D.C.: American Enterprise Institute for Public Policy Research, 1988.

MARTIN, M. D. "The Negotiation Differential for International Project Management." In P. C. DINSMORE, ed., *The AMA Handbook of Project Management.* New York: AMACOM, 1993.

MATSON, E. "Congratulations, You're Promoted" and "Project: You." *Fast Company,* as reprinted in *Engineering Management Review,* Winter 1998.

MINTZBERG, H. *The Nature of Managerial Work.* New York: Harper & Row, 1973.

NIXON, M. A. "Legal Lights: Business Ethics." *Project Management Journal,* September 1987.

PASTIN, M. *The Hard Problems of Management.* San Francisco: Jossey-Bass, 1986.

PATTERSON, N. "Selecting Project Managers: An Integrated List of Predictors." *Project Management Journal,* June 1991.

PHILLIPS, R. C. "How to Build a Low-Cost Black Box: Practical Tips for Owners." *PM Network,* October 1995.

PILL, J. *Technical Management and Control of Large Scale Urban Studies: A Comparative Analysis of Two Cases,* Ph.D. dissertation. Cleveland: Case Western Reserve University, 1971.

PINTO, J. K. *Power and Politics in Project Management.* Upper Darby, PA, Project Management Institute, 1996.

PINTO, J. K., and S. J. MANTEL, JR. "The Causes of Project Failure." *IEEE Transactions on Engineering Management,* November 1990.

PINTO, M. B., and J. K. PINTO. "Determinants of Cross-Functional Cooperation in the Project Implementation Process." *Project Management Journal,* June 1991.

PINTO, J. K., and D. P. SLEVIN "The Project Champion: Key to Implementation Success." *Project Management Journal,* December 1989.

ROBB, D. J. "Ethics in Project Management: Issues, Practice, and Motive." *PM Network,* December 1996.

ROSEGGER, G., and S. J. MANTEL, JR. "Competitors as Consultants: Collaboration and Technological Advance." In J. Allesch, ed., *Consulting In Innovation: Practice, Methods, Perspectives.* Amsterdam: Elsevier, 1990.

SAHLIN, J. P. "How Much Technical Training Does a Project Manager Need?" *PM Network,* May 1998.

SCHAEFER, A. G., and A. J. ZALLER. "The Ethics Audit for Nonprofit Organizations." *PM Network,* March 1998.

SCOTT, S. G., and R. A. BRUCE. "Following the Leader in R&D: The Joint Effect of Subordinate Problem-Solving Style and Leader-Member Relations on Innovative Behavior." *IEEE Transactions on Engineering Management,* February 1998.

SHENHAR, A. J. "From Theory to Practice: Toward a Typology of Project-Management Styles." *IEEE Transactions on Engineering Management,* February 1998.

SLEVIN, D. P. *The Whole Manager.* New York: AMACOM, 1989.

SLEVIN, D. P., and J. K. PINTO "Project Leadership: Understanding and Consciously Choosing Your Style." *Project Management Journal,* March 1991.

SMITH, L. A., and J. HAAR. "Managing International Projects." In P. C. Dinsmore, ed., *The AMA Handbook of Project Management.* New York: AMACOM, 1993.

SOUDER, W. E. "Autonomy, Gratification, and R & D Output: A Small-Sample Field Study." *Management Science,* April 1974.

STARR, M. K. "The Role of Project Management in a Fast Response Organization." *Journal of Engineering and Technology Management,* September 1990.

TANNENBAUM, R., and F. MASSARICK. "Leadership: A Frame of Reference." *Management Science,* October 1957.

The World Book. Chicago: Field Enterprises, 1997.

VAN GIGCH, J. P. *Applied General Systems Theory.* 2nd ed., New York: Harper & Row, 1978.

WHITTEN, N. "Attributes of the Successful Project Leader." *PM Network,* June 1996.

WYNTER, L. E. "Business and Race." *Wall Street Journal,* January 1, 1994.

ZIMMERER, T. W., and M. M. YASIN. "A Leadership Profile of American Project Managers." *Project Management Journal,* March 1998.

The following case involves a project manager who stumbles into a public project somewhat by accident. The project starts out as one thing and evolves into something else. Acquiring sufficient resources for the project is a major difficulty, and competition may be troublesome also. A consultant is hired who conducts two surveys to gather more information and makes recommendations based on the survey evidence and experience. The case illustrates the varied skills necessary to be a successful project manager and the myriad opportunities/difficulties some projects entail.

C A S E

THE NATIONAL JAZZ HALL OF FAME*
Cornelis A. de Kluyver, J. Giuliano, J. Milford, and B. Cauthen

Mr. Robert Rutland, founder of the National Jazz Hall of Fame, poured himself another drink as he listened to some old jazz recordings and thought about the decisions facing him. Established about one year ago, the National Jazz Hall of Fame (NJHF) had achieved moderate success locally but had not yet attracted national recognition. Mr. Rutland wondered how much support existed nationally, what services the NJHF should provide and for whom, and what the NJHF should charge for those services. He also thought about other jazz halls of fame and their implications for the NHJF. Although he had engaged an independent consultant to find some answers, the questions still lingered.

Jazz

The word "jazz," according to Dr. David Pharies, a linguistics scholar at the University of Florida, originally meant copulation, but later identified a certain type of music. Amid the march of funeral bands, jazz music began in New Orleans in the early 1900s by combining Black spirituals, African rhythms, and Cajun music; Dixieland jazz became the sound of New Orleans. Jazz traveled from New Orleans, a major trade center, on river boats and ships and reached St. Louis, Kansas City, Memphis, Chicago and New York. Musicians in these cities developed local styles of jazz, all of which remained highly im-

provisational, personal, and rhythmically complex. Over the years, different sounds emerged—swing, big band, be bop, fusion, and others—indicating the fluidity and diversity of jazz. Jazz artists developed their own styles and competed with one another for recognition of their musical ability and compositions. Such diversity denied jazz a simple definition, and opinions still differed sharply on what exactly jazz was. It was difficult, however, to dispute Louis Armstrong's statement that "if you have to ask what jazz is, you'll never know."

Origins of the National Jazz Hall of Fame

Mr. Rutland, a history professor at the University of Virginia, which is in Charlottesville, discovered that renovation plans for the city's historic district excluded the Paramount Theatre, a local landmark. The Paramount was constructed in the 1930s and used as a performance center and later as a movie theatre. It was closed in the 1970s and now was in danger of becoming dilapidated. Alarmed by the apparent lack of interest in saving the Paramount, Mr. Rutland began to look for opportunities to restore and eventually use the theatre. The most attractive option to him was to establish a jazz hall of fame that would use the theatre as a museum and performance center; this would capitalize on the theatre's name, because the Paramount Theatre in New York City was a prominent jazz hall during the 1930s and 1940s. Mr. Rutland mentioned his idea—saving the theatre by establishing a jazz hall of fame—to several friends in Charlottesville.

---

*Copyright © 1984 by the Darden Graduate Business School Foundation, Charlottesville, VA.

They shared his enthusiasm, and together they incorporated the National Jazz Hall of Fame and formed the board of directors in early 1983. A few prominent jazz musicians, such as Benny Goodman and Chick Corea, joined the NJHF National Advisory Board. The purpose of the NJHF was to establish and maintain a museum, archives, and concert center in Charlottesville to sponsor jazz festivals, workshops, and scholarships, and to promote other activities remembering great jazz artists, serving jazz enthusiasts, and educating the public on the importance of jazz in American culture and history.

The First Year's Efforts

Immediately after incorporation, the directors began their search for funds to save the Paramount and to establish the NJHF, and soon encountered two difficulties. Philanthropic organizations refused to make grants because no one on the board of directors had experience in a project like the NJHF. In addition, government agencies such as the National Endowment for the Arts and the National Endowment for the Humanities considered only organizations in operation for at least two years. However, some small contributions came from jazz enthusiasts who had read stories about the NJHF in *Billboard*, a music industry magazine, and in the Charlottesville and Richmond newspapers.

By mid-1983, the board of directors discovered that to save the Paramount at least $600,000 would be needed, a sum too large for them to consider. They decided, however, that out of their love for jazz they would continue to work to establish the NJHF in Charlottesville.

Despite these setbacks, Mr. Rutland and the other directors believed that the first year's activities showed promise. The NJHF sponsored three concerts at local high schools. The concerts featured such jazz greats as Maxine Sullivan, Buddy Rich, and Jon Hendricks and Company, and each concert attracted more than 500 people. Although the NJHF lost some money on each concert, the directors thought that the concerts succeeded in publicizing and promoting the NJHF. In addition, a fundraiser at a Charlottesville country club brought $2,000 to the NJHF, and Mr. Rutland started the NJHF newsletter. The collection of objects for the museum was en-

larged, and Louis Armstrong and Duke Ellington were posthumously inducted into the NJHF. At the end of the first year, enthusiasm among board members was still high, and they believed that the NJHF could survive indefinitely, albeit on a small scale.

But a Hall of Fame in Charlottesville . . .

Mr. Rutland believed that a hall of fame could succeed in Charlottesville, though other cities might at first seem more appropriate. More than 500,000 tourists annually were attracted to Charlottesville (1980 population: 40,000) to visit Thomas Jefferson's home at Monticello, James Monroe's home at Ash Lawn, and the Rotunda and the Lawn of the University of Virginia, where total enrollment was 16,000. Mr. Jefferson designed the Rotunda and the buildings on the Lawn and supervised their construction. The Virginia Office of Tourism promoted these national landmarks as well as the city's two convention centers. In addition, 13 million people lived within a three-hour drive of Charlottesville. If Charlottesville seemed illogical for a hall of fame, Mr. Rutland reasoned, so did Cooperstown, New York, home of the Baseball Hall of Fame and Canton, Ohio, location of the Professional Football Hall of Fame. He thought that successful jazz festivals in such different places as Newport, Rhode Island, and French Lick, Indiana, showed that location was relatively unimportant for jazz. Moreover, a Charlottesville radio station recently switched to a music format called "Memory Lane," which featured classics by Frank Sinatra, Patti Page, the Mills Brothers, the Glenn Miller Orchestra, and numerous others. The station played much jazz, and won the loyalty of many jazz enthusiasts in the Charlottesville area. The success of "Memory Lane" indicated to Mr. Rutland that the Charlottesville community could provide the NJHF with a base of interest and loyalty. Most important, Mr. Rutland believed that he and his friends possessed the commitment necessary to make a jazz hall of fame succeed.

. . . And Halls of Fame in Other Cities?

Although no national organization operated successfully, several local groups claimed to be *the* Jazz Hall of Fame, as Billboard magazine reported.

***

Billboard 4/28/84

HALL OF FAME IN HARLEM
by Sam Sutherland and Peter Keepnews

CBS Records and the Harlem YMCA have joined forces to establish a Jazz Hall of Fame. The first induction ceremony will take place on May 14 at Avery Fisher Hall, combined with a concert featuring such artists as Ramsey Lewis, Hubert Laws, Ron Carter, and an all-star Latin Jazz ensemble. Proceeds from the concert will benefit the Harlem YMCA.

Who will the initial inductees be, and how will they be chosen? What's being described in the official literature as "a prestigious group of jazz editorialists, critics, producers, and respected connoisseurs" (and, also, incidentally, musicians—among those on the panel are Miles Davis, Dizzy Gillespie, Cab Calloway, Max Roach and the ubiquitous Dr. Billy Taylor) will do the actual selecting, but nominations are being solicited from the general public. Jazz lovers are invited to submit the names of six artists, three living and three dead, to: The Harlem YMCA Jazz Hall of Fame, New York, NY 10030. Deadline for nominations is May 1.

Billboard, 5/19/84

ONE, TWO, MANY HALLS OF FAME?
by Sam Sutherland and Peter Keepnews

Monday night marks the official launch of the Harlem YMCA Jazz Hall of Fame (Billboard, April 28), a project in which CBS Records is closely involved. The Hall's first inductees are being unveiled at an Avery Fisher Hall concert that also includes performances by, among others, Sarah Vaughan and Branford Marsalis.

The project is being touted as the first jazz hall of fame, a statement that discounts a number of similar projects in the past that never quite reached fruition. But first or not, the good people of CBS and the Harlem YMCA are apparently in for some competition.

According to a new publication known as JAMA, the Jazz Listeners/Musicians Newsletter, Dizzy Gillespie—who also is a member of the Harlem YMCA Jazz Hall of Fame committee—"promised in Kansas City, Mo. To ask musicians for help in establishing an International Jazz Hall of Fame" in that city. The newsletter quotes Gillespie, whom it describes as "honorary chairman of the proposed hall," as vowing to ask "those musicians who were inspired by jazz"—among them Stevie Wonder, Quincy Jones and Paul McCartney (?)—to contribute financially to the Kansas City project, which, as envisioned by the great trumpeter, would also include a jazz museum, classrooms and performance areas.

Is there room for two Jazz Halls of Fame? Do the people involved in the New York city project know about the Kansas City project, and vice versa? (Obviously Gillespie does, but does anyone else?) Remember the New York Jazz Museum? Remember the plaques in the sidewalk on 52nd Street (another CBS Records brainchild)?

The notion of commemorating the contributions of the great jazz musicians is a noble one. It would be a shame to see the energies of the jazz community get diverted into too many different endeavors for accomplishing the same admirable goal—which, unfortunately, is what has tended to happen in the past.

Billboard, 5/26/84

Also noted: the first inductees in the Harlem YMCA Jazz Hall of Fame (Billboard, May 19) have been announced. The posthumous inductees are, to nobody's great surprise, Louis Armstrong, Duke Ellington, Count Basie, Charlie Parker, and—a slight surprise, perhaps—Mary Lou Williams. The living honorees are Roy Eldridge, Dizzy Gillespie, Miles Davis, Ella Fitzgerald and Art Blakey.

***

The New York Jazz museum (which the 5/19/84 article referred to) was established in the early 1970s but quickly ran out of money and was closed a few years later. In the early 1960s, a jazz museum was established in New Orleans and because of insufficient funds, all that remained was the Louis Armstrong Memorial Park, the site of an outdoor jazz festival each summer. Tulane and Rutgers universities each possessed extensive archives containing thousands of phonograph records, tape recordings, posters, books, magazines, journals, and other historic pieces and memorabilia. Neither university, however, considered its archives a hall of fame.

Other Halls of Fame

The more prominent halls of fame in the U.S. were the Baseball, the Professional Football, the College Football, and the Country Music Hall of Fame. These and many other halls of fame were primarily concerned with preserving history by collecting and displaying memorabilia, compiling records, and inducting new members annually.

Mr. Rutland visited most of the other halls of fame and learned that they were usually established by a significant contribution from an enthusiast. In the case of the Country Music Hall of Fame, some country music stars agreed to make a special recording of country hits and to donate the royalties to the organization.

Mr. Rutland was especially interested in The Country Music Hall of Fame because of similarities between country music and jazz. Country music, like jazz, had a rich cultural history in America, and neither type of music was the most popular in the U.S.

The Country Music Hall of Fame (CMHF) was established in 1967 in Nashville after a coooperative fundraising effort involving the city, artists, and sponsors. By 1976, the CMHF included a museum, an archives, a library, and a gift shop. More than one-half million people visited the CMHG in 1983, partly because of the nearby Grand Ole Opry, the premier concert hall for country music where the Grand Ole Opry cable radio broadcasts originated. Of the CMHF's $2.1 million annual budget, 85 percent came from admissions, 10 percent from sales at the gift shop and by mail, and 5 percent from donations. In the past two years, the CMHF had formed the Friends of Country Music, now more than 2,000 people who donated $25 each per year and who received a country music newsletter every three months and discounts on CMHF merchandise.

The National Association of Jazz Educators

Mr. Rutland was uncertain how much and what type of support he could get from the National Association of Jazz Educators. This organization, with 5,000 members, primarily coordinated and promoted jazz education programs.

Performance programs were normally offered through music departments. Most high schools and colleges had bands that played a variety of jazz arrangements as part of their repertoire. Band conductors usually had a music degree from a major university and belonged to the National Association of Jazz Educators.

Most of the jazz appreciation courses offered in schools throughout the U.S. treated jazz as a popular art form, as a barometer of society, rather than as a subject of interest in itself. Some educators believed that jazz greats such as Louis Armstrong and Duke Ellington should be honored not as jazz musicians, but as composers like George Gershwin and Richard Rogers. Indeed, a prominent jazz historian told Mr. Rutland that jazz might benefit more from breaking down this distinction between jazz artists and composers than from reinforcing it.

The National Survey

To get some of the answers to his many questions, Mr. Rutland engaged an independent consultant who conducted two surveys; the first was a national survey and the second a tourist survey. For the national survey (Appendix A), the consultant designed a questionnaire to gauge the respondent's level of interest in both jazz and the concept of a National Jazz Hall of Fame, and to determine the respondent's demographics. A sample size of 1,300 was used and the mailing covered the entire continental United States. The mailing list, obtained from the Smithsonian Institution in Washington, DC, contained names and addresses of people who had purchased the "Classic Jazz Record Collection," as advertised in *Smithsonian* magazine. Of the 1,300 questionnaires, 440 were sent to Virginia residents and 860 to residents of other states in order to provide both statewide and national data. Of the questionnaires

Exhibit 1. Survey Results: Demographics of Respondents

Demographics	Percentage of Respondents	Percentage of All Record Buyers*	Census Data**
Age—35+	79	37	43
Sex—Male	73	82	49
Education—Grad.+	54	24 ***	31
Job—Professional	57	26	22
Income—$50,000+	50	23	7
Non-profit Contr. $200/year+	75		

*Source: Consumer Purchasing of Records and Pre-recorded Tapes in the U.S., 1970–1983, Recording Industry Association of America.

**Source: U.S. Department of Commerce, Bureau of the Census, 1982.

***Source: Simmons Market Research Bureau, 1982.

that went to other states, the majority was targeted toward major cities and apportioned according to the interest level for jazz in each city as indicated by the circulation statistics of *Downbeat,* a jazz magazine. Of the 860 questionnaires sent to the other states, 88 were sent to residents of Chicago, 88 to Detroit, 83 to New York City, 60 to San Francisco, 56 to Philadelphia, 56 to Washington, DC, 52 to Los Angeles, 46 to Charlotte, 46 to Miami, 45 to Dallas, 42 to Atlanta, 42 to Houston, 30 to Denver, 28 to Kansas City, 28 to New Orleans, 28 to St. Louis, 27 to Boston, and 15 to Seattle. Of the 1,300 questionnaires, 165, or 12.7 percent, were returned.

As shown in Exhibit 1, 79 percent of the respondents were 35 years of age or older, 73 percent were male, and the majority were well-educated, professionals, and had an annual income of more than $50,000. Of interest also was that 75 percent of the respondents contributed $200 or more per year to different non-profit organizations. Since the sample included a large number of record buyers of age 50 or older, the consultant weighted the survey results with age data obtained from the Recording Industry Association of America to make the survey results representative of all jazz-record buyers.

The survey also showed in Exhibit 2 that swing was the most popular form of jazz, followed by Dixieland, and then more traditional forms of jazz, from which the consultant concluded that a nostalgic emphasis should gather support from jazz enthusiasts of all ages, and that later, the National Jazz Hall of Fame could promote more contemporary forms of jazz.

Exhibit 2. Survey Results: Preferences for Different Styles of Jazz

Type of Interest	Percentage of Respondents Answering with a 4 or 5 Rating	Weighted Percentage of Respondents Answering with a 4 or 5 Rating
General Interest in Music	62	71
Dixieland	62	70
Swing	87	81
Traditional	63	66
Improvisational	41	48
Jazz Rock	25	47
Fusion	15	9
Pop Jazz	27	53
Classical	68	73

Exhibit 3.   Survey Results: Preferences for Services Offered

Service	Percentage of Respondents Answering with a 4 or 5 Rating	Weighted Percentage of Respondents Answering with a 4 or 5 Rating
Performance Center	70	83
Concert Hall	66	79
Artist Seminars	50	62
Nightclub	52	57
Museum	57	57
Tourist Center	42	48
Audio-Visual Exhibitions	57	55
Shrine	55	52
Educational Programs	48	51
Record Information	71	69
History Seminars	38	54
Member Workshops	25	34
Lounge	37	45
Financial Support:		
at $10.00/year	17	13
at $20.00/year	30	26
at $30.00/year	15	25
Number of Contributors	62	64

As for services, the survey suggested in Exhibit 3 that respondents most wanted a performance center or concert hall. A museum and seminars were also popular choices. The consultant was surprised by the strong interest in information about jazz recordings because the average respondent did not buy many records. A newsletter was rated relatively unimportant by most respondents. Most gratifying for Mr. Rutland was that respondents on average were willing to contribute between $20.00 and $30.00 per year to the National Jazz Hall of Fame, with a weighted average contribution of $23.40.

The Tourist Survey

In addition to conducting the National Survey, the consultant developed a questionnaire (Appendix 2) and interviewed approximately 100 tourists to the Charlottesville area at the Western Virginia Visitors Center near Monticello. About 140,000 tourists stopped at the center annually to collect information on attractions nearby and throughout the state. The respondents came from all areas of the country, and most were traveling for more than one day. Almost 70 percent said they like jazz, mostly Dixieland and big band, and more than 60 percent indicated they would visit a Jazz Hall of Fame. The average admission they suggested was $3.50 per person.

The Consultant's Recommendations

The consultant limited his recommendations to the results of the two surveys. As a result, the question of whether the efforts in other cities to establish a National Jazz Hall of Fame would make the Charlottesville project infeasible was still unresolved. In a private discussion, however, the consultant intimated that "if the other efforts are as clumsily undertaken as many of the previous attempts, you will have nothing to worry about." He thought it was time that a professional approach was taken toward this project. Specifically, he made three recommendations:

1. Launch a direct mail campaign to the 100,000 people on the Smithsonian jazz mailing list. The focus of the mailing should be an appeal by a jazz great such as Benny Goodman to become a Founding Sponsor of the National Jazz Hall of Fame. He estimated that the cost of the campaign would range between $25,000 and $30,000; however, with an average contribution of $25.00 per respondent, a response rate of only 2 percent would allow the National Jazz Hall of Fame to break even.

2. Appoint a full-time executive director with any funds exceeding the cost of the mailing. The principal responsibilities of the executive director would be to organize and coordinate fundraising activities, to establish a performance center and museum, and to coordinate the collection of memorabilia and other artifacts.

3. Promote the National Jazz Hall of Fame at strategic locations around Charlottesville to attract tourists and other visitors. The Western Virginia Visitors Center was a prime prospect in his view for this activity. He calculated that 50,000 tourists annually at $3.00 each would provide sufficient funds to operate and maintain the National Jazz Hall of Fame.

The consultant also identified what he considered the critical elements for his plan's success. First, the National Jazz Hall of Fame should be professional in all of its services and communications to jazz enthusiasts. Second, the executive director should have prior experience in both fundraising and direct mail; he should have a commitment to and love for jazz, as well as administrative skill and creativity. Third, the National Jazz Hall of Fame should communicate frequently with Founding Sponsors to keep their interest and excitement alive. Finally, to ensure the enthusiastic cooperation of city officials, local merchants and the Charlottesville community, he thought that more local prominence for the National Jazz Hall of Fame would prove indispensable.

The National Jazz Hall of Fame—
Dream of Reality

As he paged through the consultant's report, Mr. Rutland wondered what to make of the recommendations. While he was encouraged by a national base of support for his idea, he was unsure how the Board of Directors would react to the consultant's proposals. With less than $2,500 in the bank, how would they get the necessary funds to implement the plan? Yet he knew he had to make some tough decisions, and quickly, if he wanted to make his dream a reality.

Appendix A
NATIONAL JAZZ HALL OF FAME SURVEY

1. How would you classify your interest in jazz? (Please circle)

Not interested		Moderate interest	Very enthusiastic	
1	2	3	4	5

1. _____

2. Rate your interest in the following categories of jazz. (Circle your answer)

	No Interest		Some Interest		Very Interested	
Dixieland/New Orleans (K. Oliver, P. Fountain)	1	2	3	4	5	2. _____
Big Band/Swing (B. Goodman, G. Miller)	1	2	3	4	5	3. _____
Traditional (A. Tatum, E. Garner)	1	2	3	4	5	4. _____
Improvisational (C. Parker, D. Gillespie)	1	2	3	4	5	5. _____
Jazz/Rock (M. Ferguson, P. Metheny)	1	2	3	4	5	6. _____
Fusion (M. Davis, S. Clarke)	1	2	3	4	5	7. _____
Pop Jazz	1	2	3	4	5	8. _____

(B. James, G. Benson)

3. Besides Jazz, what other types of music do you usually like to listen to? (Circle your answer)

	Never				Often	
Popular/Top 40	1	2	3	4	5	9. _____
Classical	1	2	3	4	5	10. _____
Easy Listening	1	2	3	4	5	11. _____
Rock and Roll	1	2	3	4	5	12. _____
Country	1	2	3	4	5	13. _____
Soul/Disco	1	2	3	4	5	14. _____
Nostalgia	1	2	3	4	5	15. _____

4. How many jazz albums have you bought in the last 3 months? _____   16. _____

         In the past year? _____   17. _____

5. Do you play a musical instrument?   18. _____

    Yes _____   How many? _____   Hours per week _____   No _____   19. _____

    20. _____

    Do you sing?   Yes _____   Hours per week _____   No _____   21. _____

    22. _____

    23. _____

    Do you compose music?   Yes _____   Hours per week _____   No _____   24. _____

6. Are there any Jazz nightclubs/concert halls in your area?   Yes _____   No _____   25. _____

  If yes, how many times have you been there in the last 3 months?
      0–1 _____   2–4 _____   5–9 _____   10 or more _____   26. _____

7. How many hours per week do you listen to the radio?
      0–5 _____   5–10 _____   10–15 _____   15–20 _____   More than 20 _____   27. _____

  What format(s) do you listen to most often?
  Popular/Top 40 _____   Rock and Roll _____
  Classical _____   Jazz _____
  Easy Listening _____   Country _____
  Soul/Disco _____   Nostalgia _____
  Talk Show _____   All News _____

8. Have you ever visited a Hall of Fame?   Yes _____   No _____   28. _____

9. The following section is an attempt to determine the services you would expect from a National Jazz Hall of Fame. Please circle the level of your interest in each of the following services.

	Low				high	
Performance center	1	2	3	4	5	29. _____
Concert Hall	1	2	3	4	5	30. _____
Seminars by Jazz artists	1	2	3	4	5	31. _____
Seminars by Jazz historians	1	2	3	4	5	32. _____
Student workshops	1	2	3	4	5	33. _____
Member workshops	1	2	3	4	5	34. _____
Jazz nightclub	1	2	3	4	5	35. _____
Museum with memorabilia	1	2	3	4	5	36. _____
Tourist Center	1	2	3	4	5	37. _____
Audio/Visual exhibits	1	2	3	4	5	38. _____
Recording studio	1	2	3	4	5	39. _____
Music chart library	1	2	3	4	5	40. _____
Shrine for Jazz greats	1	2	3	4	5	41. _____
Souvenir shop with mail order	1	2	3	4	5	42. _____
Jazz lounge	1	2	3	4	5	43. _____
School education programs	1	2	3	4	5	44. _____
Newsletter	1	2	3	4	5	45. _____
Jazz journal/Magazine	1	2	3	4	5	46. _____
Concert update	1	2	3	4	5	47. _____
Record information	1	2	3	4	5	48. _____
Musician referral center	1	2	3	4	5	49. _____
Toll free jazz "hot line"	1	2	3	4	5	50. _____
Other (Describe below)	1	2	3	4	5	51. _____

10. We would now like to ask you how much you would be willing to pay for the services you feel are essential. Please check the box below for the annual contribution you would be willing to pay for the items you circled "4" or "5" above.
      $10 _____ $20 _____ $30 _____ $40 _____ $50 _____ $100 _____   52. _____

  Please check here if you would NOT be willing to financially contribute to a National Jazz Hall of Fame.   _____

11. Would you consider donating any of your Jazz albums or memorabilia to the National Jazz Hall of Fame?

    Yes _____   No _____   Do not own any _____   53. _____

12. Please circle the number indicating how often you read each of the following magazines:

	Never				Often	
Time	1	2	3	4	5	54. _____
Barron's	1	2	3	4	5	55. _____
Esquire	1	2	3	4	5	56. _____
Harper's Bazaar	1	2	3	4	5	57. _____
Jet	1	2	3	4	5	58. _____
Inside Sports	1	2	3	4	5	59. _____
Money	1	2	3	4	5	60. _____
Omni	1	2	3	4	5	61. _____
New Republic	1	2	3	4	5	62. _____
Psychology Today	1	2	3	4	5	63. _____
Playboy	1	2	3	4	5	64. _____
Down Beat	1	2	3	4	5	65. _____
Rolling Stone	1	2	3	4	5	66. _____
Musician	1	2	3	4	5	67. _____
The New Yorker	1	2	3	4	5	68. _____
The National Enquirer	1	2	3	4	5	69. _____

13. How many movies have you been to in the last 3 months?

    0–1 _____   2–4 _____   5–9 _____   10 or more _____   70. _____

14. How many books have you read during the past year?

    0–2 _____   3–6 _____   7–10 _____   More than 10 _____   71. _____

    What types of books do you like to read? (Answer below)

15. What other hobbies/activities do you regularly engage in?

16. Do you belong to any clubs or community organizations? If so, please list them in the space below.

17. Our group is considering locating the National Jazz Hall of Fame in Charlottesville, Virginia. Some other attractions in the area are the home of Thomas Jefferson, Monticello, the University of Virginia and the Blue Ridge Mountains. Would you plan a vacation to include a visit to Charlottesville and the Hall of Fame?

    Yes _____   No _____   72. _____

18. What do you think about the idea of locating the Hall of Fame in Charlottesville?

19. If the Hall of Fame was located in Charlottesville, and if it offered the services you felt were essential (Question 9), would you support it?

        Yes _____   No _____   73. _____

****

The following questions will enable us to better compare you to the nation at large. Your responses will help us very much, and will be kept STRICTLY CONFIDENTIAL.

20. In what city and state do you live? _____   74–75. _____

21. What is your age?   76. _____

      Less than 20 _____   20 to 24 _____
      25 to 29 _____   30 to 34 _____
      35 to 39 _____   40 to 49 _____
              50 and older _____

22. What is your sex?   Male _____   Female _____   77. _____

23. What is your race?   Caucasian _____   Black _____   Hispanic _____   Other _____   78. _____

24. What is your marital status?   Married _____   Single _____   79. _____

25. How many people are in your household? _____   80. _____

26. What is your highest level of education? _____   81. _____
    Have not received high school diploma _____
    High school graduate _____
    Some post-high school education _____
    Associate's Degree _____
    College graduate _____   What Degree? _____
    University work beyond Bachelor's degree _____   What Degree: _____

27. What type of job do you have?   82. _____
    Student _____   Sales/Clerical _____
    Semi/Unskilled Labor _____   Professional _____
    Skilled Labor _____   Managerial _____
    Technical _____   Retired _____

28. What is your total household income?   83. _____
    Under $5,000 _____ $5,000 to $15,000 _____
    $15,000 to $25,000 _____ $25,000 to $35,000 _____
    $35,000 to $50,000 _____ $50,000 and above _____

29. How much do you contribute to non-profit organizations annually?   84. _____
    Under $25 _____ $25 to $50 _____
    $51 to $75 _____ $76 to $100 _____
    $101 to $200 _____ $200 and above _____

30. We would appreciate any other comments or suggestions.

_____

_____

_____

_____

_____

_____

_____

31. Please write your name and address below if you wish to be added to our mailing list:

THANK YOU VERY MUCH!

NO POSTAGE
NECESSARY
IF MAILED
IN THE
UNITED STATES

BUSINESS REPLY MAIL

FIRST CLASS PERMIT NO. 545 CHARLOTTESVILLE. VIRGINIA

POSTAGE WILL BE PAID BY ADDRESSEE

JAZZ HALL OF FAME
EXECUTIVE PROGRAMS
The Colgate Darden Graduate Business School Sponsors
University of Virginia
P. O. Box 6550
Charlottesville, Virginia 22906-6550

Appendix B

Hello, My name is _____. I am a Graduate Student at the University of Virginia and am conducting a survey. Could I ask you a few questions?

We are conducting a survey for a group here in Charlottesville who is considering the establishment of a National Jazz Hall of Fame. We would like to get some information from you about your visit to Charlottesville and the tourist sites you plan to visit.

1. Where are you from? _____
   How far is that from Charlottesville?

   0–50 _____   50–150 _____   150–300 _____   300+ _____

2. Have you visited Charlottesville before?   yes _____   no _____

3. How long do you plan to stay here?

   One hour _____   1/2 day _____   overnight _____   more _____

4. Are you stopping here on your way to another destination?   yes _____   no _____

5. What places do you plan to visit in Charlottesville?

   Monticello _____   Ash Lawn _____   Michie Tavern _____
   U. Va. _____   Downtown _____   Castle Hill _____
   Mountains _____   Other _____

   Now, I'd like to ask you some questions about the music you like to listen to.

6. What is your favorite type of music?

   Popular/Top 40 _____   Classical _____   Easy Listening _____
   Rock and Roll _____   Country _____   Soul/Disco _____
   Nostalgia _____   Jazz _____   Other _____

7. Do you have an interest in Jazz music?   yes _____   no _____

8. If yes, how often do you listen to Jazz?

   Seldom   Always
     1   2   3   4   5

9. If yes, what is your favorite type of Jazz?

   Dixieland _____   Big Band _____   Traditional _____
   Improvisational _____   Jazz/Rock _____   Fusion _____   Pop/Jazz _____

10. Have you ever visited a Hall of Fame?   yes _____   no _____

11. The people who are considering opening a National Jazz Hall of Fame in Charlottesville plan a building which would house a collection of memorobilia, audio/visual displays, a gift shop which would sell magazines, books and records, and perhaps a performing arts center. Would you be interested in visiting such an attraction: yes _____   no _____

12. If YES, we are trying to determine what effect the location of the Hall of Fame would have on your decision to visit it. Would you visit the Hall of Fame if it was located
    more than 10 minutes from the Visitors Center?   yes _____   no _____
    5 to 10 minutes away from the Visitors Center?   yes _____   no _____
    less than 5 minutes away from the Center?   yes _____   no _____

13. Finally, how much do you think you would be willing to pay (per person) to visit a National Jazz Hall of Fame as described above?

     1   2   3   4   5   6   7   8   9   10

QUESTIONS

1. What is the project Mr. Rutland is trying to manage? Has it stayed the same?
2. Identify the various stakeholders in the project, including the competition.
3. Of the skills mentioned in the chapter that a project manager needs, which are most important here? Why?
4. What credibility does Mr. Rutland have? Is he a leader?
5. What cultures are relevant to this project? Describe the project environment.

6. What should Mr. Rutland do? Include the following issues:
   - Budget: acquiring adequate resources
     -philanthropic organizations
     -governmental agencies
     -donations
     -memberships
     -visitors
   - Budget: expenditures (consider Paramount theater)
   - Performance: services/activities to offer
   - Competition
   - Schedule: deadlines, windows, milestones

The following reading integrates two views about the requirements for good project managers. One view concerns the personal and managerial characteristics of PMs and their ability to lead a team, regardless of the project. The other view considers the critical problems in the project in question and the PM's talents relative to these problems. A survey is first described and then the critical problems that projects face are identified from the survey responses. Next, the skills required of project managers, as indicated by the survey respondents, are detailed. Last, the skills are related back to the critical project problems for an integrated view of the requirements for a successful project manager.

R E A D I N G

WHAT IT TAKES TO BE A GOOD PROJECT MANAGER
B. Z. Posner

Selecting a good project manager is not a simple task. Being an effective project manager is an ongoing challenge. The complex nature and multifaceted range of activities involved in managing projects precludes easily identifying managerial talent and continually stretches the capabilities of talented project managers. Two seemingly contradictory viewpoints have been advanced about what is required to be a good project manager.

One perspective prescribes a set of *personal characteristics* necessary to manage a project [1]. Such personal

What it takes to be a good project manager. *Project Management Journal,* March 1987. (c)1987 by the Project Management Institute. Reprinted by permission.

attributes include aggressiveness, confidence, poise, decisiveness, resolution, entrepreneurship, toughness, integrity, versatility, multidisciplinary, and quick thinking.

However, Daniel Roman [2] maintains that it would take an extraordinary individual to have all of these critical personal characteristics. A more practical solution, he suggests, would be to determine the *critical problems* faced by project managers and to select a person who can handle such difficulties. The shortcoming with this second perspective, argue those like Michael Badaway [3], is that the primary problems of project managers are really not technical ones. The reason managers fail at managing projects, he contends, is because they lack critical organization and management skills.

Scholars like Roman and Badaway—as well as practitioners—may actually be raising different issues. On the one hand, good project managers understand the critical problems which face them and are prepared to deal with them. On the other hand, managing projects well requires a set of particular attributes and skills. But, are these two viewpoints really at odds with one another? In this study they were discovered to be two sides of the *same* coin!

Study of Project Manager Problems and Skills

Questionnaires were completed by project managers during a nationwide series of project management seminars. Project managers attending these seminars came from a variety of technology-oriented organizations. Responses to the survey instrument were both voluntary and confidential.

Information about the respondents and the nature of their projects was collected. The typical project manager was a 37-year-old male, had nine people reporting to him, and was responsible for a small to moderate size project within a matrix organization structure. More specifically, there were 189 men and 98 women in the sample (N = 287) and their ages ranged from 22 to 60 years of age (X = 37.4, S.D. = 8.3). Fifty-six percent indicated that they were the formal manager of the project. The size of their immediate project group ranged from 2 to over 100 people (median = 8.9). Fifty-nine percent reported that they worked primarily on small projects (involving few people or functions, with a short time horizon) as compared to large projects (involving many people or functions, with a long time horizon). More than 63 percent indicated they were working within a matrix organization structure. No information was collected about the specific nature (e.g., new product development, R & D, MIS) of their projects.

Two open-ended questions were asked (their order was randomized). The first asked about the skills necessary to be a successful project manager. The second question investigated the most likely problems encountered in managing projects. Responses to these questions were content analyzed. Content analysis is a systematic approach to data analysis, resulting in both qualitative assessments and quantitative information. Each respondent comment was first coded and then re-coded several times as patterns of responses became apparent. The two questions were:

1. What factors or variables are *most* likely to cause you problems in managing a project?

2. What *personal* characteristics, traits, or skills make for "above average" project managers? What specific behaviors, techniques, or strategies do "above average" project managers use (or use better than their peers)?

Problems in Managing Projects. There were nearly 900 statements about what factors or variables created "problems" in managing a project. Most of these statements could be clustered into eight categories as shown in Table 1. Inadequate resources was the issue most frequently mentioned as causing problems in managing a project. "No matter what the type or scope of your project," wrote one engineering manager, "if insufficient resources are allocated to the project, you have to be a magician to be successful." Not having the necessary budget or personnel for the project was a frequent complaint. However, the specific resource of time—and generally the lack thereof—was mentioned just about as often as the general inadequate resource lament. Typically, the problem of time was expressed as "having to meet unrealistic deadlines."

That resources are inadequate is caused by many factors, not the least of which being that resources are generally limited and costly. Before this hue is dismissed by veteran project managers as just so much bellyaching—"after all, there are never enough resources to go around"—it is important to examine the cause(s) of this problem. Respondents pointed out that resource allocation problems were usually created by senior management's failure to be clear about project objectives, which in turn, resulted in poor planning efforts. These two problems—lack of clear goals and effective planning—were specifically mentioned by more than 60 percent of the respondents. It is painfully

Table 1. Project Management Problems

1. Resources inadequate (69)
2. Meeting ("unrealistic") deadlines (67)
3. Unclear goals/direction (63)
4. Team members uncommitted (59)
5. Insufficient planning (56)
6. Breakdown of communications (54)
7. Changes in goals and resources (42)
8. Conflicts between departments or functions (35)

Note: Numbers in parentheses represent percentage of project managers whose response was included in this cluster.

obvious that vague goals and insufficient planning lead to mistakes in allocating the resources needed by project managers.

The three most significant problems reported by first-line research, development, and engineering supervisors in Lauren Hitchcock's [4] study parallels those identified by project managers. He found "insufficient definition of policy from top downward, how to define the goal of a problem, and budgeting and manpower assignments" to be the major problems confronting supervisors. It remains true that senior management needs to articulate clearly where the project should be going, why, and what it expects from project personnel.

When project goals are not clear, it is difficult (if not impossible) to plan the project efficiently. The lack of planning contributes directly to unrealistic resource allocations and schedules. People assigned to the project are unlikely, therefore, to commit energetically to the endeavor. The lack of commitment (and poor motivation) among project personnel was reported as emerging more from the problems already mentioned than from issues associated with the project's technology or organizational structure (e.g., matrix form).

The communication breakdowns (problems which occur during the life of a project) were often referred to as "inevitable." These breakdowns occur as a result of the ambiguity surrounding the project, but also result from difficulties in coordinating and integrating diverse perspectives and personalities. The project manager's challenge is to handle communication breakdowns as they arise rather than being able to predict (and control) communication problems before they happen.

How the problems confronting project managers were interrelated is exemplified by how frequently problems of communication and dealing with conflicts were linked by respondents. The linkage between these two issues was demonstrated in statements like: "My problem is being able to effectively communicate with people when we disagree over priorities." "Conflicts between departments end up as major communication hassles." Conflicts between departments were also linked to earlier problems of poor goal-setting and planning.

Managing changes (e.g., in goals, specifications, resources) contributed substantially to project management headaches. This was often mentioned as "Murphy's Law," highlighting the context or environment in which project management occurs. Planning cannot accurately account for future possibilities (or better yet, unknowns). Interestingly, less than one in ten project

managers mentioned directly a "technological" factor or variable as significantly causing them problems in managing a project.

Project Manager Skills

The second issue investigated was what project manager skills—traits, characteristics, attributes, behaviors, techniques—make a difference in successfully managing projects. Most respondents easily generated four to five items which they believed made the difference between average and superior project performance. The result was nearly 1400 statements. These statements were summarized into six skill areas as shown in Table 2. Several factors within each are highlighted.

Eighty-four percent of the respondents mentioned "being a good communicator" as an essential project manager skill. Being persuasive or being able to sell one's ideas was frequently mentioned as a characteristic of a good communicator within the project management context. Many people also cited the importance of receiving information, or good listening skills. As one systems engineer exclaimed: "The good project managers manage not by the seat of their pants but by the soles of their feet!"

Organizational skills represented a second major set of competencies. Characteristics included in this category were planning and goal-setting abilities, along with the ability to be analytical. The ability to priori-

Table 2. Project Management Skills

1. Communication Skills (84)	4. Leadership Skills (68)
• Listening	• Sets an example
• Persuading	• Energetic
	• Vision (big picture)
2. Organizational Skills (75)	• Delegates
• Planning	• Positive
• Goal-setting	5. Coping Skills (59)
• Analyzing	• Flexibility
3. Team Building Skills (72)	• Creativity
• Empathy	• Patience
• Motivation	• Persistence
• Esprit de corps	6. Technological Skills (46)
	• Experience
	• Project knowledge

Note: Numbers in parentheses represent percentage of project managers whose response was included in this cluster.

tize, captured in the phrases "stays on track" and "keeps the project goals in perspective," was also identified as significant.

While successful project managers were viewed as good problem solvers, what really differentiated them from their so-so counterparts was their problem *finding* ability. Because of their exceptional communication skills, goal clarity and planning, effective project managers were aware of issues *before* they became problems. Problem finding gave them greater degrees of freedom, enabling them to avoid being seriously sidetracked by problems caused by unforeseen events.

The important team building skills involved developing empathetic relationships with other members of the project team. Being sensitive to the needs of others, motivating people, and building a strong sense of team spirit were identified as essential for effectively managing a project. "The best project managers use a lot of 'we' statements in describing the project," wrote one computer programmer. Being clear about the project's objectives and subsequently breaking down the project into its component parts (e.g., schedules) helped project participants to understand their interdependencies and the need for teamwork.

Several different attributes and behaviors were catalogued under leadership skills. These included setting a good example, seeing the big picture, being enthusiastic, having a positive outlook, taking initiative, and trusting people. Having a vision is closely related to goal clarity (which was included as an organizational skill). The leadership component of this competency was best expressed by one financial analyst as "the ability to see the forest through the trees." Since, as is often lamented, the only constant in managing a project is change, successful project managers require coping or stress-management skills. Respondents indicated that both flexibility and creativity were involved in effectively dealing (or coping) with change, as were patience and persistence. What project managers experience are generally high levels of stress. How well they handle stress ("grace under pressure") significantly affects their eventual success or failure.

The final cluster of skills was labeled technological. Successful project managers were seen as having relevant experience or knowledge about the technology required by the project. Seldom, however, were effective project managers seen as technological "experts." Indeed, expertise was often felt to be detrimental because it decreased flexibility and the willingness to consider alternative perspectives. Project managers do need to be sufficiently well versed in the technology to be able to ask the right questions because, as one senior military officer pointed out, "you've got to be able to know when people are blowing smoke at you."

Skills and Problems: Fundamentally Interconnected

It has been argued in the literature that project managers require certain skills in order to be effective. It has also been argued that project managers need to be able to handle certain problems in order to be effective. The results of this study suggest that these two perspectives are not contradictory but are fundamentally compatible. When the set of required skills is considered side-by-side with the set of critical problems project managers face, the complementary nature of these two perspectives is evident. This is illustrated in Table 3.

Without arguing which comes first, it is clear that either (a) project managers require certain skills in order to deal effectively with the factors most likely to create problems for them in managing the project, or (b) because certain problems are most likely to confront project managers, they require particular skills in order to handle them.

While this one-on-one matching in Table 3 obviously oversimplifies the dynamic nature of project management, it does have an inherent logical appeal. Since communication breakdowns are likely to create project management problems, effective project managers need to cultivate their communications (persuading and listening) skills. Project managers with good organizational skills are likely to be more effective at planning and subsequently allocating resources. Unless project managers are able to build strong project teams they are likely to be plagued by problems

Table 3. Skills ↔ Problems: Interconnected in Project Management

Communication	Breakdowns in communications
Organizational	Insufficient planning
	Resources inadequate
Team Building	Team members uncommitted
	Weak inter-unit integration
Leadership	Unclear goals/direction
	Interpersonal conflicts
Coping	Handling changes
Technological	Meeting ("unrealistic") deadlines

caused by poorly committed team members and inter-departmental conflict. Project goals are likely to be more easily understood when the project manager's leadership is consistent. Interpersonal conflicts will likely diminish when project managers set clear standards of performance and demonstrate their trust in, and respect for, others. The inevitable changes which accompany any project will be less problematic when not only coped with calmly, but also when handled with flexibility and creativity. Finally, problems created when deadlines and schedules are unrealistic may be minimized through a project manager's problem finding ability and experience in getting things back on track.

What was found underscores the claim that the primary problems of project managers are not technical, but human. Improving project managers' technological capabilities will be helpful only to the extent that this improves their ability to communicate, be organized, build teams, provide leadership, and deal comfortably with change. The challenge for technical managers, or for those moving from technical into managerial positions, is to recognize the need for, and to develop where necessary, their interpersonal skills.

References

1. ARCHIBALD, R. D. *Managing High-Technology Programs and Projects.* New York: John Wiley & Sons, 1976; KERZNER, H. *Project Management for Executives.* New York: Van Nostrand Reinhold, 1982; STUCKENBRUCK, L., "Ten Attributes of the Proficient Project Manager." *Proceedings of the Project Management Institute,* Montreal, 1976, 40–47; and THAMHAIN, H., and WILEMON, D., "Skill Requirements of Engineering Project Managers." *Twenty-Sixth IEEE Joint Engineering Management Conference,* 1978.

2. ROMAN, D. D. *Managing Projects: A Systems Perspective.* New York: Elsevier Science Publishing, 1985.

3. BADAWAY, M. *Developing Managerial Skills in Scientists and Engineers.* New York: Van Nostrand Reinhold, 1982.

4. HITCHCOCK, L. "Problems of First-Line Supervisors." *Research Management* Vol. 10, No. 6, 1967, 385–397.

Questions

1. What primary characteristic distinguishes the very successful project managers from the more mediocre project managers?

2. In Table 3, match the rankings between skills and problems. Why aren't the top skills matched to the main problems?

3. In Table 1, which of the problems are related to project setup (perhaps occurring before a project manager was selected) and which are related to the project manager's skills?

4. How does Table 1 compare to the discussion in the chapter?

5. How does Table 2 compare to the discussion in the chapter?

4

Project Organization

A firm, if successful, tends to grow, adding resources and people, developing an organizational structure. Commonly, the focus of the structure is specialization of the human elements of the group. As long as its organizational structure is sufficient to the tasks imposed on it, the structure tends to persist. When the structure begins to inhibit the work of the firm, pressures arise to reorganize along some other line. The underlying principle will still be specialization, but the specific nature of the specialization will be changed (see Greiner, 1972).

Any elementary management textbook covers the common bases of specialization (see Holt, 1993, for example). In addition to the ever-popular functional division, firms organize by product line, by geographic location, by production process, by type of customer, by subsidiary organization, by time, and by the elements of vertical or horizontal integration. Indeed, large firms frequently organize by several of these methods at different levels. For example, a firm may organize by major subsidiaries at the top level; the subsidiaries organize by product groups; and the product groups organize into customer divisions. These, in turn, may be split into functional departments that are further broken down into production process sections, which are set up as three-shift operating units.

Since the last edition of this book, a new kind of organization structure has appeared in growing numbers—the project organization, a.k.a. "enterprise project management" (Dinsmore, 1998; Levine, 1996, 1998; and Williams, 1997), the "managing organizations by projects" (Boznak, 1996 and Dinsmore, 1998), the "project-oriented firm," and other names. Such organizations have been described as applying "project management practices and tools across an enterprise" Levine, 1998). The source of these organizations is probably in the software industry that has long made a practice of developing major software application programs by decomposing them into a series of comparatively small software projects. Once the projects are completed, they are integrated into the whole application system. A great many firms, both software and nonsoftware firms alike, have now adopted a system whereby their traditional business is carried out in the traditional way, but anything that represents a change is carried out as a project. One hospital, for example, operates the usual departments in what, for them, are the usual ways. At the same time, the hospital supports several dozen projects oriented toward developing new health care products, or changing various aspects of standard medical and administrative methods.

There are many reasons for the rapid growth of project-oriented organizations, but most of them can be subsumed in four general areas. First, speed and market responsiveness have become absolute requirements for successful competition. It is no longer competitively acceptable to develop a new product or service using traditional methods in which the potential new product is passed from functional area to functional area until it is deemed suitable for production and distribution. (See below for a description of how Chrysler (now Daimler-Chrysler) shortened the design-production cycle for new automobile models.) *First-to-market* is a powerful competitive advantage. Further, in many industries it is common (and necessary) to tailor products specifically for individual clients. Suppliers of hair care products or cosmetics, for example, may supply individual stores in a drug chain with different mixes of products depending on the purchase patterns, ethnic mix of customers, and local style preferences for each store.

Second, the development of new products, processes, or services regularly requires inputs from diverse areas of specialized knowledge. Unfortunately, the exact mix of specialties appropriate for the design and development of one product or service is rarely suitable for another product or service. Teams of specialists that are created to accomplish their ad hoc purpose and disband typify the entire process.

Third, the rapid expansion of technological possibilities in almost every area of enterprise tends to destabilize the structure of organizations. Consider communications, entertainment, banks, consumer product manufacturing and sales, the automotive industry, aircraft manufacture, heavy electrical equipment, machine tools, and so forth without end. Mergers, downsizing, reorganizations, spin-offs, new marketing channels, and other similar major disturbances all require system-wide responsiveness from the total organization. Again, no traditional mechanism exists to handle change on such a large scale satisfactorily—but project organization can.

Finally, TV, movies, novels, and other mythology to the contrary, a large majority of senior managers we know rarely feel much confidence in their understanding of and control over a great many of the activities going on in their organizations. The hospital mentioned just above became a project-oriented organization because the new CEO strongly felt that she had no way of understanding, measuring, or controlling anything going on in the hospital except for the most routine, traditional activities. Transforming nonroutine activities into projects allowed her to ensure that accountability was established, projects were properly planned, integrated with other related activities, and reported routinely on their progress.

Moving from a nonproject environment to one in which projects are organized and used to accomplish special tasks to a full-fledged project-oriented organization presents senior management of a firm with an extraordinarily difficult transition. A full treatment of this subject is beyond the scope of this book, but several observations are in order. First, the process is time consuming. Even when the required resources are available and senior management is fully committed to the transition, it is still an arduous process. Our experience indicates that when all goes well, the transition rarely requires less than three years. In an excellent article on the process of leading fundamental change in a complex organization, Kotter (1997) lists eight steps that must be successfully completed if the change is to be accomplished. Most of these are dependent on active leadership from top management. Fusco (1997), who lists eight different steps, comes to much the same conclusion.

Whether the organization is conducting a few occasional projects or is fully project-oriented and carrying on scores of projects, any time a project is initiated, three organizational issues immediately arise. First, a decision must be made about how to tie the project to the parent firm. Second, a decision must be made about how to organize the project itself. Third, a decision must be made about how to organize activities that are common to other projects.

In the previous chapter we discussed the selection of the project manager (PM) and described the difficulties and responsibilities inherent in the PM's role. This chapter focuses on the interface between the project and its parent organization (i.e., how the project is organized as a part of its host). In the latter part of this chapter, we begin a discussion of how the project itself is organized, a discussion that will be continued in the next chapter.

First we look at the three major organizational forms commonly used to house projects and see just how each of them fits into the parent organization. We examine the advantages and disadvantages of each form, and discuss some of the critical factors that might lead us to choose one form over the others. We then consider some combinations of the fundamental forms and briefly examine the implications of using combination structures. Finally, we discuss some of the details of organizing the project team, describing the various roles of the project staff. We then turn to the formation and operation of two groups that may provide important services for all projects, the *risk management group*, and the *project management office*. We also describe some of the behavioral problems that face any project team. Finally, we discuss the impact that various ways of structuring projects may have on intraproject conflict in project-oriented firms.

To our knowledge, it is rare for a PM to have much influence over the interface between the organization and the project, choice of interface usually being made by senior management. The PM's work, however, is strongly affected by the project's structure, and the PM should understand its workings. Experienced PMs do seem to mold the project's organization to fit their notions of what is best. One project team member of our acquaintance remarked at length about how different life was on two projects (both matrix organized) run by different PMs. Study of the subtle impacts of the PM on project structure deserves more attention from researchers in the behavioral sciences. (For an excellent review of relevant research, see Hodge, Anthony, and Gales, 1996.)

4.1 THE PROJECT AS PART OF THE FUNCTIONAL ORGANIZATION

As one alternative for giving the project a "home," we can make it a part of one of the functional divisions of the firm. Figure 4-1 is the organizational chart for the University of Cincinnati, a functionally organized institution. If U.C. undertook the develop-

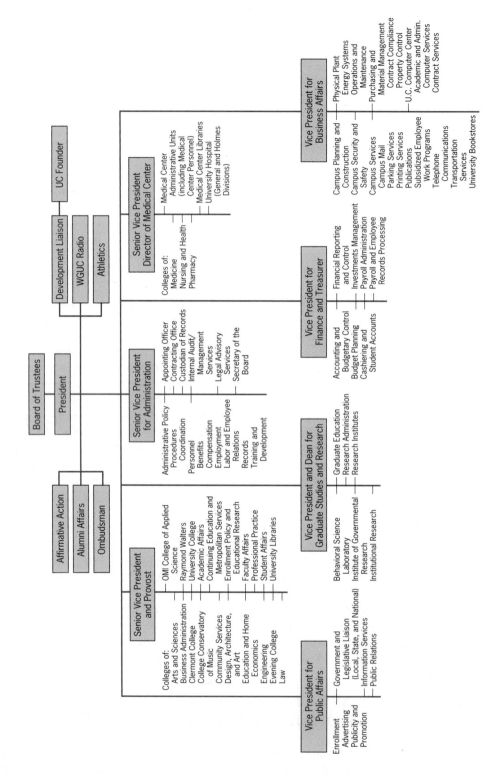

Figure 4-1 University of Cincinnati organization chart.

ment of a Master of Science program in Project Management (or perhaps an MPM), the project would probably be placed under the *general supervision* of the senior vice president and provost, under the *specific supervision* of the dean of the College of Business Administration (and/or College of Engineering), and would be managed by a senior faculty member with a specialty in operations management. (It might also be placed under the general supervision of the V.P. and dean for Graduate Studies and Research.) A project involving the construction of a new parking garage would fall under the V.P. for Business Affairs, as would a project to construct a local area network for all computers on the university campus. For functionally organized projects, the project is assigned to the functional unit that has the most interest in ensuring its success or can be most helpful in implementing it. As we noted in the case of the proposed MPM, more than one choice of parent may exist.

There are advantages and disadvantages of using functional elements of the parent organization as the administrative home for a project—assuming that one has chosen an appropriate function. The major advantages are:

1. There is maximum flexibility in the use of staff. If the proper functional division has been chosen as the project's home, the division will be the primary administrative base for individuals with technical expertise in the fields relevant to the project. Experts can be temporarily assigned to the project, make the required contributions, and immediately be reassigned to their normal work.

2. Individual experts can be utilized by many different projects. With the broad base of technical personnel available in the functional divisions, people can be switched back and forth between the different projects with relative ease.

3. Specialists in the division can be grouped to share knowledge and experience. Therefore, the project team has access to whatever technical knowledge resides in the functional group. This depth of knowledge is a potential source of creative, synergistic solutions to technical problems.

4. The functional division also serves as a base of technological continuity when individuals choose to leave the project, and even the parent firm. Perhaps just as important as technological continuity is the procedural, administrative, and overall policy continuity that results when the project is maintained in a specific functional division of the parent firm.

5. Finally, and not the least important, the functional division contains the normal path of advancement for individuals whose expertise is in the functional area. The project may be a source of glory for those who participate in its successful completion, but the functional field is their professional home and the focus of their professional growth and advancement.

Just as there are advantages to housing the project in a functional area, there are also disadvantages:

1. A primary disadvantage of this arrangement is that the client is not the focus of activity and concern. The functional unit has its own work to do, which usually takes precedence over the work of the project, and hence over the interests of the client.

2. The functional division tends to be oriented toward the activities particular to its function. It is not usually problem oriented in the sense that a project must be to be successful.

3. Occasionally in functionally organized projects, no individual is given full responsibility for the project. This failure to pinpoint responsibility usually means that the PM is made accountable for some parts of the project, but another person is made accountable for one or more other parts. Little imagination is required to forecast the lack of coordination and chaos that results.

4. The same reasons that lead to lack of coordinated effort tend to make response to client needs slow and arduous. There are often several layers of management between the project and the client.

5. There is a tendency to suboptimize the project. Project issues that are directly within the interest area of the functional home may be dealt with carefully, but those outside normal interest areas may be given short shrift, if not totally ignored.

6. The motivation of people assigned to the project tends to be weak. The project is not in the mainstream of activity and interest, and some project team members may view service on the project as a professional detour.

7. Such an organizational arrangement does not facilitate a holistic approach to the project. Complex technical projects such as the development of a jet transport aircraft or an emergency room in a hospital simply cannot be well designed unless they are designed as a totality. No matter how good the intentions, no functional division can avoid focusing on its unique areas of interest. Cross-divisional communication and sharing of knowledge is slow and difficult at best.

Project Management in Practice
Reorganizing for Project Management at Prevost Car

In July 1994, the vice-president of production at Prevost Car in Quebec City, Canada, was told that he would have to expand production capacity 31 percent in the next five months. In the past, such a task would start with a bulldozer the next day and the work would be under way, but no one knew at what cost, what timetable, or what value to the firm. Realizing that he needed some fresh ideas, a structured approach, and that there was no allowance for a mistake, the VP contacted a project management consulting firm to help him.

The consulting firm set up a five-day meeting between their project managers, a value engineering expert, and the seven foremen from Pre-

vost's main factory to scope out the project. The group produced a report for senior management outlining a $10 million project to expand the main factory by 60,000 square feet, and a follow-on potential to make a further expansion of 20 percent more. The detail of the plan came as a revelation to top management who approved it after only two days of study. After it was completed on time and on budget, the firm also committed to the additional 20 percent expansion which also came in as planned.

The success of this project resulted in "infecting" Prevost Car with the project management "bug." The next major task, an initiative to reduce workplace injuries, was thus organized as a project and was also highly successful. Soon, all types of activities were being handled as projects at Prevost. The use of project management in manufacturing firms is highly appropriate given their need to adapt quickly to ferocious international competition, accelerating technological change, and rapidly changing market conditions. In addition, Prevost has found that project management encourages productive cooperation between departments, fresh thinking and innovation, team approaches to problems, and the highly valued use of outside experts to bring in new ideas, thereby breaking current short-sighted habits and thinking. As Prevost's VP states: "Right now it's a question of finding what couldn't be better managed by project."

Source: M. Gagne, "Prevost Car—The Power of Project Management," *PM Network,* August 1997, pp. 35–36.

4.2 PURE PROJECT ORGANIZATION

At the other end of the organizational spectrum is pure project organization. The project is separated from the rest of the parent system. It becomes a self-contained unit with its own technical staff, its own administration, tied to the parent firm by the tenuous strands of periodic progress reports and oversight. Some parent organizations prescribe administrative, financial, personnel, and control procedures in detail. Others allow the project almost total freedom within the limits of final accountability. There are examples of almost every possible intermediate position. Figure 4-2 illustrates this pure project organization.

As with the functional organization, the pure project has its unique advantages and disadvantages. The former are:

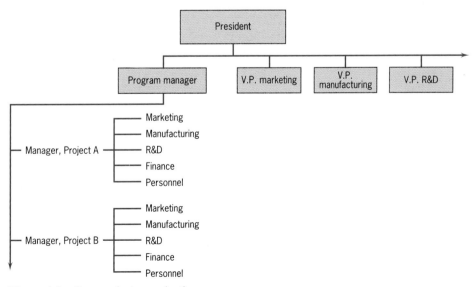

Figure 4-2 Pure project organization.

1. The project manager has full line authority over the project. Though the PM must report to a senior executive in the parent organization, there is a complete work force devoted to the project. The PM is like the CEO of a firm that is dedicated to carrying out the project.

2. All members of the project work force are directly responsible to the PM. There are no functional division heads whose permission must be sought or whose advice must be heeded before making technological decisions. The PM is truly the project director.

3. When the project is removed from the functional division, the lines of communication are shortened. The entire functional structure is bypassed, and the PM communicates directly with senior corporate management. The shortened communication lines result in faster communications with fewer failures.

4. When there are several successive projects of a similar kind, the pure project organization can maintain a more or less permanent cadre of experts who develop considerable skill in specific technologies. Indeed, the existence of such skill pools can attract customers to the parent firm. Lockheed's famous "Skunk Works" was such a team of experts who took great pride in their ability to solve difficult engineering problems. The group's name, taken from the Li'l Abner comic strip, reflects the group's pride, irreverent attitude, and strong sense of identity.

5. The project team that has a strong and separate identity of its own tends to develop a high level of commitment from its members. Motivation is high and acts to foster the task orientation discussed in Chapter 3.

6. Because authority is centralized, the ability to make swift decisions is greatly enhanced. The entire project organization can react more rapidly to the requirements of the client and the needs of senior management.

7. Unity of command exists. While it is easy to overestimate the value of this particular organizational principle, there is little doubt that the quality of life for subordinates is enhanced when each subordinate has one, and only one, boss.

8. Pure project organizations are structurally simple and flexible, which makes them relatively easy to understand and to implement.

9. The organizational structure tends to support a holistic approach to the project. A brief explanation of the systems approach was given in Chapter 3, and an example of the problems arising when the systems approach is not used appears in Section 4.3 of this chapter. The dangers of focusing on and optimizing the project's subsystems rather than the total project are often a major cause of technical failure in projects.

While the advantages of the pure project organization make a powerful argument favoring this structure, its disadvantages are also serious:

1. When the parent organization takes on several projects, it is common for each one to be fully staffed. This can lead to considerable duplication of effort in every area from clerical staff to the most sophisticated (and expensive) technological support units. If a project does not require a full-time personnel manager, for example, it must have one nonetheless because personnel managers come in integers, not fractions, and staff are not shared across projects.

2. In fact, the need to ensure access to technological knowledge and skills results in an attempt by the PM to stockpile equipment and technical assistance in order to be certain that it will be available when needed. Thus, people with critical technical skills may be hired by the project when they are available rather than when they are needed. Similarly, they tend to be maintained on the project longer than needed, "just in case." Disadvantages 1 and 2 combine to make this way of organizing projects very expensive.

3. Removing the project from technical control by a functional department has its advantages, but it also has a serious disadvantage if the project is characterized as "high technology." Though individuals engaged with projects develop considerable depth in the technology of the project, they tend to fall behind in other areas of their technical expertise. The functional division is a repository of technical lore, but it is not readily accessible to members of the pure project team.

4. Pure project groups seem to foster inconsistency in the way in which policies and procedures are carried out. In the relatively sheltered environment of the project, administrative corner-cutting is common and easily justified as a response to the client or to technical exigency. "They don't understand our problems" becomes an easy excuse for ignoring dicta from headquarters.

5. In pure project organizations, the project takes on a life of its own. Team members form strong attachments to the project and to each other. A disease known as *projectitis* develops. A strong we–they divisiveness grows, distorting the relationships between project team members and their counterparts in the parent organization. Friendly rivalry may become bitter competition, and political infighting between projects is common.

6. Another symptom of projectitis is the worry about "life after the project ends." Typically, there is considerable uncertainty about what will happen when the project is completed. Will team members be laid off? Will they be assigned to low-prestige work? Will their technical skills be too rusty to be successfully integrated into other projects? Will our team (that old gang of mine) be broken up?

4.3   THE MATRIX ORGANIZATION

In an attempt to couple some of the advantages of the pure project organization with some of the desirable features of the functional organization, and to avoid some of the disadvantages of each, the matrix organization was developed. In effect, the functional and the pure project organizations represent extremes. The matrix organization is a combination of the two. It is a pure project organization overlaid on the functional divisions of the parent firm.

Being a combination of pure project and functional organization structures, a matrix organization can take on a wide variety of specific forms, depending on which of the two extremes (functional or pure project) it most resembles. The "project" or "strong" matrix most resembles the pure project organization. The "coordination" or "functional" or "weak" matrix most resembles the functional form of organization.

Finally, the "balanced" matrix lies in between the other two. In practice, there is an almost infinite variety of organizational forms between the extremes, and the primary difference between these forms has to do with the relative power/decision authority of the project manager and the functional manager. For an interesting study of the use of different structural forms used in the pharmaceutical industry, see Larson (1991).

Because it is simpler to explain, let us first consider a strong matrix, one that is similar to a pure project. Rather than being a stand-alone organization, like the pure project, the matrix project is not separated from the parent organization. Consider Figure 4-3. The project manager of Project 1, PM$_1$, reports to a program manager who also exercises supervision over other projects. Project 1 has assigned to it three people from the manufacturing division, one and one-half people from marketing, one-half of a person each from finance and personnel, four individuals from R & D, and perhaps others not shown. These individuals come from their respective functional divisions and are assigned to the project full-time or part-time, depending on the project's needs. It should be emphasized that *the PM controls when and what these people will do, while the functional managers control who will be assigned to the project and what technology will be used.*

With heavy representation from manufacturing and R&D, Project 1 might involve the design and installation of a new type of manufacturing process. Project 2 could involve a new product or, possibly, a marketing research problem. Project 3 might concern the installation of a new, computerized, financial control system. All the while, the functional divisions continue on with their routine activities.

There is no single executive to whom PMs generally report. If a project is merely one of several in a specific program, the PM typically reports to a program manager, if there is one. It is not uncommon, however, for the PM to report to the manager of the functional area that has a particular interest in the program, or an interest in the project if it is not part of a program. If several projects on mathematics are being conducted for the Office of Naval Research (ONR), for instance, it would be normal for the PMs to report to the ONR section head for Mathematical Sciences. In smaller firms with only a few projects, it is common for the PM to report directly to a senior executive.

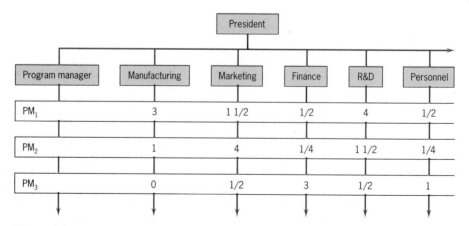

Figure 4-3   Matrix organization.

At the other end of the spectrum of matrix organizations is the functional or weak matrix. A project might, for example, have only one full-time person, the PM. Rather than having an individual functional worker actually assigned to the project, the functional departments devote *capacity* to the project, and the primary task of the PM is to coordinate the project activities carried out by the functional departments. For example, the PM of a project set up to create a new database for personnel might request that the basic design be done by the systems analysis group in the administrative division. The personnel job would then be added to the normal workload of the systems group. The priority given to the design might be assigned by senior management or might be the result of negotiations between the PM and the head of the systems group. In some cases, the systems group's charges for the job might also be subject to negotiation. The task could even be subcontracted to an outside vendor.

Between these extremes is the balanced matrix, which is typically anything but balanced. There are many different mixtures of project and functional responsibilities. When a functional group's work is frequently required by projects, it is common to operate the group as a functional unit rather than to transfer its people to the project. For instance, a toxicology unit in a cosmetic business, a quality assurance group in a multiproduct manufacturing firm, or a computer graphics group in a publishing firm might all be functionally organized and take on project work much like outside contractors. While the PM's control over the work is diminished by this arrangement, the project does have immediate access to any expertise in the group, and the group can maintain its technological integrity.

The impetus for the matrix organization was the fact that firms operating in high-technology areas had to integrate several functional specialties to work on a set of projects and wished to *time-share* expertise between individual projects in the set. Further, the technical needs of the projects often required a *systems* approach (Cleland and King, 1983). In earlier times, when a high-technology project was undertaken by a firm, it would start its journey through the firm in the R & D department. Concepts and ideas would be worked out and the result passed on to the engineering department, which would sometimes rework the whole thing. This result would then be forwarded to manufacturing, where it might be reworked once more in order to ensure that the output was manufacturable by the firm's current machinery. All of this required a great deal of time, and the emergent project might have scant resemblance to the original specifications.

In the meantime, another firm would be doing much the same thing on another project for the customer. These two projects might later have to be joined together, or to a third, and the combination was then expected to meet its intended function. For example, the first project might be a jet aircraft engine, the second a weapon system, and the third an airframe. The composite result rarely performed as originally conceived because the parts were not designed as a unified system. Military aircraft buffs may recall several World War II aircraft that used the Allison in-line engine (designed by Rolls Royce). The P-39 (Airacobra) was a mediocre combat aircraft. The P-38 (Lightning) was a fairly good plane. The P-51 (Mustang) was an outstanding combat machine. In all three cases, the engine, armament, and airframe were designed separately. In one case this approach to design worked well; in one it did not. A systems approach to design would require that engine, airframe, and weapon system be designed as a unit. The attempt is to optimize the composite system rather than the parts. This improves the chance of developing a P-51 and decreases the likelihood of making a P-39. Indeed, given the complexity of the systems going into a combat aircraft today, it is doubtful if a plane could be designed using the old methods.

The systems approach was adopted as an alternative to the traditional method described above. This did not mean that the same firm had to manufacture everything, but it did mean that one organization had to take responsibility for the integrity of project design—to make sure that the parts were compatible and that the combination would function as expected. (Note that "integrity" and "integration" come from the same word root.) This required that R & D, engineering, manufacturing, etc., work closely together, and that all these work closely with the client, all the while coordinating efforts with other firms that were supplying subsystems for the project.

Housing the project in a functional organization was simply too constraining. Setting it up as a pure project was workable but expensive because of the need to duplicate expensive technical talent when more than one project was involved. The matrix organization, which allows the PM to draw temporarily on the technological expertise and assistance of all relevant functions, was a way out of the dilemma. The effectiveness of the systems approach is well demonstrated by the success of the Chrysler Corporation in designing and bringing to market their LH sedans (as well as by their small car, the Neon, and their sports car, the Viper). The LH design was the product of a process called "concurrent" or "simultaneous" engineering or design that involves marketing, engineering, manufacturing, design, quality assurance, and other departments working together from the outset. This process not only produced designs that have been widely rated as "outstanding," it also shortened the design-to-street process by about 18 months. Quite apart from the value of a fine design, the economic value of the time saved is immense. The value derives from two sources: (1) less design labor and overhead and (2) earlier sales and return on the investment. For a more complete description of the use of design teams at Chrysler see (Raynal, 1992).

Though we deal with the subject in more detail in Section 4.8, it is well known that matrix organization results in projects characterized by high levels of conflict. Kalu (1993, p. 175) defines *virtual positions* as "task processes, the performance of which requires composite membership" in both project and functional organizations. When complex organizations conduct projects, virtual positions are typical because projects usually require input from several functional departments. This creates overlapping and shared responsibility for the work and with functional and project managers sharing responsibility for execution of the project, conflict inevitably follows. Some further specify that virtual projects exist when project team members are geographically distributed (Adams and Adams, 1997) This further exacerbates conflict. For an excellent study of this phenomenon, see (de Laat, 1994).

We have previously discussed the difference between discipline-oriented individuals and those who are problem-oriented, indicating that the latter are highly desirable as members of project teams. Both de Laat (1994) and Kalu (1993) stand as adequate testimony to the fact that discipline-oriented team members tend to become ardent supporters of their functional areas, sometimes to the detriment of the project as a whole. A study of the effects of "functional diversity" on project teams comes to much the same conclusion (Pelled and Adler, 1994). The resultant power struggles may stress the project manager's skills in conflict reduction. More will be said in Section 4.8 about the nature of these conflicts.

The matrix approach has its own unique advantages and disadvantages. Its strong points are:

1. The project is the point of emphasis. One individual, the PM, takes responsibility for managing the project, for bringing it in on time, within cost, and to specification. The matrix organization shares this virtue with the pure project organization.

2. Because the project organization is overlaid on the functional divisions, temporarily drawing labor and talent from them, the project has reasonable access to the entire reservoir of technology in all functional divisions. When there are several projects, the talents of the functional divisions are available to all projects, thus sharply reducing the duplication required by the pure project structure.

3. There is less anxiety about what happens when the project is completed than is typical of the pure project organization. Even though team members tend to develop a strong attachment for the project, they also feel close to their functional "home."

4. Response to client needs is as rapid as in the pure project case, and the matrix organization is just as flexible. Similarly, the matrix organization responds flexibly and rapidly to the demands made by those inside the parent organization. A project nested within an operating firm must adapt to the needs of the parent firm or the project will not survive.

5. With matrix management, the project will have—or have access to—representatives from the administrative units of the parent firm. As a result, consistency with the policies, practices, and procedures of the parent firm tends to be preserved. If nothing else, this consistency with parent firm procedures tends to foster project credibility in the administration of the parent organization, a condition that is commonly undervalued.

6. Where there are several projects simultaneously under way, matrix organization allows a better companywide balance of resources to achieve the several different time/cost/performance targets of the individual projects. This holistic approach to the total organization's needs allows projects to be staffed and scheduled in order to optimize total system performance rather than to achieve the goals of one project at the expense of others.

7. While pure project and functional organizations represent extremes of the organizational spectrum, matrix organizations cover a wide range in between. We have differentiated between strong and weak matrices in terms of whether the functional units supplied individuals or capacity to projects. Obviously, some functional units might furnish people and others only supply capacity. There is, therefore, a great deal of flexibility in precisely how the project is organized—all within the basic matrix structure—so that it can be adapted to a wide variety of projects and is always subject to the needs, abilities, and desires of the parent organization.

The advantages accruing to the matrix structure are potent, but the disadvantages are also serious. All of the following disadvantages involve conflict—between the functional and project managers for the most part.

1. In the case of functionally organized projects, there is no doubt that the functional division is the focus of decision-making power. In the pure project case, it is clear

that the PM is the power center of the project. With matrix organizations, the power is more balanced. Often, the balance is fairly delicate. When doubt exists about who is in charge, the work of the project suffers. If the project is successful and highly visible, doubt about who is in charge can foster political infighting for the credit and glory. If the project is a failure, political infighting will be even more brutal to avoid blame.

2. While the ability to balance time, cost, and performance between several projects is an advantage of matrix organization, that ability has its dark side. The set of projects must be carefully monitored as a set, a tough job. Further, the movement of resources from project to project in order to satisfy the several schedules may foster political infighting among the several PMs, all of whom tend to be more interested in ensuring success for their individual projects than in helping the total system optimize organizationwide goals.

3. For strong matrices, problems associated with shutting down a project are almost as severe as those in pure project organizations. The projects, having individual identities, resist death. Even in matrix organizations, projectitis is still a serious disease.

4. In matrix-organized projects, the PM controls administrative decisions and the functional heads control technological decisions. The distinction is simple enough when writing about project management, but for the operating PM the division of authority and responsibility inherent in matrix management is complex. The ability of the PM to negotiate anything from resources to technical assistance to delivery dates is a key contributor to project success. Success is doubtful for a PM without strong negotiating skills.

5. Matrix management violates the management principle of unity of command. Project workers have at least two bosses, their functional heads and the PM. There is no way around the split loyalties and confusion that results. Anyone who has worked under such an arrangement understands the difficulties. Those who have not done so cannot appreciate the discomforts it causes. To paraphrase Plato's comment on democracy, matrix management "is a charming form of management, full of variety and disorder."

4.4 MIXED ORGANIZATIONAL SYSTEMS

As noted in the introduction to this chapter, divisionalization is a means of dividing a large and monolithic organization into smaller, more flexible units. This enables the parent organization to capture some of the advantages of small, specialized organizational units while retaining some of the advantages that come with larger size.

Organizing projects by product involves establishing each product project as a relatively autonomous, integrated element within the organization as a whole. Such primary functions as engineering and finance are then dedicated to the interests of the product itself. Software projects are a common type of project organized by "product." Software projects often occur in clusters—several different projects that are parts of the same overall information system or application software. Pursuing such projects as a group tends to ensure that they will be compatible, one with another, and even increases the likelihood that they will be completed as a group.

Consider a firm making lawn furniture. The firm might be divisionalized into products constructed of plastic or aluminum. Each product line would have its own specialized staff. Assume now two newly designed styles of furniture, one plastic and the other aluminum, each of which becomes a project within its respective product division. (Should a new product be a combination of plastic and aluminum, the pure project form of organization will tend to forestall interdivisional battles for turf.)

Similarly, organization by territory is especially attractive to national organizations whose activities are physically or geographically spread, and where the products have some geographical uniqueness, such as ladies' garments. Project organization across customer divisions is typically found when the projects reflect a paramount interest in the needs of different types of customers. Here customer preferences are more substantial than either territorial or product activities. The differences between consumer and manufacturer, or civilian and military, are examples of such substantial differences.

A special kind of project organization often found in manufacturing firms develops when projects are housed in process divisions. Such a project might concern new manufacturing methods, and the machining division might serve as the base for a project investigating new methods of removing metal. The same project might be housed in the machining division but include several people from the R & D lab, and be organized as a combination of functional and matrix forms.

Pure functional and pure project organizations may coexist in a firm. This results in the *mixed* form shown in Figure 4-4. This form is rarely observed with the purity we have depicted here, yet it is not uncommon. What is done, instead, is to spin off the large, successful long-run projects as subsidiaries or independent operations. Many firms nurture young, unstable, smaller projects under the wing of an existing division, then wean them to pure projects with their own identity, and finally allow the formation of a *venture team*—or, for a larger project, *venture firm*—within the parent company. For example, Texas Instruments did this with the Speak and Spell toy that was developed by one of its employees.

The hybridization of the mixed form leads to flexibility. It enables the firm to meet special problems by appropriate adaptation of its organizational structure. There are, however, distinct dangers involved in hybridization. Dissimilar groupings within the same accountability center tend to encourage overlap, duplication, and friction because of incompatibility of interests. Again, we have the conditions that tend to result in conflict between functional and project managers.

Figure 4-5 illustrates another common solution to the problem of project organi-

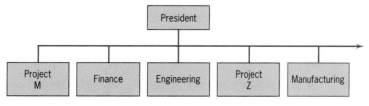

Figure 4-4   "Mixed" organization.

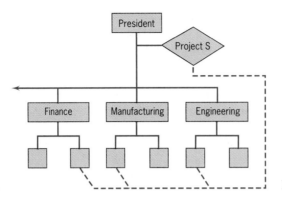

Figure 4-5   Staff organization.

zational form. The firm sets up what appears to be a standard form of functional organization, but it adds a staff office to administer all projects. This frees the functional groups of administrative problems while it uses their technical talents. In a large specialty chemical firm, this organizational form worked so well that the staff office became the nucleus of a full-scale division of the firm. The division's sole purpose is to administer projects. Much has been written about the use of a "project office" which is an equivalent structure. More will be said about the project office in Section 4.6.

In many ways this organizational form is not distinguishable from matrix management, but it is typically used for small, short-run projects where the formation of a full-fledged matrix system is not justified. This mixed form shares several advantages and disadvantages of the matrix structure, but the project life is usually so short that the disease of projectitis is rarely contracted. If the number or size of the projects being staffed in this way grows, a shift to a formal matrix organization naturally evolves.

Though the ways of interfacing project and parent organization are many and varied, most firms adopt the matrix form as the basic method of housing projects. To this base, occasional pure, functional, and hybrid projects are added if these possess special advantages in special cases. The managerial difficulties posed by matrix projects are more than offset by their relatively low cost and by their ability to get access to broad technical support. [Dinsmore (1993a) recommends "flat, flexible structures," that are, as far as we can tell, not distinguishable from matrix structures in any significant way. He strongly emphasizes "lean and mean" for projects as well as a corporate way of life.]

4.5   CHOOSING AN ORGANIZATIONAL FORM

Even experienced practitioners find it difficult to explain how one should proceed when choosing the organizational interface between project and firm. The choice is determined by the situation, but even so is partly intuitive. There are few accepted principles of design, and no step-by-step procedures that give detailed instructions for determining what kind of structure is needed and how it can be built. All we can do is consider the nature of the potential project, the characteristics of the various organizational options, the advantages and disadvantages of each, the cultural preferences of the parent organization, and make the best compromise we can.

In general, the functional form is apt to be the organizational form of choice for projects where the major focus must be on the in-depth application of a technology rather than, for example, on minimizing cost, meeting a specific schedule, or achieving speedy response to change. Also, the functional form is preferred for projects that will require large capital investments in equipment or buildings of a type normally used by the function.

If the firm engages in a large number of similar projects (e.g., construction projects), the pure project form of organization is preferred. The same form would generally be used for one-time, highly specific, unique tasks that require careful control and are not appropriate for a single functional area—the development of a new product line, for instance.

When the project requires the integration of inputs from several functional areas and involves reasonably sophisticated technology, but does not require all the technical specialists to work for the project on a full-time basis, the matrix organization is the only satisfactory solution. This is particularly true when several such projects must share technical experts. But matrix organizations are complex and present a difficult challenge for the PM.

If choice of project structure exists, the first problem is to determine the kind of work that must be accomplished. To do this requires an initial, tentative project plan. First, identify the primary deliverable(s) of the project. Next, list the major tasks associated with each deliverable. For each task, determine the functional unit that will probably be responsible for carrying out the task. These are the elements that must be involved in order to carry out the project. The problem is how best to bring them together—or, how best to integrate their work. Additional matters to be considered are the individuals (or small groups) who will do the work, their personalities, the technology to be employed, the client(s) to be served, the political relationships of the functional units involved, and the culture of the parent organization. Environmental factors inside and outside the parent organization must also be taken into account. By understanding the various structures, their advantages and disadvantages, a firm can select the organizational structure that seems to offer the most effective and efficient choice. Another view of the problem of selecting the appropriate interface between the project and its parent organization is found in (Hill and White, 1979).

Since it is our objective in this chapter to provide criteria for the selection of a project organization, we shall illustrate the process with two examples. In each case, we use the following procedure.

1. Define the project with a statement of the objective(s) that identifies the major outcomes desired.

2. Determine the key tasks associated with each objective and locate the units in the parent organization that serve as functional "homes" for these types of tasks.

3. Arrange the key tasks by sequence and decompose them into work packages.

4. Determine which organizational units are required to carry out the work packages and which units will work particularly closely with which others.

5. List any special characteristics or assumptions associated with the project—for example, level of technology needed, probable length and size of the project, any potential problems with the individuals who may be assigned to the work, possible political problems between different functions involved, and anything else that

seems relevant, including the parent firm's previous experiences with different ways of organizing projects.

6. In light of the above, and with full cognizance of the pros and cons associated with each structural form, choose a structure.

Trinatronic, Inc.

Project objective: To design, build, and market a multi-tasking portable computer containing 32- and 64-bit processors, 512 Mbytes RAM, at least 60 Gbytes HD, at least 1 GHz processing speed, have a 15 in. active matrix screen, a built-in cellular 56 Kbps modem capable of simultaneous voice and data transmission, a read/write CD/DVD drive, a 10/100 Mbps network interface card, an IEEE 1394 Firewire port, a Geoforce 4-based graphics accelerator with 128 M memory, and a battery life of at least 7 hours. The entire system built to sell at or below $2,500.

Key Tasks	Organizational Units
A. Write specifications.	Mktg. Div. and R &D
B. Design hardware, do initial tests.	R &D
C. Engineer hardware for production.	Eng. Dept., Mfg. Div.
D. Set up production line.	Eng. Dept., Mfg. Div.
E. Manufacture small run, conduct quality and reliability tests.	Mfg. Div. and Q.A. Dept., Exec. V.P. staff
F. Write (or adopt) operating systems.	Software Prod. Div.
G. Test operating systems.	Q.A. Dept., Exec. V.P. staff
H. Write (or adopt) applications software.	Software Prod. Div.
I. Test applications software.	Q.A. Dept., Exec. V.P. staff
J. Prepare full documentation, repair and user manuals.	Tech. Writing Section (Eng. Div.) and Tech. Writing Section (Software Prod. Div.)
K. Set up service system with manuals and spare parts	Service Dept., Mktg. Div.
L. Prepare marketing program.	Mktg. Div.
M. Prepare marketing demonstrations.	Mktg. Div.

Without attempting to generate a specific sequence for these tasks, we note that they seem to belong to four categories of work.

1. Design, build, and test hardware.

2. Design, write, and test software.

3. Set up production and service/repair systems with spares and manuals.

4. Design marketing effort, with demonstrations, brochures, and manuals.

Based on this analysis, it would appear that the project will need the following elements:

- Groups to design the hardware and software.
- Groups to test the hardware and software.

- A group to engineer the production system for the hardware.
- A group to design the marketing program.
- A group to prepare all appropriate documents and manuals.
- And, lest we forget, a group to administer all the above groups.

These subsystems represent at least three major divisions and perhaps a half-dozen departments in the parent organization. The groups designing the hardware and the multiple operating systems will have to work closely together. The test groups may work quite independently of the hardware and software designers, but results seem to improve when they cooperate. We can prepare a simple responsibility chart for the tasks (Figure 4-6).

Trinatronics has people capable of carrying out the project. The design of the hardware and operating systems is possible in the current state of the art,

but to design such systems at a cost that will allow a retail price of $3000 or less will require an advance in the state of the art. The project is estimated to take between 18 and 24 months, and to be the most expensive project yet undertaken by Trinatronics.

Based on the sketchy information above, it seems clear that a functional project organization would not be appropriate. Too much interaction between major divisions is required to make a single function into a comfortable organizational home for everyone. Either a pure project or matrix structure is feasible, and given the choice, it seems sensible to choose the simpler pure project organization if the cost of additional personnel is not too high. Note that if the project had required only part-time participation by the highly qualified scientific professionals, the matrix organization might have been preferable. Also, a matrix structure would probably have been chosen if this project were only one of several such projects drawing on a common staff base.

Tasks	Executive V.P. Staff		Marketing Division		Manufacturing Division		Engineering Division		Software Division		Research & Development Division
		Q.A. Dept.		Serv. Dept.		Eng. Dept.		Tech. Writ.		Tech. Writ.	
A			x								x
B											x
C						x					
D						x					
E	x				x						
F									x		
G	x										
H									x		
I	x										
J								x		x	
K				x							
L		x									
M		x									

Figure 4-6   Trinatronics, Inc. product task/organization responsibility chart.

Urban Hospital

Project objective: To develop and implement a computerized scheduling system for the hospital's operating rooms.

Key Tasks	Organizational Unit
A. Find and prioritize objectives of the system.	Systems Analysis and Dept. of Surgery
B. Build preliminary model.	Systems Analysis
C. Program and test preliminary model.	Systems Analysis
D. Use model in parallel with current scheduling system.	Systems Analysis
E. Compare results and present to Department of Surgery.	Systems Analysis and Dept. of Surgery
F. If necessary, amend model and repeat tasks D and E.	Systems Analysis and Dept. of Surgery
G. Install model, including full documentation.	Systems Analysis
H. Train Department of Surgery clerks in operation of model.	Systems Analysis and Dept. of Surgery

The order in which tasks should be performed is as shown above because all the work must be done sequentially. There are three major jobs.

1. Build the model based on input from the users.

2. Test model on an "as if" basis and amend if necessary.

3. Install model and train operators.

Only two units will be required for the project, a systems analysis group (housed in the Department of Administration) and a user group. Analysts and users will have to work together throughout the project. These groups each represent a different part of the parent organization.

Consideration was given to the use of an outside consultant to analyze the system and develop the model. The internal systems analysts are heavily involved in replacing an outside vendor's accounting software system with one of their own devising. They expect to be fully occupied for another six to eight months. On the other hand, some members of the Department of Surgery are worried that the hospital's own analysts will not be sensitive to the special needs of the department; they would be even less likely to tolerate and trust outsiders. Indeed, several of the surgeons are doubtful about the entire project. They are not sure that it makes any sense to set priorities on the objectives for scheduling the operating rooms because "quality of patient care is our only priority."

While the analysis group is currently engaged in a major project, it is estimated that they will be able to release an analyst to the OR scheduling project within three months. The project does not appear particularly difficult, and they feel it should not require more than two or three months to complete, given that the surgeons will consider cooperating in the analysis.

In this case, it seems best to house the project in the Department of Surgery. The project is small and involves only two departments. It is easy to move the analytic skill to the Department of Surgery, and there is nothing here that requires a separate project or matrix organization with the concomitant need for separate administration. Further, housing the project in Surgery would give that department a sense of control, which might act to allay their fears. It would, of course, be feasible to organize this endeavor as a staff project under the CEO of the hospital or the chief of the medical staff, but the psychological and political advantages of housing it in the Department of Surgery warrant the use of the functional organization.

Project Management in Practice
Converting to Project Management in Government Agencies

Six years into its conversion from functional management to project management of its responsibilities, the California Department of Transportation identified some of the often-painful lessons it has learned over the years. In general, an overhaul of the organizational culture is required including careful organizational planning, cultivation of project managers and staff, and proper priority in the organizational agenda.

- *Create a project office and set expectations of its role.* No single action is more telling than creating both an executive level Project Office as well as district/regional offices. These offices generally include the project general manager, the program managers, the engineering contract officer, the project managers, and the administrative and support staff. The expectations of these offices is the facilitation of project implementation and operation, as well as education and training in project management.

- *Cultivate rather than designating project managers.* Common errors are adding project management responsibilities to the duties of functional managers and redesignating the best engineers or functional managers as project managers. Instead, select individuals with the best managerial and soft skills such as team building, negotiation and conflict resolution, and communication and then educate them in the skills of managing and controlling projects.

- *Use outside resources and help.* If an organization must rely on internal staff for projects, there may be too much resistance through existing culture and policies to successfully convert to project management. In these cases, a fresh, outside perspective is needed. Consider using peer reviews, benchmarking, professional organizations

such as Project Management Institute, consultants, and existing partnerships with engineering and construction firms or other best-of-class organizations.

- *Develop a uniform work breakdown structure.* Use a multifunctional team of project managers, functional managers, and functional staff, perhaps facilitated by a consultant, to develop a comprehensive, uniform work breakdown structure that will accommodate the majority of projects anticipated by the organization. This will give a project team a jump on the task before them and help instill the project mentality in the organization.

- *Create empowered project management forums.* Early in the projectization of the organization, there will be many individuals who have been placed in project positions for which they have no formal training or relevant experience. Forums that allow these people to discuss their experiences, successes, and problems are a powerful tool to spread project management lessons throughout the firm. In addition, these people should have the authority to make organizational changes, or there should be an executive sponsor in charge of these forums who has the authority to do so, that alter policies that impede the spread of project management or their success.

- *Select project management software instead of letting it select you.* Don't let the organization be too hasty in drawing up a list of "must haves" for its project management software, thinking that using these packages is the same as project management. A better process is to determine the organizational structure, policies, people, and processes that make sense for the proj-

ects that will be undertaken and then identify software packages that support these
elements as seamlessly as possible.

- ***Involve top management.*** A change as fundamental to an organization as that of
changing its culture and policies requires
the support and commitment of top management or it simply will not happen. The
functional managers will foresee a loss of
power and influence by moving to a matrix

or projectized organization and resist the
change. Placing a top executive as approval
authority for project cost, schedule, and especially scope changes will help keep
upper management involved in the process
and supportive of the changes required.

Source: R. A. Chittenden, "Caltrans' Quest for 'True Project
Management' in Government Bureaucracy," *PM Network,*
April 1997, pp. 25–28.

4.6   TWO SPECIAL CASES—RISK MANAGEMENT AND THE PROJECT OFFICE

Thus far in this chapter it has been tacitly assumed that however the project has been
organized, it has, or has access to, sufficient skill, knowledge, and resources to accomplish any activities that may be required. As we shall see, this assumption is not
always true. A primary task of the PM is to acquire the resources, technical skills,
knowledge, and whatever is needed by the project. While this may be difficult, the acquisition of the project's technical resources is mainly dependent on the PM's skill in
negotiation—see Chapter 6.

Even if the PM has all the resources needed, two problems remain. First, in the
entire history of projects from the beginning of time until the day after tomorrow, no
project has ever been completed precisely as it was planned. Uncertainty is a way of
life for PMs and their projects. Second, the successful execution of a project is a complex managerial task and requires the use of planning, budgeting, scheduling, and
control tools with which the neophyte PM may not be completely familiar. In addition, there are contractual, administrative, and reporting duties that must be performed in accord with the law, the wishes of the client, and the rules of the organizational home of the project.

Dealing with uncertainties has come to be known as *risk management.* We introduced the subject in Chapter 2 when the uncertainties of project selection were discussed. To deal with uncertainty, the parent organization must create some mechanism
to manage risk. In order to deal with the managerial and administrative issues in a way
that meets the parent organization's rules for management and administration, many
firms have created the *project management office.* This section is devoted to the investigation of how risk management activities and project management and administration
can be organized in order to perform with efficiency, effectiveness, and consistency.

Organizing for Risk Management

The Project Management Institute's (PMI) publication *A Guide to The Project Management Body of Knowledge (PMBOK® Guide), 2000 Edition* states that risk man-

agement is "the systematic process of identifying, analyzing, and responding to project risk" and consists of six subprocesses:

1. ***Risk Management Planning***—deciding how to approach and plan the risk management activities for a project.

2. ***Risk Identification***—determining which risks might affect the project and documenting their characteristics.

3. ***Qualitative Risk Analysis***—performing a qualitative analysis of risks and conditions to prioritize their effects on project objectives.

4. ***Quantitative Risk Analysis***—measuring the probability and consequences of risks and estimating the implications for project objectives.

5. ***Risk Response Planning***—developing procedures and techniques to enhance opportunities and reduce threats to the project's objectives.

6. ***Risk Monitoring and Control***—monitoring residual risks, identifying new risks, executing risk reduction plans, and evaluating their effectiveness throughout the project life cycle.

Clearly, the six steps in the process of managing risk are not independent of one another, and the outcomes of any step may—and usually do—impact on the outcomes of other steps in the process. The outcomes of the risk management activity are also dependent on the technological nature of the project, as well as on the many environments in which the project exists. [Recall that we use the word "environment" to refer to anything outside a system (the project) that can affect or be affected by the system.] The fact that the process of risk management depends on how one or more environments impact the project may not be evident. Consider, however, the impact of a strong corporate "cost cutting" focus on how risk managers identify and deal with risks in the areas of personnel and resource allocation. Note that this refers to the *process* of risk management—carrying out the six steps—not merely to the identification of risks.

Second, the mere existence of a set of activities that must be undertaken in order to manage risk implies that some sort of organization is required to do the work of risk management. Because any individual firm might undertake a wide variety of projects based on different technologies, developed for different markets, subject to potential regulation by different levels of goverment, and with different stakeholders, no single risk management unit can be expected to deal with all projects. Routine machine repair and maintenance projects (if they are similar in size and scope to one another) might have risk management groups that are quite similar, or even composed of a group of specific individuals that carry out risk management for all such projects. In general, however, a unique risk management group is formed for each project.

Again, we stress that the specific membership of this group depends on the nature of the project. If the project's objective is to develop a new product (or product line), the risk management team might include the following: (1) a specialist in the science or technology of the proposed product; (2) a market specialist who can make an informed estimate of the total market size and amount of sales for the potential product as well as the impact that the proposed product may have on the sales of the firm's other products; (3) a manufacturing specialist who can foresee risks in the firm's (or its subcontractor's) ability to manufacture the product with an acceptable level of quality; (4) a product safety expert to foresee risks in the area of product liability as well as a public relations professional and an attorney to help deal with matters if safety claims are made against the firm; (5) a patent attorney to assess the risks of patent infringement; (6) an individual (perhaps a program manager) who understands the complete set of the firm's projects and can identify any projects that might contribute to or profit from the project in question; (7) the same or a different person who can foresee possible personnel, resource, or scheduling conflicts caused by or threatening this project; and (8) a governmental relations expert who knows what governmental licenses or approvals may be required for manufacturing processes or product release—the list can easily be extended. The group could investigate the potential product's window-of-opportunity that we discussed in Chapter 2 as a way of estimating market risk.

If we had chosen a different project, say a process improvement, the list of risk management group members would have included some with the same expertise as above and some with others. For example, the group would need to include industrial engineers who could understand risks affecting the ability to maintain current production schedules while installing a new machine in the production system, financial experts to look for potential glitches in the estimated cash flows, a specialist in air and water pollution to foresee risks in those areas, and potential users of the process.

If the risk management system had no memory, the task of risk identification would be horrendous, but the system does have memory—at least the individuals in the system have memory. Relying on the recollections of individuals, however, is a risky business in itself. The risk management system should maintain an up-to-date data bank including, but not restricted to, the following:

- identification of all environments that may impact on the project
- identification of all assumptions made in the preliminary project plan that may be the source of risk for the project
- all risks identified by the risk management group, complete with their estimated impacts on the project and probability of occurring
- a complete list of all "catagories" and "key words" used to catagorize risks, assumptions, and environments so that all risk management groups can access past work done on risk management
- the details of all qualitative and quantitative estimates made on risks, on states of the project's environment, or on project assumptions, complete with a description of the methods used to make such estimates
- minutes of all group meetings including all actions the group developed to deal with or mitigate each specific risk, including the decision to ignore a risk
- the actual outcomes of estimated risks and the results of actions taken to mitigate risk

Several comments are relevant about this process for managing risk. If all this work on data collection is going to be of value to the parent organization beyond its use on the project at hand, the database must be available to anyone proposing a project for the organization. Almost everything the risk management group does for any project should be retained in the risk database. Second, all risks must be catagorized, as must the enviroments in which projects are conducted and the methods used to deal with or mitigate them. A risk database that has been developed and is readily available at no cost is Risk Radar®. It was developed by J. E. Moore of Integrated Computer Engineering Inc. and is available at *www.spmm.com/products_software.html.* Chadbourne (2001) described this software and notes that it requires the installation of Microsoft Access®. He also describes some ways to enhance the software.

The use of multiple key words and categories is critical because risk information must be available to managers of widely varied disciplines and backgrounds. Different people often use different words to denote a single thing. Organizations may be conducting scores of projects at any given time. For large organizations, the number is apt to be in the hundreds, sometimes in the thousands. If every risk management team has to start from scratch, without reference to what has been learned by previous groups, the management of risk will be extremely expensive, take a great deal of time, and will not be particularly effective. As we will stress in later chapters, any organization expecting to conduct successful projects must allow PMs and those who work on the projects to profit from the experiences of others who have gone before. Rest assured that even with all the experience of the past readily available, mistakes will still be made. If past experience is not available, the mistakes of the past will be added to those of the future.

It is never too early in the life of a project to begin managing risk. A sensible project selection decision cannot be made without knowledge of the risks associated with the project. Therefore, the risk management plan and initial risk identification must be carried out before the project can be formally selected for support. The risk management group must, therefore, be formed as soon as a potential project is identified.

At first, project risks are loosely defined—focusing for the most part on externalities such as the state of technology in the fields that are important to the project, business conditions in the relevant industries, and so forth. The response to these external risks is usually to track the pertinent environments and try to estimate the chance that the project that the project can survive through various conditions. Not until the project is in the planning stage will such risks as those associated with project technology, schedule, budget, and resource allocation begin to take shape. The actual development of a risk management plan will be discussed in Chapter 5.

The risk management group can be a stand-alone group associated with only the project it serves. If there are several projects in a single area of technology developing similar outputs, one risk management group may serve several projects. Because risk management often involves analytic techniques not well understood by PMs who have not been trained in the area, some organizations put risk specialists in a project office and these specialists staff the project's risk management activities. For a spectacularly successful use of risk management on a major project, see Christensen and Rydberg (2001), a story of risk management in a Danish bridge construction project.

The Project Management Office

With the increasing role of projects in today's organizations and the move toward "management by projects," the need has arisen for an organizational entity to help manage these fast-multiplying forms of getting work done. This is the role of the Project Management Office (PMO), a.k.a. the Project Office, the Program Management Office, the Project Support Office, and so on. The PMO has been receiving a lot of attention lately; for example, some project management magazines have issues dedicated to topics concerning PMOs (e.g., see *PM Network*, March 1998, April 1999, and February 2001). There are a variety of forms of PMOs to serve a variety of needs. Some of these are at a low level in the organization and others report to the highest levels. Before discussing the purpose and services offered by PMOs, consider the following statistics reported by Block and Frame (2001).

As of the beginning of 2000, 85 percent of the PMOs in private firms were less than three years old and 70 percent were initiated for a specific purpose such as installing an enterprise resource planning (ERP) system or handling the Y2K problem. In public organizations, however, 75 percent of the PMOs were more than three years old. As is the case with many of the techniques and practices of project management, the PMO concept saw its start in government and military institutions before emigrating into private organizations. The great majority (80 percent) of PMOs were in organizations with over a thousand employees, with the rest evenly split between firms with less than or more than 300 employees. Two-thirds of these offices employed fewer than 5 full-time employees. Of the remainder, 22 percent had from 6 to 10 full-time employees, 8 percent had 11–20, and 3 percent had over 20. And two-thirds of the PMOs handled 11 or more projects, while a quarter managed as many as 40 projects.

When asked the reasons for initiating a PMO, almost two-thirds of the respondents indicated a need for establishing consistent project management standards and methods, and that the PMO was initiated by senior management direction. About half the respondents also indicated a need to eliminate project delays and correct poor project planning. A bit less than 40 percent wanted to improve project performance and eliminate cost overruns. Last, about a quarter of the respondents indicated they wished to reduce customer dissatisfaction.

PMOs can offer a variety of services (described in detail a bit later). As reflected by the reasons for initiating the PMOs in the first place, 78 percent of the respondents indicated that their PMO established and maintained standard project processes (practices and procedures), 64 percent offered consulting help on projects, and 58 percent offered training and mentoring services. About half performed project tracking and somewhat less conducted portfolio management. Only 28 percent maintained a stable of project managers for future project needs.

Purposes of the Project Management Office   As just noted, organizations may have many goals in mind when they establish a PMO. Although specific goals may be articulated for the PMO, the overarching purpose is often inherent in the process itself and is unarticulated—for example, ensuring that the firm's portfolio of projects supports the organization's overall goals and strategy, as described in Chapter 2. In this case, the PMO is the critical tie between strategic management and the project managers. Another overarching purpose may be the gradual assimilation of good project management practice into the entire organization, moving it from a functionally organized to a project based form, not only in structure but in culture as well.

The most commonly expressed purposes of organizations for establishing PMOs are:

- To establish and promulgate good project management processes throughout the organization and be a repository of good project management practice
- To transfer project management lessons learned to the rest of the organization
- To improve the success rate of projects
- To reduce development project lead times and get products/services to market sooner.
- To consolidate and simplify project data and provide consistent information on project progress
- To develop and maintain an "enterprise project management" system

It is important to note in the above that the role of the PMO is that of an *enabler/facilitator* of projects, not the *doer* of projects. Top management cannot allow the PMO to usurp the technical aspects—scheduling, budgeting, etc.—of running the project. Those are the project manager's responsibility. Although the PMO may, on occasion, become involved in some project management tasks, it should be for the purpose of facilitating liaison with top management, not to do the work of the project team.

Tasks of the Project Management Office   To achieve the goals detailed above, PMOs commonly perform many of the following tasks (Block, 1999):

- Establish and enforce good project management processes such as procedures for bidding, risk analysis, project selection, progress reports, executing contracts, and selecting software
- Assess and improve the organization's project management maturity
- Develop and improve an enterprise project management system
- Offer training in project management and help project managers become certified
- Identify, develop, and mentor project managers and maintain a stable of competent candidates
- Offer consulting services to the organization's project managers
- Help project managers with administrative details such as status reports
- Establish an estimation and risk evaluation process
- Determine if a new project is a good "fit" for the changing organization
- Identify downstream changes (market, organization) and their impacts on current projects: Are the projects still relevant? Is there a need to change any project's scope? Are there any cost effects on the projects?
- Review and manage the organization's project risk portfolio, including limiting the number of active projects at any given time and identifying and reining in runaway projects
- Conduct project reviews and audits, particularly early in each project's life cycle, and report project progress relative to the organization's goals

- Maintain and store project archives
- Establish a project resource database and manage the resource pool
- Assist in the launch of new projects.
- Serve as a champion to pursue project management excellence in the organization and encourage discussion on the value of individual projects in the firm
- Serve as a "home" for project managers to communicate with each other and with PMO staff
- Collect and disseminate information and techniques reported in project evaluations that can improve project management practices
- Assist in project termination

Not all of these goals can be achieved at once. In the short term, or the first few months, the PMO will only be able to assess the organization's current project management practices and perhaps evaluate the progress of each of the organization's many projects. In the midterm, the PMO can start standardizing project management processes and procedures, begin helping individual projects with risk analysis and administrative details, and initiate a strategic portfolio analysis of the current projects. In the long term, or after about a year, the more comprehensive tasks may be undertaken, such as assembling a resource database, training project managers, conducting project audits, and consulting on individual projects.

Forms of Project Management Office   Akin to the time phasing of PMO responsibilities just noted, there are various forms of PMOs that have similar responsibilities. That is, some organizations may only want a limited PMO that represents an information center, reporting on project progress and assessing the organization's project maturity. At the next level, the PMO may establish project management procedures and practices, promulgate lessons learned from prior projects, create a database for risk analysis, help project managers with administrative and managerial matters, and possibly even offer basic training in project management. At the upper level, the PMO may establish a resource database and monitor interproject dependencies, manage the project portfolio to ensure attainment of the organization's goals, audit and prioritize individual projects, and generally establish an enterprise project management system.

Another way of organizing the PMO has to do with the reporting level of the office. If top management wants to test the efficacy of a PMO at a lower level before approving it for the organization as a whole, they may place it in a functional department such as Information Technology or Engineering. In this role, the main responsibility of the PMO will be to help the department's project managers with their individual projects. If the PMO is established at the business level, it may take on more responsibility for good project management practices and possibly offer basic training. At higher organizational levels, the PMO's responsibilities will broaden and become less tactical and more strategic. If the eventual goal is to improve the organization's ability to execute projects, this is a risky way to implement a PMO. Simply because a PMO is not able to rescue a failing engineering project, for example, does not mean that it could not be extremely valuable to the organization by performing the many preceding tasks.

Implementing the Project Management Office   As was noted previously, the best way to implement a PMO is to treat it as a project and apply good project management procedures. In addition, given the role of this special type of project it is also suggested that the effort not be initiated until it has the full commitment of the top managers of the organization. It should also have a senior management sponsor/champion who is determined to see this project through to success. One way to initiate the project is through a pilot program in one of the areas that falls under the responsibility of the PMO project champion. Following its completion, the pilot project can be assessed, any mistakes corrected, and the benefits publicized to the rest of the organization. As the PMO expands and interacts with more and more projects, its benefits to the organization will increase progressively with its reach.

Unfortunately, not all PMOs are successful. According to Tennant (2001), one of the primary problems of PMOs is that the executives who establish PMOs often do not understand project management practices themselves. Thus, they have unrealistic expectations of the PMO, such as providing temporary help for a project in trouble or to obtain cost reductions from on-going projects. The PMO is not a quick fix for saving projects that are failing; its primary objective is to improve project management processes over the long run.

PMOs cannot be expected to correct upper management failures such as inappropriate project goals, insufficient project support, and inadequate resource availability. Interestingly, a recent trend in project organizations is the outsourcing of the PMO functions themselves. One has to wonder if this is a sign of impending trouble or a wise recognition of the limitations of upper management knowledge.

4.7   THE PROJECT TEAM

> "Teamwork is a lot of people doing what I say."
>
> Anonymous Boss

In this section we consider the makeup of the project team, bearing in mind that different projects have vastly different staff needs. [For an interesting discussion of the role project teams can play, see Sharifi and Pawar (1996). For a more general view, see Dewhurst (1998) and Dinsmore (1993b).] Then we take up some problems associated with staffing the team. Last, we deal with a few of the behavioral issues in managing this team.

To be concrete during our discussion of project teams, let us use the example of an engineering project to determine how to form a project team. Assume that the size of our hypothetical project is fairly large. In addition to the PM, the following key team members might be needed, plus an appropriate number of scientists, engineers, technicians, clerks, and the like. The example could be a software development project, a construction project, a medical research project, or any of a wide variety of other types of project. The titles of the individuals would change, but the roles played would be similar.

- **Project Engineer**   The project engineer is in charge of product design and development and is responsible for functional analysis, specifications, drawings, cost estimates, quality/reliability, engineering changes, and documentation.
- **Manufacturing Engineer**   This engineer's task is the efficient production of the product or process the project engineer has designed, including responsibility for manufacturing engineering, design and production of tooling/jigs/fixtures, production scheduling, and other production tasks.
- **Field Manager**   This person is responsible for the installation, testing, and support of the product/process once it is delivered to the customer.
- **Contract Administrator**   The administrator is in charge of all official paperwork, keeping track of customer changes, billings, questions, complaints, legal aspects, costs, and other matters related to the contract authorizing the project. Not uncommonly, the contract administrator also serves as project historian and archivist.
- **Project Controller**   The controller keeps daily account of budgets, cost variances, labor charges, project supplies, capital equipment status, etc. The controller also makes regular reports and keeps in close touch with both the PM and the company controller. If the administrator does not serve as historian, the controller can do so.
- **Support Services Manager**   This person is in charge of product support, subcontractors, data processing, and general management support functions.

Of these top project people, it is most important that the project engineer and the project controller report directly to the PM (see Figure 4-7). This facilitates control over two of the main goals of the project: technical performance and budget. (The project manager is usually in personal control of the schedule.) For a large project, all six project officials could work out of the project office and report directly to the PM.

To staff the project, the PM works from a forecast of personnel needs over the life cycle of the project. This is done with the aid of some special charts. First, a *work breakdown structure* (WBS) is prepared to determine the exact nature of the tasks required to complete the project. (The WBS is described in detail and illustrated in

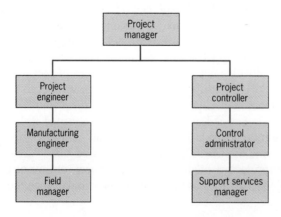

Figure 4-7   Typical organization for engineering projects.

Chapter 5.) The skill requirements for these tasks are assessed and like skills are aggregated to determine work force needs. From this base, the functional departments are contacted to locate individuals who can meet these needs.

On occasion, certain tasks may be subcontracted. This option may be adopted because the appropriately skilled personnel are unavailable or cannot be located, or even because some special equipment required for the project is not available in-house. The need to subcontract is growing as firms "downsize." If the proper people (and equipment) are found within the organization, however, the PM usually must obtain their services from their home departments. Many firms insist on using "local" resources when they are available, in order to maintain better control over resource usage and quality. Typically, the PM will have to negotiate with both the department head and the employee, trying to "sell" the employee on the challenge and excitement of working on the project and trying to convince the department head that lending the employee to the project is in the department head's best interest.

There are some people who are more critical to the project's success than others and should report directly to the PM or to the PM's deputy (often the project engineer):

- Senior project team members who will be having a long-term relationship with the project
- Those with whom the PM will require continuous or close communication
- Those with rare skills necessary to project success

Remember that the PM must depend on reason when trying to convince a department head to lend these valuable people to the project. The department head, who sees the project as a more or less glamorous source of prestige in which the department cannot share, has little natural motivation to be cooperative. Once again, it is obvious that success depends on the political skill of the PM as much as on the technical skill of the team.

Thus far, we have tacitly assumed a fairly strong matrix organization for the project in our example. In recent years, the use of weaker matrices has become more and more frequent. In many firms, when project managers are asked for the number of people who report directly to them, the answer "None!" is not uncommon. Most common of all, it seems to us, is the matrix organization with a project manager, one or two key skilled contributors who may be full-time members of the project, and a wide variety of services or capacity supplied to the project by functional groups in the parent organization. Such structures are often found in software projects that are part of larger programs being carried out by a parent firm. One or two programmers may be assigned to the project, but the work involved in integrating and testing the software, etc. is supplied to the project in the form of deliverables rather than people assigned to the project to carry out their work.

Although the project manager has to bargain for fewer individuals than in the case of stronger matrices, the PM's negotiating skills are just as critical. It is typical for the success of weak-matrix projects to be dependent on the skills of the few technical specialists who are assigned directly to the project. The ability of the PM to negotiate for skilled technicians as well as for the *timely* delivery of services from functional departments is a key determinant of success.

4.8   HUMAN FACTORS AND THE PROJECT TEAM

With a reminder of the need for the PM to possess a high level of political sensitivity, we can discuss some other factors in managing project teams, all the while remembering that the principles and practices of good, general management also apply to the management of projects. We discuss them from the viewpoint of the PM as an individual who must cope with the personal as well as the technical victories and frustrations of life on a project.

Meeting schedule and cost goals without compromising performance appears to be a technical problem for the PM. Actually, it is only partly technical because it is also a human problem—more accurately, a technical problem with a human dimension. Project professionals tend to be perfectionists. It is difficult enough to meet project goals under normal conditions, but when, out of pride of workmanship, the professionals want to keep improving (and thus changing) the product, the task becomes almost impossible. Changes cause delays. Throughout the project, the manager must continue to stress the importance of meeting due dates. It also helps if the PM establishes, at the beginning of the project, a technical change procedure to ensure control over the incidence and frequency of change. (It would not, however, be wise for the PM to assume that everyone will automatically follow such a procedure.) More on this subject in Chapters 5 and 11.

Another problem is motivating project team members to accomplish the work of the project. As we noted in Chapter 3 and in the discussion of matrix organizations in this chapter, the PM often has little control over the economic rewards and promotions of the people working on the project. this is certainly true when the matrix is weak. This does not, however, mean that the PM cannot motivate members of the project team. Frederick Herzberg, who studied what motivates technical employees such as engineers, scientists, and professionals on a project team, contends that recognition, achievement, the work itself, responsibility, advancement, and the chance to learn new skills are motivators (see Fedor and Werther (1996) in Chapter 3). It is the PM's responsibility to make sure that project work is structured in such a way as to emphasize these motivational factors. We have also found that the judicious use of "thank you" notes from the PM to those functional managers who have supplied the project with capable and committed individuals and/or effective and efficient capacity is a potent motivator—copies to the relevant individuals, of course. It is also important not to write such notes for mediocre or poor performance. Indeed, an occasional "non-thank you" note may be in order.

The use of participative management is also a way of motivating people. This is not a new theory. It originated in the work of Argyris, Likert, McGregor, and others in the 1950s and 1960s. The concept suggests that the individual worker (or team) should play a significant role in deciding what means should be employed in meeting desired ends, and in finding better ways of accomplishing things. Management By Objectives (MBO) was an early mechanism designed to develop participative management. Suggested by Drucker (1986) initially in 1954, and advocated by others (e.g., Odiorne, 1965), MBO allowed the worker to take responsibility for the design and performance of a task under controlled conditions. More recently, such programs as

Employee Involvement (EI) and Total Quality Management (TQM) have been developed that do not suffer from some of the problems associated with MBO. [There is a large body of literature on EI and TQM. Readers who are not familiar with these techniques might see Dean and Evans (1994) and Evans and Lindsay (1993), especially Chapters 5, 10, and 11 for excellent descriptions of both EI and TQM together with the associated behavioral theory and a discussion of implementing EI and TQM teams.]

In addition to TQM and EI, a.k.a. continuous improvement teams (CIT), we also have observed the rise of self-directed teams (SDT), a.k.a. self-directed work teams (SDWT), and/or self-managed teams (SMT). While these teams may have slightly different structures and may vary somewhat in the amount of decision-making authority and autonomy exercised by the team, they are all aimed at improving worker performance as well as improving production methods and product quality. In a multiplant study comparing three team structures, CIT, QC, and SDWT, Bailey (1998, p. 30) found that SDWTs "did not perform as well as more traditionally organized and supervised workgroups whose members participate in" QCs or CITs. This finding was in conflict with several other researches, all of which were single-site studies (e.g., Moravec, Johannessen, and Hjelmas, 1997). While Bailey's (1998, p. 31) results are not clearly understood, she argues that they could easily be due to "poor design of team involvement," "lack of information infrastructure," and a management structure that may not have fully supported the teams.

The adoption of such methods *empowers* the team (as well as its individual members) to take responsibility and to be accountable for delivering project objectives. Some advantages of empowerment for project teams are:

1. It harnesses the ability of the team members to manipulate tasks so that project objectives are met. The team is encouraged to find better ways to do things.
2. Professionals do not like being micromanaged. Participative management does not tell them how to work but, given a goal, allows them to design their own methods (usually within some constraints on their authority).
3. The team members know they are responsible and accountable for achieving the project deliverables.
4. There is a good chance that synergistic solutions will result from team interaction.
5. Team members get timely feedback on their performance.
6. The PM is provided a tool for evaluating the team's performance.

All of these items serve to increase motivation among members of the project team. Informal discussions with many project team leaders lead us to the same conclusions, but the success of SDWTs (and all other teams) is ultimately dependent on a clear statement of what the team is expected to accomplish, when, and at what cost. Senior management must "make the effort to clearly delineate project goals, responsibilities, and authority" in order to reap the advantages of project teams (Ford and McLaughlin, 1992, p. 316; Nelson, 1998, p. 43). Finally, it is important to remember that giving a project to a team does not supersede the need for competent project management skills (Levine, 1996).

In Chapter 5, we cover the process of planning projects in detail, and we emphasize the use of an *action plan* (WBS), a concept borrowed directly from MBO. It is a detailed planning and scheduling technique directed toward achievement of the objectives of the project. The PM works with members of the project team and a comprehensive set of written plans is generated by this process. The resulting document is not only a plan, but also a control mechanism. Because the system of developing the plan is participative and makes team members accountable for their specific parts of the overall plan, it motivates them, and also clearly denotes the degree to which team members are mutually dependent. The importance of this latter outcome of the planning process is not well recognized in the literature on team building.

There are a number of excellent works on team building: for example, see Cleland, 1997; Dyer, 1987; Ford and McLaughlin, 1992; Katzenbach and Smith, 1993; Pinto and Pinto, 1991; Rossy and Archibald, 1992; and Todryk, 1990. They cover a wide range of issues that affect team building and team operation. Such works, however, rarely mention a precondition that greatly eases the process of team formation, *mutual dependence required and recognized,* though this concept is, perhaps, implied by Katzenbach and Smith's (1993, p. 112) emphasis on the fact that teams (rather than "working groups") "hold themselves mutually accountable" for reaching the team's performance goals.

Bringing people together, even when they belong to the same organization and contribute their efforts to the same objectives, does not necessarily mean that they will behave like a team. Organizing the team's work in such a way that team members are mutually dependent and recognize it, will produce a strong impetus for the group to form a team. Project success will be associated with teamwork, and project failure will surely result if the group does not work as a team.* If many or most of the team members are also problem-oriented (see also Chapter 3, Section 3.2), the likelihood of the group forming an effective team is further increased. In an extensive research on the matter, Tippet and Peters conclude that overall results show that companies are generally doing a poor job of team building. Lack of effective rewards, inadequate individual and team performance feedback mechanisms, and inadequate individual and team goal-setting are all weak areas (Tippet and Peters, 1995, p. 35).

Another behavioral problem for the PM is interpersonal conflict. The problem is so pervasive that conflict between project team members, and between team members and outsiders (including the client) seems to be the natural state of existence for projects. It is our strong feeling that the PM who cannot manage conflict is doomed to failure.

In 1975, Thamhain and Wilemon (1975) published the definitive work on the focus and nature of conflict in projects. We have found their insights just as relevant today as they were in 1975. Table 4-1, based on Thamhain and Wielmon, relates the most likely focus of conflict to specific stages of the project life cycle. The table also

---

*Though team formation is not even mentioned, a reading of A. S. Carlisle's (1976) article, "MacGregor" is instructive. The article is a classic on the power of delegation and was clearly the inspiration for Blanchard and Johnson's *The One Minute Manager.* The Carlisle paper reports on a plant manager who delegates most operating decisions to his subordinates and insists that they help in solving one another's problems. As a result, they form a team that would be the envy of any project manager.

Table 4–1. Major Sources of Conflict during Various Stages of the Project Life Cycle

Life Cycle Phase	*Major Conflict Source and Recommendations for Minimizing Dysfunctional Consequences*	
	Conflict Source	*Recommendations*
Project formation	Priorities	Clearly defined plans. Joint decision making and/or consultation with affected parties. Stress importance of project to organization goals.
	Procedures	Develop detailed administrative operating procedures to be followed in conduct of project.
		Secure approval from key administrators.
		Develop statement of understanding or charter.
	Schedules	Develop schedule commitments in advance of actual project commencement.
		Forecast other departmental priorities and possible impact on project.
Buildup phase	Priorities	Provide effective feedback to support areas on forecasted project plans and needs via status review sessions.
	Schedules	Schedule work breakdown packages (project subunits) in cooperation with functional groups.
	Procedures	Contingency planning on key administrative issues.
Main program	Schedules	Continually monitor work in progress.
		Communicate results to affected parties.
		Forecast problems and consider alternatives.
		Identify potential trouble spots needing closer surveillance.
	Technical	Early resolution of technical problems.
		Communication of schedule and budget restraints to technical personnel.
		Emphasize adequate, early technical testing.
		Facilitate early agreement on final designs.
	Labor	Forecast and communicate staffing requirements early.
		Establish staffing requirements and priorities with functional and staff groups.
Phaseout	Schedules	Close schedule monitoring in project life cycle.
		Consider reallocation of available staff to critical project areas prone to schedule slippages.
		Attain prompt resolution of technical issues that may affect schedules.
	Personality and labor	Develop plans for reallocation of people upon project completion.
		Maintain harmonious working relationships with project team and support groups. Try to loosen up high-stress environment.

Source: Thamhain and Wilemon 1975.

suggests some solutions. When the project is first organized, priorities, procedures, and schedules all have roughly equal potential as a focus of conflict. During the buildup phase, priorities become significantly more important than any other conflict factor; procedures are almost entirely established by this time. In the main program phase, priorities are finally established and schedules are the most important cause of trouble within the project, followed by technical disagreements. Getting adequate support for the project is also a point of concern. At project finish, meeting the schedule is the critical issue, but interpersonal tensions that were easily ignored early in the project can suddenly erupt into conflict during the last hectic weeks of the life cycle. Worry about reassignment exacerbates the situation. Both Tables 4-1 and 4-2 show

Table 4-2.   Number of Conflicts during a Sample Project

Phase of Project				
Start	*Early*	*Main*	*Late*	*Sources of Conflict*
27	35	24	16	Project priorities
26	27	15	09	Admin. procedures
18	26	31	11	Technical trade-offs
21	25	25	17	Staffing
20	13	15	11	Support cost estimates
25	29	36	30	Schedules
16	19	15	17	Personalities

Source: Thamhain and Wilemon 1975.

conflict as a function of stage in the project life cycle as well as by source of the conflict, but Table 4-2 also shows the *frequency* of conflict by source and stage of the life cycle. Figure 4-8 illustrates these tables.

It seems clear to us that most of the conflict on project teams is the result of individuals focusing on the project through the eyes of their individual discipline or department (de Laat, 1994; Hughes, 1998; and Pelled and Adler, 1994). Such people are not problem oriented and thus are rarely effective members of project teams. Dewhirst (1998, p. 34) defines a group of individuals working independently as a "Name-Only-Team" or a "NOT." If teamwork is vital to success, then for a NOT, the "work

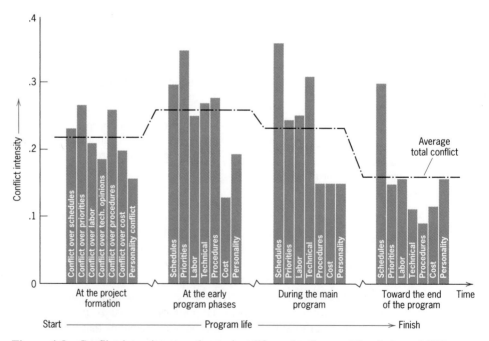

Figure 4-8   Conflict intensity over the project life cycle. *Source*: Thamhain and Wilemon, 1975.

group math (is) 2 + 2 = 3 or less." The infighting that results when discipline-oriented individuals introduce conflict to a project team is perceived by most team members to be "political." If the PM allows project decisions to be dictated by the infighting, the project is apt to fail (de Laat, 1994; Pinto, 1997, p. 31).

Conflict can be handled in several ways, but one thing is certain: Conflict avoiders do not make successful project managers. On occasion, compromise appears to be helpful, but most often, gently confronting the conflict is the method of choice. Much has been written about conflict resolution and there is no need to summarize that literature here beyond noting that the key to conflict resolution rests on the manager's ability to transform a win-lose situation into win-win. The Likerts (1976) have written an interesting work on the nature and management of conflict, and Hill and White (1979) report on how one particular project manager handled a difficult conflict.

The project manager did not flinch in the face of negative interpersonal feelings when listening to differences between people. "You have to learn to listen, keep your mouth shut, and let the guy get it off his chest."

- The project manager encouraged openness and emotional expression.
- The manager set a role model for reacting to personality clashes. It was observed that a peer would often intercede and act out a third-party conciliation role much like the manager.
- The manager seemed to exhibit the attitude that conflict could be harnessed for productive ends.
- Although managers usually confronted conflicts, they also avoided face-to-face meetings when the outside pressure was too high.

Project Management in Practice
South African Repair Success through Teamwork

On March 8, 1994, a fire broke out in the carbonate regeneration column in the Benfield facility of Sasol, a leading South African coal, chemical, and crude-oil company. It was determined that the damaged portion of the 19-foot-wide, 231-foot-long column would have to be cut out and replaced before the facility could operate again. Time was of the essence, and only 40 days were allowed for the repair project.

To achieve this unheard-of schedule, a number of special ground rules were established:

- The project is to be schedule-driven, not cost-driven

- There is no float anywhere on the project
- Always plan to reduce scheduled times, not meet them
- Resources are not to be considered as a limitation
- Communication will be continuous across all levels
- Safety will not be compromised
- Quality will not be compromised

In addition, special effort was directed toward making the project team strive to reduce time on

Benfield facility, with columns at the left and right.

the project. First, it was made clear that a higher premium would be placed on team performance than on individual performance. The "soft" aspects of management were always taken into consideration: making sure transport was available, accommodations were acceptable, food was available, excessive overtime was avoided, communication forms matched each member's preferences (verbal, phone, written, etc.), and so on. A communication board was installed and updated twice daily to communication project progress, and especially time saved on the schedule with the person's name who achieved it. There were both twice-daily shift change meetings, where each shift communicated with the previous shift about progress and problems, and twice-daily planning meetings where the work activities of the next two days were planned in minute detail.

The response to this level of project team attention was overwhelming. People raised ideas for saving even five minutes on the schedule. Enthusiasm for the project, and saving project time, became the dominant culture. As a result, the project was completed in only 25 days, 15 days early, with a corresponding cost savings of over $21 million out of an $85 million budget.

Source: I. Boggon, "The Benfield Column Repair Project," *PM Network,* February 1996, pp. 25–30.

 ## SUMMARY

This chapter described the various organizational structures that can be used for projects, and detailed their advantages. An appropriate procedure for choosing the best form was described and two examples were given. The chapter then moved into a discussion of risk management and the role of the Project Management Office. Following this, discussion turned to the project team itself, describing the organization of the project office staff and the human issues, such as motivation and conflict, the project manager will face. Specific points made in the chapter were these:

If the project is to be included in a functional organization, it should be placed in that unit with the greatest interest in its success or the unit that can provide the most help. Though there are advantages in this mode of organizing, the disadvantages are greater.

The project form of organizing has its advantages and disadvantages. Though the disadvantages are not as severe as with the functional form, they are nevertheless significant.

The matrix organization combines the functional and project forms in an attempt to reap the advantages of each. While this approach has been fairly successful, it also has its own unique disadvantages. There are many variants of the pure forms of organization, and special hybrids are commonly used to handle special projects. The best form for a particular case requires consideration of the characteristics of the project compared with the various advantages and disadvantages of each form.

A useful procedure for selecting an organizational form for a project is:

1. Identify the specific outcomes desired.
2. Determine the key tasks to attain these outcomes and identify the units within the parent organization where these tasks would normally be assigned.
3. Sequence the key tasks and group them into logical work steps.
4. Determine which project subsystems will be assigned which steps and which subsystems must closely cooperate.
5. Identify any special firm or project characteristics, constraints, or problems that may affect how the project should be organized.
6. Consider all the above relative to the pros and cons of each organizational form as a final decision is made.

Every project should have a project office, even if it must be shared with another project.

Larger, more complex projects may include, in addition to the PM, a project engineer, manufacturing engineer, field manager, contract administrator, project controller, and support service manager. If an organization engages in multiple projects, a Project Management Office may also be warranted.

Those on the project team who should report directly to the PM are the project engineer and project controller as well as:

1. Senior team members who will have a long-term relationship with the project.
2. Those with whom the PM will be continuously or closely communicating.
3. Those with rare skills needed for project success.

Perfectionism, motivation, and conflict are often the major behavioral problems facing the PM. Management by Objectives (MBO) can be a useful tool for addressing the first two, while gentle confrontation usually works best for the latter.

Sources of project conflict are often priorities and policies at first, schedule and technical problems during the main phase, and schedule and personal issues near termination.

In the next chapter, we move from organizational issues to project planning tasks. We address the topics of coordination, interface management, and systems engineering. We also present some extremely useful concepts and tools such as the work breakdown structure and linear responsibility chart.

GLOSSARY

Action Plan   A detailed plan of what needs to be done and when (see Chapter 5 for more discussion and some examples).

Concurrent/Simultaneous Engineering   Originally, the use of a design team that included both design and manufacturing engineers, new expanded to include staff from quality control, purchasing, and other relevant areas.

Functional Management   The standard departments of the organization that represent individual disciplines such as engineering, marketing, purchasing, and so on.

Holistic   The whole viewed at one time rather than each piece individually.

Management by Objectives (MBO)   A management approach popular during the 1960s that encouraged managers to give their subordinates more freedom in determining how to achieve task objectives.

Matrix Organization   A method of organizing that maintains both functional supervisors as well as project supervisors. A strong matrix operates closer to a pure project organization while a weak matrix operates more like a functional organization.

Mixed Organization   This approach includes both functions (disciplines) and projects in its hierarchy.

Parent Organization   The firm or organization within which the project is being conducted.

Program Manager   This person is typically responsible for a number of related projects, each with its own project manager.

Project Management Office   An office to deal with multiple projects and charged with improving the project management maturity and expertise of the organization, as well as increasing the success rate of projects.

Projectitis   A social phenomenon, inappropriately intense loyalty to the project.

Subcontract   Subletting tasks out to smaller contractors.

Suboptimization   The optimization of a subelement of a system, perhaps to the detriment of the overall system.

War Room   A project office where the latest detail on project progress is available. It may also be a source of technical assistance in managing the project.

Work Breakdown Structure   A basic project document that describes all the work that must be done to complete the project and forms the basis for costing, scheduling, and work responsibility (see Chapter 5).

 ## QUESTIONS

Material Review Questions

1. What is a program manager? How does this job differ from that of a project manager?

2. Identify the advantages and disadvantages of the matrix form of organization.

3. Name the four basic types of project organization and list at least one characteristic, advantage, and disadvantage of each.

4. Give some major guidelines for choosing an organizational form for a project.

5. Why is the project management office so important?

6. Identify three ways of dealing with a conflict associated with projects. Does dealing with conflict always need to be a zero-sum game?

7. What are some advantages and disadvantages of housing a project in a functional form?

8. What are the project engineer's duties?

9. What are the major sources of conflict throughout the life cycle?

10. Describe risk management and how it applies to projects.

11. What are the major tasks of a Project Management Office?

Class Discussion Questions

12. Discuss some of the differences between managing professionals and managing other workers or team members.

13. Human and political factors loom large in the success of projects. Given the general lack of coverage of this subject in engineering and science education, how might a PM gain the ability to deal with these issues?

14. A disadvantage of the pure project organization has to do with the tendency of project professionals to fall behind in areas of technical expertise not used on the project. Name several ways that a project manager might avoid this problem.

15. Discuss the effects of the various organizational forms on coordination and interaction, both within the project team and between the team and the rest of the firm.

16. Can you think of any advantages other than those

listed in the text associated with using MBO, etc. for empowerment? Disadvantages?

17. How would you organize a project to develop a complex new product such as a new color fax–copy machine? How would you organize if the product was simpler, such as a new disk drive?

18. How should the following be organized?
   (a) A bank's investment banking department
   (b) A firm's basic research laboratory
   (c) An international construction firm's project
   (d) A city's bus transportation project
   (e) A state's health service organization
   (f) A management consulting firm's project

Questions for Project Management in Practice

Reorganizing for Project Management at Prevost Car

24. Surely this was not the first time Prevost needed to make a significant change in their firm. Why do you think this was the first time the VP called upon a project management consulting firm?

25. Do you expect there was some concern among top management that no bulldozer was working the next day?

26. This example well illustrates the trend to using project management to do everything in organizations that used to be done in other ways. Can everything be better executed using project management? If not, what are the characteristics of those tasks that cannot?

Converting to Project Management in Government Agencies

27. Which of the lessons seems most important to you?

19. What do you think may be the purpose of a work breakdown structure? How might it aid the PM in organizing the project?

20. Why do you think the average total conflict increases during the "early program phase" (Figure 4-8)?

21. What should be the role of the project manager in conflict management?

22. Is it ethical to employ participative management solely as a way to motivate employees?

23. What are the pros and cons of the head of a Project Management Office reporting to senior management? To departmental management?

28. Which lesson would be easiest to implement? Which the hardest? Which would bring the most value for the time involved?

29. Would you expect this government department to be one of the early or late adopters of project management? Why?

South African Repair Success through Teamwork

30. Of the special ground rules, which ones do you think really gave impetus to the speed of the project?

31. What do you think was the primary factor that changed the culture for this project?

32. Given that this project cut about 40 percent off the schedule and 25 percent off the cost, what is the message about the importance of teamwork?

▨ INCIDENTS FOR DISCUSSION

Shaw's Strategy

Colin Shaw has been tapped to be an accounting project manager for the second time this year. Although he enjoys the challenges and opportunity for personal development afforded to him as a project manager, he dreads the interpersonal problems associated with the position. Sometimes he feels like a glorified baby-sitter handing out assignments, checking on progress, and making sure everyone is doing his or her fair share. Recently

Colin read an article that recommended a very different approach for the project manager in supervising and controlling team members. Colin thought this was a useful idea and decided to try it on his next project.

The project in question involved making a decision on whether to implement an activity-based costing (ABC) system throughout the organization. Colin had once been the manager in charge of implementing a process costing system in this same division, so he felt very comfortable about his ability to lead the team and resolve this question. He defined the objective of the project and detailed all the major tasks involved, as well as most of the subtasks. By the time the first meeting of the project team took place, Colin felt more secure about the control and direction of the project than he had at the beginning of any of his previous projects. He had specifically defined objectives and tasks for each team member and had assigned completion dates for each task. He had even made up individual "contracts" for each team member to sign as an indication of their commitment to completion of the assigned tasks per schedule dates. The meeting went very smoothly, with almost no comments from team members. Everyone picked up a copy of his or her "contract" and went off to work on the project. Colin was ecstatic about the success of this new approach.

Question: Do you think he will feel the same way six weeks from now? Compare this approach with his previous approach.

Hydrobuck

Hydrobuck is a medium-sized producer of gasoline-powered outboard motors. In the past it has successfully manufactured and marketed motors in the 3- to 40-horsepower range. Executives at Hydrobuck are now interested in larger motors and would eventually like to produce motors in the 50- to 150-horsepower range.

The internal workings of the large motors are quite similar to those of the smaller motors. However, large, high-performance outboard motors require power trim. Power trim is simply a hydraulic system that serves to tilt the outboard motor up or down on the boat transom. Hydrobuck cannot successfully market the larger outboard motors without designing a power trim system to complement the motor.

The company is financially secure and is the leading producer of small outboard motors. Management has decided that the following objectives need to be met within the next two years:

1. Design a quality power trim system.

2. Design and build the equipment to produce such a system efficiently.

3. Develop the operations needed to install the system on the outboard motor.

The technology, facilities, and marketing skills necessary to produce and sell the large motors already exist within the company.

Questions: What alternative types of project organization would suit the development of the power trim system? Which would be best? Discuss your reasons for selecting this type of organization.

BIBLIOGRAPHY

ADAMS, J. R., and L. L. ADAMS. "The Virtual Project: Managing Tomorrow's Team Today." *PM Network,* January 1997.

BAILEY, D. E. "Comparison of Manufacturing Performance of Three Team Structures in Semiconductor Plants." *IEEE Transactions on Engineering Management,* February 1998.

BLOCK, T. R. "The Project Office Phenomenon." *PM Network,* March 1998.

BLOCK, T. R. "The Seven Secrets of a Successful Project Office." *PM Network,* April 1999.

BLOCK, T. R., AND J. D. FRAME. "Today's Project Office: Gauging Attitudes," *PM Network,* August 2001.

BOLLES, D. "The Project Support Office." *PM Network,* March 1998.

BOZNAK, R. G. "Management of Projects: A Giant Step Beyond Project Management." *PM Network,* January 1996.

CARLISLE, A. S. "MacGregor," *Organizational Dynamics.* New York: AMACOM, Summer 1976.

CHADBOURNE, B. "Put Risk Management Training Wheel on Your Project Office," *PM Network,* February 2001.

CHAMBERS, G. J. "The Individual in a Matrix Organization," *Project Management Journal,* December 1989.

CHRISTENSEN, P. J., and RYDBERG, J. "Overcoming Obstacles." *PM Network,* November 2001.

CLELAND, D. I. "Team Building: The New Strategic Weapon." *PM Network,* January 1997.

CLELAND, D. I. *Strategic Management of Teams.* New York: Wiley, 1996.

CLELAND, D. I. *Matrix Management Systems Handbook.* New York: Van Nostrand Reinhold, 1983.

CLELAND, D. I. "The Age of Project Management," *Project Management Journal,* March 1991.

CLELAND, D. I., and W. R. KING. *Systems Analysis and Project Management, 3rd ed.* New York: McGraw-Hill, 1983.

DEAN, J. W., JR., and J. R. EVANS. *Total Quality: Management, Organization, and Strategy.* St. Paul, MN: West, 1994.

DE LAAT, P. B. "Matrix Management of Projects and Power Struggles: A Case Study of an R&D Laboratory." *IEEE Engineering Management Review,* Winter 1995, reprinted from *Human Relations,* Vol. 47, No. 9, 1994.

DEWHURST, H. D. "Project Teams: What Have We Learned?" *PM Network,* April 1998.

DINSMORE, P. C. "On the Leading Edge of Management: Managing Organizations By Projects." *PM Network,* March 1996.

DINSMORE, P. C. "Converging on Enterprise Project Management." *PM Network,* October 1998.

DINSMORE, P. C. "Flat, Flexible Structures: The Organizational Answer to Changing Times," in P. C. Dinsmore, ed., *The AMA Handbook of Project Management.* New York: AMACOM, 1993.

DINSMORE, P. C. "A Conceptual Team-Building Model: Achieving Teamwork Through Improved Communication and Interpersonal Skills," in P. C. Dinsmore, ed., *The AMA Handbook of Project Management.* New York: AMACOM, 1993.

DRUCKER, P. *The Practice of Management.* New York: HarperCollins, 1986.

DYER, W. G. *Team Building: Issues and Alternatives,* 2nd ed. Reading, MA: Addison-Wesley, 1987.

EVANS, J. R., and W. M. LINDSAY. *The Management and Control of Quality,* 2nd ed. St. Paul, MN: West, 1993.

FORD, R. C., and F. S. MCLAUGHLIN. "Successful Project Teams: A Study of MIS Managers," *IEEE Transactions on Engineering Management,* November 1992.

FRAME, J. D. "Risk Assessment Groups: Key Component of Project Offices." *PM Network,* March 1998.

FUSCO, J. C. "Better Policies Provide the Key to Implementing Project Management." *Project Management Journal,* September 1997.

GREINER, L. E. "Evolution and Revolution as Organizations Grow." *Harvard Business Review,* July–August 1972.

HAMMER, M., and J. CHAMPY. *Reengineering The Corporation: A Manifesto for Business Revolution.* New York: Harper Business, 1993.

HILL, R., and B. J. WHITE. *Matrix Organization and Project Management.* Michigan Business Paper #64. Ann Arbor: University of Michigan, 1979.

HOBBS, B., and P. MÉNARD, "Organizational Choices for Project Management." in P. C. Dinsmore, ed., *The AMA Handbook of Project Management.* New York: AMACOM, 1993.

HODGE, B. J., W.P. ANTHONY, and L. M. GALES. *Organizational Theory: a Strategic Approach,* 5th ed. Englewood Cliffs, NJ: Prentice-Hall, 1996.

HOLT, D. H. *Management Principles and Practices,* 3rd ed. Englewood Cliffs, NJ: Prentice-Hall, 1993.

HUGHES, T. P. *Rescuing Prometheus.* New York, Pantheon, 1998.

ISGAR, T. *The Ten Minute Team: How Team Leaders Can Build High Performing Teams.* Longmont, CO: Seluera Press, 1989.

KALU, T. CH. U. "A Framework for the Management of Projects in Complex Organizations." *IEEE Transactions on Engineering Management,* May 1993.

KATZENBACH, J. R., and D. K. SMITH. "The Discipline of Teams," *Harvard Business Review,* March–April 1993.

KERZNER, H., and D. I. CLELAND. *Project/Matrix Management Policy and Strategy: Case and Situations.* New York: Van Nostrand Reinhold, 1984.

KETCHAM, L., and E. TRIST. *All Teams Are Not Created Equal: How Employee Empowerment Really Works.* Beverly Hills, CA.: Sage, 1992.

KNUTSON, J. "Developing a Team Charter." *PM Network,* August 1997.

KOTTER, J. P. "Leading Change: Why Transformation Efforts Fail." *Harvard Business Review,* March/April 1995. Reprinted in *IEEE Engineering Management Review,* Spring 1997.

LARSON, E. W. "Project Management in Pharmaceutical R&D." *Product & Process Innovation,* March/April 1991.

LARSON, E. W., and D. H. GOBELI. "Significance of Project Management Structure on Development Success," *IEEE Transactions on Engineering Management,* May 1989.

LEVINE, H. A. "Teamocracy and Project Management: A Conundrum." *PM Network,* September 1996.

LEVINE, H. A. "Minnesota Smith and The Temple of Unrealized Dreams." *PM Network,* October 1996.

LEVINE, H. A. "Enterprise Project Management: What Do Users Need? What Can They Have?" *PM Network,* July 1998.

LIKERT, R., and J. G. LIKERT. *New Ways of Managing Conflict.* New York: McGraw-Hill, 1976.

McCOLLUM, J. K., and J. D. SHERMAN. "The Effects of Matrix Organization Size and Number of Project Assignments on Performance." *IEEE Transactions on Engineering Management,* February 1991.

MORAVEC, M., O. JOHANNESSEN, and T. A. HJELMAS. "We Have Seen the Future and It Is Self-Managed." *PM Network,* September 1997.

NELSON, B. "Energized Teams: Real World Examples." *PM Network,* July 1998.

ODIORNE, G. S. *Managing by Objectives: A System of Management Leadership.* New York: Pitman, 1965.

PADGHAM, H. E. "Choosing the Right Project Management Organization." *Project Management Journal,* June 1989.

PELLED, L. H., and P. S. ADLER. "Antecedents of Intergroup Conflict in Multifunctional Product Development Teams: A Conceptual Model." *IEEE Transactions on Engineering Management,* January 1994.

PINTO, M. B., and J. K. PINTO. "Determinants of Cross-Functional Cooperation in the Project Implementation Process." *Project Management Journal,* June 1991.

PINTO, J. K. "Twelve Ways to Get the Least From Yourself and Your Project." *PM Network,* May 1997.

Project Management Institute, *A Guide to the Project Management Body of Knowledge (PMBOK® Guide),* 2000 ed. Newtown Square, PA: Project Management Institute, 2001.

RAYNAL, W. "Teaming With Enthusiasm." *AutoWeek,* May 4, 1992.

ROSSY, G. L., and R. D. ARCHIBALD. "Building Commitment in Project Teams." *Project Management Journal,* June 1992.

SHARIFI, S., and K. S. PAWAR. "Product Design as a Means of Integrating Differentiation." *Technovation,* May 1996.

SHAW, M. E. *Group Dynamics,* 3rd ed. New York: McGraw-Hill, 1981.

SNOW, H. *The Power of Teambuilding Using Ropes Techniques.* San Diego, CA: Pfeffer, 1992.

TENNANT, D. "PMO Failure: An Observation," *PM Network,* October 2001.

THAMHAIN, H. J., and D. L. WILEMON. "Conflict Management in Project Life Cycles." *Sloan Management Review,* Summer 1975.

TIPPET, D. D., and J. F. PETERS. "Team Building and Project Management: How Are We Doing?" *Project Management Journal,* December 1995.

TODRYK, L. "The Project Manager as Team Builder: Creating An Effective Team." *Project Management Journal,* December 1990.

WILLIAMS, G. "Implementing an Enterprise Project Management Solution." *PM Network,* October 1997.

WREN, D. A., and D. VOICH, JR. *Management: Process, Structure and Behavior.* New York: Wiley, 1984.

The following case describes an unusual organizational arrangement for an actual manufacturing firm. The company is largely run by the employees through teams. When projects are instituted, it is common to pass the idea through the relevant teams first, before any changes are made. However, not everything can be passed through all the teams that may be involved in the change and this can be a source of trouble.

C A S E

OILWELL CABLE COMPANY, INC.
Jack R. Meredith

As Norm St. Laurent, operations manager for Oilwell Cable Company, pulled his Bronco 4x4 onto Kansas' Interstate 70, he heard on the CB about the traffic jam ahead of him due to icy road conditions. Although the traffic was moving some, Norm decided to get off at the eastern offramp for Lawrence, rather than the more direct western offramp, to save time. While waiting for the offramp to come up, Norm's mind drifted back to his discussion with Bill Russell, the general manager, on the previous day. Norm had been contemplating adding microprocessors to their rubber mixing equipment in order to save manual adjustments on these machines. This would improve throughput and reduce costs simultaneously, though without displacing any employees. Based on the data Norm had seen, it appeared that the microprocessors could cut the production time by 1 percent and reduce scrap from the current rate of 1 percent down to one-half of 1 percent.

However, it seemed that this might be an issue that should first be submitted to the production team in charge of rubber mixing for their thoughts on the idea. Once before, an even simpler change had been made without their knowledge and it wound up causing considerable trouble.

As the traffic wound around two cars in the ditch by the highway, Norm reflected on how difficult it was to make changes at this plant with their team management process, though there were advantages too. It probably stemmed from the way the company was originally set up.

History of Oilwell Cable Company (OCC)

Originally known as the Chord Cable Company and located in New Jersey, the firm had been experiencing severe management difficulties. When acquired by new management in 1983, they renamed it Oilwell Cable Company and relocated in Lawrence, Kansas to be closer to their primary customers in northeastern Oklahoma. Their product line consisted primarily of flat and round wire and cables for submersible pumps in oil wells.

The manager chosen to head up the new enterprise, Gino Strappoli, gave considerable thought to the organization of the firm. Gino envisioned a company where everyone took some responsibility for their own management and the success of the business. Gino preferred this approach not only for personal reasons but because cable manufacturing is a continuous process rather than a job shop-type of activity. The dedicated allegiance of the relatively few employees in a process firm is crucial to staying competitive. In such industries, direct labor commonly constitutes only 5 percent of the cost of the product, with indirect labor being another 5 percent. By contrast, in a job shop the wages paid for labor are a major determinant to being cost-competitive, often running 30 percent of product cost, thus introducing a potential conflict between labor and management. Gino reasoned that if he could obtain the employees' commitment to improving productivity, reducing scrap, being innovative with new technologies, and staying competitive in general, he would have a very viable firm.

With the approval of the new owners, Gino initiated his plan. Of the original labor force, only a few moved to Kansas, including Gino and the firm's controller, Bill Safford. All new equipment was purchased for the firm, and a local labor force was selectively recruited. As the firm was organized, the team management process was developed. Eleven teams were formed, six of which constituted the production area. The remainder included the management team; the resource team (support functions such as computing services, accounting, etc.); the technical team (including the lab employees, R&D, and so on); the administrative team (office and clerical); and the maintenance team.

These teams basically set their own work schedules, vacation schedules, and job functions. They addressed common problems in their work area and interfaced with other teams when needed to solve problems or improve processes. With Gino's enthusiastic encouragement, the team approach grew and took on more responsibility such as handling grievances and reprimanding team members when needed.

In January 1985 the firm became profitable and later that year came fully on-stream. Gino soon thereafter left for another position, and the operations manager, Bill Russell, was selected to succeed him. At this point, Norm was brought in to replace Bill as operations manager. Norm had years of experience in manufacturing and was a degreed mechanical engineer. (See Exhibit 1 for the organization structure.)

As Norm recalled, from 1985 to 1989 the firm rapidly increased productivity, improving profits significantly in the process and increasing in size to 140 employees. In so doing, they became the low-cost leader in the industry and gained a majority of the market share. This resulted in a virtual fourfold increase in sales since the days of Chord Cable Co. They were now approaching almost $25 million in annual sales.

In 1989, however, the recession hit the oilwell industry. Added to this was the slowdown in energy consumption, effective conservation, and the oil glut. For almost a year the company bided time and idle employees were paid for minimal production. Management felt a commitment to the employees to avoid a cutback, more so than in a normally organized firm. But finally, in 1990, top management told the teams that they would have to choose a method for handling this problem. Alternatives were shortened work-weeks, layoffs, and other such measures. The teams chose layoffs. Next, management drew up a list of names of "recommended" layoff personnel representing a vertical slice through the organization—a top management employee, some professional and technical people, and a number of production employees. These lists were given to the teams who then decided what names to change and what names to keep. Management largely went along with the teams' recommendations, and the layoffs (about 20) took place.

With a slimmer work force, the division increased their productivity even more significantly (see Exhibit 2), allowing them to cut their product prices from between 10 and 20 percent. As the country climbed out of the stagnant economy in 1991, the division was excellently poised to capitalize on the increased economic activity, although oil itself was still largely in the doldrums. Increased demand in mid-1991 forced the division to use overtime, and

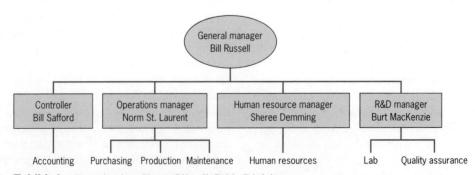

Exhibit 1   Organization Chart: Oilwell Cable Division

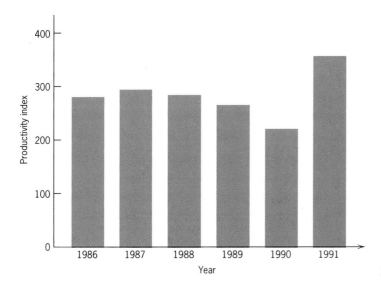

Exhibit 2 Productivity History

then temporary help. They didn't want to get back in the same workforce predicament they were in earlier.

The Team Management Process

The 1990 layoff was a traumatic situation for the teams and the team process. Following that episode, the employees were unsure whether the team management process might require too much responsibility on their part. They had faced reprimanding employees in the past, and had even asked one employee to leave who tried to deceive them. In general, they were very receptive to employees' individual problems and had helped their colleagues through tough times on many occasions, but now they were unsure.

Team size varied from a low of 3 to a high of 17. The advantages of the team process to the firm seemed significant, in the minds of the team members and area managers. One member of the maintenance team noted that the team process gave much more responsibility to the employee and allowed the firm to obtain the maximum talent from each person. The firm, in response, spends $1,000 per person per year on upgrading the skills of the employees in such areas as team effectiveness training, technical skill acquisition, communication skills, and general skill building. Bill Russell sees the major benefit of the team process as its production flexibility. Employees are also very receptive to change. Since the 1990 lay-

offs, the employees have become much more sensitive to outside threats to their jobs. This spurred quality and productivity gains of over 30 percent in 1991.

The primary benefit of the team process to the employees is having a say in their own work schedule. A typical secondary benefit was the elimination of penalties for making an error. The employees feel that this is an excellent place to work; absenteeism is only 0.7 percent, and only two people have left voluntarily since 1988.

Overall, the employees seemed to feel that this process worked well but wasn't utopian. "It doesn't give away the store," one employee commented. Two disadvantages of the process, according to the employees, were the time and energy it required on their part to make decisions. As an example, they noted that it required three full days for the teams to come up with the revised layoff lists. Normally the teams met once a week for an hour and a half.

But when the teams made a decision, the implementation of the decision was virtually immediate, which was a big advantage over most management decisions. Although this process required more time on the part of the employees, the total amount of time from idea to full implementation was probably less than that in a traditional organization, and it was clearly more successful. When asked if he would ever be willing to work in a regular work environment again, one team member voiced the opinion that this process while very good, really wasn't that much different from a well-run, open, traditional organization.

Teams realized that not every decision was put through them. They felt that this was appropriate, however. They also recognized the difficulty facing management when trying to decide whether something should come through the teams or if it was unnecessary to consult them. Though the teams met on company time, they were not eager to spend more time on team meetings. Especially after the layoff crisis, the teams realized that self-management was a two-way street and frequently hoped that upper management would make the tough decisions for them.

In summary, the teams felt that the process was based on trust, in both directions, and was working pretty well.

The Cable Production Process

As Norm pulled his truck into the OCC parking lot, he noticed that there were quite a few empty spaces. This 1992 winter had been more severe than most people had expected, based on the November

and December weather. The snow was almost over Norm's boots as he slogged his way to the buildings. Upstairs in his small, jumbled office, Norm pulled out the microprocessor file from his desk drawer and sat down to review the production process.

Their primary raw materials, which made up about 60 percent of the products' cost, included copper rods, lead, polypropylene, nylon, and rubber. Inspection consisted of submerging the cable in water and charging it with 30,000 volts. To date, none of their products had ever been returned. However, just in case they were ever queried about a cable they had produced, they kept samples of all their cables for five years back.

The firm considered itself very vulnerable to new technology, and hence kept an active R & D lab in continuous operation. Simple advances in process technology or insulation and jacketing materials could wipe out their market overnight, so they didn't want to be caught napping. Other methods of oil extraction were also a constant threat. Since they competed in a world market, they were highly exposed to foreign competition, and the location of their competitors was often a major factor in sales.

QUESTIONS

1. If Norm chooses to go ahead with the microprocessor conversion on the machinery, what are the potential conflicts that might arise? What are the advantages of such a move?

2. If Norm decides to put the decision to the appropriate production team, what are the potential problems? What would be the advantages?

3. If the production team chooses to approve and implement this microprocessor conversion project, what form of project organization will this represent?

4. Given the size of this organization and the number of projects they deal with, would it make sense to

institute a Project Management Office? Is there another arrangement that might be a good alternative?

5. How much impact might microprocessors have on production costs? Assume that variable overhead represents the same percentage of costs as fixed overhead. Find the net present value if the microprocessors cost $25,000 and their installation runs another $5,000.

6. Compare Norm's recollection of the division's productivity gains between 1985 and 1989 to Exhibit 2. Explain the inconsistency.

7. What would you recommend that Norm do?

The following reading discusses a new phenomenon in the increasingly global competitive environment— geographically dispersed project teams. The competitiveness of global firms is often facilitated by new electronic technologies and these technologies are also useful to the success of globally dispersed project teams, as described in the article. However, other aspects of such dispersed teams are more problematic, and the article illustrates these, as well as approaches used by project managers for circumventing them. Finally, some of the advice given in the article should be useful as well for project teams that aren't geographically dispersed.

R E A D I N G

THE VIRTUAL PROJECT: MANAGING TOMORROW'S TEAM TODAY*
J. R. Adams and L. L. Adams

Extraordinary demands are placed on project personnel—demands that require extraordinary commitments in order to accomplish the task at hand. Generating this commitment through the process of team building is a primary responsibility of any project manager. The processes of team building have been studied extensively by both academics and practitioners for decades, but until recently nearly all of these studies were conducted within the bureaucratic setting: that is, the team members shared a common workplace, saw each other frequently, knew each other well, and expected to continue working together for an extended period of time. The team building concepts developed within such an environment naturally reflect these working conditions as either stated or implied assumptions, and the concepts derived from these studies can be assumed to hold only as long as these assumptions hold.

These concepts still hold for projects intended to support and improve bureaucratic organizations. In the vast majority of cases, however, the working conditions experienced by modern projects differ greatly from those surrounding traditional bureaucratic work. Nevertheless, the basic definitions of team building continue to emphasize the assumption of typical bureaucratic working conditions. For example, one leading textbook in the field (Kast and Rosenzweig's *Organization and Management: A Systems and Contingency Approach,* McGraw-Hill, 1985) states that "actual teamwork involves small groups of three to fifteen people that meet face-to-face to carry out their assignments." Even in PMI's current *PMBOKGuide* (pp. 99–100), one of the five basic "tools and techniques" of team development is called "collocation," which involves ". . . placing all, or almost all, of the most active project team members in the same physical location to enhance their ability to perform as a team." In both of these publications, the concept of the virtual project is clearly ignored.

In the new, "virtual project" environment, team members seldom share a common workplace, may rarely see each other, may never have worked together before, and may never work together again after the project is complete. For an ever-increasing number of organizations, the world is represented by an environment of rapid technological advancement, particularly in the area of communications; complex organizational structures needed to deal with tough global competition; and dynamic markets that demand short production runs of unique products. Downsizing, outsourcing, and employee empowerment have become facts of life in the climate of many organizations, while job security is rapidly becoming a thing of the past. The survival of many organizations depends on the ability of the organization to rapidly change its structure, culture and products to match the changing demands of the environment.

Let's explore the conditions faced by the modern project manager in developing an effective and productive project team within a "virtual project."

The Virtual Project. The virtual project, also known as a "distributed team," is one in which the participants are geographically distributed to an extent that they may seldom, if ever, meet face-to-face as a team. The geographical distances involved do not have to be great; individuals who work in the same industrial complex may be functioning in a virtual project if their schedules do not allow them to meet face-to-face. As distances increase, however, the difficulties of communicating and building teams increase significantly. When team members are spread across several time zones, opportunity for direct communication is severely limited, and the associated costs of both face-to-face and electronic communications increase dramatically. Electronic communication takes on much more importance in virtual projects because electronic systems must assume the burden of making the development of effective project teams possible.

---

*Reprinted from *PM Network,* Project Management Institute, Inc., January 1997, Vol. 11, Number 1. © 1997, Project Management Institute Inc. All rights reserved.

It is beyond the scope of this article to discuss at length the issues that are generating the need for virtual projects. Suffice it to say that the environmental conditions described above are precisely those that require project teams to be dispersed.

Jaclyn Kostner has written extensively on the virtual project. In *Knights of the TeleRound Table* (Warner Books, 1994), she documents the unique issues faced by project managers who must manage such a virtual or distributed project. The issues she defines are shown in the left-hand column of the accompanying sidebar.

Developing trust is the greatest challenge to the remote project manager. It's difficult for distant team members to get to know each other well; consequently, they tend to communicate poorly because they often are less than comfortable with each other. Both of these situations destroy the trust that is so essential to creating good teamwork. Developing a group identity across

Virtual Project Management Suggestions

Issues	Problems	Suggestions
Developing Trust	Irregular, inconsistent communication; lower level of comfort and familiarity among team members; "us vs. them" attitude.	Provide and use a variety of communication alternatives. Communicate electronically except when signatures are required. Make project management software available to all team members.
Developing Group Identity	Fewer shared experiences; lack of cohesion; little understanding of other members' roles and responsibilities.	Conduct regular teleconference meetings when the need warrants. Manage the agenda to include a variety of participants and ensure everyone is involved in the discussion. Use logos, mottoes, and creative humor. Stay in contact when meetings are not required. Note: Do not exclude anyone from group discussions.
Sharing Information	Difficulty sharing adequate levels of information across distances; lack of formal opportunities to discuss work-related issues; lack of a common system to transmit information across distances.	Use technology to develop additional information-sharing opportunities: cellular phones, pagers, faxes, telephones, e-mail, Internet, and computer-to-computer. Distribute all key reports to all team members. Put information at one central access point, e.g., a project Web page, a LAN account.
Developing Clear Structures	Uncertain roles and responsibilities of team members; clashing cultures create different expectations, few clearly defined processes for decision making.	Use standard formats for meetings. Define goals, objectives, problems, and concerns at the kickoff meeting, and reiterate them frequently. Have participants describe and define potential problems and concerns, and evaluate risks as a group.

Issues	Problems	Suggestions
Formation of "Cliques" or Informal Subgroups	Cliques tend to create antagonism and competition between the team and the project manager, between team members, or among the cliques themselves.	The project manager can't prevent them from forming, but can manage these subgroups. Identify and keep track of them. Create subcommittees for dealing with problems, drawing members from the different cliques. Look for opportunities to mix participants from the different cliques, and initiate or create these opportunities when necessary.
Understanding Information	Each team member has different information (inconsistent); each member has varying levels of information (incomplete); each member has a different perspective of the information. All = inequities of information.	Ask members to explain their viewpoints. Ask members to describe the actions they plan to take, and solicit possible impacts to other involved parties. Use different levels of information for different participants, as appropriate.

distances is also difficult because people normally associate with events that occur at their local level. Teams tend to have a problem sharing information effectively across distances. One reason for this may be the lack of informal opportunities for discussion at lunches or during coffee breaks. Developing clear structures is an issue for the virtual project manager because distant work groups need more than the traditional vision, mission, and goals that are important for all project groups. Members of virtual teams tend to develop relationships with those who are located with them rather than with those who are at distant sites. The formation of such "cliques" can create competition or antagonism between the project manager and/or team members located elsewhere. Lastly, each distributed team member tends to have information that is somewhat different from that held by others. More important, each team member views information from a different perspective. Such inequities of information frequently increase the opportunity for miscommunication among team members.

If issues such as these are not dealt with, the virtual project experiences management difficulties far in excess of the more "typical" project with higher levels of collocation. Fortunately, the technology that has made virtual projects both possible and necessary also provides opportunities for dealing progressively with these problems.

Implementing Virtual Project Teams. The sidebar includes suggestions created by virtual project managers for using the advantages of project management team building to overcome virtual team difficulties. Generally, these suggestions encourage project managers to make creative use of modern communication technologies to bring the team together and encourage the participation and sense of ownership that generates commitment to the project and team objectives.

Since it's seldom possible in the virtual project to meet face-to-face, experienced project managers recommend using a variety of electronic communications. Trust seems to develop as the individual team member learns more about the project manager, other team members, and the project. It's therefore essential that team members be encouraged to communicate with each other frequently, as well as with the project manager and the team as a whole. Virtual project managers use all forms of electronic communication—cellular phones, pagers, faxes, e-mail, Web pages, and computer-to-computer transmissions across local area and wide area networks—to distribute everything from key reports to jokes, logos, and mottoes. These communications are specifically intended to increase the common experiences shared by the team members and thus increase the bonds among them. Regularly scheduled video and telephone conference calls increase team members' exposure to project information, as well as to each other.

When cliques form as subgroups of the project team, these subgroups are managed, not ignored. Subcommittees are created to resolve project problems, specifically drawing members from different cliques together so that they learn more about each other. Team members are frequently asked to explain their viewpoints and to discuss their plans with the team at large to improve the common understanding of information about the project, its progress, and its prospects.

Four specific types of electronic communication, which didn't even exist just a few years ago, are being used extensively by managers of virtual projects to help overcome the lack of formal and informal personal contact among the team members.

The Internet. As technology creates conditions that demand faster reactions, team building over extensive distances, and ever-more-extensive communications, that same technology provides new approaches with which to deal with these issues. The Internet provides a means for communicating quickly and inexpensively throughout the world. It is essential for all participants in virtual project teams to have access to the Internet and e-mail. The virtual project manager relies on e-mail to exchange project data with the dispersed team, especially when team members or clients are internationally located. E-mail is a particularly good tool for exchanging the detailed information necessary to update the status of project activities. This task is difficult to accomplish verbally via telephone or videoconference because of the detail involved and the difference in time zones. Transmitting such data by facsimile can be expensive due to the volume of data involved, the frequency of needed updates, and the requirement for consistent information flows.

With e-mail as the primary mode of communication, information flows easier and faster, and the difference in time zones is less likely to be a critical failure factor. The ease of communication encourages the team to communicate more often and in more detail. Team members get to know each other more personally, and therefore develop more cohesive working relationships. One word of caution, however; many companies, in a misguided attempt to economize, are limiting the use of e-mail to "official" business, and eliminating personal comments, jokes, and other "nonessential" communications. It is precisely these "informal" transmissions that can at least partially make up for the lack of personal contact. Informal e-mail communications can replace some face-to-face contact and help generate the close working relationships, commitments, and friendships that are traditionally considered to be characteristic of successful project teams.

The Pager. A byproduct of today's business environment is that technical specialists (team members) frequently are working on multiple projects, and are considered highly valuable resources. The time of these "highly valuable resources" may be quite limited. Though regularly scheduled project meetings are critical throughout the project life cycle, these valuable resources may often be required elsewhere, and the project manager may need to help conserve their time.

One way to make the best use of a team member's time is to use a paging system. Each team member carries a pager, and the pager numbers are published with the team roster. When agenda topics don't directly relate to a particular team member or function, that person can be released from attendance, freeing up time that can then be used more productively. If an issue surfaces that requires that person's attention, he or she can be "paged" into the teleconference call. This allows for quick responses to problems and issues, and limits the number of "open action items" on meeting minutes. This procedure must be established at the project's kickoff meeting, when the project manager discusses team roles, responsibilities and expectations. A culture must be developed within the project where each team member is expected to respond quickly to paging, especially when a 911 code, meaning an emergency needing immediate response, is attached to the pager number.

Teleconferencing. Teleconferencing is not as new as some of the techniques noted above, but its use has expanded dramatically in recent years along with the increase of virtual projects. Everyone thinks they understand teleconferencing, but few are able to use it effectively. The lack of visual communication means that only the spoken word is available for the transfer of information, so individual speakers must identify themselves when contributing to the discussion. The medium was originally designed to provide communications between two people. When more people are added to the conference, managing the conversation flow rapidly becomes a complex issue. The goal is to assure that everyone has an opportunity to contribute and that all issues are dealt with in a reasonable period of time.

Using telephony technology for communicating among several people requires careful management and control of the communication process. The project manager cannot manage the results of the communications, but must manage the process of getting to those results. The conference needs to be well-organized and structured. A detailed agenda is essential to a productive conference call. The project manager should schedule the call in advance so that an agenda can be published and distributed at least two to three days prior to the meeting. The agenda should always include specific items of information: purpose of the teleconference, day-date-time of the call, call-in number, expected duration of the call, chair of the meeting (the project manager), a detailed listing of items to be discussed and *the key participants for each item noted.* The project manager can then facilitate discussion among these key players, solicit input from other team members, and maintain a solution-oriented attitude. This structure allows all essential persons to share in the conversation and present their viewpoints, while keeping the team focused on the critical issues at hand. The structure also prevents side conversations and keeps the team from straying from the intended topic until a solution has been achieved.

The checklist in the accompanying sidebar is useful for developing a successful teleconference.

- Have one major agenda topic called "deliverables," where the deliverables that are due or past-due are listed, along with who is responsible for completing those items. The items can be statused and assistance can be solicited from the team to expedite completion.

- Always have an "open discussion" section at the end of the agenda. Do a round-table roll call of each person to see if anyone has comments or concerns that need to be discussed or documented in the minutes. Putting the open discussion section last also keeps the focus on issues that are critical to the project, rather than on issues that may be critical to an individual. If time runs out, at least the necessities have been covered.

- Invite team members to call in or e-mail additional agenda topics, and then add these topics to the agenda for discussion. If people can't submit topics prior to agenda distribution, introduce new items only during the open discussion section so that the flow of the meeting is not disrupted.

- Talk about any major changes to the schedule, such as slippages or early completions that affect the schedule or multiple departments, at the beginning of the conference. These changes could drastically affect the items on the agenda, the flow of the conference call, or even the flow of work for your whole project.

Teleconferencing Tips

- Include an overall time limit for scheduling purposes (for yourself and for your team). Anything over 1.5 hours tends to become unproductive because of the high level of concentration required to communicate in an audio-only format.

- Organize the meeting in two sequential categories. In Category 1 are those activities that on the project plan should be completed by the time the meeting occurs. In Category 2 are those activities that need to be completed prior to the next meeting.

Videoconferencing. With a geographically dispersed team, the cost of travel, including the cost of team members' time during travel, is too high to justify having the team involved in periodic face-to-face status meetings. However, current issues may be too critical to rely on e-mail, teleconferencing, and one-on-one voice contact. This is a time when videoconferencing is the most appropriate form of communication.

A capability not present in other forms of electronic communication, videoconferencing allows participants to feel more involved with each other because they can communicate on many different levels. Body language and facial expressions can be observed and interpreted, in many cases transferring more meaning than the actual words. Full team participation in developing the initial work breakdown structure and the project plan, both of which occur in the kickoff meeting, is crucial to developing the commitment to the virtual project team. It is particularly appropriate to have the kickoff meeting in a site that is videoconference-accessible, if possible, so that if some people can't attend then they can still be involved.

Despite all its good points, there is a downside to videoconferencing. Some of the common problems and barriers are logistical. For example, all participants must be located at pre-arranged receiving/transmitting sites; and, although the cost has been decreasing slowly, videoconferencing is still quite expensive, especially when numerous sites and satellite-based communications are involved, so these sites may not be readily accessible.

Also, even though technology is gradually moving forward and the signal transmission speed is increasing, videoconferencing uses a wide bandwidth, which translates into a significant delay in viewing the movements and expressions of participants. This delay as well as an individual's tendency to be uncomfortable in front of a camera frequently combine to make the whole process somewhat stiff and stilted. This seems to be a particular problem in systems where the participants can see themselves and worry about how they look to the others.

Since the purpose of this extraordinary use of electronic communications is to increase the stability of the virtual project, it is particularly important that all team members be able to work with the detailed project plan. All team members should have access to whatever software is being used to plan and control project activities. They should also have easy access to the project files. The liberal distribution of project documentation provides enhanced communication as well as an exposure to the project cultural structure.

A basic knowledge of team building is essential to the effective management of any project. With the advent of the virtual project, however, the methods and techniques necessary for implementing the project team building process have changed. Face-to-face communications are obviously desirable, but they may no longer be possible because of time or cost constraints. Fortunately, the same technologies that have made the virtual project a possibility also provide the methods for developing effective teams of dispersed project participants.

Virtual project managers must be both knowledgeable and creative in using the modern communication technologies available to them for the purpose of enhancing the common experiences of their project team members, and hence the commitment that can be generated for the project's objectives and goals. Perhaps more important, however, is to recognize that the ability to effectively use all of the current electronic communication techniques available to the project manager is rapidly becoming a mandatory skill for anyone likely to be involved in virtual projects.

This topic deserves some extensive research in order to help the virtual project manager develop more effective methods and techniques for dealing with the task of building effective project teams from dispersed project participants.

Questions

1. Which virtual project problems are unique to the phenomenon of being dispersed and which are common project problems in any project?

2. What new electronic technologies have contributed to the problems, and solutions, of virtual project teams?

3. Of the solutions to virtual team problems, which would apply to regular project teams also?

4. Which problems described in the article are the most serious for virtual projects? Which might be fatal?

5. How might the difficulties of matrix organization change when implementing virtual projects?

CHAPTER

5

Project Planning

In the *Reader's Digest* (March 1998, p. 49) Peter Drucker is quoted on planning: "Plans are only good intentions unless they immediately degenerate into hard work." To make such a transformation possible is no easy task. Inadequate planning is a cliché in project management. Occasionally, articles appear in project management periodicals attesting to the value of good planning. Project managers pay little attention. PMs say, or are told, that planning "takes too much time," "customers don't know what they want," "if we commit we will be held accountable," and a number of similar weak excuses (Bigelow, 1998, p. 15). Tom Peters, well-known seeker of business excellence, was quoted in the *Cincinnati Post:* "Businesses [believe] a lot of dumb things. . . . .The more time you spend planning, the less time you'll need to spend on implementation. Almost never the case! Ready. Fire. Aim. That's the approach taken by businesses I most respect." We strongly disagree and, as we will report below (and in Chapter 13), there is a great deal of research supporting the view that careful planning is solidly associated with project success—and none, to our knowledge, supporting the opposite position. On the other hand, sensible planners do not kill the plan with overanalysis. This leads to a well-known "paralysis by analysis." In an excellent article, Langley (1995) finds a path in between the two extremes. It is now time to consider how to plan the work of the project in such a way that it may be translated into "hard work" that actually leads to a successful completion of the project.

There are several reasons why we must use considerable care when planning projects. The primary purpose of planning, of course, is to establish a set of directions in sufficient detail to tell the project team exactly what must be done, when it must be done, and what resources to use in order to produce the deliverables of the project successfully. As we noted in Chapter 1, the deliverables (or scope, or specifications, or objectives) of a project are more than mere descriptions of the goods and/or services we promise to deliver to the client at a quality level that will meet client expectations. They also include the time and cost required to complete the project to the client's satisfaction. The plan must be designed in such a way that the project outcome also meets the objectives of the parent organization, as reflected by the project portfolio or other strategic selection process used to approve the project. Because the plan is only an estimate of what must be done, it is always carried out in an environment of uncertainty. Therefore, the plan must include allowances for risk and features that allow it to be *adaptive,* i.e., to be responsive to things that might disrupt it while it is being carried out. One such disruption—"scope creep"—is particularly common in software projects and will be discussed further in Chapter 11. Finally, the plan must also contain methods to ensure its integrity, which is to say it must include means of controlling the work it prescribes.

There is an extensive literature on project planning. Some of it is concerned with the strategic aspects of planning, being focused on the choice of projects that are consistent with the organization's goals (e.g., Archibald, 1988; Cleland and Kimball, 1987; Englund and Graham, 1999; Liberatore, 1988; Tan, Hayes, and Shaw, 1996). Another group of works is aimed at the process of planning individual projects, given that they have been chosen as strategically acceptable (e.g., Bennigson, 1972; Pells, 1993; Prentis, 1989; Westney, 1993). Laufer (1991), in particular, offers an interesting discussion on the theory of planning that includes some practical implications. Most fields have their own accepted set of project planning processes, though they are all similar, as we shall soon see. For example, in the field of Information Systems they refer to the standard "systems development cycle" for software projects, consisting of four or six or seven "phases," depending on which author is being consulted (e.g., see Rakos, 1990). For a different view of the software planning process, see Boehm, 1988). Prentis (1989) breaks the general planning process into seven steps, while Roman (1968) describes it as a set of six planning sequences.

The purpose of planning is to facilitate later accomplishment. The world is full of plans that never become deeds. The planning techniques covered here are intended to smooth the path from idea to accomplishment. It is a complicated process to manage a project, and plans act as a map of this process. The map must have sufficient detail to determine what must be done next but be simple enough that workers are not lost in a welter of minutiae.

In the pages that follow we discuss a somewhat formal method for the development of a project plan. Almost all project planning techniques lead to plans that contain the same basic elements. They differ only in the ways they approach the process of planning. We have adopted an approach that we think makes the planning process straightforward and fairly systematic, but it is never as systematic and straightforward as planning theorists would like. At its best, planning is tortuous. It is an iterative process yielding better plans from not-so-good plans, and the iterative process of improvement seems to take place in fits and starts. The process may be described formally, but it does not occur formally. Bits and pieces of plans are developed by individuals, by informal group meetings, or by formalized planning teams (Paley, 1993), and then improved by other individuals, groups, or teams, and improved again, and again. Both the plans themselves and the process of planning should start simple and then become more complex.

If the appropriate end product is kept firmly in mind, this untidy process yields a *project plan.* In this chapter we focus on designing the physical aspects of the project, defining what it is the project is supposed to accomplish, and who will have to do what for the project's desired output to be achieved. The project's budget and schedule are major parts of the project plan, but we delay discussion of them until Chapters 7 and 8. Indeed, what must be done to test and approve project outputs at both interim and final stages, and what records must be kept are both parts of the project plan and these are covered in later chapters, as is the part of the plan that covers ending the project. There is nothing sacrosanct about this sequence. It is simply in the order that these parts of the project plan tend to develop naturally.

Project plans may take many forms and in the coming pages we will mention several of these. A *project plan* should include the elements described in the next section. As we will see later, it should also include a record of all changes and adjustments that were made to the project during its life because it can then serve as the primary document of project termination, the *project history* (see Chapter 13). The project plan will include a complete set of schedules together with the associated resources and personnel needed to perform all of the tasks required to complete the project. For many purposes, we sometimes use an *action plan,* a portion of the project plan detailing the activities, their schedules, and resources, including personnel. Like a project plan, an action plan can take many forms and we illustrate a few of these somewhat later. The focus of an action plan, however, is on the schedule/resource/personnel elements of the activities and/or events required by the project. In the case of both the project plan and the action plan, we may use a partial version or enhanced version of either at any time, depending on the need.

In Section 5.4, we describe the project *work breakdown structure* (WBS) that is another (usually hierarchical) way of viewing the activities in the action plan. Often, the WBS consists of a simple list of all project activities with major activities broken down into subactivities, and these broken down still further. Schedules may also be shown, and resources, budget account numbers, and other specific aspects of the project may be displayed. The project *linear responsibility chart* (or *table*) is another specialized view of the action plan and focuses on who has what responsibility (e.g., performing, approving, communicating, supporting) associated with each project task. Many different forms may be used for both the WBS and responsibility charts.

It is appropriate to ask, "Why so many different ways of showing similar types of information?" As is true of so many things, tradition is probably the major reason. The project plan is usually a large and complex document. PMs need fast and simple ways of communicating specific kinds of information about their projects. Action plans, WBSs, and responsibility charts are simple and highly flexible ways of doing this.

5.1   INITIAL PROJECT COORDINATION

It is crucial that the project's objectives be clearly tied to the overall mission, goals, and strategy of the organization, such as might be reflected in the project portfolio process. Senior management should delineate the firm's intent in undertaking the project, outline the scope of the project, and describe how the project's desired results reinforce the organization's goals. Without a clear beginning, project planning (and later progress) can easily go astray. It is also vital that a senior manager call and be present at the *project launch meeting,* an initial coordinating meeting, as a visible symbol of top management's commitment to the project.

The individual leading the launch meeting is first to define the scope of the project. The success of the project launch meeting is absolutely dependent on the existence of a well-defined set of objectives. Unless all parties to the planning process have a clear understanding of precisely what it is the project is expected to deliver, planning is sure to be inadequate. The precise nature of the scope statement depends on the nature of the project itself, and because of this, it reflects the fact that all projects are, to some extent, unique. For some useful comments on the scope statement, see Duncan (1994). We will have more to say about project scope and its management in Chapters 6 and 11.

At the launch meeting, the project is discussed in sufficient detail that potential contributors develop a general understanding of what is needed. If the project is one of many similar projects, the meeting will be short and routine, a sort of "touching base" with other interested units. If the project is unique in most of its aspects, extensive discussion may be required.

It is useful to review the major risks facing the project during the launch meeting. The known risks will be those identified during the project selection process. These are apt to focus largely on the market reaction to a new process/product, the potential feasibility of an innovation, and like matters. The risk management plan for the project must be started at the launch meeting so that further risk identification can be extended to include the technology of the process/product, the project's schedule, resource base, and a myriad of other risks facing the project but not really identifiable until the project plan has begun to take form. In addition to the matters discussed below, one of the outcomes of the project planning process will be the formulation of the project's risk management group and the initial risk management plan that the group develops during the process of planning the project.

While various authors have somewhat different expectations for the project launch meeting (e.g., see Knutson, 1995; Martin and Tate, 1998), we feel it is important not to allow plans, schedules, and budgets to go beyond the most aggregated level (Level 1), possibly Level 2 if the project deliverables are fairly simple and do not

Source: DILBERT reprinted by permission of United Feature Syndicate, Inc.

require much interdepartmental coordination. To fix plans in more detail at this initial meeting will tend to prevent team members from integrating the new project into their ongoing activities and from developing creative ways of coordinating activities that involve two or more organizational units. Worse still, departmental representatives will be asked to make "a ballpark estimate of the budget and time required" to carry out this first-blush plan. Everyone who has ever worked on a project is aware of the extraordinary propensity of preliminary estimates to metamorphose instantaneously into firm budgets and schedules. Remember that this is only one of a series of meetings that will be required to plan projects of more than minimal complexity. It is critical to the future success of the project to take the time required to do a technically and politically careful job of planning. "If this means many meetings and extensive use of participatory decision making, then it is well worth the effort" (Ford and McLaughlin, 1992, p. 316).

Whatever the process, the outcome must be that: (1) technical scope is established (though perhaps not "cast in concrete"); (2) basic areas of performance responsibility are accepted by the participants; (3) some tentative overall schedules and budgets are spelled out; and (4) a risk management group is created. Each individual/unit accepting responsibility for a portion of the project should agree to deliver, by the next project meeting, a preliminary but detailed plan about how that responsibility will be accomplished. Such plans should contain descriptions of the required tasks, and estimates of the budgets and schedules.

Simultaneous with these planning activities, the risk management group develops a risk management plan that includes proposed methodologies for managing risk, the group's budget, schedule, criteria for dealing with risk, and required reports. Further, necessary inputs to the risk data base are described and various roles and responsibilities for group members are spelled out (Project Management Institute, 2001, p. 130). It must be emphasized that the process of managing risk is not a static process. Rather, it is ongoing, with constant updating as more risks are identified, as some risks vanish, as others are mitigated—in other words as reality replaces conjecture—and new conjecture replaces old conjecture.

The various parts of the project plan, including the risk management plan, are then scrutinized by the group and combined into a composite project plan. The composite plan, still not completely firm, is approved by each participating group, by the project manager, and then by senior organizational management. Each subsequent approval hardens the plan somewhat, and when senior management has endorsed it, any further changes in the project's scope must be made by processing a formal *change order.* If the project is not large or complex, informal written memoranda can substitute for the change order. The main point is that no *significant* changes in the project are made, without written notice, following top management's approval. The definition of "significant" depends on the specific situation and the people involved.

The PM generally takes responsibility for gathering the necessary approvals and assuring that any changes incorporated into the plan at higher levels are communicated to, and approved by, the units that have already signed off on the plan. Nothing is as sure to enrage functional unit managers as to find that they have been committed by someone else to alterations in their carefully considered plans without being informed. Violation of this procedure is considered a betrayal of trust. Several incidents of this kind occurred in a firm during a project to design a line of children's clothing. The anger at this *change without communication* was so great that two chief designers resigned and took jobs with a competitor.

Because senior managers are almost certain to exercise their prerogative to change the plan, the PM should always return to the contributing units for consideration and reapproval of the plan as modified. The final, approved result of this procedure is the project plan, also sometimes known as the *master plan,* the *baseline plan,* or the *project charter* (discussed later). When the planning phase of the project is completed, it is valuable to hold one additional meeting, a postplanning review (Martinez, 1994). This meeting should be chaired by an experienced project manager who is not connected with the project (Antonioni, 1997). The major purpose of the postplanning review is to make sure that all necessary elements of the project plan have been properly developed and communicated.

Outside Clients

When the project is to deliver a product/service to an outside client, the fundamental planning process is unchanged except for the fact that the specifications cannot be altered without the *client's* permission. A common "planning" problem in these cases is that marketing has promised deliverables that engineering may not know how to produce on a schedule that manufacturing may be unable to meet. This sort of problem usually results when the various functional areas are not involved in the planning process at the time the original proposal is made to the potential client. We cannot overstate the importance of a carefully determined set of *deliverables,* accepted by both project team and client (Martin, 1998).

Two objections to such early participation by engineering and manufacturing are likely to be raised by marketing. First, the sales arm of the organization is trained to sell and is expected to be fully conversant with all technical aspects of the firm's products/services. Further, salespeople are expected to be knowledgeable about design and manufacturing lead times and schedules. On the other hand, it is widely assumed by marketing (with some justice on occasion) that manufacturing and design engineers do not understand sales techniques, will be argumentative and/or pessimistic about client needs in the presence of the client, and are generally not "housebroken" when customers are nearby. Second, it is expensive to involve so much technical talent so early in the sales process—typically, prior to issuing a proposal. It can easily cost a firm more than $10,000 to send five technical specialists on a trip to consider a potential client's needs. The willingness to accept higher sales costs puts even more emphasis on the selection process.

The rejoinder to such objections is simple. It is usually cheaper, faster, and easier to do things right the first time than to redo them. When the product/service is a complex system that must be installed in a larger, more complex system, it is appropriate to treat the sale like a project, which deserves the same kind of planning. A great many firms that consistently operate in an atmosphere typified by design and manufacturing crises have created their own panics. (Software producers and computer system salespeople take note!) In fairness, it is appropriate to urge that anyone meeting customers face to face should receive some training in the tactics of selling.

A potential remedy for these problems is the use of multifunctional teams, also known in this context as *concurrent engineering*. This latter term, born in the 1980s, has been applied to product/service development "where, typically, a product design and its manufacturing process are developed simultaneously, cross-functional groups are used to accomplish integration, and the voice of the customer is included in the product development process" (Smith, 1997, p. 67). Multifunctional teaming may also be applied to the software design and development process. In software projects it is critically important to keep the customer involved in the process of developing software requirements from the start of the project. Clients often ask such questions as "While you're at it, can you fix it so the software will also. . . ?" Software writers tend to focus on technical feasibility when dealing with these questions and not uncommonly fail to note the additional time and cost required. More will be said about multifunctional teaming later in this chapter. In any event, if multifunctional planning is not utilized, the risk management group should be informed. The group will have addtional work to do.

Project Plan Elements

Given the project plan, approvals really amount to a series of authorizations. The PM is authorized to direct activities, spend monies (usually within preset limits) request resources and personnel, and start the project on its way. Senior management's approval not only signals its willingness to fund and support the project, but also notifies subunits in the organization that they may commit resources to the project.

The process of developing the project plan varies from organization to organization, but any project plan must contain the following elements:

- *Overview*   This is a short summary of the objectives and scope of the project. It is directed to top management and contains a statement of the goals of the project, a brief explanation of their relationship to the firm's objectives, a description of the managerial structure that will be used for the project, and a list of the major milestones in the project schedule.

- *Objectives*   This contains a more detailed statement of the general goals noted in the overview section. The statement should include profit and competitive aims as well as technical goals.

- *General Approach*   This section describes both the managerial and the technical approaches to the work. The technical discussion describes the relationship of the project to available technologies. For example, it might note that this project is an extension of work done by the company for an earlier project. The subsection on the managerial approach takes note of any deviation from routine procedure—for instance, the use of subcontractors for some parts of the work.

- *Contractual Aspects*   This critical section of the plan includes a complete list and description of all reporting requirements, customer-supplied resources, liaison arrangements, advisory committees, project review and cancellation procedures, proprietary requirements, any specific management agreements (e.g., use of subcontractors), as well as the technical deliverables and their specifications, delivery schedules, and a specific procedure for changing any of the above. (Project change orders will be discussed in Chapter 11.) Completeness is a necessity in this section. If in doubt about whether an item should be included or not, the wise planner will include it.

- *Schedules*   This section outlines the various schedules and lists all milestone events. Each task is listed, and the estimated time for each task should be obtained from those who will do the work. The project master schedule is constructed from these inputs. The responsible person or department head should sign off on the final, agreed-on schedule.

- *Resources*   There are two primary aspects to this section. The first is the budget. Both capital and expense requirements are detailed by task, which makes this a *project budget* (discussed further in Chapter 7). One-time costs are separated from recurring project costs. Second, cost monitoring and control procedures should be described. In addition to the usual routine elements, the monitoring and control procedures must be designed to cover special resource requirements for the project, such as special machines, test equipment, laboratory usage or construction, logistics, field facilities, and special materials.

- *Personnel*   This section lists the expected personnel requirements of the project. Special skills, types of training needed, possible recruiting problems, legal or policy restrictions on work force composition, and any other special requirements, such as security clearances, should be noted here. (This reference to "security" includes the need to protect trade secrets and research targets from competitors as well as the need to protect the national security.) It is helpful to time-phase personnel needs to the project schedule. This makes clear when the various types of contributors are needed and in what numbers. These projections are an important element of the budget, so the personnel, schedule, and resources sections can be cross-checked with one another to ensure consistency.

- *Evaluation Methods*   Every project should be evaluated against standards and by methods established at the project's inception. This section contains a brief description of the procedure to be followed in monitoring, collecting, storing, and evaluating the history of the project.

- *Potential Problems*   This is the province of risk management. Sometimes it is difficult to convince planners to make a serious attempt to anticipate potential difficulties. One or more such possible disasters such as subcontractor default, technical failure, strikes, bad weather, sudden required breakthroughs, critical sequences of tasks, tight deadlines, resource limitations, complex coordination requirements, insufficient authority in some areas, and new, complex, or unfamiliar tasks are certain to occur. The only uncertainties are which ones will occur and when. In fact, the timing of these disasters is not random. There are times, conditions, and events in the life of every project when progress depends on subcontractors, or the weather, or coordination, or resource availability, and plans to deal with unfavorable contingencies should be developed early in the project's life cycle. Some PMs avoid dealing with risk because "Trying to list everything that can go wrong gets everyone in a negative state of mind. I want my people to be positive!" Some PMs disdain this section of the plan on the grounds that crises cannot be predicted. Further, they claim to be very effective firefighters. (It is quite possible that when one finds such a PM, one has discovered an arsonist.) No amount of current planning can solve the current crisis, but preplanning may avert some.

These are the elements that constitute the project plan and are the basis for a more detailed planning of the budgets, schedules, work plan, and general management of the project. Once this basic plan is fully developed and approved, it is disseminated to all interested parties. This approved document is also known, as noted earlier, as the *project charter*. Because the project charter is generated through negotiations involving the many parties-at-interest in the project (usually under the leadership of the PM), we discuss the charter in Chapter 6.

Before proceeding, we should make explicit that this formal planning process is required for relatively large projects that cannot be classified as "routine" for the organization. The time, effort, and cost of the planning process we have described is not justified for routine projects, for example, most plant or machine maintenance projects. Admittedly, no two routine maintenance projects are identical, but they do tend to be quite similar. It is useful to have a complete plan for such projects, but it is meant to serve as a template that can easily be modified to fit the specific maintenance project at hand. The template also can serve as a benchmark in a continuous improvement program.

Project Management in Practice
Extensive Project Planning for Kodak's New Photographic System

After five years of secret planning involving five major worldwide film and camera companies, the Kodak System Developing Companies announced the new *Advantix* photographic system on February 1, 1996. The project, code-named Orion, was among the most ambitious new product development projects ever undertaken by Kodak. The initial brainstorming of concepts began in the mid-1980s and the search for partners in the late 1980s. By November 1991, an agreement had been reached on how Kodak, Fuji, Canon, Minolta, and Nikon—the System Developing Companies—would work together to develop this new system.

The main project plan consisted of a four-stage, eight-gate process as illustrated next.

- **Stage 1: Define and Refine Value Proposition**

    Gate 0: Project Inception
    Gate 1: Project Assessment

- **Stage 2: Product and Market Launch Design**

    Gate 2: Project Commitment
    Gate 3: Design Readiness

- **Stage 3: Marketing and Manufacturing Implementation**

    Gate 4: Project Verification
    Gate 5: Launch Readiness

An array of Advantix cameras to capitalize on their system.

- **Stage 4: Production and Sales**
  Gate 6: Manufacturing Readiness
  Gate 7: Marketing and Manufacturing Re-Review

As an example of the elements of the project plan, a 25 page "Concept Document" was a deliverable at Gate 0 by December 1992. The document included the identified consumer needs, benefits to Kodak and the industry, strategies, requirements, product descriptions, technology and manufacturing approaches, business case, schedule, and key risk areas. With significant changes occurring later on in the project, the Concept Document was modified and re-approved in mid-1994. The Gates represented major project milestones and always involved a major, top management review for verifying status and discussing upcoming issues.

Eleven months after the announcement, *Business Week* selected the Advanced Photo System (APS) as one of the best new products on the market. *Consumers Digest* selected the Kodak Advantix 3700ix camera as a best buy in its 1997 annual buying guide. However, by 2002 digital camera sales largely replaced APS in the mass market.

Source: C. Adams, "A Kodak Moment: *Advantix* Named 1997 International Project of the Year," *PM Network,* January 1998, pp. 21–27.

Project Planning in Action

Project plans are usually constructed by listing the sequence of activities required to carry the project from start to completion. This is not only a natural way to think about a project; it also helps the planner decide the necessary sequence of things—a necessary consideration for determining the project schedule and duration. In a fascinating paper, Aaron and his colleagues (1993) describe the planning process used at a telecommunications firm.

Using a planning process oriented around the life-cycle events common for software and hardware product developers, they divide the project into nine segments:

- Concept evaluation
- Requirements identification
- Design
- Implementation
- Test
- Integration
- Validation
- Customer test and evaluation
- Operations and maintenance

Each segment is made up of activities and milestones (significant events). As the project passes through each of the segments, it is subjected to a series of "quality gates" that must be successfully passed before proceeding to the next segment. Note that the planning process must pass through the quality gates as must the physical output of the project itself. For example, the requirements identification segment must meet the appropriate quality standards before the design segment can be started, just as design must be approved before implementation can be commenced. See Section 5.5 for more on this system.

Beginning in Chapter 1, we have argued that quality should be an inherent part of the project's specification/deliverables. The approach taken by Aaron, et al. (1993) is a direct embodiment of our position. Indeed, it "goes us one better," by applying quality standards to the process of managing the project as well as to the project's deliverables.

5.2 SYSTEMS INTEGRATION

Systems integration (sometimes called *systems engineering* or *concurrent engineering*) is one part of *integration management,* discussed further in Section 5.5, and plays a crucial role in the performance aspect of the project. We are using this phrase to include any technical specialist in the science or art of the project who is capable of integrating the technical disciplines to achieve the customer's objectives, and/or integrating the project into the customer's system. As such, systems integration is concerned with three major objectives.

1. *Performance*   Performance is what a system does. It includes system design, reliability, quality, maintainability, and repairability. Obviously, these are not separate, independent elements of the system, but are highly interrelated qualities. Any of these system performance characteristics are subject to overdesign as well as underdesign but must fall within the design parameters established by the client. If the client approves, we may give the client more than the specifications require simply because we have already designed to some capability, and giving the client an overdesigned system is faster and less expensive than delivering precisely to specification. At times, the aesthetic qualities of a system may be specified, typically through a requirement that the appearance of the system must be acceptable to the client.

2. *Effectiveness*   The objective is to design the individual components of a system to achieve the desired performance in an optimal manner. This is accomplished through the following guidelines:

   - Require no component performance specifications unless necessary to meet one or more systems requirements.
   - Every component requirement should be traceable to one or more systems requirements.
   - Design components to optimize system performance, not the performance of subsystems.

   It is not unusual for clients or project teams to violate any or all of these seemingly logical dicta. Tolerances specified to far closer limits than any possible system requirement, superfluous "bells and whistles," and "off the shelf" components that do not work well with the rest of the system are so common they seem to be taken for granted by both client and vendor. The causes of these strange occurrences are probably associated with some combination of inherent distrust between buyer and seller, the desire to overspecify in order "to be sure," and the feeling that "this part will do just as well." As we will see in Chapter 6, these attitudes can be softened and replaced with others that are more helpful to the process of systems integration.

3. *Cost*   Systems integration considers cost to be a design parameter, and costs can be accumulated in several areas. Added design cost may lead to decreased component cost, leaving performance and effectiveness otherwise unchanged. Added design cost may yield decreased production costs, and production cost may be traded off against unit cost for materials. *Value engineering* (or *value analysis*) examines all these cost trade-offs and is an important aspect of systems integration (Morris, 1979). It can be used in any project where the relevant cost trade-offs can be estimated. It is simply the consistent and thorough use of cost/effectiveness analysis.

Multifunctional teaming (see Section 5.5) is a way of achieving systems integration and, as such, may play a major role in the success or failure of any complex project. If a risky approach is taken by systems integration, it may delay the project. If the approach is too conservative, we forego opportunities for enhanced project capabilities or advantageous project economics. A good design will take all these trade-offs into account in the initial stages of the technical approach. A good design will also avoid locking the project into a rigid solution with little flexibility or adaptability in case problems occur later or changes in the environment demand changes in project performance or effectiveness. Multifunctional teams are also valuable for assessing and mitigating risk in the project, particularly in anticipating crises during the execution of the project (refer to the Directed Reading: "Planning for Crises in Project Management" at the end of this chapter).

The details of systems integration are beyond the scope of this book. The interested reader is referred to Badiru (1988) or Blanchard and Fabrycky (1990). In any case, the ability to do systems integration/engineering depends on at least a minimal level of technical knowledge about most parts of the project. It is one of the reasons project managers are expected to have some understanding of the technology of the projects they head.

5.3 SORTING OUT THE PROJECT

In this and the following sections of this chapter, and in Chapters 7 and 8 on budgeting and scheduling, we move into a consideration of the details of the project. We need to know exactly what is to be done, by whom, and when. All activities required to complete the project must be precisely delineated and coordinated. The necessary resources must be available when and where they are needed, and in the correct amounts. Some activities must be done sequentially, but some may be done simultaneously. If a large project is to come in on time and within cost, a great many things must happen when and how they are supposed to happen. Yet each of these details is uncertain and thus each must be subjected to risk management. In this section, we propose a conceptually simple method to assist in sorting out and planning all this detail. It is a *hierarchical planning system*—a method of constructing an action plan and, as we will see shortly, a WBS. We have also named it the "*even planning process.*"

To accomplish any specific project, a number of major activities must be undertaken and completed. Make a list of these activities in the general order in which they would occur. This is Level 1. A reasonable number of activities at this level might be anywhere between 2 and 20. (There is nothing sacred about these limits. Two is the minimum possible breakdown, and 20 is about the largest number of interrelated items that can be comfortably sorted and scheduled at a given level of aggregation.) Now break each of these Level 1 items into 2 to 20 tasks. This is Level 2. In the same way, break each Level 2 task into 2 to 20 subtasks. This is Level 3. Proceed in this way until the detailed tasks at a level are so well understood that there is no reason to continue with the work breakdown.

It is important to be sure that all items in the list are at roughly the same level of task generality. In writing a book, for example, the various chapters tend to be at the same level of generality, but individual chapters are divided into finer detail. Indeed, subdivisions of a chapter may be divided into finer detail still. It is difficult to overstate the significance of this simple dictum. It is central to the preparation of most of the planning documents that will be described in this chapter and those that follow.

The logic behind this simple rule is persuasive. We have observed both students and professionals in the process of planning. We noted that people who lack experience in planning tend to write down what they perceive to be the first activity in a sequence of activities, begin to break it down into components, take the first of these, break it further, until they have reached a level of detail they feel is sufficient. They then take the second step and proceed similarly. If they have a good understanding of a basic activity, the breakdown into detail is handled well. If they are not expert, the breakdown lacks detail and tends to be inadequate. Further, we noted that integration of the various basic activities was poor. An artist of our acquaintance explained: When creating a drawing, the artist sketches in the main lines of a scene, and then builds up the detail little by little over the entire drawing. In this way, the drawing has a "unity." One cannot achieve this unity by drawing one part of the scene in high detail, then moving to another part of the scene and detailing it. He asked a young student to make a pen-and-ink sketch of a fellow student. Her progress at three successive stages of her drawing is shown in Figure 5-1.

This illustrates the "even planning process." The PM will probably generate the most basic level (Level 1) and possibly the next level as well. Unless the project is

Figure 5-1   The "even planning process."

quite small, the generation of additional levels will be delegated to the individuals or groups who have responsibility for doing the work. Maintaining the "even planning" discipline will help keep the plan focused on the project's deliverables rather than on the work at a subsystem level.

Sometimes a problem arises because some managers tend to think of outcomes (events) when planning and others think of specific tasks (activities). Many mix the two. The problem is to develop a list of both activities and outcomes that represents an exhaustive, nonredundant set of results to be accomplished (outcomes) and the work to be done (activities) in order to complete the project.

In this hierarchical planning system, the objectives are taken from the project plan. This aids the planner in identifying the set of required activities for the objectives to be met, a critical part of the action plan. Each activity has an outcome (event) associated with it, and these activities and events are decomposed into subactivities and subevents, which, in turn, are subdivided again.

Assume, for example, that we have a project whose purpose is to acquire and install a large machining center in an existing plant. In the hierarchy of work to be accomplished for the installation part of the project, we might find such tasks as "Develop a plan for preparation of the floor site" and "Develop a plan to maintain plant output during the installation and test period." These tasks are two of a larger set of jobs to be done. The task "... preparation of the floor site" is subdivided into its elemental parts, including such items as "Get specifics on machine center mounting points," "Check construction specifications on plant floor," and "Present final plan for floor preparation for approval." A form that may help to organize this information is shown in Figure 5-2. (Additional information about each element of the project will

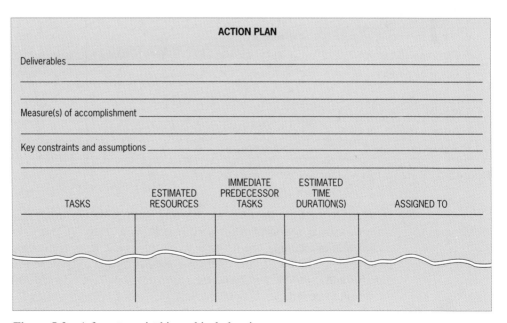

Figure 5-2   A form to assist hierarchical planning.

ACTION PLAN

Objective Career Day				
Steps	**Responsibility**	**Time (weeks)**	**Prec.**	**Resources**
1. Contact Organizations				
a. Print forms	Secretary	6	–	Print shop
b. Contact organizations	Program manager	15	1.a	Word processing
c. Collect display information	Office manager	4	1.b	
d. Gather college particulars	Secretary	4	1.b	
e. Print programs	Secretary	6	1.d	Print shop
f. Print participants' certificates	Graduate assistant	8	–	Print Shop
2. Banquet and Refreshments				
a. Select guest speaker	Program manager	14	–	
b. Organize food	Program manager	3	1.b	Caterer
c. Organize liquor	Director	10	1.b	Dept. of Liquor Control
d. Organize refreshments	Graduate assistant	7	1.b	Purchasing
3. Publicity and Promotion				
a. Send invitations	Graduate assistant	2	–	Word processing
b. Organize gift certificates	Graduate assistant	5.5	–	
c. Arrange banner	Graduate assistant	5	1.d	Print shop
d. Contact faculty	Program manager	1.5	1.d	Word processing
e. Advertize in college paper	Secretary	5	1.d	Newspaper
f. Class announcements	Graduate assistant	1	3.d	Registrar's Office
g. Organize posters	Secretary	4.5	1.d	Print shop
4. Facilities				
a. Arrange facility for event	Program manager	2.5	1.c	
b. Transport materials	Office manager	.5	4.a	Movers

Figure 5-3   Partial action plan for college "Career Day."

be added to the form later when budgeting and scheduling are discussed.) Figure 5-3 shows a partial action plan for a college "Career Day." (Clearly, Figure 5-3 is not complete. For example, the list of activities does not show such items as "setting and decorating the tables." In the interest of simplicity and in order to avoid doubling the length—and cost—of this book, the examples shown in this and following chapters are meant to be indicative, not exhaustive.)

A short digression is in order before continuing this discussion on action plans.

The actual form the action plan takes is not sacrosanct. As we will show in this and the coming chapters, not even all elements of the action plan shown in Figure 5-2 may be shown in all cases. In some cases, for example, the amounts of specific resources required may not be relevant. In others, "due dates" may be substituted for activity durations. The appearance of an action plan will probably differ in different organizations, and may even differ between departments or divisions of the same organization (though standardization of format is usual, and probably desirable in any given firm). In some plans, numbers are used to identify activities; in others, letters. In still others, combinations of letters and numbers are used. In this chapter, we will illustrate several different forms of action plans drawn from "real life." Our purpose is not to confuse the reader, but to focus the reader's attention on the *content* of the plan, not its *form.*

A tree diagram can be used to represent a hierarchical plan as in Figure 5-4. Professor Andrew Vazsonyi has called this type of diagram a *Gozinto chart,* after the famous Italian mathematician Prof. Zepartzat Gozinto of Vazsonyi's invention. Readers familiar with the Bill of Materials in a Materials Requirements Planning (MRP) system will recognize the parallel to nested hierarchical planning.

If the project does not involve capital equipment and special materials, estimates may not be necessary. Some projects require a long chain of tasks that are mostly sequential—for example, the real estate syndication of an apartment complex or

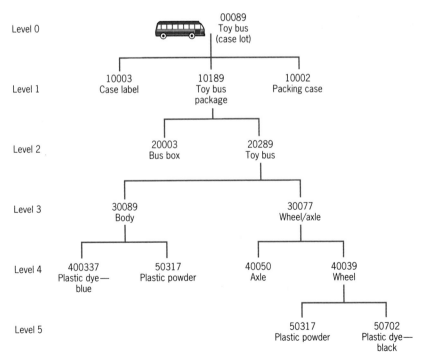

Figure 5-4   Gozinto chart for a toy bus. *Source:* Harris and Gonzalez 1981.

the development and licensing of a new drug. Other projects require the coordination of many concurrent tasks that finally come together—for example, the design and manufacture of an aircraft engine or the construction of a house. Still others have the characteristics of both. An example of a plan to acquire a subsidiary is illustrated in Figures 5-5a and 5-5b. A verbal "action plan" was written in the form of a memorandum, Figure 5-5a, and was followed by the more common, tabular plan shown in Figure 5-5b. Only one page of a five-page plan is shown. The individuals and groups

---

MEMO

To allow Ajax to operate like a department of Instat by April 1, 1996, we must do the following by the dates indicated.

September 24

Ajax Management to be advised of coming under Instat operation. The Instat sales department will begin selling Ajax Consumer Division production effective Jan. 1, 1996. There will be two sales groups: (1) Instat, (2) Ajax Builder Group.

October 15

Instat Regional Managers advised—Instat sales department to assume sales responsibility for Ajax products to distribution channels, Jan. 1, 1996.

October 15

Ajax regional managers advised of sales changes effective Jan. 1, 1996.

October 15

Instat Management, Bob Carl, Van Baker, and Val Walters visit Ajax management and plant. Discuss how operations will merge into Instat.

October 22

Ajax regional managers advise Ajax sales personnel and agents of change effective Jan. 1, 1996.

October 24

Brent Sharp and Ken Roadway visit Instat to coordinate changeover.

October 29

Instat regional managers begin interviewing Ajax sales personnel for possible positions in Instat's sales organization.

November 5

Instat regional managers at Ajax for sales training session.

November 26

Walters visits Ajax to obtain more information.

November 30

Data Processing (Morrie Reddish) and Mfg. Engineering (Sam Newfield):Request DP tapes from Bob Cawley, Ajax, for conversion of Ajax to Instat eng. records: master inventory file, structure file, bill of materials file, where-used file, cross-reference Instat to Ajax part numbers, etc.

Allow maximum two weeks until December 14, 1995, for tapes to be at Instat.

December 3

ADMINISTRATIVE (Val Walters): Offer Norwood warehouse for sublease.

December 3

SALES (Abbott and Crutchfield): Week of sales meeting . . . Instruction of salespeople in Ajax line . . . including procedure in writing Ajax orders on separate forms from Instat orders . . . temporarily, adding weight and shipping information, and procedure below:

Crutchfield to write procedure regarding transmission of orders to Instat, credit check, and transmission of order information to shipping point, whether Norwood, San Francisco, or, later, Instat Cincinnati.

Figure 5-5a Partial action plan for merger of Ajax Hardware into Instat Corp (page 1 of 5).

ACTION PLAN

Objective: Merger of Ajax Hardware into Instat Corp. by April 1, 1996			
Steps	**Due Date**	**Responsibility**	**Precedent**
1. Ajax management advised of changes	September 24	Bob Carl, Van Baker	–
2. Begin preparing Instat sales dept. to sell Ajax Consumer Division products effective 1/1/96	September 24	Bob Carl	1
3. Prepare to create two sales groups: (1) Instat, (2) Ajax Builder Group effective 1/1/96	September 24	Bob Carl	1
4. Advise Instat regional managers of sales division changes	October 15	Bob Carl	2,3
5. Advise Ajax regional managers of sales division changes	October 15	Van Baker	2,3
6. Visit Ajax management and plan to discuss merger of operations	October 15	Bob Carl, Van Baker, Val Walters	4,5
7. Advise Ajax sales personnel and agents	October 22	Van Baker	6
8. Visit Instat to coordinate changeover	October 24	Brent Sharp, Ken Roadway	6
9. Interview Ajax sales personnel for possible position	October 29	Instat regional managers	7
10. Sales training sessions for Ajax products	November 5	Instat regional managers	9
11. Visit Ajax again	November 26	Val Walters	8,10
12. Request DP tapes from Bob Cawley for conversion	November 30	Morrie Reddish, Sam Newman	6
13. Offer Norwood warehouse for sublease	December 3	Val Walters	11
14. Write order procedures	December 3	Doug Crutchfield	10
15. Sales meeting (instruction— product line and procedures)	December 3	Fred Abbott, Doug Crutchfield	14
16. DP tapes due for master inventory file, bill of materials, structure file	December 14	Bob Cawley	12
. . .			
. . .			
. . .			

Figure 5-5b Tabular partial action plan for Ajax-instat merger based on Figure 5-4a.

mentioned developed similar plans at a greater level of detail. (Names have been changed at the request of the firm.)

As we have noted several times, the importance of careful planning can scarcely be overemphasized. Pinto and Slevin (1987, 1988) developed a list of ten factors that should be associated with success in implementation projects. The factors were split into strategic and tactical clusters. Of interest here are the strategic factors:

1. *Project mission.* It is important to spell out clearly defined and agreed-upon objectives in the project plan.

2. *Top management support.* It is necessary for top managers to get behind the project at the outset and make clear to all personnel involved that they support successful completion.

3. *Project's action plan.* A detailed, scheduled plan of the required steps in the implementation process needs to be developed, including all resource requirements (money, raw materials, staff, etc.).

Extensive empirical testing showed these factors to be required for implementation project success. (Tactical factors are also necessary for success, but they are not a consideration here.)

At this point, it might be helpful to sum up this section with a description of how the planning process actually works in many organizations. Assume that you, the PM, have been given responsibility for developing the computer software required to transmit a medical X-ray from one location to another over a telephone line. There are several problems that must be solved to accomplish this task. First, the X-ray image must be translated into computer language. Second, the computerized image must be transmitted and received. Third, the image must be displayed (or printed) in a way that makes it intelligible to the person who must interpret it. You have a team of four programmers and a couple of assistant programmers assigned to you. You also have a specialist in radiology assigned part-time as a medical advisor.

Your first action is to meet with the programmers and medical advisor in order to arrive at the technical requirements for the project. From these requirements, the project mission statement and detailed specifications will be derived. (Note that the original statement of your "responsibility" is too vague to act as an acceptable mission statement.) The basic actions needed to achieve the technical requirements for the project are then developed by the team. For example, one technical requirement would be to develop a method of measuring the density of the image at every point on the X-ray and to represent this measurement as a numerical input for the computer. This is the first level of the project's action plan.

Responsibility for accomplishing the first level tasks is delegated to the project team members who are asked to develop their own action plans for each of the first level tasks. These are the second level action plans. The individual tasks listed in the second level plans are then divided further into third level action plans detailing how each second level task will be accomplished. The process continues until the lowest level tasks are perceived as "units" or "packages" of work.

Early in this section, we advised the planner to keep all items in an action plan at the same level of "generality" or detail. One reason for this is now evident. The tasks at any level of the action plan are usually monitored and controlled by the level just above. If senior managers attempt to monitor and control the highly detailed work packages several levels down, we have a classic case of micromanagement. Another reason for keeping all items in an action plan at the same level of detail is that planners have an unfortunate tendency to plan in great detail all activities they understand well, and to be dreadfully vague in planning activities they do not understand well. The result is that the detailed parts of the plan are apt to be carried out and the vague parts of the plan are apt to be given short shrift.

In practice, this process is iterative. Members of the project team who are assigned responsibility for working out a second, third, or lower-level action plan generate a tentative list of tasks, resource requirements, task durations, predecessors, etc., and bring it to the delegator for discussion, amendment, and approval. This may require several amendments and take several meetings before agreement is reached. The result is that delegator and delegatee both have the same idea about what is to be done, when, and at what cost. Not uncommonly, the individuals and groups that make commitments during the process of developing the action plan actually *sign-off* on their commitments. The whole process involves negotiation and will be further developed in the chapters to follow. Of course, like any managers, delegators can micromanage their delegatees, but micromanagement cannot be mistaken for negotiation—especially by the delegatee.

Project Management in Practice
Disaster Project Planning in Iceland

Natural hazards abound in the remote island nation of Iceland. Not only is it one of the most volcanically active countries in the world but its remote and exposed location in the North Atlantic Ocean leaves it vulnerable to gales, landslides, snow avalanches, and other such natural disasters.

There are three phases of a natural disaster: the disaster itself, the response in terms of planning for the future, and the actual rebuilding project phase. Based on previous disasters such as the 1995 avalanche in Suodavik which claimed 15 lives, it has been proposed that the response phase be moved up in terms of contingency planning so the rebuilding phase can begin immediately after the disaster.

The normal stakeholders in an Icelandic disaster typically include the population experiencing the disaster, the local government, the insurance bodies, Iceland Catastrophe Insurance, the Landslide and Avalanche Fund, and the consulting and contracting repair organizations. In the past, these bodies have not been coordinated so every natural disaster had a delayed response to the event until all the political issues could be resolved, which often took months.

The proposal for reorganizing the response phase includes such items as:

- Documenting the response plans in a compulsory project handbook

- Charging the financing bodies with directing the actual rebuilding process
- Identifying an appropriate coordinating body for each disaster type and location
- Identifying a process for the appointment of a project manager independent, both financially and emotionally, of all the main stakeholders.

Source: G. Torfason, "Lessons from a Harsh Land: Project Management and Disaster Preparedness in Iceland," *PM Network,* February 1998, pp. 39–42.

Buried homes in Heimaey, Iceland from 1973 volcano.

5.4   THE WORK BREAKDOWN STRUCTURE AND LINEAR RESPONSIBILITY CHARTS

As was the case with project action plans and contrary to popular notion, the Work Breakdown Structure (WBS) is not one thing. It can take a wide variety of forms that, in turn, serve a wide variety of purposes. The WBS often appears as an outline with the Level 1 tasks on the left and successive levels appropriately indented. The WBS may also picture a project subdivided into hierarchical units of tasks, subtasks, work packages, etc. as a type of Gozinto chart or tree constructed directly from the project's action plan. Most current project management software will generate a WBS on command. Microsoft's Project 2002®, for example, links the indented activity levels with a Gantt chart (see Chapter 10, Figure 10-16) that visually shows the activity durations at any level.

Another type of WBS shows the organizational elements associated with specific categories of tasks. Figure 5-6 is such a WBS. The project is to build a robot. The control group of the Electronics Department of the organization has responsibility for developing control systems for the robot. Five different control functions are shown, each of which is presumably broken down into more detailed tasks. In this case, the account numbers for each task are shown so that proper charges can be assigned for each piece of work done on the project.

Some writers recommend using the WBS as the fundamental tool for planning (Hubbard, 1993, for instance). We find nothing logically wrong with this approach, but it seems overly structured when compared to the way that firms noted for high-quality planning actually proceed. If this approach is used, the PM is well advised to adopt the general philosophy of building the WBS that was used when building the action plan (see Section 5.3). Other writers pay scant attention to the WBS, giving the subject little more than a mention (Badiru, 1988; Love, 1989; and others). We do not find this a fatal error as long as the planning activity is otherwise carried out to an appropriate level of detail.

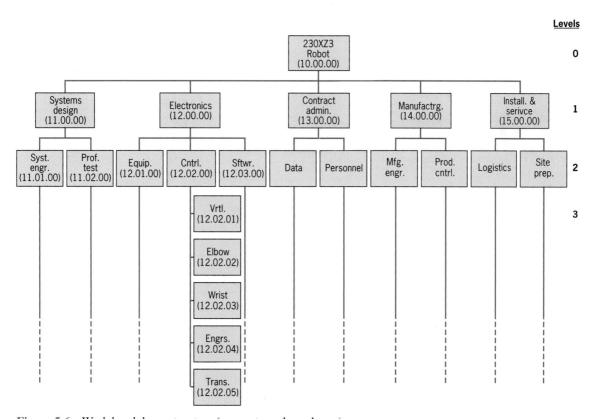

Figure 5-6   Work breakdown structure (account numbers shown).

In general, the WBS is an important document and can be tailored for use in a number of different ways. It may illustrate how each piece of the project contributes to the whole in terms of performance, responsibility, budget, and schedule. It may, if the PM wishes, list the vendors or subcontractors associated with specific tasks. It may be used to document that all parties have signed-off on their various commitments to the project. It may note detailed specifications for any work package, establish account numbers, specify hardware/software to be used, and identify resource needs. It may serve as the basis for making cost estimates (see Chapter 7) or estimates of task duration (see Chapter 8). Its uses are limited only by the needs of the project and the imagination of the PM. No one version of the WBS will suit all needs, so the WBS is not *a* document, but any given WBS is simply one of many possible documents.

The following general steps explain the procedure for designing and using the WBS. For small- or moderate-size projects, and depending on the use for which the WBS is designed, some of the following steps might be skipped, combined, extended, and handled less formally than our explanation indicates, particularly if the project is of a type familiar to the organization.

1. Using information from the action plan, list the task breakdown in successively finer levels of detail. Continue until all meaningful tasks or work packages have been identified and each task can be individually planned, budgeted, scheduled, monitored, and controlled.

WBS / Responsibility		Project Office				Field Oper.
Subproject	Task	Project Manager	Contract Admin.	Project Eng.	Industrial Eng.	Field Manager
Determine	A1	○		●	▲	
need	A2	■	○	▲	●	
Solicit	B1	○	■	▲		●
quotations						
Write approp.	C1	■	▲	○	●	
request.	C2		●	○	▲	
	C3	●	■	▲		■
"	"					
"	"					
"	"					

Legend:
▲ Responsible
● Support
■ Notification
○ Approval

Figure 5-7   Linear responsibility chart.

2. For each such work package, identify the data relevant to the WBS (e.g., vendors, durations, equipment, materials, special specifications). List the personnel and organizations responsible for each task. It is helpful to construct a *linear responsibility chart* (sometimes called a *responsibility matrix*) to show who is responsible for what. This chart also shows critical interfaces between units that may require special managerial coordination. With it, the PM can keep track of who must approve what and who must report to whom. Such a chart is illustrated in Figure 5-7. If the project is not too complex, the responsibility chart can be simplified (see Figure 5-8). Figure 5-9 shows one page of a verbal responsibility chart developed by a firm to reorganize its distribution system. In this case, the chart takes the form of a 30-page document covering 116 major activities.

3. All work package information should be reviewed with the individuals or organizations who have responsibility for doing or supporting the work in order to verify the WBS's accuracy. Resource requirements, schedules, and subtask relationships

	Vice-president	General manager	Project manager	Manager engineering	Manager software	Manager manufacturing	Manager marketing	Subprogram manager manufacturing	Subprogram manager software	Subprogram manager hardware	Subprogram manager services
Establish project plan	6	2	1	3	3	3	3	4	4	4	4
Define WBS		5	1	3	3	3	3	3	3	3	3
Establish hardware specs		2	3	1	4	4	4				
Establish software specs		2	3	4	1		4				
Establish interface specs		2	3	1	4	4	4				
Establish manufacturing specs		2	3	4	4	1	4				
Define documentation		2	1	4	4	4	4				
Establish market plan	5	3	5	4	4	4	1				
Prepare labor estimate			3	1	1	1		4	4	4	4
Prepare equipment cost estimate		3	1	1	1			4	4	4	4
Prepare material costs			3	1	1	1		4	4	4	4
Make program assignments			3	1	1	1		4	4	4	4
Establish time schedules		5	3	1	1	1	3	4	4	4	4

1 Actual responsibility   4 May be consulted
2 General supervision   5 Must be notified
3 Must be consulted   6 Final approval

Figure 5-8   Simplified linear responsibility chart.

Activities	Initiate Action	Responsible Individuals	
		Work with	Clear Action with
Distribution System and Its Administration			
1. Recommend distribution system to be used.	Mktg Officers	ILI & IHI LOB MCs M-A Cttee VP&Agcy Dir	Sr VP Mktg
	Mktg Officers	Group LOB MC M-A Cttee VP & Agcy Dir	Sr VP Mktg
	Mktg Officers	IA LOB MC M-A Cttee VP&Agcy Dir	Sr VP Mktg
Compensation			
2. Determine provisions of sales-compensation programs (e.g., commissions, subsidies, fringes).	Compensation Task Force	Mktg, S&S & Eqty Prod Offrs	President
	Compensation Task Force	Mktg, S&S & Eqty Prod Offrs	
	Compensation Task Force	Mktg, S&S & Eqty Prod Offrs	President
3. Ensure cost-effectiveness testing of sales compensation programs.	Compensation Task Force	Mktg, S&S & Eqty Prod Offrs	President
Territory			
4. Establish territorial strategy for our primary distribution system.	VP&Agcy Dir	Dir MP&R M-A Cttee	Sr VP Mktg
5. Determine territories for agency locations and establish priorities for starting new agencies.	VP&Agcy Dir	Dir MP&R M-A Cttee	Sr VP Mktg
6. Determining agencies in which advanced sales personnel are to operate.	Dir Ret Plnng Sls Dir Adv Sls	VP S & S	Sr VP Mktg

Legend: IA, ILI, IHI: Product lines
LOB: Line of business
MC: Management committee
M-A Cttee: Marketing administration committee
S&S: Sales and service
MP&R: Marketing planning and research

Figure 5-9 Verbal responsibility chart.

can now be aggregated to form the next higher level of the WBS, continuing on to each succeeding level of the hierarchy. At the uppermost level, we have a summary of the project, its budget, and an estimate of the duration of each work element. For the moment, we are ignoring uncertainty in estimating the budget and duration of work elements. We will deal with these subjects in Chapters 7 and 8.

4. For the purpose of pricing a proposal, or determining profit and loss, the total project budget should consist of four elements: direct budgets from each task as just described; an indirect cost budget for the project, which includes general and administrative overhead costs (G&A), marketing costs, potential penalty charges, and other expenses not attributable to particular tasks; a project "contingency" reserve for unexpected emergencies; and any residual, which includes the profit derived from the project, which may, on occasion, be intentionally negative. In Chapter 7 we argue that the budget used for pricing or calculation of profit should not be the same budget that the PM uses to control the project.

5. Similarly, schedule information and milestone (significant) events can be aggregated into a *project master schedule.* The master schedule integrates the many different schedules relevant to the various parts of the project. It is comprehensive and may include contractual commitments, key interfaces and sequencing, milestone events, and progress reports. In addition, a time contingency reserve for unforeseeable delays might be included. A graphic example of a master schedule is shown in Figure 5-10.

Listed items 1 to 5 focus on the WBS as a planning tool. It may also be used as an aid in monitoring and controlling projects. Again, it is important to remember that no single WBS contains all of the elements described and any given WBS should be designed with specific uses in mind.

6. As the project is carried out, step by step, the PM can continually examine actual resource use, by work element, work package, task, and so on up to the full project level. By comparing actual against planned resource usage at a given time, the PM can identify problems, harden the estimates of final cost, and make sure that relevant corrective actions have been designed and are ready to implement if needed. It is necessary to examine resource usage in relation to results achieved because, while the project may be over budget, the results may be farther along than expected. Similarly, the expenses may be exactly as planned, or even lower, but actual progress may be much less than planned. Control charts showing these *earned values* are described in more detail in Chapter 10. In Chapters 7 and 8, as we have just noted, the details of how to include risk in the budget and in the schedule will be covered.

7. Finally, the project schedule may be subjected to the same comparisons as the project budget. Actual progress is compared to scheduled progress by work element, package, task, and complete project, to identify problems and take corrective action. Additional resources may be brought to those tasks behind schedule to expedite them. These added funds may come out of the budget reserve or from other tasks that are ahead of schedule. This topic is discussed further in Chapter 9.

Subproject		Task	Responsible Dept.	Dependent Dept.	2002												2003											
					J	F	M	A	M	J	J	A	S	O	N	D	J	F	M	A	M	J	J	A	S	O	N	D
Determine need	A1	Find operations that benefit most	Industrial						△ ▲																			
	A2	Approx. size and type needed	Project Eng.	I.E.		-	-	-	△	▲																		
Solicit quotations	B1	Contact vendors & review quotes	P.E.	Fin., I.E., Purch.						O	- ●	△		O	▲	□												
Write appropriation request	C1	Determine tooling costs	Tool Design	I.E.									O	-	●	△												
	C2	Determine labor savings	I.E.	I.E.									-	-	△ ▲													
	C3	Actual writing	P.E.	Tool Dsgn., Fin., I.E.													-	△ O										
Purchase machine tooling, and gauges	D1	Order robot	Purchasing	P.E.													-	- △										
	D2	Design and order or manufacture tooling	Tool Design	Purch., Tooling																		-	- △					
	D3	Specify needed gauges and order or mfg.	Q.C.	Tool Dsgn., Purch.																		-	- △ O					
Installation and startup	E1	Install robot	Plant Layout	Millwrights																		-	△					
	E2	Train employees	Personnel	P.E. Mfg.																		-	△					
	E3	Runoff	Mfg.	Q.C.																							- △ □

Legend:
* Project completion
□ Contractual commitment
△ Planned completion
▲ Actual completion
∧ Status date
O Milestone planned
● Milestone achieved
--- Planned progrss
— Actual progress

Note: As of Jan. 31, 2003, the project is one month behind schedule. This is due mainly to the delay in task C1, which was caused by the late completion of A2.

Figure 5-10   Project master schedule.

5.5   INTERFACE COORDINATION THROUGH INTEGRATION MANAGEMENT

The most difficult aspect of implementing the plan for a complex project is the coordination and integration of the various elements of the project so that they meet their joint goals of performance, schedule, and budget in such a way that the total project meets its goals.

As projects become more complex, drawing on knowledge and skills from more areas of expertise—and, thus, more subunits of the parent organization as well as more outsiders—the problem of coordinating multidisciplinary teams (MTs) becomes more troublesome. At the same time, and as a result, uncertainty is increased. As the project proceeds from its initiation through the planning and into the actual process of trying to generate the project's deliverables, still more problems arise. One hears, "Why didn't you tell us that when we could have done something about it?" One hears, "We tried to tell you that this would happen, but you didn't pay any attention to us." These, as well as less printable remarks, are what one hears when the members of an MT do not work and play well together—in other words, when the various individuals and groups working on the project are not well integrated. Rather than operating as a team, they work as separate and distinct parts, each of which has its own tasks and is not much interested in the other parts.

The intricate process of coordinating the work and timing of the different groups is called *integration management.* The term *interface coordination* is used to denote the process of managing this work across multiple groups. The linear responsibility chart discussed above is a useful aid to the PM in carrying out this task. It displays the many ways the members of the project team (which, as usual, includes all of the actors involved, not forgetting the client and outside vendors) must interact and what the rights, duties, and responsibilities of each will be.

An early approach to this problem was developed by Benningson (1972). Called TREND (Transformed Relationships Evolved from Network Data), the analysis was designed to illustrate important linkages and dependencies between work groups. The aim was to alert the PM to potential problems associated with cross-functional interfaces and to aid in the design of effective ways to avoid or deal with potential interface problems. Benningson added interdependence, uncertainty, and prestige to the mix. The precise way in which these elements were attached to the relationships delineated in the project plan is best seen by reference to Bennigson (1972). (A brief explanation of TREND also appeared in the third edition of this work, pp. 221–24.) A key point is that mapping all dependencies in the project can show a complete description of project interfaces.

Recent work on managing the interfaces focuses on the use of MTs to plan the project as well as design the products/services the project is intended to produce. There is general agreement that MT has a favorable impact on product/service design and delivery. As we noted in Chapter 4, Section 4.3, the Chrysler Corporation's use of concurrent engineering (CE), one form of MT, not only resulted in excellent design, it also produced major economic benefits by shortening the design cycle. Work by Hauptman and Hirji (1996, p. 161) shows that CE has had a "favorable impact . . . on attainment of project budget goals, but achieves this without any adverse impact on quality, cost or schedule." [Note: this entire issue of *IEEE Transactions on Engineering Management* is devoted to CE.] The process also was associated with higher levels of team job satisfaction.

The use of MTs in product development and planning is not without its difficulties. Successfully involving cross-functional teams in project planning requires that some structure be imposed on the planning process. The most common structure is simply to define the task of the group as having the responsibility to generate a plan to accomplish whatever is defined as the project scope. There is considerable evidence that this is not sufficient for complex projects. Using MT creates what Kalu (1993) has defined as a virtual project. In Section 4.3, we noted the high level of conflict in many virtual projects (cf. de Laat, 1994). It follows that MT tends to involve conflict. Conflict raises uncertainty and thus requires risk management. Obviously, many of the risks associated with MT involve intergroup political issues. The PM's negotiating skill will be tested in dealing with intergroup problems, but the outcomes of MT seem to be worth the risks. At times, the risks arise when dealing with an outside group. For an interesting discussion of such issues and their impact on project scope, see Siegle (2001).

In an interesting attempt to give structure to the product design and planning problem and to make creative use of the conflict inherent in MT, Tan, Hayes, and Shaw (1996) proposed a planning model with four components: (1) an integrated base of information about the product plus design and production constraints, both technical and human; (2) software to aid the process of detecting conflicts in the information base, and to aid in the process of resolving those conflicts; (3) software that, given a product design, could generate a production plan and could also simulate changes in the plan suggested by design changes resulting from resolving conflicts; and (4) a model incorporating the knowledge base of the autonomous project team members and a network linking them, their intelligent-agents (computerized assistants), and their computers. The components all use an electronic blackboard for communication so the participants do not need to be in a common location. We suggest that risk identification and assessment be added.

With these parts, the design/planning process is conceptually straightforward. Team members with different technical backgrounds will view the product design task differently. Therefore, initial design ideas will be in conflict. Conflict resolution will result in design improvement, which alters the production plans that are simulated to test manufacturing feasibility. At base, the approach suggested by Tan and her colleagues (1996) uses MT to generate conflicts on the design of a product, and uses the resolution of the conflicts to suggest feasible design improvements.

Bailetti, Callahan, and DiPietro (1994) make a different attack on the problem of interface management. They define and map all interdependencies between various members of the project team. The concept of mapping interdependencies recalls TREND, but TREND maps interfaces on the firm's organization chart while Bailetti, et al. map the interdependencies directly. Because the nature of these interfaces may differ during different phases of the product/service design/production process, they map each major phase separately. Figure 5-11 shows the mapping for the design of a silicon chip.

The logic of this approach to structuring MT is strong. The WBS and linear responsibility charts are a good initial source of information on interfaces, but they do not reflect the uncertainty associated with tasks on large, complex projects. Further, they implicitly assume that interfaces are stable within and across project phases—an assumption often contrary to fact. This does not ignore the value of the WBS, PERT/CPM networks, and similar tools of longstanding use and proven value in project management. It simply uses interface maps as a source of the coordination re-

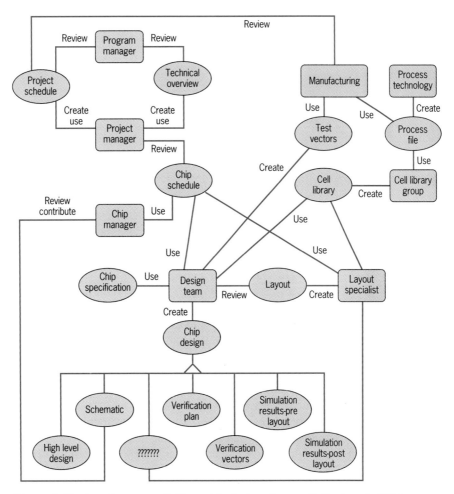

Figure 5-11   Interface map of silicon chip design. *Source*: Bailetti et al., 1994.

quirement to manage the interdependencies. The fundamental structure of this approach to interface management is shown in Figure 5-12.

Managing Projects by Phases and Phase-Gates

The subsection just above notes several ways of attacking the problems that result when the interfaces are not well coordinated. It is clear that they are quite helpful but, alone, are not enough to solve the problems. In addition to mapping the interfaces, a necessary but not sufficient condition for MT peace, the process of using MTs on complex projects must be subject to some more specific kinds of control. Stressing the project's overall objective(s) seems to be inadequate as a unifying force for most teams.

One of the ways to control any process is to break the overall objectives of the process into shorter term subobjectives and to focus the MT on achieving the sub-

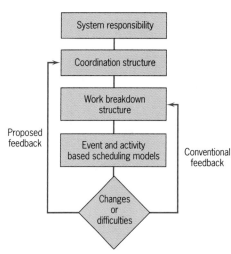

Figure 5-12   Coordination structure model of project management. *Source*: Bailetti et al., 1994.

objectives, often in a preset sequence. If this could be done, and if multidisciplinary cooperation and coordination were required in order to be successful in accomplishing the project, the level of conflict would surely fall. At least there is evidence that if team members work cooperatively and accomplish their short-term goals, the project will manage to meet its long-term objectives; moreover, the outcome of any conflict that does arise will be creative work on the project. This was one of the lessons learned from the concurrent engineering work at Chrysler and from similar successful experiments done elsewhere.

The project life cycle serves as a readily available way of breaking a project up into component parts, each of which has a unique, identifiable output. Cooper and Kleinschmidt (1993) developed such a system with careful reviews conducted at the end of each "stage" of the life cycle. A feature of this system was feedback given to the entire project each time a project review was conducted.

Another attack on the same problem was tied to project quality, again, via the life cycle (Aaron, Bratta, and Smith, 1993). They created 10 phase-gates associated with milestones for a software project. To move between phases, the project had to pass a review. (They even note that in the early stages of the project when there is no "inspectable product," that "... *managing quality on a project means managing the quality of the subprocesses* that produce the delivered product." Emphasis in the original.) While feedback is not emphasized in this system, reports on the finding of project reviews are circulated. The quality-gate process here did not allow one phase to begin until the previous phase had been successfully completed, but many of the phase-gate systems allow sequential phases to overlap in an attempt to make sure that the output of one phase is satisfactory as an input to the next.

There are many such control systems, but the ones that appear to work have two elements in common. First, they focus on relatively specific, short-term, interim outputs of a project with the reviews including the different disciplines involved with the project. Second, feedback (and feedforward) between these disciplines is emphasized. No matter what they are called, they use the fundamental approach of concurrent engineering. When using CE, it must be made clear to all involved that cooperation between the multiple disciplines is required for success, that all parties to the project are mutually dependent on one another.

Finally, it should be stressed that phase-gate management systems were not meant as substitutes for the standard time, cost, and performance controls usually used for project management. Instead, phase-gate and similar systems are intended to create a rigorous set of standards against which to measure project progress. Their primary purpose is to keep senior management informed about the current state of projects being carried out.

SUMMARY

In this chapter we initiated planning for the project in terms of identifying and addressing the tasks required for project completion. We emphasized the importance of initial coordination of all parties involved and the smooth integration of the various systems required to achieve the project objectives. Last, we described some tools such as the Work Breakdown Structure (WBS), the linear responsibility chart, the action plan, and the Gozinto chart to aid in the planning process. We also briefly investigated several methods for controlling and reducing conflict in complex projects that use multidisciplinary teams.

Specific points made in the chapter were these:

- The preliminary work plans are important because they serve as the basis for personnel selection, budgeting, scheduling, and control.

- Top management should be represented in the initial coordinating meeting where technical objectives are established, participant responsibility is accepted, and preliminary budgets and schedules are defined.

- The approval and change processes are complex and should be handled by the project manager.

- Common elements of the project plan are the overview, statement of objectives, general approach, contractual requirements, schedules, budget, cost control procedures, evaluation procedures, and potential problems.

- Systems integration concerns the smooth coordination of project systems in terms of cost, performance, and effectiveness.

- The hierarchical approach (even planning process) to project planning is most appropriate and can be aided by a tree diagram of project subsets, called a Gozinto chart, and a Work Breakdown Structure (WBS). The WBS relates the details of each subtask to its task and provides the final basis for the project budget, schedule, personnel, and control.

- A linear responsibility chart is often helpful to illustrate the relationship of personnel to project tasks and to identify where coordination is necessary.

- When multifunctional terms are used to plan complex projects, their work must be integrated and coordinated. Interface maps are a useful way of identifying the interdependencies that must be managed.

Based on the now-established project plan and WBS, we can consider the task of negotiating for the resources to implement the project. This topic completes Part I of the text.

GLOSSARY

Action Plan   The set of activities, their schedules, and the resources needed to complete the project.

Bill of Materials   The set of physical elements required to build a product.

Control Chart A graph showing how a statistic is changing over time compared to its average and extreme values.

Deliverables The physical items to be delivered from a project. This typically includes reports and plans as well as physical objects.

Earned Value A measure of project progress, frequently related to tasks accomplished and milestones achieved.

Effectiveness Achieving the objectives set beforehand; to be distinguished from efficiency, which is measured by the output realized for the input used.

Engineering Change Orders Product improvements that engineering has designed after the initial product design was released.

Gozinto Chart A pictorial representation of a product that shows how the elements required to build a product fit together.

Hierarchical Planning A planning approach that breaks the planning task down into the activities that must be done at each managerial level. Typically, the upper level sets the objectives for the next lower level.

Interface Management Managing the problems that tend to occur between departments and disciplines, rather than within individual departments.

Material Requirements Planning (MRP) A planning and material ordering approach based on the known or forecast final demand requirements, lead times for each fabricated or purchased item, and existing inventories of all items.

Project Plan The nominal plan to which deviations will be compared.

Systems Engineering The engineering tasks involved in the complete system concerning the project and the integration of all the subsystems into the overall system.

Value Engineering An approach that examines each element of a product or system to determine if there is a better or cheaper way of achieving the same function.

Work Statement A description of a task that defines all the work required to accomplish it, including inputs and desired outputs.

 QUESTIONS

Material Review Questions

1. List the nine component planning sequences of software project planning.

2. Any successful project plan must contain nine key elements. List these items and briefly describe the composition of each.

3. What are the basic guidelines for systems design which assure that individual components of the system are designed in an optimal manner?

4. What are the general steps for managing each work package within a specific project?

5. Describe the "even planning process" and explain why it is helpful.

6. What is shown on a linear responsibility chart? How is it useful to a PM?

7. What should be accomplished at the initial coordination meeting?

8. Why is it important for the functional areas to be involved in the project from the time of the original proposal?

9. What are the three major objectives of systems integration?

10. What are the basic steps to design and use the Work Breakdown Structure?

11. What is the objective of interface management?

Class Discussion Questions

12. What percentage of the total project effort do you think should be devoted to planning? Why?

13. Why do you suppose that the coordination of the various elements of the project is considered the most difficult aspect of project implementation?

14. What kinds of problem areas might be included in the project plan?

15. What is the role of systems integration in project management? What are the three major objectives of systems integration?

16. In what ways may the WBS be used as a key document to monitor and control a project?

17. Describe the process of subdivision of activities and events that composes the tree diagram known as the Work Breakdown Structure or Gozinto chart. Why is the input of responsible managers and workers so important an aspect of this process?

18. Why is project planning so important?

19. What are the pros and cons concerning the early participation of the various functional areas in the project plan?

20. What trade-offs might exist among the three objectives of system integration?

21. Task 5-C is the critical, pacing task of a rush project. Fred always nitpicks anything that comes his way, slowing it down, driving up its costs, and irritating everyone concerned. Normally, Fred would be listed as "Notify" for task 5-C on the responsibility matrix but the PM is considering "forgetting" to make that notation on the chart. Is this unethical, political, or just smart management?

Questions for Project Management in Practice

Extensive Project Planning for Kodak's New Photographic System

22. Compare and contrast Kodak's project plan with the description in the chapter.

23. How do you think Kodak kept a project of this magnitude and involving so many major photographic firms a secret for over a decade?

24. How is this "photographic system" different from another advanced camera?

Disaster Project Planning in Iceland

25. The United States emergency body FEMA (Federal Emergency Management Act) was formed for much the same reasons as Iceland's disasters. How do the two approaches appear to differ?

26. Given a nation so prone to disasters, why do you think it took so long to formulate a contingency disaster plan?

27. The directed reading at the end of this chapter describes four tools for crises in projects. Might any of these be useful to Iceland in their planning?

■ INCIDENTS FOR DISCUSSION

Ringold's Pool and Patio Supply

John Ringold, Jr., just graduated from a local university with a degree in industrial management and joined his father's company as executive vice-president of operations. Dad wants to break John in slowly and has decided to see how he can do on a project that John Sr. has never had time to investigate. Twenty percent of the company's sales are derived from the sale of above-ground swimming pool kits. Ringold's does not install the pools. John Sr. has asked John Jr. to determine whether or not they should get into that business. John Jr. has decided that the easiest way to impress Dad and get the project done is personally to estimate the cost to the company of setting up a pool and then call some competitors and see how much they charge. That will show whether or not it is profitable.

John Jr. remembered a method called the work break-

down structure (WBS) that he thought might serve as a useful tool to estimate costs. Also, the use of such a tool could be passed along to the site supervisor to help evaluate the performance of work crews. John Jr.'s WBS is shown in Table A. The total cost John Jr. calculated was $185.00, based on 12.33 labor-hours at $15.00/labor-hour. John Jr. found that, on average, Ringold's competitors charged $229.00 to install a similar pool. John Jr. thought he had a winner. He called his father and made an appointment to present his findings the next morning. Since he had never assembled a pool himself, he decided to increase the budget by 10 percent, "just in case."

Questions: Is John Jr.'s WBS projection reasonable? What aspects of the decision will John Sr. consider?

Table A. Pool Installation WBS

Works Tasks	Labor-Hours (estimated)
Prepare ground surface	2.67
Clear — 1	
Rake — 1/3	
Level — 1	
Sand bottom — 1/3	
Lay out pool frame	2.50
Bottom ring — 1	
Side panels — 1/2	
Top ring — 1	
Add plastic liner	0.50
Assemble pool	1.66
Build wooden support	3.00
Layout — 1	
Assemble — 2	
Fill and test	2.00
Total	12.33

Better-Built

Better-Built Burner Company of Cleveland, Ohio, is planning to manufacture a new line of mini-CD burners to compete with the small burners made by competitors. The company currently manufactures about 10,000 regular size CD burners per year and hopes to be manufacturing 5000 of the smaller version beginning in two years. The new burner will require a 25 percent enlargement of the existing facility. The company has already selected the project manager and the project team. The project manager is ready to get the project under way. The three aspects she is most concerned about are schedules, resources, and personnel.

Questions: If you were the project manager, which project planning tools would you start with to resolve your concerns? Do these tools relate to each other? Explain.

BIBLIOGRAPHY

AARON, J. M., C. P. BRATTA, AND D. P. SMITH. "Achieving Total Project Control Using the Quality Gate Method." *Proceedings of the Annual Symposium of the Project Management Institute,* San Diego, October 4, 1993.

ANTONIONI, D. "Post-Planning Review Prevents Poor Project Performance." *PM Network,* October 1997.

ARCHIBALD, R. D. "Projects: Vehicles for Strategic Growth." *Project Management Journal,* September 1988.

BADIRU, A. B. *Project Management in Manufacturing and High Technology Operations.* New York: Wiley, 1988.

BAILETTI, A. J., J. R. CALLAHAN, AND P. DI-PIETRO. "A Coordination Structure Approach to the Management of Projects." *IEEE Transactions on Engineering Management,* November 1994.

BENNINGSON, L. A. "TREND: A Project Management Tool." *Proceedings of the Project Management Conference,* Philadelphia, October 1972.

BIGELOW, D. "Planning Is Important—Why Don't We Do More of It?" *PM Network,* July 1998.

BLANCHARD, B. S., AND W. FABRYCKY. *Systems Engineering and Analysis,* 2nd ed. Englewood Cliffs, NJ: Prentice Hall, 1990.

BOEHM, B. W. "A Spiral Model of Software Development and Enhancement." *IEEE Engineering Management Review,* Winter 1995, reprinted from *Computer,* May 1988.

CLELAND, D. I., AND R. K. KIMBALL. "The Strategic Context of Projects." *Project Management Journal,* August 1987.

COOPER, R.G., AND E. J. KLEINSCHMIDT, "Stage-Gate Systems for New Product Success," *Marketing Management,* Vol. 1, No. 4, 1993.

DE LAAT, P. B. "Matrix Management of Projects and Power Struggles: A Case Study of an R & D Laboratory." *IEEE Engineering Management Review,* Winter 1995, reprinted from *Human Relations,* Vol. 47, No. 9, 1994.

DUNCAN, W. R. "Scoping Out A Scope Statement." *PM Network,* December 1994.

ENGLUND, R. L., AND R. J. GRAHAM. "From Experience: Linking Projects to Strategy, *"Journal of Product Innovation Management,* Vol. 16, No. 1, 1999.

FORD, R. C., AND F. S. MCLAUGHLIN. "Successful Project Teams: A Study of MIS Managers." *IEEE Transactions on Engineering Management,* November 1992.

HARRIS, R. D., AND R. F. GONZALEZ. *The Operations Manager.* St. Paul: West, 1981.

HAUPTMAN, O., AND K. K. HIRJI. "The Influence of Process Concurrency on Project Outcomes in Product Development: An Empirical Study of Cross-Functional Teams." *IEEE Transactions on Engineering Management,* May 1996.

HUBBARD, D. G. "Work Structuring," in P. C. Dinsmore, ed., *The AMA Handbook of Project Management.* New York: AMACOM, 1993.

KALU, T. CH. U. "A Framework for the Management of Projects in Complex Organizations." *IEEE Transactions on Engineering Management,* May 1993.

KERZNER, H. *Project Management: A Systems Approach to Planning, Scheduling, and Controlling,* 6th ed. New York: Wiley, 1998.

KNUTSON, J. "How to Manage a Project Launch Meeting." *PM Network,* July 1995.

LANGLEY, A. "Between 'Paralysis by Analysis' and 'Extinction by Instinct.'" *IEEE Engineering Management Review,* Fall 1995, reprinted from *Sloan Management Review,* Spring 1995.

LAUFER, A. "Project Planning: Timing Issues and Path of Progress." *Project Management Journal,* June 1991.

LAVOLD, G. D. "Developing and Using the Work Breakdown Structure," in D. I. Cleland, and W. R. King, *Project Management Handbook.* New York: Van Nostrand Reinhold, 1983.

LIBERATORE, M. J. "A Decision Support System Linking Research and Development Project Selection with Business Strategy." *Project Management Journal,* November, 1988.

LOVE, S. F. *Achieving Problem Free Project Management.* New York: Wiley, 1989.

MARTIN, M. G. "Statement of Work: The Foundation for Delivering Successful Service Projects." *PM Network,* October 1998.

MARTIN, P. K., AND K. TATE. "Kick Off the Smart Way." *PM Network,* October 1998.

MARTINEZ, E. V. "Executives to Project Manager: Get a Plan." *PM Network,* October 1994.

MORRIS, W. T. *Implementation Strategies for Industrial Engineers.* Columbus, OH: Grid, 1979.

PALEY, A. I. "Value Engineering and Project Management: Achieving Cost Optimization," in P. C. Dinsmore, ed., *The AMA Handbook of Project Management.* New York: AMACOM, 1993.

PELLS, D. L. "Project Management Plans: An Approach to Comprehensive Planning for Complex Projects," in P. C. Dinsmore, ed., *The AMA Handbook of Project Management.* New York: AMACOM, 1993.

PINTO, J. K., AND D. P. SLEVIN. "Critical Factors in Successful Project Implementation." *IEEE Transactions on Engineering Management,* February 1987.

PINTO, J. K., AND D. P. SLEVIN. "Project Success: Definitions and Measurement Techniques." *Project Management Journal,* February 1988.

PRENTIS, E. L. "Master Project Planning: Scope, Time and Cost." *Project Management Journal,* March 1989.

Project Management Institute, *A Guide to the Project Management Body of Knowledge* (*PMBOK® Guide*), 2000 ed. Newtown Square, PA: Project Management Institue, 2001.

RAKOS, J. J. *Software Project Management.* Englewood Cliffs, NJ: Prentice Hall, 1990.

ROMAN, D. *R & D Management.* New York: Appleton-Century-Crofts, 1968.

SCHULTZ, R. L., D. P. SLEVIN, and J. K. PINTO. "Strategy and Tactics in a Process Model of Project Implementation." *Interfaces,* May–June 1987.

SEIGLE, G., "Government Projects: Expect the Unexpected," *PM Network,* November, 2001.

SMITH, R. P. "The Historical Roots of Concurrent Engineering Fundamentals." *IEEE Transactions on Engineering Management,* February 1997.

TAN, G. W., C. C. HAYES, and M. SHAW. "An Intelligent-Agent Framework for Concurrent Product Design and Planning." *IEEE Transactions on Engineering Management,* August 1996.

WEBSTER, J. L., W. E. REIF, and J. S. BRACKER. "The Manager's Guide to Strategic Planning Tools and Techniques." *Planning Review*, November/December 1989, reprinted in *Engineering Management Review,* December 1990.

WESTNEY, R. E. "Paradigms for Planning Productive Projects," in P. C. Dinsmore, ed., *The AMA Handbook of Project Management.* New York: AMACOM, 1993.

The following case illustrates the development of a project planning, management, and control system for large capital engineering projects. Senior management's goal in developing the system was primarily financial, in terms of keeping projects from exceeding budget and optimally allocate increasingly scarce investment funds. It is interesting to compare this system to that of Hewlett-Packard in the reading in Chapter 2.

C A S E

A Project Management and Control System for Capital Projects
Herbert F. Spirer and A. G. Hulvey

Introduction

Heublein, Inc., develops, manufactures, and markets consumer food and beverage products domestically and internationally. The business of Heublein, Inc., their sales revenue, and some of their better known products are shown in Figure 1. Highlights of Figure 1 include: The four major businesses ("Groups") use different manufacturing plants, equipment, and processes to produce their products. In the Spirits Group large, continuous-process bottling plants are the rule; in the Food Service and Franchising Group,

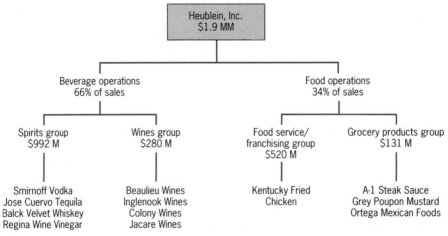

Figure 1   Heublein, Inc.

small fast food restaurants are the "manufacturing plants."

The amount of spending for capital projects and support varies greatly among the Groups, as would be expected from the differences in the magnitude of sales revenues.

The engineering departments of the Groups have responsibility for operational planning and control of capital projects, a common feature of the Groups. However, the differences among the Groups are reflected in differences in the sizes of the engineering departments and their support services. Similarly, financial tracking support varies from full external support to self-maintained records.

Prior to the implementation of the Project Management and Control System (PM&C) described in this paper, the capital project process was chiefly concerned with the financial justification of the projects, as shown in Figure 2. Highlights include:

- A focus on cost-benefit analysis.
- Minimal emphasis on execution of the projects; no mechanism to assure that non-financial results were achieved.

The following factors focused attention on the execution weaknesses of the process:

- Some major projects went over budget.
- The need for optimal utilization of capital funds intensified since depreciation legislation was not keeping pace with the inflationary rise in costs.

Responding to these factors, Heublein's corporate management called for a program to improve execution of capital projects by implementing PM&C. Responsibility for this program was placed with the Corporate Facilities and Manufacturing Department, which, in addition to reviewing all Capital Appropriation Requests, provided technical consulting services to the corporation.

Feasibility Study

Lacking specialized expertise in project management, the Director of Facilities and Manufacturing Planning decided to use a consultant in the field. In-

Figure 2   Capital project progress prior to PM&C.

terviewing of three consultants was undertaken to select one who had the requisite knowledge, compatibility with the style and goals of the firm, and the ability to communicate to all levels and types of managers. The latter requirement was important because of the diversity of the engineering department structures and personnel involved. The first author was selected as the consultant.

With the consultant selected, an internal program manager for PM&C was selected. The deferral of this choice until after selection of the consultant was deliberate, to allow for development of interest and enthusiasm among candidates for this position and so that both the selected individual and the selection committee would have a clear picture of the nature of the program. A program manager was chosen from the corporate staff (the second author).

Having the key staff in place, ground rules were established as follows:

- The PM&C program would be developed internally to tailor it to the specific needs of the Groups. A "canned" or packaged system would limit this flexibility, which was deemed essential in this application of project management principles.
- The directors of the engineering departments of each of the Groups were to be directly involved in both the design and implementation of the PM&C system in total and for their particular Group. This would assure the commitment to its success that derives from ownership and guarantees that those who know the needs best determine the nature of the system.

To meet the above two ground rules, a thorough fundamental education in the basic principles of project management would be given to all involved in the system design.

The emphasis was to be project planning as opposed to project control. The purpose of PM&C was to achieve better performance on projects, not catch mistakes after they have occurred. Success was the goal, rather than accountability or identification of responsibility for failure.

Program Design

The option of defining a uniform PM&C system, to be imposed on all engineering departments by corporate mandate was rejected. The diversity of projects put the weight in favor of individual systems, provided planning and control was such that success of the projects was facilitated. The advantage to corporate staff of uniform planning and reporting was given second place to accommodation of the unique needs of each Group and the wholehearted commitment of each engineering manager to the effective use of the adopted system. Thus, a phased implementation of PM&C within Heublein was planned in advance. These phases were:

Phase 1. Educational overview for engineering department managers. A three-day seminar with two top-level educational objectives: (1) comprehension by participants of a maximal set of project

management principles and (2) explanation of the corporate objectives and recommended approach for any PM&C system.

Phase II. PM&C system design. A "gestation period" of three weeks was deliberately introduced between Phases I and II to allow for absorption, discussion, and review of the project management principles and objectives by the engineering department managers. At the end of this period a session was called for the explicit purpose of defining the system. The session was chaired by the consultant, a deliberate choice to achieve the "lightning rod" effect whereby any negative concern was directed to an outsider. Also, the consultant—as an outsider—could criticize and comment in ways that should not be done by the engineering department managers who will have long-term working relationships among each other. It was agreed in advance that a consensus would be sought to the greatest possible extent, avoiding any votes on how to handle particular issues which leaves the "nay" votes feeling that their interests have been overridden by the majority. If consensus could not be achieved, then the issue would be sidestepped to be deferred for later consideration; if sufficiently important then a joint solution could be developed outside the session without the pressure of a fixed closing time.

Phase III. Project plan development. The output of Phase II (the set of consensus conclusions) represented both guidelines and specific conclusions concerning the nature of a PM&C system. Recognizing that the PM&C program will be viewed as a model project and that it should be used as such, serving as an example of what is desired, the program manager prepared a project plan for the PM&C program. The remainder of this paper is primarily concerned with the discussion of this plan, both as an example of how to introduce a PM&C system and how to make a project plan. The plan discussed in this paper and illustrated in Figures 3 to 11 is the type of plan that is now required before any capital project may be submitted to the approval process at Heublein.

Phase IV. Implementation. With the plan developed in Phase III approved, it was possible to move ahead with implementation. Implementation was in accordance with the plan discussed in the balance of this paper. Evaluation of the results was considered a part of this implementation.

Project Plan

A feature of the guidelines developed by the engineering managers in Phase II was that a "menu" of component parts of a project plan was to be established in the corporate PM&C system, and that elements of this menu were to be chosen to fit the situational or corporate tracking requirements. The menu is:

1. Introduction
2. Project Objectives
3. Project/Program Structure
4. Project/Program Costs
5. Network
6. Schedule
7. Resource Allocation
8. Organization and Accountability
9. Control System
10. Milestones or Project Subdivisions

In major or critical projects, the minimal set of choices from the menu is specified by corporate staff (the definition of a "major" or "critical" project is a part of the PM&C procedure). For "routine" projects, the choice from the menu is left to the project manager.

In the PM&C plan, items 6 and 7, Schedule and Resource Allocation, were combined into one section for reasons which will be described as part of the detailed discussions of the individual sections which follow.

Introduction

In this PM&C system, the Introducton is an executive summary, with emphasis on the justification of the project. This can be seen from the PM&C Program Introduction shown in Figure 3. It is to the advantage of everyone concerned with a project to be fully aware of the reasons for its existence. It is as important to the technicians as it is to the engineers or the corporate financial department. When the project staff clearly comprehends the reason for the project's existence it is much easier to enlist and maintain their support and wholehearted efforts. In the Heublein PM&C system, it is expected that the intro-

---

External and internal factors make it urgent to ensure most efficient use of capital funds. Implementation of a project management and control ("PM&C") system has been chosen as one way to improve the use of capital funds. In March the Corporate Management Committee defined this need.

Subsequently, Corporate Facilities and Manufacturing Planning performed a feasibility study on this subject. A major conclusion of the study was to develop the system internally rather than use a "canned" system. An internally developed system can be tailored to the individual Groups, giving flexibility which is felt to be essential to success. Another conclusion of the study was to involve Group engineering managers in the design and implementation of the system for better understanding and acceptance.

This is the detailed plan for the design and implementation of a corporate-wide PM&C System. The short-term target of the system is major capital projects; the long term target is other types of projects, such as new product development and R&D projects. The schedule and cost are:
   Completion Date: 1 year from approval.
   Cost: $200,000, of which $60,000 is out of pocket.

Figure 3   Introduction to PM&C program project plan.

duction section of a project plan will include answers to these questions: What type of project is involved? What is the cost-benefit relationship? What are the contingency plans? Why is it being done this way (that is, why were alternatives rejected)? Figure 3 not only illustrates this approach, but is the executive summary for the Heublein PM&C system.

Objectives

Goals for a project at Heublein must be stated in terms of deliverable items. To so state a project objective forces the definition of a clear, comprehensible, measurable and tangible objective. Often, deliverable items resulting from a project are documents. In constructing a residence, is the deliverable item "the house" or is it "the certificate of occupancy"? In the planning stages of a project (which can occur during the project as well as at the beginning), asking this question is as important as getting the answer. Also, defining the project in terms of the deliverables tends to reduce the number of items which are forgotten. Thus, the Heublein PM&C concept of

objectives can be seen to be similar to a "statement of work" and is not meant to encompass specifications (detailed descriptions of the attributes of a deliverable item) which can be included as appendices to the objectives of the project.

Figure 4 shows the objectives stated for the Heublein PM&C program. It illustrates one of the principles set for objective statement: that they be hierarchically structured, starting with general statements and moving to increasingly more detailed particular statements. When both particular and general objectives are defined, it is imperative that there be a logical connection; the particular must be in support of the general.

Project Structure

Having a definition of deliverables, the project manager needs explicit structuring of the project to:

- Relate the specific objectives to the general.
- Define the elements which comprise the deliverables.

General Objectives
1. Enable better communication between Group and Corporate management with regard to the progress of major projects.
2. Enable Group management to more closely monitor the progress of major projects.
3. Provide the capability for Group personnel to better manage and control major projects.

Specific Objectives[a]
1. Reporting and Control System
   - For communication of project activity within Group and between Group and Corporate.
   - Initially for high-cost capital projects, then for "critical," then all others.
2. Procedures Manual
   - Document procedures and policies.
   - Preliminary manual available by October 20, 1979, for use in general educational seminars.
3. Computer Support Systems
   - Survey with recommendations to establish need for and value of computer support.
4. General Educational Package
   - Provide basic project planning and control skills to personnel directly involved in project management, to be conducted by academic authority in field.
   - Technical seminars in construction, engineering, contract administration, and financial aspects of project management.

[a]Defined at the PM&C Workshop, attended by representatives of Operating Groups.

Figure 4   Objectives of PM&C program.

- Define the activities which yield the elements and deliverables as their output.
- Show the hierarchical relationship among objectives, elements, and activities.

The work breakdown structure (WBS) is the tool used to meet these needs. While the WBS may be represented in either indented (textual) or tree (graphical) formats, the graphic tree format has the advantage of easy comprehension at all levels. The tree version of the WBS also has the considerable advantage that entries may be made in the nodes ("boxes") to indicate charge account numbers, accountable staff, etc.

Figure 5 is a portion of the indented WBS for the

PM&C Program, showing the nature of the WBS in general and the structure of the PM&C Program project in particular. At this point we can identify the component elements and the activities necessary to achieve them. A hierarchical numbering system was applied to the elements of the WBS, which is always a convenience. The 22 Design Phase Reports (2100 series in Figure 5) speak for themselves, but it is important to note that this WBS is the original WBS: All of these reports, analyses, and determinations were defined prior to starting the program and there were no requirements for additional items.

Project Costs

The WBS provides a listing of the tasks to be performed to achieve the project objectives; with only the WBS in hand it is possible to assemble a preliminary project estimate. The estimates based only on the WBS are preliminary because they reflect not only uncertainty (which varies considerably among types of projects), but because the allocation of resources to meet schedule difficulties cannot be determined until both the network and the schedule and resource evaluations have been completed. However, at this time the project planner can begin to hierarchically assemble costs for use at any level. First the lowest level activities of work (sometimes called "work packages") can be assigned values. These estimates can be aggregated in accordance with the WBS tree structure to give higher level totals. At the root of the tree there is only one element-the project-and the total preliminary estimated cost is available.

Figure 6 shows the costs as summarized for the

Work Breakdown Structure

HEUBLEIN PM&C PROGRAM
1000 Program Plan
2000 PM&C System
  2100 Design-Phase Reports
    2101 Analyze Project Scope
    2102 Define Performance Reports
    2103 Define Project Planning
    2104 Define Revision Procedure
    2105 Define Approval/Signoff Procedure
    .
    .
    .
    2121 Define Record Retention Policy
    2122 Define Computer Support Systems
      Requirements
  2200 Procedures Manual
    2201 Procedures Manual
    2202 Final Manual
  2300 Reporting and Control System
    2400 Computer Support Survey
    2401 PERT/CPM
    2402 Scheduling
    2403 Accounting
3000 General Training
  3100 Project Planning and Control Seminar
    3101 Objective Setting
    3102 WBS
    .
    .
    .

Figure 5 Project structure.

Labor costs	
Development & Design	$ 40,000
Attendees' time in sessions	60,000
Startup time of PM&C in Group	40,000
Basic Educational Package	
Consultants' fees	20,000
Attendees' travel & expenses	30,000
Miscellaneous	10,000
Total Program Cost	$200,000

Out-of-pocket costs: $60,000

Figure 6 Program costs.

PM&C program plan. This example is supplied to give the reader an idea of the nature of the costs to be expected in carrying out such a PM&C program in this type of situation. Since a project-oriented cost accounting system does not exist, out-of-pocket costs are the only incremental charges. Any organization wishing to cost a similar PM&C program will have to do so within the framework of the organizational approach to costing indirect labor. As a guide to such costs, it should be noted that in the Heublein PM&C Program, over 80 percent of the costs—both out-of-pocket and indirect—were in connection with the General Training (WBS code 3000).

Seminars were limited to two and two-and-a-half days to assure that the attendees perceived the educational process as efficient, tight, and not unduly interfering with their work; it was felt that it was much better to have them leaving with a feeling that they would have liked more rather than the opposite.

Knowing the number of attendees, it is possible to determine the labor-days devoted to travel and seminar attendance; consultant/lecturer's fees can be obtained (expect preparation costs) and the incidentals (travel expenses, subsistence, printing, etc.) are easily estimated.

Network

The PM&C system at Heublein requires networks only for major projects, but encourages their use for all projects. Figure 7 shows a segment of the precedence table (used to create the network) for the PM&C Plan. All the usual principles of network creation and analysis (for critical path, for example) may be applied by the project manager to the extent that it facilitates planning, implementation, and control. Considerable emphasis was placed on network creation and analysis techniques in the educational

Act'y Short Descr.	Time (weeks)	Immediate Predecessors
4000 prepare final rpt	2	2000, 2122, 3200
2000 monitor system	6	2000: hold group workshops
2000 hold group w'shps	2	2000: obtain approval
2000 prepare final proc	2	2000: monitor system
2000 prepare final proc manual, revise syst	2	2116–2121: approvals
2000 monitor system	8	2000: hold group workshops
2000 prepares for impl'n	2	3100: hold PM&C seminar
2122 get approval	2	2122: define com & supp needs
2122 def comp supp needs	4	3100: hold PM&C sem
3200 hold tech seminars	4	3200: prepare seminars
3200 prepare seminars	8	3200: obtain approvals
3200 obtain approvals	2	3200: def tech sem needs
3200 def tech sem needs	2	3100: hold PM& C sem
3100 hold PM&C seminar	3	3100: integrate proc man in sem
		2201: revise prel proc man
3100 int. proc man in sem	1	2201: prel. proc manual
2201 revise prel proc man	.6	2201–2300: get approval
.		
.		
.		

Note: Because of space limitations, the network is given in the form of a precedence table. An activity-on-node diagram may be directly constructed from this table. Numerical designations refer to the WBS in Figure 5.

Figure 7   Network of PM&C program.

phases of the PM&C Program because the network is the basis of the scheduling methods presented, is potentially of great value and is one of the hardest concepts to communicate.

In the Heublein PM&C system, managerial networks are desired—networks which the individual project managers will use in their own management process and which the staff of the project can use to self-direct where appropriate. For this reason, the view toward the network is that no one network should exceed 50 nodes. The top-level network represents the highest level of aggregation. Each activity on that network may well represent someone else's next lower level network consisting of not more than 50 nodes. This is not to say that there are not thousands of activities possible in a Heublein project, but that at the working managerial level, each manager or project staff person responsible for a networked activity is expected to work from a single network of a scope that can be easily comprehended. It is not an easy task to aggregate skillfully to reduce network size, but the exercise of this discipline has value in planning and execution in its own right.

The precedence table shown reflects the interdependencies of activities for Heublein's PM&C Program; they are dependent on the design of the Program and the needs of the organization. Each organization must determine them for themselves. But what is important is that institution of a PM&C Program be planned this way. There is a great temptation in such programs to put all activities on one path and not to take advantage of parallel activities and/or not to see just what is the critical path and to focus efforts along it.

Schedule and Resource Allocation

The network defines the mandatory interdependency relationships among the tasks on a project; the schedule is the realization of the intent of the project manager, as it shows when the manager has determined that tasks are to be done. The schedule is constrained in a way that the network is not, for the schedule must reflect calendar limitations (vacations, holidays, plant and vendor shutdowns, etc.) and also the limitations on resources. It is with the schedule that the project manager can develop the resource loadings and it is the schedule which ultimately is determined by both calendar and resource constraints.

Organization and Accountability

Who is responsible for what? Without clear, unambiguous responses to this question there can be no assurance that the task will be done. In general, committees do not finish projects and there should be one organizational unit responsible for each element in the work breakdown structure and one person in that organizational unit who holds final responsibility. Thus responsibility implies a single name to be mapped to the task or element of the WBS, and it is good practice to place the name of the responsible entity or person in the appropriate node on the WBS.

However, accountability may have multiple levels below the top level of complete responsibility. Some individuals or functions may have approval power, veto power without approval power, others may be needed for information or advice, etc. Often, such multilevel accountability crosses functional and/or geographical boundaries and hence communication becomes of great importance.

A tool which has proved of considerable value to Heublein where multilevel accountability and geographical dispersion of project staff is common is the "accountability matrix," which is shown in Figure 8.

The accountability matrix reflects considerable thought about the strategy of the program. In fact, one of its great advantages is that it forces the originator (usually the project manager) to think through the process of implementation. Some individuals must be involved because their input is essential. For example, all engineering managers were essential inputs to establish the exact nature of their needs. On the other hand, some individuals or departments are formally involved to enlist their support, even though a satisfactory program could be defined without them.

Control System

The basic loop of feedback for control is shown in Figure 9. This rationale underlies all approaches to

Activity	PM&C Mgr	Consultant	Mgrs. of Eng.				Dir F&MP
			FS/F	*GPG*	*Wines*	*Spirits*	
Program Plan	I	P					A
Design-Phase Reports	I	P	P	P	P	P	
Procedures Manual	I						A
Reporting & Control System	I	P	P	P	P	P	
Computer Support Survey	I	P					P
Project Planning & Control Seminar	A	I					P
Technical Seminars	I		P	P	P	P	A

Legend: I: Initiate/Responsibility
           A: Approve
           P: Provide input

Figure 8   Accountability matrix for PM&C program.

controlling projects. Given that a plan (or budget) exists, we then must know what is performance (or actual); a comparison of the two may give a variance. If a variance exists, then the cause of the variance must be sought. Note that any variance is a call for review; as experienced project managers are well aware, underspending or early completions may be as unsatisfactory as overspending and late completions.

The PM&C program did not involve large purchases, or for that matter, many purchases. Nor were large numbers of people working on different tasks to be kept track of and coordinated. Thus, it was possible to control the PM&C Program through the use of Gantt conventions, using schedule bars to show plan and filling them in to show performance. Progress was tracked on a periodic basis, once a week.

Figure 10 shows the timing of the periodic reviews for control purpose and defines the nature of the reports used.

Milestones and Schedule Subdivisions

Milestones and Schedule Subdivisions are a part of the control system. Of the set of events which can be, milestones form a limited subset of events, in practice rarely exceeding 20 at any given level. The

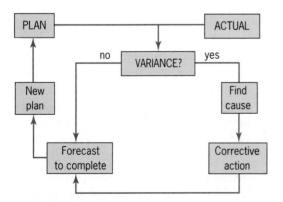

Figure 9   The basic feedback loop of control.

1. Periodic status checking will be performed monthly.
2. Labor costs will be collected manually and estimated where necessary from discussion with Group engineering management.
3. Out-of-pocket costs will be collected through commitments and/or invoice payment records.
4. Monthly status reports will be issued by the PM&C Program project manager including:
   a. Cost to date summaries.
   b. Cost variances.
   c. Schedule performance relative to schedule in Gantt format.
   d. Changes in scope or other modifications to plan.
5. Informal control will be exercised through milestone anticipation by the PM&C Program project manager.

Figure 10   Control system.

milestones are predetermined times (or performance states) at which the feedback loop of control described above (Figure 9) should be exercised. Other subdivisions of the project are possible, milestones simply being a subdivision by events. Periodic time subdivisions may be made, or division into phases, one of the most common. Figure 11 shows the milestones for the PM&C Program.

Summary

The Heublein PM&C Program met the conditions for a successful project in the sense that it was completed on time and within the budgeted funds. As is so often the case, the existence of a formal plan and continuing reference to it made it possible to deal with changes of scope. Initial reaction to the educational package was so favorable that the population

of attendees was increased by Group executives and engineering managers.

To deliver on time and within budget, but to deliver a product which does not serve the client's needs is also unsatisfactory. Did this PM&C Program achieve the "General Objectives" of Figure 5? As is so often the case in managerial systems and educational programs, we are forced to rely on the perceptions of the clients. In this PM&C Program, the clients are Corporate Management, Group Management, and most importantly, the Managers of Engineering and their staffs. In the short run, the latter two operational clients are primary. In addition to informal feedback from them, formal feedback was obtained in the form of Impact Statements (item number 4000 in the WBS of Figure 5). The Impact Statements concerned the impact of the PM&C Program on the concerned organization ("How many

Date	Description
09/05/79	Program plan approved by both Corporate & Groups
09/26/79	Reporting and control system approved by Corporate and Groups
10/05/79	Organizational impact analysis report issued
11/07/79	Basic project planning and control seminars completed
01/07/80	Reporting and control system implemented
03/24/80	Final procedures manual approved
	Technical Seminars completed
	Computer support systems survey completed
06/30/80	Final impact assessment report issued

Figure 11   Milestones.

labor-hours are expected to be devoted to the PM&C System?) and response to the PM&C Program ("Has this been of value to you in doing your job better?").

Clearly, the response of perceived value from the operating personnel was positive. Can we measure the improvement which we believe to be taking place in the implementation of capital and other projects? It may be years before the impact (positive or negative) can be evaluated, and even then there may be such confounding with internal and external variables that no unequivocal, quantified response can be defined.

At this point we base our belief in the value of the PM&C Program on the continuing flow-starting

with Impact Statements-of positive perceptions. The following is an example of such a response, occurring one year after the exposure of the respondent:

> . . . find attached an R&D Project Tracking Diagram developed as a direct result of the [PM&C] seminar . . . last year. [In the seminar we called it] a Network Analysis Diagram. The Product Development Group has been using this exclusively to track projects. Its value has been immeasurable. Since its inception, fifteen new products have gone through the sequence. . . .

QUESTIONS

1. Which of the project planning aids (WBS, etc.) described in the chapter was used in the case?
2. For each of the aids used in the case, describe how they were constructed and if there were any modifications in form.
3. Compare this project with the Project Portfolio Process and Hewlett-Packard's project management process in the reading for Chapter 2.

4. What was the purpose of the PM&C project? Was it successful?
5. What was wrong with the previous focus on cost-benefit? Does the PM&C system still include a cost-benefit analysis?
6. Why did lagging depreciation legislation increase the importance of using capital funds optimally?

The following reading applies the planning tools from emergency management to projects with their inevitable crises. The application of risk analysis, contingency plans, logic charts, and tabletop exercises is discussed in terms of both planning for and managing crises when they actually occur. Examples such as the 1996 Atlanta Olympic Games are used to illustrate the effectiveness of crisis planning tools.

R E A D I N G

PLANNING FOR CRISES IN PROJECT MANAGEMENT*
L. M. Mallak, H. A. Kurstedt, Jr., G. A. Patzak

Project managers can't always foresee every contingency when planning and managing their projects. Many spurious events affecting project milestones and

*Project Management Institute, Inc., *Project Management Journal,* June 1997, Vol. 28, Number 2. ©1997, Project Management Institute, Inc. All rights reserved.

resource allocations can surface once the project is under way. Experienced project managers find crises, miscommunications, mistakes, oversights, and disasters must be managed as part of successful project management.

Project managers need effective tools to plan for and anticipate these crises. These are tools project managers may not use every day, yet they need these tools to serve them in time of emergency. The ideas and information in this paper will help project managers identify the appropriate crisis planning tools and how to use them. The project manager's experience, training, and skills should allow the understanding and use of these emergency management tools to support quicker and better decision making. In a crisis the worst decision is no decision and the second worst decision is a late one (Sawle, 1991). Managing crises better means mitigating and preparing for crises so we can reduce their occurrence and manage the consequences better if crises do occur. Based on the authors' experience in emergency management for the public and private sectors and several experiences shared in the literature, we recommend ways of planning for crises in projects.

We offer a brief list of emergency management planning tools and skills for project managers: risk analyses, contingency plans, logic charts, and tabletop exercises. These tools have different uses in different types of crises, whether they are natural, chemical/technological, or security types of crises. They also require different kinds of support—police, fire, medical, rescue, etc.

Crises are analyzed from the project management perspective, identifying the similarities and differences between crises in project management and crises in general. We discuss crisis planning strategies and tools by looking at the tools used for emergency management and investigating how we can modify them or design new tools for crisis management in projects.

Framing the Crisis

Many crises become projects once the deleterious effects are gone. A commercial airline crash, such as TWA 800 in summer 1996, where all passengers and crew died, is managed as a project once the threat of explosion and other immediate dangers diminish. However, we're concerned with crises occurring within an existing project, rather than a crisis or emergency that becomes a project.

In many of emergency management's phases and types, the primary skills required are project management skills we're already familiar with. When we're in an emergency situation and we're in the mitigation, preparedness, or recovery phase in a chronic, long-term emergency, we can readily apply our project management skills. The focus of this paper is the use of emergency management tools to aid in anticipating and

planning for crises in projects. Project managers need additional tools to respond to acute emergencies—here is where emergency management tools become paramount.

The scope of application for emergency management tools will vary based on the size of the project. The tools can be quite elaborate, such as volumes for a risk analysis or reserved space for an emergency operations center (EOC) with many dedicated phone lines. The tools can also be quite simple, such as a one- to two-page list of risks in priority order or a designated office or conference room (to function as a mini-EOC) with the ability to bring in portable phones. All the tools should be used, even if just in simple form. In a small project, using one hour of a staff meeting to assign roles in the event of a crisis may suffice for more elaborate means in a larger project. The elaborateness of tools should be balanced with the cost and time required for preparation.

Typical project management requires attention to issues of cost, schedule, and quality. As the customer demands for quality increase, either the cost or the schedule must yield to balance these new demands. But at what point do increased demands reach a crisis point? Increased demands may lead to a perplexity. A perplexity is "an event with an unknown start and an unknown end." An example of a perplexity is an earthquake centered around the New Madrid (Mo.) fault line—we don't know when the earthquake will occur, for how long, nor what the extent of damage will be. In fact, the earthquake may not occur in our lifetime. The opposite of a perplexity is a process, an event with a known start and a known end and the cycle is constantly repeated (as in a manufacturing process). The concept of perplexity helps in understanding the amount and level of uncertainty faced in emergency planning for projects.

In this paper, a crisis could be externally generated, as in an earthquake, deregulation, loss of key executives through accidental death (airplane or automobile crash), or internally generated, as in a plant explosion or a strike. We use Lagadec's (1993) definition of a crisis as being an incident that upsets normal conditions, creating a disturbance that cannot be brought back to normal using existing or specialized emergency functions. A crisis, according to Lagadec, can occur when the incident passes a certain level or when the system is unstable or close to the breaking point before the incident took place. Consequently, crises considered in this paper disrupt project activities to the point where new (and typically unanticipated) decisions must be made to continue the project.

Projects have characteristics that make the design and preparation of elaborate tools difficult. First, many projects lack the permanence of a large plant, mine, or government installation. Second, emergencies in smaller projects tend to be more constrained to the site, while larger projects must deal with emergencies of greater scope and impact, such as chemical and radiological releases. Third, in a plant, a large number of people are affected by an emergency—especially the public as opposed to the workers. When the public or a large number of workers are involved, the organization's confidence in safe operations has a heavy influence, and this begets elaborateness. A simple tool can afford us most of the protection we need (for example, 70% of maximum), while a more elaborate tool will buy us more confidence and protection (perhaps up to 99% of maximum). The more elaborate tool is worth the investment when confidence is at stake.

Tools to Help Project Managers Plan for Crises

We've chosen four types of tools used primarily in emergency management to help project managers plan for crises better. We'll describe and show how to apply risk analyses, contingency plans, logic charts, and tabletop exercises.

Risk Analysis.   An essential crisis planning tool is risk analysis. Risk analysis helps us find out what can go wrong, what's most probable, and what has the greatest impact. The combination of an event's probability of occurrence and severity of consequences (e.g., catastrophic failure) determines priorities. Incident analysis can also help us understand the lessons learned in an actual crisis and develop plans to mitigate the effects of similar incidents in the future.

The 1996 Olympic Games in Atlanta presented many potential disruptions to area businesses (Bradford, 1996). Comprehensive contingency plans were needed to increase the potential for business continuity. Atlanta-based BellSouth Business Systems' Director of Business Continuity Services John Copenhaver stated, "If you plan for a medium-case scenario and a worst-case scenario happens, it's like having no plans at all." BellSouth's plan attempted to minimize disruptions during the Olympics through special arrangements for deliveries, telecommuting, and increased modem pools so employees could work from home. BellSouth conducted a vulnerability assessment and then put systems into place to avoid interruptions to service or minimize the impact of interruptions.

Another Bell company, BellSouth Advertising and Publishing Co. (BAPCO), saw the need to develop a plan to deal with the human side of crises (traumatic stress), because those could disable a firm just as well as interruption of normal business operations (e.g., phone, equipment, facilities) (Kruse, 1993). BAPCO brought in a consultant team to deliver a one-day crisis management training session. The training was given to members of a human resources crisis team and other members of management who wanted to participate. Through counseling, housing, "BellMart," rental cars, and other support mechanisms, BAPCO weathered Hurricane Andrew much better than most South Florida organizations. BellMart was a stocked warehouse of essentials that BAPCO employees (and even their non-BAPCO neighbors) were invited to visit to take whatever they needed. Eighty-five percent of BAPCO employees were affected by the hurricane, although none were killed by the hurricane. The company pointed to several initiatives that were taken to reduce traumatic stress so that people could return to work sooner and with fewer worries. These initiatives included a rapid deployment system to immediately attend to their employees' needs, determining those needs in advance, heading off traumatic stress with constant information (daily bulletin, people sought out on phone, foot, car, etc.), bringing in BAPCO volunteers from other areas, making cash available immediately, and giving employees time off from work to get their personal lives together.

Sometimes nature surprises us and sometimes nature just tests us. The Virginia Department of Transportation (VDOT) had an opportunity to test its emergency preparedness in a potential disaster that never materialized (Slack, 1996). Hurricane Bertha threatened to slam into Virginia as a full-force hurricane, but then weakened into a tropical gale with heavy winds and rain—not the widespread destruction of a hurricane. Bertha served as a drill for VDOT's Emergency Operations Center (EOC), which used a new computer system designed to keep various safety agencies up to date with the latest information during a crisis. One of the problems VDOT faced during many natural disasters was conflicting information among VDOT, state police, local police, and other state agencies involved in emergency response. All parties now have the same information via a real-time connection, rather than each agency gathering its own information.

The availability of accurate, real-time information is

not enough to mitigate crises in project management. Good implementation of risk analysis helps to plan and properly prepare for crises in projects and take steps to reduce the occurrences of crises. Engineering analyses support this process of risk analysis and make up the quantitative portion of mitigation. Cause-and-effect analyses make up the qualitative portion of mitigation and help us assess the systematic effects both forward and backward.

In emergency management, we use risk analysis to find out the risks beforehand. The use of risk analysis in this paper should be differentiated from a probabilistic risk analysis. Establishing consequences of accidents or incidents by deterministic or risk analysis provides effective tools in emergency management. In project management, we concentrate on planning and sequencing activities to maximize our efficiencies and effectively schedule resources.

Illinois Power (IP) has a risk analysis process, called the Risk Register, that was developed and implemented in 1988 and serves as a comprehensive risk assessment system. "The Risk Register is a formal process that identifies, quantifies, and categorizes the risks facing Illinois Power, develops cost-effective methods to control them, and positions the company to achieve its stated goals" (Leonard, 1995). The system continually assesses new risks, generates information for decision-making and supports employees at all levels.

IP's Risk Register process has five phases: risk analysis, mitigation development, mitigation selection, implementation, and monitoring. In conjunction with the Risk Register, IP has a Corporate Disaster Recovery Plan. This plan is designed to "obtain information on levels of damage, resource availability, and the status of restoration activities; provide timely and accurate information to the media, government officials, regulatory authorities, employees, and the general public; give guidance on restoration activities; coordinate acquisition and allocation of resources and coordinate operations with city, county, state and federal emergency-service operations" (Leonard, 1995).

For each identified risk, IP decides on a post-loss goal—in other words, the minimum acceptable capabilities following an event. The post-loss goal sets the target for what the crisis management tool should help IP achieve and helps reduce uncertainty during and after an event.

Contingency Plans. Once the risk analysis is performed, project managers must translate those risks into contingency plans. Project managers need to sit down and ask, "What can go wrong with my project?" Once identified, the project manager has a list of risks associated with a particular project—the output of a risk analysis. Then they should ask, "Which of these risks is most likely to happen?" and "Which of these will have the greatest impact?" "On what or whom?" This last question implies the vulnerability of the organization to the identified risks. Project managers should develop plans that use the data from a risk analysis to prepare them and their organizations for the broadest range of emergencies.

Appointing a person to be in charge of crisis planning puts responsibility and resources together, thereby reducing the need to overload already busy executives with planning for a low-probability event. Nestle U.S.A., Inc.'s headquarters are in Glendale, California, a suburb of Los Angeles. To support its contingency planning efforts, Nestle has appointed a director of business interruption planning (Ceniceros, 1995). As part of its contingency plan, Nestle has a contract with the Stouffer Renaissance Esmeralda, a resort hotel in the desert near Palm Springs, stipulating that the hotel has three days to empty out its ballroom if Nestle needs the space to resume business. The hotel was selected because it is already set up to provide comfort, food, and beverages—and that relieves the demands on Nestle managers and counselors, so they can get back into serving their customers more rapidly and effectively. "Concern for personnel in planning for business resumption is just as important as facilities or data recovery" (Ceniceros, 1995). Nestle has contracts with work-area-recovery vendors that have 72 hours to deliver office materials to the hotel. The hotel is accessible from an airport in Palm Springs, which expands access from Phoenix, should supplies need to come from elsewhere.

Nestle's contingency plan was tested with good results: "With the help of two furniture installation specialists and some hotel staff, the ballroom can quickly convert into 300 workstations complete with copy machines, computers, telecommunication cables, double-circuited power distribution panels, and everything else workers usually take for granted, such as sound barriers so business can be conducted with minimal distractions. . . . At our last exercise, we pulled together 100 workstations in 20 clock hours" (Ceniceros, 1995).

Risk analyses support planning by helping project managers pick the most probable and most severe events combined with a vulnerability assessment to see who or what is vulnerable and what will be affected. Therefore, when the crisis occurs, the project manager has thought about the crisis and what can be affected. Plans incorporating this thinking help the project manager be ready when the crisis occurs and do what is necessary to fix it. If a manager is responsible for a project, he or she should require that someone conduct a risk analysis. The risk analysis improves early recognition of warning signs; the vulnerability assessment helps identify whom to notify and how to start support to them early.

Logic Charts. Logic charts employ project flow logic to show the project flow with all dependencies in an extremely flexible, time-scale-independent diagram. Logic charts are a form of expert system because they embody the decision-making knowledge of the expert in a system that can be followed procedurally. Project flow logic is the basis for any personal computer-assisted project management tool. Project managers are skilled at charting. But, in times of crisis, different types of charts are needed.

When a crisis occurs, people need procedures to follow. Logic charts form the basis for writing these procedures. In project management, the most commonly used charts are Gantt charts for looking at activities against time and networks for looking at precedence. Emergency logic charts depend heavily on logic because of branching due to chained contingencies (e.g., "if event A and event B happened, then event C is likely").

Logic charts provide an overview of principal emergency response events and recovery operations. The charts also depict decisions, notifications, support requests, and public information actions. Use of properly prepared charts take the affected site personnel through event discovery, event assessment, identification of emergency classification level, and to the activation of on-site response actions.

Logic charts force project managers to think through the critical decisions necessary in a crisis. Project managers won't have time to go through the logic chart when the actual emergency occurs—the project manager must learn from the preparation and thinking required to construct a logic chart and feed this into or reinforce it through a tabletop exercise. When the crisis occurs, the project manager isn't thinking as clearly as usual, and the more that has been done before the crisis occurs, the better action the project manager can take.

The Oak Ridge Office (ORO) of the U.S. Depart-ment of Energy (DOE) used logic charts in its emergency response and recovery operations. ORO's logic charts offered specific steps to take based on the type of event. The first step was event discovery, where provisions for an initial response were depicted. This resulted in an event assessment leading to an initial emergency classification. Four levels of emergency classification followed, each evoking a particular response: a hazardous materials Usual Event (non-radiological), a hazardous materials Alert, a Site Emergency, and a General Emergency. A logic chart corresponding to the event discovery and initial response logic is shown in Figure 1.

Tabletop Exercises. Tabletops and other exercises use the information from the risk analysis in the mitigation phase to simulate the decision-making and action-taking occurring in an actual crisis. A tabletop exercise involves assembling the people who will be responding to a crisis and acting out possible scenarios in advance, usually in a conference room or similar space. There, without the pressure of time or the actual crisis, people have the freedom to discuss alternatives and decide on the best courses of action in a given situation. Tabletops also provide the opportunity to rehearse the steps to take in a potential crisis. These same techniques can help project managers prepare for possible crises that may occur in their projects.

The events or crises occurring to project managers won't be the things being tracked. What we don't track is what will go wrong. The need for tracking illustrates the use of a structured management process to catch the small problems through a thorough, systematic, and frequent review of relevant indicators (Kurstedt, Mallak & Pacifici, 1992).

Gershanov (1995) offers a five-stage process for holding tabletop exercises. Stage 1 is to identify significant policy issues surrounding disasters in the organization. This identification may be done using an assessment tool, reviewing documents on responses to previous disasters, researching competitors' experiences, and reviewing debriefings of past exercises. Stage 2 examines these issues and isolates appropriate discussion questions. These discussion questions must be appropriate to the participants' level of responsibility in the organization. Discussion questions should address policy-level rather than operations-level concerns. Stage 3 is the tabletop exercise itself. According to Gershanov, one realistic scenario that encompasses the essential issues and problems should drive the exer-

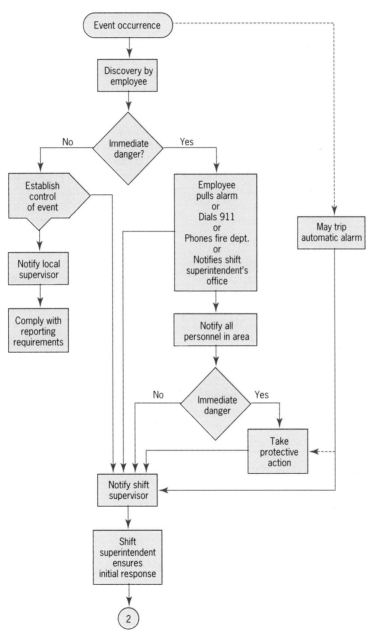

Figure 1   Event Discovery and Initial Response Logic Chart.

cise. A written version of the scenario should be available for the participants to refer to during the exercise. An outside facilitator with experience in emergency preparedness planning should run the exercise. Stage 4 is the debriefing of the exercise, providing a basis for further action and bringing a sense of closure to the exercise. Stage 5, follow-up planning, concerns how the outcomes of the debriefing will be handled and getting commitment to developing plans based on the tabletop exercise.

Tabletop exercises were used in planning for security for the 1996 Democratic National Convention (DNC) in Chicago (O'Connor, 1996). The Federal Emergency Management Agency (FEMA) facilitated tabletop exercises with members of the Chicago Police Department, the FBI, and the Secret Service to examine various scenarios and work out what would be done. Chicago Police also observed training and security practices for the 1996 Atlanta Olympic Games for lessons they could bring back to the DNC in Chicago.

Tabletop exercises are generally used in the beginning of crisis planning and focus on managerial information flows—who we talk to, what we do, who needs what information, and so forth. Issues surface in tabletops. Tabletops are a training device used to elicit understanding by carefully guiding the participants through a simulated emergency requiring a response. Although tabletop exercises are typically less expensive to conduct than drills or field exercises, they cannot substitute for the simulation of actual emergency events available through drills and field exercises.

Tabletop exercises should be conducted every quarter to keep emergency plans, procedures, and necessary thinking fresh in project managers' minds. Thinking through the decisions beforehand in an evaluative session such as a tabletop pays off when a real crisis occurs.

Tabletop exercises force managers to think through the decisions made during a crisis in advance, thereby reducing the need for decision-making during the crisis and reducing the time needed to make those decisions. "A tabletop is accomplished in controlled phases to allow discrete, individual answers, which focuses group attention on each point and thereby promotes a common understanding of roles and responsibilities and the entire response sequence by all participants" (Walker & Middleman, 1988). The tabletop exercise is a versatile tool that can be applied to all phases of project management. The overarching benefit of tabletops is they require people and systems to pay attention both during development and as the system evolves (Walker & Middleman).

One essential element to have in place for effective crisis management is a notification system. An effective notification system not only provides for contacting emergency response units, authorities, and key decision-makers, but also provides for accounting for personnel whereabouts and disposition.

After the 1996 Atlanta Olympics bombing, a plan to track the whereabouts of U.S. athletes and officials was deployed within 15 minutes of the blast (Lloyd, 1996). Dick Schultz, executive director of the U.S. Olympic Committee, stated: "In a two-hour time span, we not only determined the location of everybody, we had them secured. We had put together a crisis management plan for as many situations as we needed to" (Lloyd, 1996). Each U.S. Athlete was issued a pager, the first time that this was ever done in an Olympics. The ability to account for all athletes and their whereabouts provides evidence for the effectiveness of their crisis plan.

Risk analysis, contingency planning, logic charts, and tabletop exercises represent several of the more common tools to help plan for crises in projects. Table 1 summarizes these tools by output. Project managers should think through their projects, in consultation with other project personnel, to select and use the tools judged to be most effective for the specific project. Once selected, these tools should be developed and tested to ensure people understand how to use them and what types of outcomes will result. Most certainly, any test of the tools results in refinement of the tools and learning on participants' behalf.

Recommendations for Project Managers

While we don't have a closed set of comprehensive strategies to offer other project managers to better plan for crises, we do have several recommendations to offer based on experience in emergency management.

Table 1.   Summary of Crisis Planning Tools

Tools	Output
Risk analysis	Identification of risks
Contingency plan	Steps to take based on identified risks
Logic chart	Specific steps to take in a crisis
Tabletop exercise	Rehearse, discuss, and solidify a specific emergency response

Considering the uncertainty involved in crisis management, we would be wary of any closed set of strategies. Crisis management, by definition, is perplexing, constantly changing, full of uncertainties, and challenging to any manager, especially the project manager. Crisis planning logically parallels the uncertain nature of crisis management. Although there is no simple solution to the complex problems posed by crises, here are our recommendations:

- Even for small projects, assign the job of developing at least a two-page risk analysis and contingency plan before the project begins. This is similar to a company appointing a manager of business interruption planning.

- Assign the job of producing a notification sequence.

- Use logic charts to design procedures that won't go awry during a crisis.

- Use tabletop exercises, because few people will look at a logic chart or even a procedure when a crisis occurs. Project managers will depend on what they've practiced, and this underscores the need and value of tabletops.

- Conduct these tabletop exercises quarterly to ensure readiness and to update procedures and responsibilities.

- Establish authority for crisis management before the crisis. The project manager isn't always the best emergency manager, so choose the person who has greatest knowledge of the operational issues associated with the crisis.

- Use emergency planning processes in projects, including risk analysis and contingency planning.

- Design effective, accurate, and timely feedback systems to provide early warning signs of failure and impending crises. A structured management process can help in focusing attention on regular tracking of relevant and critical indicators to surface the little problems before they become big ones. Become sensitive to indicators of impending project failure. Pay special attention to untracked indicators, because these are the most likely to cause trouble. Develop antennae and know when the project is going wrong.

- Choose a project manager indigenous to the country where the project is being conducted. An indigenous project manager will be sensitive to the social and political aspects of the project and its peripheral issues and will catch more problems while they're small or otherwise undetectable to the outsider.

- Be mindful of the social and political consequences of crises or events. Critics, or stakeholders, bear significant influence on project success regardless of what the indicators of cost, schedule, and quality show. Learn how to satisfy stakeholders (Mallak, Patzak & Kurstedt,1991). Identify one spokesperson as a liaison with the public and prepare a procedure for quick dissemination of information to all affected parties.

- Adopt a systems view and separate the crisis from the origin of the crisis. Consider the basic performance principles and problem analysis techniques popularized in total quality management programs. Look forward and backward to access the potential overall effects of the crisis.

These tools, recommendations, and strategies should help project managers to manage their crises better and perhaps to avoid some crises altogether. Making time and resources available to those in charge of crisis planning is essential; otherwise these critical tasks will be subordinated to the day-to-day activities, a vicious circle that can increase the likelihood for a larger crisis going undetected until it's too late. The regular and proper use and testing of risk analyses, contingency plans, logic charts, and tabletop exercises should surface the information, discussion of decisions and actions, and mitigation techniques that may reduce the occurrence and impact of crises in projects.

Acknowledgments

The preparation of this paper was partially funded by U.S. Department of Energy (DOE) Grant No. DE-FG05-86DP70033.

References

Bradford, M. (1996, February 2). Firms may be caught in a five-ring circus: With games on, planning will pay off. *Business Insurance,* P. 3.

Ceniceros, R. (1995, October 23). Nestle resorts to crisis. *Business Insurance*, p. 83.

GERSHANOV, K. M. (1995). Emergency preparedness in five easy steps. *Occupational Health and Safety,* 64 (3), 51–53.

KRUSE, C. (1993, June). Disaster plan stands test of hurricane. *Personnel Journal,* 36–43.

KURSTEDT, H. A., JR., MALLAK, L. A., & PACIFICI, L. C. (1992). Expand quality management into the customer's environment to establish effective measures and standards. *Proceedings of the 1st International Symposium on Productivity and Quality Improvement,* February 1992, 478–485.

LAGADEC, P. (1993). *Preventing chaos in a crisis.* London: McGraw-Hill.

LEONARD, J. B. (1995). Assessing risk systematically: Illinois Power's risk assessment system. *Risk Management,* 42:1, p. 12.

LLOYD, J. (1996, July 28). U.S. official says athletes were safe—and feel safe. *USA Today,* p. 3C.

MALLAK, L. A., PATZAK, G. R., & KURSTEDT, JR., H. A. (1991). Satisfying stakeholders for successful project management. *Computers and Industrial Engineering,* 21, 429–433.

O'CONNOR, P. J. (1996, May 23). Security practice for convention called a success. *Chicago Sun-Times,* p. 23.

SAWLE, W. S. (1991). Concerns of project managers: Crisis project management. *PM Network,* 5(1), 25–29.

SLACK, C. (1996, July 15). Bertha gives VDOT center real-life situation to test computer system. *Richmond Times Dispatch,* p. D–13.

WALKER, J. A., & MIDDLEMAN, L. I. (1988). Tabletop exercise programs complement any emergency management system. *Proceedings of the ANS Topical Meeting on Emergency Response—Planning, Technologies, and Implementation.* Charleston, SC.

Questions

1. Planning for inevitable crises seems to be quite logical, yet is rarely done in projects. Why?

2. Would some of these tools have been of value to Iceland in the Project Management in Practice example?

3. Scenario analysis—the brainstorming of possible crises and anticipation of their outcomes—seems like another useful tool here. How does this approach compare to the tools described?

4. Which of the four tools would have the most value? Which would be easiest to implement?

5. In their recommendations to project managers regarding implementing these tools, which recommendations are most important?

CHAPTER

6

Conflict and Negotiation

Conflict has been mentioned many times thus far in this book. This chapter is about conflict. It is also about negotiation—the skill required to resolve most conflicts. The question arises, why should there be so much conflict on projects? One of several causes is that conflict arises when people working on the same project have somewhat different ideas about how to achieve project objectives. But why should such a disagreement occur? Is there not "one best way?" There may be one best way, but exactly which way is the "one best" is a matter surrounded by uncertainty. Most conflicts have their roots in uncertainty, and negotiation is a way of managing the resultant risk. Therefore, this chapter is also about risk management, about dealing with conflicts that often arise from uncertainty.

As we noted in Chapter 5, the process of planning a project usually requires inputs from many people. Even when the project is relatively small and simple, planning involves the interaction of almost every functional and staff operation in the organization. It is virtually impossible for these interactions to take place without conflict, and when a conflict arises, it is helpful if there are acceptable methods to reduce or resolve it.

This chapter thus represents somewhat of an aside in our progress through the project management life cycle, the organizational principle of this book. Planning would normally be followed by budgeting and scheduling, but during the planning process the need for some rational means of addressing interpersonal/intergroup conflicts arises. The matters discussed in this chapter all impact on the plan and the planning process, and do so in ways that are not obvious until both the planning process and the output of that process are well understood.

Conflict has been defined as "the process which begins when one party perceives that the other has frustrated, or is about to frustrate, some concern of his" (Thamhain and Wilemon, 1975a, p. 891). While conflict can arise over issues of belief or feelings or behavior, our concern in this chapter is focused for the most part on goal conflicts that occur when an individual or group pursues goals different from those of other individuals or groups (Raiffa, 1982, Chapter 12). A party to the conflict will be satisfied when the level of frustration has been lowered to the point where no action, present or future, against the other party is contemplated. When all parties to the conflict are satisfied to this point, the conflict is said to be resolved.

There are, of course, many ways to resolve conflict. Brute force is a time-honored method, as is the absolute rule of the monarch, but the rule of law is the method of choice for modern societies—in spite of occasional lapses. Conflict resolution is the ultimate purpose of law.

Organizations establish elaborate and complex sets of rules and regulations to settle disputes between the organization itself and the individuals and groups with whom it interacts. Contracts between a firm and its suppliers, its trade unions, and its customers are written to govern the settlement of potential conflicts. But the various parties-at-interest (stakeholders) do not always agree about the meaning of a law or a provision in a contract. No agreement, however detailed, can cover all the circumstances that might arise in the extensive relationships between the buyer and the seller of complicated industrial equipment, between the user and the supplier of engineering consulting services, between the producer and user of computer programs—the list of potential conflicts is endless. Our overcrowded courts are witness to the extent and variety of conflict. According to the web page of the New York State Bar Association, there are approximately 850,000 lawyers in the United States. The great majority of this group that numbers between 25 and 35 percent of the world's supply of lawyers are employed in helping conflicting parties to adjudicate or settle their differences.

In this chapter, we examine the nature of negotiation as a means of reducing or resolving the kinds of conflict that typically occur within projects. But before we begin the discussion, it must be made quite clear that *this chapter is not a primer on how to negotiate;* a course in negotiation is beyond the scope of this book and beyond our expertise (for such information, the reader is referred to the bibliography). Rather, this chapter focuses on the roles and applications of negotiation in the management of projects. Note also that we have excluded negotiations between the organization and outside vendors. In our experience, this type of negotiation is conducted sometimes by the project manager, sometimes by the project engineer, but most often by members of the organization's purchasing department. In any case, negotiations between buyer and seller are admirably covered by Hajek (1984) and Raiffa (1982).

As we noted in the previous chapter, conflict can play a creative role in the planning process. Debate over the proper technical approach to a problem often generates a collaborative solution that is superior to any solution originally proposed. Conflict often educates individuals and groups about the goals/objectives of other individuals and groups in the organization, thereby satisfying a precondition for valuable win-win negotiations (see Section 6.3). Indeed, the act of engaging in win-win negotiations serves as an example of the positive outcomes that can result from such an approach to conflict resolution.

In Chapter 3 we noted that negotiation was a critical skill required of the project manager. In this chapter, we describe typical areas of project management where this skill is mandatory. In addition, we will cover some of the appropriate and inappropriate approaches to negotiation, as well as a few of the characteristics of successful negotiation suggested by experts in the field or indicated by our experience. We will also note some ethical issues regarding negotiation. There are probably more opportunities for ethical missteps in handling conflicts and negotiations than in any other aspect of project management. Unlike other chapters, we will use comparatively few illustrative examples. Successful negotiation tends to be idiosyncratic to the actual situation, and most brief examples do little to help transform theory into practice. We have, however, included a vignette at the end of the chapter. This vignette was adapted from "real life"; the names were changed to protect innocent and guilty alike.

No project manager should attempt to practice his or her trade without explicit training in negotiation. We are appalled that the subject is rarely mentioned in books on project management, excepting Hajek (1984) on buyer-seller negotiations.

Project Management in Practice
Selling New Area Codes to Consumers Who Don't Want Them

After analyzing the area code problem for some time, BellSouth received permission from all regulatory and organizational authorities in December 1994 to proceed with splitting South Carolina into two area codes and install the new code, 864, in the upper northwest region of the state. The project task was massive, yet the conversion of all equipment, databases, and associated systems had to be completed before the existing prefixes ran out in 12–18 months.

However, in spite of the demanding technical challenges, one of the most difficult tasks facing the project team was confronting the dilemma that this conversion was a product that South Carolina's phone customers absolutely did not want! Nevertheless, the exploding demand for fax machines, cellular telephones, pagers, additional residential phone lines, Internet service, and other such recent technological innovations required additional area codes to make them op-

erative. Here was a basic conflict: "selling" a populace on the need to change their area code so they can use the new innovations they are purchasing.

The problem was exacerbated by the lack of time to involve the populace in the decision-making process and options available: changing the area code boundaries, using multiple area codes in the same region, splitting an area code region and adding a new code, and a few others. BellSouth thus adopted a variety of measures to communicate the need for the new area code to their customers:

- Developing a regional advertising campaign
- Sending out promotional brochures
- Putting inserts into customer bills
- Contract with an inbound telemarketing company to handle calls and provide information

This map reflects the large number of new area codes introduced in 1995–96 alone.

- Informing all employees who had customer contact about how to explain the need
- Establishing a "South Carolina Area Code Assistance Hotline"

As the new system went live on May 1, 1996, the changeover was smooth and uneventful, a tribute not only to the technical ability of the project team but also their marketing prowess.

Source: M.W. Strickland, "'Mission Possible': Managing an Area Code Relief Project," *PM Network,* March 1997, pp. 39–46.

6.1   THE NATURE OF NEGOTIATION

The favored technique for resolving conflict is *negotiation.* What is negotiation? Wall (1985, preface) defines negotiation as "the process through which two or more parties seek an acceptable rate of exchange for items they own or control." Dissatisfied with this definition, he spends part of a chapter extending and discussing the concept (Chapter 1), without a great deal of improvement. Cohen (1980, p. 15) says that "Negotiation is a field of knowledge and endeavor that focuses on gaining the favor of people from whom we want things." Other authors define negotiation differently, but do not appreciably extend Cohen's definition. Even if no single definition neatly fits all the activities we label "negotiation," we do recognize that such terms as "mediate," "conciliate," " make peace," "bring to agreement," "settle differences," "moderate," "arbitrate," "adjust differences," "compromise," "bargain," "dicker," and "haggle" (*Roget's International Thesaurus,* 1993) are synonyms for " negotiate" in some instances.

Most of the conflicts that involve the organization and outsiders have to do with property rights and contractual obligations. In these cases, the parties to negotiation see themselves as opponents. Conflicts arising inside the organization may also appear to involve property rights and obligations, but they typically differ from conflicts with outsiders in one important way: As far as the firm is concerned, they are conflicts between allies, not opponents. Wall (1985, pp. 149–150) makes this point neatly:

> Organizations, like groups, consist of interdependent parts that have their own values, interests, perceptions, and goals. Each unit seeks to fulfill its particular goal . . . and the effectiveness of the organization depends on the success of each unit's fulfillment of its specialized task. Just as important as the fulfillment of the separate tasks is the integration of the unit activities such that each unit's activities aid or at least do not conflict with those of the others.

One of the ways in which organizations facilitate this integration is to establish *"lateral relations* [which] allow decisions to be made horizontally across lines of authority" (Wall, 1985, p. 150). Because each unit will have its own goals, integrating the activities of two or more units is certain to produce the conflicts that Wall says should not take place. The conflicts may, however, be resolved by negotiating a solution, if one exists, that produces gains (or minimizes losses) for all parties. Raiffa (1982, p. 139) defines a Pareto-optimal solution to the two-party conflict and discusses the nature of the bargaining process required to reach optimality, a difficult and time-consuming process. While it is not likely that the conflicting parties will know and understand the complex trade-offs in a real-world, project management, many-persons/many-issues conflict (see Raiffa, 1982, Chapters 17–23), the general objective is to find a solution such that no party can be made better off without making another party worse off by the same amount or more—i.e., a Pareto-optimal solution.

The concept of a Pareto-optimal solution is important. Approaching intraproject conflicts with a desire to win a victory over other parties is inappropriate. The PM must remember that she will be negotiating with project stakeholders many times in the future. If she conducts a win-lose negotiation and the other party loses, from then on she will face a determined adversary who seeks to defeat her. This is not helpful. The proper outcome of this type of negotiation should be to optimize the outcome in terms of overall organizational goals. Although it is not always obvious how to do this, negotiation is clearly the correct approach.

During the negotiation process, an ethical situation often arises that is worth mentioning. Consider the situation where a firm requests an outside contractor to develop a software package to achieve some function. When the firm asks for a specific objective to be accomplished, it frequently does not know if that is a major job or a trivial task because it lacks technical competence in that area. Thus, the contractor has the opportunity to misrepresent the task to its customer, either inflating the cost for a trivial task or minimizing the impact of a significant task in order to acquire the contract and then boosting the cost later. The ethics of the situation require that each party in the negotiation be honest with the other, even in situations where it is clear there will not be further work between the two.

6.2 PARTNERING, CHARTERING, AND CHANGE

Projects provide ample opportunity for the project manager (PM) to utilize her or his skills at negotiation. There are, however, three situations commonly arising during projects that call for the highest level of negotiating skill the PM can muster: the use of subcontractors, the use of input from two or more functional units to design and develop the project's mission, and the management of changes ordered in the project's deliverables and/or priorities after the project is underway (de Laat, 1995; Hughes, 1998; Tan, Hayes, and Shaw, 1996). The former probably accounts for more litigation than all other aspects of the project combined. The latter two are, in the authors' experience, by far the most common and most troublesome issues project managers report facing.

Partnering

In recent years there has been a steady growth in the frequency of outsourcing parts of projects (Smith, 1998). External suppliers, increasingly, are delivering parts of projects, including tangible products and services as well as intangible knowledge and skills. There are many reasons beyond avoidance of litigation that firms enter partnering arrangements with each other, for example, diversification of technical risk, avoidance of capital investment, reducing political risk on multinational projects, shortening the duration of the project, and pooling of complementary knowledge, among others (Beecham and Cordey-Hayes, 1998, p. 192).

Generally, relations between the organization carrying out a project and a subcontractor working on the project are best characterized as adversarial. The parent organization's objectives are to get the deliverable at the lowest possible cost, as soon as possible. The subcontractor's objectives are to produce the deliverable at the highest possible profit with the least effort. These conflicting interests tend to lead both parties to work in an atmosphere of mutual suspicion and antagonism. Indeed, it is almost axiomatic that the two parties will have significantly different ideas about the exact nature of the deliverable, itself. The concept of "partnering" has been developed to replace this atmosphere with one of cooperation and mutual helpfulness, but the basically adversarial relationship makes cooperation difficult in the best of cases (Larson and Drexler, 1997).

Cowan, Gray, and Larson (1992, p. 5, italics in original) define partnering as follows:

> *Project partnering is a method of transforming contractual relationships into a cohesive, cooperative project team with a single set of goals and established procedures for resolving disputes in a timely and effective manner.*

They present a multistep process for building partnered projects. First, the parent firm must make a commitment to partnering, select subcontractors who will also make such a commitment, engage in joint team-building exercises, and develop a "charter" for the project. (See the next subsection for a description of such a charter.) Second, both parties must implement the partnering process with a four-part agreement on: (1) "joint evaluation" of the project's progress; (2) a method for resolving any problems or disagreements; (3) acceptance of a goal for continuous improvement (also known as TQM) for the joint project; and (4) continuous support for the process of partnering from senior management of both parties. Finally, the parties commit to a joint review of "project execution" when the project is completed. Beecham and Cordey-Hayes (1998, p. 194ff; see also Walles, 1998) note several things that can "doom" partnering agreements and they develop several "propositions" that lead to success. Partnering is an attempt to mitigate the risks associated with subcontracting. Consider the nature of the steps listed above. Clearly, there are specific risks that must be managed in each of them.

Each step in this process must be accompanied by negotiation, and the negotiations must be nonadversarial. The entire concept is firmly rooted in the assumption of mutual trust between the partners, and this assumption, too, requires nonadversarial negotiation. Finally, these articles focus on partnering when the partners are members of different organizations. We think the issue is no less relevant when the partners are from different divisions or departments of the same parent organization. Identical assumptions hold, identical steps must be taken, and interparty agreements must be reached for partnering to succeed [see also Baker (1990)].

There can be no doubt that those who have not had much experience with partnering underrate its difficulty. Partnering requires strong support from senior management of both firms, and it requires continuous support of project objectives and partnering agreements (Moore, Maes, and Shearer, 1995). Above all, and most difficult of all, it requires open and honest communication between the partners. With all of its problems, however, partnering yields benefits great enough to be worth the efforts required to make it work correctly (Baker, 1996; Larson, 1997).

Chartering

A project charter is simply a written agreement between the PM, senior management, and the functional managers who are committing resources and/or people to the project (Love, 1989). Like planning documents, WBSs, and responsibility charts, the charter may take many different forms. Typically, it details the expected project deliverables, often including the project's schedule and budget. It attests to the fact that senior management, functional managers, and the PM are "on the same page," agreeing about what is to be done, when, and at what cost. Note that if there is such an agreement, there is also an implication that none of the parties will change the agreement unilaterally, or, at least, without prior consultation with the other parties. Most projects do not have charters, which is one reason for observing that most projects are not completed on specification, on time, and on budget. Also note the additional fact that project managers are among the most frustrated people in American industry.

In the previous chapter, we described an iterative process for developing project action plans wherein individuals responsible for a task or subtask provided an action plan for completing it. We noted that it is not uncommon for the individuals or groups who make commitments during the process of developing the project's action plan to sign-off on their commitments. The signed-off project plan or set of action plans might constitute a project charter, particularly if senior management has signed-off on the overall mission statement, *and if it is recognized as a charter by all parties to the plan.*

A somewhat less specific charter appears in Cowen, Gray, and Larson (1992, Figure 2, p. 8), in which the various members of the partnering team sign a commitment to

- Meet design intent
- Complete contract without need for litigation
- Finish project on schedule:
  —Timely resolution of issues
  —Manage joint schedule
- Keep cost growth to less than 2 percent . . . etc.

Of course, even this charter assumes some agreement on the "design intent," the schedule, and costs.

Scope Change

No matter how carefully a project is planned, it is almost certain to be changed before completion. No matter how carefully defined at the start, the scope of most projects is subject to considerable uncertainty. There are three basic causes for change in projects. Some changes result because planners erred in their initial assessment about how to achieve a given end or erred in their choice of the proper goal for the project. Technological uncertainty is the fundamental causal factor for either error. The foundation for a building must be changed because a preliminary geological study did not reveal a weakness in the structure of the ground on which the building will stand. An R & D project must be altered because metallurgical test results indicate another approach should be adopted. The project team becomes aware of a recent innovation that allows a faster, cheaper solution to the conformation of a new computer.

Other changes result because the client/user or project team learns more about the nature of the project deliverable or about the setting in which it is to be used. An increase in user or team knowledge or sophistication is the primary factor leading to change. A computer program must be extended or rewritten because the user thinks of new uses for the software. Physicians request that intensive care units in a hospital be equipped with laminar air-flow control in order to accommodate patients highly subject to infection who might otherwise not be admissible in an ICU. The fledgling audio-addict upgrades the specifications for a system to include very high frequencies so that his dog can enjoy the music, too.

A third source of change is the mandate. This is a change in the environment in which the project is being conducted. As such, it cannot be controlled by the PM. A new law is passed. A government regulatory unit articulates a new policy. A trade association sets a new standard. The parent organization of the user applies a new criterion for its purchases. In other words, the rules of conduct for the project are altered. A state-approved pollution control system must be adopted for each chemical refinery project. The state government requires all new insurance policies to conform to a revised law specifying that certain information must be given to potential purchasers.

At times, mandates affect only priorities. The mandate in question might move a very important customer to the "head of the line" for some scarce resource or service.

To some extent, risk management techniques can be applied to scope change. Technological uncertainty can be mitigated by careful analysis of the technologies involved, including the use of technological forecasting. Risk of scope change caused by increased user knowledge can only be managed by improving the up-front communication with the client and then establishing a formal process to handle change. See Chapter 11 for more about this. Finally, mandates are, for the most part, unpredictable. These can be "managed" only by having some flexibility built into the budget and schedule of the project. Ways of doing this sensibly will be discussed in the following two chapters.

As Greek philosopher Heraclitus said, "Nothing endures but change." It is thus with projects, but whatever the nature of the change, specifications of the deliverables must be altered, and the schedule and budget recalculated. Obviously, negotiation will be required to develop new agreements between the parties-at-interest to the project. These negotiations are difficult because most of the stakeholders will have a strong interest in maintaining the status quo. If the proposed change benefits the client and increases the cost of the project, the producer will try to sequester some of the user's potential benefit in the form of added charges to offset the added cost. The client will, of course, resist. All parties must, once again, seek a Pareto-optimal solution—always a difficult task.

Change by mandate raises an additional problem. Not only are the project's deliverables, budget, and schedule usually changed, the *priorities* of other projects are typically changed too, if only temporarily while the mandate receives the system's full attention. Suddenly, a PM loses access to key resources, because they are urgently required elsewhere. Key contributors to a project miss meetings or are unable to keep promised task-delivery dates. All too often, the PM's response to this state of affairs is anger and/or discouragement. Neither is appropriate.

> This project is so important, we can't let things that are more important interfere with it.
>
> Anonymous

After discussing priorities with both PMs and senior managers, it has become clear to us that most firms actually have only three levels of priority (no matter how ornate the procedure for setting project priorities might seem to be). First, there are the high-priority projects, that is, the "set" of projects currently being supported. When resource conflicts arise within this high-priority set, precedence is typically given to those projects with the earliest due date. (More about this is in Chapter 9.) Second, there are the lower-priority projects, the projects "we would like to do when we have the time and money." Third, occasionally, there are urgent projects, mandates, that must be done immediately. "Customer A's project must be finished by the end of the month." "The state's mandate must be met by June 30." Everything else is delayed to ensure that mandates are met. As noted earlier, we will have more to say on this subject in Chapter 11.

While project charters and partnerships would certainly help the PM deal with conflicts that naturally arise during a project, the use of charters and partnering is growing slowly—though outsourcing is growing rapidly. It is understandably difficult to convince senior managers to make the firm commitments implied in a project charter in the face of a highly uncertain future. Functional managers are loath to make firm commitments for precisely the same reason. So, too, the client, aware of her or his own ignorance about the degree to which the project output will meet his or her needs, is cautious about commitment—even when a procedure for negotiating change exists.

Partnering is a recently developed concept, and in our litigious society any system for conflict resolution that asks parties to forego lawsuits is viewed with considerable suspicion. Indeed, we find that a great many organizations preach "team building," "TQM," and "employee involvement," but many fail to practice what they preach. For each participative manager you find, we can show you a dozen micromanagers. For each team player ready to share responsibility, we can show you a dozen "blame placers." The era of project charters and partnering is approaching, but it is not yet here.

6.3   CONFLICT AND THE PROJECT LIFE CYCLE

In this section, following a brief discussion of the project life cycle, we will categorize the types of conflicts that frequently occur in the project environment, and then amplify the nature of these conflicts. Finally, we will link the project life cycle with the fundamental conflict categories and discover that certain patterns of conflict are associated with the different periods in the life of a project. With this knowledge, the PM can do a faster and more accurate job of diagnosing the nature of the conflicts he or she is facing, thereby reducing the likelihood of escalating the conflict by dealing with it ineffectually.

More on the Project Life Cycle

Various authors define the stages of the project life cycle (see Figures 1-3, 1-4, and 1-5) in different ways. Two of the most commonly cited definitions are those of Thamhain and Wilemon (1975a) and Adams and Barndt (1983). The former use a four-stage model with project formation, buildup, main program, and phaseout identified as the stages of the life cycle. Adams and Barndt also break the project life cycle into four stages: conceptualization, planning, execution, and termination.

For our purposes, these two views of the cycle are not significantly different. During the first stage, senior management tentatively, sometimes unofficially, approves preliminary planning for a project. Often, this management recognition is preceded by some strictly unofficial "bootleg" work to test the feasibility of an idea. Initial planning is undertaken, basic objectives are often adopted, and the project may be "scoped out." The second stage is typified by detailed planning, budgeting, scheduling, and the aggregation of resources. In the third stage, the lion's share of the actual work on the project is accomplished. During the final stage of the life cycle, work is completed and products are turned over to the client or user. This stage also includes disposition of the project's assets and personnel. It may even include preparation for the initial stage of another related project to follow.

Categories of Conflict

All stages of the project life cycle appear to be typified by conflict. In Chapter 4, we discussed some of the human factors that require the PM to be skilled at reducing interpersonal tensions. In that chapter, we also introduced the work of Thamhain and Wilemon (1975a, 1975b) on conflict in the project. These conflicts center on such matters as schedules, priorities, staff and labor requirements, technical factors, administrative procedures, cost estimates, and, of course, personality conflicts. Thamhain and Wilemon collected data on the frequency and magnitude of conflicts of each type during each stage of the project life cycle. Multiplying conflict frequency by a measure of conflict magnitude and adjusting for the proportion of PMs who reported each specific type of conflict, they derived an estimate of the "intensity" of the conflicts (see Tables 4-1 and 4-2). Figure 4-8 illustrates these conflicts and is repeated here as Figure 6-1 for the reader's convenience.

On examination of the data, it appears that the conflicts fall into three fundamentally different categories:

1. Groups working on the project may have different goals and expectations.

2. There is considerable uncertainty about who has the authority to make decisions.

3. There are interpersonal conflicts between people who are parties-at-interest in the project.

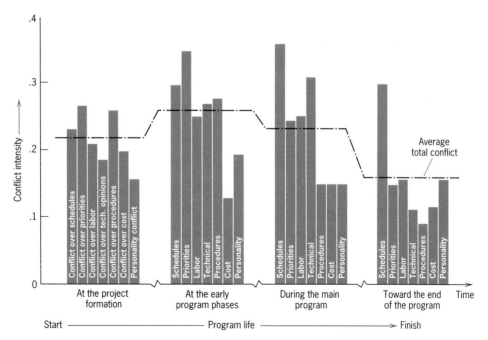

Figure 6–1   Conflict intensity over the project life cycle. *Source:* Thamhain and Wilemon (1975a).

Some conflicts reflect the fact that the day-to-day work on projects is usually carried out by many different units of the organization, units that often differ in their objectives and technical judgments. The result is that these units have different expectations about the project, its costs and rewards, its relative importance, and its timing. Conflicts about schedules, intra-and interproject priorities, cost estimates, and staff time tend to fall into this category. At base, they arise because the project manager and the functional managers have very different goals. The PM's concern is the project. The primary interest of the functional manager is the daily operation of the functional department.

Other conflicts reflect the fact that both technical and administrative procedures are important aspects of project management. Uncertainty about who has the authority to make decisions on resource allocation, on administrative procedures, on communication, on technological choices, and on all the other matters affecting the project produces conflict between the PM and the other parties. It is simple enough (and correct) to state that in a matrix organization, the functional manager controls who works on the project and makes technical decisions, while the project manager controls the schedule and flow of work. In practice, in the commonly hectic environment of the project, amid the day's countless little crises faced by project and functional manager alike, the distinction is rarely clear.

Finally, some conflicts reflect the fact that human beings are an integral part of all projects. In an environment that depends on the cooperation of many persons, it seems inevitable that some personalities will clash. Also, in conflicts between the project and the client, or between senior management and the project, it is the project manager who personifies the project and thus is generally a party to the conflict.

We can categorize these conflicts as conflict over differing goals, over uncertainty about the locus of authority, and between personalities. For the entire array of conflict types and parties-at-interest, see Table 6-1.

The three types of conflict seem to involve the parties-at-interest to the project in identifiable ways. the different goals and objectives of the project manager, senior management, and functional managers are a major and constant source of conflict. For example, senior management (at times, arbitrarily) is apt to fix all three parameters of the project—time, cost, and performance—and then to assume that the PM will be able to achieve all the preset targets. As we will see in Chapter 7 on budgeting, underestimation of cost and time is a natural consequence of this practice, and it leads

Table 6-1. Project Conflicts by Category and Parties-at-Interest

	Categories of Conflict		
Parties-at-Interest	*Goals*	*Authority*	*Interpersonal*
Project team	Schedules Priorities	Technical	Personality
Client	Schedules Priorities	Technical	
Functional and senior management	Schedules Priorities Labor Cost	Technical Administrative	Personality

directly to conflict between the PM, as a representative of the project team, and senior management. A second consequence is that the PM tries to pass the stringent cost and time estimates along to functional managers whose units are expected to perform certain work on the project. More conflict arises when the functional managers complain that they cannot meet the time and cost restrictions. All this tends to build failure into the job of managing a project, another source of conflict between the PM and senior management.

Functional managers also may not see eye-to-eye with the PM on such issues as the project's priority or the desirability of assigning a specifically named individual to work on the project, or even the applicability of a given technical approach to the project. In addition, the client's priorities and schedule, whether an inside or outside client, may differ radically from those of senior management and the project team. Finally, the project team has its own ideas about the appropriateness of the schedule or level of project staffing. The Thamhain and Wilemon (1975a) data show that these goal-type conflicts occur in all stages of the project's life cycle, though they are particulary serious in the early stages (see Figure 6-1). Regardless of the timing, in many cases it is not certain just whose priorities are ruling.

There are, of course, a number of methods for settling conflicts about priorities between projects, as well as intraproject conflicts. Often, the project selection model used to approve projects for funding will generate a set of projects ranked by some measure of value. It is also common for senior management to determine interproject priorities. The relative importance of the various tasks in an individual project is set by the project manager, who allocates scarce resources depending on the requirements of schedule, task difficulty, resource availability, and similar considerations. The existence of these methods for resolving priority conflicts is all too often irrelevant, because there is a powerful tendency for both project and functional managers to optimize their individual interests, with little regard for the total organization.

In matrix organizations, the center of authority is particularly unclear. Locus-of-authority conflicts are endemic to matrix-organized projects. The project team and the client tend to focus on the technical procedures, debating the proper approach to the project, or perhaps how to solve individual problems that can occur at any stage. Senior management has other fish to fry. Not only do they insist that the project manager adopt and maintain a set of administrative procedures that conform to organizational and legal standards, but they also are quite concerned with who reports to whom and whose permission is required to take what action. The astute reader will note that such concerns are not entirely appropriate for matrix-organized projects. Our discussions with senior managers lead us to the obvious conclusion that it is common for senior management to want the efficiency and other advantages of matrix management but simultaneously to attempt to maintain the managerial comforts of traditional hierarchical structures—a sure source of conflict.

The conflict-resolution potential of partnering and project charters should be quite clear. Neither technique will stop conflicts from arising, but they will sharply lower the intensity of the conflicts as well as provide a framework for resolving conflict. They will even allow an environment in which the PM and functional managers can take positions that support the total organization rather than suboptimizing the project or the function.

Project managers will often find themselves arguing for scheduling or resource priorities from functional managers who outrank them by several levels. Neither the functional nor the project managers are quite sure about who has what authority. (The reader will recall that the pure project form of organization has a tendency to breed deviant administrative behaviors, and that matrix organization is characterized by superior–subordinate confusion.) A constant complaint of project managers is "I have to take the responsibility, but I have no authority at all."

People problems arise, for the most part, within the project team, though functional managers may clash with PMs—the former accusing the latter of being "pushy," and the latter accusing the former of "foot dragging." In our experience, most personality clashes on the project team result from differences in technical approach or philosophy of problem solving, and in the methods used to implement the project results. Of course, it is quite possible that a personality conflict causes a technical conflict. It is also possible that any type of conflict will appear, at first blush, to be a personality clash.

Next we put these conflicts into the chronological perspective of the project life cycle.

Project Formation

In the initial stage of the project life cycle, most of the conflict centers around the inherent confusion of setting up a project in the environment of matrix management. Almost nothing about the project or its governance has been decided. Even the project's technical objectives, not clearly defined or established, are apt to be understood only in the most general sense. Moving from this state of semi-chaos to the relatively ordered world of the buildup stage is difficult. To make this transition, four fundamental issues must be handled, although not necessarily in the order presented here.

First, the technical objectives of the project must be specified to a degree that will allow the detailed planning of the buildup stage to be accomplished. Second, commitment of resources to the project must be forthcoming from senior management and from functional managers. Third, the priority of the project, relative to the priorities of the parent organization's other projects, must be set and communicated. (Our comments about priorities at the end of Section 6.2 notwithstanding, we feel the project's priority must be set as early as possible in the life of the project. While it will probably not save the project from delay in the event of a mandate, it stands as an important political signal to functional managers about which projects take precedence in case of resource conflicts.) Fourth, the organizational structure of the project must be established to an extent sufficient for the WBS and a linear responsibility chart, or its equivalent, to be prepared during the next stage of the life cycle.

These conditions are not sufficient, but they are most certainly necessary if the conflicts typical of the formation stage are to be resolved—at least at a reasonable level—and not simply carried forward to the buildup stage in an exacerbated state.

The project manager who practices conflict avoidance in this stage is inviting disaster in the next. The four fundamental issues above underlie such critical but down-to-earth matters as these: Which of the functional areas will be needed to accomplish project tasks? What will be the required level of involvement of each of the functional areas? How will conflicts over resources/facility usage between this and other projects be settled? What about those resource/facility conflicts between the project and the routine work of the functions? *Who* has the authority to decide the technical, scheduling, personnel, and cost questions that will arise? Most important, how will changes in the parent organization's priorities be communicated to everyone involved?

Note that three of the four fundamental issues—delimiting the technical objectives, getting management commitment, and setting the project's relative priority—must be resolved irrespective of what organizational form is selected for the project. It should also be noted that the organizational structure selected will have a major impact on the ways in which the conflicts are handled. The stronger the matrix, having the pure project as its limit, the more authoritative the role played by the PM. The weaker the matrix, having functional organization as its limit, the more authority is embedded in the functional managers. Lack of clarity about the relative power/influence/authority of the PM and the functional managers is a major component of all conflicts involving technical decisions, resource allocation, and scheduling.

Project Buildup

Thamhain and Wilemon (1975a, p. 39) note that conflict occurring in the buildup stage "over project priorities, schedules, and administrative procedures . . . appears as an extension from the previous program phase." This is the period during which the project moves (or should move) from a general concept to a highly detailed set of plans. If the project's organizational format is a strong matrix, the PM seeks a commitment of *people* from the functional departments. If the project is organized as a weak matrix, the PM seeks a commitment of *work* from the functional departments. In either case, the PM seeks commitment from functional managers who are under pressure to deliver support to other projects, in addition to the routine, everyday demands made on their departments.

As the project's plans become detailed, conflicts over technical issues build—again, conflicts between the PM and the functional areas tend to predominate. Usually, the functional departments can claim more technical expertise than the PM, who is a "generalist." On occasion, however, the PM is also a specialist. In such situations, discussions between the functional manager and the project manager about the best technical approach often result in conflict. The total level of conflict is at its highest in this transition period.

Main Program

Schedules are still a major source of conflict in the main program phase of the project life cycle, though the proximate cause of schedule-related conflict is usually different than in the earlier stages. Project plans have been developed and approved by everyone involved (although, perhaps, grudgingly), and the actual work is under way. Let us make an assumption that is certain to be correct; let us assume that some activity runs into difficulty and is late in being completed. Every task that is dependent on this late activity will also be delayed. Some of these subsequent activities will, if sufficiently late and if the late work is not made up, delay the entire project.

In order to prevent this consequence, the PM must try to get the schedule back on track. But catching up is considerably more difficult than falling behind. Catching up requires extra resources that the functional groups who are doing the "catching up" will demand, but which the PM may not have.

The more complex the project, the more difficult it is to trace and estimate the impact of all the delays, and the more resources that must be consumed to get things back on schedule. Throughout this book we have referred to the PM's job of managing time/cost/performance trade-offs. Maintaining the project schedule is precisely an exercise in managing trade-offs, but adding to the project's cost or scaling down the project's technical capabilities in order to save time are trade-offs the PM will not take if there is any viable alternative. The PM's ability to make trade-offs is often constrained by contract, company policy, and ethical considerations. In reality, trade-off decisions are extremely difficult.

Like schedule conflicts, technical conflicts are frequent and serious during the main program stage. Also like schedule conflicts, the source of technical conflict is somewhat different than in earlier stages. Just as a computer and a printer must be correctly linked together in order to perform properly, so must the many parts of a project. These linkages are known as *interfaces*. The number of interfaces increases rapidly as the project gets larger, which is to say that the system gets more complex. As the number of interfaces increases, so does the probability that problems will arise at the interfaces. The need to manage these interfaces and to correct incompatibilities is the key to the technical conflicts in the main program phase.

Project Phaseout

As in the main program stage, schedule is the major source of conflict during project phaseout. If schedule slippage has occurred in the main program stage (and it probably has), the consequences will surely be felt in this final stage. During phaseout, projects with firm deadlines develop an environment best described as hectic. The PM, project team, and functional groups often band together to do what is necessary to complete the project on time and to specification. Cost overruns, if not outrageously high, are tolerated—though they may not be forgiven and they will certainly be remembered.

Technical problems are comparatively rare during phaseout because most have been solved or bypassed earlier. Similarly, working interfaces have been developed and put in place. If the project involves implementing a technology in an outside client's system, technical conflicts will probably arise, but they are usually less intense.

Thamhain and Wilemon (1975b, p. 41) note that personality conflicts are the second-ranked source of conflict during phaseout. They ascribe these conflicts to interpersonal stress caused by the pressure to complete the project, and to individuals' natural anxiety about leaving the project either to be assigned to another, or be returned to a functional unit. In addition, we have observed conflict, sometimes quite bitter, focused on the distribution of the project's capital equipment and supplies when the project is completed. Conflict also arises between projects phasing out and those just starting, particularly if the latter need resources or personnel with scarce talents being used by the former.

The way in which Thamhain and Wilemon have defined conflict as having its source in differences about goals/expectations, uncertainty about authority, and interpersonal problems, precludes identifying conflict as occurring between discipline-oriented and problem-oriented team members. Recall our discussions of Hughes (1998), de Laat (1994), and Pill (1971) among several others. We do not argue that Thamhain and Wilemon are in error, but merely that their classification does not specifically include a type of conflict we feel is both frequent and important. Much of the conflict identified during our discussion of planning in Chapter 5, it seems to us, is due to discipline/problem-orientation differences. A clear example comes from an interview recorded during Pelled and Adler's (1994, p. 23) research on conflict in multifunctional design teams. One team member speaking of another said, "He will do whatever he thinks is right to get his [own] job done, whether or not it's good for [the company] or anyone else." In context, it is clear that this conflict was between a problem-oriented individual and one who was discipline-oriented.

The upshot is simple. As we noted in the first section of Chapter 1, conflict is an inherent characteristic of projects, and the project manager is constantly beset by conflict. The ability to reduce and resolve conflict in ways that support achievement of the project's goals is a prime requisite for success as a PM. The primary tool to accomplish conflict resolution and reduction is negotiation, and the method of handling conflict established in the project formation stage will set the pattern for the entire project. Therefore, the style of negotiation adopted by the PM is critical.

Much has been written on conflict resolution. Burke's classic paper on the confrontation-problem solving method of resolving conflicts is offered as a "Reading" at the end of this chapter. The similarities between the confrontation-problem solving technique for conflict resolution and win-win negotiation covered in the following section are quite striking. Pinto and Kharbanda (1995) also approach conflict resolution in the spirit of win-win negotiation. Dyer (1987) writes of resolving conflicts, focusing on conflict between members of a team, and Afzalur (1992) is a general work on the subject.

Project Management in Practice
A Consensus Feasibility Study for Montreal's Archipel Dam

To assess the desirability of a feasibility study evaluating the costs and benefits of constructing a dam for watershed development within the St. Lawrence river basin in the Montreal metropolitan area, Quebec initiated an interdepartmental evaluation. The evaluation concluded that a feasibility study that considered the hydroelectric power generated, the flood control possible, and the shoreline restoration for recreation for the 3 million local area residents was justified. It was recommended that a central authority act as project manager for the study and that arbitration procedures be instituted for the interests of all affected parties.

Thus, a new body called "Secretariat Archipel" was created to directly supervise the feasibility study. Secretariat Archipel, however, rejected the recommendations of the prior evaluation and chose to use a more democratic "consensus" approach between all involved agencies rather than a central authority approach. Doing so avoided the need for arbitration procedures as well. In addition, a matrix structure was put in place to guarantee a veto right to each of the ten governmental departments involved in the process. It was believed that this consensus approach would lead to a solution acceptable to all, while protecting the jurisdictional responsibilities of all departments.

Although this approach apparently avoided difficult conflicts, and the concomitant need to arbitrate them, a post-study evaluation of the process concluded that it was neither effective nor efficient. By discarding the recommendation for a central authority body, a leadership gap arose in the decision framework and veto rights were abused by many of the participants. The leadership gap led, for example, to no one identifying incompatible objectives, rules for making decisions, or common priorities.

In terms of effectiveness, the recommendations of the study are questionable: that the dam be postponed until the year 2015 while only $35 million—less than the cost of the feasibility study—be spent on recreational facilities. Considering efficiency, it was found that many of the expensive support studies authorized by the Secretariat did not add significantly to the feasibility process. Also, the study appeared to take one to two years longer than necessary, with a correspondingly higher cost.

The evaluation proposed three probable causes of the lack of decisiveness in this study process:

1. Fear of litigation between the governmental departments and municipalities,

2. Difficulty comparing positive and negative impacts due to a lack of decision rules, and

3. Long delays and unavoidable sacrifices through a failure of the consensus process.

In retrospect, the consensus approach appeared to have been selected to protect the fields of jurisdiction of each governmental department rather than for defining the best project for the community. Since many of the goals were incompatible to start with, a consensual decision process with veto override would simply have to reject any recommendation—no matter how appropriate for the community—that was incompatible with another goal or disliked by any of the ten departments involved in the study. Although consensus is a highly desirable goal for public studies, leadership cannot be abandoned in the process. Attempting to avoid conflict through mandated consensus simply defeats the purpose of any study in the first place, except a study to determine what everyone commonly agrees upon.

Source: R. Desbiens, R. Houde, and P. Normandeau, "Archipel Feasibility Study: A Questionable Consensus Approach," *Project Management Journal*, March 1989.

6.4   SOME REQUIREMENTS AND PRINCIPLES OF NEGOTIATION

The word "negotiation" evokes many images: the United States President and Congress on the annual federal budget, the "Uruguay Round" of the GATT talks, a player's agent and the owner of an NFL team, the buyer and seller of an apartment complex, attorneys for husband and wife in a divorce settlement, union and management working out a collective bargaining agreement, tourist and peddler haggling over a rug in an Ankara market. But as we noted in the introduction to this chapter, none of these images is strictly appropriate for the project manager who must resolve the sorts of conflicts we have considered in the previous section.

The key to understanding the nature of negotiation as it applies to project management is the realization that few of the conflicts arising in projects have to do with *whether* or not a task will be undertaken or a deliverable produced. Instead, they have to do with the precise *design* of the deliverable and/or *how* the design will be achieved, by *whom, when,* and at *what cost.* The implication is clear: *The work of the project will be done.* If conflicts between any of the parties to the project escalate to the point where negotiations break down and work comes to a halt, everyone loses. *One requirement* for the conflict reduction/resolution methods used by the PM is that *they must allow the conflict to be settled without irreparable harm to the project's objectives.*

A closer consideration of the attorneys negotiating the divorce settlement makes clear a second requirement for the PM negotiating conflicts between parties-at-interest to the project. While the husband and wife (or the rug peddler and tourist) may employ unethical tactics during the negotiation process and, if not found out, profit from them at the expense of the other party, it is much less likely for the attorneys representing the husband and wife to do so—particularly if they practice law in the same community. The lawyers know they will have to negotiate on other matters in the future. Any behavior that breeds mistrust will make future negotiations extremely difficult, perhaps impossible. The rug peddler assumes no further contact with the tourist, so conscience is the sole governor of his or her ethics. A *second requirement* for the conflict resolution/reduction methods used by the PM is that *they allow (and foster) honesty between the negotiators.*

The conflicting parties-at-interest to a project are not enemies or competitors, but rather allies—members of an alliance with strong common interests. It is a *requirement of all conflicting parties to seek solutions to the conflict that not only satisfy their own individual needs, but also satisfy the needs of other parties to the conflict, as well as the needs of the parent organization.* In the language of negotiation, this is called a win-win solution. Negotiating to a win-win solution is the key to conflict resolution in project management.

Fisher and Ury (1983, p. 11) have developed a negotiation technique that tends to maintain these three requirements. They call it "principled negotiation," that is, win-win. The method is straightforward; it is defined by four points.

1. *Separate the people from the problem.*   The conflicting parties are often highly emotional. They perceive things differently and feel strongly about the differences. Emotions and objective fact get confused to the point where it is not clear which is which. Conflicting parties tend to attack one another rather than the problem. To minimize the likelihood that the conflict will become strictly interpersonal, the substantive problem should be carefully defined. Then everyone can work on it rather than each other.

2. *Focus on interests, not positions.*   Positional bargaining occurs when the PM says to a functional manager: "I need this subassembly by November 15." The functional manager responds: "My group can't possibly start on it this year. We might be able to deliver it by February 1." These are the opening lines in a dialogue that sounds suspiciously like the haggling of the tourist and the rug peddler. A simple "Let's talk about the schedule for this subassembly" would be sufficient to open

the discussion. Otherwise each party develops a high level of ego involvement in his or her position and the negotiation never focuses on the real interests and concerns of the conflicting parties—the central issues of the conflict. The exchange deteriorates into a series of positional compromises that do not satisfy either party and leave both feeling that they have lost something important.

In positional negotiation, the "positions" are statements of immediate wants and assume that the environment is static. Consider these positional statements: "I won't pay more than $250,000 for that property." Or, as above, "We might be able to deliver it by February 1." The first position assumes that the bidder's estimates of future property values are accurate, and the second assumes that the group's current workload (or a shortage of required materials) will not change. When negotiation focuses on interests, the negotiator must determine the underlying concern of the other party. The real concerns or interests of the individuals stating the positions quoted above might be to earn a certain return on the investment in a property, or to not commit to delivery of work if delivery on the due date cannot be guaranteed. Knowledge of the other party's interests allows a negotiator to suggest solutions that satisfy the other party's interests without agreeing with the other's position.

3. *Before trying to reach agreement, invent options for mutual gain.*   The parties-in-conflict usually enter negotiations knowing the outcome they would like. As a result, they are blind to other outcomes and are not particulary creative. Nonetheless, as soon as the substantive problems are spelled out, some effort should be devoted to finding a wide variety of possible solutions—or elements thereof—that advance the mutual interests of the conflicting parties. Success at finding options that produce mutual gain positively reinforces win-win negotiations. Cohen (1980) reports on a conflict between a couple in which "he" wanted to go to the mountains and "she" wanted to go to the shore. A creative win-win solution sent them both to Lake Tahoe.

4. *Insist on using objective criteria.*   Rather than bargaining on positions, attention should be given to finding standards (e.g., market value, expert opinion, law, company policy) that can be used to determine the quality of an outcome. Doing this tends to make the negotiation less a contest of wills or exercise in stubbornness. If a functional manager wants to use an expensive process to test a part, it is acceptable for the PM to ask if such a process is required to ensure that the parts meet specified quality standards.

Fisher and Ury (1983) have had some success with their approach, "principled negotiation," in the Harvard (Graduate School of Business) Negotiation Project. Use of their methods increases the chance of finding win-win solutions.

There are many books on negotiation, some of which are listed in the bibliography of this chapter. Most of these works are oriented toward negotiation between opponents, not an appropriate mindset for the project manager, but all of them contain useful, tactical advice for the project manager. Wall's book (1985) is an excellent academic treatment of the subject. Fisher and Ury (1983) is a clear presentation of principled negotiation, and contains much that is relevant to the PM. In addition, Herb Cohen's *You Can Negotiate Anything* (1980) is an outstanding guide to win-win negotiation. The importance of negotiation is beginning to be recognized by the project management profession (Dodson, 1998; Grossman, 1995; Long, 1997; and Robinson, 1997), but the subject has not yet found its way into the Project Management Body of Knowledge.

Among the tactical issues covered by most books on negotiation are things the project manager, as a beginning negotiator, needs to know. For example, what should a negotiator who wishes to develop a win-win solution do if the other party to the conflict adopts a win-lose approach? What do you do if the other party tries to put you under psychological pressure by seating you so that a bright light shines in your eyes? What do you do if the other party refuses to negotiate in order to put you under extreme time pressure to accept whatever solution he or she offers? How do you settle what you perceive to be purely technical disputes? How should you handle threats? What should be your course of action if a functional manager, with whom you are trying to reach agreement about the timing and technology of a task, goes over your head and attempts to enlist the aid of your boss to get you to accept a solution you feel is less than satisfactory? How can you deal with a person you suspect dislikes you?

Almost every writer on negotiation emphasizes the importance of understanding the interests of the person with whom you are negotiating. As we noted above, the positions taken by negotiators are not truly understandable without first understanding the interests and concerns that prompt those positions. The statement that a test requested for May 15 cannot be run until June 2 may simply mean that the necessary test supplies will not be delivered until the latter date. If the PM can get the supplies from another source in time for the May 15 deadline, the test can be run on schedule. But the ability to do this depends on knowing *why* the test was to be delayed. If the negotiation remains a debate on positions, the PM will never find out that the test could have been run on time. *The key to finding a negotiator's interests and concerns is to ask "Why?" when he or she states a position.* The following vignette demonstrates the maintenance of a nonpositional negotiating style. This vignette is based on an actual event and was described to the authors by an "actor" in the case.

6.5   NEGOTIATION IN ACTION—THE QUAD SENSOR PROJECT

Dave Dogers, an experienced project manager, was assigned the project of designing and setting up a production system for an industrial instrument. The instrument would undoubtedly be quite delicate, so the design and fabrication methods for the shipping container were included in the project. Production of containers capable of meeting the specifications in this case were outside the experience of the firm, but one engineer in the container group had worked with this type of package in a previous job. This engineer, Jeff Gamm, was widely recognized as the top design engineer in the container group.

During the initial meetings on the project, which was organized as a weak matrix, Dogers asked Tab Baturi, manager of the Container Group, to assign Gamm to the project because of his unique background. Baturi said he thought they could work it out, and estimated that the design, fabrication of prototypes, and testing would require about four weeks. The package design could not start until several shape parameters of the instrument had been set and allowable shock loadings for the internal mechanisms had been determined. The R&D group responsible for instrument design thought it would require about nine months of work before they could complete specifications for the container. In addition to the actual design, construction, and test work, Gamm would have to meet periodically with the instrument design team to keep track of the project and to consult on design options from the container viewpoint. It was estimated that the entire project would require about 18 months.

Seven months into the project, at a meeting with Dave Dogers, the senior instrument design engineer, Richard Money casually remarked: "Say, Dave, I thought Jeff Gamm was going to do the package for the Quad Sensor."

"He is, why?" Dogers replied.

"Well," said the engineer, "Gamm hasn't been coming to the design team meetings. He did come a couple of times at the start of the project, but then young McCutcheon showed up saying that he would substitute for Gamm and would keep him informed. I don't know if that will work. That package is going to be pretty tricky to make."

Dogers was somewhat worried by the news the engineer had given him. He went to Gamm's office, as if by chance, and asked, "How are things coming along?"

"I'm up to my neck, Dave," Gamm responded. "We've had half a dozen major changes ordered from Baker's office (V.P. Marketing) and Tab has given me the three toughest ones. I'm behind, getting behinder, and Baker is yelling for the new container designs. I can't possibly do the Quad Sensor package unless I get some help—quick. It's an interesting problem and I'd like to tackle it, but I just can't. I asked Tab to put McCutcheon on it. He hasn't much experience, but he seems bright."

"I see," said Dogers. "Well, the Quad Sensor package may be a bit much for a new man. Do you mind if I talk to Tab? Maybe I can get you out from under some of the pressure."

"Be my guest!" said Gamm.

The next day Dogers met with Tab Baturi to discuss the problem. Baturi seemed depressed. "I don't know what we're supposed to do. No sooner do I get a package design set and tested than I get a call changing things. On the Evans order, we even had production schedules set, had ordered the material, and had all the setups figured out. I'm amazed they didn't wait till we had completed the run to tell us to change everything."

Baturi continued with several more examples of changed priorities and assignments. He complained that he had lost two designers and was falling further and further behind. He concluded: "Dave, I know I said you could use Gamm for the Quad Sensor job, but I simply can't cut him loose. He's my most productive person, and if anyone can get us out from under this mess, he can. I know McCutcheon is just out of school, but he's bright. He's the only person I can spare, and I can only spare him because I haven't got the time to train him on how we operate around here—if you can call this 'operating.'"

The two men talked briefly about the poor communications and the inability of senior management to make up its collective mind. Then Dogers suggested, "Look, Tab, Quad Sensor is no more screwed up than usual for this stage of the project. How about this? I can let you borrow Charlotte Setter for three or four weeks. She's an excellent designer and she's working on a low-priority job that's not critical at the moment. Say, I'll bet I can talk Anderson into letting you borrow Levy, too, maybe half time for a month. Anderson owes me a favor."

"Great, Dave, that will help a lot, and I appreciate the aid. I know you understand my problem and you know that I understand yours." Baturi paused and then added, "You realize that this won't take much pressure off Jeff Gamm. If you can get him the designing help he needs he can get more done, but I can't release him for the amount of time you've got allocated for the Quad Sensor."

They sat quietly for a while, then Dogers said, "Hey, I've got an idea. Container design is the hard problem. The production setup and test design isn't all that tough. Let me have Gamm for the container design. I'll use McCutcheon for the rest of the project and get him trained for you. I can get Carol Mattson to show him how to set up the shock tests and he can get the word on the production setup from my senior engineer, Dick Money."

Baturi thought a moment. "Yeah, that ought to work," he said. "But Gamm will have to meet with your people to get back up to speed on the project. I think he will clean up Baker's biggest job by Wednesday. Could he meet with your people on Thursday?"

"Sure, I can arrange that," Dogers said.

Baturi continued. "This will mean putting two people on the package design. McCutcheon will have to work with Gamm if he is to learn anything. Can your budget stand it?"

"I'm not sure," Dogers said, "I don't really have any slack in that account, but . . ."

"Never mind," interrupted Baturi, "I can bury the added charge somewhere. I think I'll add it to Baker's charges. He deserves it. After all, he caused our problem."

SUMMARY

This chapter addressed the need for negotiation as a tool to resolve project conflicts. We discussed the nature of negotiation and its purpose in the organization. We also described various categories of conflict and related them to the project life cycle. We followed this by identifying a number of requirements and principles of negotiation. Finally, we presented a short vignette illustrating an actual negotiation situation.

Specific points made in the chapter were these:

- Negotiation within the firm should be directed at obtaining the best outcome for the organization, not winning.
- There are three traditional categories of conflict: goal-oriented, authority-based, and interpersonal.

- There are also three traditional sources of conflict. They are the project team itself, the client, and functional and senior management. We added the problem/discipline-orentation of people working on the project.
- Critical issues to handle in the project formation stages are delimiting technical objectives, getting management commitment, setting the project's relative priority, and selecting the project organizational structure.
- The total level of conflict is highest during the project buildup stage.
- Scheduling and technical conflicts are most frequent and serious in the project buildup and

main program stages, and scheduling conflicts in particular during the phaseout stage.

- Project negotiation requirements are that conflicts must be settled without permanent damage, the methodology must foster honesty, and the solution must satisfy both individuals' and the organization's needs.

- One promising approach to meeting the requirements of project negotiation is called principled negotiation.

This chapter concludes the subject of project initiation. In the next part of the text, we address project implementation, starting with the subject of budgeting. We look at various budgeting methods. The chapter also addresses the issue of cost estimation and its difficulty.

 GLOSSARY

Interfaces   The boundaries between departments or functions.

Lateral Relations   Communications across lines of equivalent authority.

Pareto-Optimal Solution   A solution such that no party can be made better off without making another party worse off by the same amount or more.

Positional Negotiation   Stating immediate wants on the assumption that the environment is static.

Principled Negotiation   A process of negotiation that aims to achieve a win-win result.

Parties-at-interest   Those who have a vested interest in the outcome of the negotiations.

Win-win   When both parties are better off in the outcome.

 QUESTIONS

Material Review Questions

1. Review and justify the placement of the seven types of conflicts into the nine cells of Table 6-1.

2. Discuss each of the four fundamental issues for potential conflict during the project formation stage.

3. Identify the types of likely conflicts during the project buildup, main program, and phaseout stages.

Class Discussion Questions

9. Summarize the vignette in the chapter in terms of the negotiation skill used. Comment on the appropriateness and ethical aspects related to "burying" the cost.

10. What will be the likely result of a win-win style manager negotiating with a win-lose style manager? What if they are both win-lose styled?

11. Reallocate the placement of the seven types of conflicts into the nine cells of Table 6-1 according to your own logic.

4. What are the three main requirements of project negotiation?

5. Describe the four points of principled negotiation.

6. What is the objective of negotiation?

7. What are the four categories of conflict?

8. What is "principled negotiation"?

12. How does the type of project organization affect each of the types of conflicts that occur over the project life cycle?

13. Project managers are primarily concerned with project interfaces. At what rate do these interfaces increase with increasing project size?

14. The critical term in the concept of principled negotiation is "position." Elaborate on the multiple meanings of this term relative to negotiation. Can you think of a better term?

15. Give an example of a Pareto-optimal solution in a conflict.

16. Given that many conflicts are the result of different parties having different interests, is it possible to achieve a win-win situation?

Questions for Project Management in Practice

Selling New Area Codes to Consumers Who Don't Want Them

18. Did BellSouth's customers want new area codes or not? What was the true nature of the problem here?

19. Why did BellSouth have to change all the area codes instead of simply using the new codes for the new devices?

20. BellSouth employed a number of measures to communicate the need for change. In the end, what was probably the main reason their customers accepted the change?

17. The chairman of Cadbury Schweppes PLC, G.A.H. Cadbury suggests (1987) the following test for an ethical action: Would you be embarrassed to have it described in the newspaper? Is this a sufficient test for ethics? Can you think of any others?

A Consensus Feasibility Study for Montreal's Archipel Dam

21. Given the results of the study, did the consensus approach indeed lead to a solution acceptable to all? Why wasn't everyone happy with this outcome?

22. Based on this case situation, does the consensus approach lead to what is best for the overall community? Why (not)?

23. What approach should have been adopted to determine what was best for the overall community?

■ INCIDENTS FOR DISCUSSION

Pritchard Soap Co.

Samantha ("Sam") Calderon is manager of a project that will completely alter the method of adding perfume to Pritchard Soap's "Queen Elizabeth" gift soap line. The new process will greatly extend the number of available scents and should result in a significant increase in sales. The project had been proceeding reasonably well, but fell several weeks behind when the perfume supplier, the Stephen Marcus Parfumissary, was unable to meet its delivery deadline because of a wildcat strike.

Under normal circumstances this would not have caused problems, but the project had been subject to a particularly long evaluation study and now was in danger of not being ready for the Christmas season. The major scheduling problem concerned Pritchard's toxicity lab. Kyle Lee, lab manager, had been most cooperative in scheduling the Queen Elizabeth perfumes for toxicity testing. He had gone out of his way to rearrange his own schedule to accommodate Sam's project. Because of the strike at Marcus, however, Sam cannot have the perfumes ready for test as scheduled, and the new test date Lee has given Sam will not allow

her to make the new line available by Christmas. Sam suspects that the project might not have been approved if senior management had known that they would miss this year's Christmas season.

Questions: What are Sam's alternatives? What should she do?

Sutton Electronics

Eric Frank was still basking in the glory of his promotion to marketing project manager for Sutton Electronics Corporation, manufacturer of electronic fire alarm systems for motels, offices, and other commercial installations. Eric's first project involved the development of a marketing plan for Sutton's revolutionary new alarm system based on sophisticated circuitry that would detect and identify a large number of dangerous gases as well as smoke and very high temperatures. The device was the brainchild of Ira Magee, vice-president of research and the technical wizard responsible for many of Sutton's most successful products

It was unusual for so young and relatively inexperienced an employee as Eric to be given control of such a potentially important project, but he had shown skill in handling several complex, though routine, marketing assignments. In addition, he had the necessary scientific background to allow him to understand the benefits of Magee's proposed gas detection system.

Four weeks into the project, Eric was getting quite worried. He had tried to set up an organizational and planning meeting several times. No matter when he scheduled the meeting, the manager of the manufacturing department, Jaki Benken, was unable to attend. Finally, Eric agreed that manufacturing could be represented by young Bill Powell, a Benken protégé who had just graduated from college and joined Sutton Electronics. However, Eric was doubtful that Powell could contribute much to the project.

Eric's worry increased when Powell missed the first planning meeting completely and did not appear at the second meeting until it was almost over. Powell seemed apologetic and indicated that plant floor crises had kept him away from both meetings. The project was now five weeks old, and Eric was almost three weeks late with the marketing master plan. He was thinking about asking Ira Magee for help.

Questions: Do you think that Eric should involve Magee at this point? If so, what outcome would you expect? If not, what should he do?

 # BIBLIOGRAPHY

ADAMS, J. R., and S. E. BARNDT. "Behavorial Implications of the Project Life Cycle." In D. I. Cleland, and W. R. King, eds., *Project Management Handbook.* New York: Van Nostrand Reinhold, 1983.

AFZALUR, R. M. *Managing Conflict in Organizations.* Westport, CT: Praeger, 1992.

BAKER, K. R. "Measuring the Benefits of Partnering." *PM Network,* June 1996.

BAKER, S. T. "Partnering: Contracting for The Future." *Cost Engineering,* April 1990.

BEECHAM, M. A., and M. CORDEY-HAYES. "Partnering and knowledge transfer in the U.K. motor industry." *Technovation,* March 1998.

BROCKS, E., and G. S. ODIORNE. *Managing by Negotiation.* Melbourne, FL: Krieger 1990.

BURTON, J. *Conflict Resolution and Prevention.* New York: St. Martins, 1990.

CADBURY, G. A. H. "Ethical Managers Make Their Own Rules." *Harvard Business Review,* September–October 1987.

COHEN, H. *You Can Negotiate Anything.* Secaucus, NJ: Lyle Stuart Inc., 1980.

COWEN, C., C. GRAY, and E. W. LARSON. "Project Partnering." *Project Management Journal,* December 1992.

DE LAAT, P. B. "Matrix Management of Projects and Power Struggles: A Case Study of an R&D Laboratory." *IEEE Engineering Management Review,* Winter 1995, reprinted from *Human Relations,* Vol. 47, No. 9, 1994.

DODSON, W. R. "Virtually International." *PM Network,* April 1998.

DYER, W. G. *Team Building,* 2nd ed. Reading, MA: Addison-Wesley, 1987.

FISHER, R., and W. URY. *Getting to Yes.* Harmondsworth, Middlesex, G.B.: Penguin Books, 1983.

GROSSMAN, J. "Resolve Conflicts So Everybody Wins." *PM Network,* September 1995.

HAJEK, V. G. *Management of Engineering projects,* 3rd ed. New York: McGraw Hill, 1984.

HELPERN, A. *Negotiating Skills.* Holmes Beach, FL: W. W. Gaunt, 1992.

HUGHES, T. P. *Rescuing Prometheus,* New York: Pantheon, 1998.

JANDT, F. E. *Win-Win Negotiating.* New York: Wiley, 1987.

LARSON, E. W., and J. A. DREXLER, Jr. "Barriers to Project Partnering: Reports from the Firing Line." *Project Management Journal,* March 1997.

LARSON, E. W. "Partnering on Construction projects: A Study of the Relationship between Partnering Activities and Project Success." *IEEE Transactions on Engineering Management,* May 1997.

LONG, A. "Negotiating the Right Decision." *PM Network,* December 1997.

LOVE, S. F. *Achieving Problem Free Project Management.* New York: Wiley, 1989.

MOORE, C. C., J. D. MAES, and R. A. SHEARER. "Recognizing and Responding to the Vulnerabilities of Partnering." *PM Network,* September 1995.

NIERENBERG, G. I. *Fundamentals of Negotiating.* New York: HarperCollins, 1987.

OBRODOVITCH, M. M., and S. E. STEPHENOU. *Project Management: Risks and Productivity* (see Chapter 11, "Ethics"). Bend, OR: Daniel Spencer Pub., 1990.

PELLED, L. H., and P. S. ADLER. "Antecedents of Intergroup Conflict in Multifunctional Product Development Teams: A Conceptual Model." *IEEE Transactions on Engineering Management,* February 1994.

PILL, J. *Technical Management and Control of Large Scale Urban Studies: A Comparative Analysis of Two Cases.* Ph.D. dissertation, Cleveland: Case Western Reserve University, 1971.

PINTO, J. K., and O. P. KHARBANDA. "Project Management and Conflict Resolution." *Project Management Journal,* December 1995.

RAIFFA, H. *The Art and Science of Negotiation.* Cambridge: Belknap/Harvard Press, 1982.

RECK, R., and B. G. LONG. *The Win-Win Negotiator: How to Negotiate Favorable Agreements that Last.* Portage, MI: Spartan, 1987.

ROBINSON, T. "When Talking Makes Things Worse!" *PM Network,* March 1997.

Roget's International Thesaurus. New York: Thomas Y. Crowell, 1993.

SMITH, M. B. "Financial Constraints on Service and Outsourcing Projects." *PM Network,* October 1998.

TAN, G. W., C. C. HAYES, and M. SHAW. "A Intelligent-Agent Framework for Concurrent Product Design and Planning." *IEEE Transactions on Engineering Management,* August 1996.

THAMHAIN, H. J., and D. L. WILEMON. "Conflict Management in Project Life Cycles." *Sloan Management Review,* Summer 1975a.

THAMHAIN, H. J., and D. L. WILEMON. "Diagnosing Conflict Determinants in Project Management." *IEEE Transactions on Engineering Management,* February 1975b.

WALL, J. A., Jr. *Negotiation: Theory and Practice.* Glenview, IL: Scott, Foresman, 1985.

WALLES, T. K. "Enhancing Supplier Relationships." *PM Network,* October 1998.

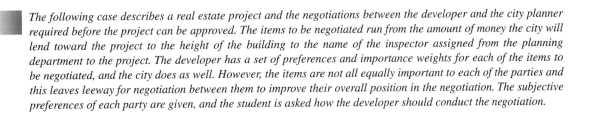

The following case describes a real estate project and the negotiations between the developer and the city planner required before the project can be approved. The items to be negotiated run from the amount of money the city will lend toward the project to the height of the building to the name of the inspector assigned from the planning department to the project. The developer has a set of preferences and importance weights for each of the items to be negotiated, and the city does as well. However, the items are not all equally important to each of the parties and this leaves leeway for negotiation between them to improve their overall position in the negotiation. The subjective preferences of each party are given, and the student is asked how the developer should conduct the negotiation.

C A S E

PELICAN LANDING: BENDER CORPORATION*
Susan E. Brodt

Chris Corbett, Vice President of the Bender Corporation, was guardedly optimistic about the upcoming meeting with Lee Lawson, Chief Planner for the City of Springfield. Corbett hoped they would be able to resolve the eight remaining issues that had stalled the approval of Pelican Landing, a residential community proposed for Springfield's "Old Town," so that construction could soon begin. A project such as Pelican Landing would go a long way toward revitalizing the Bender Corporation and reversing its depressed earnings. The stockholders were demanding action.

Historic Old Town

Old Town was the historic district, along the east bank of the Green River, that had formed the core of the original Springfield settlement. As the community flourished over the years following its founding, almost all the new growth had taken place just across the river in what was now identified in everyone's mind, and on most maps, as Springfield. Downtown Springfield bordered the Green River, with the rest of Springfield spreading west beyond it. This divergence of growth was probably as much a result of a feud between two of the families that had settled Springfield as it was the topography east of Old Town.

Although still linked to downtown Springfield by two old bridges, Old Town had been largely ignored as a commercial area. For decades, in fact, Old Town had been characterized as "light industrial" or "the warehouse district." Eventually, however, even

those uses had been discontinued, and Old Town now contained little more than old vacant buildings and empty lots littered with broken glass, weeds, and abandoned vehicles. The City of Springfield owned much of the property in Old Town.

Pelican Landing and the Bender Corporation

The Bender Corporation, a real estate development and property management company based 20 miles upstream from Springfield in Kentwood, also owned a lot of the property in Old Town, and it was now interested in turning Old Town into a residential community containing a combination of condominiums and rental units. Pelican Landing, as the project was to be called, was designed to include a small marina also. The proposed development had been tentatively endorsed by The Downtown Springfield Merchants Association and the local media.

The Bender Corporation had recently completed a similar development, called Miraloma Pointe, in Kentwood. After a shaky beginning, Miraloma Pointe now seemed to be doing well. Corbett thought that Pelican Landing was just the type of development that could stimulate the Bender Corporation and generate much needed new business. The past decade had not been kind to the company. Corbett leaned back and briefly reflected upon the events that had contributed to Bender's present financial plight.

When Corbett first became Vice President, the Bender Corporation was relatively small but very dynamic. The corporation had earned its reputation by specializing in urban residential development projects—condominiums, apartment buildings, or a combination of the two. After completion, the prop-

---

erty management division would take care of selling or renting the units. Even if the entire development had been built for or sold to a third party, the property management division would often be retained to manage the project.

Interest in the Bender Corporation was high, as were the profits. A lot of growth was taking place in Kentwood and the cities nearby, and Bender could boast of a dozen medium- or large-scale projects in various stages of planning or construction at any one time—developments such as the Divisadero Center, or the award winning Latimer Towers. Not only were the buildings full (thus generating large rents or management fees for the Bender Corporation), but the demand for more construction was high. It seemed that everyone wanted to live in "a Bender building."

Unfortunately, and suddenly (as it appeared to Corbett in retrospect), everything came to a standstill. Not only did new urban construction slow down, but people and companies started leaving the cities for other states or the less expensive suburbs. The opening of the interstate highway west of Kentwood, instead of bringing people to the city, seemed to have the opposite effect. Bedroom communities sprang up overnight along the interstate corridor.

Not only did Corbett find suburban tract houses and shopping malls aesthetically displeasing, Corbett knew they represented a loss of the company's income. As demand for urban living had dropped, so had rents, sales, and new construction. Corbett had been severely criticized for failing to anticipate and to capitalize on urban flight by building in the suburbs, but that was water over the dam.

What was important now was that cities once again represented opportunities for growth, and workers were again looking for homes near the city center. The Bender Corporation, after surviving some lean years, was now posed to take advantage of the young professionals' renewed interest in living and working in the city. That was why Corbett was excited about Pelican Landing.

Many cities, although welcoming new projects in their area, were also eager to seek concessions from a developer before agreeing to pursue a project.

The Bender Corporation/City of Springfield Discussions

As Corbett reviewed the status of the discussions with the City of Springfield, it appeared that eight issues still needed to be resolved with Lawson.

(1) **City Financing**—Corbett knew that government financing was almost always less expensive for a project such as Pelican Landing than financing by banks or other commercial lenders. Also, because of the Bender Corporation's current financial condition, Corbett did not expect the corporation to still qualify for the "preferred customer" rate that it had obtained from most banks in the past.

(2) **Retail Space**—Until the Bender Corporation built Miraloma Pointe, "a Bender building" had been exclusively residential. Corbett had discovered, however, that the square-footage rental value of the commercial space that had been included at Miraloma Pointe was almost 35% greater than the residential square-footage value. The Bender Corporation's property management division was anxious to duplicate that return at Pelican Landing, although Corbett did not know how that would go over with the Downtown Springfield Merchants Association.

(3) **Local Subcontractors**—The Bender Corporation had developed a strong relationship with many Kentwood subcontractors during its years in the construction business, and Corbett attempted, whenever possible, to use those subcontractors. However, Corbett understood that employing some local subcontractors was often part of the cost of doing business with some cities. Corbett knew, from past experience, that Kentwood subcontractors would not be considered "local" for the Pelican Landing development.

(4) **Open Space**—Urban residential developments were more and more frequently committing a percentage of their real estate to an open area, accessible to the public as well as the residents. Generally the open space would be nicely landscaped and lighted, and it would often include park benches and paths. Corbett, however, viewed open space as wasted space; i.e., space that the Bender Corporation would be unable to build on. Additionally, although the incident had been quietly settled, a

nonresident was mugged a year ago while enjoying the sunshine at the Divisadero Center and had sued the Bender Corporation and its property management division alleging a negligent lack of security.

(5) **Condominium/Apartment Ratio**—Although Corbett knew that condominiums represented an immediate return on investment, the property management division's experience had shown that a rental community, if well managed, would be more profitable over the long term. The corporation could maintain greater control over the community, and, if the financial need arose in the future, rental units could be converted to condominiums and sold, thereby providing additional capital. Obviously, the reverse was not true—once sold, a unit could not be so readily converted to a rental unit by the corporation.

(6) **Low/Moderate Income Units**—Another trend was for large urban residential developments to commit a percentage of total units to low/moderate-income families. Some kind of government funding would be available to families that qualified. Corbett recognized the public relations benefit from such an arrangement, not to mention the tax advantages; however, the reality was often lower overall sales prices or rents for the Bender Corporation.

(7) **Height**—People were almost always willing to pay a premium (on increased sales price or rent)

Exhibit 1
Pelican Landing Bender Corporation

Corbett's Payoff Schedule

CONFIDENTIAL—Do Not Share With Lawson

City financing	Points	Condo/apartment ratio	Points
$500,000	50	3:1	50
$625,000	150	2:1	130
$750,000	250	1:1	210
$875,000	350	1:2	290
$1,000,000	450	1:3	370

Retail space		Low/moderate-income units	
0 sq. ft.	−190	10%	50
1500 sq. ft.	−130	8%	70
3000 sq. ft.	−70	6%	90
4500 sq. ft.	−10	4%	110
6000 sq. ft.	50	2%	130

Local subcontractors		Height	
4	50	2 stories	−550
3	90	3 stories	−400
2	130	4 stories	−250
1	170	5 stories	−100
0	210	6 stories	50

Open space		Building inspector	
30%	50	Wottle	50
25%	110	DeWitt	80
20%	170	Gellespie	110
15%	230	Hawes	140
10%	290	Conibear	170

to be higher up. Corbett knew that this would be especially true at Pelican Landing with a westward view over the river of Springfield and beyond.

(8) **Planning Department Building Inspector**—Lawson would be able to assign one inspector from the staff of the Planning Department to work with the Bender Corporation on Pelican Landing. Corbett knew quite well, from past experience, that some staff members were "pro-development," some were "slow-growth," and others were somewhere in between. Corbett also knew that the indi-

vidual selected could significantly affect the project in terms of time and cost for the Bender Corporation.

Corbett considered alternative resolutions for each of the issues and thought about their importance. In order to better understand these tradeoffs, Corbett assigned relative points to each alternative (**Exhibit 1**) and noted the highest and lowest attainable values were 1,720 and –440, respectively. Clearly, the goal was to maximize these points in the discusssions with Lawson.

PELICAN LANDING REPORTING FORM

Your Name and Role _____

Your Counterpart _____

AGREEMENT		POINTS
Building inspector	_____	_____
City financing	_____	_____
Condo/apartment ratio	_____	_____
Height	_____	_____
Local subcontractor	_____	_____
Low-/moderate-income units	_____	_____
Open space	_____	_____
Retail space	_____	_____
	TOTAL	_____

QUESTIONS

1. In what ways are Corbett and Larson partners? Adversaries?

2. Interpret this situation in terms of the four points of principled negotiation.

3. If Corbett's estimate of the importance of each of the resolutions to the eight issues in Exhibit 1 is accurate, does it appear that a win-win scenario is feasible? Why? If so, would it be acceptable for Corbett to reveal his position on the eight issues to Lawson in order to speed up the negotiations and start of the project?

4. Given the data in Exhibit 1, how would you suggest Corbett proceed with the negotiations?
   — Which issues should be discussed first?
   — Which last?

— What position should Corbett take on each of the issues?

5. Consider one negotiation approach of coming to a strict compromise on each issue, resolved one at a time. Would another negotiation approach such as considering two or more issues at once, offer a better solution for both parties? If so, how?

6. Could numbers be inserted for the measures and the process converted into a problem of maximizing the sums for each of the negotiators? If all possible outcomes were then plotted in two-dimensional space, with each axis being the sum of the results for each negotiator, what would the plot look like? What would the outer boundary represent?

The following classic article describes a number of methods for negotiating and handling conflicts. The author identifies effective and ineffective methods ranging from withdrawal to forcing. Each method is then illustrated with a number of examples. Finally, the most effective method, Confrontation Problem Solving, *is described in terms of its many characteristics.*

R E A D I N G

METHODS OF RESOLVING INTERPERSONAL CONFLICT*
R. J. Burke

The management of conflict in creative and useful ways, rather than its containment or abolition, has been proposed by many writers. Various strategies for dealing with conflict at different levels and for managing disagreements have also been proposed. Most of these methods have not been experimentally evaluated. Given the central and inevitable role of conflict in human affairs, a high priority of importance is to be placed on learning the most effective way to resolve it.

Purpose of This Study

In a previous investigation, Burke (1969a) collected questionnaire data from 74 managers, in which they described the way they and their superiors dealt with conflict between them. It was possible to relate five different methods of conflict resolution originally proposed by Blake and Mouton (1964)—Withdrawing, Smoothing, Compromising, Forcing, and Confrontation or Problem Solving—to two major areas of the

*Methods of Resolving Interpersonal Conflict. *Personnel Administration,* July–August 1969. ©1969 by the International Personnel Management Association. Reprinted by permission.

superior-subordinate relationship. These were (1) constructive use of differences and disagreements, and (2) several aspects of the superior-subordinate relationship in planning job targets and evaluating accomplishments.

In general, the results showed that Withdrawing and Forcing behaviors were consistently negatively related to these two areas. Compromising was not related to these two areas. Use of Smoothing was inconsistently related, sometimes positive and sometimes negative. Only Confrontation-Problem Solving was always related positively to both. That is, use of Confrontation was associated with constructive use of differences and high scores on various measures of the superior-subordinate relationship.

This study has the dual purpose of attempting to specify more precisely the characteristics of the Confrontation-Problem Solving method of conflict resolution, and replicating the earlier study (Burke, 1969a) using different methodology.

Method

Subjects: The respondents were managers from various organizations who were enrolled in a university course emphasizing behavioral science concepts relevant to the functions of management. Their organizational experience ranged from one year to over 30 years.

Procedure: Each respondent was asked to describe a time when he felt particularly GOOD (or BAD) about the way in which an interpersonal conflict was resolved. The specific instructions stated:

"Think of a time when you felt especially GOOD (or BAD) about the way an interpersonal conflict or disagreement (e.g., boss-subordinate, peer-peer, etc.) in which you were involved was resolved. It may have been on your present job, or any other job, or away from the work situation.

"Now describe it in enough detail so a reader would understand the way the conflict or differences were handled."

This statement appeared at the top of a blank sheet of paper.

Approximately half the respondents were first to describe the instance when they felt particularly good, followed by the instance when they felt particularly bad. The remaining respondents described the instances in the reverse order. No apparent effects were observed from the change in order, so the data from both groups will be considered together in this report.

Results

Fifty-three descriptions of effective resolution of conflict (felt especially GOOD) and 53 descriptions of ineffective resolutions of conflict (felt especially BAD) were obtained. These were provided by 57 different individuals. Some individuals provided only one example. The response rate was about 70 percent of the total available population.

The written descriptions were then coded into one of the five methods of conflict resolution proposed by Blake and Mouton (1964).

1. *Withdrawing*—easier to refrain than to retreat from an argument; silence is golden. "See no evil, hear no evil, speak no evil."

2. *Smoothing*—play down the differences and emphasize common interests; issues that might cause divisions or hurt feelings are not discussed.

3. *Compromising*—splitting the difference, bargaining, search for an intermediate position. Better half a loaf than none at all; no one loses but no one wins.

4. *Forcing*—a win-lose situation; participants are antagonists, competitors, not collaborators. Fixed positions, polarization. Creates a victor and a vanquished.

5. *Confrontation-Problem Solving*—open exchange of information about the conflict or problem as each sees it, and a working through of their differences to reach a solution that is optimal to both. Both can win.

Table 1 presents the method of conflict resolution associated with effective resolution (left half of Table 1) and ineffective resolution (right half of Table 1). Considering the left half of the table, Confrontation-Problem Solving was the most common method for effective resolution (58.5%), followed by Forcing (24.5%), and Compromise (11.3%). The prominence of Confrontation as an effective method is consistent with the earlier study (Burke, 1969a) but the value for Forcing was higher than expected. When these 13 cases are considered as a group, 11 of them are similar in that the party providing the written description benefited as a result of the Forcing. That is, Forcing was perceived as an effective method of resolving conflict by the victor, but not by the vanquished.

Moving to the right half of Table 1, Forcing was the most commonly used method for ineffective resolution,

Table 1. Methods Associated with Effective and Ineffective Conflict Resolution

	Effective Resolution (N = 53)		Ineffective Resolution (N = 53)	
	N	%	N	%
Withdrawal	0	0.0*	5	9.4*
Smoothing	0	0.0	1	1.9
Compromise	6	11.3	3	5.7
Forcing	13	24.5*	42	79.2*
Confrontation- problem solving	31	58.5*	0	0.0*

Other (still unresolved;
    unable to determine
    how resolved;
    irrelevant to
    assignment; etc.)
	3	5.7	2	3.8

*Percentage difference between groups is significant at the .05 level of confidence.

followed in second place by Withdrawal with only 9.4 percent. The vast majority of individuals providing written descriptions of Forcing methods were victims or "losers" as a result of Forcing behavior.

In summary, the major differences in methods of conflict resolution found to distinguish effective versus ineffective examples were: (1) significantly greater use of Confrontation in the effective examples (58.5% vs. 0.0%); (2) significantly less use of Forcing in the effective examples (24.5% vs. 79.2%); and (3) significantly less use of Withdrawing in the effective examples (0.0% vs. 9.4%).

When Forcing was seen to be effective, the authors of the examples were "winners" of a win-lose conflict; when Forcing was seen to be ineffective, the authors of the examples were "losers" of a win-lose conflict. Whether the resolution of conflict via Forcing would actually be perceived to be effective by members of the organization outside the conflict (i.e., objectively seen as effective), as it was perceived to be effective by the "winners," remains to be determined by future research.

Effective Conflict Resolution

A few of the examples of effective conflict resolution are provided to highlight specific features of Confrontation. These were taken verbatim from the written descriptions.

1. *This example highlights the presentation of a problem of mutual interest—meeting deadlines more often at the earliest opportunity (when the problem is observed). Superior is open-minded and asking for help.*

"I once was given the responsibility for managing a small group of technicians engaged in turning out critical path schedules. I spent some time trying to get organized and involved with the group, but I sensed a hostile atmosphere, accompanied by offhand sarcastic remarks. At the end of the day very little work had been accomplished.

"The next day when I came in, I called the group together and told them that we were falling behind, and asked them to help me find a solution. After the initial distrust had been dissipated, the group produced some good ideas on work reallocation, office arrangement, priorities and techniques. I told the group that all of their agreed-upon suggestions would be implemented at once, and their reply was that the backlog would be cleared in three days and would not build up again.

"Within three days the backlog was gone, the group worked together better, and for the six months I was in charge, schedules were always ready before they were required."

2. *This example highlights emphasis on facts in determining the best resolution of conflict. Both had strong convictions but one willingly moved to the other's position when facts indicated that this position was best.*

"The project engineer and I disagreed about the method of estimating the cost of alternative schemes in a highway interchange. Neither of us could agree on the other's method. Eventually I was able to satisfy him using algebra. We were both happy with the result."

3. *Like Example 2, this one highlights an emphasis on facts and the conviction that by digging and digging, the truth will be discovered. Although the superior had a vested interest in the "old" system (a product of his thinking), the discussion was never personalized. That is, it did not involve "me" versus "you," but rather a comparison of two systems, two concepts or two ideas.*

"About a year ago I developed a new system for processing the accounting of the inventory of obsolete material on hand in our plant. It was my estimation that it would prove to be an easier system to operate and control and would also involve a considerable monetary saving for the company.

"When I approached my boss with the system, he immediately turned it down as he had developed the present system and was sure it was the best possible system. As I was sure my new system was superior to the present one, I then convinced him to join me in analyzing a comparison of the two systems, pointing out the strengths and weaknesses of the two. After a period of evaluation involving many differences of opinion, we were able to resolve that my system had definite merit and should be brought into operation."

4. *This example highlights the fact that through problem solving both parties can benefit. Instead of compromising, the issues are discussed until a solution completely satisfactory to both is found. Often this is superior to the ones initially favored by the separate parties.*

"In the—Board of Education, there were eight inspectors of Public Schools and four superintendents. Last February the inspectors were given the assignment of developing an in-service plan for the training of teachers for the school year 1968–69. The inspectors gave the assignment to a group of three of their number who were to bring a report to the next inspectors' meeting. I was not a member of the in-service committee but in conversations with the committee members I discovered that they contemplated having an in-service program for two teachers from each school (there are about 85 schools) once a month for the entire year in mathematics. I felt that this would be a very thin coverage of our 2000 or so teachers.

"Consequently I worked on a plan whereby utilizing two Thursday mornings a month and the specialized teaching help available in—, every teacher would have the opportunity to become involved in an in-service training session in a subject of his or her choice once during the year. At the inspectors' meeting the sub-committee presented its report and after some procedural wrangling I was permitted to present my plan. The two were diametrically opposed and it looked as if my plan would be voted down except the chairman suggested that both plans be presented to the superintendents.

"At the meeting of the superintendents, the subcommittee made its report and I presented my plan. As the meeting progressed there was some give and take and instead of one or the other being discarded both plans were adopted. For this school year mathematics is stressed for the first eight Thursday mornings (their plan in a rather concentrated form); then for the next eight months on the second and fourth Thursday my

plan is used. We came out of this meeting with a combination of the two plans which was better than either one individually."

Ineffective Conflict Resolution

Examples 5, 6, and 7 illustrate Forcing methods of conflict resolution. A win-lose situation is set up, and usually the superior wins. The individual with the greater power triumphs (a personalized disagreement) rather than the one whose position is supported by the most factual evidence.

5. "In a previous job, I worked for a major management consulting group as a consultant. One assignment, lasting four months, was to use a simulation technique to evaluate the most preferable investment decision using defined quantitative criteria. At the end of the job two alternatives were shown to be marginally better than the other. However, later sensitivity tests also showed that the analytical technique could not rate one to be substantially better than the other.

"Therefore, I wrote a 'technically honest' report stating that our analysis could not provide the one best alternative. My manager, feeling that we were hired to recommend a 'one best' alternative, wanted to cover up the limitations of our methodology.

"We disagreed and I was overruled. The manager wrote a 'technically dishonest' version of the report and the revised report was sent to the client indicating the 'one best' alternative."

6. "Recently in my firm, management had sprung a secrecy agreement contract upon all of the technical people. No word of introduction or explanation was given. It was simply handed out and we were asked to sign it. Most of us found objection in several clauses in the agreement. However, management officials stated that the agreement would probably not stand up in a court of law. They further stated that it was something that was sent from corporate in the United States and was not their idea. The employees continued to show reluctance.

"The vice-president called on everyone individually and stated that there would be no room for advancement for anyone who did not sign the contract. As a result everyone signed."

7. "I was assigned a project by my boss to determine the optimum way, using predetermined times, to lay out an assembly line. It would have to provide optimum efficiency with the following variables: (a) different hourly production rates (e.g., 100/hr. Mon., 200/hr.

Tues.) which would mean different numbers of operators on the line; (b) different models of the product (electric motors). The group was on group incentive.

"After much research and discussion, the system was installed utilizing the floating system of assembly (operators could move from station to station in order to keep out of the bottleneck operation). This system was working out well. However, at this time I was informed by my boss that he and the foreman of the area decided that they wished to use the 'paced' system of assembly. This would mean the conveyor belt would be run at set speeds and that the stripes would be printed on the belt indicating that one device would have to be placed on each mark and operators would not float.

"I was dead against this since I had considered it and rejected it in favor of the implemented method. I was, however, given the order to use their proposed system or else. There was no opportunity for discussion or justification of the method."

8. *This example is a classic description of Withdrawal as a mode of conflict resolution. Clearly the problem is not resolved.*

"On the successful completion of a project which involved considerable time and effort, I was praised and thanked for a job well done by my immediate supervisor and his supervisor, the vice-president in charge of manufacturing. They promised me that on my next salary review I would receive a substantial increase.

"The next salary review came up and my immediate supervisor submitted an amount that he and I felt was a good increase. The amount I received was one-third of this figure. I felt insulted, cheated, and hurt that the company considered I was worth this 'token' amount.

"I had a personal interview with the vice-president where I argued that I felt I should receive more. He agreed in sort of an offhanded way—he felt the whole salary schedule should be reviewed and that my area of responsibility should be increased. He said the company wants people to 'prove themselves' before they give them increases; and he suggested a salary review. I felt I had just done this in my last project—I felt I was being put off, but agreed to the salary review.

"One month passed and nothing happened. I became frustrated—I purposely slowed down the amount of work I turned out.

"Another month passed and still no action. I became disillusioned with the company and resolved at this point to look for another position. Several months later with still no action, I resigned and accepted another position."

Inability to Resolve Conflict

These descriptions of ineffective resolution of conflict indicate that an impressive number of respondents included termination or change of employment of one member in the situation (19 of 53, 26%). These cases tended to be of two types.

The first is represented by Example 8. Here an employee decides to quit because he felt the problem was not resolved in a satisfactory manner. Forcing is likely to be associated with instances of voluntary termination.

The second centered around an inability to resolve the conflict. Then the "problem employee" (a visible symptom of the conflict) was dismissed.

9. *The following example illustrates this:*

"This concerned a young girl about 18 years old who was a typist in our office. This girl lacked a little maturity, but was not really all that bad. She was tuned to all the latest fashions in both dress and manners.

"I felt and still feel that this girl was a potentially good employee. But it was decided that she should be let go. The argument used was that she was not a good worker and lacked the proper attitude for office work. Rather than spend a little time and effort to understand the girl and perhaps develop her into a good employee, the easy way was taken and the girl was fired."

There were two other clear cases of "effective" conflict resolution resulting in voluntary employee terminations. In both instances a Forcing mode was employed and the "loser" resigned from the organization soon after. Our finding is that these were given as examples of effective conflict resolution by the "winner." In another effective example of Forcing, the "loser" was dismissed.

Conclusions

The results of this investigation are consistent with an earlier study (Burke, 1969a), and the data of Lawrence and Lorsch (1967a, 1967b) in showing the value of Confrontation-Problem Solving as a method of conflict resolution. About 60 percent of the examples of effective conflict resolution involved use of the method, while no examples of ineffective conflict resolution did. The poorest method of conflict resolution was Forcing. This method accounted for 80 percent of the examples of ineffective conflict resolution and only 24 percent of the examples of effective conflict resolution.

The latter conclusion is somewhat at odds with Lawrence and Lorsch's findings that Forcing was an effective backup method to Confrontation, from an organizational effectiveness standpoint. In fact, the earlier study (Burke, 1969a) found that the use of these methods tended to be negatively correlated. Managers high in use of one of them tended to be low in use of the other.

Characteristics of Problem Solving

Let us now consider more specific features of Confrontation, the most effective method of resolving interpersonal conflict. Insights from the present investigation and the writings of others (e.g., Blake, Shepard and Mouton, 1964; Maier, 1963; Maier and Hoffman, 1965) becomes relevant. The following then are characteristics of Confrontation as a method of managing conflict:

(1) Both people have a vested interest in the outcome. (Examples 1, 2, 3, and 4).

(2) There is a belief on the part of the people involved that they have the potential to resolve the conflict and to achieve a better solution through collaboration.

(3) There is a recognition that the conflict or the problem is mainly in the relationship between the individuals and not in each person separately. If the conflict is in the relationship, it must be defined by those who have the relationship. In addition, if solutions are to be developed, the solutions have to be generated by those who share the responsibility for assuring that the solution will work and for making the relationship last.

(4) The goal is to solve the problem, not to accommodate different points of view. This process identifies the causes of reservation, doubt, and misunderstanding between the people confronted with conflict and disagreement. Alternative ways of approaching conflict resolution are explored and tested (Examples 2 and 3).

(5) The people involved are problem-minded instead of solution-minded; "fluid" instead of "fixed" positions. Both parties jointly search out the issues that separate them. Through joint effort, the problems that demand solutions are identified, and later solved.

(6) There is a realization that both aspects of a controversy have potential strengths and potential weaknesses. Rarely is one position completely right and the other completely wrong. (Example 4).

(7) There is an effort to understand the conflict or problem from the other person's point of view, and from the standpoint of the "real" or legitimate needs that must be recognized and met before problem solving can occur. Full acceptance of the other is essential.

(8) The importance of looking at the conflict objectively rather than in a personalized sort of way is recognized. (Example 3).

(9) An examination of one's own attitudes (hostilities, antagonisms) is needed before interpersonal contact on a less effective basis has a chance to occur.

(10) An understanding of the less effective methods of conflict resolution (e.g., win-lose, bargaining, etc.) is essential.

(11) One needs to present "face-saving" situations. Allow people to "give" so that a change in one's viewpoint does not suggest weakness or capitulation.

(12) There is need to minimize effects of status differences, defensiveness, and other barriers which prevent people from working together effectively.

(13) It is important to be aware of the limitations of arguing or presenting evidence in favor of your own position while downgrading the opponent's position. This behavior often stimulates the opponent to find even greater support for his position (increased polarization). In addition, it leads to selective listening for weaknesses in the opponent's position rather than listening to understand his or her position.

Attitude, Skill, and Creativity

Two related themes run through these characteristics, one dealing with attitudes, and the other with skills (interpersonal, problem solving) of the individuals involved. As the research of Maier and his associates has shown, differences and disagreements need not lead to dissatisfaction and unpleasant experiences but rather can lead to innovation and creativity. One of the critical variables was found to be the leader's attitudes toward disagreement. The person with different ideas, especially if he or she is a subordinate, can be seen as a problem employee and troublemaker or as an innovator, depending on the leader's attitude.

There are some people that go through life attempting to sell their ideas, to get others to do things they do not want to do. They set up a series of win-lose situations, and attempt to emerge victorious. Many of these people are able to accomplish their ends. There are others who are more concerned with the quality and effectiveness of their operations, and who, with creative solutions to problems, are genuinely openminded and able and willing to learn from others (and to teach others), in a collaborative relationship.

The interpersonal skills are related to the development of a "helping relationship" and include among other things, mutual trust and respect, candid communication, and awareness of the needs of others. The problem solving skills center around locating and stating the problem, seeking alternatives, exploring and testing alternatives, and selecting the best alternative. Knowledge and insight gained through experience with the benefits of problem solving and the dysfunctional effects of other strategies would be valuable in developing interpersonal skills.

Further Research Needed

Two additional areas need immediate research consideration. The first needs to explore the notions of conflict resolution from the organizational as well as the individual viewpoint. Lawrence and Lorsch report that Forcing was an effective back-up mode to Confrontation from the organization's standpoint, because at least things were being done. Our data in two separate investigations indicate that this mode of conflict resolution is very unsatisfactory from the standpoint of the one forced, the "loser," and may also have dysfunctional consequences.

The second research area concerns the application of these principles of effective conflict resolution (Confrontation-Problem Solving, with their more specific attitudinal and skill components) in an attempt to arrive at more constructive use of disagreement. Preliminary results from an experiment simulating conflict situations using role playing suggest that knowledge of these principles and some limited practice in their use increases one's ability to use differences constructively in obtaining a quality solution, and decreases the tendency to engage in "limited war" (Burke, 1969b).

References

BLAKE, R. R., and J. S., MOUTON. *The Managerial Grid,* Houston: Gulf Publishing Company, 1964.

BLAKE, R. R., H. A. SHEPARD, and J. S MOUTON. *Managing Intergroup Conflict in Industry,* Houston: Gulf Publishing Company, 1964.

BOULDING, K. "A pure theory of conflict applied to organization." In R. I. Kahn and E. Boulding (eds.), *Power and Conflict in Organizations.* New York: Basic Books, Inc., 1964, pp. 136–145.

BURKE, R. J. "Methods of managing superior-subordi-

nate conflict: Their effectiveness and consequences." Unpublished manuscript, 1969a.

BURKE, R. J. "Effects of limited training on conflict resolution effectiveness." Unpublished manuscript, 1969b.

KATA, D. "Approaches to managing conflict." In R. L. Kahn and E. Boulding (eds.), *Power and Conflict in Organizations.* New York: Basic Books, Inc., 1964, pp. 105–114.

LAWRENCE, P. R., and J. W. LORSCH. "Differentiation and intergration in complex organizations." *Administrative Science Quarterly,* 1967a, 12, 1–47.

LAWRENCE, P. R., and J. W LORSCH. *Organization and Environment,* Boston: Division of Research, Harvard Business School, Harvard University, 1967b.

MAIER, N. R. F. *Problem-Solving Discussions and Conferences.* New York: McGraw-Hill, 1963.

MAIER, N. R. F., and L. R. HOFFMAN. "Acceptance and quality of solutions as related to leaders' attitudes toward disagreement in group problem-solving." *Journal of Applied Behavioral Science,* 1965, 1, pp. 373–386.

MCGREGOR, D. *The Professional Manager.* New York: McGraw-Hill, 1967.

SHEPARD, H. A. "Responses to situations of competition and conflict." In R. L. Kahn and E. Boulding (eds.), *Power and Conflict in Organizations.* New York: Basic Books, Inc., 1964, pp. 127–135.

Questions

1. In Table 1, what was the second best resolution technique? What was the worst resolution technique? What do you conclude from this?

2. Which of the four examples of conflict resolution is the best example, in your opinion, of effective resolution? Why?

3. Of the ineffective resolution examples, which was the worst, in your opinion? Why?

4. Summarize or condense the 13 characteristics of Confrontation as a conflict-resolving method.

5. The article concludes on the note that conflict need not be a bad thing. Compare this view with that in the chapter concerning the win-win approach to negotiation.

7

Budgeting and Cost Estimation

In Chapter 5, we reviewed the planning process and gave some guidelines for designing the project plan; in Chapter 6, we discussed the conflicts arising around the project plan and its implementation. We proposed win-win negotiation and other conflict resolution techniques to deal with these conflicts.

We are now ready to begin implementation. First priority is, of course, obtaining resources with which to do the work. Senior management approval of the project budget does exactly that. A budget is a plan for allocating resources. Thus, the act of budgeting is the allocation of scarce resources to the various endeavors of an organization. The outcomes of the allocation process often do not satisfy managers of the organization who must live and work under budget constraints. It is, however, precisely the pattern of constraints in a budget that embodies organizational policy. The degree to which the different activities of an organization are fully supported by an allocation of resources is one measure of the importance placed on the outcome of the activity. Most of the senior managers we know try hard to be evenhanded in the budgetary process, funding each planned activity at the "right" level—neither overfunding, which produces waste and encourages slack management, nor underfunding, which inhibits accomplishment and frustrates the committed. (This is not to suggest that subordinate managers necessarily agree with our assessment.)

The budget is not simply one facet of a plan, nor is it merely an expression of organizational policy; it is also a control mechanism. The budget serves as a standard for comparison, a baseline from which to measure the difference between the actual and planned uses of resources. As the manager directs the deployment of resources to accomplish some desired objective, resource usage should be monitored carefully. This allows deviations from planned usage to be checked against the progress of the project, and exception reports can be generated if resource expenditures are not consistent with accomplishments. Indeed, the pattern of deviations (variances) can be examined to see if it is possible, or reasonable, to forecast significant departures from budget. With sufficient warning, it is sometimes possible to implement corrective actions. In any event, such forecasting helps to decrease the number of undesirable surprises for senior management.

Budgets play an important role in the entire process of management. It is clear that budgeting procedures must associate resource use with the achievement of organizational goals or the planning/control process becomes useless. If budgets are not tied to achievement, management may ignore situations where funds are being spent far in advance of accomplishment but are within budget when viewed by time period. Similarly, management may misinterpret the true state of affairs when the budget is overspent for a given time period but outlays are appropriate for the level of task completion. Data must be collected and reported in a timely manner, or the value of the budget in identifying and reporting current problems or anticipating upcoming problems will be lost. The reporting process must be carefully designed and controlled. It is of no value if the data are sent to the wrong person or the reports take an inordinately long time to be processed through the system. For example, one manager of a now defunct, large, computer company complained that, based on third-quarter reports, he was instructed to act so as to alter the fourth-quarter results. However, he did not receive the instructions until the first quarter of the following year.

In Chapter 5, we described a planning process that integrated the planning done at different levels of the project. At the top level is the overall project plan, which is then divided and divided again and, perhaps, still again into a "nest" of plans. Project plans were shown to be the verbal equivalents of the WBS. If we cost the WBS, step by step, we develop a project budget. If we cost project plans, we achieve exactly the same end. Viewed in this way, *the budget is simply the project plan in another form.*

Let us now consider some of the various budgeting methods used in organizations. These are described in general first, then with respect to projects. We also address some problems of cost estimation, with attention to the details and pitfalls. We consider some of the special demands and concerns with budgeting for projects. Throughout the chapter attention is paid to dealing with budgetary risk, although the methods of handling risk will be covered in greater detail in Chapter 8. Finally, we present a method for reducing the risk in making estimations, and improving one's skills at budget estimation, or estimation and forecasting of any kind. Printouts of project budgets from PM software packages will be shown in Chapter 10 where we cover project management information systems.

Project Management in Practice
Pathfinder Mission to Mars—on a Shoestring

The Pathfinder Rover explores Martian terrain.

In 1976, NASA's two Viking Mars-lander missions took six years and $3 billion (in 1992 dollars) to develop. Twenty-one years later, on July 4, 1997, Mars Pathfinder and Sojourner Rover landed on Mars once again, but at a development cost of only $175 million, representing a whopping 94 percent cost reduction over the earlier mission. This amazing cost reduction was achieved through a variety of means but the most important was perhaps the philosophical one that this was a design-to-cost project rather than a design-to-performance project. Given this philosophy, the scope of the mission was intentionally limited and "scope-creep" was never an issue:

- to achieve a successful landing
- return of engineering telemetry

- acquisition and transmission of a *single,* partial panoramic image
- successful rover deployment and 7 sol (Martian day) operation on the surface
- completion of a 30 sol lander mission meeting all engineering, science, and technology objectives
- *one* successful alpha proton X-ray spectrometer measurement of a Martian rock and soil sample.

The means of limiting the cost of the mission were multiple and creative:

- development was cost-capped, with no opportunity for more funds

- identifying a set of "de-scope" options which could be implemented in case the cost grew beyond the fixed budget
- mission, flight, and ground systems designs were driven by existing hardware and system capability
- a project cash reserve of 27 percent of the total budget was held back and carefully planned for time-phased release throughout the duration of the project
- mission designers/builders transitioned into the testers/operators to save documentation, time, labor cost, and chance of error
- existing NASA mission infrastructure was used rather than designing new systems
- instituting time-phased "what if" and lien lists for real or potential current and anticipated items of cost growth during the project
- choosing to use a "single-string" but higher

risk design and offsetting the risk by using more reliable parts

- 70 percent of major procurements contracts were fixed-price rather than cost-plus
- creative procurement, such as existing equipment spares, and accounting, such as lower burden rate personnel

On July 5, the Mars Sojourner Rover rolled down its deployment ramp and the resulting pictures made the headlines on newspapers around the world. The mission continued for almost three months and returned 2.6 gigabites of scientific and engineering data, 16,000 lander camera images, 550 rover camera images, 8.5 million environmental measurements, and the results of 16 chemical rock/soil experiments and 10 technology rover experiments.

Source: C. Sholes and N. Chalfin, "Mars Pathfinder Mission," *PM Network,* January 1999, pp. 30–35.

7.1   ESTIMATING PROJECT BUDGETS

In order to develop a budget, we must forecast what resources the project will require, the required quantity of each, when they will be needed, and how much they will cost—including the effects of potential price inflation. Uncertainty is involved in any forecast, though some forecasts have less uncertainty than others. An experienced cost estimator can forecast the number of bricks that will be used to construct a brick wall of known dimensions within 1 to 2 percent. (The estimator knows almost exactly how many bricks are needed to build the wall and must simply add a small allowance for broken or discolored bricks being delivered to the job, plus a few more for bricks broken during construction work.) On the other hand, the errors are apt to be much larger for an estimate of the number of programmer hours or lines of code that will be required to produce a specific piece of software (see Section 7.2). While the field of software science makes such estimates quite possible, the level of uncertainty is considerably higher and the typical error size is much larger.

In many fields, cost-estimating methods are well codified. The office walls of organizational purchasing departments are lined with catalogues detailing what materials, services, and machines are available, and from whom. Also on the bookshelves are volumes devoted to the techniques of estimating the quantities of materials and labor required to accomplish specific jobs. Every business has its own rules of thumb for cost estimating. These usually distill the collective experience gained by many estimators over many years. An experienced producer of books, for example, can leaf through a manuscript and, after asking a few questions about the number and type of illustrations and the quality of paper to be used, can make a fairly accurate estimate of what it will cost to produce a book.

At times, the job of cost estimation for entire complex projects may be relatively simple because experience has shown that some formula gives a good *first approximation* of the project's cost. For example, the Goodyear Aircraft Company makes an initial estimate of the cost of building a blimp by multiplying the estimated weight of the blimp by a specific dollar factor. (The weight is estimated in pounds, presumably prior to the blimp's inflation with helium.) The cost of buildings is commonly estimated as dollars per square foot times the square feet of floor area. Obviously these approximations must be adjusted for any special characteristics associated with each individual project, but this adjustment is far easier than making an estimate from scratch.

We will have more to say about gathering data shortly. Before doing so, however, and before discussing budget construction and presentation, it is helpful to understand that developing project budgets is much more difficult than developing budgets for more permanent organizational activities. The influence of history is strong in the budget of an ongoing activity, and many entries may ultimately become just "last year's figure plus X percent," where X is any number the budgeter feels "can be lived with" and is probably acceptable to the person or group who approves the budgets. No single item in the budget for an ongoing activity is apt to be crucial, because over the course of years the budget has gained sufficient slack that internal adjustments will probably take care of minor shortages in the key accounts—which is to say that budget uncertainty is significantly greater for projects than for traditional operations.

The project budgeter cannot depend on tradition. At project inception, there may be no past budgets to use as a base. At times, the budgeter may have budgets and audit reports for similar projects to serve as guides, but these are rough guides at best. In any case, all projects are unique and all project budgets are based on *forecasts* of resource usage and the associated costs. Thus, estimating the cost for any project involves risk. Tradition, however, has another impact on budgeting, this time a helpful one. In the special case of R & D projects, it has been found (Dean, Mantel, and Roepcke, 1969) that project budgets are stable over time when measured as a percent of the total allocation to R & D from the parent firm, though within the project the budget may be reallocated among activities. There is no reason to believe that the situation is different for other kinds of projects, and we have some evidence that shows stability similar to R & D projects.

For multiyear projects, another problem is raised. The plans and schedules for such projects are set at the beginning of project life, but over the years, the forecast resource usage may be altered by the availability of alternate or new materials, machinery, or personnel—available at different costs than were estimated, giving rise to both the risk of inflation and technological risk. The longer the project life, the less the PM can trust that traditional methods and costs will be relevant. As if that were not enough, the degree of executive oversight and review is usually much higher for projects than for ongoing operations, so the budgeter must expect to defend any and all budget entries.

Tradition has still another impact on project budgeting. Every organization has its idiosyncrasies. One firm charges the project's R & D budget with the cost of training sales representatives on the technical aspects of a new product. Another adopts special property accounting practices for contracts with the government. Unless the PM understands the organizational accounting system, there is no way to exercise budgetary control over the project. The methods for project budgeting described below are intended to avoid these problems as much as possible, but complete avoidance is out of the question. Further, it is not politically feasible for the PM to plead a special case with the accountants, who have their own problems. The PM simply must be familiar with the organization's accounting system!

One aspect of cost estimation and budgeting that is not often discussed has to do with the *actual* use of resources as opposed to the accounting department's assumptions about how and when the resources will be used. For instance, presume that you have estimated that $5,000 of a given resource will be used in accomplishing a task that is estimated to require five weeks. The actual use of the resource may be none in the first week, $3,000 worth in the second week, none in the third week, $1,500 in the fourth week, and the remaining $500 in the last week. Unless this pattern of expenditure is detailed in the plan, the accounting department, which takes a linear view of the world, will spread the expenditure equally over the five-week period. This may not affect the project's budget, but it most certainly affects the project's cash flow. The PM must be aware of both the resource requirements and the specific time pattern of resource usage. This subject will be mentioned again in Chapter 9.

Another aspect of preparing budgets is especially important for project budgeting. Every expenditure (or receipt) must be identified with a specific project task (and with its associated milestone, as we will see in the next chapter). Referring back to Figure 5-6, we see that each element in the WBS has a unique account number to which charges are accrued as work is done. These identifiers are needed for the PM to exercise budgetary control.

With these things in mind, the issue of how to gather input data for the budget becomes a matter of some concern. There are two fundamentally different strategies for data gathering, top-down and bottom-up.

Top-Down Budgeting

This strategy is based on collecting the judgments and experiences of top and middle managers, and available past data concerning similar activities. These managers estimate overall project cost as well as the costs of the major subprojects that comprise it. These cost estimates are then given to lower-level managers, who are expected to continue the breakdown into budget estimates for the specific tasks and work packages that comprise the subprojects. This process continues to the lowest level.

The process parallels the hierarchical planning process described in the last chapter. The budget, like the project, is broken down into successively finer detail, starting from the top, or most aggregated level following the WBS. It is presumed that lower-level managers will argue for more funds if the budget allocation they have been granted is, in their judgment, insufficient for the tasks assigned. This presumption is, however, often incorrect. Instead of reasoned debate, argument sometimes ensues, or simply sullen silence. When senior managers insist on maintaining their budgetary positions—based on "considerable past experience"—junior managers feel forced to accept what they perceive to be insufficient allocations to achieve the objectives to which they must commit.

Discussions between the authors and a large number of managers support the contention that lower-level managers often treat the entire budgeting process as if it were a zero-sum game, a game in which any individual's gain is another individual's loss. Competition among junior managers is often quite intense.

The advantage of this top-down process is that aggregate budgets can often be developed quite accurately, though a few individual elements may be significantly in error. Not only are budgets stable as a percent of total allocation, the statistical distribution of the budgets is also stable, making for high predictability (Dean, Mantel, and Roepcke, 1969). Another advantage of the top-down process is that small yet costly tasks need not be individually identified, nor need it be feared that some small but important aspect has been overlooked. The experience and judgment of the executive is presumed automatically to factor all such elements into the overall estimate. Questions put to subordinates, however, indicate that senior management has a strong bias toward underestimating costs.

Bottom-Up Budgeting

In this method, elemental tasks, their schedules, and their individual budgets are constructed, again following the WBS. The people doing the work are consulted regarding times and budgets for the tasks to ensure the best level of accuracy. Initially, estimates are made in terms of resources, such as labor hours and materials. These are later converted to dollar equivalents. Standard analytic tools such as learning curve analysis (discussed in the next section) and work sampling are employed where appropriate to improve the estimates. Differences of opinion are resolved by the usual discussions between senior and junior managers. If necessary, the project manager and the functional manager(s) may enter the discussion in order to ensure the accuracy of the estimates. The resulting task budgets are aggregated to give the total direct costs of the project. The PM adds such indirect costs as general and administrative (G&A), possibly a project reserve for contingencies, and then a profit figure to arrive at the final project budget.

Bottom-up budgets should be, and usually are, more accurate in the detailed tasks, but it is critical that all elements be included. It is far more difficult to develop a complete list of tasks when constructing that list from the bottom up than from the top down. Just as the top-down method may lead to budgetary game playing, the bottom-up process has its unique managerial budget games. For example, individuals overstate their resource needs because they suspect that higher management will probably cut all budgets. Their suspicion is, of course, quite justified, as Gagnon (Gagnon, 1982; Gagnon and Mantel, 1987) and others have shown. Managers who are particularly persuasive sometimes win, but those who are consistently honest and have high credibility win more often.

The advantages of the bottom-up process are those generally associated with participative management. Individuals closer to the work are apt to have a more accurate idea of resource requirements than their superiors or others not personally involved.

In addition, the direct involvement of low-level managers in budget preparation increases the likelihood that they will accept the result with a minimum of grumbling. Involvement also is a good managerial training technique, giving junior managers valuable experience in budget preparation as well as the knowledge of the operations required to generate a budget.

While top-down budgeting is common, true bottom-up budgets are rare. Senior managers see the bottom-up process as risky. They tend not to be particularly trusting of ambitious subordinates who may overstate resource requirements in an attempt to ensure success and build empires. Besides, as senior managers note with some justification, the budget is the most important tool for control of the organization. They are understandably reluctant to hand over that control to subordinates whose experience and motives are questionable. This attitude is carried to an extreme in one large corporation that conducts several dozen projects simultaneously, each of which may last five to eight years and cost millions of dollars. Project managers do not participate in the budgeting process in this company, nor do they have access to project budgets during their tenure as PMs. (In the past few years, the firm has decided to give PMs access to project budgets, but they are still not allowed to participate in the budgetary process.)

Work Element Costing

The actual process of building a project budget—either top-down or bottom-up or, as we will suggest, a combination of both—tends to be a straightforward but tedious process. Each work element in the action plan or WBS is evaluated for its resource requirements, and the cost of each resource is estimated.

Suppose a work element is estimated to require 25 hours of labor by a technician. The specific technician assigned to this job is paid $17.50/hr. Overhead changes to the project are 84 percent of direct labor charges. The appropriate cost appears to be

$$25 \text{ hr} \times \$17.50 \times 1.84 = \$805.00$$

but the accuracy of this calculation depends on the precise assumptions behind the 25-hr estimate. Industrial engineers have noted that during a normal eight hour day, no one actually works for all eight hours. Even on an assembly line, workers need breaks called "personal time." This covers such activities as visiting the water cooler, the toilet, having a cigarette, blowing one's nose, and all the other time consuming activities engaged in by normal people in a normal workplace. A typical allowance for personal time is 12% of total work time. If personal time was not included in the 25 hr estimate made above, then the cost calculation becomes

$$1.12 \times 25 \text{ hr} \times \$17.50 \times 1.84 = \$901.60*$$

The uncertainty in labor cost estimating lies in the estimate of hours to be expended. Not including personal time ensures an underestimate.

---

*In a weak matrix project, the Technical Assistance Group (TAG) would submit a lump-sum charge to the project, calculated in much the same way. The charge would, of course, include the costs noted in the rest of this section.

Direct costs for resources and machinery are charged directly to the project, and are not usually subject to overhead charges. If a specific machine is needed by the project and is the property of a functional department, the project may "pay" for it by transferring funds from the project budget to the functional department's budget. The charge for such machines will be an operating cost ($/hr or $/operating cycle), plus a depreciation charge based on either time or number of operating cycles. Use of general office equipment, e.g., copy machines, drafting equipment, and coffeemakers, is often included in the general overhead charge.

In addition to these charges, there is also the *General and Administrative (G&A)* charge. This is composed of the cost of senior management, the various staff functions, and any other expenses not included in overhead. G&A charges are a fixed percent of either the direct costs or the total of all direct and indirect costs.

Thus, a fully costed work element would include direct costs (labor, resources, and special machinery) plus overhead and G&A charges. We advise the PM to prepare two budgets, one with overheads and G&A charges, and one without. The full cost budget is used by the accounting group to estimate the profit earned by the project. The budget that contains only direct costs gives the PM the information required to manage the project without being confounded with costs over which the PM has no control. Let us now consider a combination of top-down and bottom-up budgeting.

An Iterative Budgeting Process—Negotiation-in-Action

In Chapter 5, we recommended an iterative planning process with subordinates* developing action plans for the tasks for which they were responsible. Superiors review these plans, perhaps suggesting amendments. (See also the latter part of Section 5.3.) The strength of this planning technique is that primary responsibility for the design of a task is delegated to the individual accountable for its completion, and thus it utilizes participative management (or "employee involvement"). If done correctly, estimated resource usage and schedules are a normal part of the planning process at all planning levels. Therefore, the individual concocting an action plan at the highest level would estimate resource requirements and durations for each of the steps in the highest level action plan. Let us refer to these as r_i and t_i, the resource level and task time requirements for the ith task, respectively. Similarly, the subordinate estimates the resource and time requirements for each step of the lower-level action plan. Let us denote the *aggregate* resource and time requirements for the lower level action plan as r_i' and t_i', respectively.

In a perfect world, r_i would equal r_i'. (As regards t_i and t_i', our argument holds for duration estimates as well as resource estimates.) We do not, however, live in a perfect world. As a matter of fact, the probable relationship between the original estimates made at the different levels is $r_i \ll r_i'$. This is true for several reasons, three of which are practically universal. First, as Gagnon (1982) has found, the farther one moves up the organizational chart away from immediate responsibility for doing the

---

*We use the terms "superior" and "subordinate" here for the sole purpose of identifying individuals working on different relative levels of a project's set of action plans. We recognize that in a matrix organization it is not uncommon for PMs ("superiors") to delegate work to individuals ("subordinates") who do not report to the PM and who may even be senior to the PM on the parent firm's organizational chart.

work, the easier, faster, and cheaper the job looks to the superior than to the one who has to do it. This is because the superior either does not know the details of the task, or has conveniently forgotten the details, as well as how long the job takes and how many problems can arise. Second, wishful thinking leads the superior to underestimate cost (and time), because the superior has a stake in representing the project to senior management as a profitable venture. Third, the subordinate is led to build-in some level of protection against failure by adding an allowance for "Murphy's Law" onto a budget that already has a healthy contingency allowance.

Assuming that the superior and subordinate are reasonably honest with one another (any other assumption leads to a failure in win-win negotiations), the two parties meet and review the subordinate's action plan. Usually, the initial step toward reducing the difference in cost estimates is made by the superior who is "educated" by the subordinate in the realities of the job. The result is that r_i rises. The next step is typically made by the subordinate. Encouraged by the boss's positive response to reason, the subordinate surrenders some of protection provided for by the budgetary "slop," and r_i' falls. The subordinate's cost estimate is still greater than the superior's, but the difference is considerably decreased.

The pair now turn their attention to the technology of the task at hand. They carefully inspect the subordinate's work plan, trying to find a more efficient way to accomplish the desired end; that is, they practice total quality management (TQM) and/or value engineering. It may be that a major change can be made that allows a lower resource commitment than either originally imagined. It may be that little or no further improvement is possible. Let us assume that moderate improvement is made, but that r_i' is still somewhat greater than r_i, although both have been altered by the negotiations thus far. What should the superior do, accept the subordinate's estimate or insist that the subordinate make do with r_i? In order to answer this question, we must digress and reconsider the concept of the project life cycle.

In Chapter 1, we presented the usual view of the project life cycle in Figure 1-3, shown here as Figure 7-1 for convenience. This view of the life cycle shows decreasing returns to inputs as the project nears completion. Figure 1-5 is also shown here as Figure 7-2 for convenience. In this case, the project shows increasing return to inputs as the project nears completion. In order to decide whether to adopt the subordinate's resource estimate, r_i', or the superior's, r_i, we need to know which picture of the life cycle represents the task under consideration. Note that we are treating the subordinate's action plan as if it were a project, which is perfectly all right because it has the characteristics of a project that were described in Chapter 1. Also note that we do not need to know the shape of the life cycle with any precision, merely if its last stage is concave or convex to the horizontal axis.

Remember that the superior's and subordinate's resource estimates are not very far apart as a result of the negotiations preceding this decision. If the latter part of the life-cycle curve is concave (as in Figure 7-1), showing diminishing marginal returns, we opt for the superior's estimate because of the small impact on completion that results from withholding a small amount of resources. The superior might say to the subordinate, "Jeremy, what can you get me for r_i? We will have to live with that." If, on the other hand, the life cycle curve is convex, showing increasing marginal returns as in Figure 7-2, the subordinate's estimate should be chosen because of the potentially drastic effect a resource shortage would have on project completion. In this

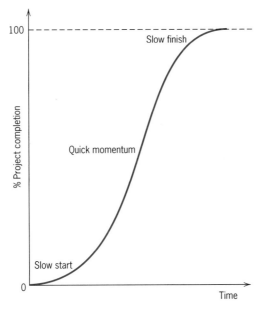

Figure 7-1   The project life cycle. (Figure 1-3 reproduced.)

event, the superior might say, "OK, Brandon, we have got to be sure of this job. We'll go with your numbers." If the disagreement had concerned schedule (duration) instead of resources, the negotiation process and underlying logic would be unaltered.

This is a time-consuming process. At the same time the PM is negotiating with the several subordinates responsible for the pieces of the PM's action plan, each of the subordinates is negotiating with their subordinates, and so on. This multilevel process is messy and not particularly efficient, but it allows a free-flow of ideas up and down the system at all levels. This iterative process tends to reduce the uncertainty in budget estimations. The debate over processes and their associated costs means that the uncertainty in budget estimates is very likely to be reduced.

It is worth noting that ethics is just as important in negotiations within an organization as in negotiations between an organization and an outside party. In this case, the superior and subordinate have the responsibility to be honest with each other. For one thing, they must continue to work together in the future under the conditions of mutual trust. Second, it is ethically necessary to be honest in such negotiations.

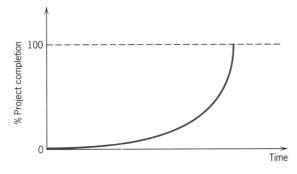

Figure 7-2   Another possible project life cycle. (Figure 1-5 reproduced.)

Source: DILBERT reprinted by permission of United Feature Syndicate, Inc.

Comments on the Budget Request Process

The budget process often begins with an invitation from top management for each division to submit a *budget request* for the coming year. Division heads pass the invitation along to departments, sections, and subsections, each of which presumably collects requests from below, aggregates them, and passes the result back up the organizational ladder.

This sounds like bottom-up budgeting, but there is an important difference between this procedure and a true bottom-up system. Along with the formal invitation for submission of a budget request, in the iterative system another message is passed down—a much less formal message that carries the following kinds of information: the percent by which the wage bill of the organization will be allowed to be increased, organizational policy on adding to the work force, the general attitude toward capital expenditures, knowledge about which projects and activities are considered to be high priority and which are not, and a number of other matters that, in effect, prescribe a set of limits on lower-level managers. As the budget requests are passed back up the organization, they are carefully inspected for conformity to guidelines. If they do not conform, they are "adjusted," often with little or no consultation with the originating units.

Senior management tends to adopt an autocratic stance on budget making for many reasons, but two are very common: the need to feel in control of the budget, and the feeling that a tight budget will somehow motivate subordinates to perform more efficiently. We know of no particular evidence to support such views, but they are quite common. Moreover, they lead to budgetary game playing and increase the uncertainty surrounding the budgetary process.

The less autocratic the organization (and the less pressured it is by current financial exigencies), the greater the probability that this process will allow dialogue and some compromise between managerial levels. Even the most *participative* firms, however, will not long tolerate lower-level managers who are not sensitive to messages relating to budget limitations. It makes little difference whether budget policy is passed down the system by means of formal, written policy statements or as a haphazard set of oral comments informally transmitted by some senior managers and practically neglected by others; the PM's budget request is expected to conform to policy. Ignorance of the policy is no excuse. Repeated failure to conform will be rewarded with a ticket to "corporate Siberia." It is the budget originator's responsibility to find out about budget policy. Again we see the importance of political sensitivity. The PM's channels of communication must be sensitive enough to receive policy signals even in the event that a noncommunicative superior blocks those signals.

Category/Activity Budgeting vs. Program Budgeting

Thus far we have discussed one facet of an organization's philosophy of budgeting. Another facet has to do with the degree to which a budget is category/activity-oriented or program-oriented, a distinction we have mentioned before. The traditional organizational budget is either category-oriented or activity-oriented, often based upon historical data accumulated through an accounting system such as *activity-based costing* (Coburn, 1997; Vandament and Jones, 1993). Individual expenses are classified and assigned to basic budget *lines* such as phone, materials, personnel-clerical, utilities, direct labor, etc. or to production centers or processes (Brimson, 1993). These expense lines are gathered into more inclusive categories, and are reported by organizational unit—for example, by section, department, and division. In other words, the budget can be overlaid on the organizational chart. Table 7-1 shows one page of a typical, activity-oriented monthly budget report for a real estate project.

With the advent of project organization, it became necessary to organize the budget in ways that conformed more closely to the actual pattern of fiscal responsibility. Under traditional budgeting methods, the budget for a project could be split up among many different organizational units, which diffused control so widely that it was frequently nonexistent. It was often almost impossible to determine the actual size of major expenditure categories in a project's budget. In light of this problem, ways were sought to alter the budgeting process so that budgets could be associated directly with the projects that used them. This need gave rise to *program budgeting*. Table 7-2 shows a program-oriented project budget divided by task and expected time of expenditure. In an interesting paper, Brimson (1993) critiques both systems separately, and then combines them.

Program budgeting aggregates income and expenditures across programs (projects). In most cases, aggregation by program is in addition to, not instead of, aggregation by organizational unit. The project has its own budget. The physical arrangement of such budget reports varies widely, but usually takes the form of a spreadsheet with the standard budget categories listed down the left-hand side of the sheet and category totals disaggregated into "regular operations" and charges to the various projects. For example, the columns shown in Table 7-1 would be repeated for each project.

The estimation of capital costs raises special problems. Accounting systems in different industries handle capital costs differently. Further, estimation requires highly specialized knowledge because the prices of some durable goods, e.g., machine tools, rise and fall in response to much different forces than affect the prices of other equipment, e.g., computer systems or aircraft. In an interesting two-part article, Sigurdsen (1996a, 1996b) notes that capital costs are variant with quantity of output and compares two methods of making capital cost estimates.

Table 7-1. Typical Monthly Budget for a Real Estate Project (page 1 of 6)

	Current			
	Actual	*Budget*	*Variance*	*Pct.*
Corporate—Income Statement				
Revenue				
8430 Management fees				
8491 Prtnsp reimb—property mgmt	7,410.00	6,222.00	1,188.00	119.0
8492 Prtnsp reimb—owner acquisition	.00	3,750.00	3,750.00–	.0
8493 Prtnsp reimb—rehab	.00	.00	.00	.0
8494 Other income	.00	.00	.00	.0
8495 Reimbursements—others	.00	.00	.00	.0
Total revenue	7,410.00	9,972.00	2,562.00–	74.3
Operating expenses				
Payroll &P/R benefits				
8511 Salaries	29,425.75	34,583.00	5,157.25	85.0
8512 Payroll taxes	1,789.88	3,458.00	1,668.12	51.7
8513 Group ins & med reimb	1,407.45	1,040.00	387.45–	135.3
8515 Workmen's compensation	43.04	43.00	.04–	100.0
8516 Staff apartments	.00	.00	.00	.0
8517 Bonus	.00	.00	.00	.0
Total payroll & P/R benefits	32,668.12	39,124.00	6,457.88	83.5
Travel & entertainment expenses				
8512 Travel	456.65	300.00	156.65–	152.2
8522 Promotion, entertainment & gift	69.52	500.00	430.48	13.9
8523 Auto	1,295.90	1,729.00	433.10	75.0
Total travel & entertainment exp	1,822.07	2,529.00	706.93	72.1
Professional fees				
8531 Legal fees	419.00	50.00	369.00–	838.0
8532 Accounting fees	289.00	.00	289.00–	.0
8534 Temporary help	234.58	200.00	34.58–	117.2

Table 7-2. Project Budget by Task and Month

Task	I	J	Estimate	Monthly Budget (£)							
				1	2	3	4	5	6	7	8
A	1	2	7000	5600	1400						
B	2	3	9000		3857	5143					
C	2	4	10000		3750	5000	1250				
D	2	5	6000		3600	2400					
E	3	7	12000				4800	4800	2400		
F	4	7	3000				3000				
G	5	6	9000			2571	5143	1286			
H	6	7	5000					3750	1250		
I	7	8	8000						2667	5333	
J	8	9	6000								6000
			75000	5600	12607	15114	14193	9836	6317	5333	6000

Source: Harrison, 1983.

Project Management in Practice
Completing the Limerick Nuclear Facility Under Budget

On January 8, 1990, the Limerick nuclear power generating facility in Pennsylvania began commercial operation, thereby setting a construction record for nuclear facilities. In an era when it is common to hear of nuclear plants that massively overrun their budgets and completion schedules, Limerick was completed eight months ahead of its 49-month schedule and came in $400 million under its $3.2 billion budget. Limerick has truly set a standard for the industry.

It was no accident that Limerick was completed ahead of schedule and under budget. When construction started in February 1986, a project goal was to complete the project eight months ahead of the planned completion, which would help keep the costs under the budget limit as well. To achieve this early target, a series of innovative approaches were taken. Two of the major ones were to accelerate ramp-up staffing and to use an extensive, fully-supported second shift. The momentum of the speedy start-up set the fast pace for the remainder of the project. The second shift earned a very favorable premium, as well as having a full complement of managers and engi-

neers to work with the manual workers. In this fashion, the second shift productivity was equal to, if not higher than, the first shift's.

Other decisions and actions further helped either the cost or the schedule. For example, it was decided that overtime would not be worked since a second shift was being used. And as a condition of the project approval, a project labor agreement with the local unions (rather than the national) had to be developed that would eliminate strikes, lockouts, and delays and provide for peaceful resolution of disputes. Also, an incentive fee contract with the building contractor was signed whereby the contractor would share equally in cost/schedule overruns or underruns, with limits set.

With such attention to the goal of an early and underbudget completion, the team, numbering almost 3000 workers by June 1987, worked diligently and with high morale, meeting the goal in January 1990.

Source: T. P. Gotzis, "Limerick Generating Station No. 2," *PM Network,* January 1991.

7.2 IMPROVING THE PROCESS OF COST ESTIMATION

The cooperation of several people is required to prepare cost estimates for a project. If the firm is in a business that routinely requires bids to be submitted to its customers, it will have "professional" (experienced) cost estimators on its staff. The major responsibility of the professional estimators is to reduce the level of uncertainty in cost estimations so that the firm's bids can be made in the light of expert information about its potential costs. In these cases, it is the job of the PM to generate a description of the work to be done on the project in sufficient detail that the estimator can know what cost data must be collected. Frequently, the project will be too complex for the PM to generate such a description without considerable help from experts in the functional areas.

Even with the finest of experts working to estimate resource usage, the one thing that is certain is that things will not go precisely as planned. There are two fundamentally different ways to manage the risks associated with the chance events that occur on every project. The simpler and far more common way is to make an allowance for contingencies—usually 5 or 10 percent of the estimated cost. Just why these numbers are chosen in preference to $6\frac{7}{8}$ or $9\frac{1}{4}$ for instance, we do not know. We strongly prefer another method in which the forecaster selects "most likely, optimistic, and pessimistic" estimates. We adopted this method in Chapter 2 when we applied simulation to the discounted cash flow problem in the PsychoCeramic Sciences case. The method is described in detail in Chapter 8 when we cover the issue of estimating the duration of elements in the action plan. The method described in Chapter 8 is applicable, unchanged, to the estimation of resource requirements and costs for the determination of project budgets.

Turning now to the problem of estimating direct costs,* project managers often find it helpful to collect direct cost estimates on a form that not only lists the estimated level of resource needs, but also indicates when each resource will be needed, and notes if it is available (or will be available at the appropriate time). Figure 7-3 shows such a form. It also has a column for identifying the person to contact in order to get specific resources. This table can be used for collating the resource requirements for each task element in a project, or for aggregating the information from a series of tasks onto a single form.

Note that Figure 7-3 contains no information on overhead costs. The matter of what overhead costs are to be added and in what amounts is unique to the firm, beyond the PM's control, and generally a source of annoyance and frustration to one and all. The allocation of overhead is arbitrary by its nature, and when the addition of overhead cost causes an otherwise attractive project to fail to meet the organization's economic objectives, the project's supporters are apt to complain bitterly about the "unfairness" of overhead cost allocation.

At times, firms support projects that show a significant incremental profit over direct costs but are not profitable when fully costed. Such decisions can be justified for a number of reasons, such as:

- To develop knowledge of a technology
- To get the organization's "foot in the door"
- To obtain the parts or service portion of the work
- To be in a good position for a follow-on contract
- To improve a competitive position
- To broaden a product line or a line of business

All of these are adequate reasons to fund projects that, in the short term, may lose money but provide the organization with the impetus for future growth and profitability. It is up to senior management to decide if such reasons are worth it.

---

*Our emphasis on estimating direct costs and on focusing on resources that are "direct costed" in the action plan is based on our belief that the PM should be concerned with only those items over which he or she has some control—which certainly excludes overheads. The PM, however, may wish to add some nonchargable items to the resource column of the action plan simply to "reserve" that item for use at a specific time.

Project Name _____

Date _____

Task Number _____

RESOURCES NEEDED

Resources	Person to Contact	How Many/ Much Needed	When Needed	Check (✔) If Available
People: Managers, Supervisors				
Professional & Technical				
Nontechnical				
Money				
Materials: Facilities				
Equipment				
Tools				
Power				
Space				
Special Services: Research & Test				
Typing/clerical				
Reproduction				
Others				

Figure 7-3   Form for gathering data on project resource needs.

Learning Curves

If the project being costed is one of many similar projects, the estimation of each cost element is fairly routine. If the project involves work in which the firm has little experience, cost estimation is more difficult, particularly for direct labor costs. For example, consider a project that requires 25 units of a complex electronic device to be assembled. The firm is experienced in building electronic equipment but has never before made this specific device, which differs significantly from the items routinely assembled.

Experience might indicate that if the firm were to build many such devices, it would use about 70 hours of direct labor per unit. If labor is paid a wage of $12 per hour, and if benefits equal 28 percent of the wage rate, the estimated labor cost for the 25 units is

$$(1.28)(\$12/hr)(25 \text{ units})(70 \text{ hr/unit}) = \$26,880$$

In fact, this would be an underestimate of the actual labor cost because more time per unit output is used early in the production process. Studies have shown that human performance usually improves when a task is repeated. In general, performance improves by a fixed percent each time production doubles. More specifically, *each time the output doubles, the worker hours per unit decrease to a fixed percentage of their previous value.* That percentage is called the *learning rate.* If an individual requires 10 minutes to accomplish a certain task the first time it is attempted and only 8 minutes the second time, that person is said to have an 80 percent learning rate. If output is doubled again from two to four, we would expect the fourth item to be produced in

$$8(0.8) = 6.4 \text{ min}$$

Similarly, the eighth unit of output should require

$$6.4(0.8) = 5.12 \text{ min}$$

and so on. The time required to produce a unit of output follows a well-known formula:

$$T_n = T_1 n^r$$

where

T_n = the time required for the nth unit of output,
T_1 = the time required for the initial unit of output,
n = the number of units to be produced, and
r = log decimal learning rate/log 2.

The total time required for all units of a production run of size N is

$$\text{total time} = T_1 \sum_{n=1}^{N} n^r$$

Tables are widely available with both unit and total values for the learning curves, and have been calculated for many different improvement ratios (learning rates—e.g., see Shafer and Meredith, 1998).

In the example of the electronic device just given, assume that after producing the twentieth unit, there is no significant further improvement (i.e., assembly time has reached a steady state at 70 hours). Further assume that previous study established that the usual learning rate for assemblers in this plant is about 85 percent. We can estimate the time required for the first unit by letting $T_n = 70$ hours by the unit $n = 20$. Then

$$r = \log 0.85/\log 2$$
$$= -0.1626/0.693$$
$$= -0.235$$

and

$$70 = T_1(20)^r$$
$$T_1 = 141.3 \text{ hr}$$

Now we know the time for the initial unit. Using a table that shows the total time multipler (see Shafer and Meredith, 1998, pp. 343–346, for example), we can find the appropriate total time multiplier for this example—the multiplier for 20 units given a learning rate of 85 percent. With this multiplier, 12.40, we can calculate the total time required to build all 20 units. It is

$$(12.40)(141.3 \text{ hr}) = 1752.12 \text{ hr}$$

The last five units are produced in the steady-state time of 70 hours each. Thus the total assembly time is

$$1752.12 + 5(70 \text{ hr}) = 2102.12 \text{ hr}$$

We can now refigure the direct labor cost.

$$2102.12(\$12)(1.28) = \$32,288.56$$

Our first estimate, which ignored learning effects, understated the cost by

$$\$32,288.56 - \$26,880 = \$5,408.56$$

or about 17 percent. Figure 7-4 illustrates this source of the error.

In recent years, learning curves have received increasing interest from project managers, particularly in the construction industry. Methods have been developed for

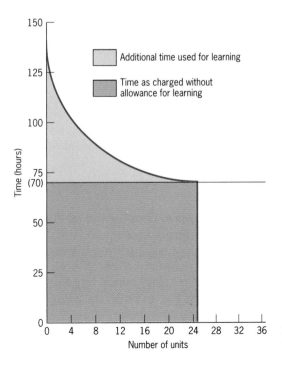

Figure 7-4 Effects of ignoring learning curve.

the approximation of composite learning curves for entire projects (Amor and Teplitz, 1998), and for the approximation of total cost from the unit learning curve (Camm, Evans, and Womer, 1987). Badiru (1995) has included learning curve effects in his critical resource diagramming, which is discussed in Chapter 8.

Remember that we are attempting to reduce the risk inherent in estimating costs. Therefore, for any task where labor is a significant cost factor and the production run is reasonably short, the PM should take the learning curve into account when estimating costs.

The implications of this conclusion should not be overlooked. We do not often think of projects as "production," but they are. While the construction, electronics, and aircraft assembly industries have used learning curves for many years, other industrial areas have been slow to follow. For example, research (Gagnon and Mantel, 1987) has shown that the learning curve effect is important to decisions about the role of engineering consultants on computer-assisted design (CAD) projects. The same is assuredly true for the design of advertizing campaigns or charity drives. The failure to consider performance improvement is a significant cause of project cost underestimation.

A Special Case of Learning—Technological Shock

If the parent organization is not experienced in the type of project being considered for selection, performance measures such as time to installation, time to achieve 80 percent efficiency, cost to install, and the like are quite uncertain and often will be underestimated. It is interesting to observe that an almost certain, immediate result of installing a new, cost-saving technology is that costs rise. Sometimes we blame the cost increases on resistance to change, but a more sensible explanation is that when we alter a system, we disturb it and it reacts in unpredictable ways. A steelmaker recalling the installation of the then new technology for manufacturing tinplate by electrolysis remarked, "We discovered and installed the world's first electrolytic method for making scrap. It took a year before we had that line running the way it was designed." Of course, if the organization is experienced, underestimation is not likely to be a serious problem. The Reliance Electric Company undertook several "18-month" plant construction projects that they predicted, accurately, would require 36 months to build from decision to the point when the plant was capable of operating at or above three-fourths capacity. (Note the potential for ethical problems here.) To the extent possible, past knowledge of system actions and reactions should be built into estimates of future project performance.

Other Factors

Depending on the reference, anywhere from about three-fifths to five-sixths of projects fail to meet their time, cost, and/or specification objectives. (See, for example, Frame, 1998.) The record of IS projects is particularly poor, according to article after article in the journals of the Project Management Institute. Possibly the problem is that Dilbert's pointy-haired boss sets arbitrary and impossible goals. Possibly scope-creep impacts all projects [though cost overruns are not necessarily associated with changing scope (Christensen and Gordon, 1998)]. Possibly PMs use wildly optimistic estimates in order to influence the project selection process. Or maybe they are simply unaware of good cost (or time) estimating practices. For example, there are at least 45 estimating models available for IS projects, but few IS project managers use any of them (Lawrence, 1994; Martin, 1994). Possibly all of these things, and even others, act together to produce this unenviable track record.

While the number of things that can increase risk by producing errors in cost estimates is almost without limit, some problems occur with particularly high frequency. Changes in resource prices are one of these. The most commonly used solution to this problem is to increase all cost estimates by some fixed percentage. A more useful approach is to identify each input that accounts for a significant portion of project cost and estimate the direction and rate of price change for each.

The determination of which inputs account for a "significant" portion of project cost is not difficult, although it may be somewhat arbitrary. Suppose, for example, that our initial, rough cost estimate (with no provision for future price changes) for a project with an objective of setting up a small storefront accounting office is $1 million and is to be spent over a three-year period in approximately equal amounts per year. If we think personnel costs will comprise about 60 percent of that total, also spread equally over time, the wage/salary bill will be about $600,000. Split into three equal amounts, we have expenditures of $200,000 per year. If we estimate that wage/salary rates will increase by 6 percent per year, our expense for the second year rises to $212,000 (an increase of $12,000), and to $224,720 in the third year (a further increase of $12,720). Failure to account for wage/salary inflation would result in an underestimate of project cost of $24,720. This is an error of slightly more than 4 percent of the estimated personnel cost and almost 2.5 percent of the total project budget.

Further improvements can be made by taking into account the fact that the prices of different inputs often change at very different rates and sometimes in different directions. A quick examination of the Bureau of Labor Statistics (BLS) wage and price indices, which cover a very large number of specific commodities and wage rates, will reveal that even in periods of stable prices, the prices of some things rise while others fall and still others do not change appreciably. Thus, the PM may wish to use different *inflators/deflators* for each of several different classes of labor or types of commodities. While most PMs are concerned only with price increases, any industry submitting competitive bids on projects must remember that failure to be aware of falling prices will lead to cost overestimation and uncompetitive bids.

The proper level of breakdown in estimating the impact of price changes simply depends on the organization's willingness to tolerate error. Assume that management is willing to accept a 5 percent difference between actual and estimated cost for each major cost category. In the example above, expected increases in wage/salary costs will use more than four-fifths of that allowance. That leaves less than one-fifth (about $5,300) of the allowable error, and the need to add one part-time clerk to the project for a single year would more than use the remaining allowance.

Other elements that need to be factored into the estimated project cost include an allowance for waste and spoilage. No sane builder would order "just enough" lumber to build a house. Also, personnel costs can be significantly increased by the loss and subsequent replacement of project professionals. Not only must new people go through a learning period—which, as we have seen, will have a negative effect on production—but professional starting salaries often rise faster than the general rate of annual salary increases. Thus, it may well cost more to replace a person who leaves the project with a newcomer who has approximately the same level of experience.

We have already mentioned the inclination PMs have toward understating the costs of a project in order to make it appear more profitable to senior managers, as well as the proclivity of lower-level project workers to overestimate costs in order to protect themselves. If the project is in its initial planning stage as a response to a Request for Proposal (RFP) from an outside organization, over- and underestimation of cost can have a serious impact on the probability of winning the contract—or on the level of profit, if a win occurs.

Serious ethical problems may arise during the process of estimating costs and submission of bids in response to an RFP. If the job is to be paid on a cost-plus basis, or even if it is a fixed-fee project, with fee increases allowed for special circumstances, some bidders may "low ball" a contract (submit underestimated costs). By doing this, they hope to win the bid, counting on the opportunity to increase costs or to plead special circumstances once the job is underway. At times, clients have been known to give favored bidders a "last look" at supposedly sealed bids so that the favored bidder can submit a winning bid, often with an unwritten agreement to allow some cost escalation at a later date. There is considerable opportunity for unethical behavior during cost estimation and bidding. Further, estimation and bidding practices vary widely from industry to industry.

Finally, there is plain bad luck. Delays occur for reasons that cannot be predicted. Machinery with the reliability of a railroad spike suddenly breaks down. That which has never failed fails. Every project needs an "allowance for contingencies."

Some writers and instructors differentiate four bases for estimating costs: experience, quantitative (statistical) methods, constraints, and worksheets. They discuss the advantages and disadvantages of each and then, typically, decide that one or another gives the best results. We feel strongly that all four are useful and that no single approach to cost estimation should be accepted as the best or rejected out of hand. The best estimators seem to employ an eclectic approach that uses, as one said, "anything that works." The wise PM takes into account as many known influences on the project budget as can be predicted. What cannot be predicted must then, by experience, simply be "allowed for." There are two other factors, particularly common to projects involving intangible outputs such as software programming, that need to be mentioned relating to cost-estimation and the schedule. These two factors have been identified in a classic and highly readable work—*The Mythical Man-Month*—by Brooks (1975).

First, most projects involve a tangible medium that tends not to be under our control—the wood splits, the paint smears—and thus we blame implementation problems of our "good" ideas on these physical elements. So, when we are working with a purely intellectual medium that has no physical elements, such as computer code, we are highly optimistic and foolishly assume that all will go well. However, when any project consisting of a series of components can only be successful if all of the components are successful, and each component has a small probability of failing, the chances of the overall project being successful are in fact very poor. Consider, for example, a software program consisting of 1000 lines of code, each of which is 99.9 percent reliable. The chance of the program itself working is only about 36 percent! Brooks' experience has led him to the following rule of thumb for software projects. As a fraction of the total time of the project, planning consumes about $\frac{1}{3}$, coding consumes $\frac{1}{6}$, component test consumes $\frac{1}{4}$, and system test consumes $\frac{1}{4}$. Thus, if a project estimate is made based on the expected coding time (the main element for which we can derive an estimate), this in reality will usually represent only about 17 percent of the entire project time rather than the 80 to 90 percent commonly assumed.

The second factor is what Brooks calls "the mythical man month" and relates to our tendency to assume that workers and time are interchangeable. Thus, when a schedule slips, the traditional response is to add labor which is like trying to douse a fire with gasoline. Our assumption that workers and time are interchangeable is correct only when a task can be partitioned such that there is no communication needed between the workers, such as in picking cotton by hand. Most projects, however, especially computer programming, are not set up that way and the more workers that are added require even more workers to train, as well as lines of communication to coordinate their efforts. Thus, three workers require three times as much pairwise intercommunication as two, and four require six times as much, etc. This result is captured in Brooks' law: *Adding manpower to a late software project makes it later.*

The Emanon Aircraft Corporation

Emanon Aircraft is a major manufacturer of aircraft parts, specializing in landing gear parts and assemblies. They are located in a highly industrialized midwestern state. The local area suffers from somewhat higher than average unemployment, partly because Emanon has experienced a downturn in business. In the past three years, they have lost out on a number of landing gear contracts, being underbid by competitors from other areas of the country. Senior management studied the problem, but has come to no conclusion about what can be done. They have hired a consulting team from a nearby university to study the situation and make a recommendation.

Business in the aircraft industry is not significantly different than in many other industries specializing in the building of complex machines. Aircraft builders are primarily assembly operations. They build planes from subassemblies and parts manufactured by themselves or by subcontractors who, in turn, specialize in specific subassemblies; for example, landing gear, avionics, passenger seats, heating and air conditioning, etc. When an order is received to build some number of a given type of plane, the builder (prime contractor) requests bids for the proper number of a certain part or subassembly from appropriate subcontractors. All relevant specifications for the part or subassembly are included in the RFP. The subcontractors who wish to participate in the project submit proposals that include a complete description of the proposed subassembly together with price information, delivery dates, and any other pertinent conditions of sale.

The university consulting team studied three aspects of Emanon's landing gear operation: the manufacturing process, the cost structure, and the bidding behavior and profit structure on landing gear bids. They determined that the manufacturing process was reasonably efficient and not significantly different from Emanon's competitors. Second, they found that all competitors were using approximately the same level of mark-up when determining their cost-plus price. When examining the cost structure, however, they noted that in the past three years, the firm consistently ran negative cost variances in material accounts. That is, the amount of material actually used in the construction of landing gears was approximately 10 percent less than the plan indicated. The team was unsure of this finding because there were only a few winning contracts for landing gears during the past three years.

An investigation was conducted on the estimation and purchase of materials for this department. It exposed the following facts. Three and one-half years ago, Emanon was late making a delivery of landing gear parts. The firm paid a large penalty and was threatened with loss of further business with the prime contractor. The late delivery resulted when Emanon ordered an insufficient quantity of a special steel alloy used in landing gear struts, and was unable to purchase any on the open market. The steel company required a manufacturing lead time of more than 90 days, so Emanon's delivery was late.

As a result, the purchasing official who had responsibility for this contract was demoted. The new purchasing official handled the problem in a straightforward fashion by inflating the material estimates by approximately 10 percent. The cost of material is about half of the total cost of landing gear production, which resulted in bids that were approximately 5 percent above the competition.

On Making Better Estimates

Let us begin with the assumption that budget estimation errors are not the result of deliberate dishonesty, but derive from honest errors on the part of the PM, project cost estimators, or anyone else involved. We have already noted that there are many reasons why "honest" errors occur—that projects look easier, faster, and cheaper to senior managers than to those who must do the work—that nonexpert estimators tend to overlook details required to do a complete job—that everyone seems to assume that Murphy's law has been repealed for their personal project. But these things should be learned by experience. Why do experienced managers err on their budget and schedule estimates?

Ambrose Bierce, in *The Devil's Dictionary,* defined "experience" as "The wisdom that enables us to recognize as an undesirable old acquaintance the folly that we have already embraced." It is axiomatic that we should learn through experience. It is a truism that we do not. Nowhere is this more evident than in project management, and yet it is not difficult to improve one's estimation/forecasting skills.

Recall that there are two generic types of estimation error. First, there is random error in which overestimates and underestimates are equally likely. Second, there is bias, which is systematic error. For biased estimates, the chance of over- and underestimates are not equally likely. Using the ubiquitous Excel® we can construct a spreadsheet that captures the essence of a person's performance as an estimator. Two simple statistical measures are used: the mean absolute deviation (MAD), and the tracking signal (TS). The printout* of such a spreadsheet is shown in Figure 7-5. Appendix B and Meredith, Shafer, and Turban (2002) include information on probability, statistics, and forecasting.

Figure 7-5 assumes that for each period (Column A) someone has made an estimate of a variable (Column B), and that the actual value of that variable is, sooner or later, known (Column C). (It should be noted that Column A need not be time periods. This column simply counts the number of estimates made and links estimates with their respective actuals.) Column D calculates the difference between the actual value, A(t), and the estimate or forecast for that period, F(t). Column E contains the absolute value of that difference. We can now calculate a statistic known as the *mean absolute deviation* (MAD).

As the information in Row 3 of the spreadsheet shows,

$$MAD = \sum (|A(t) - F(t)|)/n$$

where n is the number of differences. The MAD is therefore the arithmetic average of the absolute values of the differences—the mean absolute deviation.

---

*Any of the common spreadsheet programs can easily handle all of the calculations shown in this chapter and will accept formulas and calculations from any of the others.

	A	B	C	D	E	F	G
1	This is a template for improving one's estimating skills						
2							
3	MAD = SUM ($|A(t) - F(t)|$)/n The Average Absolute Error						
4	Tracking Signal = SUM(A(t) − F(t))/MAD A Measure of Bias						
5							Tracking
6	Period	Estimate	Actual	A(t) – F(t)	$|A(t) - F(t)|$	MAD	Signal
7	======	========	========	========	========	========	========
8							
9	1	155	163	8	8		
10	2	242	240	−2	2	5.00	1.20
11	3	46	67	21	21	10.33	2.61
12	4	69	78	9	9	10.00	3.60
13	5	75	71	−4	4	8.80	3.64
14	6	344	423	79	79	20.50	5.41
15	7	56	49	−7	7	18.57	5.60
16	8	128	157	29	29	19.88	6.69
17							
18				133	159		

Figure 7-5   Excel® template for cost estimation.

Students of statistics may note that the MAD has certain logical similarities to the standard deviation. Assuming that the forecast errors are normally distributed, the MAD is approximately 80 percent of a standard deviation (see Chase and Aquilano, 1989 and elsewhere). Thus, if the MAD is a sizable fraction of the variable being estimated, the average error is large and the forecast or estimate is not very accurate.

Now, consider Column D. The sum of the entries in this column for any number of periods is the sum of the forecast errors, often referred to as the "running sum of the forecast errors" (RSFE). If the estimator's errors are truly random, their sum should approach zero; that is, the RSFE should be a small number because positive errors should be offset by negative errors. If either positive or negative errors are more numerous or consistently larger than the other, the estimation process is said to be biased and the errors are not random. In Figure 7-5, RSFE = 133, so the forecast is quite positively biased.

The tracking signal measures the estimator's bias. It is easily found:

$$TS = RSFE/MAD$$

Note that it calculates the number of MADs in the RSFE (see column G in Figure 7-5, and recall the similarity between MAD and standard deviation). If the RSFE is small, approaching zero, the TS will also approach zero. As the RSFE grows, the TS will grow, indicating bias. Division of the RSFE by the MAD creates a sort of "index number," the TS, that is independent of the size of the variables being considered. We cannot say just how much bias is acceptable in an estimator/forecaster. We feel that a TS $\geq$ 3 is too high unless the estimator is a rank beginner. Certainly, an experienced estimator should have a much lower TS. (It should be obvious that the TS may be either negative or positive. Our comment actually refers to the absolute value of the TS.) Perhaps more important than worrying about an acceptable limit on the size of the tracking signal is the practice of tracking it and analyzing why the estimator's bias, if there is one, exists. Similarly, the estimator should consider how to reduce the MAD, the average estimation error. Such analysis is the embodiment of "learning by experience." The Excel® template makes the analysis simple to conduct, and should result in descreasing the size of both the MAD and the TS. (The formulae used in Figure 7-5 are shown in Figure 7-6. Similar formulae can be used in other popular spreadsheets.)

Some estimators would like to speed up the process of improving their estimation skills by grouping forecasts of different resources to generate more data points when calculating their MADs and TSs. Use of the tracking signal requires that the input data, estimates (forecasts) and actuals, be collected and processed separately for each variable being estimated. Cost estimates and actuals for different resources, for instance, would be used to find the MAD and TS for each individual resource. The reason for this inconvenience is that resources come in different units and the traditional caution about adding apples and oranges applies. (Even if all resources are measured in dollars, we still have scale problems when we mix resource costs of very different sizes.) Fortunately, there is a way around the problem.

Instead of defining the estimation error as the *difference* between actual and forecast, we can define it as the *ratio* of actual to forecast. Therefore, the new error for the first forecast (Period 1) in Figure 7-5 is not eight units, but rather is

$$A(t)/F(t) = 163/155 = 1.052$$

or a 5.2 percent error. In order to produce measures similar in nature and concept to the MAD and TS, we will subtract 1 from the ratio. Thus, when the actual is greater than the forecast, the measure (i.e., the error ratio minus 1) will be positive, and if the actual is *less* than the forecast, the measure will be negative. Figure 7-7 shows the calculations of $\{A(t)/F(t) - 1\}$ for the data used in Figure 7-5. The formulas are shown in Figure 7-8. Column E shows the absolute value of column D, and column F lists the MAR (mean absolute ratio). The tracking signal is calculated as usual by dividing the "running sum of the forecast ratios" (RSFR) by the MAR,

$$TS = RSFR/MAR$$

Notice that this calculation does not suffer from unit or scale effects because the ratio of actual to forecast is a dimensionless number and we are finding the percent error rather than the "real" error.

One caution remains. While this technique will allow one to aggregate dissimilar data and, thereby, measure the degree of random error and bias faster than when using differences, care must be exercised to aggregate only data for which there is good reason to believe that the amount of bias and uncertainty is roughly the same for all resource estimates.

At the beginning of this discussion, we made the assumption that estimation errors were "honest." That assumption is not necessary. If a manager suspects that costs are purposely being under- or overestimated, it is usually not difficult to collect

	A	B	C	D	E	F	G
1							
2							
3							
4							
5							Tracking
6	Period	Estimate	Actual	A(t) − F(t)	|A(t) − F(t)|	MAD	Signal
7	=====	=======	======	==========	==========	==========	===========
8							
9	1	155	163	= C9 − B9	= ABS(C9 − B9)		
10	2	242	240	= C10 − B10	= ABS(C10 − B10)	= (SUM($E$9:E10))/A10	= (SUM($D$9:D10))/F10
11	3	46	67	= C11 − B11	= ABS(C11 − B11)	= (SUM($E$9:E11))/A11	= (SUM($D$9:D11))/F11
12	4	69	78	= C12 − B12	= ABS(C12 − B12)	= (SUM($E$9:E12))/A12	= (SUM($D$9:D12))/F12
13	5	75	71	= C13 − B13	= ABS(C13 − B13)	= (SUM($E$9:E13))/A13	= (SUM($D$9:D13))/F13
14	6	344	423	= C14 − B14	= ABS(C14 − B14)	= (SUM($E$9:E14))/A14	= (SUM($D$9:D14))/F14
15	7	56	49	= C15 − B15	= ABS(C15 − B15)	= (SUM($E$9:E15))/A15	= (SUM($D$9:D15))/F15
16	8	128	157	= C16 − B16	= ABS(C16 − B16)	= (SUM($E$9:E16))/A16	= (SUM($D$9:D16))/F16
17							
18				= SUM(D9:D17)	= SUM(E9:E17)		

Figure 7-6 Excel® formulas for Figure 7-5.

	A	B	C	D	E	F	G
1	This is a template for improving one's estimating skills						
2							
3	MAR = SUM {|(A(t) / F (t)) − 1|} /n						
4	Tracking Signal = SUM{(A(t) / F (t)) − 1}/MAR						
5							Tracking
6	Period	Estimate	Actual	(A(t)/F(t)) − 1	|(A(t)/F(t)) − 1|	MAR	Signal
7	====	=======	=======	========	==========	========	========
8							
9	1	155	163	0.052	0.052		
10	2	242	240	−0.008	0.008	0.030	1.448
11	3	46	67	0.457	0.457	0.172	2.904
12	4	69	78	0.130	0.130	0.162	3.898
13	5	75	71	−0.053	0.053	0.140	4.120
14	6	344	423	0.230	0.230	0.155	5.205
15	7	56	49	−0.125	0.125	0.151	4.523
16	8	128	157	0.227	0.227	0.160	5.670
17							
18				0.908	1.281		

Figure 7-7   Estimation template using ratios.

appropriate data and calculate the tracking signal for an individual estimator—or even for an entire project team. If it is known that such information is being collected, one likely result is that the most purposeful bias will be sharply reduced.

It may occur to the reader that we have not applied simulation analysis, similar to that illustrated in Chapter 2, to deal with budgetary uncertainty. It should be obvious that such an application is appropriate. For example, in addition to optimistic, pessimistic, and most likely cost estimates, a number of other variables are uncertain — the inflation rate for various cost elements, the learning rate, the amount of resource usage for individual tasks, and the timing of expenditures, to mention a few. As we have noted above, we are saving this application for a detailed description for the scheduling problem in Chapter 8. Its application to budgeting is quite similar.

A final note: In the next chapter, we discuss a method for managing schedule and budget risk. We also describe some software used for risk management. Most of the useful methods require that the forecaster specify the mode and range of the variable being forecast. These models tacitly assume that the data supplied represent unbiased estimates. As we noted previously, if the input estimates are biased, the output will incorporate that error and the danger is not "Garbage in, garbage out" but "Garbage in, gospel out."

	A	B	C	D	E	F	G
1							
2							
3							
4							
5							Tracking
6	Period	Estimate	Actual	(A(t)/F(t)) − 1	|(A(t)/F (t)) − 1|	MAR	Signal
7	======	========	======	========	=========	=====	=======
8							
9	1	155	163	= (C9/B9) − 1	= ABS((C9/B9) − 1)		
10	2	242	240	= (C10/B10) − 1	= ABS((C10/B10) − 1)	= (SUM($E$9:E10))/A10	= (SUM($D$9:D10))/F10
11	3	46	67	= (C11/B11) − 1	= ABS((C11/B11) − 1)	= (SUM($E$9:E11))/A11	= (SUM($D$9:D11))/F11
12	4	69	78	= (C12/B12) − 1	= ABS((C12/B12) − 1)	= (SUM($E$9:E12))/A12	= (SUM($D$9:D12))/F12
13	5	75	71	= (C13/B13) − 1	= ABS((C13/B13) − 1)	= (SUM($E$9:E13))/A13	= (SUM($D$9:D13))/F13
14	6	344	423	= (C14/B14) − 1	= ABS((C14/B14) − 1)	= (SUM($E$9:E14))/A14	= (SUM($D$9:D14))/F14
15	7	56	49	= (C15/B15) − 1	= ABS((C15/B15) − 1)	= (SUM($E$9:E15))/A15	= (SUM($D$9:D15))/F15
16	8	128	157	= (C16/B16) − 1	= ABS((C16/B16) − 1)	= (SUM($E$9:E16))/A16	= (SUM($D$9:D16))/F16
17							
18				= SUM(D9:D16)	= SUM(E9:E16)		

Figure 7-8 Formulas for Figure 7-7.

SUMMARY

This chapter initiated the subject of project implementation by focusing on the project budget, which authorizes the project manager to obtain the resources needed to begin work. Different methods of budgeting were described along with their impacts on project management. Then, a number of issues concerning cost estimation were discussed, particularly the effect of learning on the cost of repetitive tasks and how to use the concept of the learning curve. Finally, methods for improving cost estimation skills were described.

Specsific points made in the chapter were these:

- The intent of a budget is to communicate organizational policy concerning the organization's goals and priorities.

- There are a number of common budgeting methods: top-down, bottom-up, the program budget.

- A form identifying the level of resource need, when it will be needed, who the contact is, and its availability is especially helpful in estimating costs.

- It is common for organizations to fund projects whose returns cover direct but not full costs in order to achieve long-run strategic goals of the organization.

- If projects include repetitive tasks with significant human input, the learning phenomenon should be taken into consideration when preparing cost estimates.

- The learning curve is based on the observation

that the amount of time required to produce one unit decreases a constant percentage every time the cumulative output doubles.

- A method for determining whether or not cost estimates are biased is described. The method can be used to improve any estimation/forecasting process.

- Other major factors, in addition to learning, that should be considered when making proj-

ect cost estimates are inflation, differential changes in the cost factors, waste and spoilage, personnel replacement costs, and contingencies for unexpected difficulties.

In the next chapter, we address the subject of task scheduling, a topic of major importance in project management. More research and investigation have probably been conducted on the subject of scheduling than any other element of project management.

 GLOSSARY

Bottom-up Budgeting   A budgeting method that begins with those who will be doing the tasks estimating the resources needed. The advantage is more accurate estimates.

Learning Rate   The percentage of the previous worker hours per unit required for doubling the output.

Program Budgeting   Aggregating income and expenditures by project or program, often in addition to aggregation by organizational unit or activity.

Top-Down Budgeting   A budgeting method that begins with top managers' estimates of the resources needed for a project. Its primary advantage is that the aggregate budget is typically quite accurate because no element has been left out. Individual elements, however, may be quite inaccurate.

Variances   The pattern of deviations in costs and usage used for exception reporting to management.

 QUESTIONS

Material Review Questions

1. What are the advantages of top-down budgeting? Of bottom-up budgeting? What is the most important task for top management to do in bottom-up budgeting?

2. In preparing a budget, what indirect costs should be considered?

3. Describe the purpose and use of a tracking signal.

4. Describe the top-down budgeting process.

5. What is a variance?

6. Describe the learning curve phenomenon.

7. How might you determine if cost estimates are biased?

8. What is "program budgeting"?

9. What is the difference between activity- and program-oriented budgets?

Class Discussion Questions

10. Discuss ways in which to keep budget planning from becoming a game.

11. List some of the pitfalls in cost estimating. What steps can a manager take to correct cost overruns?

12. Why do consulting firms frequently subsidize some projects? Is this ethical?

13. What steps can be taken to make controlling costs easier? Can these steps also be used to control other project parameters, such as performance?

14. Which budgeting method is likely to be used with which type of organizational structure?

15. What are some potential problems with the top-down and bottom-up budgeting processes? What are some ways of dealing with these potential problems?

16. How is the budget planning process like a game?

17. Would any of the conflict resolution methods described in the previous chapter be useful in the budget planning process? Which?

18. How does the fact that capital costs vary with different factors complicate the budgeting process?

19. Why is learning curve analysis important to project management?

Questions for Project Management

Pathfinder Mission to Mars—On a Shoestring

21. How did a change in philosophy make such a drastic difference in project cost?

22. Why was the mission scope so limited? Why even spend the money to go to Mars with such limited objectives?

23. Describe their "de-scope," "lien list," and "cash reserve" approaches.

24. Recent design-to-cost interplanetary projects have also had some spectacular failures. Is this the natural result of this new philosophy?

Completing the Limerick Nuclear Facility Under Budget

25. What "trick" did the construction firm use to come in ahead of schedule and under budget?

20. Why is it "ethically necessary to be honest" in negotiations between a superior and subordinate?

26. What extra expenses did the contractor incur in order to finish ahead of schedule? How can one tell whether they are spending too much to finish early, thereby saving not only time but also overhead costs?

Managing Costs at Massachusetts' Neighborhood Health Plan

27. Wouldn't higher eligibility requirements for subscribers cut NHP's health care costs? Why did this exacerbate NHP's situation?

28. Explain the trade-off between hospital utilization and contract rates.

29. How did changing from a line item pay plan to an episode plan allow comparisons and save costs?

 ## INCIDENTS FOR DISCUSSION

Preferred Sensor Company

Sean Cole has been appointed project manager of the Preferred Sensor Company's new sensor manufacturing process project. Sensors are extremely price-sensitive, and Preferred has done a great deal of quantitative work so it can accurately forecast changes in sales volume relative to changes in pricing.

The company president, "Dude" Sensor, has considerable faith in the firm's sensitivity model and insists that all projects that affect the manufacturing cost of sensors be run against the sensitivity model in order to generate data to calculate the return on investment. The net result is that project managers, like Sean, are under a great deal of pressure to submit realistic budgets so go/no-go project decisions can be made quickly. Dude has canceled several projects that appeared marginal during their feasibility stages and recently fired a project manager for overestimating project costs on a new model sensor. The project was killed very early in the design stage and six months later a competitor introduced a similar sensor that proved to be highly successful.

Sean's dilemma is how to go about constructing a budget that accurately reflects the cost of the proposed new manufacturing process. Sean is an experienced executive and feels comfortable with his ability to come close to estimating the cost of the project. However, the recent firing of his colleague has made him a bit gunshy. Only one stage out of the traditional four-stage sensor manufacturing process is being changed, so he has detailed cost information about a good percentage of the process. Unfortunately, the tasks involved in the process stage being modified are unclear at this point. Sean also believes that the new modification will cause some minor changes in the other three stages, but these changes have not been clearly identified. The stage being addressed by the project represents almost 50 percent of the manufacturing cost.

Questions: Under these circumstances, would Sean be wise to pursue a top-down or a bottom-up budgeting approach? Why? What factors are most relevant here?

General Ship Company

General Ship Company has been building nuclear destroyers for the Navy for the last 20 years. It has recently completed the design of a new class of nuclear destroyer and will be preparing a detailed budget to be followed during construction of the first destroyer.

The total budget for this first destroyer is $90 million. The controller feels the initial project cost estimate prepared by the planning department was too low because the waste and spoilage allowance was underestimated. Thus, she is concerned that there may be a large cost overrun on the project and wants to work closely with the project manager to control the costs.

Question: How would you monitor the costs of this project?

BIBLIOGRAPHY

AGGARWAL, R. *Capital Budgeting Under Uncertainty.* Englewood Cliffs, NJ: Prentice-Hall, 1993.

AMOR, J. P., and C. J. TEPLITZ. "An Efficient Approximation for Project Composite Learning Curves." *Project Management Journal,* September 1998.

BADIRU, A. B. "Incorporating Learning Curve Effects Into Critical Resource Diagramming." *Project Management Journal*, June 1995.

BIERMAN, H. *The Capital Budgeting Decision: Economic Analysis of Investment Projects,* 7th ed. New York: Macmillan, 1988.

BOQUIST, J. A. "How do you win the capital allocation game?" *Sloan Management Review,* Winter 1998.

BRIMSON, J. A. "Activity Product Cost." *IEEE Engineering Management Review,* Spring 1993.

BROOKS, F. P. *The Mythical Man-Month.* Reading, MA: Addison-Wesley, 1975.

CAMM, J. D., J. R. EVANS, and N. K. WOMER. "The Unit Learning Curve Approximation of Total Cost." *Computers in Industrial Engineering.* Vol. 12, No. 3, 1987.

CASE, J. "Opening the books." *Harvard Business Review,* March/April 1997.

CHASE, R. B., and N. J. AQUILANO. *Production and Operations Management,* 5th ed. Homewood, IL: Irwin, 1989.

CHILDS, P. D., S. H. OTT, and A. J. TRIANTIS. "Capital Budgeting for Interrelated Projects: A Real Options Approach." *Journal of Financial and Quantitative Analysis,* September 1998.

CHRISTENSEN, D. S., and GORDON, J. A. "Does a Rubber Baseline Guarantee Cost Overruns on Defense Acquisition Contracts?" *Project Management Journal,* September 1998.

COBURN, S. "How Activity Based Costing was used in Capital Budgeting." *Management Accounting,* May 1997.

COOPER, R. "The Promise—and the Peril—of Integrated Cost Systems." *Harvard Business Review,* July/August 1998.

DEAN, B. V., S. J. MANTEL, Jr., and L. A. Roepcke. "Research Project Cost Distributions and Budget Forecasting." *IEEE Transactions on Engineering Management,* November 1969.

FRAME, J. D. "Risk Assessment Groups: Key Component of Project Offices." *PM Network,* March 1998.

GAGNON, R. J. *An Exploratory Analysis of the Relevant Cost Structure of Internal and External Engineering Consulting,* Ph.D. dissertation. Cincinnati: University of Cincinnati, 1982.

GAGNON, R. J., and S. J. Mantel, Jr. "Strategies and Performance Improvement for Computer-Assisted Design." *IEEE Transactions on Engineering Management,* November 1987.

GLASS, G. W. *Assessing the Effectiveness of Milestone Budgeting.* Washington, DC: U.S. Congress, 1987.

HARRISON, F. L. *Advanced Project Management.* Hants, England: Gower, 1983.

LAWRENCE, A. O. "Using Automated Estimating Tools to Improve Project Estimating." *PM Network,* December 1994.

LAYARD, P. R. G. *Cost-Benefit Analysis.* Cambridge, England: Cambridge University Press, 1994.

LUEHRMAN, T. A. "Investment Opportunities as Real Options: Getting Started on the Numbers." *Harvard Business Review,* July/August 1998.

MARTIN, J. E. "Selecting an Automated Estimating Tool for IS Development Projects." *PM Network*, December 1994.

MEREDITH, J. R., S. M. Shafer, and E. Turban. *Quantiative Business Modeling*, Cincinnati: South-Western, 2002.

MOOLMAN, G. C. "A Capital Budgeting Model Based on the Project Portfolio Approach: Avoiding Cash Flows per Project." *The Engineering Economist,* Winter 1997.

RAY, A. *Cost-Benefit Analysis: Issues and Methodologies.* Baltimore, MD: Johns Hopkins Press,1984.

REIMUS, B. "The IT System that Couldn't Deliver." *Harvard Business Review,* May/June 1997.

SHAFER, S. M., and J. R. Meredith. *Operations Management: A Process Approach with Spreadsheets.* New York: Wiley, 1998.

SIGURDSEN, A. "Principal Errors in Capital Cost Estimating Work, Part 1: Appreciate the Relevance of the Quantity-Dependent Estimating Norms." *Project Management Journal,* September 1996a.

SIGURDSEN, A. "Principal Errors in Capital Cost Estimating, Part 2: Appreciate the Relevance of the Objective Cost Risk Analysis Method." *Project Management Journal,* December 1996b.

TOWN, C. "Project Control and Earned Value Management." *Management Accounting*, September 1998.

UMAPATHY, S. *Current Budgeting Practices in U.S. Industry: The State of the Art.* New York: Quorum Books, 1987.

VANDAMENT, W. F., and D. P. JONES. *Financial Management: Progress and Challenges.* San Francisco: Jossey-Bass, 1993.

The following case and the answers to the questions at the end describe the stringent criteria this disguised but well-known firm uses to select among projects that offer major profit opportunities for the firm. In addition, the firm intentionally ties the criteria to their strategic goals so that each adopted project moves the organization farther in the competitive direction they have chosen by adding to their core competencies. The case also illustrates how the firm integrates their marketing, operations, engineering, and finance functions to forge a competitive advantage for the firm in the marketplace.

C A S E

AUTOMOTIVE BUILDERS, INC.: THE STANHOPE PROJECT
Jack Meredith

It was a cold, gray October day as Jim Wickes pulled his car into ABI's corporate offices parking lot in suburban Detroit. The leaves, in yellows and browns, swirled around his feet as he walked into the wind toward the lobby. "Good morning, Mr. Wickes," said his secretary as he came into the office. "That proposal on the Stanhope project just arrived a minute ago. It's on your desk." "Good morning, Debbie. Thanks. I've been anxious to see it."

This was the day Jim had scheduled to review the 1986 supplemental capital request and he didn't want any interruptions as he scrutinized the details of the flexible manufacturing project planned for Stanhope, Iowa. The Stanhope proposal, compiled by Ann Williamson, PM and managerial "champion" of this effort, looked like just the type of project to fit ABI's new strategic plan, but there was a large element of risk in the project. Before recommending the project to Steve White, executive vice president of ABI, Jim wanted to review all the details one more time.

History of ABI

ABI started operations as the Farm Equipment Company just after the First World War. Employing new technology to produce diesel engine parts for tractors, the firm flourished with the growth of farming and became a multimillion dollar company by 1940.

During the Second World War, the firm switched to producing tank and truck parts in volume for the military. At the war's end, the firm converted its equipment to the production of automotive parts for the expanding automobile industry. To reflect this major change in their product line, the company was renamed Automotive Builders, Inc. (ABI), though they remained a major supplier to the farm equipment market.

A Major Capital Project

The farm equipment industry in the 1970s had been doing well, but there were some disturbing trends. Japanese manufacturers had entered the industry and were beginning to take a significant share of the domestic market. More significantly, domestic labor costs were significantly higher than overseas and resulted in price disadvantages that couldn't be ignored any longer. Perhaps most important of all, quality differences between American and Japanese farm equipment, including tractors, were becoming quite noticeable.

To improve the quality and costs of their incoming materials, many of the domestic tractor manufacturers were beginning to single-source a number of their tractor components. This allowed them better control over both quality and cost, and made it easier to coordinate delivery schedules at the same time.

In this vein, one of the major tractor engine manufacturers, code-named "Big Red" within ABI, let its suppliers know that it was interested in negotiating a contract for a possible 100 percent sourcing of 17 versions of special piston heads destined for a new line of high-efficiency tractor engines expected to replace the current conventional engines in both new and existing tractors. These were all six-cylinder diesel engines and thus would require six pistons each.

This put ABI in an interesting situation. If they

failed to bid on this contract, they would be inviting competition into their very successful and profitable diesel engine parts business. Thus, to protect their existing successful business, and to pursue more such business, ABI seemed required to bid on this contract. Should ABI be successful in their bid, this would result in 100 percent sourcing in both the original equipment market (OEM) as well as the replacement market with its high margins. Furthermore, the high investment required to produce these special pistons at ABI's costs would virtually rule out future competition.

ABI had two plants producing diesel engine components for other manufacturers and believed they had a competitive edge in engineering of this type. These plants, however, could not accommodate the volume Big Red expected for the new engine. Big Red insisted at their negotiations that a 100 percent supplier be able to meet peak capacity at their assembly plant for this new line.

As Jim reviewed the proposal, he decided to refer back to the memos that restated their business strategy and started them thinking about a new Iowa plant located in the heart of the farm equipment industry for this project. In addition, Steve White had asked the following basic, yet rather difficult questions about the proposal at their last meeting and Jim wanted to be sure he had them clearly in mind as he reviewed the files.

- ABI is already achieving an excellent return on investment (ROI). Won't these investments simply tend to dilute it?

- Will the cost in new equipment be returned by an equivalent reduction in labor? Where's the payoff?

- What asset protection is there? This proposal requires an investment in new facilities before knowing whether a long-term contract will be procured to reimburse us for our investment.

- Does this proposal maximize ROI, sales potential, or total profit?

To address these questions adequately, Jim decided to recheck the expected after-tax profits and average rate of return (based on sales of 70,000 engines per year) when he reached the financial portion of the proposals. These figures should give a clear indication of the "quality" of the investment. There were, however, other aspects of capital resource allocation to consider besides the financial elements. One of these was the new business strategy of the firm, as recently articulated by ABI's executive committee.

The Business Strategy

A number of elements of ABI's business strategy were directly relevant to this proposal. Jim took out a note pad to jot down each of them and assign them a priority as follows:

1. Bid only on good margin products that have the potential for maintaining their margins over a long term.
2. Pursue only new products whose design or production process is of a proprietary nature and that exist in areas where our technical abilities enable us to maintain a long-term position.
3. Employ, if at all possible, the most advanced technology in new projects that is either within our experience or requires the next step up in experience.
4. Foster the "project champion" approach to innovation and creativity. The idea is to encourage entrepreneurship by approving projects to which individual managers are committed and that they have adopted as personal "causes" based on their belief that the idea, product, or process is in our best interest.
5. Maintain small plants of no more than 480 employees. These have been found to be the most efficient, and they enjoy the best labor relations.

With these in mind, Jim reopened the proposal and started reading critical sections.

Demand Forecasts and Scenarios

For this proposal, three scenarios were analyzed in terms of future demand and financial impacts. The baseline "Scenario I" assumed that the new line would be successful. "Scenario II" assumed that the Japanese would soon follow and compete successfully with Big Red in this line. "Scenario III" assumed that the new

Table 1. Demand Forecasts (000s engines)*

Year	Baseline I	Scenario II	Scenario III
1987	69	69	69
1988	73	72	72
1989	90	81	77
1990	113	95	68
1991	125	87	62
1992	145	74	47

*Each engine requires six pistons.

line was a failure. The sales volume forecasts under these three scenarios are shown in Table 1.

There was, however, little confidence in any of these forecasts. In the preceding few years Japan had become a formidable competitor, not only in price but also in more difficult areas of competition, such as quality and reliability. Furthermore, the economic situation in 1986 was taking a severe toll on American farmers and economic forecasts indicated there was no relief in sight. Thus, as stated in the proposal:

> The U.S. farm market will be a difficult battleground for world farm equipment manufacturers and any forecast of a particular engine's potential in this market must be considered as particularly risky. How much risk do we want to accept? Every effort should be made to minimize our exposure on this investment and maximize our flexibility.

Manufacturing Plan

The proposal stressed two primary aspects of the manufacturing process. First, a learning curve was employed in calculating production during the 1000-unit ramp-up implementation period in order to not be overly optimistic. A learning rate of 80 percent was assumed. Second, an advanced technology process using a flexible manufacturing system, based largely on turning centers, was recommended since it came in at $1 million less than conventional equipment and met the strategy guidelines of using sophisticated technology when appropriate.

Since ABI had closely monitored Big Red's progress in the engine market, the request for bids had been foreseen. In preparation for this, Jim had authorized a special manufacturing-process study to determine more efficient and effective ways of producing piston heads. The study considered product design, process selection, quality considerations, productivity, and manufacturing system planning. Three piston manufacturing methods were considered in the study: (1) batch manufacture via computer numerically controlled (CNC) equipment; (2) a flexible manufacturing system (FMS); and (3) a high-volume, low-unit-cost transfer machine.

The resulting recommendation was to install a carefully designed FMS, if it appeared that additional flexibility might be required in the future for other versions, or even other manufacturers. Though such a system would be expensive, the volume of production over the FMS's longer lifetime would offset that expense. Four preferred machine builders were contacted for equipment specifications and bids. It was ABI's plan to work closely with the selected vendor in designing and installing the equipment, thus building quality and reliability into both the product and the process and learning about the equipment at the same time.

To add further flexibility for the expensive machinery, all design features that would facilitate retool or changeover to other products were incorporated. For example, the machining centers would also be capable of machining other metals, such as aluminum or nodular iron, and would be fitted with variable feed and speed motors, feed-force monitors, pressure-controlled clamping of workpieces, and air-leveling pallets. Also, fully interchangeable chucks, spindles, pallets, tooling, and risers would be purchased to minimize the spare parts inventories.

Plant Operation and Organization

As stated in the proposal, many innovative practices were to be employed at the new plant:

- Machine operators will be trained to do almost all of their own machine maintenance.
- All employees will conduct their own statistical process control and piston heads will be subject to 100 percent inspection.
- There will only be four skill classes in the plant. Every employee in each of those classes will be trained to do any work within that class.
- There will not be any time clocks in the plant.

The organizational structure for the 11 salaried workers in the new plant is shown in Figure 1, and

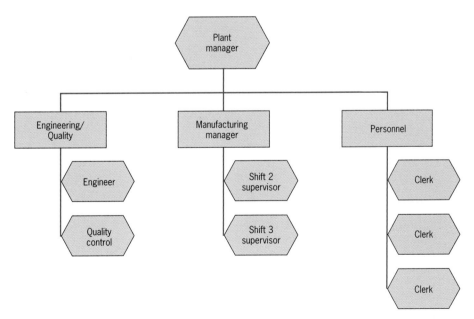

Figure 1 Stanhope organization.

the complete labor summary is illustrated in Figure 2, including the shift breakdown. As can be seen, the plant will be relatively small, with 65 employees in the ratio of 1:5 salaried to hourly. The eight-month acquisition of the employees during the ramp-up is illustrated in Figure 3, with full employment occurring by March 1987.

Financial Considerations

Financial aspects of new proposals at ABI were considered from a number of perspectives, in part because of the interdependent nature of many proposals. The results of not investing in a proposal are normally compared with the results of investing and the differences noted. Variations on the investment assumptions are also tested, including errors in the forecast sales volumes, learning rates, productivities, selling prices, and cancellations of both current and future orders for existing and potential business.

For the Stanhope proposal, the site investment required is $3,012,000. The details of this investment are shown in Table 2. The total investment re-

Salaried Labor	Number of Staff
Plant manager	1
Manufacturing managers (3 shifts)	3
Quality control manager	1
Engineering	2
Personnel manager	1
Clerical	3
	11

Hourly Labor	Days	Afternoons	Night
Direct	14	14	10
Inspection	1	1	1
Maintenance	2	1	1
Tooling	2	2	1
Rec./shp./mtl.	2	1	1
Total	21	19	14

Summary

Salary	11
Hourly	54
Total	65

Figure 2 Stanhope labor summary.

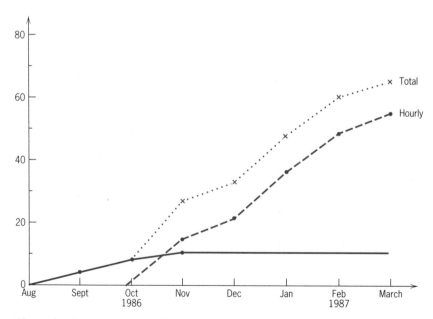

Figure 3 Stanhope labor buildup.

Table 2. Stanhope Site Capital Costs

Land and Site Preparation

land	$246,000
access roads/parking lot	124,000
landscaping	22,000

Building Costs

building (67,000 sq ft)	1,560,000
air conditioning	226,000
power	205,000
employee services	177,000
legal fees and permits	26,000

Auxiliary Equipment

ABI company sign	25,000
containers, racks, etc.	33,000
flume	148,000
coolant disposal	97,000
furnishings	51,000
forklift trucks	72,000
Total	3,012,000

quired amounts to $7,108,000 (plus required working capital of $1,380,000). The equipment is depreciated over an eight-year life. ABI, under the revised tax laws, is in the 34 percent tax bracket. The price of the piston heads has been tentatively set at $25.45 apiece. ABI's expected costs are shown in Table 3.

Table 3. Piston Head Cost Summary

Material	$8.47
Labor	1.06
Variable overhead	2.23
Fixed overhead	2.44
Freight	0.31
Total Factory Cost	14.51
General & administrative	1.43
Scrap	0.82
Testing	0.39
Total Cost	17.15

Some Concerns

Jim had spoken with some of his colleagues about the FMS concept after the preliminary financial results had been tabulated. Their concerns were what now interested him. For example, he remembered one manager asking: "Suppose Big Red's sales only reach 70 percent of our projections in the 1989–90 time period, or say, perhaps as much as 150 percent; how would this affect the project? Does the FMS still apply or would you consider some other form of manufacturing equipment, possibly conventional or CNC with potential aftermarket application in the former case or a transfer machine in the latter case?"

Another manager wrote down his thoughts as a memo to forward to Jim. He had two major concerns:

- "Scenario II" analysis assumes the loss of substantial volume to competition. This seems rather unlikely.

- After-tax margins seem unreasonably high. Can we get such margins on a sole-source contract?

Jim wondered what these changes in their assumptions would do to the ROI of the proposal and its overall profitability.

Conclusion

Jim had concerns about the project also. He wondered how realistic the demand forecasts were, given the weak economy and what the Japanese might do. If the demand didn't materialize, ABI might be sorry they had invested in such an expensive piece of equipment as an FMS.

Strategically, it seemed like ABI had to make this investment to protect its profitable position in the diesel engine business; but how far should this argument be carried? Were they letting their past investments color their judgment on new ones? He was also concerned about the memo questioning the high profit margins. They did seem high in the midst of a sluggish economy.

QUESTIONS

1. What are the answers to Steve White's questions?
2. What other factors are relevant to this issue?
3. How do the changes in assumptions mentioned by the other managers affect the proposal?
4. What position should Jim take? Why?

This article clearly describes the importance and impact of cost-related issues on a project. These issues can significantly alter the profitability and even success of a project. Costs are discussed from three viewpoints: that of the project manager, the accountant, and the controller. Not only are the amounts of expenditures and encumbrances important, but their timing is critical also. Perhaps most important is having a project cost system that accurately reports costs and variances in a way that can be useful for managerial decisions.

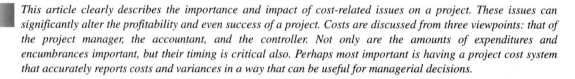

R E A D I N G

THREE PERCEPTIONS OF PROJECT COST*
D. H. Hamburger

Project cost seems to be a relatively simple expression, but "cost" is more than a four letter word. Different elements of the organization perceive cost differently, as the timing of project cost identification affects their particular organizational function. The project manager charged with on-time, on-cost, on-spec execution of a project views the "on cost" component of his responsibility as a requirement to stay within the allocated budget, while satisfying a given set of specified conditions (scope of work), within a required time frame (schedule). To most project managers this simply means a commitment to project funds in accordance with a prescribed plan (time-based budget). Others in the organization are less concerned with the commitment of funds. The accounting department addresses expense recognition related to a project or an organizational profit and loss statement. The accountant's ultimate goal is reporting profitability, while positively influencing the firm's tax liability. The comptroller (finance department) is primarily concerned with the organiza-

tion's cash flow. It is that person's responsibility to provide the funds for paying the bills, and putting the unused or available money to work for the company.

To be an effective project manager, one must understand each cost, and also realize that the timing of cost identification can affect both project and corporate financial performance. The project manager must be aware of the different cost perceptions and the manner in which they are reported. With this knowledge, the project manager can control more than the project's cost of goods sold (a function often viewed as the project manager's sole financial responsibility). The project manager can also influence the timing of cost to improve cash flow and the cost of financing the work, in addition to affecting revenue and expense reporting in the P&L statement.

Three Perceptions of Cost

To understand the three perceptions of cost—commitments, expenses, and cash flow—consider the purchase of a major project component. Assume that a $120,000 compressor with delivery quoted at six months was purchased. Figure 1 depicts the order execution cycle. At time 0 an order is placed. Six months later the vendor makes two shipments, a large box containing the

*Three Perceptions of Project Cost—Cost Is More Than a Four Letter Word. *Project Management Journal,* June 1986. ©1987 by the Project Management Institute. Reprinted by permission.

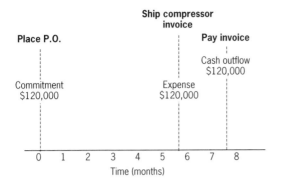

Figure 1 Three perceptions of project cost.

compressor and a small envelope containing an invoice. The received invoice is processed immediately, but payment is usually delayed to comply with corporate payment policy (30, 60, 90, or more days may pass before a check is actually mailed to the vendor). In this example, payment was made 60 days after receipt of the invoice or 8 months after the order for the compressor was given to the vendor.

Commitments—The project Manager's Concern

Placement of the purchase order represents a *commitment* to pay the vendor $120,000 following satisfactory delivery of the compressor. As far as the project manager is concerned, once this commitment is made to the vendor, the available funds in the project budget are reduced by that amount. When planning and reporting project costs the project manager deals with commitments. Unfortunately, many accounting systems are not structured to support project cost reporting needs and do not identify commitments. In fact, the value of a purchase order may not be recorded until an invoice is received. This plays havoc with the project manager's fiscal control process, as he cannot get a "handle" on the exact budget status at a particular time. In the absence of a suitable information system, a conscientious project manager will maintain personal (manual or computer) records to track his project's commitments.

Expenses—The Accountant's Concern

Preparation of the project's financial report requires identification of the project's revenues (when applicable) and all project *expenses*. In most conventional accounting systems, expenses for financial reporting purposes are recognized upon receipt of an invoice for a purchased item (not when the payment is made—a common misconception). Thus, the compressor would be treated as an expense in the sixth month.

In a conventional accounting system, revenue is recorded when the project is completed. This can create serious problems in a long-term project in which expenses are accrued during each reporting period with no attendant revenue, and the revenue is reported in the final period with little or no associated expenses shown. The project runs at an apparent loss in each of the early periods and records an inordinately large profit at the time revenue is ultimately reported—the final reporting period. This can be seriously misleading in a long-term project which runs over a multiyear period.

To avoid such confusion, most long-term project P&L statements report revenue and expenses based on a "percentage of completion" formulation. The general intent is to "take down" an equitable percentage of the total project revenue (approximately equal to the proportion of the project work completed) during each accounting period, assigning an appropriate level of expense to arrive at an acceptable period gross margin. At the end of each accounting year and at the end of the project, adjustments are made to the recorded expenses to account for the differences between actual expenses incurred and the theoretical expenses recorded in the P&L statement. This can be a complex procedure. The misinformed or uninformed project manager can place the firm in an untenable position by erroneously misrepresenting the project's P&L status; and the rare unscrupulous project manager can use an arbitrary assessment of the project's percentage of completion to manipulate the firm's P&L statement.

There are several ways by which the project's percentage of completion can be assessed to avoid these risks. A typical method, which removes subjective judgments and the potential for manipulation by relying on strict accounting procedures, is to be described. In this process a theoretical period expense is determined, which is divided by the total estimated project expense budget to compute the percentage of total budget expense for the period. This becomes the project's percentage of completion which is then used to determine the revenue to be "taken down" for the period. In this process, long delivery purchased items are not expensed on receipt of an invoice, but have the value of their purchase order prorated over the term of order execution. Figure 2 shows the $120,000 compressor in the example being expensed over the six-month delivery period at the rate of $20,000 per month.

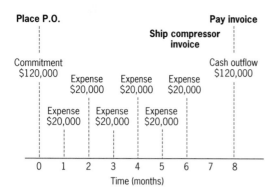

Figure 2   Percentage of completion expensing.

Cash Flow—The Comptroller's Concern

The comptroller and the finance department are responsible for managing the organization's funds, and also assuring the availability of the appropriate amount of cash for payment of the project's bills. Unused funds are put to work for the organization in interest-bearing accounts or in other ventures. The finance department's primary concern is in knowing when funds will be needed for invoice payment in order to minimize the time that these funds are not being used productively. Therefore, the comptroller really views project cost as a *cash outflow*. Placement of a purchase order merely identifies a future cash outflow to the comptroller, requiring no action on his part. Receipt of the invoice generates a little more interest, as the comptroller now knows that a finite amount of cash will be required for a particular payment at the end of a fixed period. Once a payment becomes due, the comptroller provides the funds, payment is made, and the actual cash outflow is recorded.

It should be noted that the compressor example is a simplistic representation of an actual procurement cycle, as vendor progress payments for portions of the work (i.e., engineering, material, and delivery) may be included in the purchase order. In this case, commitment timing will not change, but the timing of the expenses and cash outflow will be consistent with the agreed-upon terms of payment.

The example describes the procurement aspect of project cost, but other project cost types are treated similarly. In the case of project labor, little time elapses between actual work execution (a commitment), the recording of the labor hours on a time sheet (an expense), and the payment of wages (cash outflow).

Therefore, the three perceptions of cost are treated as if they each occur simultaneously. Subcontracts are treated in a manner similar to equipment purchases. A commitment is recorded when the subcontract is placed and cash outflow occurs when the monthly invoice for the work is paid. Expenses are treated in a slightly different manner. Instead of prorating the subcontract sum over the performance period, the individual invoices for the actual work performed are used to determine the expense for the period covered by each invoice.

Thus the three different perceptions of cost can result in three different time-based cost curves for a given project budget. Figure 3 shows a typical relationship between commitments, expenses, and cash outflow. The commitment curve leads and the cash outflow curve lags, with the expense curve falling in the middle. The actual shape and the degree of lag/lead between the curves are a function of several factors, including: the project's labor, material, and subcontract mix; the firm's invoice payment policy; the delivery period for major equipment items; subcontract performance period and the schedule of its work; and the effect of the project schedule on when and how labor will be expended in relation to equipment procurement.

The conscientious project manager must understand these different perceptions of cost and should be prepared to plan and report on any and all approaches required by management. The project manager should also be aware of the manner in which the accounting department collects and reports "costs." Since the project manager's primary concern is in the commitments, he or she should insist on an accounting system which is compatible with the project's reporting needs. Why must a project manager resort to a manual control system when the appropriate data can be made available

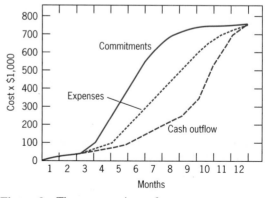

Figure 3   Three perceptions of cost.

through an adjustment in the accounting department's data processing system?

Putting Your Understanding of Cost to Work

Most project managers believe that their total contribution to the firm's profitability is restricted by the ability to limit and control project cost, but they can do much more. Once the different perceptions of cost have been recognized, the project manager's effectiveness is greatly enhanced. The manner in which the project manager plans and executes the project can improve company profitability through influence on financing expenses, cash flow, and the reporting of revenue and expenses. To be a completely effective project manager one must be totally versed in the cost accounting practices which affect the firm's project cost reporting.

Examination of the typical project profit & loss statement (see Table 1) shows how a project sold for profit is subjected to costs other than the project's costs (cost of goods sold). The project manager also influences other areas of cost as well, addressing all aspects of the P&L to influence project profitability positively.

Specific areas of cost with examples of what a project manager can do to influence cost of goods sold, interest expense, tax expense, and profit are given next.

Cost of Goods Sold (Project Cost)

- Evaluation of alternate design concepts and the use of "trade-off" studies during the development phase of a project can result in a lower project cost, without sacrificing the technical quality of the project's output. The application of value engineering principles during the initial de-

Table 1. Typical Project Profit & Loss Statement

Revenue (project sell price)	$1,000,000
(less) cost of goods sold (project costs)	($ 750,000)
Gross margin	$ 250,000
(less) selling, general & administrative expenses	($ 180,000)
Profit before interest and taxes	$ 70,000
(less) financial expense	($ 30,000)
Profit before taxes	$ 40,000
(less) taxes	($ 20,000)
Net profit	$ 20,000

sign period will also reduce cost. A directed and controlled investment in the evaluation of alternative design concepts can result in significant savings of project cost.

- Excessive safety factors employed to ensure "on-spec" performance should be avoided. Too frequently the functional members of the project team will apply large safety factors in their effort to meet or exceed the technical specifications. The project team must realize that such excesses increase the project's cost. The functional staff should be prepared to justify an incremental investment which was made to gain additional performance insurance. Arbitrary and excessive conservatism must be avoided.

- Execution of the project work must be controlled. The functional groups should not be allowed to stretch out the project for the sake of improvement, refinement, or the investigation of the most remote potential risk. When a functional task has been completed to the project manager's satisfaction (meeting the task's objectives), cut off further spending to prevent accumulation of "miscellaneous" charges.

- The project manager is usually responsible for controlling the project's contingency budget. This budget represents money that one expects to expend during the term of the project for specific requirements not identified at the project onset. Therefore, these funds must be carefully monitored to prevent indiscriminate spending. A functional group's need for a portion of the contingency budget must be justified and disbursement of these funds should only be made after the functional group has exhibited an effort to avoid or limit its use. It is imperative that the contingency budget be held for its intended purpose. Unexpected problems will ultimately arise, at which time the funds will be needed. Use of this budget to finance a scope change is neither advantageous to the project manager nor to management. The contingency budget represents the project manager's authority in dealing with corrections to the project work. Management must be made aware of the true cost of a change so that financing the change will be based on its true value (cost-benefit relationship).

- In the procurement of equipment, material and subcontract services, the specified requirements should be identified and the lowest priced, qualified supplier found. Adequate time for price "shopping" should be built into the project schedule. The Mercury project proved to be safe and successful even though John Glenn, perched in the Mercury capsule atop the Atlas rocket prior to America's first earth orbiting flight, expressed his now famous concern that "all this hardware was built by the low bidder." The project manager should ensure that the initial project budget is commensurate with the project's required level of reliability. The project manager should not be put in the position of having to buy project reliability with unavailable funds.

- Procurement of material and services based on partially completed drawings and specifications should be avoided. The time necessary for preparing a complete documentation package before soliciting bids should be considered in the preparation of the project schedule. Should an order be awarded based on incomplete data and the vendor then asked to alter the original scope of supply, the project will be controlled by the vendor. In executing a "fast track" project, the project manager should make certain that the budget contains an adequate contingency for the change orders which will follow release of a partially defined work scope.

- Changes should not be incorporated in the project scope without client and/or management approval and the allocation of the requisite funds. Making changes without approval will erode the existing budget and reduce project profitability; meeting the project manager's "on-cost" commitment will become extremely difficult, if not impossible.

- During periods of inflation, the project manager must effectively deal with the influence of the economy on the project budget. This is best accomplished during the planning or estimating stage of the work, and entails recognition of planning in an inflationary environment for its effect by estimating the potential cost of two distinct factors. First, a "price protection" contingency budget is needed to cover the cost increases that will occur between the time a vendor provides a firm quotation for a limited period and the actual date the order will be placed.

(Vendor quotations used to prepare an estimate usually expire long before the material is actually purchased.) Second, components containing certain price-volatile materials (e.g., gold, silver, etc.) may not be quoted firm, but will be offered by the supplier as "price in effect at time of delivery." In this case an "escalation" contingency budget is needed to cover the added expense that will accrue between order placement and material delivery. Once the project manager has established these inflation related contingency budgets, the PM's role becomes one of ensuring controlled use.

Financial Expense

- The project's financial cost (interest expense) can be minimized by the project manager through the timing of order placement. Schedule slack time can be used to defer the placement of a purchase order so that the material is not available too early and the related cash outflow is not premature. There are several risks associated with this concept. Delaying an order too long could backfire if the desired material is unavailable when needed. Allowing a reasonable margin for error in the delivery cycle, saving some of the available slack time for potential delivery problems, will reduce this risk. Waiting too long to place a purchase order could result in a price increase which can more than offset the interest savings. It is possible to "lock-up" a vendor's price without committing to a required delivery date, but this has its limitations. If vendor drawings are a project requirement, an "engineering only" order can be placed to be followed by hardware release at the appropriate time. Deferred procurement which takes advantage of available slack time should be considered in the execution of all projects, especially during periods when the cost of money is excessively high.

- Vendors are frequently used to help "finance the project" by placing purchase orders which contain extended payment terms. Financially astute vendors will build the cost of financing the project into their sell price, but only to the extent of remaining competitive. A vendor's pricing structure should be checked to determine if progress payments would result in a reduced price and a net project benefit.

A discount for prompt payment should be taken if the discount exceeds the interest savings that could result from deferring payment.

- Although frequently beyond the project manager's control, properly structured progress payment terms can serve to negate most or all project financial expenses. The intent is simple. A client's progress payment terms can be structured to provide scheduled cash inflows which offset the project's actual cash outflow. In other words, maintenance of a zero net cash position throughout the period of project execution will minimize the project's financial expense. In fact, a positive net cash position resulting from favorable payment terms can actually result in a project which creates interest income rather than one that incurs an interest expense. Invoices to the client should be processed quickly, to minimize the lost interest resulting from a delay in receiving payment.

- Similarly, the project manager can influence receipt of withheld funds (retention) and the project's final payment to improve the project's rate of cash inflow. A reduction in retention should be pursued as the project nears completion. Allowing a project's schedule to indiscriminately slip delays project acceptance, thereby delaying final payment. Incurring an additional expense to resolve a questionable problem should be considered whenever the expense will result in rapid project acceptance and a favorable interest expense reduction.

- On internally funded projects, where retention, progress payments, and other client related financial considerations are not a factor, management expects to achieve payback in the shortest reasonable time. In this case, project spending is a continuous cash outflow process which cannot be reversed until the project is completed and its anticipated financial benefits begin to accrue from the completed work. Unnecessary project delays, schedule slippages, and long-term investigations extend system startup and defer the start of payback. Early completion will result in an early start of the investment payback process. Therefore, management's payback goal should be considered when planning and controlling project work, and additional expenditures in the execution of the work should be considered if a shortened schedule will adequately hasten the start of payback.

Tax Expense and Profit

- On occasion, management will demand project completion by a given date to ensure inclusion of the project's revenue and profit within a particular accounting period. This demand usually results from a need to fulfill a prior financial performance forecast. Delayed project completion by only a few days could shift the project's entire revenue and profit from one accounting period to the next. The volatile nature of this situation, large sums of revenue and profit shifting from one period to the next, results in erratic financial performance which negatively reflects on management's ability to plan and execute their efforts.

- To avoid the stigma of erratic financial performance, management has been known to suddenly redirect a carefully planned, cost-effective project team effort to a short-term, usually costly, crash exercise, directed toward a project completion date, artificially necessitated by a corporate financial reporting need. Unfortunately, a project schedule driven by influences external to the project's fundamental objectives usually results in additional cost and reduces profitability.

- In this particular case, the solution is simple if a percentage of completion accounting process can be applied. Partial revenue and margin take-down during each of the project's accounting periods, resulting from this procedure (rather than lump sum take down in a single period at the end of the project, as occurs using conventional accounting methods) will mitigate the undesirable wild swings in reported revenue and profit. Two specific benefits will result. First, management's revenue/profit forecast will be more accurate and less sensitive to project schedule changes. Each project's contribution to the overall forecast will be spread over several accounting periods and any individual performance change will cause the shift of a significantly smaller sum from one accounting period to the next. Second, a project nearing completion will have had 90–95 percent of its revenue/profit taken down in earlier periods which will lessen or completely eliminate management pressure to complete the work to satisfy a financial reporting demand.

Inordinate, unnecessary spending to meet such unnatural demands can thereby be avoided.

- An Investment Tax Credit,* a net reduction in corporate taxes gained from a capital investment project (a fixed percentage of the project's installed cost), can be earned when the project actually provides its intended benefit to the owner. The project manager should consider this factor in scheduling the project work, recognizing that it is not necessary to complete the entire project to obtain this tax benefit as early as possible. Failure to substantiate beneficial use within a tax year can shift this savings into the next tax year. The project manager should consider this factor in establishing the project's objectives, diligently working toward attainment by scheduling the related tasks to meet the tax deadline. Consideration should also be given to expenditures (to the extent they do not offset the potential tax savings) to reach this milestone by the desired date.

- In managing the corporate P&L statement, the need to shift revenue, expenses, and profit from one tax period to the next often exists. By managing the project schedule (expediting or delaying major component procurements or shifting expensive activities) the project manager can support this requirement. Each individual project affords a limited benefit, but this can be maximized if the project manager is given adequate notice regarding the necessary scheduling adjustments.

- Revenue/profit accrual based on percentage of completion can create a financial problem if actual expenses greatly exceed the project budget. In this case the project's percentage of completion will accumulate more quickly than justified and the project will approach a theoretical 100 percent completion before all work is done. This will "front load" revenue/profit take down and will ultimately require a profit reversal at project completion. Some managers may find this desir-

able, since profits are being shifted into earlier periods, but most reputable firms do not wish to overstate profits in an early period which will have to be reversed at a later time. Therefore, the project manager should be aware of cost overruns and, when necessary, reforecast the project's "cost on completion" (increasing the projected cost and reducing the expected profit) to reduce the level of profit taken down in the early periods to a realistic level.

Conclusion

Cost is not a four letter word to be viewed with disdain by the project manager. It is a necessary element of the project management process which the project manager must comprehend despite the apparent mysteries of the accounting systems employed to report cost. The concept of cost is more than the expenses incurred in the execution of the project work: the manner in which cost is treated by the organization's functional elements can affect project performance, interest expenses and profitability. Therefore, the conscientious project manager must develop a complete understanding of project cost and the accounting systems used to record and report costs. The project manager should also recognize the effect of the timing of project cost, and the differences between commitments, expenses, and cash flow. The project manager should insist on the accounting system modifications needed to accommodate project cost reporting and control requirements. Once an appreciation for these concepts has been gained, the project manager can apply this knowledge towards positively influencing project and organizational profitability in all areas of cost through control of the project schedule and the execution of the project's work.

Questions

1. What is the major point of the article?
2. How does the accountant view project costs?
3. How does the controller view project costs?
4. How does the project manager view project costs?
5. What other costs does the project manager need to be cognizant of? What actions should the PM take concerning these other costs?

---

*The proposed tax law revisions under consideration in Congress at the time this article was written include a provision which eliminates the Investment Tax Credit.

CHAPTER

8

Scheduling

The previous chapter initiated our discussion of project implementation. In this and the following three chapters, we continue with the implementation of the project plans we made in Chapter 5. In this chapter, we examine some scheduling techniques that have been found to be useful in project management. We cover the Program Evaluation and Review Technique (PERT), the Critical Path Method (CPM), Gantt charts, and briefly discuss Precedence Diagramming, the Graphical Evaluation and Review Technique (GERT), Critical Resource Diagramming, and report-based methods. Risk analysis and management will be considered as an inherent feature of all scheduling methods, and a simulation of a project schedule will be demonstrated.

In Chapter 9, we consider the special problems of scheduling when resource limitations force conflicts between concurrent projects, or even between two or more tasks in a single project. We also look at Goldratt's "critical chain" (1997) and ways of expediting activities by adding resources. Following a discussion of the monitoring and information system function in Chapter 10, we discuss the overall topic of project control in Chapter 11.

8.1 BACKGROUND

A schedule is the conversion of a project action plan into an operating timetable. As such, it serves as the basis for monitoring and controlling project activity and, taken together with the plan and budget, is probably the major tool for the management of projects. In a project environment, the scheduling function is more important than it would be in an ongoing operation because projects lack the continuity of day-to-day operations and often present much more complex problems of coordination. Indeed, project scheduling is so important that a detailed schedule is sometimes a customer-

Source: By permission of Johnny Hart and Creators Syndicate, Inc.

specified requirement. In later chapters, we discuss the fact that a properly designed, detailed schedule can also serve as a key input in establishing the monitoring and control systems for the project.

Not all project activities need to be scheduled at the same level of detail. In fact, there may be several schedules (e.g., the master schedule, the development and testing schedule, the assembly schedule). These schedules are typically based on the previously determined action plan and/or work breakdown structure (WBS), and it is good practice to create a schedule for each major task level in the WBS that will cover the work packages. It is rarely necessary, however, to list all work packages. One can focus mainly on those that need to be monitored for maintaining adequate control over the project. Such packages are usually difficult, expensive, or have a relatively short time frame for their accomplishment.

The basic approach of all scheduling techniques is to form a network of activity and event relationships that graphically portrays the sequential relations between the tasks in a project. Tasks that must precede or follow other tasks are then clearly identified, in time as well as function. Such a network is a powerful tool for planning and controlling a project, and has the following benefits:

- It is a consistent framework for planning, scheduling, monitoring, and controlling the project.
- It illustrates the interdependence of all tasks, work packages, and work elements.

Project Management in Practice
Replacing the Atigun Section of the TransAlaska Pipeline

In June of 1977, the TransAlaska Pipeline was put into service as the successful conclusion of one of the most difficult projects in history. As part of the maintenance of the 48-inch diameter pipeline, instrumented "pigs" are run along the pipeline every year to detect both internal and external corrosion. In the fall of 1988, data from the pig run indicated that excessive external corrosion had occurred in an 8.5 mile section of the pipeline located in the Atigun River flood plain, 135 miles north of the Arctic Circle (see map). Thus, in the spring of 1989 a project team was formed to take total responsibility for replacing this portion of the buried pipeline with another buried pipe that had much better external corro-

sion protection, fusion bonded epoxy covered with 1.25 inches of concrete, an articulated concrete mat, and then five to fifteen feet of dirt. As part of the project objectives, the oil flow of two million barrels per day at pressures exceeding 800 psi was *not* to be interrupted, and there could be absolutely no oil spills!

This meant that a bypass system had to be constructed while the pipe was being replaced, all in a very hostile work environment. The site is subject to flooding, rockslides, avalanches, mudslides, temperatures that reach −60°F in the winter (tires break like glass and gasoline turns to jelly at that temperature), and as little as three hours of sunshine in which to work during the

Young grizzly bear at construction site—Atigun section of TransAlaska Pipeline.

Repairing and maintaining the Pipeline requires constant vigilance.

winter months. To minimize exposure to the springtime avalanches, they worked in another area first and then used explosives to trigger potential avalanches and unstable snow deposits. Also, a full-time avalanche control and forecasting expert was present during construction in the danger area. Blasting was also used to dig the ditch, ironically, to protect the existing pipeline which was only 30 feet away. Another ironic aspect of the project was the constant curiosity of the wildlife in the area: "What impressed me most was completing this project right there in the middle of all these animals, and seeing that we didn't affect them at all—that was gratifying."

The project began in September of 1989 and was completed in December 1991, a 27-month duration. Scheduling was a major facet of the project, not just due to the limited hours of sunshine, but also in obtaining facilities and materials for the project. For example, some elements of the replacement pipeline had to be shipped to Saudi Arabia for corrosion treatment and then shipped back, all just prior to the Persian Gulf war. Yet, the project met or exceeded all expectations, without one oil spill. More surprisingly, the project was completed 34 percent under budget through careful analysis of the financial and physical risks and assignment to the most appropriate contractor.

Source: Project Team, "Atigun Mainline Reroute Project," *PM Network,* January 1993.

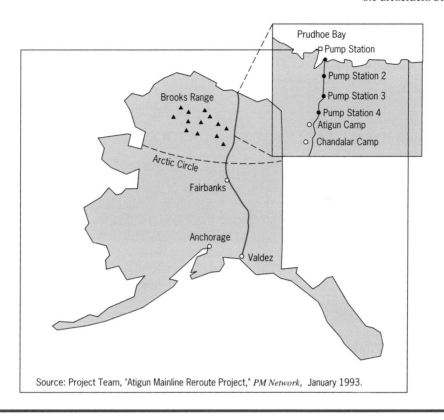

Source: Project Team, "Atigun Mainline Reroute Project," *PM Network*, January 1993.

- It denotes the times when specific individuals and resources must be available for work on a given task.
- It aids in ensuring that the proper communications take place between departments and functions.
- It determines an expected project completion date.
- It identifies so-called critical activities that, if delayed, will delay the project completion time.
- It also identifies activities with slack that can be delayed for specified periods without penalty, or from which resources may be temporarily borrowed without harm.
- It determines the dates on which tasks may be started—or must be started if the project is to stay on schedule.
- It illustrates which tasks must be coordinated to avoid resource or timing conflicts.
- It also illustrates which tasks may be run, or must be run, in parallel to achieve the predetermined project completion date.

- It relieves some interpersonal conflict by clearly showing task dependencies.
- It may, depending on the information used, allow an estimate of the probability of project completion by various dates, or the date corresponding to a particular a priori probability.

8.2   NETWORK TECHNIQUES: PERT AND CPM

With the exception of Gantt charts, to be discussed below, the most common approach to project scheduling is the use of network techniques such as PERT and CPM. The Program Evaluation and Review Technique was developed by the U.S. Navy in cooperation with Booz-Allen Hamilton and the Lockheed Corporation for the Polaris missile/submarine project in 1958. The Critical Path Method was developed by DuPont, Inc., during the same time period.

In application, PERT has primarily been used for R&D projects, the type of projects for which it was developed, though its use is more common on the "development" side of R&D than it is on the "research" side. CPM was designed for construction projects and has been generally embraced by the construction industry. (There are many exceptions to these generalities. The Eli Lilly Company, for example, uses CPM for its research projects.)

The two methods are quite similar and are often combined for educational presentation. Throughout most of this chapter we will not distinguish between them except where the differences are of direct interest to us. We will write "PERT/CPM" whenever the distinction is not important. Originally, however, PERT was strictly oriented to the time element of projects and used probabilistic activity time estimates to aid in determining the probability that a project could be completed by some given date. CPM, on the other hand, used deterministic activity time estimates and was designed to control both the time and cost aspects of a project, in particular, time/cost trade-offs. In CPM, activities can be "crashed" (expedited) at extra cost to speed up the completion time. Both techniques identified a project *critical path* with activities that could not be delayed, and also indicated activities with *slack* (or *float*) that could be somewhat delayed without lengthening the project completion time. Some writers insist on a strict differentiation between PERT and CPM. This strikes us as unnecessary. One can estimate probabalistic CPM times, and can "crash" PERT networks.

We might note in passing that the *critical* activities in real-world projects typically constitute less than 10 percent of the total activities. In our examples and simplified problems in this chapter, the critical activities constitute a much greater proportion of the total because we use smaller networks to illustrate the techniques.

Before explaining the mechanics of these methods, we must note that their value in use was not totally accepted by everyone. Research on the use of PERT/CPM conducted in the 1960s and early 1970s (e.g., Davis, 1974) found that there was no significant difference in the technological performance on projects where PERT/CPM was used and where it was not. This research found, however, that there was a significantly lower probability of cost and schedule overruns when PERT/CPM was used. In our experience, the use of network scheduling techniques has increased markedly in recent years, particularly with the proliferation of project management software pack-ages that are inexpensive and reasonably friendly to PMs who are familiar with the fundamental concepts of PERT/CPM, and who are also sensible enough to avoid try-ing to construct complex networks by hand.

Research (Badiru, 1993) finds that a greater use of "project management tech-niques" (PERT/CPM among a number of others) occurs on R&D type projects, on projects with greater levels of complexity, and on projects with resource limitations, than on other types of projects or those with lower levels of complexity and fewer re-source limitations. Unfortunately, this otherwise excellent research did not investigate whether or not the use of project management software influenced the number of project management techniques used. The use of project management software for scheduling projects will be discussed and illustrated a bit later in this chapter.

Terminology

Let us now define some terms used in our discussion of networks.

Activity   A specific task or set of tasks that are required by the project, use up resources, and take time to complete.

Event   The result of completing one or more activities. An identifiable end state occurring at a particular time. Events use no resources.

Network   The arrangement of all activities (and, in some cases, events) in a project arrayed in their logical sequence and represented by arcs and nodes. This arrangement (network) defines the project and the activity precedence relation-ships. Networks are usually drawn starting on the left and proceeding to the right. Arrowheads placed on the arcs are used to indicate the direction of flow—that is, to show the proper precedences. Before an event can be *realized*—that is, achieved—all activities that immediately precede it must be completed. These are called its *predecessors.* Thus, an event represents an instant in time when each and every predecessor activity has been finished

Path   The series of connected activities (or intermediate events) between any two events in a network.

Critical   Activities, events, or paths which, if delayed, will delay the completion of the project. A project's *critical path* is understood to mean that sequence of critical activities (and critical events) that connects the project's start event to its finish event and which cannot be delayed without delaying the project.

To transform a project plan into a network, one must know what activities com-prise the project and, for each activity, what its predecessors (or successors) are. An activity can be in any of these conditions: (1) it may have a successor(s) but no prede-cessor(s); (2) it may have a predecessor(s) but no successor(s); and (3) it may have both predecessor(s) and successor(s). The first of these is an activity that starts a net-work. The second ends a network. The third is in the middle. Figure 8-1 shows each of the three types of activities. Activities are represented here by rectangles (one form of what in a network are called "nodes") with arrows to show the precedence relation-ships. In this activity-on-node (AON) notation, when there are multiple activities with

Figure 8-1 Three sequential activities, AON format.

no predecessors, it is usual to show them all emanating from a single node called "START," as in Figure 8-2. Similarly, when multiple activities have no successors, it is usual to show them connected to a node called "END."

The interconnections depend on the technological relationships described in the action plan. For example, when one paints a room, filling small holes and cracks in the wall and masking windows and woodwork are predecessors to painting the walls. Similarly, removing curtains and blinds, as well as pictures and picture hooks from the wall are predecessors to spackling and masking. It is the nature of the work to be done that determines predecessor–successor relationships.

> As of tomorrow, employees will only be able to access the building using individual security cards. Pictures will be taken next Wednesday, and employees will receive their cards in two weeks.

In the preceding examples, rectangles (nodes) represent the activities, hence it is called an activity-on-node (AON) network. Another format for drawing networks is AOA (activity-on-arrow), as shown in Figure 8-3. Here, the activities are shown on the arrows and the (circular) nodes represent events. If the project begins with multiple activities, they can all be drawn emanating from the initial node and multiple activities can terminate in a single node at the end of the project.

Throughout most of this chapter we adopt the AON format. This chapter is intended as an introduction to project scheduling at a level sufficient for the PM who wishes to use most commercial computerized project scheduling packages. For a deeper understanding of PERT/CPM, we refer the reader to Dean (1985); Moder, Phillips, and Davis (1983); Naik (1984); and Weist and Levy (1977).

Recall the planning documents we developed in Chapter 5. In particular, the action plan contains the information we need. It is a list of all activities that must be undertaken in order to complete a specified task, the time each activity is expected to

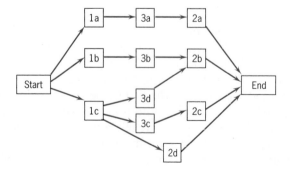

Figure 8-2 Activity network, AON format

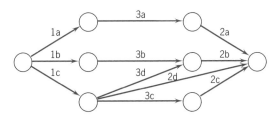

Figure 8-3   Activity network, AOA format.

take, any nonroutine resources that will be used by the activity, and the predecessor activities for each activity. For example, we might have an action plan like that shown in Figure 8-4.

Constructing the Network, AON Version

We begin with the node called "START." Activities **a** and **b** have no predecessors, so we draw arrows out of START to each of them (Figure 8-5a). As explained above, the arrowheads show the direction of precedence. Activity **c** follows **a**, activity **d** follows **b**, and activity **e** also follows **b**. Let's add these to our network in Figure 8-6a. Now, activity **f** follows both **c** and **d**. The action plan does not indicate any further activity is required to complete the task, so we have reached the end of this particular plan. We thus draw arrows from activities **e** and **f** to the node END, as shown in Figure 8-7a. Many of the project management software packages will generate these networks on request.

Constructing the Network, AOA Version

Again, we begin with a node (event) called "START." Activities **a** and **b** have no predecessors, so we draw arrows labeled "**a**" and "**b**" from START and terminating in circle-shaped nodes numbered "1" and "2" for easy identification (Figure 8-5b). Ac-

ACTION PLAN

Objective: To complete . . . .
. . . .

Measures of Performance . . . .
. . . .

Constraints . . . .

Tasks	Precedence	Time	Cost	Who Does
a	—	5 days	—	—
b	—	4 days	—	—
c	a	6 days	—	—
d	b	2 days	—	—
e	b	5 days	—	—
f	c,d	8 days	—	—

Figure 8-4   Sample action plan.

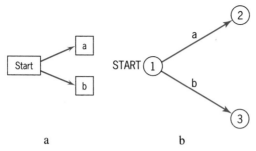

Figure 8-5 Sample of network construction.

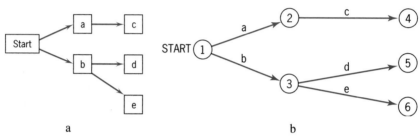

Figure 8-6 Sample of network construction.

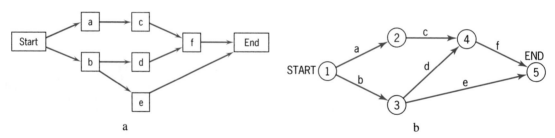

Figure 8-7 Sample of network construction.

tivity **c** follows **a**, activity **d** follows **b**, and activity **e** also follows **b**. Let's add these arrows to our AOA network, labeling the arrows and nodes sequentially as we go (Figure 8-6b).

Note that activity **f** must follow both **c** and **d**, but *any given activity must have its source in one and only one node.* Therefore, **c** and **d** must terminate at the same node. Erase activity **d** and its node—it is now clear that hand-drawn networks should be drawn in pencil—and redraw **d** to end at the same node that terminates **c**. We now add activity **e** following **b**, and **f** following **c** and **d**. Because **e** and **f** have no successors, they will terminate at the END node (Figure 8-7b).

The choice between AOA and AON representation is largely a matter of personal preference. Our impression is that users of PERT favor AOA and users of CPM favor AON, but both approaches appear in the educational literature. AON is typically used

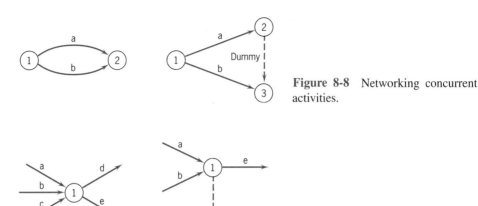

Figure 8-8 Networking concurrent activities.

Figure 8-9 Activity **c** not required for **e.**

in the most popular PC-based commercially available computer software, and AON networks are easier to draw. AOA networks are slightly harder to draw because they sometimes require the use of *dummy* activities to aid in indicating a particular precedence, via a dashed arc. A dummy activity has no duration and uses no resources. Its sole purpose is to indicate a technological relationship. (AON networks do not require the use of dummy activities.) AOA networks clearly identify events in the network. These must be added as "zero-duration" activities (or *milestones*) in AON networks.

Figure 8-8 illustrates the proper way to use a dummy activity if two activities occur between the same *two* events. Figure 8-8 also shows why dummy activities may be needed for AOA networks. An activity is identified by its starting and ending nodes as well as its "name." For example, activities **a** and **b** both start from node 1 and end at node 2. Many computer programs that are widely used for finding the critical path and time for networks require the nodes to identify which activity is which. In our example, **a** and **b** would appear to be the same, both starting at node 1 and ending at node 2. Figure 8-9 illustrates how to use a dummy activity in AOA format when activities **a, b,** and **c** must precede activity **d,** but only **a** and **b** must precede activity **e.** Last, Figure 8-10 illustrates the use of dummy activities in a more complex setting.

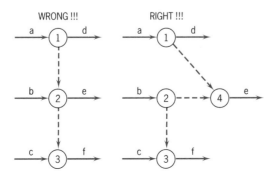

Figure 8-10 **a** precedes **d; a** and **b** precede **e; b** and **c** precede **f** (**a** does not precede **f**).

Because both AOA and AON networks are widely used, the PM must be familiar with both types.

Gantt Charts and Microsoft Project® (MSP)

One of the oldest and still one of the most useful methods of presenting schedule information is the Gantt chart, developed around 1917 by Henry L. Gantt, a pioneer in the field of scientific management. The Gantt chart shows planned and actual progress for a number of tasks displayed against a horizontal time scale. It is a particularly effective and easy-to-read method of indicating the actual current status for each of a set of tasks compared to the planned progress for each item of the set. As a result, the Gantt chart can be helpful in expediting, sequencing, and reallocating resources among tasks, as well as in the valuable but mundane job of keeping track of how things are going. In addition, the charts usually contain a number of special symbols to designate or highlight items of special concern to the situation being charted.

There are several advantages to the use of Gantt charts. First, even though they may contain a great deal of information, they are easily understood. While they do require frequent updating (as does any scheduling/control device), they are easy to maintain *as long as task requirements are not changed or major alterations of the schedule are not made.* Gantt charts provide a picture of the current state of a project. Gantt charts, however, have a serious weakness. If a project is complex with a large set of activities, it may be very difficult to follow multiple activity paths through the project. Gantt charts are powerful devices for communicating to senior management, but networks are usually more helpful in the hands-on task of managing the project.

Another significant feature of Gantt charts is that they are as easy to construct as an AON network. While they may be constructed without first drawing a PERT diagram, there is a close relationship between the PERT/CPM network and the Gantt chart. We use the example in the previous subsection to illustrate this relationship and, at the same time, demonstrate how to construct such a chart.

As is true of many things, it is important for the student to be able to understand just what it is that networks and Gantt charts show (and what they do not show) before using MSP or other software to draw complex networks and Gantt charts that the student will have to understand and use. Drawing networks and charts by hand is a quick way to develop that understanding. Once understanding is gained, however, software is easier, faster, and given a project of a size that reflects reality, far more cost effective.

Consider the example in Figure 8-7 that was just used to illustrate how to draw a network. If we open MSP we see the form that is used to enter action plan (or WBS) data into the program. (You may have to close the MSP help box to see the whole form.) Entering the data is straightforward. We begin by entering an activity named "START." We assign it a duration of 0 days which makes it a "milestone" rather than a true "activity." We now enter activity **a** with a duration of five days, and then continue with the rest of the activities. At the end of the list, we add FINISH with zero days duration, the project ending milestone.

The software automatically assigns a WBS (ID) number to each activity as you enter it. You may delete or add columns if you wish. If you do not enter a specific start date, the MSP will default to the present date for its start date. As you enter data from the action plan, MSP will draw an AON network and a Gantt chart automatically. (The Gantt chart will be visible to the right of the action plan information.) If the activity names and durations are entered without noting the appropriate predecessor information, all activities will be assumed to start on the same start date. As the predecessor information is entered, the proper relationships between the activities are shown, see Figures 8-11 and 8-12.

Our concern so far has simply been to show the technological dependencies in a network or Gantt chart. A glance at the AON network or the Gantt chart shows something interesting. If we sum up the activity times for all activities in the action plan, we see that there are 30 days of work to schedule. But, as the network and chart show, the project is scheduled to start on January 21, 2002 and will be completed on February 14, 2002. That is 25 days, not 30. Further, MSP defaults to a work calendar with a five-day week. (Note that Saturday and Sunday are lightly shaded on the Gantt chart to indicate they are nonwork days.) If the calendar is adjusted to a seven-day week, the project will require only 19 days to be completed. It can be finished as early as February 8. Calculation of project duration has not yet been discussed, though it will be very shortly. Calculation-by-hand is not at all difficult, but MSP can do it faster and easier. It is important, however, to remember that software makes assumptions

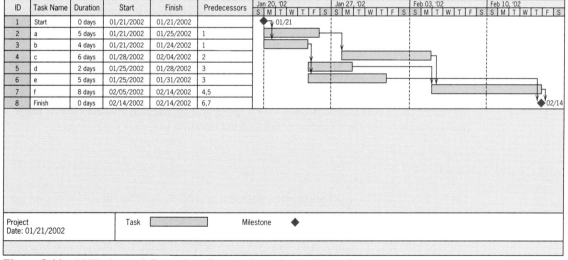

Figure 8-11   MSP plan and Gantt chart for sample project in Figure 8-4.

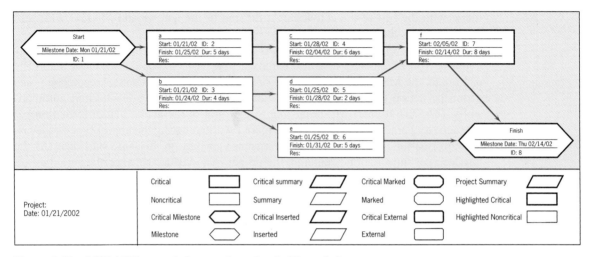

Figure 8-12   MSP AON network for sample project in Figure 8-4.

about such things as the number of days worked in a week, the number of hours per day that are worked, and several other matters that will be considered later. These assumptions may be changed if one wishes, but they must be considered every time the software is used to map a project.

This example illustrates both the strength and weakness of the Gantt chart. Its major strength is that it is easy to read. All popular project management software will prepare Gantt charts, and most have some options available for customization. On balance, ease of construction and ease of use have made the Gantt chart the most popular method for displaying a project schedule. Nonetheless, a PERT/CPM network is still needed for the PM to exercise control over the schedule, and the viewer may be misled if the Gantt chart is not read carefully or if it does not contain all appropriate information (Wilkins, 1997).

In many ways, the Gantt chart is similar to the project master schedule described in Chapter 5. Both are types of bar charts and are used similarly. The major difference is that the Gantt chart is intended to monitor the detailed progress of work, whereas the master schedule contains only major tasks and is oriented toward overall project management rather than precise control of the detailed aspects of the project.

Solving the Network

Let us now consider a small project with ten activities in order to illustrate the network technique. Table 8-1 lists the activities, their most likely completion times, and the activities that must precede them. The table also includes optimistic and pessimistic estimates of completion time for each activity in the list. Actual activity time

Table 8-1. Project Activity Times and Precedences

Activity	Optimistic Time	Most Likely Time	Pessimistic Time	Immediate Predecessor Activities
a	10	22	22	—
b	20	20	20	—
c	4	10	16	—
d	2	14	32	a
e	8	8	20	b,c
f	8	14	20	b,c
g	4	4	4	b,c
h	2	12	16	c
i	6	16	38	g,h
j	2	8	14	d,e

is expected rarely to be less than the optimistic time or more than the pessimistic time. (More on this matter shortly.)

Beginning with a node named START, connect the three activities with no predecessors (**a, b,** and **c**) to the Start node as in Figure 8-13.

Activity **d** has a predecessor of **a**, and thus it follows **a**. Activities **e, f,** and **g** all must follow both **b** and **c** as predecessors. Activity **h** follows **c**. Activity **j** follows both **d** and **e**. Activity **i** follows **g** and **h**. Because there are no more activities, we must be at the end of the network. Add a node labeled "END" and connect any nodes without successor activities, in this case, **j, f,** and **i**, reading from top to bottom. As stated earlier, always show the direction of a connection with an arrowhead.

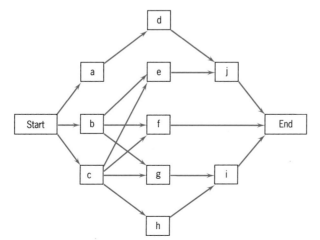

Figure 8-13 The AON network from Table 8-1.

Calculating Activity Times

The next step is to calculate expected activity completion times from the data in Table 8-1. These expected completion times are found by using the three time estimates (optimistic, pessimistic, and most likely) in the table. Remember that these estimates are an expression of the risk associated with the time required for each activity. (The optimistic, pessimistic, and most likely estimates made for activity times are equally applicable to the estimates of resource usage made in Chapter 7, as are the calculations that follow.)

Once again, a short digression is helpful. Precisely what is meant by "optimistic," "pessimistic," and "most likely"? Assume that all possible times for some specific activity might be represented by a statistical distribution (e.g., the asymmetrical distribution in Figure 8-14) The "most likely" time, m, for the activity is the mode of this distribution. In theory, the "optimistic" and "pessimistic" times are selected in the following way. The PM, or whoever is attempting to estimate a and b, is asked to select a such that the actual time required by the activity will be a or greater about 99 percent of the time. Similarly, b is estimated such that about 99 percent of the time the activity will have a duration of b or less. (Some project managers or workers may be uncomfortable making estimates at this level of precision, but we will delay dealing with this problem for the moment.)

The expected time, TE, is found by

$$TE = (a + 4m + b)/6$$

where

    a = optimistic time estimate

    b = pessimistic time estimate

    m = most likely time estimate, the mode

Note in Table 8-1 that some activity durations are known with certainty, which is to say that a, b, and m are the same (see activity **g**, for instance). Note further that the most likely time may be the same as the optimistic time ($a = m$) as in activity **e**, or that the most likely time may be identical to the pessimistic time ($m = b$) as in activity **a**. The range about m may be symmetric where

$$m - a = b - m$$

as in activity **c**, or may be quite asymmetric, as in activities **h** and **i**.

The above formula for calculating expected times is based on the beta statistical distribution.* This distribution is used rather than the more common normal distribu-

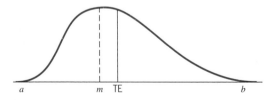

a m TE b

Figure 8-14   Distribution of all possible activity times for an activity.

---

*We remind readers who would like a short refresher on elementary statistics and probability that one is available in the Appendix at the end of this book.

tion because it is highly flexible in form and can take into account such extremes as where $a = m$ or $b = m$.

TE is an estimate of the mean of the distribution. It is a weighted average of a, m, and b with weights of 1-4-1, respectively. Again, we emphasize that this *same method can be applied to finding the expected level of resource usage given the appropriate estimates of the modal resource level as well as optimistic and pessimistic estimates.*

This process of estimating activity times occasionally comes under criticism. In general, critics argue that when activity times are set, these come to be considered as targets, leading to a comparison with Management by Objectives (MBO) (Littlefield and Randolph, 1987). This argument maintains that PERT/CPM success is due to the *process* of estimating times rather than to the estimates themselves. That is, like MBO, the estimates are said to become self-fulfilling prophecies. An additional argument (Williams, 1995) is that actual activity times are rarely less than the estimate of the mode, and are often greater, accounting for the right skew of the distribution. The cause is attributed to Parkinson's law—that work expands to fill the allotted time. If problems occur, the activity may require more time, but it will almost never require less. While no one, to the best of our knowledge, had proven this empirically, there is some anecdotal evidence that supports this notion. There is, however, also anecdotal evidence that supports the traditional assumption, that PERT/CPM estimates are the "best guesses" of people who have experience in similar activities. In any event, our purpose here is to estimate the range of time required for each activity rather than argue with the underlying logic of the estimation process.

> "Doing it right is no excuse for not meeting the schedule. No one will believe you solved this problem in one day! Now, go act busy for a few weeks and I'll let you know when it's time to tell them."

Sasieni (1986) noted that writers (including himself) have long been using the formula given here to estimate TE. He pointed out that it could not be derived from the formula for the beta distribution without several assumptions that were not necessarily reasonable, and he wondered about the original source of the formula. As it happens, Littlefield and Randolph (1987) cite a U.S. Navy paper that derives the approximation used here and states the reasonable assumptions on which it is based. Gallagher (1987) also derives the formula using a slightly different set of assumptions.

The results of the expected value calculations are shown in Table 8-2 and are included in the activity nodes of Figure 8-14 as well. Also included in the table and in the nodes are measures of the uncertainty for the duration of each activity, the *variance,* σ^2, that is,

$$\sigma^2 = ((b - a)/6)^2$$

and the *standard deviation*, σ, which is given by

$$\sigma = \sqrt{\sigma^2}$$

Table 8-2. Expected Activity Times (TE),
Variances (σ^2), and Standard Deviations (σ)

Activity	Expected Time, TE	Variance σ^2	Standard Deviation, σ
a	20	4	2
b	20	0	0
c	10	4	2
d	15	25	5
e	10	4	2
f	14	4	2
g	4	0	0
h	11	5.4	2.32
i	18	28.4	5.33
j	8	4	2

This calculation of σ is based on the assumption that the standard deviation of a beta distribution is approximately one-sixth of its range, $(b - a)/6$.

Sasieni's inquiry (1986) caused a flurry of research on the estimation of activity times for PERT analysis. For example, Keefer and Verdini report on the error associated with several different ways of approximating the mean and variance of activity times (Keefer and Verdini, 1993). Kamburowski (1997) validates the methods used here. (Both Kamburowski (1997) and Keefer and Verdini (1993) have excellent bibliographies for anyone interested in investigating or pursuing the debate.) Later in this chapter, we will argue for an amendment to the estimation procedure for the variance of activity times if the estimates of a and b are not made at the 99 percent level. Note that the format and calculations of Tables 8-1 and 8-2 lend themselves to the use of a spreadsheet program such as Excel® (XL), as we did in Chapter 7. The equations for TE, σ^2, and σ can be entered once and copied to the rest of the rows.

Critical Path and Time

Consider again the project shown in Figure 8-15. Assume, for convenience, that the time units involved are days, that the first figure is the expected time, and that the second figure is the variance. How long will it take to complete the project? (For the moment we will treat the expected times as if they were certain.) If we start the project on day 0, shown as ES (earliest start) at the upper left of each node in Figure 8-16, we can begin simultaneously working on activities **a, b,** and **c,** each of which has no predecessor activities. We will complete activity **a** in 20 days, activity **b** in 20 days, and activity **c** in 10 days, shown as EF (earliest finish) at the upper right of each of their respective nodes. These early finish times represent the earliest times that the following activities can begin.

Note that activity **e** not only requires the completion of activity **b,** but also requires the completion of activity **c,** as shown by the two incoming arrows. Activity **e** cannot begin until all paths leading to it have been completed. Therefore, the ES for activity e is equal to the EF of the *latest* activity leading to it, 20 for activity **b.**

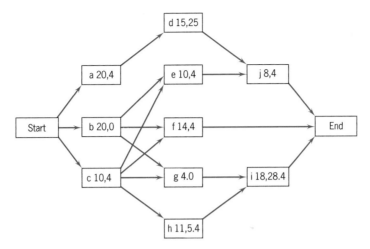

Figure 8-15   The AON network from Table 8-1, showing activity durations and variances.

Proceeding similarly, we see that activity **j** has two predecessor activities, **d** and **e**. Activity **d** cannot start until day 20, (ES = 20) and it requires 15 days to complete. Thus, it will end (EF) a total of 35 days from the start of the project. Activity **e** may also start after 20 days but it requires only ten days, a total of 30 days from the project start. Because activity **j** requires the completion of both activities **d** and **e**, its ES is 35 days, the longest of the paths to it. Activity **i** has an ES of 24 days, the longest of the two paths leading to it, and END, the completion of the network, has a time of 43 days. The remaining ESs and EFs are shown in Figure 8-16.

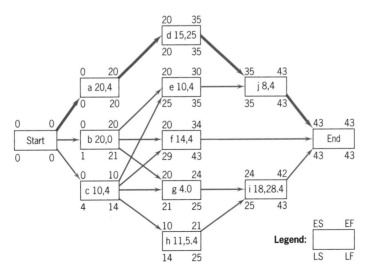

Figure 8-16   AON network showing earliest and lastest start and finish times.

As can be seen, the longest of the paths through the network is **a-d-j** using 43 days, which means that 43 days is the shortest time in which the entire network can be completed. This is called the *critical time* of the network, and **a-d-j** is the *critical path,* usually shown as a heavy line as in Figure 8-16.

In a simple network such as our example, it is easy to find and evaluate every path between start and finish to find the longest path. However, many real networks are considerably more complex, and finding all the paths can be taxing. Using the method illustrated above, there is no need to worry about the problem. Every node is characterized by the fact that one or more activities lead to it. Each of these activities has an expected duration and originates in an earlier node. As we proceed to calculate the ES and EF of each node, beginning at the start, we are *actually finding the critical path and time to each of the nodes* in the network. Note that activity **i** has an ES of 24 days, and its critical path is **b-g** rather than **c-h** which requires 21 days, or **c-g**.

Although we will assume throughout this chapter that we always employ the "as-soon-as-possible" approach to scheduling tasks ("early start"), there are situations where other approaches are sometimes used. One example is the simultaneous start, where all resources are launched at the beginning. Another is the simultaneous finish, where a facility can be moved to its next location once all the tasks are finished. Of course, delay early on in a project runs the risk of delaying the overall project if some other activities inadvertently become delayed. One important reason for using an "as-late-as-possible" approach, described below, is that it delays the use of resources as much as possible, thereby optimizing the cash flow of the project, but again at some risk of delay.

Slack

We will now focus on the latest possible starting times (LS) for the activities. As noted in the previous section, the ES for an activity is equal to the largest EF for its preceding activities. An important question for the PM is this: What is the latest time (LS) activity **i** could start without making the entire project late?

Refer again to Figure 8-16. The project has a critical time of 43 days. Activity **i** must therefore be finished by day 43, indicated by LF (latest finish time), placed at the bottom right of its node. Also, activity **i** requires 18 days to be accomplished. Therefore, **i** *must* be started no later than day 25 (43 − 18 = 25) if the project is to be complete on day 43. The LS for activity **i** is thus 25, placed at the lower left corner of the node. Because **i** cannot begin until activities **g** and **h** have finished, the latest time (LF) for each of these is also day 25. The difference between the LS and the ES for an activity is called its *slack* or *float*. In the case of activity **i,** it must be started no later than day 25, but *could* be started as early as day 24, so it has one day of slack. It should be immediately obvious that all activities on the critical path have zero slack. They cannot be delayed without making the project late.

For another example, consider activity **f**. Its ES is day 20, which is equal to the EF of its predecessor activity **b**. The LS for activity **f** is 43 − 14 = 29. If **f** is started later than day 29, it will delay the entire project. Activity **f** has slack of LS − ES = 29 − 20 = 9 days.

To find the slack for any activity, we make a backward pass (right to left) through the network just as we made a forward pass (left to right) to find the critical path and time and the ESs and EFs for successor activities. There is one simple convention we must adopt: *When there are two or more noncritical activities on a path, it is conventional to calculate the slack for each activity as if it were the only activity in the path.* Thus, when finding the slack for activity **i**, for example, we assume that none of **i**'s predecessors are delayed. Of course, if some activity, **x**, had six days of slack, and if an earlier activity was late, causing the event to be delayed say two days, then activity **x** would have only four days of slack, having lost two days to the earlier delay.

It is simple to calculate slack for activities that are immediate predecessors of the final node. As we move to earlier activities, it is just a bit more complicated. Consider activity **g.** Remembering our assumption that the other activities in the same path use none of the available slack, we see that activity **i** must follow **g**, and that **g** follows activities **b** and **c**. Starting with activity **i**'s LS of 25, we subtract four days for **g** ($25 - 4 = 21$). Thus **g** can begin no later than day 21 without delaying the network. The ES for **g** is day 20, so **g** has one day of slack.

As another example, consider activity **e**. Activity **e** must be completed by day 35, the LS of activity **j**. The LS for **e** is thus $35 - 10 = 25$. Its ES is day 20, so activity **e** has five days of slack. Table 8-3 shows the LS, ES, and slack for all activities.

On occasion, the PM may negotiate an acceptable completion date for a project which allows for some slack in the entire network. If, in our example, an acceptable date was 50 working days after the project start, then the network would have a total of $50 - 43 = 7$ days of slack.

Once again, Microsoft Project®

Entry of data into MSP for a three-time network is almost as easy as for a single-time network, but first you must add another toolbar to MSP's array of tools. This is easily done by clicking on **View**. Choose **Toolbars** from the list that appears, then click on **PERT Analysis**. A short row of seven buttons will be added at the lower left side of

Table 8-3. Times and Slacks for Network in Figure 8-16

Activity	LS	ES	Slack
a	0	0	0
b	1	0	1
c	4	0	4
d	20	20	0
e	25	20	5
f	29	20	9
g	21	20	1
h	14	10	4
i	25	24	1
j	35	35	0

Table 8-4.   MSP Gantt Chart Version of Project Described in Table 8-1.

ID	Task Name	Predecessors	Duration	Optimistic Duration	Expected Duration	Pessimistic Duration
1	Start		0 days	0 days	0 days	0 days
2	a	1	20 days	10 days	22 days	22 days
3	b	1	20 days	20 days	20 days	20 days
4	c	1	10 days	4 days	10 days	16 days
5	d	2	15 days	2 days	14 days	32 days
6	e	3,4	10 days	8 days	8 days	20 days
7	f	4,3	14 days	8 days	14 days	20 days
8	g	3,4	4 days	4 days	4 days	4 days
9	h	4	11 days	2 days	12 days	16 days
10	i	9,8	18 days	6 days	16 days	38 days
11	j	5,6	8 days	2 days	8 days	14 days
12	Finish	10,11,7	0 days	0 days	0 days	0 days

the toolbar area. Click on **PERT entry sheet** (the right-most button), and a form such as that in Table 8-4 will appear. The numbers shown in Table 8-4 are those shown in Table 8-1. A "predecessor" column has been added.

The "optimistic" and "pessimistic" columns mean exactly what we have described them to mean, as does the "predecessor" column. Unfortunately, this is not true for the "duration" and "expected duration" columns. MSP's "expected duration" column shows what we, and most other writers, call the "most likely" or "normal" time estimates. This is an estimate of the most frequently occurring (or modal) time. Microsoft gives the title "duration" to what we and others call "the expected duration." MSP calculates their "duration" in the same way we found our "expected duration," that is, by the $(a + 4m + b) / 6$ weighted average. (Right next to the MSP button that calls up the PERT entry sheet is another button that appears to be a balance type scale. This can be used to reset the a, m, and b weights to those of your own choosing. We will make use of other weights when we illustrate simulation later in this chapter.)

Once the data in Table 8-4 have been entered, click on the button labeled **Calculate PERT** and you will get a Gantt chart (Figure 8-17) and a PERT network (Figure 8-18) that show an expected duration of 43 days, a "duration" of 43 days in MSP's language. (NOTE: We have set the calendar for this project to a seven-day work week.)

In the next section we show how to determine the probability that a project will be completed in a specified time. To do this, the standard deviation, σ, and variance, σ^2, for each activity duration is needed. MSP does not calculate these numbers. The variances and standard deviations for the activities in the project demonstrated here are shown in Table 8-2. They are easily calculated by hand for small projects or on an Excel® (XL) spreadsheet for larger ones. Recall that

$$\sigma = (b-a) / 6$$

and

$$\sigma^2 = ((b-a) / 6)^2$$

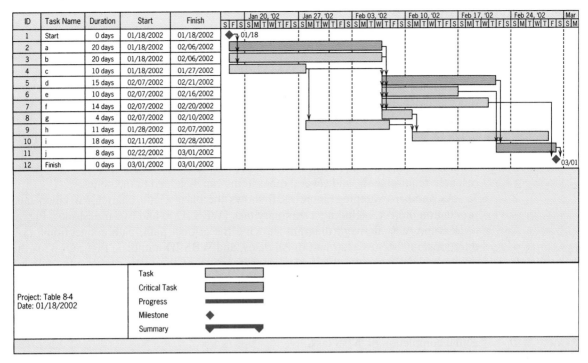

Figure 8-17 Gantt Chart of Table 8-4.

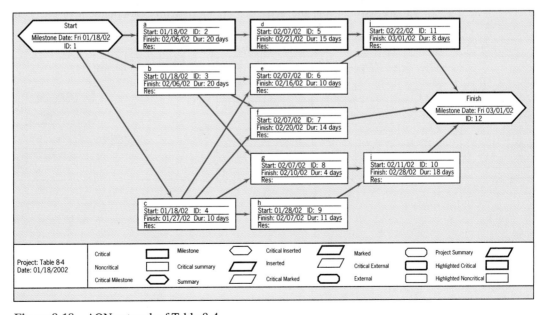

Figure 8-18 AON network of Table 8-4.

401

Exhibits Available from Software, a Bit More MSP

As we noted earlier and you have seen just above, project management software can illustrate the project as a Gantt chart and, in addition, show precedences, times, and other activity elements directly on the chart. Moreover, PERT/CPM network diagrams, calendars, and other displays and reports can also be shown. For example, Figure 8-19 shows an MSP Gantt chart for the project of Table 8-1 with the critical path, path connections, and ES and EF times depicted on the chart. It is simple to customize the information shown; for instance, late start and finish times, slack, special resource requirements, and several other items can be added to the nodes.

As another example, Figure 8-20 shows the basic Gantt chart for a video tape production project, including a summary task (WBS ID 3) and two milestones. Figure 8-21 is the AON network diagram showing the critical path, path connections, task durations, milestones, start and finish dates, and WBS ID numbers. Figure 8-22 is the project calendar showing the calendar scheduling of the tasks (weekends included here) and highlighting the critical path tasks. Project progress should also be monitored and input to the software for updating the charts and reports. Such progress is indicated directly on the Gantt chart, such as that shown in Figure 8-23 for the video project. Note in the figure how the completed milestone has been delayed to match actual completion of WBS task 3.4.

Uncertainty of Project Completion Time

When discussing project completion dates with senior management, the PM should try to determine the probability that a project will be completed by the suggested deadline—or find the completion time associated with a predetermined level of risk. With the information in Table 8-2, this is not difficult.

If we assume that the activities are statistically independent of each other, then

WBS	Task Name	Expected Duration	Start	Finish	Late Start	Late Finish
1	a	20 days	1/30/02	2/26/02	1/30/02	2/26/02
2	b	20 days	1/30/02	2/26/02	1/31/02	2/27/02
3	c	10 days	1/30/02	2/12/02	2/5/02	2/18/02
4	d	15 days	2/27/02	3/19/02	2/27/02	3/19/02
5	e	10 days	2/27/02	3/12/02	3/6/02	3/19/02
6	f	14 days	2/27/02	3/18/02	3/12/02	3/29/02
7	g	4 days	2/27/02	3/4/02	2/28/02	3/5/02
8	h	11 days	2/13/02	2/27/02	2/19/02	3/5/02
9	i	18 days	3/5/02	3/28/02	3/6/02	3/29/02
10	j	8 days	3/20/02	3/29/02	3/20/02	3/29/02

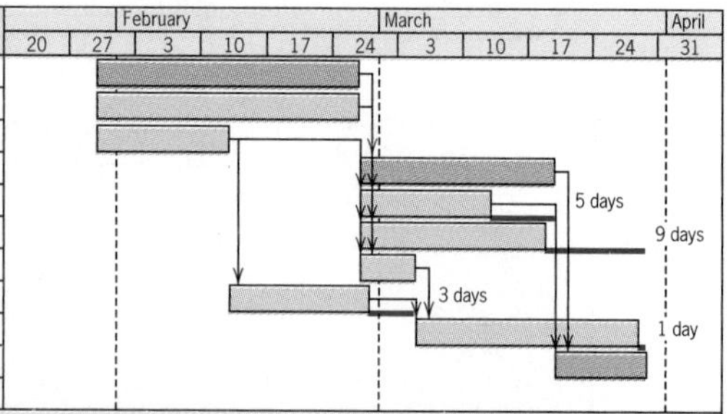

Start Date: Wed 1/30/02

Task — Critical Task — Slack — Milestone — Summary

Figure 8-19 An MSP Gantt chart of the project in Table 8-1 showing activity durations and schedule, critical path, path connections, slack, and earliest and latest start and finish times.

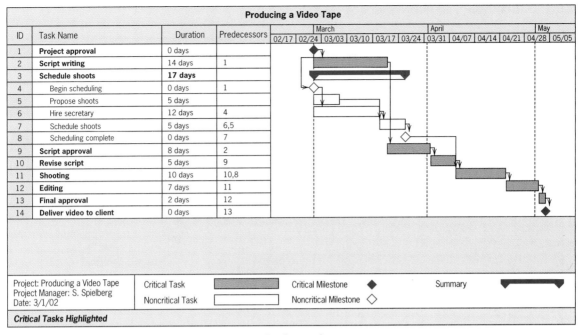

Figure 8-20 MSP Gantt chart for a video tape production project.

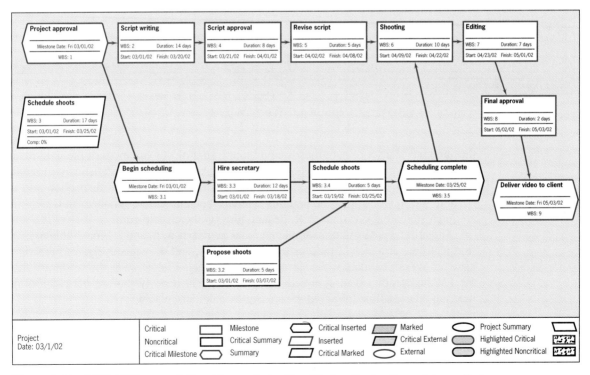

Figure 8-21 MSP AON network for video project with critical path, durations, dates, milestones, and WBS ID numbers.

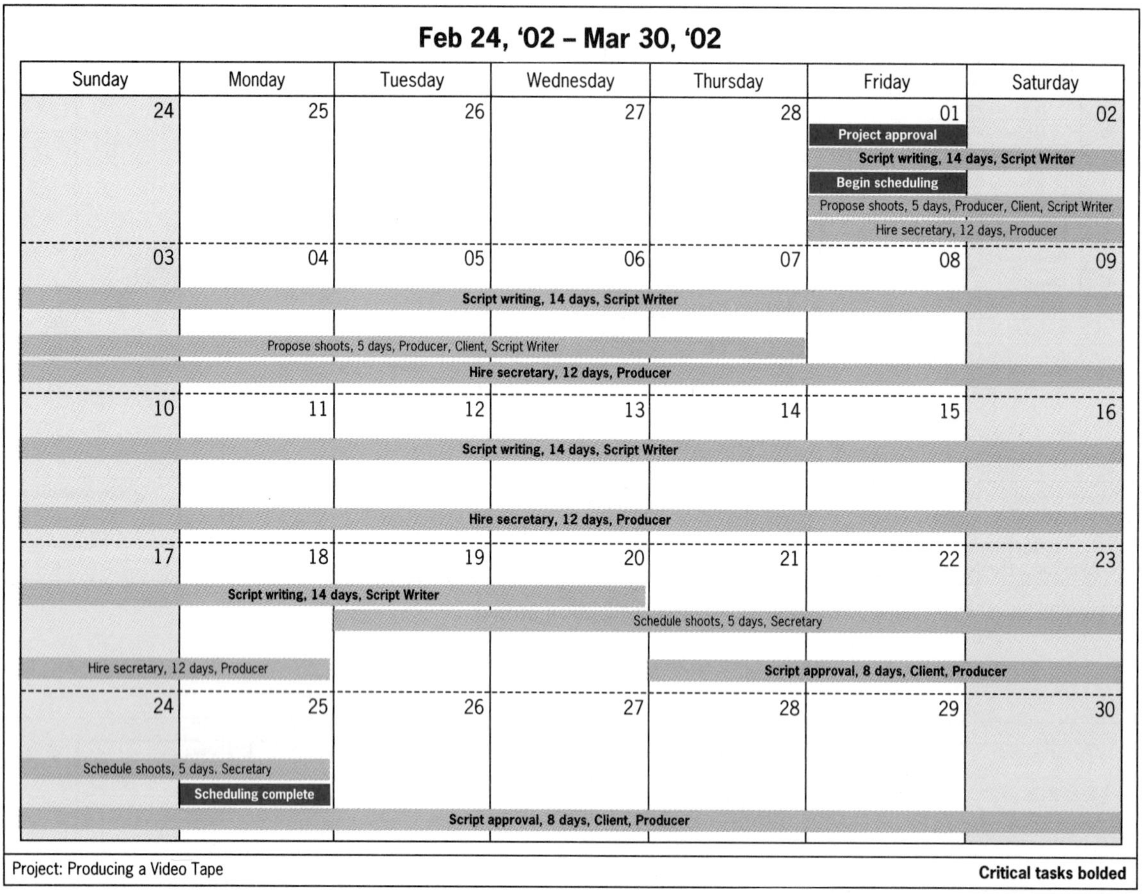

Figure 8-22   MSP calendar for video project, critical path is in bold print.

the variance of a set of activities is equal to the sum of the variances of the individual activities comprising the set. Those who have taken a course in statistics will recall that the variance of a population is a measure of the population's dispersion and is equal to the square of the population's standard deviation. The variances in which we are interested are the variances of the activities on the critical path.

The critical path of our example includes activities **a, d,** and **j.** From Table 8-2 we find that the variances of these activities are 4, 25, and 4, respectively; and the variance for the critical path is the sum of these numbers, 33 days. Assume, as above, that the PM has promised to complete the project in 50 days. What are the chances of meeting that deadline? We find the answer by calculating Z, where

$$Z = (D - \mu)/\sqrt{\sigma_\mu^2}$$

and

D = the desired project completion time

μ = the critical time of the project, the sum of the TEs for activities on the critical path

Mar 31, '02 – May 04, '02

Sunday	Monday	Tuesday	Wednesday	Thursday	Friday	Saturday
31	01	02	03	04	05	06
		Revise script, 5 days, Producer, Script Writer				
Script approval, 8 days, Client, Producer						
07	08	09	10	11	12	13
Revise script, 5 days, Producer, Script Writer		Shooting, 10 days, Editor, Client, Production Staff [300%]				
14	15	16	17	18	19	20
		Shooting, 10 days, Editor, Client, Production Staff [300%]				
21	22	23	24	25	26	27
Shooting, 10 days, Editor, Client, Production Staff [300]			Editing, 7 days, Editor, Editing Staff, Editing Room			
28	29	30	01	02	03	04
	Editing, 7 days, Editor, Editing Staff, Editing Room			Final approval, 2 days, Client, Producer, Editor		
					Deliver video to client	

Project: Producing a Vedio Tape | Critical tasks bolded

Figure 8-22 (*Continued*)

WBS	Task Name	Act. Start	Act. Finish	Baseline Duration	Act. Dur.	Rem. Dur.	March / April / May
1	Project approval	03/01/02	03/01/02	0 days	0 days	0 days	
2	Script writing	03/01/02	03/19/02	14 days	13 days	0 days	
3	**Schedule shoots**	**03/01/02**	**03/28/02**	**17 days**	**20 days**	**0 days**	
3.1	Begin scheduling	03/01/02	03/01/02	0 days	0 days	0 days	
3.2	Propose shoots	03/01/02	03/07/02	5 days	5 days	0 days	
3.3	Hire secretary	03/01/02	03/21/02	12 days	15 days	0 days	
3.4	Schedule shoots	03/22/02	03/28/02	5 days	5 days	0 days	3 days
3.5	Scheduling complete	03/28/02	03/28/02	0 days	0 days	0 days	2 days
4	Script approval	03/20/02	03/29/02	8 days	8 days	0 days	
5	Revise script	04/01/02	NA	5 days	9 days	3 days	
6	Shooting	NA	NA	10 days	0 days	10 days	6 days
7	Editing	NA	NA	7 days	0 days	7 days	6 days
8	Final approval	NA	NA	2 days	0 days	2 days	6 days
9	Deliver video to client	NA	NA	0 days	0 days	0 days	6 days

Project: Producing a Video Tape
Updated as of: 04/12/02

Task	▬	Completed Milestone ◆	Slippage ▬▬
Progress	▬▬	Baseline Milestone ◇	Summary ◣▬◢
Baseline	▭	Milestone ◇	Summary Progress ▭

Figure 8-23 MSP Gantt chart for video project tracking progress to date.

σ_μ^2 = the variance of the critical path, the sum of the variances of activities on the critical path

Z = the number of standard deviations of a normal distribution (the *standard normal deviate*)

Z, as calculated above, can be used to find the probability of completing the project on time. Using the numbers in our example, $D = 50$, $\mu = 43$, and $\sigma_\mu^2 = 33$ (the square root of σ_μ^2 is 5.745), we have

$$Z = (50 - 43)/5.745$$

$$= 1.22 \text{ standard deviations}$$

We turn now to Table 8-5, which shows the probabilities associated with various levels of Z. (Table 8-5 also appears on the rear cover. It is shown here for the reader's convenience.) We go down the left column until we find $Z = 1.2$, and then across to column .02 to find $Z = 1.22$. The probability value of $Z = 1.22$ shown in the table is .8888, or almost 89 percent, which is the likelihood that we will complete the critical path of our sample project within 50 days of the time it is started. Figure 8-24 shows the resulting probability distribution of the project completion times.*

We can work the problem backward, too. What deadline is consistent with a .95 probability of on-time completion? First, we go to Table 8-4 and look through the table until we find .95. The Z value associated with .95 is 1.645. (The values in the table are not strictly linear, so our interpolation is only approximate.) We know that μ is 43 days, and that $\sqrt{\sigma_\mu^2}$ is 5.745. Solving the equation for D, we have

$$D = \mu + 5.745(1.645)$$

$$= 43 + 9.45$$

$$= 52.45 \text{ days.}$$

Thus, we conclude that here is a 95 percent chance of finishing the project by 52.45 days. However, that is not quite true. There is a 95 percent chance of finishing path **a-d-j** in 52.45 days. Remember that this is a stochastic network. ("Stochastic"—sta kas' tik—is much nicer to say than "probabilistic" and means the same thing.) If the activities of the project are of uncertain duration, no one knows how long it will take to complete each of them. Therefore, no one knows how long any path through the network might take—except that it will undoubtedly be equal to or less than the sum of the pessimistic estimates of all activities in the path and will be equal to or greater than the sum of the optimistic estimates of all activities in the path. When the project is initially analyzed, the path that originally appeared to be the critical path may or may not actually be critical. We will return to this issue several times before Chapter 8 is complete.

Note that as D approaches μ, Z gets smaller, approaching zero. Table 8-5 shows that for $Z = 0$, the chance of on-time completion is 50–50. The managerial implications are all too clear. If the PM wants a reasonable chance of meeting a project dead-

---

* Our use of the normal distribution is allowed by the Central Limit Theorem which attests to the fact that the sum of independent activity times is normally distributed if the number of activities is large.

Table 8-5 Cumulative (Single Tail) Probabilities of the Normal Probability Distribution (Areas under the Normal Curve from $-\infty$ to Z)

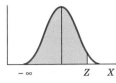

Example: the area to the left of $Z = 1.34$ is found by following the left Z column down to 1.3 and moving right to the .04 column. At the intersection read .9099. The area to the right of $Z = 1.34$ is $1 - .9099 = .0901$. The area between the mean (dashed line) and $Z = 1.34 = .9099 - .5 = .4099$.

z	.00	.01	.02	.03	.04	.05	.06	.07	.08	.09
.0	.5000	.5040	.5080	.5120	.5160	.5199	.5239	.5279	.5319	.5359
.1	.5398	.5438	.5478	.5517	.5557	.5596	.5636	.5675	.5714	.5753
.2	.5793	.5832	.5871	.5910	.5948	.5987	.6026	.6064	.6103	.6141
.3	.6179	.6217	.6255	.6293	.6331	.6368	.6406	.6443	.6480	.6517
.4	.6554	.6591	.6628	.6664	.6700	.6736	.6772	.6808	.6844	.6879
.5	.6915	.6950	.6985	.7019	.7054	.7088	.7123	.7157	.7190	.7224
.6	.7257	.7291	.7324	.7357	.7389	.7422	.7454	.7486	.7517	.7549
.7	.7580	.7611	.7642	.7673	.7704	.7734	.7764	.7794	.7823	.7852
.8	.7881	.7910	.7939	.7967	.7995	.8023	.8051	.8078	.8106	.8133
.9	.8159	.8186	.8212	.8238	.8264	.8289	.8315	.8340	.8365	.8389
1.0	.8413	.8438	.8461	.8485	.8508	.8531	.8554	.8577	.8599	.8621
1.1	.8643	.8665	.8686	.8708	.8729	.8749	.8770	.8790	.8810	.8880
1.2	.8849	.8869	.8888	.8907	.8925	.8944	.8962	.8980	.8997	.9015
1.3	.9032	.9049	.9066	.9082	.9099	.9115	.9131	.9147	.9162	.9177
1.4	.9192	.9207	.9222	.9236	.9251	.9265	.9279	.9292	.9306	.9319
1.5	.9332	.9345	.9357	.9370	.9382	.9394	.9406	.9418	.9429	.9441
1.6	.9452	.9463	.9474	.9484	.9495	.9505	.9515	.9525	.9535	.9545
1.7	.9554	.9564	.9573	.9582	.9591	.9599	.9608	.9616	.9625	.9633
1.8	.9641	.9649	.9656	.9664	.9671	.9678	.9686	.9693	.9699	.9706
1.9	.9713	.9719	.9726	.9732	.9738	.9744	.9750	.9756	.9761	.9767
2.0	.9772	.9778	.9783	.9788	.9793	.9798	.9803	.9808	.9812	.9817
2.1	.9821	.9826	.9830	.9834	.9838	.9842	.9846	.9850	.9854	.9857
2.2	.9861	.9864	.9868	.9871	.9875	.9878	.9881	.9884	.9887	.9890
2.3	.9893	.9896	.9898	.9901	.9904	.9906	.9909	.9911	.9913	.9916
2.4	.9918	.9920	.9932	.9925	.9927	.9929	.9931	.9932	.9934	.9936
2.5	.9938	.9940	.9941	.9943	.9945	.9946	.9948	.9949	.9951	.9952
2.6	.9953	.9955	.9956	.9957	.9959	.9960	.9961	.9962	.9963	.9964
2.7	.9965	.9966	.9967	.9968	.9969	.9970	.9971	.9972	.9973	.9974
2.8	.9974	.9975	.9976	.9977	.9977	.9978	.9979	.9979	.9980	.9981
2.9	.9981	.9982	.9982	.9983	.9984	.9984	.9985	.9985	.9986	.9986
3.0	.9987	.9987	.9987	.9988	.9988	.9989	.9989	.9989	.9990	.9990
3.1	.9990	.9991	.9991	.9991	.9992	.9992	.9992	.9992	.9993	.9993
3.2	.9993	.9993	.9994	.9994	.9994	.9994	.9994	.9995	.9995	.9995
3.3	.9995	.9995	.9995	.9996	.9996	.9996	.9996	.9996	.9996	.9997
3.4	.9997	.9997	.9997	.9997	.9997	.9997	.9997	.9997	.9997	.9998

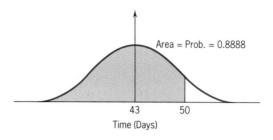

Figure 8-24   Probability distribution of project completion times.

line, there must be some slack in the project schedule. When preparing a project budget, it is quite proper to include some allowance for contingencies. The same principle holds for preparing a project schedule. The allowance for contingencies in a schedule is *network slack,* and the wise PM will insist on some.

Finally, to illustrate an interesting point, let's examine an apparently noncritical path, activities **b-g-i**. The variance of this path (from Figure 8-16) is $0 + 0 + 28.4 = 28.4$, which is slightly less than the variance of the critical path. The path time is 42 days. The numerator of the fraction $(D - \mu)/\sqrt{\sigma_\mu^2}$ is larger, and in this case the denominator is smaller. Therefore, Z will be larger, and the probability of this path delaying project completion is less than for the apparently critical **a-d-j** path. But consider the noncritical path **c-h-i** with a time of $10 + 11 + 18 = 39$ days, and a total variance of 37.8. (Remember, we are trying to find the probability that this noncritical path with its higher variance but shorter completion time will make us late, given that the critical path is 43 days.)

$$Z = (50 - 39)/6.15$$
$$Z = 1.79$$

The result is that we have a 96 percent chance for this noncritical path to allow the project to be on time.

If the desired time for the network equaled the critical time, 43 days, we have seen that the critical path has a 50–50 chance of being late. What are the chances that the noncritical path **c-h-i** will make the project late? D is now 43 days, so we have

$$Z = (43 - 39)/6.15$$
$$= .65$$

$Z = .65$ is associated with a probability of .74 of being on time, or $1 - .74 = .26$ of being late.

Assuming that these two paths (**a-d-j** and **c-h-i**) are independent, the probability that *both* paths will be completed on time is the product of the individual probabilities, $(.50)(.74) = .37$, which is considerably less than the 50–50 we thought the chances were. If the paths are not independent, the calculations become more complicated. We will describe a more accurate way to determine project completion probabilities using *simulation* in the next section. Therefore, it is a good idea to consider noncritical paths that have activities with large variances and/or path times that are close to critical in duration (i.e., those with little slack).

This leads us to what is often referred to as *merge bias* (Hulett, 1996). Any time two or more paths of a network come together or merge we have the case noted just above, the probability of both paths being on time is the product of the probabilities for the individual paths. If one of the paths is critical and the others have a reasonable amount of slack (and/or low path variance compared to the critical path), the problem of merge bias is rarely serious. If, however, a second path has low slack and significant path variance, we cannot ignore it and should use simulation.

Simulation is an obvious way to check the nature and impacts of interactions between probabilistic paths in a network. While this used to be difficult and time consuming, software has now been developed which simplifies matters greatly. There are several excellent risk management and simulation software packages that link directly to one or more of the popular spreadsheet application packages. We prefer Crystal Ball®, a copy comes with this book, but Risk+®, and @Risk® are also well regarded. All the above allow easy simulation of network interactions and yield data that show the probability of completing the networks by specific times (Levine, 1996). These simulations, of course, include the results of potential path mergers. As we have stated earlier, the methods noted here can also be applied to risk analysis for resources. If resource usage is related to the time required by an activity, then the uncertainty about time means that there is also uncertainty about resource use. If the relationship between activity time and resource use is known or can be assumed to be roughly linear, it is not difficult to estimate the resource equivalents of the simulation. The likelihood of a strictly linear relationship is very low unless one gets the data from the accounting department. Hulett (1996) mentions integrated cost/schedule risk, and notes that most software does not deal with this issue.

SOLVED PROBLEM

Consider the following project (times given in days).

Activity	a	m	b	Predecessors
a	1	4	7	—
b	2	2	2	—
c	2	5	8	a
d	3	4	5	a
e	4	6	8	c,b
f	0	0	6	c,b
g	3	6	9	d,e

Find:

1. The network.
2. All expected activity times, variances, and slacks.
3. The critical path and expected completion time.
4. The probability the project will be done in 23 days.
5. The completion time corresponding to 95% probability.

Answer

1.

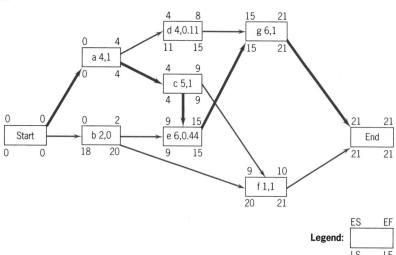

2. Activity

Activity	TE	σ^2	Slack
a	4	1.00	0
b	2	0	7
c	5	1.00	0
d	4	0.11	7
e	6	0.44	0
f	1	1	11
g	6	1	0

3. Critical path is a-c-e-g for a time of 21 days.

4. $z = (23 - 21)/\sqrt{3.44} = 1.078$ for a probability of 85.9%.

5. P = 0.95 corresponds to $z = 1.65 = (T - 21)/1.855$, or T = 24.06 days.

Toward Realistic Time Estimates

The calculations of expected network times, and the uncertainty associated with those time estimates performed in the preceding sections are based, as we noted, on estimating optimistic and pessimistic times at the .99 level. That is, *a* is estimated such that the actual time required for an activity will be *a* or higher 99 percent of the time and will be *b* or lower 99 percent of the time. We then noted, parenthetically, that sometimes project managers are uncomfortable making estimates at that level of precision.

Fortunately, in practice it is not necessary to make estimates at the one-in-a-hundred level. Unless the underlying distribution is very asymmetric, no great error is introduced in finding TE if the pessimistic and optimistic estimates are made at the 95 percent, or even at the 90 percent levels; that is to say, only once in 20 times (or ten times for the 90 percent level) will the actual activity time be greater than or less than the pessimistic or optimistic estimates, respectively. *The formula for calculating the variance of an activity, however, must be modified.*

Recall that the calculation of variance is based on the assumption that the standard deviation of a beta distribution is approximately one-sixth of its range. Another way of putting this assumption is that a and b are estimated at the -3σ and $+3\sigma$ limits respectively—roughly at the 99+ percent levels. Let the 95 percent estimates be represented by a' and b' and 90 percent estimates by a'' and b''. If we use a 95 or 90 percent estimation level, we are actually moving both a and b in from the distribution's tails so that the range will no longer represent $\pm3\sigma$. See Figure 8-25.

It is simple to correct the calculation of variance for this error. Consider the 95 percent estimates. Referring to Table 8-5 we can find the Z associated with .95 of the area under the curve from a' to ∞. For .95, Z is approximately -1.65. (Of course, this applies to the normal distribution rather than to the beta distribution, but this heuristic appears to work quite well in practice.) Similarly, Z = 1.65 for the area under the curve from $-\infty$ to b'.

The range between b' and a' represents $2(1.65)\sigma = 3.3\sigma$, rather than the 6σ used in the traditional estimate of the variance. Therefore, when estimating a' and b' at the 95 percent level, we should change the variance calculation formula to read

$$\sigma^2 = ((b' - a')/3.3)^2$$

For estimates at the 90 percent level (a'' and b'' in Figure 8-25), Z is approximately 1.3 and the variance calculation becomes

$$\sigma^2 = ((b'' - a'')/2.6)^2$$

In order to verify that this modification of the traditional estimator for the variance of a beta distribution gave good estimates of the true variance, we ran a series of trials using Statistical Analysis Systems' (SAS) PROC IML for beta distributions of different shapes and estimated a and b at the 95 and 90 percent levels. We then compared these estimates of a and b with the true variance of the distribution and found the differences to be quite small, consistently under 5 percent.

It is important to repeat that some managers do not have confidence in making estimates at the 99 percent level and prefer the 90 or 95 percent levels. If estimates are made at these levels, however, use of the traditional calculation for variance ($\{[b - a]/6\}^2$) will result in a serious underestimation of path variances and introduce considerable error into estimates of the probabilities of completing projects by specific dates. [A similar warning holds when one uses a triangular distribution as shown in Hulett (1995, pp. 22ff).] Some writers recommend the use of contingency allowances. While we applaud Eichhorn's approach (1997) that clearly identifies such allowances by introducing them as activities that show up on networks or Gantt charts, we think that such allowances are not particularly helpful. They simply codify the "padding"

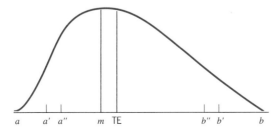

Figure 8-25 *a, m,* and *b* estimates at the 99, 95, and 90 percent levels.

that is typical in organizations in which workers avoid measurement of work, largely because they distrust their managers.

Once again, we caution readers. Neither statistical analysis (e.g., Hare, Hoerl, Hromi, and Snee, 1995; Robinson, 1997) nor simulation (e.g., Levine, 1996; Pascale, Carland, and Lorenz, 1998) nor contingency allowances (Eichhorn, 1997) will help the PM manage risk if the input data are biased or carelessly developed. One suggestion made by several writers is to use specialized teams to assess risk and make estimates (Frame, 1998; Martin and Tate, 1998). Another writer suggests a "10-step miniprocess" for estimating (DeYoung-Currey, 1998). Still another recommends a group of experts who will use the Delphi process (Campanis, 1997). Any of these may help increase care and reduce bias when making estimates.

An alternate method for approximating the mean and variance of a beta distribution when a and b are estimated at the 95 percent level is given in the last section of Appendix B. For the full exposition of the method, see the Neter et al. (1987) reference of Appendix B.

8.3   RISK ANALYSIS USING SIMULATION WITH CRYSTAL BALL® 2000

As we have emphasized often in this book, life with projects is characterized by uncertainty. The time required to carry out an activity, the cost and availability of a resource, the success of a research experiment, the wishes of the client, and the actions of a competitor, as well as the vagaries of the weather, ups and downs of interest rates, and the dyspepsia of a senior manager are typical of the things that can upset the most carefully planned and managed project. While it is possible through careful preplanning to reduce somewhat the degree of uncertainty surrounding any project, uncertainty can never be eliminated. We can, however, manage the uncertainty so as to reduce the impact of the ambiguities existing in our uncertain world.

As we noted in Section 2-4 in Chapter 2, one method of managing the uncertainty is to perform risk analysis on such data as we have involved in our managerial decisons. This requires us to make assumptions about the probability distributions of the varaibles and parameters affecting our decisions. These assumptions allow us to adopt Monte Carlo simulation models and evaluate the impact of given managerial decisions. The decision is modeled mathematically. Individual values for each variable in the model are selected at random from the probability distributions we specified, and the outcome of the model is calculated. This process is repeated many times, and the model's output for each repetition is used to construct a statistical distribution of all of the outcomes. This distribution shows the *risk profile* of the decison. The risk profile is considered along with the parent organization's strategies and policies, the wishes of the client, and many other factors when making the decision.

In Chapter 2, we used Crystal Ball® 2000 (CB) to simulate a decision process that measured whether or not a project was above an organization's hurdle rate of return. We have noted several times that the same kind of simulation might be used to manage the uncertainty involved in deciding at what level to budget a project. We can now examine its use in scheduling projects.

Let us reconsider the data we have previously analyzed from Table 8-1. The analytical approach to finding the duration of the critical path of the network as well as path times for the network's other paths is based on our assumption that the probability distribution used for activity times was best described as a beta distribution. CB can use the beta distribution to generate random numbers for a simulation, but for each assumption cell we must be able to specify two shape-variables for the beta distribution, and this, in turn, requires an advanced understanding of statistical topics beyond our scope. Remember that the problem we are attacking here is the process of simulating project completion times. The problem of finding the proper distribution to model activity completion times should be addressed in a formal statistics and probability course.

Our solution is to adopt the triangular distribution, a solution also suggested by Evans and Olson (1998) and many others.* Figure 8-26 shows a model for simulating project completion times. It is surprisingly simple for what seems to be such a complex problem. Having entered XL and CB, we label the columns, first one for each activity, and then one for each path through the network, and finally one for "completion time." The most difficult job one faces is identifying all of the paths to be evaluated. For small networks, this is not difficult, but for large networks, it may be. The MSP PERT network of the problem can be a major help.

Recalling that it is easier to follow instructions if the software is running, entering the data into the spreadsheet that XL and CB present to you is simple.

1. After entering the appropriate column labels, click on space **A3** with the cursor and enter "20." Click on that number to fix the entry in place.

2. Click on **Cell** at the top of the toolbar. Click on **Define Assumption** in the dropdown menu.

3. The gallery of distributions will appear, click on **Triangular**, and then on **OK**.

4. In the **Triangular Distibution** box, enter the pessimistic, most likely, and optimistic estimates for activity **a** and click on **OK**. Note that assumption cells are colored green.

Before continuing, there are two things that should be noted. First, the number you originally entered in **A3** was "20," the expected duration of activity **a** calculated earlier. You, or MSP, or XL had calculated this by the $(a + 4m + b) / 6$ rule. When you entered the data on the triangular distribution form for space **A3**, you entered, we trust, 10, 22, and 22 in the appropriate spaces. To find the expected duration for an activity with those three time estimates, CB applied the correct formula for this distribution, $(a + m + b) / 3$. TE is therefore, 18, not 20. CB properly changes the cell accordingly. You cannot leave the cell A3 blank and click on **Cell/Define assumption** because CB won't allow it. Just put any old number in the cell, click on it to fix it, and proceed. CB will change it to the correct number automatically.

The second anomaly worth mentioning concerns activity **b**. If you call up the triangular distribution and attempt to enter 20-20-20, the three times given in the problem, CB will not allow it, because these numbers will not define a triangle. Do not de-

---

*If you intend to solve the problem analytically, the triangular distribution requires different ways of estimating the expected time for an activity and of estimating the activity's statistical variance; TE = $(a + m + b)/3$ and $\sigma^2 = (a^2 + m^2 + b^2 - ab - am - bm)/18$. Once you have adopted the triangular distribution for the assumption cells, CB will take care of this matter for you.

	A	B	C	D	E	F	G	H	I	J	K	L	M	N	O	P	Q	R	S
1	Activity	Activity	Activity	Activity	Activity	Activity	Activity	Activity	Activity	Activity	Path	Path	Path	Path	Path	Path	Path	Path	Completion
2	a	b	c	d	e	f	g	h	i	j	a-d-j	b-e-j	b-f	b-g-i	c-e-j	c-f	c-g-i	c-h-i	Time
3	18	20	10	16	12	14	4	10	20	8	42	40	34	44	30	24	34	40	44
4																			
5																			
6	**Key**																		
7	*Formulas:*																		
8	Cell K3	=A3 + D3 + J3																	
9	Cell L3	=B3 + E3 + J3																	
10	Cell M3	=B3 + F3																	
11	Cell N3	=B3 + G3 + I3																	
12	Cell O3	=C3 + E3 + J3																	
13	Cell P3	=C3 + F3																	
14	Cell Q3	=C3 + G3 + I3																	
15	Cell R3	=C3 + H3 + I3																	
16	Cell S3	=MAX(K3:Q3)																	

Figure 8-26 Crystal Ball® 2000 simulation-ready spreadsheet for project described in Table 8-1.

fine cell B3 as an assumption cell. Merely enter 20 in the cell and continue with the next entry. It will be treated by CB as a "constant," which, of course, it is. Activity **g** is also a cell listing a constant or deterministic time. These cells will not be colored.

5. Continue entering data until you have completed all activities.

6. If you counted carefully, you found eight paths through the network. Enter the path identification for each and then enter the formula for path duration for each of the paths. Note that these formulas simply sum the activity TEs for each path.

7. Now enter the formula that calculates the project duration in cell S3, labeled "Completion time." Click on **Cell** and then on **Define Forecast**. Type in "Project Completion Time," or whatever you select for a title, and click **OK**. The formula will find the longest of the paths for each simulation. That will be the critical path for any given trial.

8. Now click on **Run** and choose **Run preferences** from the drop-down menu. Ask for 1000 trials. Click **OK**.

9. Now click on **Run**, and then again on **Run** from the drop-down menu. You can watch the results being shown on your screen in the form of a statistical distribution.

Before discussing the results of the simulation, it should be noted that altering the assumption about the probability distribution of the activity times from the beta to the triangular distribution has had an interesting effect. Using the new TEs, the critical path of the network has been changed from **a-d-j** under the beta assumption to **b-g-i** for the triangular assumption. This shift is solely the result of the different formula for calculating activity TEs.

The statistical distribution you see when running a simulation will be similar to Figure 8-27, the project completion time frequency chart. If you wish to find out the likelihood of completing the project in 52 days, for example, simply enter the number

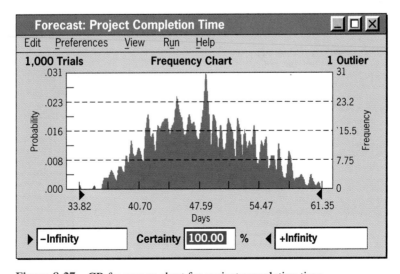

Figure 8-27   CB frequency chart for project completion time.

52, or number of your choice, in the box that reads "+ Infinity." Then press **Enter.** The probability you seek will appear in the **Certainty** cell.

If you click on **View** in the short toolbar at the top of the **Forecast: Project Completion Time** box, you can see other information. For example, click on **View** and then on **Statistics** in the drop-down list. Figure 8-28 shows several interesting statistics about the distribution in Figure 8-27. The distribution of 1000 completion times had a mean of 47.8 days and a median of 47.6 days. Recall that the expected completion time with the beta distribution was 43 days and the expected time with the triangular assumption was 44 days. The greater mean time found by simulation is almost certainly due to the impact of path mergers.

The **Percentiles** data in Figure 8-29 show the percent of the trials completed at or below the completion shown. The **Cumulative Chart** shown in Figure 8-30 shows graphically the probability that a project will be completed in 52 days or less. (The "52" was simply entered in the cell of the **Forecast: Project Completion Time** chart where shown.)

The value of simulation is well demonstrated by this simple example. The problem of gathering a large amount of information about path mergers, the probability of completion for a number of different times, and the impact of different assumptions about activity distributions by use of analytical methods is formidable even with spreadsheets to handle the calculations. Simulation handles these issues easily.

At times, PMs avoid the whole issue by suggesting that all they "really need to know" is the expected time of completion, the fastest time the project could be completed, and the latest possible time for completion. If one examines the optimistic and pessimistic times for each activity, we can readily find those times. The fastest time is 30 days and the critical path is **b-e-j**; the slowest time is, 70 days with critical path **c-h-i**. The likelihood of either path occurring, that is, that activities **b,e,** and **j** all take minimum values at the same time (or that **c, h,** and **i** take on their maximum values) is

Forecast: Project Completion Time	
Cell S3	**Statistics**

Statistic	Value
Trials	1,000
Mean	47.78
Median	47.62
Mode	—
Standard Deviation	5.39
Variance	29.03
Skewness	0.18
Kurtosis	2.35
Coeff. of Variability	0.11
Range Minimum	33.82
Range Maximum	61.50
Range Width	27.68
Mean Std. Error	0.17

Figure 8-28 CB summary statistics for project completion time.

Percentile	Days
0%	33.82
10%	40.87
20%	42.85
30%	44.49
40%	45.91
50%	47.62
60%	48.90
70%	50.83
80%	52.77
90%	55.11
100%	61.50

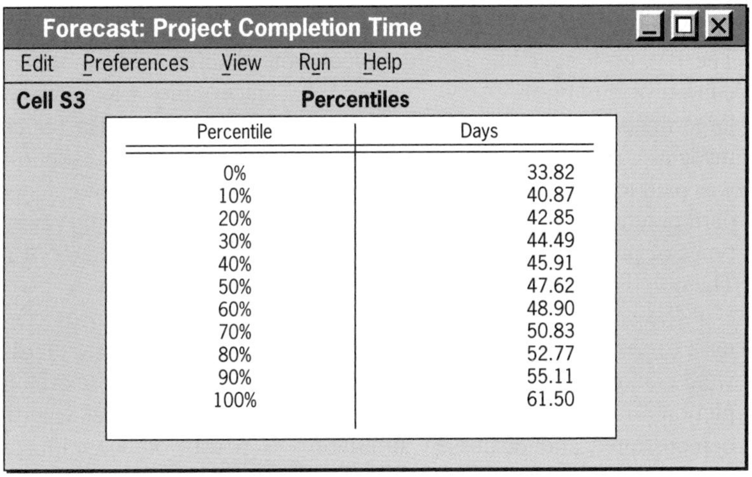

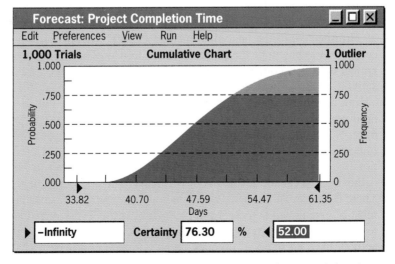

Figure 8-29 CB percentile probabilities of completing project in n days.

so small as to be negligible. (If the estimates are made at the 3σ level, the probability that an activity would have a duration at or less than the optimistic estimate is (1 – .9987) = .0013. The probability that all three activities would simultaneously be at or below their estimates is $.0013^3 = .000000002$, and this ignores the more improbable condition that all other activities would simultaneously maintain the required small values.) The project could, of course, be delayed for far more than 70 days, but that would be caused by some external, catastrophic event not contemplated when generating the original time estimates. (The possibility that this type of event may occur is precisely why we will advise PMs to continue to update risk identification, assessment, and analysis as long as the project is underway.)

Figure 8-30 CB cumulative probability chart of project completion time.

Traditional Statistics or Simulation?

The PM no longer has much choice about dealing with uncertainty. When the first edition of this book was written in 1985, uncertainty was more or less ignored by a large majority of those involved with projects. "Allowances for contingencies" were made as a sort of insurance against time and budget overruns, but little more attention was paid to risk. Times have changed. Formal risk management systems are now standard practice in many firms, and risk management is used by many others on specific types of projects that are considered "risky." The management of risk is not an issue. The only issue is how to do it.

The subject of project scheduling brings the problem of choosing the methods used to perform quantitative risk analysis into focus. The standard statistical methods were explained and demonstrated in the subsection on "Uncertainty in Project Completion Time," in this chapter. Following the section on traditional methods, we demonstrated and discussed simulation as a way of accomplishing essentially the same analysis. For a number of reasons, we suggest that simulation is the preferred method—*but only after the analyst has a good understanding of the traditional statistical approach.*

Both methods require that the three-time estimates be made and that the TE be found for each activity. TE (and variance) is easily calculated on almost any commercially availbable spreadsheet. Using statistics, TE and variance must also be found for each path—again, easily done by computer. Most real projects, however, are larger than the hypothetical projects we used to explain and illustrate the techniques of project management. When dealing with larger projects and their many paths, it is difficult merely to find those paths that may be critical or near critical. This must be done whether using statistics or simulation. But the statistical method requires one to analyze potential path mergers by hand. This increases the difficulty to extraordinary levels, not to mention adding a horrendous level of tedium. Of course, whichever method is chosen, it is rarely required to evaluate every path carefully. Paths that are significantly shorter than the critical path can usually be safely ignored. Unless their variance is extremely high, there is little chance they will affect the project duration.

Irrespective of the analytical method chosen, the PM will not know much about activity durations until the project gets underway. The actual critical path cannot be known until it becomes an historical fact. Even if we make three-time estimates for activities and then calculate TE for each, that does not make the TEs certain. If we cannot determine which path through a project will turn out to be the critical path until after the fact, we also cannot determine how much slack any given path will have. Nonetheless, careful analysis, be it by traditional statistics or by simulation, is important. It provides much better insight into the risks associated with project duration than the PM can get in any other way—including a call to Miss Cleo. The result is that the PM cannot devote his or her managerial attention solely to the critical path. There is no way of knowing which path will turn out to be critical, and thus attention must be given to all activities and paths. It is useful, every once in a while, for the PM to remember that if an activity has a great deal of slack, the people working on that activity have no sense of urgency about completing it. The activity is apt to lose its slack rapidly.

Project Management in Practice
Hosting the Annual Project Management Institute Symposium

Planning and implementing a national conference for a society that will draw about 1000 attendees is a major project. The tasks involved in hosting such an event are considerable and involve se-lecting a program committee, choosing a theme, contacting exhibitors, making local arrangements, planning the program, and on and on.

Pittsburgh was selected as host city/chapter

WORK BREAKDOWN STRUCTURE AND TASKS

S/S Project Management
Recruit Project Team
Establish Organizational
Procedures
Establish CAO Support
Levels and Budget
Issue Reports to VP-Tech
and Board of Directors
Develop S/S Goals and
Objectives
Assemble and Issue Post-
S/S Report

Technical Program
Develop S/S Theme
Strategize Tracks and SIGs
Recruit Technical Program
Team
Develop Selection Process
Procedures
Interface with Education
Committee on Workshops
Plan and Issue Call for
Papers/Panel Discussion
Recruit Invited Papers/
Panel Discussions
Recruit Moderators
Develop and Issue Master
Schedule for Presenta-
tions
Select Printer
Plan and Issue Abstract
Books and Proceedings
Organize Awards for
Speakers' Breakfasts

Identify Audio/Visual
Requirements
Develop and Issue Post-S/S
Technical Report

Social Guest Program
Establish Objectives
Identify Available
Activities
Analyze Cost-Benefit
Identify Recommendations
Complete Contracts
Recruit Staff

Speakers
Identify Candidates and
Related
Benefits and Costs
Make Recommendations
and
Obtain Approval
Complete Contracts
Maintain Periodic Contact
Host Speakers

Publicity/Promotion
Theme Establishment and
Approval
Logo Development and
Approval
Video Production
Promotional Materials
Identification and Approval
Advertising: PMI, Public
and Trade Media Releases

Regional Newsletter Articles

Finance
Initiate Code of Accounts
Develop Procedures of
Financial Operation
Develop Independent
Auditing Procedure
Initiate Separate Banking
Account
Develop Cash Flow
Estimates/Projections
Develop and Issue Standard
Reports
Interact with CAO on
Account Reconciliation
Develop and Issue Post-S/S
Financial Report

Corporate Sponsorship
Establish Participation
Philosophy
Target Prime Corporations
Solicit Participation
Recognition

Facilities Vendor/COA Support
Contract with Host and
Backup Hotels
Staff Recruiting
(Details to be Identified
and Scheduled with PMI
Exective Director and
Events Manager)

Figure A   The work breakdown structure.

for the 1992 Project Management Institute's annual September seminar/symposium. The objectives for the event were three: (1) to deliver a high-quality, value-added program that would be useful and last for years to come, (2) to offer a social and guest program that would reflect well on the host city, and (3) to meet strict financial criteria. The first task after selecting the city and hotel facilities was to put together the project team and chairperson. This included managers in charge of each of the tracks, the social program, the local arrangements, and all the other details.

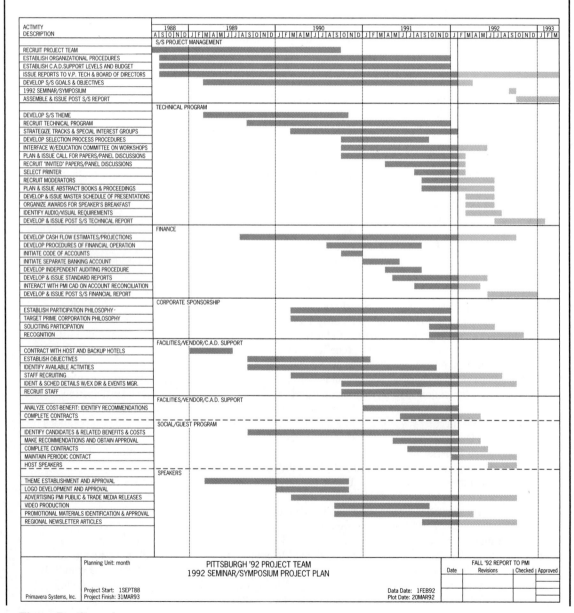

Figure B Gantt chart.

The project team was organized using a functional approach. Pittsburgh PMI Chapter officers had most of the primary responsibilities, with members from nine other chapters assisting in other duties.

Next was the development of the work breakdown structure, shown in Figure A, and the Gantt chart of activity schedules, shown in Figure B. As seen in the Gantt chart, scheduling all the work for a major conference such as this is an overwhelming effort. In the WBS, the major task was the development of the technical program. For PMI '92, the technical program offered 22 workshops composed of 70 technical papers, special panel discussions, and case studies. The technical tracks included engineering and construction, pharmaceuticals, utilities, software, automotive, R&D, defense, education, and manufacturing.

The workshops included sessions on preparing for the PMI certification examinations, learning about Taguchi concepts of statistical quality control, and future practice in project management. All of these also required careful scheduling.

The vendor program included exhibits by dozens of vendors and a large number of showcase sessions for in-depth demonstrations of their wares. The social program included a golf tournament, numerous social activities to meet with colleagues, tours of Pittsburgh's attractions, and a wide variety of entertainment opportunities.

All in all, a conference such as PMI's is as difficult a project as many firms face in their competitive markets.

Source: PMI Staff, "Catch the Spirit . . . at Pittsburgh," *PM Network,* May 1992.

Pittsburgh—host city for the PMI Annual Symposium.

Crystal Ball® 2000 is an excellent piece of software and makes simulation a reasonably easy tool with which to simulate project durations. XL also can be used to simulate project schedules with its own built-in programs. [For a full description of how to use XL for simulation, cf. Mantel, Meredith, Shafer, and Sutton (2001, pp. 132–140)]. We prefer CB because it is somewhat more user friendly, and also because it can display its results in a wide variety of formats. CB also allows the user to interact with the software by responding immediately to changes in the parameters of a simulation.

8.4   EXTENSIONS AND APPLICATIONS

There have been a large number of extensions to the basic ideas of PERT and CPM. These extensions are often oriented toward handling rather specific problem situations through additional program flexibility, computerizing some of the specific problems, fine-tuning some of the concepts for special environments, and combining various management approaches with the PERT/CPM concepts.

One interesting extension deals with the case when it is very difficult to estimate activity times because no one has experience with the activity, or because the activity is ill-defined. In this case, the concepts of fuzzy-set theory are applied (McCahon, 1993). In this section we discuss some of these extensions and look at the utility of network scheduling models in general. However, we delay our coverage of extensions aimed primarily at resource allocation and formal applications of CPM until Chapter 9. Specifically, we will briefly discuss Critical Resource Diagramming (Badiru, 1993, 1995)], Goldratt's "critical chain" (1997), and resource constrained scheduling (Tukel, 1996) in Chapter 9.

Precedence Diagramming

One shortcoming of the PERT/CPM network method is that it does not allow for leads and lags between two activities without greatly increasing the number of subactivities to account for this. In construction projects, in particular, it is quite common for the following restrictions to occur. (Node designations are shown in Figure 8-31.)

- **Finish to Start**   Activity 2 must not start before Activity 1 has been completed. This is the typical arrangement of an activity and its predecessor. Other finish–start arrangements are not uncommon. If the predecessor information had been written "1FS + 2 days," Activity 2 would be scheduled to start two days after the completion of Activity 1. For instance, if Activity 1 was the pouring of a concrete sideway, Activity 2 might be any activity that used the sidewalk.

- **Start to Start**   Activity 5 cannot begin until Activity 4 has been underway for 2 days. Setting electrical wires in place cannot begin until 2 days after framing has begun.

- **Finish to Finish**   Activity 7 and Activity 8 should be completed at the same time. If Activity 7 is priming the walls of a house, Activity 8 might be the pur-

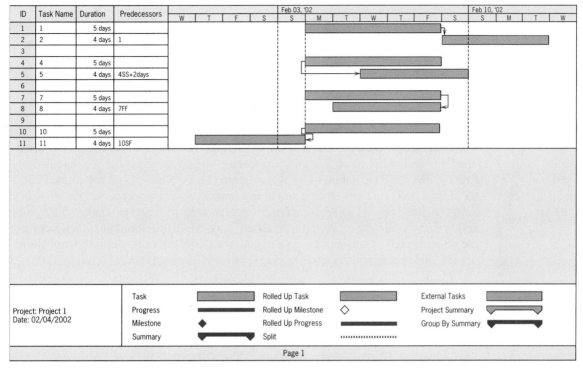

ID	Task Name	Duration	Predecessors
1	1	5 days	
2	2	4 days	1
3			
4	4	5 days	
5	5	4 days	4SS+2days
6			
7	7	5 days	
8	8	4 days	7FF
9			
10	10	5 days	
11	11	4 days	10SF

Figure 8-31   Precedence diagramming conventions.

chase and delivery of wallpaper. It is desirable to hang the paper immediately after the walls have been primed.

- **Start to Finish**   Activity 11 should be complete before Activity 10 is started. If Activity 11 is an automobile trip, it should not be started until the car has been repaired and inspected (Activity 10.) The S-F relationship is rare because there are usually simpler ways to map the required relationship.

Precedence diagramming is an AON network method that easily allows for these leads and lags within the network. MSP handles leads and lags without problems. However, some anomalies tend to occur in precedence diagramming that are not encountered in PERT/CPM. For example, because of the lead and lag requirements, activities may appear to have slack when they really do not. Also, the critical path of the network will frequently go backward through an activity, with the result that increasing the activity time may actually decrease the project completion time. Such an activity is called *reverse critical*. This happens when the critical path enters the completion of an activity through a finish constraint, continues backward through the activity, and leaves through a start constraint (see Activities 7–8 and Activities 10–11 in Figure 8-31).

Network node times are calculated in a manner similar to PERT/CPM times. Because of the lead and lag restrictions, it is often helpful to lay out a Gantt chart to see what is actually happening.

Precedence diagramming seems to be gaining in popularity. The richer set of precedence relationships it allows is pertinent for a variety of projects, particularly construction projects. [For more details on this technique, see Al-Hammed and Assaf (1998), Dean (1985, Chapters 6 and 17), and Moder, Phillips, and Davis (1983)]. Most current project management software will allow leads, lags, delays, and other constraints in the context of their standard AON network and Gantt chart programs.

GERT

The Graphical Evaluation and Review Technique (GERT) is a network model developed to deal with more complex modeling situations than can be handled by PERT/CPM. GERT combines signal flowgraph theory, probabilistic networks, PERT/CPM, and decision trees all in a single framework. Its components consist of *logical nodes* (defined below) and *directed arcs* (or branches) with two parameters; the probability that a given arc is taken (or "realized") and the distribution function describing the time required by the activity. Evaluation of a GERT network yields the probability of each node being realized and the elapsed time between all nodes.

At this point, it may be useful to compare GERT and PERT/CPM in order to focus on what is different about GERT.

GERT	**PERT/CPM**
Branching from a node is probabilistic.	Branching from a node is deterministic.
Flexibility in node realization.	No flexibility in node realization.
Looping back to earlier events is acceptable.	Looping back is not allowed.
Difficult to use as a control tool.	Easy to use for control.
Arcs may represent time, cost, reliability, etc.	Arcs represent time only.

While there are computer programs that optimize PERT/CPM problems, GERT and its various enhancements are computer simulations. Most of the programs (and the enhancements) are the result of work conducted by Pritsker (1968). His modeling package called Q-GERT simulates queues, or waiting lines, in the network. (There are other extensions of PERT that have some features similar to GERT and Q-GERT—VERT, for example—but GERT seems to be the most widely used extension.)

These are the steps employed in using GERT:

1. Convert the qualitative description of the project action plan into a network, just as in the use of PERT/CPM.

2. Collect the necessary data to describe the arcs of the network, focusing not only on the specific activity being modeled, but also on such characteristics of the activity as the likelihood it will be realized, the chance it might fail, any alternative activities that exist, and the like.

3. Determine the *equivalent function* of the network.

4. Convert the equivalent function of the network into the following two performance measures:

The probability that specific nodes are realized.

The *moment generating function* of the arc times.

5. Analyze the results and make inferences about the system.

It is not appropriate to deal here with the complex solution techniques employed for GERT networks. They make use of topology equations, equivalent functions, moment generating functions, and extensive calculation. The interested reader is urged to consult the papers of Pritsker (1968) and others (Al-Hammed and Assaf, 1998; Silverberg, 1991) for formal descriptions of the methods involved in formulating and solving GERT networks. Instead, we will describe how to construct a GERT network of a simple situation.

The list of common GERT symbols, together with a few examples, is given in Figure 8-32. This figure describes the left, or input side of the nodes first, and then the right-hand output side next. All combinations of input and output symbols are feasible, as shown in the examples.

Now let us describe a manufacturing project situation developed by Pritsker and portray it through the GERT approach. This situation concerns the initiation of a new

Symbol	Name	Explanation
		INPUT
K	Exclusive—or	Any branch leading into the node causes the node to be realized, but only one branch can occur.
$<$	Inclusive—or	Any branch causes the node to be realized and at the time of the earliest branch.
$($	And	The node is realized only after ALL branches have occurred.
		OUTPUT
$)$	Deterministic	All branches out must occur if the node is realized.
$>$	Probabilistic	Only one of the branches may occur if the node is realized.
		EXAMPLES
 $\rhd$		Beginning node with branches that must occur.
 a b $\lhd$		Ending node that occurs whenever **a** or **b** occurs.
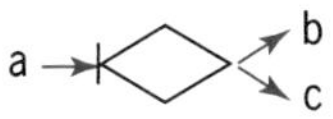 a → ◇ < b c		Intermediate node that occurs if **a** occurs with either **b** or **c** following.
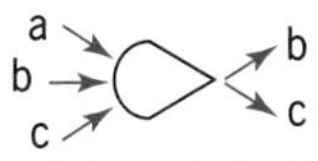 a b c ◯ < b c		Intermediate node that occurs when all **a**, **b**, and **c** occur with either **d** or **e** following.

Figure 8-32   GERT symbols.

production process developed by manufacturing engineering for an electronic component. The resulting GERT model could just as well describe an R & D project, a government project, or a Girl Scout project.

Sample Problem, Modeled with GERT

A part is manufactured on a production line in four hours. Following manufacture, parts are inspected. There is a 25 percent failure rate, and failed parts must be reworked. Inspection time is a stochastic variable, exponentially distributed, with a mean of 1 hour. Rework takes 3 hours, and 30 percent of the reworked parts fail the next inspection and must be scrapped. Parts that pass their original inspection or pass inspection after rework are sent to finishing, a process that requires 10 hours 60 percent of the time and 14 hours otherwise. A final inspection rejects 5 percent of the finished parts, which are then scrapped.

We can now model this situation as a GERT network so that it can be solved for the expected percentage of good parts and the expected time required to produce a good part. This GERT network is illustrated in Figure 8-33.

Activity **a** represents the output of the four-hour manufacturing process. The outputs enter an inspection from which 75 percent are passed, **c**, and 25 percent fail, **b**. The latter go to rework, with flow **d** emerging. Another inspection takes place—**e** (30 percent of 25 percent = 7.5%) flows to scrap, while the successfully reworked parts (70 percent of 25 percent = 17.5 percent), represented by **f**, go with the other good parts, **c**, to the finishing process. Sixty percent of this input requires 10 hours of work, **g**, and the remainder (40 percent) needs 14 hours, **h**. The final inspection process discards 5 percent of the output, **i** which goes to scrap, and the remainder (which is 87.875 percent of the original input) is sent to "good parts," **j**.

The time for an "average" part to proceed through the network can be found in much the same way as we calculated the output. The result of the entire analysis is therefore considerably richer than the simpler PERT/CPM. It should, however, be obvious that the input information requirements for GERT are more extensive and the computational requirements are far more extensive than for PERT/CPM, particularly for large networks. As always, the PM should adopt the simplest scheduling technique consistent with the needs of the project.

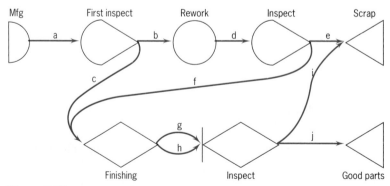

Figure 8-33   Sample GERT network.

Other Methods

Two straightforward methods for project scheduling that do not use networks or Gantt charts are employed by some agencies of the U.S. government. The Goddard Space Flight Center develops its project schedules in three phases. Phase I is advanced schedule planning, where the basic project schedule is developed directly from the work breakdown structure. Phase I also lists all major elements of the project. This is used for presenting the proposed project to NASA and to the congress and its many committees.

Phase II consists of the preparation of the operational schedule. This is the equivalent of the project master schedule. Phase III is schedule administration. In this last phase, the project is monitored and the master schedule is updated through the use of biweekly reports. Any necessary corrections and alterations to the project master schedule are made as a result of this process.

The Department of General Services uses a project scheduling system that provides planning, scheduling, and control in three distinct but closely related stages. Activity scheduling is the initial stage. At this point the planner attempts to develop optimum timing for the start and completion of all tasks associated with the project. Labor-hour and progress scheduling is carried out in the second stage. This identifies the labor (and other resources) required to initiate project activities on time and to sustain the necessary rate of progress to keep the project on schedule. Progress reporting takes place in the final stage. In this third stage, the project is monitored and a more or less constant stream of reports is filed so that appropriate action can be taken to keep the project on schedule. The information reported to senior management shows the project status relative to activity milestones and actual progress relative to planned progress. The value of the progress achieved as well as the estimated value of progress remaining is used to calculate (forecast) the labor-hours required to complete the remaining work on schedule.

Note that these methods parallel the basic concept of the project action plan with its specific steps to be taken, its estimate of resource requirements, times, and precedences, and most important, with each step in the higher-level plans broken down into lower-level action plans.

Using These Tools

We have heard differing opinions on the value of each of the tools we have described, including many of the computerized project management information systems (PMISs). We have been told, "No one uses PERT/CPM/Precedence diagramming," "No one uses three-time PERT," and "No one uses _____ computer package." But we have first-hand knowledge of PERT users, of CPM users, and of precedence diagram users. We know PMs who collect and use three-time PERT. For example, refer to the boxed Apartment Complex example (Figure 8-34).

Figure 8-34 is a portion of a 48-step action plan for the syndication of an apartment complex. Note that several of the steps are obvious composites of multistep action plans designed for a lower level (e.g., see steps 1–4). Figure 8-35 is an AON network of Figure 8-34. The firm also has a Gantt chart version of the network that is

Task	a (days, hours)	m (days)	b (days)	TE (hr)	σ² (hr)	TE	σ²
1. Product package received by Secy. in Real Estate (R.E.) Dept.	n/a	(.3)	(.4)				
2. Secy. checks for duplicates, and forwards all packages in Atlanta region (but not ad-dressed to R.E staff member) to Atl. via fast mail. Atl. office sends copy of submittal log to L.A. office on weekly basis.	n/a	(.2)	(.3)				
3. Secy. dates, stamps, logs, checks for duplication, makes new file, checks for contact source, adds to card file all new packages. Sends criteria letter to new source. Send duplication letter. Forwards package to Admin. Asst. (AA).	(.7)	(.7)	(.9)				
4. AA reviews package, completes Property Summary Form, forwards to L.A. Reg. Acquisit. Director officer or to R.E. staff member to whom package is addressed (RAD).	(.5)	(.5)	(.7)				
Total 1–4	1(1.7)	1(1.7)	3(2.3)	1.3	0.11	1.80	0.01
5. Person to whom package forwarded determines action. (May refer to other or retain for further review.) "Passes" sent to Secy. for files. "Possibles" retained by RAD for further review.	1(.5)	1(.5)	1(1)	1.0		.58	0.01
6. RAD gets add'l data as needed, gets demographic and comparables. Rough numbers run. Looks for the "opportunities." If viable, continue.	4(3)	5(3)	3(2.3)	5.5	0.69	3.83	0.69
•				•	•	•	
•				•	•	•	
•				•	•	•	
45. Prop. Mgt./Fin. prepares for closing and take-over. At closing, prorations of taxes, rents, service contracts.	3(4)	5(8)	10(24)	5.5	1.36	10.00	11.11
46. PM final inspect. On-site at close.	1(4)	1(8)	2(12)	1.2	0.03	8.00	1.78
47. Legal closes.	2(8)	2(14)	4(25)	2.3	0.11	14.83	8.03
48. Legal issues Post Closing Memo-randum.	2(5)	5(8)	10(10)	5.3	1.78	7.83	0.69

Figure 8-34   Action plan for syndication of an apartment complex.

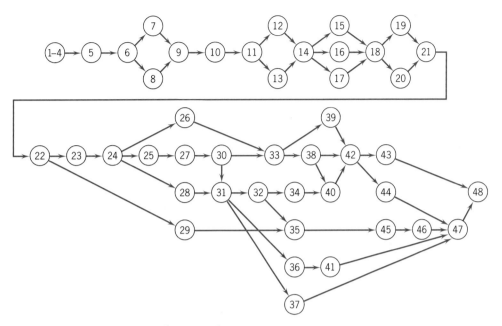

Figure 8-35   Apartment complex network.

used for tracking each project. Figure 8-34 also contains three time estimates of the "calendar" time used for each step (in days) and of the "resource" time used for each step (in hours). The time estimate 2(10) is read, "2 days, 10 labor-hours." The duplicate data are useful for scheduling workloads.

We are reluctant to give advice about which tools to use. If the PM indulges in a bit of experimentation with the major systems, their relative advantages and disadvantages in a given application will become evident. We have noted Bubshait and Selen's work (1992) on the use of project management techniques. Digman and Green (1981) have also developed an interesting and useful framework for evaluating the various planning and control techniques. As discussed earlier in Chapter 2, interest has been growing in the development of models for measuring the "maturity level" of an organization's practice of project management (e.g., Cabanis, 1998; Combe, 1998; Remy, 1997; Schlicter, 1999) and to develop benchmarks of "best practice" in the field (Gupta and Graham, 1997; Ibbs and Kwak, 1998; Thamhain, 1996; Toney, 1997). In one particularly well developed model, Ibbs and Kwak (1998) measured and published scores of the level of project management maturity in 38 firms representing several industries.

There are several forces driving this effort. First, and most obvious, is the desire of professionals in the field to develop standards by which practice of the art can be measured. Second, senior management, considering investment in project management, has a need to know what level of competency they are buying. Third, the Software Engineering Institute developed a Capability Maturity Model that served as an indication that the development of such a model was feasible. Fourth, it was generally felt that such models would allow individual firms to document a level of excellence in project management that would be attractive to potential customers. Fifth, some consulting firms felt that such models would be saleable. While the logic of some of the reasons for developing a maturity model may seem questionable (Cabanis, 1998, p. 54), the work is well underway. Several consulting firms claim to have developed models (see Ibbs and Kwak, 1998 for one example) and the Project Management Institute's Standards Committee has established a "working group" (Comb, 1998, p. 21) to pursue the matter.

Although the effort is still developing, so are the several efforts to measure the return on investment (ROI) assignable to investing in project management (e.g., Knutson, 1999). (Those trying to measure the ROI from project management would do well to review efforts in the 1950s and 1960s to determine the ROI from investments in R&D.) Until generally acceptable standards for maturity and methods for calculating the ROI from project management are developed, the PM should opt for the simplest method sufficient to the needs of the project and its parent firm.

SUMMARY

In this chapter the scheduling aspect of project implementation was addressed. Following a description of the benefits of using a network for planning and controlling a project, the PERT/CPM approach was described, as were Gantt charts. Finally, precedence diagramming, GERT, and a few other extensions were discussed.

Specific points covered in the chapter were these:

- Scheduling is particularly important to projects because of complex coordination problems.
- The network approach to scheduling offers a number of specific advantages of special value for projects.
- Critical project tasks typically constitute fewer than 10 percent of all the project tasks.
- Although research indicates technological performance is not significantly affected by the use of PERT/CPM, there did seem to be a significantly lower probability of cost and schedule overruns.
- Network techniques can adopt either an activity-on-node or activity-on-arc framework without significantly altering the analysis.
- Networks are usually constructed from left to right, indicating activity precedence and event times as the network is constructed. Through use of the network, critical activities and events are identified, early and late activity start times are found, available slacks for each activity are determined, and probabilities of project completion by various times are calculated.

- Gantt charts, a monitoring technique, are closely related to network diagrams, but are more easily understood and provide a clearer picture of the current state of the project. However, while offering some advantages, they also have some drawbacks, such as not clearly indicating task precedence and dependencies.
- Precedence diagramming is a useful extention of Gantt charts. It is particularly useful when lead or lag relationships between activities is common.
- GERT is also a useful extension of PERT/CPM and allows: probabilistic branching from nodes, various probability distributions for the activity times, looping in the network, and representation of project elements other than time, such as cost or reliability.

In the next chapter, we investigate the scheduling problem further when multiple projects require a set of common resources to be shared. Again, a number of techniques are useful for resource allocation and activity expediting under such circumstances.

GLOSSARY

Activity A specific project task that requires resources and time to complete.

Activity-On-Arrow (Activity-on-Node) The two ways of illustrating a network: placing the activities on the arcs or on the nodes.

Arc The line connecting two nodes.

Crash In CPM, an activity can be conducted at a normal pace or at an expedited pace, known as crashing, at a greater cost.

Critical An activity or event that, if delayed, will delay project completion.

Event An end state for one or more activities that occurs at a specific point in time.

Gantt Chart A manner of illustrating multiple, time-based activities on a horizontal time scale.

Milestone A clearly identifiable point in a project or set of activities that commonly denotes a reporting requirement or completion of a large or important set of activities.

Network A combination of interrelated activities and events depicted with arcs and nodes.

Node An intersection of two or more lines or arrows, commonly used for depicting an event or activity.

Path A sequence of lines and nodes in a network.

Project Management Information System (PMIS) The systems, activities, and data that allow information flow in a project, frequently computerized but not always.

Trade-off The amount of one factor that must be sacrificed in order to achieve more or less of another factor.

QUESTIONS

Material Review Questions

1. Define *activity, event*, and *path* as used in network construction. What is a dummy activity?

2. What characteristic of the critical path times makes them critical?

3. What two factors are compared by Gantt charting? How does the Gantt chart differ in purpose from the project master schedule?

4. How is the GERT technique different from the PERT technique?

5. When is each scheduling technique appropriate to use?

6. What is the difference between activity-on-node and activity-on-arrow diagrams?

7. How does simulation determine the probabilities of various project completion times?

8. Briefly summarize how a network is drawn.

9. Define "late start time," "early start time," and "early finish time."

10. How is the critical path determined?

11. What is "slack"?

Class Discussion Questions

12. How do you think the network technique could be used to estimate costs for manufacturing?

13. What are some benefits of the network approach to project planning? What are some drawbacks?

14. What is your position on the statements in the Using These Tools section?

15. Why is PERT of significant value to the project manager?

16. How is uncertainty in project scheduling dealt with?

17. Are there any drawbacks to using GERT?

18. How are activity times estimated?

19. Should the critical path activities be managed differently from noncritical path activities? Explain.

Questions for Project Management in Practice

Replacing the Atigun Section of the TransAlaska Pipeline

20. How do you imagine the polar bear got on top of the pipe?

21. One requirement of the project was to keep the oil flowing while replacing the pipeline section. How do you think they managed to do this?

22. Did the project team always have to work in 3-hour segments? What would you expect their longest shifts to run?

Hosting the Annual Project Management Institute Symposium

23. Elaborate on the uniqueness of this work breakdown structure.

24. Based on the Gantt chart, when did the symposium actually occur?

25. Why are there activities scheduled after the symposium? When is the project finally done?

PROBLEMS

1. Given the following information, draw the PERT/CPM diagram:

Activity	Immediate Predecessor
1	—
2	—
3	1,4
4	2
5	2
6	3,5

2. Convert the AON diagram below to an AOA diagram.

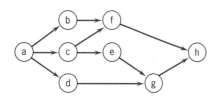

3. Find three errors in the diagram below.

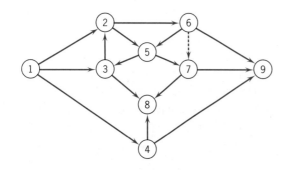

4. Given the diagram below, find:
(a) The critical path.
(b) How long it will take to complete the project.

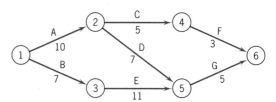

5. Convert the AOA diagram in Problem 4 to an AON diagram. How would the AON diagram change if there had been a dummy from node 2 to node 3 in Problem 4?

6. Convert each of the following AOA diagrams into AON diagrams.

a.

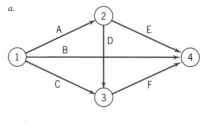

b.

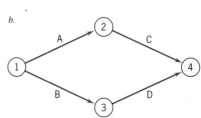

7. Given the following activities and precedences, draw a PERT/CPM diagram:

Activity	Immediate Predecessor
A	—
B	—
C	A
D	A,B
E	A,B
F	C
G	D,F
H	E,G

8. Given the following network,
(a) What is the critical path?
(b) How long will it take to complete this project?
(c) Can activity **B** be delayed without delaying the completion of the project? If so, how many days?

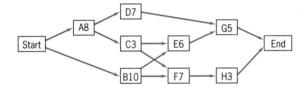

9. Given the estimated activity times below and the network in Problem 8 above,

Activity	a	m	b
A	6.5	7.5	14.5
B	8.5	10.5	12.5
C	2.5	3.5	4.5
D	6.5	7.5	8.5
E	5.5	5.5	9.5
F	5.5	7.5	9.5
G	4.5	6.5	8.5
H	2.5	3.5	3.5

what is the probability that the project will be completed within:
(a) 21 days?
(b) 22 days?
(c) 25 days?

10.

Activity*	a	m	b
AB	3	6	9
AC	1	4	7
CB	0	3	6
CD	3	3	3
CE	2	2	8
BD	0	0	6
BE	2	5	8
DF	4	4	10
DE	1	1	1
EF	1	4	7

Find
(a) the critical path;
(b) all event slacks;
(c) critical path to event D;
(d) probability of completion in 14 days; and
(e) the effect if CD slips to 6 days; to 7 days; to 8 days.

11.

Activity*	TE
AB	1
AC	2
AD	3
DC	4
CB	3
DE	8
CF	2
BF	4
IJ	2
CE	6
EF	5
FG	10
FH	11
EH	1
GH	9
EJ	3
GI	8
HJ	6

(a) Draw the PERT diagram.
(b) Find the critical path.
(c) Find the completion time.

12. The Denver Iron & Steel Company is expanding its operations to include a new drive-in weigh station. The weigh station will be a heated/air-conditioned building with a large floor and small office. The large room will have the scales, a 15-foot

---
*The nomenclature AB means the activity *between* nodes A and B.

Table A.

#	Activity	Times			Preceding Tasks
		Optimistic	Most Likely	Pessimistic	
1	Lay foundation	8	10	13	—
2	Dig hole for scale	5	6	8	—
3	Insert scale bases	13	15	21	2
4	Erect frame	10	12	14	1,3
5	Complete building	11	20	30	4
6	Insert scales	4	5	8	5
7	Insert display cases	2	3	4	5
8	Put in office equipment	4	6	10	7
9	Finishing touches	2	3	4	8,6

counter, and several display cases for its equipment.

Before erection of the building, the project manager evaluated the project using PERT/CPM analysis. The activities with their corresponding times were recorded in Table A.

Using PERT/CPM analysis, find the critical path, the slack times, and the expected completion time.

13. Miracle Marketing has received a contract from a large pharmaceutical firm to design a nationwide advertising campaign for their recently approved cancer drug. The drug is easily taken, compared with current intravenous drugs, and can be administered from home. Miracle Marketing has assigned to the task a project manager who, in turn, has delegated minor subprojects to subordinate managers.

The project was evaluated using PERT/CPM analysis. Due to the extensive length of the project, many activities were combined: The following is the result.

Activity*	Time (months)
AB	3
BC	6
BD	2
BF	5
BE	4
CD	9
DG	20
FG	6

*See nomenclature note in Problem 10.

Activity*	Time (months)
EH	11
EI	19
GJ	1
HK	3
IL	9
LM	12
KN	7
JO	4
MN	15
NP	13
OP	10

Find the critical path and expected completion date.

14. The following PERT chart was prepared at the beginning of a HRM crash hiring project. The project begins with two activities: Assemble interview team (A) and Budget resources (B).

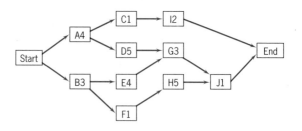

The duration, in days, follows the letter of each activity. What is the critical path? Which activities should be monitored most closely?

At the end of the first week of construction, it was noted that activity **A** was completed in 2.5

days, but activity **B** required 4.5 days. What impact does this have on the project? Are the same activities critical?

15. Given the following financing project being considered by a venture firm, find the probability of completion by 17 weeks. By 24 weeks. By what date is management 90 percent sure completion will occur?

Times (weeks)

Activity*	Optimistic	Most Likely	Pessimistic
1–2	5	11	11
1–3	10	10	10
1–4	2	5	8
2–6	1	7	13
3–6	4	4	10
3–7	4	7	10
3–5	2	2	2
4–5	0	6	6
5–7	2	8	14
6–7	1	4	7

If the venture firm can complete the project for the customer within 18 weeks it will receive a bonus of $10,000. But if the project delays beyond 22 weeks, it must pay a penalty of $5,000 due to lost customer impact. If the firm can choose whether or not to bid on this project, what should its decision be if the project is only a breakeven one normally?

16. Given an auditing project with the following activities,

Activity	Standard Deviation	Critical?	Duration
a, add	2	yes	2
b, balance	1		3
c, count	0	yes	4
d, deduct	3		2
e, edit	1	yes	1
f, finance	2		6
g, group	2	yes	4
h, hold	0	yes	2

*See nomenclature note in Problem 10.

Find:
(a) The probability of completing this project in 12 weeks (or less), as the client desires.
(b) The probability of completing this project in 13 weeks (or less).
(c) The probability of completing this project in 16 weeks (or less), the client's drop-dead date.
(d) The number of weeks required to assure a 92.5 percent chance of completion, as guaranteed by the auditing firm.

17. The following PERT network is a compressed representation of the prospectus of a start-up firm that plans to develop a new, bio-electronic computer chip.

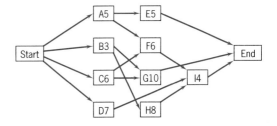

Note that four activities, the biological elements, can start immediately.

Find:
(a) The critical path.
(b) The earliest time to complete the project.
(c) The slack on activities **E**, **F**, and **H**.

18. The events of the project below are designated as 1, 2, and so on.
(a) Draw the PERT network.
(b) Find the critical path.
(c) Find the slacks on all the activities.

Activity	Prec. Evt.	Suc. Evt.	TE (weeks)	Prec. Activ.
a	1	2	3	none
b	1	3	6	none
c	1	4	8	none
d	2	5	7	a
e	3	5	5	b
f	4	5	10	c
g	4	6	4	c
h	5	7	5	d,e,f
i	6	7	6	g

19. Given the following PERT network (times are in weeks),

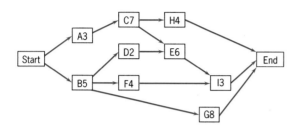

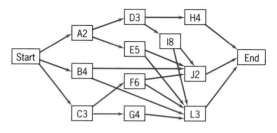

determine:
(a) The ES, LS, EF, and LF for each activity.
(b) The slacks on all activities.
(c) The critical activities and path.

20. Given the schedule in Table B for a liability work package done as part of an accounting audit in a corporation, find:
(a) The critical path.
(b) The slack time on "process confirmations."
(c) The slack time on "test pension plan."
(d) The slack time on "verify debt restriction compliance."

Table B.

Activity	Duration (days)	Preceding Activities
a. Obtain schedule of liabilities	3	none
b. Mail confirmation	15	a
c. Test pension plan	5	a
d. Vouch selected liabilities	60	a
e. Test accruals and amortization	6	d
f. Process confirmations	40	b
g. Reconcile interest expense to debt	10	c,e
h. Verify debt restriction compliance	7	f
i. Investigate debit balances	6	g
j. Review subsequent payments	12	h,i

21. In the Web site development project network, shown in the following figure, the number alongside each activity designates the activity duration (TE) in weeks.

Determine:
(a) The ES and LS for each activity.
(b) The earliest time that the Web site can be completed.
(c) The slack on all activities.
(d) The critical activities.
(e) The critical path.

22. Given the following information regarding a project concerning an initial public offering (IPO),

Activity	TE (weeks)	Preceding Activities
a	3	none
b	1	none
c	3	a
d	4	a
e	4	b
f	5	b
g	2	c,e
h	3	f

(a) Draw the PERT network.
(b) What is the critical path?
(c) When will the offering be available (completion of the project)?
(d) What is the effect on the project if activity **e** (approvals) takes an extra week? Two extra weeks? Three extra weeks?

23. Construct a network for the aerospace launch project below and find its critical path.

Activity	TE (weeks)	Preceding Activities
a	3	none
b	5	a
c	3	a
d	1	c
e	3	b
f	4	b,d

Activity	TE (weeks)	Preceding Activities
g	2	c
h	3	g,f
i	1	e,h

24. Construct a network for the following training and development project.

Activity	TE (weeks)	Preceding Activities
a	3	none
b	5	none
c	14	a
d	5	a
e	4	b
f	7	b
g	8	d,e
h	5	g,f

(a) Draw the PERT network.
(b) Find the critical path.
(c) Assume activity **a** (hire trainers) took 5 weeks. Replan the project.
(d) From where would you suggest transferring resources, and to what activities, so that the original target training date may be maintained?

25. Resolve part (d) of Problem 10 assuming the values of a and b are given at the 95 percent level. Repeat, assuming the values are given at the 90 percent level.

26. Using the landscaping information below, draw an AOA network. Find the critical path and compute the number of days you would be 95 percent sure the garden would be completed. Calculate the slack, earliest start, and latest start times for each activity and show in table form. Does any path come close to causing a problem in determining the probability of project completion based on the critical path alone?

Activity	Time (days)		
	a	m	b
1–2	6	8	10
1–3	5	6	7
1–4	6	6	6
2–6	0	0	0

Activity	Time (days)		
	a	m	b
2–7	10	11	12
3–6	12	14	16
4–5	5	8	11
4–9	7	9	11
5–6	8	10	12
5–9	0	0	0
6–7	14	15	16
6–8	10	12	14
7–10	9	12	15
8–10	0	4	14
9–11	5	5	5
10–11	7	8	9

27. Given the following information about staging a community play on Independence Day,
(a) Construct an AON diagram.
(b) Determine the earliest completion time for advertising the play and the critical path.
(c) What completion date are you 80% confident of achieving? 40% confident?
(d) Will a 1-day delay in this project be serious?

Activity	Predecessor	Time (days)		
		a	m	b
1	—	2	4	6
2	—	5	5	5
3	2	3	5	7
4	1	7	10	13
5	1	11	12	13
6	2,4	5	6	7
7	3	9	10	11
8	3,6	5	7	9
9	4	7	9	11
10	5	3	3	3
11	7	15	17	19
12	8	6	8	10
13	9,10	7	8	15
14	7	12	14	16
15	12,13	16	17	18

28. Draw an AON network using the following data and find the probability of completing the critical path of the operatic project in 44 days, the official opening date.

Activity	Predecessor	Time (days) a	m	b
1	—	6	10	14
2	1	0	1	2
3	1	16	20	30
4	2	3	5	7
5	4	2	3	4
6	3	7	10	13
7	4	1	2	3
8	7	0	2	4
9	3,7	2	2	2
10	9	2	3	4
11	8	0	1	2
12	10, 11	1	2	3

29. Simulate Problem 27 to find the probabilities of project completion. Preset the calendar to a 7-day workweek. Use a triangular distribution for defining activity time distributions. After a 1000-trial simulation, examine the statistical information generated and compare the output of the simulation with your findings in Problem 27. Briefly explain the significant similarities and differences.

30. Simulate Problem 28 to find the probabilities of project completion. Preset the calendar to a 7-day workweek. Use a triangular distribution for defining activity time distributions. After a 1000-trial simulation, examine the statistical information generated and compare the output of the simulation with your findings in Problem 28. Briefly explain the significant similarities and differences.

31. In the following table are listed tasks, duration in weeks, and predecessors.

Task	Predecessors	Duration
a	—	2
b	—	2
c	a,b	4
d	c	3
e	a,b,c	1
f	d,e	2
g	f	3
h	g	1

(a) Construct a Gantt chart using MSP.
(b) Assuming the default 5-day workweek, calculate the critical path of the project.
(c) Calculate the project duration.

32. In the following table, project activities in days are listed with three time estimates for duration in days and predecessors for the activities.

Activity	Optimistic Time	Most Likely Time	Pessimistic Time	Predecessors
a	5	7	12	—
b	8	8	8	—
c	2	6	10	a
d	12	14	19	a, b
e	6	6	12	c, d
f	3	12	18	b, e
g	6	8	10	f

(a) Calculate the expected time of each activity using MSP.
(b) Construct a Gantt chart using MSP.
(c) Use MSP to draw a network diagram.
(d) Assuming the default 5-day workweek, calculate the critical path of the project.
(e) Calculate the slack for the activities.

INCIDENTS FOR DISCUSSION

Yankee Chair Company

The Yankee Chair Company was anxious to get a new model rocking chair onto the market. Past efforts to introduce new models had resulted in frustrating failures. Bret Ricks, president of Yankee Chair, was determined that it would not happen again with the newest model. He had no confidence in his current management team, so he hired Jan Dymore, a local consultant, to organize and manage this project. He assigned a Yankee Chair manager, Tom Gort, to work with Dymore to start developing some talent for project management within the company. Dymore decided to set up a PERT network and guided Gort through the process of listing activities, assigning precedence, and estimating completion times. She also explained the critical path concept to Gort, who by this time had a reasonable grasp of the project direction. At the first review session with Mr. Ricks, the PERT approach was accepted enthusiastically, but toward the end of the review Dymore made some critical remarks about the product design and was subsequently released from the project.

Ricks then asked Gort if he could carry on the PERT approach by himself. Gort jumped at the chance, but later in his office he began to question whether or not he really could use the PERT network effectively. Dymore had made a guess at what the critical path would be and how long the project would take, but she had also told Gort that several other calculations had to be made in order to calculate the exact time estimates for each activity and the variances of those activity times. Gort really did not understand the mathematics involved and certainly did not want to look bad in Ricks' eyes, so he decided to take Dymore's guess at the critical path and get the best possible estimates of those activity times. By concentrating his attention on the critical path activities and ignoring the variance issues, he figured he could bring the project in on time.

Questions: Will Gort's approach work? How much more of a gamble is Gort taking than any project manager normally takes? What should Gort watch out for?

Cincinnati Software

Cincinnati Software, which currently specializes in the installation of manufacturing resource planning (MRP II) systems in small firms, is planning a major expansion into installing the new enterprise resource planning (ERP) systems. This major expansion into the hottest software area will be organized as an in-house project of strategic importance. The company has selected a project manager and team to follow the project through to completion. The project team is very interested in selecting an appropriate scheduling technique for the project. The project manager has thus set the following guidelines for the selection process: simple; able to show durations of events, the flow of work, and the relative sequence of events; able to indicate planning and actual flow, which items may proceed at the same time, and how far they are from completion. The assistant project manager favors the Gantt chart, the finance representative likes PERT, and the information technology department head prefers CPM.

Questions: If you were the project manager, which method would you use, and why?

BIBLIOGRAPHY

AL-HAMMED, A., and S. ASSAF. "A Survey of Cost Reduction Techniques Used by Construction Firms in Saudi Arabia."*American Association of Cost Engineers Transactions,* 1988.

BADIRU, A. B. "Incorporating Learning Curve Effects Into Critical Resource Diagramming." *Project Management Journal,* June 1995.

BADIRU, A. B. "Activity-Resource Assignments Using Critical Resource Diagramming." *Project Management Journal,* September 1993.

BUBSHAIT, K. A., and W. J. SELEN. "Project Characteristics That Influence The Implementation of Project Management Techniques: A Survey." *Project Management Journal,* June 1992.

CABANIS, J. "Show Me the Money." *PM Network,* September 1998.

CAMPANIS, N. A. "Delphi: Not the Greek Oracle, but Close." *PM Network,* February 1997.

COMBE, M. W. "Standards Committee Tackles Project Management Maturity Models." *PM Network,* August 1998.

DAVIS, E. W. "Networks: Resource Allocation." *Industrial Engineering,* April 1974.

DEAN, B. V. *Project Management: Methods and Studies.* New York: Elsevier, 1985.

DEYOUNG-CURREY, J. "Want Better Estimates? Let's Get to Work." *PM Network,* December 1998.

DIGMAN, L. A., and G. I. GREEN. "A Framework of Evaluating Network Planning and Control Tecniques." *Research Management,* January 1981.

EICHHORN, B. R. "Manage Contingencies, Reduce Risk: The PCA Technique." *PM Network,* October 1997.

EVANS, J. R., and D. L. OLSON, *Introduction to Simulation and Risk Analysis,* Upper Saddle River, NJ: Prentice-Hall, 1998.

FRAME, J. D. "Risk Assessment Groups: Key Component of Project Offices." *PM Network,* March 1998.

GALLAGHER, C. "A Note on Pert Assumptions." *Management Science,* October 1987.

GIDO, J. *Successful Project Management,* Cincinnati, OH: South-Western, 1999.

GOLDRATT, E. M. *Critical Chain,* Great Barrington, MA, North River, 1997.

GUPTA, V. K., and D. J. GRAHAM. "A Customer-Driven Quality Improvement and Management Project at Diamond Offshore Drilling." *Project Management Journal,* September 1997.

HARE, L. B., R. W. HOERL, J. D. HROMI, and R. D. SNEE. "The Role of Statistical Thinking in Management." *IEEE Engineering Management Review,* Fall 1998, reprinted with permission of the American Society for Quality (1995).

HULETT, D. T. "Schedule Risk Analysis Simplified." *PM Network,* July 1996.

HULETT, D. T. "Project Schedule Risk Assessment." *Project Management Journal,* March 1995.

IBBS, C. W., and Y.-H. KWAK. "Benchmarking, Project Management Organizations." *PM Network,* February 1998.

KAMBUROWSKI, J. "New Validations of PERT Times." *Omega, International Journal of Management Science,* Vol. 25, No. 3, 1997.

KEEFER, D. L., and W. A. VERDINI. "Better Estimation of PERT Activity Time Parameters." *Management Science,* September 1993.

KERZNER, H. *Project Management: A Systems Approach to Planning, Scheduling, and Controlling,* 6th ed. New York: Wiley, 1998.

KNUTSON, J. "From Making Sense to Making Cents: Measuring Project Management ROI—Part 1." *PM Network,* January 1999.

LEVINE, H. A. "Risk Management for Dummies, Part 2." *PM Network,* April 1996.

LIBERATORE, M. J., and G. J. TITUS. "The Practice of Management Science in R & D Project Management." *Management Science,* August 1983.

LITTLEFIELD, T. K., JR., and P. H. RANDOLPH. "An Answer to Sasieni's Question on PERT Times." *Management Science,* October 1987.

MALLON, J. C. "Verifying Cost and Schedule During Design." *Project Management Journal,* March 1992.

MANTEL, S. J., Jr., J. R. MEREDITH, S. M. SHAFER, and M. M. SUTTON, *Project Management in Practice,* New York: Wiley, 2001.

MARTIN, P., and K. TATE. "Team-Based Risk Assessment." *PM Network,* February 1998.

MCCAHON, C. S. "Using PERT as an Approximation of Fuzzy Project-Network Analysis." *IEEE Transactions on Engineering Management,* May 1993.

MILLS, N. L. "The Development of a University Sports Complex: A Project Management Application." *Computers and Industrial Engineering,* 17:149–153, 1989.

MODER, J. J., C. R. PHILLIPS, and E. W. DAVIS. *Project Management with CPM, PERT, and Precedence Diagramming,* 3rd ed. New York: Van Nostrand Reinhold, 1983.

NAIK, B. *Project Management: Scheduling and Monitoring by PERT/CPM.* Advent Books, 1984.

ORCZYK, J. J., and L. CHANG. "Parametric Regression Model for Project Scheduling." *Project Management Journal,* December 1991.

PASCALE, S., J. CARLAND, and C. LORENZ. "Risk Analysis: Making the Right Call, Part 2." *PM Network,* March 1998.

POWERS, J. R. "A Structured Approach to Schedule Development and Use." *Project Management Journal,* November 1988.

PRITSKER, A. A. B. "GERT Networks." *The Production Engineer,* October 1968.

REMY, R. "Adding Focus to Improvement Efforts with PM[3]." *PM Network,* July 1997.

ROBINSON, P. B. "The Performance Measurement Baseline—A Statistical View." *Project Management Journal,* June 1997.

SANTELL, M. P., J. R. JUNG, and J. C. WARNER. "Optimization in Project Coordination Scheduling through Application of Taguchi Methods." *Project Management Journal,* September 1992.

SASIENI, M. W. "A Note on PERT Times." *Management Science,* December 1986.

SCHLICTER, J. An Organizational PM Maturity Model. *PM Network,* February 1999.

SHAFER, S. M., and J. R. MEREDITH. *Operations Management: A Process Approach with Spreadsheets,* New York: Wiley, 1998.

SILVERBERG, E. C. "Predicting Project Completion." *Research-Technology Management,* May–June 1991.

THAMHAIN, H. J. "Best Practices for Controlling Technology-Based Projects." *Project Management Journal,* December 1996.

TOELLE, R. A., and J. WITHERSPOON. "From 'Managing the Critical Path' to 'Managing Critical Activities.'" *Project Management Journal,* December 1990.

TONEY, F. "What the Fortune 500 Know about PM Best Practices." *PM Network,* February 1997.

TUKEL, O. I. "Scheduling Resource-Constrained Projects When Non-conformities Exist." *Project Management Journal,* September 1996.

VAZSONYI, A. "L'Histoire de Grandeur et la Decadence de la Methode PERT." *Management Science,* April 1979.

WEIST, J. D., and F. K. LEVY. *A Management Guide to PERT/CPM,* 2nd ed. Englewood Cliffs, NJ: Prentice Hall, 1977.

WILKENS, T. T. "Are You Being Misled by Your Progress Gantt Chart?" *PM Network,* August 1997.

WILLIAMS, T. M. "What are PERT Estimates?" *Journal of the Operational Research Society,* Vol. 44, No. 12, 1995.

The following case presents a realistic situation facing a construction firm that has just won a competitive contract. The realistic conditions complicating the project are described in detail, as are the alternatives offered by the staff for dealing with these complexities.

C ' A S E

THE SHARON CONSTRUCTION CORPORATION
E. Turban and J. R. Meredith

The Sharon Construction Corporation has been awarded a contract for the construction of a 20,000-seat stadium. The construction must start by February 15 and be completed within one year. A penalty clause of $15,000 per week of delay beyond February 15 of next year is written into the contract.

Jim Brown, the president of the company, called a planning meeting. In the meeting he expressed great satisfaction at obtaining the contract and revealed that the company could net as much as $300,000 on the project. He was confident that the project could be completed on time with an allowance made for the usual delays anticipated in such a large project.

Bonnie Green, the director of personnel, agreed that in a normal year only slight delays might de-

velop due to a shortage of labor. However, she reminded the president that for such a large project, the company would have to use unionized employees and that the construction industry labor agreements were to expire on November 30. Past experience indicated a fifty–fifty chance of a strike.

Jim Brown agreed that a strike might cause a problem. Unfortunately, there was no way to change the contract. He inquired about the prospective length of a strike. Bonnie figured that such a strike would last either eight weeks (70 percent chance) or possibly 12 weeks (30 percent chance).

Jim was not pleased with these prospects. However, before he had a chance to discuss contingency plans he was interrupted by Jack White, the vice-president for engineering. Jack commented that a colder December than had been assumed was now being predicted. This factor had not been taken into consideration during earlier estimates since previous forecasts called for milder weather. Concrete pouring in December might thus require in one out of every three cases (depending on the temperature) special heating that costs $500 per week.

This additional information did not please Jim at all. The chances for delay were mounting. And an overhead expense of $500 per week would be incurred in case of any delay. The technical details of the project are given in the appendix to this case.

The management team was asked to consider alternatives for coping with the situation. At the end of the week, five proposals were submitted.

1. Expedite the pouring of seat gallery supports. This would cost $20,000 and cut the duration of the activity to six weeks.

2. The same as proposal 1, but in addition, put a double shift on the filling of the field. A cost of $10,000 would result in a five-week time reduction.

3. The roof is very important since it precedes several activities. The use of three shifts and some overtime could cut six weeks off the roofing at an additional cost of only $9,000.

4. Do nothing special until December 1. Then, if December is indeed cold, defer the pouring of the seat gallery supports until the cold wave breaks, schedule permitting, and heat whenever necessary. If a strike occurs, wait until it is over (no other choice) and then expedite all remaining activities. In that case, the duration of any activity could be cut but to no less than one-third of its normal duration. The additional cost per activity for any week which is cut would be $3,000.

5. Do not take any special action, that is, hope and pray that no strike and no cold December occur (no cost).

Appendix: Technical Details of the Stadium

The stadium is an indoor structure with a seating capacity of 20,000. The project begins with clearing the site, an activity that lasts eight weeks. Once the site is clear, the work can start simultaneously on the structure itself and on the field.

The work in the field involves subsurface drainage which lasts eight weeks, followed by filling for the playing field and track. Only with the completion of the filling (14 weeks) can the installation of the artificial playing turf take place, an activity that consumes 12 weeks.

The work on the structure itself starts with excavation followed by the pouring of concrete footings. Each of these activities takes four weeks. Next comes the pouring of supports for seat galleries (12 weeks), followed by erecting pre-cast galleries (13 weeks). The seats can then be poured (4 weeks) and are ready for painting. However, the painting (3 weeks) cannot begin until the dressing rooms are completed (4 weeks). The dressing rooms can be completed only after the roof is erected (8 weeks). The roof must be erected on a steel structure which takes 4 weeks to install. This activity can start only after the concrete footings are poured.

Once the roof is erected, work can start simultaneously on the lights (5 weeks) and on the scoreboard and other facilities (4 weeks). Assume that there are 28 days in February and that February 15 falls on a Monday.

QUESTIONS

1. Analyze the five proposals and make recommendations based on expected costs.

2. What other basis might be used to make a decision besides expected costs? What then might the decision be?

3. What other factors might enter into the decision such as behavioral, organizational, and political?

4. What decision would you make as the president?

9

Resource Allocation

In the previous chapter, we looked at a special type of resource allocation problem, that of allocating time among project tasks, better known as *scheduling.* Now we consider the allocation of physical resources as well. Also, we are concerned with using resources in both individual and in multiple, simultaneous projects. The subject relates directly to the topic of scheduling because altering schedules can alter the need for resources and—just as important—alter the timing of resource needs. At any given time, the firm may have a fixed level of various resources available for its projects. The fixed resources might include labor-hours of various types of special professional or technical services, machine-hours of various types of machinery or instrumentation, hours of computing time, specialized locations, and similar scarce resources needed for accomplishing project tasks. For example, if the need for some resource varies between 70 and 120 percent of resource capacity, then that resource will be under utilized (and wasted if no alternative use exists) at one point in the project and in insufficient supply at another. If the project schedule can be adjusted to smooth the use of the resource, it may be possible to avoid project delay and, at the same time, not saddle the project with the high cost of excess resources allocated "just to make sure."

This chapter addresses situations that involve resource problems. We discuss the trade-offs involved, the difference between allocation to one project and allocation between multiple projects, the relationship between resource loading and leveling, and some of the approaches employed to solve allocation problems, including the Critical Path Method (CPM), constrained resource diagramming and scheduling, Goldratt's "critical chain," and several other approaches to the problem of scheduling under conditions of resource scarcity. We begin with resource conflicts in a single project, and extend the discussion to the multiple project case. Although CPM is not actually a resource allocation method, we include it here because we view time as a resource, and trade-offs between time and other resources are a major problem in resource management. Finally, we note the major impact that current project management software has had on the PM's ability—and willingness—to deal with resource loading and leveling.

Project Management in Practice
Expediting Los Angeles Freeway Repairs after the Earthquake

At 4:31 A.M. on January 17, 1994, a 6.8 magnitude earthquake hit Los Angeles and collapsed large sections of four major freeways, snarling one million commuters in daily gridlock for the indefinite future. Clearly, solutions to this crisis were of the highest priority. Caltrans, the California Department of Transportation, sprung into action with a three-pronged attack. First, they rushed into emergency response, fanning out to conduct visual inspections and close dangerous segments of the roads and freeways. Sec-

ond, they initiated interim traffic management strategies for all closed segments, utilizing parallel streets and old bypass roads to expand their capacity, change their signage and striping, and redirect adjacent traffic including traffic signal timing. Last, they planned for speedy demolition and rebuilding of the damaged portions of the freeways. Time was all-important and Caltrans used every tradeoff available to expedite the repairs which would normally take years to complete.

Damage to be repaired in the earthquake's aftermath.

1. California's governor signed an Emergency Declaration allowing Caltrans to streamline its contracting procedures so that RFPs, bids, and evaluations that usually took four months could be completed in five days.

2. Significant incentives/disincentives were built into the contracts, the incentive depending on the value of the construction under consideration. One firm spent heavily on overtime, extra equipment rentals, and bonuses to keep working 24 hours a day, rain or shine, and came in 74 days ahead of a contractual date of 140 days, thereby earning a $14.8 million bonus that became the talk of the town!

3. All resources of the Federal Highway Administration were made available to work with Caltrans.

4. "Force Account" contracting was employed for immediate selection of sole-source contractors. The contractor then begins work immediately under the direction of a Caltrans Resident Engineer.

5. Major project management processes were initiated including disaster response and an earthquake recovery task force consisting of top executives in local and national governmental agencies.

6. Millions in additional funds were made available through Caltrans' Director, a declaration of a state of emergency by President Clinton, and eventually Congress.

Source: J. B. Baxter, "Responding to the Northridge Earthquake," *PM Network,* November 1994, pp. 13–22.

9.1 CRITICAL PATH METHOD—CRASHING A PROJECT

In Chapter 8, we mentioned that CPM is similar to PERT. Originally, there was one important difference: CPM included a way of relating the project schedule to the level of physical resources allocated to the project. This allowed the PM to trade time for cost, or vice versa. In CPM, two activity times and two costs are specified, if appropriate, for each activity. The first time/cost combination is called *normal,* and the second set is referred to as *crash.* Normal times are "normal" in the same sense as the *m* time estimate of the three times used in PERT. Crash times result from an attempt to expedite the activity by the application of additional resources—for example, overtime, special equipment, and additional staff or material.

It is standard practice with PERT/CPM to estimate activity times under the assumption of resource loadings that are normal. To discuss a time requirement for any task without some assumption about the level of resources devoted to the task makes no real sense. At the same time, it does not make sense to insist on a full list of each and every resource that will be spent on each of the hundreds of activities that may comprise a PERT/CPM network. Clearly, there must have been some prior decision about what resources would be devoted to each task, but much of the decision making is, in practice, relegated to the common methods of standard practice and rules of thumb. The allocation problem requires more careful consideration if it is decided to speed up the accomplishment of tasks and/or the total project. We need to know what additional resources it will take to shorten completion times for the various activities making up the project.

While standard practice and rules of thumb are sufficient for estimating the resource needs for normal progress, careful planning is critical when attempting to expedite (crash) a project. Crash plans that appear feasible when considered activity by activity may incorporate impossible assumptions about resource availability. For example, we may need to crash some activities on the Wild Horse Dam Project. To do so, we have all the labor and materials required, but we will need a tractor-driven crawler crane on the project site not later than the eighth of next month. Unfortunately, our crane will be in Decatur, Illinois, on that date. No local contractor has a suitable crane for hire. Can we hire one in Decatur or Springfield and bring ours here? And so it goes. When we expedite a project, we tend to create problems; and the solution to one problem often creates several more problems that require solutions.

Difficulties notwithstanding, the wise PM adopts the Scout's motto: "Be prepared." If deterministic time estimates are used, and if project deadlines are firm, there is a high likelihood that it will be necessary to crash the last few activities of most projects. Use of the three probabilistic time estimates of PERT may reduce the chance that crashing will be needed because they include identification and estimation of risks and uncertainties that are sometimes forgotten or ignored when making deterministic time estimates. Even so, many things make crashing a way of life on some projects—things such as last-minute changes in client specifications, without permission to extend the project deadline by an appropriate increment, i.e., scope creep. An example of one of the problems that commonly result from the use of deterministic time estimates can be seen in the boxed example that follows.

Architectural Associates, Inc.

Architectural Associates, Inc. (AAI) specializes in large, industrial, retail, and public projects, including shopping malls, manufacturing complexes, convention centers, and the like. The firm is considered to be one of the region's most effective and creative design studios. Their design facility is located in a large, midwestern city and is housed on the second floor of an old building, originally used for light manufacturing. The offices are at one end of the floor, and about two-thirds of the floor space is occupied by the design staff and technicians. The entire space devoted to design is a single, open area and workstations are laid out in such a way as to encourage communication between individuals working on a common project.

A senior executive of AAI noticed that, for the past year or two, the chance of bringing design projects in on time and on budget had decreased to the point where the only uncertainty was how late and how much over budget a project would be. Architectural projects, like computer programming and a few other creative processes, seem to be typified by the need to crash projects at the last minute, but even with the usual crash, AAI was still late and, consequently, over budget.

An examination of the workplace disclosed a large, green felt display board mounted on the wall where it was visible to the entire design staff. The board listed the names of individual designers and technicians vertically, and design contract numbers across the horizontal axis. The times allocated for work on each project by appropriate staff members were shown at the intersections of the rows and columns. The time estimates were made by senior managers, themselves architects, based on their experience. The individuals with direct responsibility for design work generally felt that the time estimates were reasonable.

The work process was studied and the following problem was revealed. If the design of the electrical systems involved in a plan was estimated to take five days, for example, the individual(s) responsible for the work planned it in such a way that it used the five days allowed.

If a problem occurred on the first day, the worker(s) simply stayed late or speeded up work the next day in order to get back on schedule. Problems on the second day, and even on the third and fourth days were handled in the same way, by crashing the work. Problems occurring on the fifth day, however, could not be handled so easily and this part of the project would be late. Because most of the different systems (the mechanicals, landscape, etc.) were designed simultaneously and staffed to require about the same number of days (rather than being sequential),

and because problems were very likely to arise late in the design process of at least one of the systems, the overall design project, which required all tasks to be completed on time, was almost invariably late.

In an attempt to solve the problem, a simple checkmark to show job assignments was substituted for time allocations on the green board. Additionally, senior management made normal, optimistic, and pessimistic time estimates for each task and calculated "TE," also used to help estimate project cost. These estimates were not given to the design staff who were simply told to do the work involved as efficiently and effectively as they could. The result was that the range of task times increased slightly, but the average time required for the various tasks fell somewhat since they were now designed for efficiency rather than X days. Roughly the same number of tasks were accomplished in less than the expected time as tasks that took more than the expected time.

Consider the data in Table 9-1. First, we compute a cost/time slope for each activity that can be expedited (crashed). Slope is defined as follows:

$$\text{slope} = \frac{\text{crash cost} - \text{normal cost}}{\text{crash time} - \text{normal time}}$$

that is, the cost per day of crashing a project. The slope is negative, indicating that as the time required for a project or task is decreased, the cost is increased. Note that activity **c** cannot be expedited. Table 9-2 shows the time/cost slopes for our example.

An implication of this calculation is that activities can be crashed in increments of one day (or one period). Often, this is not true. A given activity may have only two

Table 9-1. An Example of Two-Time CPM

Activity	Precedence	Duration, Days (normal, crash)	Cost (normal, crash)
a	—	3,2	$ 40,80
b	a	2,1	20,80
c	a	2,2	20,20
d*	a	4,1	30,120
e**	b	3,1	10,80

*Partial crashing allowed

**Partial crashing *not* allowed

Table 9-2. Activity Slopes—Cost per Period for Crashing

Activity	Slope ($/day)
a	$40/-1 = -40$
b	$60/-1 = -60$
c	—
d	$90/-3 = -30$
e	-70 (2 days)

or three technically feasible durations. The "dollars per day" slope of such activities is relevant only if the whole crash increment is useful. For example, if an activity can be carried out in either eight days or four days, with no feasible intermediate times, and if an uncrashable parallel path goes critical when the first activity is reduced from eight down to six days, then the last two days (to four days) of time reduction are useless. (Of course, there are times when the PM may expedite activities that have little or no impact on the network's critical time, such as when the resources used must be made available to another project.)

One must remember that crashing a project results in a change of the technology with which something is done. In the language of economics, it is a change in the "production function." At times, crashing may involve a relatively simple decision to increase groups of resources already being used. If the project, for instance, is to dig a ditch of a certain length and depth, we might add units of labor-shovel to shorten the time required. On the other hand, we might replace labor-shovel units with a Ditch Witch. Technological discontinuities in outcomes usually result. Different amounts of labor-shovel input may result in a job that takes anywhere from one to three days. Use of the Ditch Witch may require three hours. There may be no sensible combination of resources that would complete the job in, say, six hours. In some cases, technology cannot be changed, and task duration is fixed. A 30-day toxicity test for a new drug requires 30 days—no more, no less.

Not only do changes in technology tend to produce discontinuities in outcomes, they also tend to produce discontinuities in cost. As the technology is changed to speed a project, the relationship of input cost to activity duration is apt to jump as we move from less to more sophisticated production systems. For an extended treatment of this subject, see Nicholas (1990, Chapter 13).

With CPM, our first task is to develop a table or graph of the cost of a project as a function of the project's various possible completion dates. Starting with the normal schedule for all project activities, crash selected activities, one at a time, to decrease project duration at the minimum additional cost. To crash a project, follow two simple principles: First, focus on the critical path(s) when trying to shorten the duration of a project, with the exception we noted above when a resource used by an activity not on the critical path is needed for another project. Crashing a noncritical activity will not influence project duration. Second, when shortening a project's duration, select the least expensive way to do it.

Given these guides, consider the network shown in Figure 9-1a that was constructed from the data in Table 9-1. It is easier to illustrate the impact of crashing on an activity-on-arrow (AOA) network than on an activity-on-node (AON) network, so

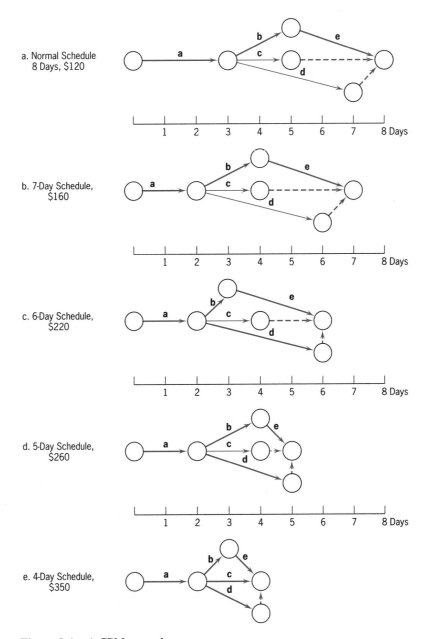

Figure 9-1   A CPM example.

we use that approach here. Also, we use dummy activities in this case not to illustrate precedence but to show time durations and slack on the time axis. As indicated in Tables 9-1 and 9-2, activity **d** can be partially crashed but activity **e** involves a technological discontinuity and must take either three days to complete at $10 or one day at $80. In general, the impact of having such a technological discontinuity is that the best solution for crashing *n* days might not be part of the best solution for crashing *n*

+ 1 days. Rather, it may be best to crash the activity with the technological discontinuity at $n + 1$ days and not crash another activity that could be crashed for n days. This situation is illustrated in the discussion that follows.

The network's critical path is **a-b-e**, the project duration is 8 days, and the normal total cost is $120, as illustrated in the network of Figure 9-1a. The decision about which activities to crash depends on how much we need to reduce the duration of the project. To reduce the total network duration by 1 day, we must reduce the time required by one of the activities along the critical path. Inspecting Table 9-2 to see which critical activity can be reduced at the least cost, we find it is activity **a** which adds $40 to the project's current cost of $120. Activity **b** could be crashed at a cost of $60 or we could even crash **e** 2 days for a cost of $70. Of course, crashing **e** would only shorten the project duration by one day because when **e** is shortened, the path **a-d-dummy**, seven days long, becomes the critical path and does not allow the project to be shortened to 6 days. Of the three options, crashing **a** is the lowest cost and therefore preferable, see Figure 9-1b. Notice that crashing **a** also shortens **a-d-dummy** and **a-c-dummy** by 1 day.

Suppose the project must be crashed by 2 days. What are the options? Reconsidering Table 9-2 and Figure 9-1a, we see that we could crash activity **e** for 2 days ($70), but path **a-d-dummy** (7-days' duration) must also be crashed at least 1 day. We choose **d** ($30/day) because it is cheaper than **a** ($40). The cost of crashing is $100, and the total project cost is $120 + $100 = $220. Alternatively, we could crash **a** and **b**, also for a cost of $100 ($40 + $60). Arbitrarily, we choose the latter option (Figure 9-1c).

Now suppose we wanted to crash the project by 3 days, from the original 8 days down to 5 days. Clearly **e** must be crashed by 2 days, costing $70, and **a** or **b** by a day. We choose **a**, the cheapest, for an additional $40. This leaves **d** to be crashed by 1 day for another $30 resulting in a total crashing cost of $140 and a project cost of $120 + $140 = $260 (Figure 9-1d). Note that we did not crash **b** this time, as we did for 6 days. This is due to the technological discontinuity in activity **e**.

Last, let us consider crashing the project by 4 days down to a project duration of four days. Since we crashed **e**, the technological discontinuity, to reach a 5-day duration, all the remaining activities can be incrementally crashed. Thus, we can simply inspect Figure 9-1d to see what else needs incremental crashing to reduce the project by another day. Notice in Figure 9-1d that **a-b-e** and **a-d-dummy** are both critical paths. Only **b** and **d** can still be crashed so we crash each by 1 day for an additional cost beyond the 5-day schedule of Figure 9-1d of $60 + $30 = $90 for a total project cost of $260 + $90 = $350 (Figure 9-1e). Note that **c** is now critical so *all* activities are critical. Since the critical paths **a-b-e** and **a-c** are at their full extent of crashing, the project duration cannot be further reduced, even though activity **d** could be crashed another day. Thus, Figure 9-1e is *not* the all-crash network, although it equals the all-crash time schedule of four days.

Another approach to CPM would have been starting with an all-crash schedule costing $380 and "relaxing" the activities one at a time. Of course, the activities relaxed first should be those that do not extend the completion date of the project. In our example, this is possible because **d** does not need to be at one day and so could be extended by one day at a cost saving of $30 without altering the project's completion date. This can be seen in Figure 9-1e, where activity **d** is shown taking two days with a project cost of $350. Continuing in this manner and relaxing the most expensive activities first would eventually result in the all-normal schedule of eight days and a cost of $120, as shown in Figure 9-1a.

Whether or not all this crashing is worthwhile is another matter. On the cost side, Figure 9-2 shows the time/cost relationship of crashing the project. On the benefit side, some projects have penalty clauses that make the parent organization liable for late delivery—and sometimes bonuses for early delivery. Starting at the right (all-normal) side of Figure 9-2, note that it becomes increasingly costly to squeeze additional time out of the project. Charts such as the one shown in Figure 9-2 are useful to the PM in exercising control over project duration and cost. They are particularly helpful in dealing with senior managers who may argue for early project completion dates with little understanding of the costs involved. Similarly, such data are of great benefit when clients plead for early delivery. If the client is willing to pay the cost of crashing, or if the firm is willing to subsidize the client, the PM can afford to listen with a sympathetic ear. (While we advise the PM to ignore overhead cost over which he or she has no control, it should be noted that indirect costs are often altered when a project is crashed.)

Some organizations have more than one level of crashing. Table 9-3 illustrates such a case. In this example, the firm has two distinct levels of expediting a project, *rush* and *blitz*. The differences in the precedence relationships between tasks are noted in the table, as are differences in resource commitments. The last two rows of the table show the expected changes in cost and time if the project is expedited.

Fast-Tracking

Another way to expedite a project is known as "fast-tracking." This term has been applied mostly to construction projects, but the technique can be used in many other types of projects. It refers to overlapping the design and build phases of a project. Be-

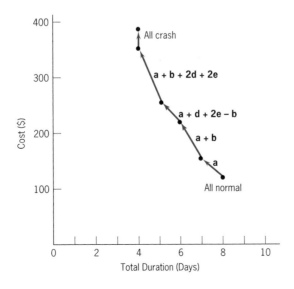

Figure 9-2 CPM cost-duration history.

Table 9-3. Official Pace of a Project

Title	Normal	Rush	Blitz
Approved Project Definition	Full	Some abbreviations from normal pace.	Only as necessary for major management decisions, purchasing and design engineering.
Study of Alternates	Reasonable	Quick study of major profitable items.	Only those not affecting schedule.
Engineering Design	Begins near end of Approved Project Definition.	Begins when Approved Project Definition 50–75% complete.	Concurrently with such approved Project Definition as is done.
Issue Engineering to Field	Allow adequate time for field to plan and purchase field items. Usually ½–2 months lead time between issue and field erection.	Little or no lead time between issue and field erection.	No lead time between issue and field erection.
Purchasing	Begins in latter stages of Approved Project Definition.	Done concurrently with Approved Project Definition. Rush purchase of all long delivery items. Many purchases on "advise price" basis.	Done concurrently with such Approved Project Definition as is done. Rush buy anything that will do job. Overorder and duplicate order to guarantee schedule.
Premium Payments	Negligible	Some to break specific bottlenecks.	As necessary to forestall any possible delays.
Field Crew Strength	Minimum practical or optimum cost.	Large crew with some spot overtime.	Large crew; overtime and/or extra shifts.
Probable Cost Difference Compared with Normal Pace, as a Result of:			
*Design and Development	Base	5–10% more	15% and up, more
*Engineering and Construction costs	Base	3–5% more	10% and up, more
Probable Time	Base	Up to 10% less	Up to 50% less

cause design is usually completed before construction starts, overlapping the two activities will result in shortening the project duration. Beginning to build before design is completed might also, however, result in an increased number of change orders, subsequent loss of productivity, increased cost, and loss of time. Studies of construction projects revealed, however, that while there were more design changes in fast-tracked projects, the total number of project change orders was not significantly different than in similar projects that were not fast-tracked (Ibbs, Lee, and Li, 1998).

Fast-tracking seems to be a reasonable way to expedite construction projects, as well as other types of projects when the early "build" or "carry out" steps are fairly routine and well understood. It is a partial use of the basic concept in phase-gate project management and is dependent on effective feed-back and feed-forward communication.

Solved Problem

Given the following network (time in days):

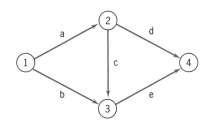

Activity	Crash Time, Cost	Normal Time, Cost	Partial Crashing?
a	3, $60	3, $60	No
b	6, 80	7, 30	Yes
c	2, 90	5, 50	No
d	5, 50	6, 30	No
e	2, 100	4, 40	Yes

Find the lowest cost to complete the project in 10 days.

Answer:
Current time and cost: 12 days and $210

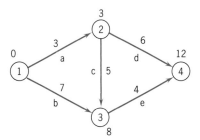

Since the critical path is **a-c-e**, we only initially need consider these three activities:

   a: cannot be crashed
   c: can cut three days at an extra cost of $40 but only results in project completion by day 11, due to **b.** To reach 10 days, cut **b** by one day, total extra cost $90.
   e: can cut **e** by two days for an extra cost of $60 and results in project completion by day 10.

Thus, cut **e** two days at a cost of $60.

9.2   THE RESOURCE ALLOCATION PROBLEM

A shortcoming of the scheduling procedures covered in the previous chapter is that they do not address the issues of resource utilization and availability. They focus on time rather than physical resources. Also, in the discussion that follows it will not be sufficient to refer to resource usage simply as "costs." Instead, we must refer to individual types of labor, specific facilities, kinds of materials, individual pieces of equipment, and other discrete inputs that are relevant to an individual project but are limited in availability. Last, we must not forget that time itself is always a critical resource in project management, one that is unique because it can neither be inventoried nor renewed.

The relationship between progress, time, and resource availability/usage is the major focus of this chapter. Schedules should be evaluated not merely in terms of meeting project milestones, but also in terms of the timing and use of scarce resources. A fundamental measure of the PM's success in project management is the skill with which the trade-offs among performance, time, and cost are managed. It is a continuous process of cost-benefit analysis: "I can shorten this project by a day at a cost of $400. Should I do it?" "If I buy 300 more hours of engineering time, I may be able to improve performance by 2 or 3 percent. Should I do it?" Of course all such estimates are uncertain. What are the risks and how should I deal with them?

Occasionally it is possible that some additional (useful) resources can be added at little or no cost to a project during a crisis period. At other times, some resources in abundant supply may be traded for scarce ones. Most of the time, however, these trades entail additional costs to the organization, so a primary responsibility for the PM is to make do with what is available.

The extreme points of the relationship between time use and resource use are these:

- *Time Limited:* The project must be finished by a certain time, using as few resources as possible. But it is time, not resource usage, that is critical.
- *Resource Limited:* The project must be finished as soon as possible, but without exceeding some specific level of resource usage or some general resource constraint.

The points between these two extremes represent time/resource-use trade-offs. As in Figure 9-2, they specify the times achievable at various resource levels. Equivalently, they specify the resources associated with various completion times. Clearly, the range of time or resource variability is limited.

Occasionally, both time and resources may be limited, but in this case, the specifications cannot also be fixed. If all three variables—time, cost, specifications—are fixed, the system is "overdetermined." The PM has lost all flexibility to perform the trade-offs that are so necessary to the successful completion of projects. Of course, it is possible that all three variables might be fixed at levels that allowed the PM plenty of maneuvering room, but this is most unlikely. Far more likely, our project manager acquaintances tell us, is the case in which senior management assigns budgets, schedules, and specifications without regard for the uncertainties of reality. It is the PM's responsibility, possibly with help from the project's champion, to warn senior management of the impropriety of such restrictions in spite of the chance that a senior manager might respond with "I'll get someone who can . . . !"

On occasion, it may be that one or more tasks in a project are *system-constrained.* A system-constrained task requires a fixed amount of time and known quantities of resources. Some industrial processes—heat treating, for instance—are system-constrained. The material must "cook" for a specified time to achieve the desired effect. More or less "cooking" will not help. When dealing with a system-constrained task or project, no trade-offs are possible. The only matter of interest in these cases is to make sure that the required resources are available when needed.

In the following sections, we discuss approaches for understanding and using these relationships in various project situations.

9.3 RESOURCE LOADING

Resource loading describes the amounts of individual resources an existing schedule requires during specific time periods. Therefore, it is irrelevant whether we are considering a single work unit or several projects; the loads (requirements) of each resource type are simply listed as a function of time period. Resource loading gives a general understanding of the demands a project or set of projects will make on a firm's resources. It is an excellent guide for early, rough project planning. Obviously, it is also a first step in attempting to reduce excessive demands on certain resources, regardless of the specific technique used to reduce the demands. Again, we caution the PM to recognize that the use of resources on a project is often nonlinear. Much of the project management software does not recognize this fact (Gilyutin, 1993).

Given an action plan, deriving a resource-loading document is not difficult. Figure 5-3 (Chapter 5, Section 5-3) shows part of an action plan for a "Career Day" at a college. The part of the plan shown lists the personnel resources needed for each activity. (The hours required are included in the plan, but were not printed in Figure 5-3.) Utilizing data in the plan, MSP generated Figure 9-3, the resource usage calendar. Each of the human resources used in the project is listed, followed by the name of the activities in which the resource is used. The total hours of work for each resource called for by the action plan are shown together with the amount planned for each activity. The schedule for resource loading is derived and the loading is then shown for each resource for each week (or day or month) of the project.

An examination of Figure 9-3 shows that the secretary is overloaded during late May and early June. Assuming that there is only one secretary, he or she must work 17+ hours per day of a 7-day week (or 24 hours per 5-day week). This is apt to try the patience of the most determined and loyal employee. Graduate assistants are certainly considered slaves by their faculty masters, but are usually indentured for only 20 hours per week of servitude. Unless there are four GAs, the project will have problems. It is the job of the PM to deal with these problems, either by adding people or by changing the schedule in such a way that the demand for resources does not exceed resource capacities.

Because the project action plan is the source of information on activity precedences, durations, and resources requirements, it is the primary input for both the project schedule and its budget. The action plan links the schedule directly to specific demands for resources. Thus, the PERT/CPM network technique can be modified to generate time-phased resource requirements. A Gantt chart could be adapted, but the PERT/CPM AOA diagram, particularly if modified to illustrate slacks as in Figure 9-1, will be helpful in the analysis used for resource leveling. Let us illustrate with the PERT/CPM network used as an example in the previous chapter, but converted to an AOA diagram. The AOA network (from Table 8-2) is illustrated in Figure 9-4, and resource usage is illustrated for two hypothetical resources, A and B, on the arcs. The expected activity time is shown above the arc, and resource usage is shown in brackets just below the arc, with the use of A shown first and B second—e.g., [5, 3] would mean that five units of A and three units of B would be used on the activity represented by the arc. Figure 9-5 shows the "calendarized" PERT/CPM diagram, similar

			May					June					July			
ID	Resource Name	Work	25	2	9	16	23	30	6	13	20	27	4	11	18	25
1	**Secretary**	**1,020 hrs**	24h	40h	40h	40h	88h	120h	102h	40h	40h	40h	40h	40h	40h	40h
	Print forms	240 hrs														
	Gather college particulars	160 hrs	24h	40h	40h	40h	16h									
	Print programs	240 hrs					24h	40h	40h	40h	40h	40h	16h			
	Advertise in college paper	200 hrs					24h	40h	36h	0h	0h	0h	24h	40h	36h	
	Organize posters	180 hrs					24h	40h	26h	0h	0h	0h	0h	0h	4h	40h
2	**Program Manager**	**1,440 hrs**	40h	40h	40h	16h	24h	40h	40h	40h	16h					
	Contact organizations	600 hrs	16h													
	Select guest speaker	560 hrs														
	Organize food	120 hrs	24h	40h	40h	16h										
	Contact faculty	60 hrs					24h	36h								
	Arrange facility for event	100 hrs						4h	40h	40h	16h					
3	**Office Manager**	**180 hrs**	24h	40h	40h	40h	16h				20h					
	Collect display information	160 hrs	24h	40h	40h	40h	16h									
	Transport materials	20 hrs									20h					
4	**Graduate Assistant**	**1,140 hrs**	24h	40h	40h	40h	64h	80h	80h	56h	40h	40h	16h			
	Print participants' certificates	320 hrs														
	Organize refreshments	280 hrs	24h	40h	40h	40h	40h	40h	40h	16h						
	Send invitations	80 hrs														
	Organize gift certificates	220 hrs														
	Arrange banner	200 hrs					24h	40h	40h	40h	40h	16h				
	Class announcements	40 hrs											24h	16h		
5	**Director**	**400 hrs**	24h	40h	40h	40h	40h	40h	40h	40h	40h	40h	16h			
	Organize liquor	400 hrs	24h	40h	40h	40h	40h	40h	40h	40h	40h	40h	16h			

Figure 9-3 Resource usage calendar for the Career Day Project.

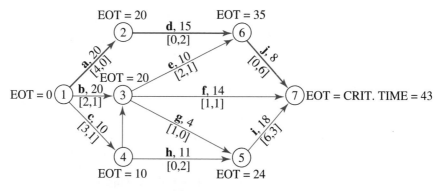

Figure 9-4 The AOA network of Table 8-2.

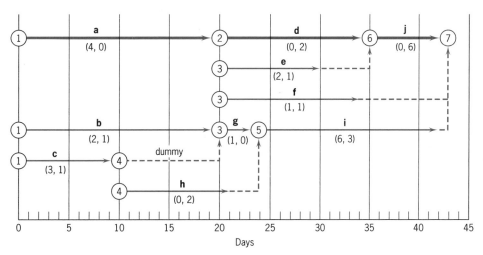

Figure 9-5   Modified PERT/CPM AOA diagram showing resource usage (from Figure 9-4).

to the familiar Gantt chart. Resource demands can now be summed by time period across all activities.

The loading diagram for resource A is illustrated in Figure 9-6a, and that for resource B in Figure 9-6b. The loads are erratic and vary substantially over the duration of the project. Resource A, used in tasks **a**, **b**, and **c**, has a high initial demand that drops through the middle of the project and then climbs again. Resource B, on the other hand, has low initial use but increases as the project develops. The PM must be aware of the ebbs and flows of usage for each input resource throughout the life of the project. It is the PM's responsibility to ensure that the required resources, in the required amounts, are available when and where they are needed. In the next three sections, we will discuss how to meet this responsibility.

9.4   RESOURCE LEVELING

In the preceding example, we noted that the project began with the heavy use of resource A, used smaller amounts during the middle of the project, and then continued with rising usage during the project's latter stages. Usage of B started low and rose throughout the project's life. Large fluctuations in the required loads for various resources are a normal occurrence—and are undesirable from the PM's point of view. Resource leveling aims to minimize the period-by-period variations in resource loading *by shifting tasks within their slack allowances.* The purpose is to create a smoother distribution of resource usage.

There are several advantages to smoother resource usage. First, much less hands-on management is required if the use of a given resource is nearly constant over its period of use. The PM can arrange to have the resource available when needed, can have the supplier furnish constant amounts, and can arrange for a backup supplier if advisable. Moreover, the PM can do this with little error. Second, if resource usage is level, the PM may be able to use a "just-in-time" inventory policy without much

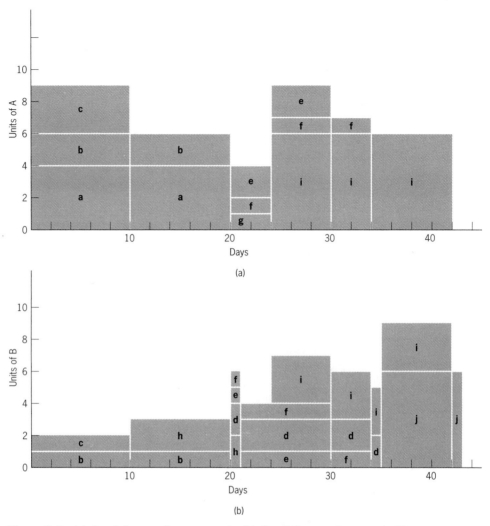

Figure 9-6   (a): Load diagram for resource A. (b): Load diagram for resource B.

worry that the quantity delivered will be wrong. If the resource being leveled is people, leveling improves morale and results in fewer problems in the personnel and payroll offices because of increasing and decreasing labor levels.

Not only are there managerial implications to resource leveling, there are also important cost implications. When resources are leveled, the associated costs also tend to be leveled. If resource use increases as time goes by, and if resources are shifted closer to the present by leveling, costs will be shifted in the same way. The opposite is true, of course, if resource usage is shifted to the future. Perhaps most important from a cost perspective is leveling employment throughout a project or task. For most organizations, the costs of hiring and layoff are quite significant. It is often less expensive to level labor requirements in order to avoid hiring and layoff, even if it means some extra wages will be paid. In any case, the PM must be aware of the cash flows associated with the project and of the means of shifting them in ways that are useful to the parent firm.

The basic procedure for resource leveling is straightforward. For example, consider the simple AOA network shown in Figure 9-7a. The activity time is shown above the arc, and resource usage (one resource, workers) is in brackets below the

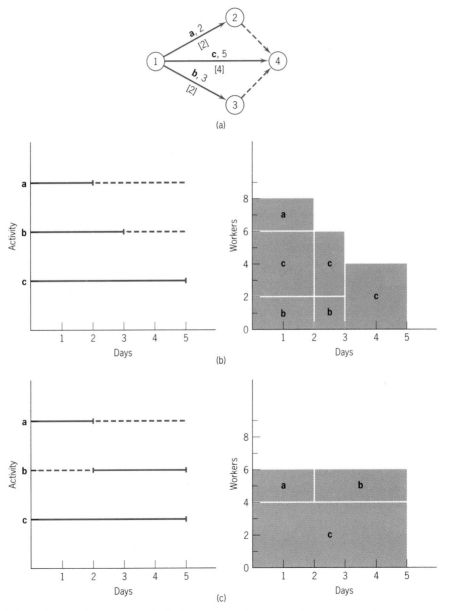

Figure 9-7 a: The network. b: Before resource leveling. c: After resource leveling.

arc. Activities **a**, **b**, and **c** follow event 1, and all must precede event 4. Activity **a** requires two workers and takes two days, **b** requires two workers and takes 3 days, and **c** needs 4 workers and 5 days. (We addressed the problem of trade-offs between labor and activity time in the first section of this chapter.) If all these tasks are begun on their early start dates, the resource loading diagram appears as shown in Figure 9-7b, steps of decreasing labor demand varying from eight workers to four workers. If, however, task **b** is delayed for 2 days, the full length of its slack in this particular case, the resource loading diagram is smoothed, as shown in Figure 9-7c. The same result would have occurred if **b** were started as early as possible and task **a** were delayed until day 3.

Resource leveling is a procedure that can be used for almost all projects, whether or not resources are constrained. If the network is not too large and there are only a few resources, the leveling process can be done manually. For larger networks and multiple resources, resource leveling becomes extremely complex, far beyond the power of manual solutions. Fortunately, a number of computer programs can handle most leveling problems efficiently (discussed in Chapter 10).

Reconsider the load diagrams of Figures 9-6a and b. Assume it is desired to smooth the loading of resource B, which is particularly jagged. both activities **e** and **f** can be delayed (**e** has 5 days of slack and **f** has 9). If we delay both for one day, we remove the peak on day 20 without increasing any of the other peaks (see Figure 9-8b). If we do this, however, it also alters the use of resource A and deepens the "valley" on day 20 (see Figure 9-8a). If we further delay **f** another 7 days in order to level the use of A toward the end of the project, we would deepen the valley between days 20 and 24, and the resultant use of A would be as shown by the dotted lines on Figure 9-8a. Activity **f** would begin on day 28 (and would become critical). The effect on the usage of B is easy to see (Figure 9-8b). The change would lower usage by one unit beginning on day 21 (remember that we have already delayed **f** one day), and increase usage by one unit beginning on day 35, continuing to the end of the project. This action increases peak use of B from nine to ten units.

It is important to emphasize that if the network under consideration is more complex and the number of resources to be leveled is realistically large, a manual leveling process is out of the question. Computer-aided leveling is not only mandatory, it is also helpful because it allows the PM to experiment with various patterns of resource usage through simulation.

In the next section, we raise the most general problem of minimizing resource usage while still achieving various completion dates—or the inverse problem, minimizing completion times while operating with specified limits on resources.

Resource Loading/Leveling and Uncertainty

Figure 9-9 is a resource loading chart for a software engineering group in a large company, constructed by importing MSP resource loading information into an Excel spreadsheet and then displaying it graphically. There are 21 engineers in the group, nominally scheduled to work 40 hours a week, resulting in a weekly capacity of

$$21 \times 40 = 840 \text{ labor-hours each week.}$$

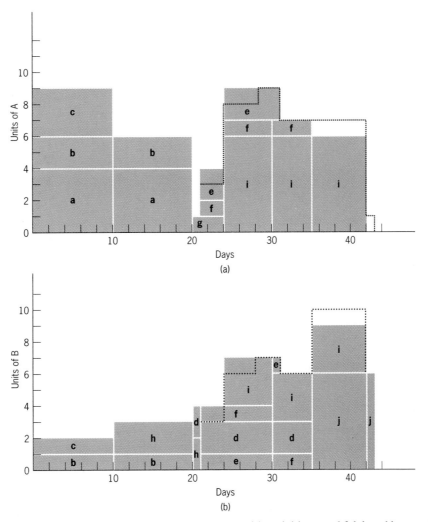

Figure 9-8 (a): Load diagram for resource A with activities e and f delayed by one day each. (b): Load diagram for resource B with activities e and f delayed by one day each.

The graph covers February through September, a period of 34 weeks. Thus, the total engineering capacity for the period shown is

$$34 \times 840 = 28,560 \text{ labor-hours.}$$

As shown, the total labor-hours required for the period is 28,282, so we see that there is excess capacity, a nice situation normally. However, there are two problems. As is clear in the loading chart, the demand for engineering labor is not evenly distributed throughout the period, hitting a major peak in the late March–early April time frame and then a few more times later in the period. This is counterbalanced by weeks

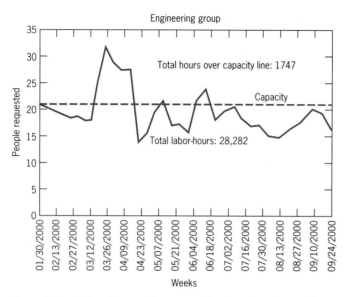

Figure 9-9 Thirty-four-week resource loading chart for a software engineering group.

throughout the time period where less-than-full capacity is required; however, this is not helpful since the engineers are employed for 40-hour weeks so the undercapacity times are wasted.

There are some alternatives used to address these kinds of situations. First, we can try to level the demand, moving some of it forward and some back, depending on our flexibility in this production environment. Second, we can try to alter the supply of engineering hours, asking the engineers to trade off time between periods of overcapacity and periods of undercapacity. We might expend additional resources, bringing in contract engineers to handle the overload period, or subcontract the workload, but such suggestions would almost certainly be rejected by senior management because of security worries by our clients. Perhaps it would be cheaper to let the work be delayed a few weeks and try to catch up later. We will identify other ways of resolving this element of uneven demand a bit later.

But there is another problem with this situation, which is that we try not to schedule a scarce resource for more than 85–90 percent capacity. The reason is due to disruptions, emergencies, maintenance requirements, personnel issues, and simple inefficiency of any resource that is scheduled for full production over an extended time period. Let us consider the case of the engineers, in particular. Over this 34-week period that includes the summer, there will probably be most of the scheduled 2-week vacations (if not longer). If 15 engineers are scheduled for vacations during this period, that will remove 15×2 weeks $\times 40 = 1200$ labor-hours from the capacity. In addition, there are three national holidays during this period: Memorial Day, the Fourth of July, and Labor Day, resulting in a further loss of $21 \times 3 \times 8$ hours $= 504$ hours.

These two scheduled sets of events have now reduced our capacity to 28,560 – 1200 – 504 = 26,856 labor-hours, 5 percent less than the demand over the period.

What about unscheduled events and disruptions? Illnesses will surely occur in this long time frame. Furthermore, will the facilities, equipment, materials, and the work itself be ready for the engineers when they become free to move to the next task? Will everything show up precisely when it is needed? Will there be no delays in the work preceding what the engineers are expected to do? Will there be no scope changes in the preceding work, thus delaying the succeeding tasks scheduled for the engineers? As you can see, we expect there to be "unexpected" delays for multiple reasons, hence the admonition to never schedule a resource for more than 85–90 percent of its capacity.

But what about manufacturing situations in which machines and processes are commonly run near capacity for extended durations? These situations are not projects but rather routine production environments. Thus, planning is extensive, maintenance is carefully scheduled, experience in what can go wrong is abundant, resources are carefully controlled and monitored, and so on. That is not the situation of projects, which by definition are nonroutine. Depending on experience, when planning routine types of manufacturing processes, we try to have line capacity just slightly in excess of our average demand for the line's output. This policy is a sure course to disaster when applied to project management.

Now, what do we do about our software engineers? As it happens, some groups of professionals, such as engineers, are employed with the understanding that there will be periods of overtime required (for which they are generally not paid) and periods when things will be slack and they are relatively free to come and go as they please. In reality, engineers often work 50 to 60 hours per week for extended periods, and if a prolonged period of insufficient work is available at the company, management may lay off some engineers. As can be seen, a workweek of, say, 55 hours × 21 engineers × 34 weeks × 85 percent capacity = 33,379 labor-hours, more than sufficient for the 28,282 labor-hours required—but not much more than sufficient.

9.5   CONSTRAINED RESOURCE SCHEDULING

There are two fundamental approaches to constrained allocation problems: heuristics and optimization models. Heuristic approaches employ rules of thumb that have been found to work reasonably well in similar situations. They seek better solutions. Optimization approaches seek the best solutions but are far more limited in their ability to handle complex situations and large problems. We will discuss each separately.

Most PC software designed for project management will level resources and solve the problems of overscheduling resources. They require priority rules to establish which activities take precedence. The priority rules the programs use vary somewhat, but most packages offer a choice. For example, reconsider the videotape project used to demonstrate MSP output forms in Chapter 8. We can include the resource requirement for each activity directly on the Gantt chart, as in Figure 9-10, but we can also show separate diagrams that illustrate the demand or "load" for each of the re-

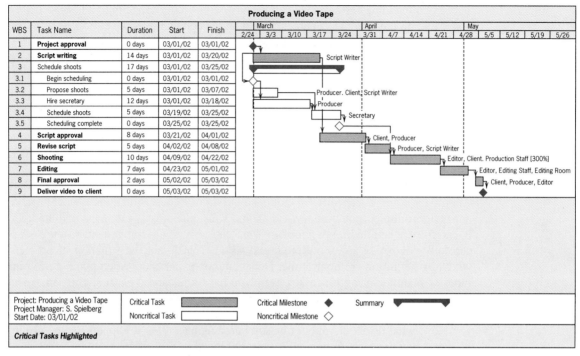

Figure 9-10   MSP Gantt chart of video tape project showing resource needs.

sources as in Figure 9-11. Figures 9-11 and 9-12 show a resource conflict for the producer and the resource leveling solution. Note the changes in the scheduled finish dates for the leveled solution.

Heuristic Methods

Heuristic approaches to constrained resource scheduling problems are in wide, general use for a number of reasons. First, they are the only feasible methods of attacking the large, nonlinear, complex problems that tend to occur in the real world of project management. Second, while the schedules that heuristics generate may not be optimal, they are usually quite good—certainly good enough for most purposes. Commercially available computer programs handle large problems and have had considerable use in industry. Further, modern simulation techniques allow the PM to develop many different schedules quickly and to determine which, if any, are significantly better than current practice. If a reasonable number of simulation runs fail to produce significant improvement, the PM can feel fairly confident that the existing solution is a good one.

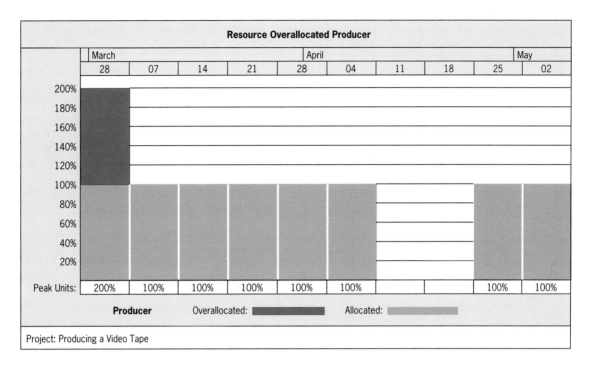

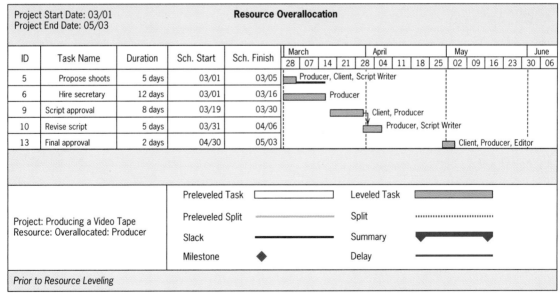

Figure 9-11 MSP load diagram showing resource conflict (producer used beyond capacity).

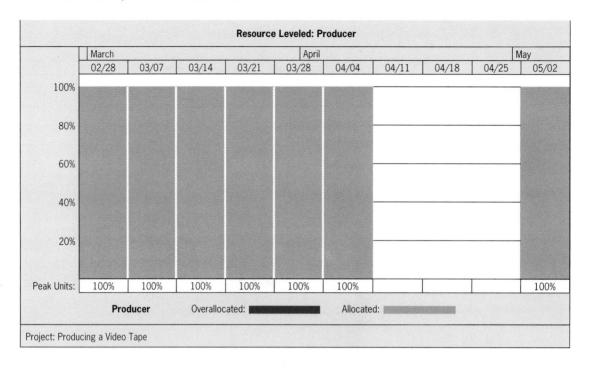

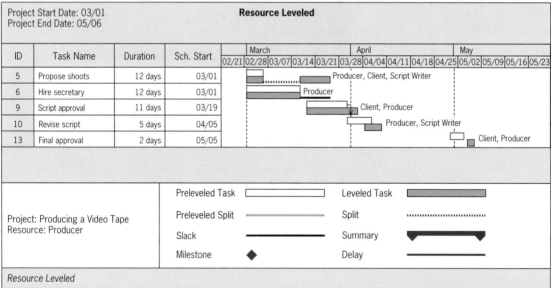

Figure 9-12 MSP rescheduling to level producer resource usage without exceeding capacity.

Most heuristic solution methods start with the PERT/CPM schedule and analyze resource usage period by period, resource by resource. In a period when the available supply of a resource is exceeded, the heuristic examines the tasks in that period and allocates the scarce resource to them sequentially, according to some priority rule. The major difference among the heuristics is in the priority rules they use. Remember that the *technological necessities always take precedence.* Some of the most common priority rules are:

As Soon as Possible The default rule for scheduling. This provides the general solution for critical path and time.

As Late as Possible all activities are scheduled as late as possible without delaying the project. The usual purpose of this heuristic is to defer cash outflows as long as possible.

Shortest Task First Tasks are ordered in terms of duration, with the shortest first. In general, this rule will maximize the number of tasks that can be completed by a system during some time period.

Most Resources First Activities are ordered by use of a specific resource, with the largest user heading the list. The assumption behind this rule is that more important tasks usually place a higher demand on scarce resources.

Minimum Slack First This heuristic orders activities by the amount of slack, least slack going first. (It is common, when using this rule, to break ties by using the shortest-task-first rule.)

Most Critical Followers Tasks are arranged by number of critical activities following them. The ones with the greatest number of critical followers go first.

Most Successors This is the same as the previous rule, except that all followers, not merely critical ones, are counted.

Arbitrary Priorities are assigned to activities according to some rule not associated with task length, slack, or resource requirements. Such rules might be that tasks on projects of higher value to the parent organization (or for the project of a favored customer) are taken before those of lower value.

There are many such priority rules employed in scheduling heuristics. From time to time researchers subject several of the more popular of the PC-based project management application programs to tests of their ability to handle such tasks as allocating constrained resources and resource leveling. They test several heuristics with each program and compare the results with optimal solutions. The results are published (e.g., Farid and Manoharan, 1996; Johnson, 1992) but are fairly short-lived, often not surviving later releases of the several software packages.

Most priority rules are simple adaptations and variations of the heuristics used for the traditional "job shop scheduling" problem of production/operations management, a problem that has much in common with multiproject scheduling and resource allocation. Also, most heuristics use a combination of rules—a primary rule, with a secondary rule used to break ties.

Several researchers (Fendley, 1968; Kurtulus and Davis, 1982; and Kurtulus and Narula, 1985) have conducted tests of the more commonly used schedule priority rules. Although their findings vary somewhat because of slightly different assumptions, the minimum slack first rule was found to be best or near-best quite often and rarely caused poor performance. It usually resulted in the minimum amount of project schedule slippage, the best utilization of facilities, and the minimum total system occupancy time.

As the scheduling heuristic operates, one of two events will result. The routine runs out of activities (for the current period) before it runs out of the resources, or it runs out of resources before all activities have been scheduled. (While it is theoretically possible for the supply of resources to be precisely equal to the demand for such resources, even the most careful planning rarely produces such a tidy result.) If the former occurs, the excess resources are left idle, assigned elsewhere in the organization as needed during the current period, or applied to future tasks required by the project—always within the constraints imposed by the proper precedence relationships. If one or more resources are exhausted, however, activities requiring those resources are slowed or delayed until the next period when resources can be reallocated.

If the minimum slack first rule is used, resources would be devoted to critical or nearly critical activities, delaying those with greater slack. Delay of an activity uses some of its slack, so the activity will have a better chance of receiving resources in the next allocation. Repeated delays move the activity higher and higher on the priority list. We consider later what to do in the potentially catastrophic event that we run out of resources before all critical activities have been scheduled.

The heuristic procedure just described is probably the most common. There are, however, other heuristic procedures that work in a similar manner. One works in reverse and schedules jobs from the end of the project instead of from its beginning. Activities that just precede the project finish are scheduled to be completed just barely within their latest finish times. Then, the next-to-last tasks are considered, and so on. The purpose of this approach is to leave as much flexibility as possible for activities that will be difficult to schedule in the middle and early portions of the project. This logic seems to rest on the idea that flexibility early in the project gives the best chance of completing early and middle activities on time and within budget, thereby improving the chances of being on time and within budget at the ending activities.

Other heuristics use the *branch and bound* approach. They generate a wide variety of solutions, discard those that are not feasible and others that are feasible but poor solutions. This is done by a *tree search* that prunes infeasible solutions and poor solutions when other feasible solutions dominate them. In this way, the heuristic narrows the region in which good, feasible solutions may be found. If the "tree" is not too large, this approach can locate optimal solutions, but more computer search time will be required. See Turban and Meredith (1994) for further details.

These heuristics are usually embedded in a computer simulation package that describes what will happen to the project(s) if certain schedules or priority rules are followed. A number of different priority rules can be tried in the simulation in order to derive a set of possible solutions. Simulation is a powerful tool and can also handle unusual project situations. Consider, for example, the following problem in *resource contouring*.

Given the network and resource demands shown in Figure 9-13, find the best

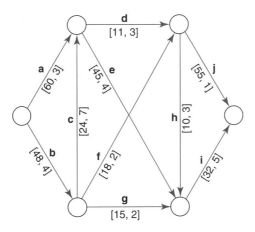

Figure 9-13   Network for resource load simulation. *Note:* The numbers on the arcs represent, respectively, worker-days, machines per day.

schedule using a constant crew size. Each day of delay beyond 15 days incurs a penalty of $1,000. Workers cost $100 per day, and machines cost $50 per day. Workers are interchangeable, as are machines. Task completion times vary directly with the number of workers, and partial work days are acceptable. The critical time for the project is 15 days, given the resource usage shown in Figure 9-13. (There are other jobs in the system waiting to be done.)

Figure 9-13 lists the total worker-days and machines per day normally required by each activity (below the activity arc). Because activity times are proportional to worker demands, path **b-c-e-i** is most demanding and this path uses 149 worker-days.

The fact that completion times vary with the number of workers means that activity **a** could be completed in 6 days with ten workers or in 10 days with six workers. Applying some logic and trying to avoid the penalty, which is far in excess of the cost of additional resources, we can add up the total worker-days required on all activities, obtaining 319. Dividing this by the 15 days needed to complete the project results in an average requirement of slightly more than 21 workers—say, 22. How should they be allocated to the activities? Figure 9-14 shows one way, arbitrarily determined. Workers are shown above the "days" axis and machines below. We have 22 workers at $100 per day for 15 days ($33,000) and 128.5 machine days at $50 per day ($6,425). The total cost of this particular solution is $39,425.

The "critical path" illustrated in Figure 9-14 is **a-g-i,** which takes 15 days. However, inspecting Figure 9-13, activity **g** does not follow activity **a** so how can this be a true "critical path"? The reason is when resources are shared among activities, the resources for one activity may not be available because an earlier activity (though not necessarily a predecessor) is still using them. Thus, in theory, **g** (and **f**, too) could have started at day 4 when **b** was completed but there were no workers available.

The availability of workers is indicated by the shaded regions in Figure 9-14. Thus, if we use the six idle workers shown between activities **f** and **h** (for 0.7 days, thereby releasing 4.2 worker-days) to reduce the length of activity **g**, we could reduce it by 4.2 worker-days/3 workers = 1.4 days, finishing now at 9.6 days. However, path **b-c-d-h** would then become critical at 10.8 days, resulting in only 0.2 days of overall project reduction. Using the 4.2 worker-days to reduce not only activity **g** but also

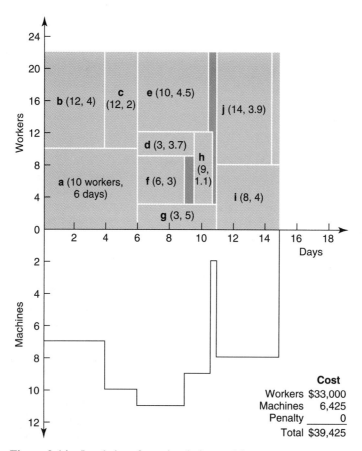

Figure 9-14   Load chart for a simulation problem.

activities **d** and **e** would allow us to complete all of activities **e, h,** and **g** at day 10.32, thereby reducing the project time by 0.68 days. The idle labor following activity **j** could be used similarly to reduce activity **i**.

After all reallocations, it is important to recalculate the demand for machines since this will also change. Note that we have assumed that machine use depends only on time and is independent of the number of workers: if this is not the case, then a different set of calculations is required to determine the machine requirements. Finally, there may be limitations on the total number of workers or machines that are available at any one time and this can affect the solution. For example, how would the solution change if only 20 workers were available?

The purpose of reassignments is not to decrease labor cost in the project. This is fixed by the base technology implied by the worker/machine usage data. The reassignments do, however, shorten the project duration and make the resources available for other work sooner than expected. If the trade-offs are among resources, for instance, trading more labor for fewer machines or more machines for less material input, the problem is handled in the same way. Always, however, the technology itself constrains what is possible. The Chinese build roads in the mountains by using labor. In the United States machines are used. Both nations exercise an option because either labor-intensive or machine-intensive technology is feasible. The ancient Israelites, however, could not substitute labor for straw in making bricks: No straw, no bricks.

On small networks with simple interrelationships among the resources, it is not difficult to perform these resource trade-offs by hand. But for networks of a realistic size, a computer is clearly required. If the problem is programmed for computer solution, many different solutions and their associated costs can be calculated. But, as with heuristics, simulation does not guarantee an optimal, or even feasible, solution. It can only test those solutions fed into it.

Another heuristic procedure for leveling resource loads is based on the concept of minimizing the sum of the squares of the resource requirements in each period. That is, the smooth use of a resource over a set of periods will give a smaller sum of squares than the erratic use of the resource that averages out to the same amount as the smooth use. This approach, called *Burgess's method,* was applied by Woodworth and Willie (1975) to a multiproject situation involving a number of resources. The method was applied to each resource sequentially, starting with the most critical resource.

In the past several years, a wide range of attacks have been made on the problems of resource allocation and scheduling when resources are constrained. Some of these depend on sophisticated mathematical and/or graphical tools and may be quite powerful in what they can do (e.g., Kumar and Ganesh, 1998). Tukel (1996) found that the minimum slack first rule and the longest path first rule both worked well for scheduling resource constrained problems when some level of rework was required. Morse, Mcintosh, and Whitehouse (1996) examined combinations of several heuristics for scheduling when there were some constrained resources. Badiru's critical resource diagramming allows the construction of a network that shows the relationships of the various resources used on a project; for example, if the use of resource 1 precedes the use of resource 2, an arrow connects the node representing resource 1 with the node representing resource 2. Given some resource availabilities, the critical resources can be found, together with project duration that depends on the availability of the critical resource(s) (Badiru, 1992). The effect of learning curves on resource usage has also been included (Badiru, 1995). Finally, simulation has been used to solve resource-constrained scheduling problems; see Gemmill and Tsai (1997) for an interesting approach.

Next, we briefly discuss some optimizing approaches to the constrained resource scheduling problem.

Optimizing Methods

The methods to find an optimal solution to the constrained resource scheduling problem fall into two categories: mathematical programming (linear programming for the most part) and enumeration. In the 1960s, the power of LP improved from being able to handle three resources and 15 activities to four resources and 55 activities. But even with this capacity, LP is usually not feasible for reasonably large projects where there may be a dozen resources and thousands of activities. (See Davis and Patterson, 1975 for more detail.)

In the late 1960s and early 1970s, limited enumeration techniques were applied to the constrained resource problem with more success. Tree search and branch and bound methods (Stinson, Davis, and Khumawala, 1978) were devised to handle up to five resources and perhaps 200 activities. Advances in LP techniques now allow LP to be used on large constrained resource scheduling problems.

Other approaches have combined programming and enumeration methods. Patterson and Huber (1974), for example, employ an integer programming approach combined with a minimum bounding procedure to reduce the computation time for minimizing project duration. Similarly, Talbot (1980) uses integer programming and implicit enumeration to formulate and solve problems where the completion time is a function of the resources allocated to the project.

One problem with even the newer combination of approaches is that the characteristics of problems that can be usefully addressed with these methods is still largely unknown. Why various methods will work on one problem and not on a similar problem is still being researched.

Project Management in Practice
Benefits of Resource Constraining at Pennsylvania Electric

Pennsylvania Electric Company, headquartered in Johnstown, PA, operates generating facilities with a capacity of 6950 megawatts to serve 547,000 customers over an area of 17,600 square miles. The Generation Division Planning Group is responsible for planning all maintenance and capital projects. In the early 1980s, the group used a manual method of planning with hand-drawn charts. The planning process has now been computerized, which is faster, allows "what-if" analyses, and controls more than just the previously monitored critical path. In bringing the planning process in-house, the group also saved $100,000 a year in service fees from an outside engineering firm who was planning their construction activities.

A special feature of the computerized system is its resource constraining module which establishes labor requirements across all jobs. In the pilot program to test the new software, $300,000 was saved when it was discovered that a job could be done with 40 percent fewer mechanics than normally used and still complete the job on time. In another application, it was found that a turbine disassembly and inspection could be added to the task list without delaying the project or exceeding the project budget.

After worker-hours are input to the program by activity, actual progress is monitored (see figure) and schedule and cost deviations are highlighted for management attention. This allows management to make adjustments to recover the schedule, slow the project down, or acquire more funds to get the project back on

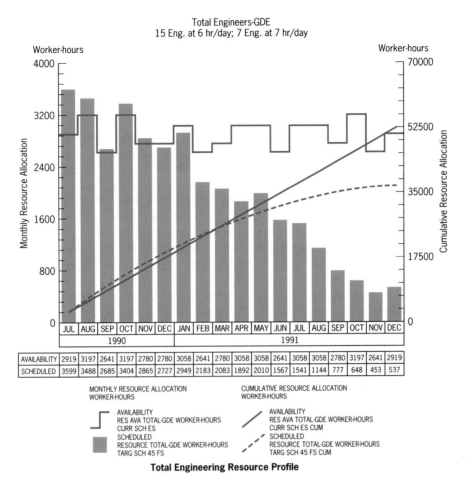

Total Engineers-GDE
15 Eng. at 6 hr/day; 7 Eng. at 7 hr/day

	JUL	AUG	SEP	OCT	NOV	DEC	JAN	FEB	MAR	APR	MAY	JUN	JUL	AUG	SEP	OCT	NOV	DEC
AVAILABILITY	2919	3197	2641	3197	2780	2780	3058	2641	2780	3058	3058	2641	3058	3058	2780	3197	2641	2919
SCHEDULED	3599	3488	2685	3404	2865	2727	2949	2183	2083	1892	2010	1567	1541	1144	777	648	453	537

MONTHLY RESOURCE ALLOCATION
WORKER-HOURS

CUMULATIVE RESOURCE ALLOCATION
WORKER-HOURS

AVAILABILITY
RES AVA TOTAL-GDE WORKER-HOURS
CURR SCH ES

SCHEDULED
RESOURCE TOTAL-GDE WORKER-HOURS
TARG SCH 45 FS

AVAILABILITY
RES AVA TOTAL-GDE WORKER-HOURS
CURR SCH ES CUM

SCHEDULED
RESOURCE TOTAL-GDE WORKER-HOURS
TARG SCH 45 FS CUM

Total Engineering Resource Profile

schedule. Obviously, there are always some emergencies outside the plan that must be handled on an exception basis. But with this software, management knows what effect different actions will have on the basic plan and can thereby make the best use of available resources to handle the emergency with minimal impact on the plan.

Source: A. J. Cantanese, "At Penelec, Project Management is a Way of Life," *Project Management Journal,* December 1990.

9.6 MULTIPROJECT SCHEDULING AND RESOURCE ALLOCATION

In Chapter 2, we described a method for strategically selecting the best set of projects that would help achieve the organization's strategic goals. This method, called the Project Portfolio Process, ended with a set of high-priority projects that could be adequately funded by the organization. However, the process did not consider the scheduling and allocation of limited, individual critical resources among the projects. In some cases, a particular machine, or skilled employee may be needed on two or more projects at the same time. This involves multiproject scheduling and resource allocation.

Scheduling and allocating resources to multiple projects are much more complicated than for the single-project case. The most common approach is to treat the several projects as if they were each elements of a single large project. (A more detailed explanation is given below when we consider a specific multiproject scheduling heuristic.) Another way of attacking the problem is to consider all projects as completely independent; see Kurtulus and Davis (1982) and Kurtulus and Narula (1985), for example. As Kurtulus and Davis (1982) show, these two approaches lead to different scheduling and allocation outcomes. For either approach, the conceptual basis for scheduling and allocating resources is essentially the same.

There are several projects, each with its own set of activities, due dates, and resource requirements. In addition, the penalties for not meeting time, cost, and performance goals for the several projects may differ. Usually, the multiproject problem involves determining how to allocate resources to, and set a completion time for, a new project that is added to an existing set of ongoing projects. This requires the development of an efficient, dynamic multiproject scheduling system.

To describe such a system properly, standards are needed by which to measure scheduling effectiveness. Three important parameters affected by project scheduling are: (1) schedule slippage, (2) resource utilization, and (3) in-process inventory. The organization (or the PM) must select the criterion most appropriate for its situation.

Schedule slippage, often considered the most important of the criteria, is the time past a project's due date or delivery date when the project is completed. Slippage may well result in penalty costs that reduce profits. Further, slippage of one project may have a ripple effect, causing other projects to slip. Indeed, expediting a project in order to prevent slippage may, and usually does, disturb the overall organization to the point where slippage due to resource shortages may then be caused in other projects. The loss of goodwill when a project slips and deliveries are late is important to all producers. As is the case with many firms, Grumman Aircraft, purchased by the Northrup Corporation in 1994, jealously guards its reputation for on-time delivery. During a project to install a new machine control system on a production line, Grumman insisted that the project be designed to minimize disturbance to operations in the affected plant and avoid late shipments. This increased the cost of the project, but the firm maintained delivery schedules.

A second measure of effectiveness, *resource utilization,* is of particular concern to industrial firms because of the high cost of making resources available. A resource allocation system that smooths out the peaks and valleys of resource usage is ideal, but it is extremely difficult to attain while maintaining scheduled performance because all the projects in a multiproject organization are competing for the same scarce resources. In particular, it is expensive to change the size of the human resource pool on which the firm draws.

While it is relatively easy to measure the costs of excess resource usage required by less than optimal scheduling in an industrial firm, the costs of uncoordinated multiproject scheduling can be high in service-producing firms, too. In the real estate syndication firm example at the end of Chapter 8, the scarce resource is executive judgment time. If two deals arrived at the same time, one would have to wait. This is undesirable because other potential buyers are seeking properties, and the process must move along without delay.

The third standard of effectiveness, the amount of *in-process inventory,* concerns the amount of work waiting to be processed because there is a shortage of some resource(s). Most industrial organizations have a large investment in in-process inventory, which may indicate a lack of efficiency and often represents a major source of expense for the firm. The remedy involves a trade-off between the cost of in-process inventory and the cost of the resources, usually capital equipment, needed to reduce the in-process inventory levels. It is almost axiomatic that the most time-consuming operation in any production system involving much machining of metals is an operation called "wait." If evidence is required, simply observe parts sitting on the plant floor or on pallets waiting for a machine, or for jigs, fixtures, and tools.

These criteria cannot be optimized at the same time. As usual, trade-offs are involved. A firm must decide which criterion is most applicable in any given situation, and then use that criterion to evaluate its various scheduling and resource allocation options.

At times, the demands of the marketplace and the design of a production/distribution system may require long production runs and sizable levels of in-process inventory. This happens often when production is organized as a continuous system, but sales are organized as projects, each customized to a client order. Items may be produced continuously but held in a semifinished state and customized in batches.

A mattress manufacturing company organized to produce part of its output by the usual continuous process; but the rest of its production was sold in large batches to a few customers. Each large order was thought of as a project and was organized as one. The customization process began after the metal frames and springs were assembled. This required extensive in-process inventories of semi-finished mattresses.

As noted earlier, experiments by Fendley (1968) revealed that the minimum-slack-first rule is the best overall priority rule, generally resulting in minimum project slippage, minimum resource idle time, and minimum system occupancy time (i.e., minimum in-process inventory) for the cases he studied. But the most commonly used priority rule is first come, first served—which has little to be said for it except that it

Source: DILBERT reprinted by permission of United Feature Syndicate, Inc.

fits the client's idea of what is "fair," if the client is at the head of the line. In any case, individual firms may find a different rule more effective in their particular circumstances and should evaluate alternative rules by their own performance measures and system objectives.

Fendley found that when a new project is added to a multiproject system, the amount of slippage is related to the average resource load factor. The load factor is the average resource *requirement* during a set time period divided by resource *availability* for that time period. When the new project is added, the load factor for a resource increases and slippage rises. analysis of resource loads is an important element in determining the amount of slippage to expect when adding projects.

Manufacturing Process Models

The general approach implied by the previous discussion is adopted from the model of a job-shop manufacturing system. The criteria for measuring schedule effectiveness are those applied to job-shops, and several approaches to resource-constrained multiple project scheduling use the job shop model. A scarce resource required for several projects or by several different activities in one project acts like a bottleneck in a manufacturing system. The bottleneck acquires a waiting line or queue. A short digression into queuing theory is in order.

Assume a random (Poisson) arrival rate, λ, of jobs to be processed by a facility, and the facility's rate of servicing jobs is also random (exponential), denoted μ. The average number of jobs, J, waiting in line for service is $J = (\lambda/\mu)/(1 - \lambda/\mu)$. Clearly, as the arrival rate approaches the service rate, the queue length heads toward infinity. The result is that to avoid long waiting lines for projects or for activities within a project, the capacity of the scarce resource must be significantly greater than the demand for it, or else the arrival rate of jobs must be tightly controlled so that it is no longer random. Even if the arrival rate is controlled, it must still be at a level that is less than the service rate (which is still random).

Adler et al. (1996) found that some highly successful firms had been applying work-process management to product development projects. Specifically, they found that projects are completed faster when the firm does fewer of them, that increasing bottleneck capacity pays large dividends to the investment, and that eliminating unnecessary workload and processes decreases the variation in service times (p. 134). Levy and Globerson (1997) also adopt queuing theory to deal with multiproduct management. They illustrate calculations for the "cost of waiting in line," the "cost of underutilizing" a facility with capacity greater than the demand for it, and "the cost of delayed projects." They also discuss ways of reducing these costs.

Given these observations, let us examine some examples of the various types of multiproject scheduling and resource allocation techniques. We begin with a short description of one optimization method, briefly cover several heuristics, and then discuss one heuristic in greater detail.

Mathematical Programming

Mathematical programming (Davis, 1983; Davis and Patterson, 1975; Turban and Meredith, 1994) can be used to obtain optimal solutions to certain types of multiproject scheduling problems. These procedures determine when an activity should be scheduled, given resource constraints. In the following discussion, it is important to remember that each of the techniques can be applied to the activities in a single project, or to the projects in a partially or wholly interdependent set of projects. Most models are based on integer programming that formulates the problem using 0–1 variables to indicate (depending on task early start times, due dates, sequencing relationships, etc.) whether or not an activity is scheduled in specific periods. The three most common objectives are these:

1. Minimum total throughput time (time in the shop) for all projects
2. Minimum total completion time for all projects
3. Minimum total lateness or lateness penalty for all projects

Constraint equations ensure that every schedule meets any or all of the following constraints, given that the set of constraints allows a feasible solution.

1. Limited resources
2. Precedence relationships among activities
3. Activity-splitting possibilities
4. Project and activity due dates
5. Substitution of resources to assign to specified activities
6. Concurrent and nonconcurrent activity performance requirements

In spite of its ability to generate optimal solutions, mathematical programming has some serious drawbacks when used for resource allocation and multiproject scheduling. As noted earlier, except for the case of small problems, this approach has proved to be extremely difficult and computationally expensive.

Heuristic Techniques

Because of the difficulties with the analytical formulation of realistic problems, major efforts in attacking the resource-constrained multiproject scheduling problem have focused on heuristics. We touched earlier on some of the common general criteria used for scheduling heuristics. Let us now return to that subject.

There are scores of different heuristic-based procedures in existence. A great many of the procedures have been published (see Davis and Patterson, 1975, for example), and descriptions of some are generally available in commercial computer programs.

The most commonly applied rules were discussed in Section 9.5. The logical basis for these rules predates PERT/CPM. They represent rather simple extensions of well-known approaches to job-shop scheduling. Some additional heuristics for resource allocation have been developed that draw directly on PERT/CPM. All these are commercially available for computers, and most are available from several different software vendors in slightly different versions.

Resource Scheduling Method   In calculating activity priority, give precedence to that activity with the minimum value of d_{ij}, where

d_{ij} = increase in project duration resulting when activity j follows activity i.

= Max $[0; (EFT_i - LST_j)]$

where

EFT_i = early finish time of activity i

LST_j = latest start time of activity j

The comparison is made on a pairwise basis among all activities in the conflict set.

Minimum Late Finish Time   This rule assigns priorities to activities on the basis of activity finish times as determined by PERT/CPM. The earliest late finishers are scheduled first.

Greatest Resource Demand   This method assigns priorities on the basis of total resource requirements, with higher priorities given for greater demands on resources. Project or task priority is calculated as

$$\text{Priority} = d_j \sum_{i=1}^{m} r_{ij}$$

where

d_j = duration of activity j

r_{ij} = per period requirement of resource i by activity j

m = number of resource types

Resource requirements must be stated in common terms, usually dollars. This heuristic is based on an attempt to give priority to potential resource bottleneck activities.

Greatest Resource Utilization   This rule gives priority to that combination of activities that results in maximum resource utilization (or minimum idle resources) during each scheduling period. The rule is implemented by solving a 0-1 integer programming problem, as described earlier. This rule was found to be approximately as effective as the minimum slack rule for multiple project scheduling, where the criterion used was project slippage. Variations of this rule are found in commercial computer programs such as RAMPS (see Moshman, Johnson, and Larsen, 1963).

Most Possible Jobs   Here, priority is given to the set of activities that results in the greatest number of activities being scheduled in any period. This rule also requires the solution of a 0-1 integer program. It differs from the greatest-resource-utilization heuristic in that the determination of the greatest number of possible jobs is made purely with regard to resource feasibility (and not with regard to any measure of resource utilization).

Heuristic procedures for resource-constrained multiproject scheduling represent the only practical means for finding workable solutions to the large, complex multiproject problems normally found in the real world. Let us examine a multiproject heuristic in somewhat more detail.

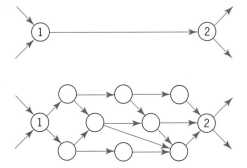

Figure 9-15   Task **a** decomposed into a network of subtasks.

A Multiproject Scheduling Heuristic

To attack this problem, recall the hierarchical approach to project planning we adopted in Chapter 5. A project plan is a nested set of plans, composed of a set of generalized tasks, each of which is decomposed into a more detailed set of work packages that are, in turn, decomposed further. The decomposition is continued until the work packages are simple enough to be considered "elemental." A PERT/CPM diagram of a project might be drawn for any level of task aggregation. A single activity (arrow) at a high level of aggregation would represent an entire network of activities at a lower level (see Figure 9-15). Another level in the planning hierarchy is shown as a Gantt chart in Figure 9-16.

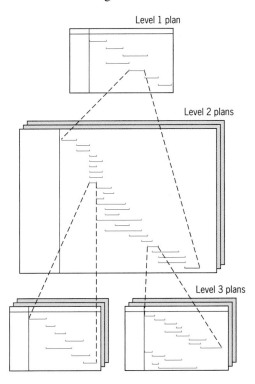

Figure 9-16   Hierarchy of Gantt charts. *Source:* Harrison (1983).

If an entire network is decomposed into subnetworks, we have the equivalent of the multiproject problem where each of the projects (subnetworks) is linked to predecessor and successor projects (other subnetworks). In this case, the predecessor/successor relationships depend on the technology of the parent project. In the true multiproject case, these relationships may still depend on technological relationships—for example, a real estate development project being dependent on the outcome of a land procurement project. The relationships may, however, be determined more or less arbitrarily, as when projects are sequenced on a first-come, first-served basis, or by any other priority-setting rule, or undertaken simultaneously in the hope that some synergistic side effects might occur. Or the relationship among the projects may simply be that they share a common pool of resources.

With this conceptual model, assume we have a set of projects. Each individual project is represented by a network of tasks. We can form a single network of these projects by connecting them with dummy activities (no resources, no duration) and/or pseudoactivities (no resources, some duration). Both dummy activities and pseudoactivities represent dependency relationships, but these dependencies, as noted above, may be technological or quite arbitrary.*

As usual, and excepting dummy and pseudoactivities, each task in each network requires time and resources. The amount of time required may or may not vary with the level of resources applied to it. The total amount of resources and/or amounts of individual resources are limited in successive scheduling periods. Our problem is to find a schedule that best satisfies the sequence and resource constraints and minimizes the overall duration of the entire network. The resulting schedule should indicate when to start any activity and at what level of resources it should be maintained while it is active.

Before undertaking the allocation of resources, it is proper to consider the quantity of resources available for allocation. (For the moment, we consider "resources" as an undifferentiated pool of assets that can be used for any purpose.) At the beginning of any period (hour, day, week, month, etc.) we have available any resources in inventory, R_I, which is to say, left over as excess from the previous allocation process. Changes in the inventory can be made from within the system of projects or by importing or exporting inventory from the outside. Excluding activities that have been completed in previous periods, every activity planned by the project is in one of four states; ongoing, stopping, waiting and technologically able to start, or waiting and technologically unable to start.

Figure 9-17 illustrates these conditions. We label ongoing activities as "resource users." Those stopping are "resource contributors." Those waiting and able to start are "resource demanders." Those waiting and unable to start can be ignored for the present. The amount of resources available for allocation is, therefore, the amount in inventory plus the amount contributed, $R_I + R_C$. If the amount demanded is less than this sum, there will be a positive inventory to start the next period. If not, some demanders will go unfunded.

---

*This exposition is based on Weist's (1967) work, and on Corwin's (1968) application of Weist's papers to resource allocation among multiple R &D projects.

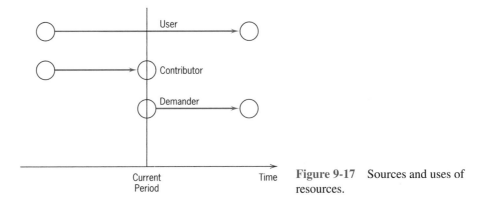

Figure 9-17 Sources and uses of resources.

Weist's heuristic (SPAR-1, Scheduling Program for Allocation of Resources) allocates resources to activities in order of their early start times. In the first period, we would list all available tasks and order them by their slack, from least to most. (Calculation of slack is based on the assumption that activities will be supported at *normal* resource levels.) Activities are selected for support and scheduling one by one, in order. As activities at the top of the list are supported, the relevant resource stocks are debited. Tasks are scheduled sequentially until the list of available jobs is completed, or until the stock of one or more necessary resources is depleted. If we deplete resources before completing the task list, remaining tasks are delayed until the next period. Postponed activities lose slack and rise toward the top of the priority list.

The information requirements for this heuristic are straightforward. Each period, we need a period-by-period updating of the list of currently active tasks continued from the previous period, including the resource usage level for each active task, the current scheduled (or expected) completion date, and the current activity slack. We need to know the currently available stocks of each type of resource, less the amounts of each in use. We also need a list of all available tasks together with their slacks and normal resource requirements. As activities are completed, their resources are "credited" to the resource pool for future use.

Thus, resources are devoted to activities until the supply of available resources or activities is exhausted. If we use up the resources before all critical activities are scheduled, we can adopt one of two subheuristics. First, we may be able to borrow resources from currently active, but noncritical, tasks. Second, we may "deschedule" a currently active, noncritical task. The former presumably slows the progress of the work, and the latter stops it. In both cases, some resources will be released for use on critical tasks. Obviously, if a critical task is slowed, descheduled, or not supported, the duration of the associated project will be extended.

The decision about which of these courses of action to take, borrowing or descheduling, can be made by adopting the same logic used in Chapter 7 when we discussed the budget negotiations between subordinate and superior. The decision to borrow or deschedule depends on our estimate of the impact either action would have on the task under consideration, given its current state of completion. Figure 9-18 shows two different versions of the project or task life cycle discussed in Chapter 7. If

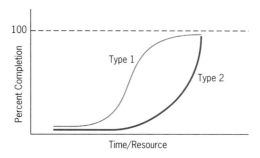

Figure 9-18   Project or task life cycles.

the task is a Type 1, borrowing would minimize the damage to the task unless it is quite near completion and we are willing to accept the outcome in its current state, in which case we can deschedule. If the task is Type 2, borrowing is apt to have a cata-strophic effect on the task and we should either deschedule it (and start it again later) or reject it as a source of resources.

If the size of the resource pool is more than sufficient for the list of active and available tasks, the extra resources may be used to crash critical activities in order to put some slack in the critical path as insurance against project delays caused by last-minute crises. In fact, it is often possible to borrow resources from tasks with plenty of slack in order to crash critical items that are frequent causes of project delay.

As a result of this scheduling process, each task from the previous period, along with any tasks newly available for support, will be:

1. Continued as is, or newly funded at a normal level
2. Continued or funded at a higher level of resources as a result of criticality
3. Continued or funded at a lower-than-normal level as a result of borrowing
4. Delayed because of a resource shortage

If there is more than one scarce resource, a separate activity can be created for each type of scarce resource. These "created" activities must be constrained to start in the same period as the parent activity, and to have the same level of resource assign-ment (normal, crash, or minimal.) Figure 9-19 shows a flow diagram for SPAR-1.

As we have noted, many commercially available software packages have the abil-ity to schedule constrained resources and deal with resource conflicts (Glauber, 1985; Johnson, 1992; Weaver, 1988). The journal *PM Network* published by the Project Management Institute is an excellent source of reviews on project management soft-ware. These reviews typically include a discussion of the package's capabilities. Many will allow the user to solve the problem either automatically, using the pro-gram's heuristics, or by hand in which case the user can adopt any method desired. If a set of projects is linked together by dummy activities so that it can be treated like a single project, the software will report resource usage conflicts; that is, cases in which the scheduled utilization of a resource is greater than the supply of that resource.

In one sense this chapter's emphasis on resource shortages is misleading. The common case of shortage applies not to resources in general, but to one or two highly specific resources. For example, an insurance firm specializing in casualty insurance

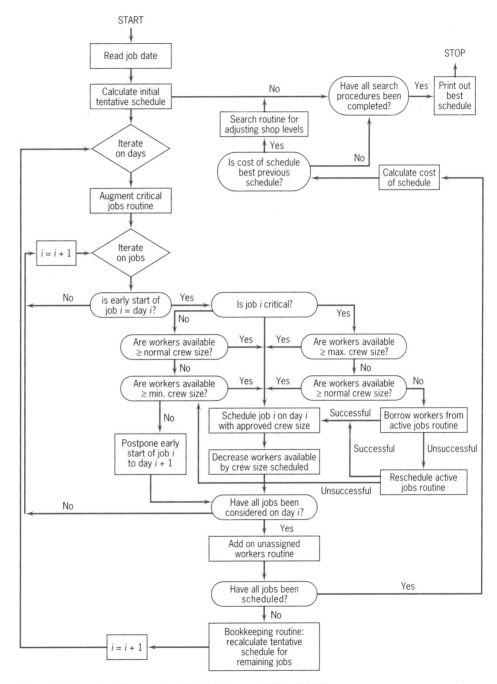

Figure 9-19   Flow diagram for SPAR-1. *Source:* Weist (1965).

Project Management in Practice
Minnesota DOT Ties Projects to Resources and Constraints

The Minnesota Department of Transportation (DOT) is responsible for facility construction and maintenance for highways, bridges, airports, waterways, railroads, and even bicycle paths. At any given time, there will be approximately 1100 projects—typically, highway improvements—in active development, with a turn-over of about 300 per year. These projects will range from $50,000 paint jobs to multimillion dollar freeway interchanges. The computerized Project Manage-

ment and Scheduling System (PMSS) used to manage these projects is based on a work breakdown structure detailing about 100 activities involving 75 functional groups, 40 of which are in-house groups and the rest being consultants.

The PMSS encompasses three major areas: scheduling, funding, and human resource planning. It allows planning, coordination, and control of the work progress and resource requirements for multiple projects over a multiyear time

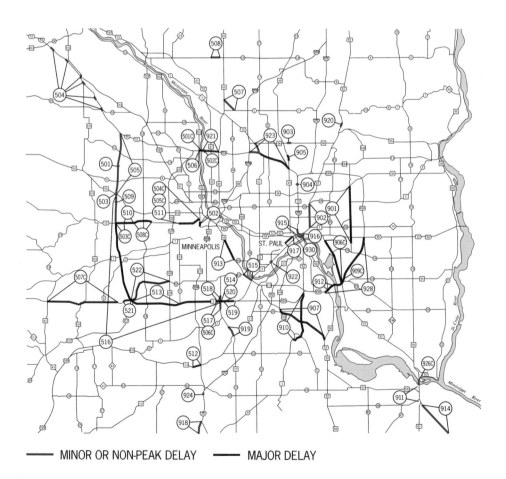

—— MINOR OR NON-PEAK DELAY　—— MAJOR DELAY

span, since projects may continue for up to four years in some cases. This integration offers the capability to relate work plans to funding availability as well as human resource availability. Conversely, resource use can be planned according to the construction project schedule. Other constraints can also be included in the system and its reports, such as avoiding projects that might overly congest a high-traffic area (see figure) or properly sequencing subprojects such as grading, surfacing, and finishing.

The PMSS system gives management a "big picture" perspective of what is happening in terms of workflow over time and geography. It has also enhanced the department's ability to answer questions about activities, funding, labor, and equipment, and to present reports in a variety of configurations to satisfy the needs of many different parties.

Source: R. Pearson, "Project Management in the Minnesota Department of Transportation," *PM Network,* November 1988.

---

has a typical kind of scarce resource, a "Walt." Walter A. is a specialist in certain types of casualty losses in the firm's commerical lines business. He is the only such specialist in the firm, and his personal knowledge is required when designing new policies in the field. His knowledge is based on years of experience and an excellent, analytical mind. It is common for projects involving the modification or creation of policies in the commercial lines area to have problems associated with the fact that the firm has one, and only one Walt. Walt-capacity cannot be hired, trained, or subcontracted within an appropriate time frame. The firm's ability to extend its Walt-capacity is not sufficient to satisfy its Walt-demand. Left with no alternative, some projects must be delayed so that others can proceed.

9.7   GOLDRATT'S CRITICAL CHAIN*

In the previous section, we showed that the problem of constrained resource scheduling of multiple projects could be reduced to the problem of scheduling activities using scarce resources in the case of a single project. We did this by joining several projects into a single network by tying them together with dummy- and pseudo-activities. Scarce resources could then be allocated to the different projects and work on the projects scheduled exactly as if they were merely different activities of a single project. The same decision criteria as those we discussed for the single project case were available for setting priorities among the different projects. Certainly the best-known attack on the resource-constrained scheduling problem is Goldratt's *Critical Chain* (1997). The celebrated author of *The Goal* (Goldratt and Cox, 1992) applies his Theory of Constraints to the constrained resource scheduling problem. The original focus of the Theory of Constraints to project management was the single project case, but it, too, is just as applicable to multiple projects.

If we consider all the comments we have heard about the problems PMs have to

---

*The authors wish to thank their friend, coauthor, and colleague Scott Shafer of Wake Forest University for his generous contributions to the ideas contained in this section.

deal with on a daily basis, many are brought up over and over again. Further, it is interesting to note that these statements are made by PMs working in construction, manufacturing, software development, R&D, marketing, communications, maintenance, . . . and the list of industries could easily be extended. For example, the following issues are raised with high frequency, and this short list is only indicative, not nearly exhaustive.

- Senior management changes the project's scope without consultation and without warning—and without changing the budget or schedule.
- Project due dates are set with little regard given to availability of resources.
- There is no possible way of accomplishing a project without exceeding the given budget.
- Project work loads and due dates are set by the sales group, not by the nature of the projects and the level of resources needed.
- Project due dates are set unrealistically short as an "incentive" for people to work harder and faster.

It appears that these, and many other, problems are generic. They are independent of the area of technology. Note that all of these issues concern trading off time, cost, and performance. To deal with the strong optimistic bias in many project schedules, let us consider just a few of the things that tend to create it.

1. **Thoughtless optimism**   Some PMs, apparently with a strong need to deny that lateness could be their fault, deal with every problem faced by their projects as strict exceptions, acts of chance that cannot be forecast and hence need not be the subject of planning. These individuals simply ignore risk management.

2. **Capacity should be set to equal demand**   Some senior managers refuse to recognize that projects are not assembly lines and are not subject to standard operations management line of balance methods. Refer back to Section 9-4, subsection "Resource Loading/Leveling and Uncertainty," for the need for capacity to exceed demand for projects.

3. **The "Student Syndrome"**   This phrase is Goldratt's name for the fact that students always want more time to complete a project. Given more time, students delay starting the project until the last possible moment. One of the common occurrences is for activities with high slack to be delayed and ignored until the slack is gone. If *any* problems arise with such activities they will be late.

4. **Multitasking to reduce idle time**   Consider a situation where there are two projects, A and B, each with three sequential activities and with you as the only resource required by both projects. Each activity requires 10 days. In Figure 9-20 see two Gantt charts for sequencing the activities in the two projects. In the first, switch from project A (red) to project B (pink) for each of the three activities, that is, carry out Activity 1 for project A, then Activity 1 for project B, then Actitity 2 for A, and so forth. In the second sequence, complete project A before starting project B. In both cases, the total time required will be 60 days. In the second,

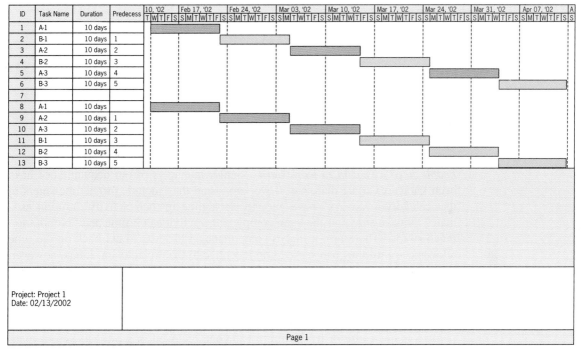

ID	Task Name	Duration	Predecess	10, '02	Feb 17, '02	Feb 24, '02	Mar 03, '02	Mar 10, '02	Mar 17, '02	Mar 24, '02	Mar 31, '02	Apr 07, '02
1	A-1	10 days										
2	B-1	10 days	1									
3	A-2	10 days	2									
4	B-2	10 days	3									
5	A-3	10 days	4									
6	B-3	10 days	5									
7												
8	A-1	10 days										
9	A-2	10 days	1									
10	A-3	10 days	2									
11	B-1	10 days	3									
12	B-2	10 days	4									
13	B-3	10 days	5									

Project: Project 1
Date: 02/13/2002

Page 1

Figure 9-20   Effect of multitasking on project completion given fixed activity times.

note that project A is completed after 30 days and B after 60 days. In the first chart, however, Project A will be finished after 50 days and B after 60 days. While the total time required is the same, project A has been delayed for 20 days by the multitasking. Further, this ignores the fact that switching back and forth between tasks is neither a particularly efficient nor effective way to complete two different jobs.

5. *Complexity of networks makes no difference*   Consider two different projects as seen in Figure 9-21. Assume that each activity requires 10 days and is known with certainty. Clearly, both projects are completed in 40 days though one is considerably more complex than the other. But let's get a bit more real. Assume that each activity is stochastic, with normally distributed times. The mean time is 10 days, and the standard deviation is 3 days. If we simulate the projects 500 times, we get the results shown in Tables 9-4 and 5. Table 9-4, covering the simulation of the simple network, shows (as we expected) a mean project completion time of about 40 days. Table 9-5 covers the simulation of the complex network and its mean completion time is about 46 days. Complexity, uncertainty and merging paths all join to make trouble.

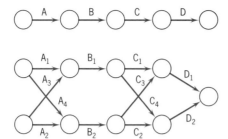

Figure 9-21 Two levels of 40-day network complexity.

6. ***People need a reason to work hard*** Senior managers of our acquaintance have been known to argue that project workers—and they include project managers in that category—"always" have enough slack time in their activity duration estimates to make sure that they can complete the activities on time and "without too much sweat." Therefore, it makes some managerial sense to cut back on the time allowances until they can serve as an incentive to the projec team. It has, however, long been known that for people with a high need for achievement, the maximum level of motivation is associated with only moderate, not high, levels of risk of failure.

7. ***Game playing*** The is possibly the most common cause of late projects. It is certainly a major cause of frustration for anyone invloved in a project. Senior managers, firm in the belief that project workers add extra time and resources to activity time and budget estimates in order to insure a safe and peaceful life on their portion of a project, routinely cut schedules and budgets. Project workers, suspecting that senior management will cut schedules and budgets without regard to any logic or reason, increase their schedules and budgets as much as they guess will be

Table 9-4. Project Simulation Statistics for Simple Network #1

Forecast: Completion Time Network #1	
Cell U3	**Statistics**

Statistic	Value
Trials	500
Mean	39.97
Median	40.23
Mode	—
Standard Deviation	5.85
Variance	34.18
Skewness	0.09
Kurtosis	2.86
Coeff. of Variability	0.15
Range Minimum	24.32
Range Maximum	56.97
Range Width	32.65
Mean Std. Error	0.26

Table 9-5.   Project Simulation Statistics for Complex Network #2

Forecast: Completion Time Network #2

Edit   Preferences   View   Run   Help

Cell V3   **Statistics**

Statistic	Value
Trials	500
Mean	46.31
Median	46.25
Mode	—
Standard Deviation	4.53
Variance	20.51
Skewness	0.05
Kurtosis	2.78
Coeff. of Variability	0.10
Range Minimum	34.83
Range Maximum	59.02
Range Width	24.18
Mean Std. Error	0.20

allowed. Each assumes that the other is not to be trusted. The outcome is simple. Rather than practice careful risk management, each blames the other for any lateness or budget overage.

Do Early Finishes and Late Finishes Cancel Out? So What?

One of the tacit assumptions of probabilistic networks is that early and late activity completions cancel out. This assumption would probably be true were it not for the matters listed in the previous subsection. Assume two activities, A and B. A is a predecessor of B. If acivity A is late, then activity B will start late by whatever amount of lateness is bequeathed to it by A. Similarly, if in spite of all the forces tending to thwart such things, activity A finishes early, B will start early. The assumption, which is also a tacit assumption of both the analytical and simulation methods of finding a path's duration, is generally true for the first case, when A is late. But for the case when A is early, the assumption is rarely true. Unfortunately, a finish by A in less than its expected duration almost never translates to a start by B before its expected start time.

With a few exceptions, the fact that early finishes do not become early starts is ignored by most people involved with projects. Goldratt writes about the phenomenon (1997, Chapter 13 and elsewhere), and a few others have also briefly discussed the matter. There is a mild debate as to the reason for this deplorable condition. Goldratt feels that project workers will avoid admitting that an activity has been completed early, again reminding us of the unknown person who uttered the famous words we have quoted in Chapter 8.

Others point out that when the activity schedule is set, it is presumed that the activity will start immediately after the most likely finish date of its (latest) predecessor. The reason is simple—its resources will not be available until that date. While we have no intention of entering the debate, we can easily demonstrate the impact of the failed assumption that early starts will follow early finishes of predecessors. Then we can investigate these two reasons why early starts rarely occur.

An Easy Simulation

Consider once more the project described by Table 8-1 that we solved analytically and then simulated in Chapter 8. We can resimulate the project, including the specification that when a predecessor finishes early, the successor activity will not begin until its predetermined ES (the predecessor's EF) has arrived. (Again, remember that when there are multiple predecessors, we require an early finish for the *latest* predecessor.) We can set up this condition by truncating the assumption distributions for each activity so that the earliest finish time is equal to the most likely time. We simply do not allow predecessors to finish early. We do this by entering the most likely time for each activity in the "truncation grabber" for each activity. The grabbers are located in boxes just above the **Min** and **Max** entry boxes in each distribution assumption entry form (see Figure 9-22). The effect of this alteration is that when the random time sample is sought for a given simulation run, if the system chooses a number less than the most likely time, the most likely time will be substituted for it. "Overs" are allowed, but "unders" are not. (Note that we cannot do this for Activity **a**. Its most likely and pessimistic times are the same—22 days—so the assumption cell should be deleted and it becomes a constant as is already the case with activites **b** and **g**.)

A 1000-trial simulation was run, and Table 9-6 shows the statistical results of the run. It is displayed with Table 8-28, renumbered below as Table 9-7 for easy comparison. Table 9-7 contains the results of the original simulation which allowed early finishes and subsequent early starts. The mean and median durations are about

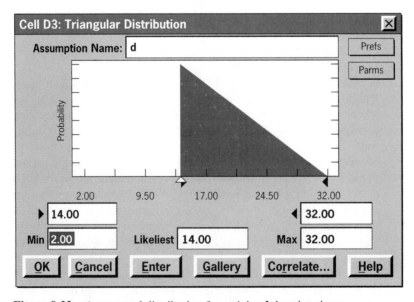

Figure 9-22 A truncated distribution for activity **d** duration times.

Table 9-6   Truncation Simulation Results for Project of Table 8-1, Early Starts Disallowed

Forecast: Project Completion Time	⬜◻❌

Edit   Preferences   View   Run   Help

Cell S3   **Statistics**

Statistic	Value
Trials	1,000
Mean	53.63
Median	53.56
Mode	—
Standard Deviation	4.39
Variance	19.26
Skewness	0.19
Kurtosis	2.31
Coeff. of Variability	0.08
Range Minimum	44.65
Range Maximum	66.23
Range Width	21.58
Mean Std. Error	0.14

12 percent higher when activity starts before the predetermined ESs are not allowed. Other reported statistics are also affected as we would expect.

There is a logical explanation of why the start of a successor is usually delayed until its predetermined expected start time. Some say that project workers will not report finishes before the most likely duration. The logic of this position depends on an inherent distrust between project workers and senior management. If an early finish is reported, workers assume that the shorter-than-normal activity duration will be the

Table 9-7   Table 8-28 Repeated: Simulation Statistics When Early Starts Allowed

Forecast: Project Completion Time	⬜◻❌

Edit   Preferences   View   Run   Help

Cell S3   **Statistics**

Statistic	Value
Trials	1,000
Mean	47.78
Median	47.62
Mode	—
Standard Deviation	5.39
Variance	29.03
Skewness	0.18
Kurtosis	2.35
Coeff. of Variability	0.11
Range Minimum	33.82
Range Maximum	61.50
Range Width	27.68
Mean Std. Error	0.17

expectation for similar activities in the future. Senior managers, the argument proceeds, do not really understand the uncertainty faced by project workers. Senior management will assume that if an activity can be finished early once, it can be finished early again, or that they were correct in their assumption that workers "pad" their time and resource estimates. The chance event of an early finish is, thus, used to substantiate a shortened duration estimate in the future.

There is also a logical explanation of why a successor activity does not receive resources until its predetermined expected start, which is, by definition, equal to the expected finish of the latest predecessor activity. A stochastic network has little in common with an assembly line; nonetheless, we find some managers attempting to delay the deployment of resources to a project as long as possible. If we agree to start a project as soon as its predecessors are completed, we must contemplate having the resources available and waiting well before the activity's expected start. Idle resources, however, are not acceptable to managers trained in a just-in-time view of the world. Assembly lines are reasonably predictable; projects are not.

Given the power of CB to develop data on activity durations, it is not particularly difficult to find the value of having resources available before the ES for a successor activity. For instance, let x be any date on which a successor activity can start. Let y be the predetermined start date for that activity, where $x < y$. Given an assumption about the distribution shape and three-time estimates for the predecessor activity (the source of information about x and y), we can determine the probability of a predecessor finishing on or before any given x. With that probability, and a carrying cost of the resources that must be held waiting for the successor start, we can find the expected value of having the resources held for the period from x to y. Similarly, if we can estimate the value of the activity finishing y-x time periods early, we can find the expected value of finishing early. This is now a relatively simple cost/benefit problem comparing the expected values of two courses of action.

The Critical Chain

In addition to the problems of multitasking, thoughtless optimism, the student syndrome, and the other things we have mentioned, Goldratt adds several more common practices (e.g., "safety time") and argues that all of these lead to a vicious cycle that makes projects substantially late. Using the logic of his Theory of Constraints, Goldratt recommends that new projects should be scheduled based on the availability of scarce resources, resources we have referred to as "Walts" at the end of the previous section. He then suggests that "time buffers" be added in the schedules of resources that feed bottleneck (scarce) resources, and the bottleneck resources themseslves.

The proper scheduling helps the problems caused by poor multitasking, but does not lead to more realistic project duration estimates. The buffers act as safety time, but here it is added to a path or two rather than to every activity or to the project as a whole. It can be shown by elementary statistics that the safety time needed to protect a path is considerably less than the sum of the safety stocks needed to protect each activity in the path, called *path buffers*. Similarly, Goldratt suggests a *project buffer*, but also suggests that activity durations be decreased to the point where the workers have no desire to act out the student syndrome. In fact, he recommends that task durations should have a high probability of being insufficient.

Finally, Goldratt argues that two activities scheduled to be carried out in parallel and using the same scarce resource are not independent as the traditional theory would assume.* If the supply of the scarce resource is not sufficient to allow both activities to be carried out simultaneously, then whichever of the two is given priority immediately lengthens the other activity's path but not its duration.

Assume that two parallel paths compose a project, A_1-B, and A_2-C. A_1 and A_2 require the same scarce resource. **B** and **C** use different resources. A_1 requires 7 days, A_2 requires 5 days, **B** needs 10 days, and **C** needs 6 days and thus, the path A_1-B is 17 days and the path A_2-C is 11 days. If there is not enough of the scarce resource to fund both **A** activities, they must be done sequentially. If A_1 is done first, A_2 cannot start until A_1 is complete, thereby adding 7 days to the A_2-C path making it 18 days long and increasing the project finish date by 1 day. If A_2 is done first, 5 days will be added to the A_1-C path, making it 22 days, a 5-day increase over its original 17-day duration. If this problem seems familiar, it is. This is precisely the issue we dealt with when we examined the process of resource leveling in Section 9-4.

Using Goldratt's meaning of the word "dependent," the activities of a project can be ordered into paths based on their resource dependencies as well as on their technological precedence requirements. The longest of these paths of sequentially dependent activities is known as the "critical chain." A project, therefore, is composed of its critical chain and of noncritical chains that feed into it—see Figure 9-23. There are two sources of delay for the project. One comes from a delay of one or more activities in the critical chain. The second results from a delay in one or more of the activities on a noncritical or "feeder" chain because such delays could delay activities on the critical chain. A project buffer protects the critical chain, and feeding buffers protect the feeder paths.

Resources used by activities on the critical chain are given priority so that they are available when required. If there are one or more truly scarce resources or Walts involved, the status of demands for any Walt must be kept up to date, and the Walts must receive immediate communication when any change in the critical chain is contemplated. Indeed, Goldratt urges that such resources be reminded of their scheduled workloads. Because any delay on the critical chain will delay the project, Walts must be available to work on critical activities when needed.

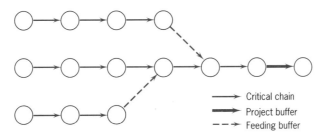

→ Critical chain
⟶ Project buffer
--→ Feeding buffer

Figure 9-23 Project and feeder buffers.

---

*The word "dependent" has two different meanings in this context. Two parallel activities using the same scarce resource depend on one another in the sense that the ability to *start* one depends on the existence of priorities indicating which of the two competing activities gets first use of the scarce resource. At the same time, they may be statistically independent which means that the *duration* of one activity does not depend on the duration of the other.

SUMMARY

In this chapter, we looked at the problem of allocating physical resources, both among the multiple activities of a project and among multiple projects. The continuous problem to the PM is finding the best trade-offs among resources, particularly time. We considered resource loading, allocation, and leveling, and presented methods and concepts to aid in all these tasks.

Specific points made in the chapter were these:

- The critical path method (CPM) is a network constructed in the same manner as PERT, but it also considers the possibility of adding resources to tasks (called crashing) to shorten their duration, thereby expediting the project.

- The resource allocation problem is concerned with determining the best trade-offs between available resources, including time, throughout the duration of a project.

- Resource loading is the process of calculating the total load from project tasks on each resource for each time period of the project's duration.

- Resource leveling is concerned with evening out the demand for various resources required in a project by shifting tasks within their slack allowances. The aid of a computer is mandatory for realistic projects.

- There are two basic approaches to addressing the constrained resources allocation problem:

  — *Heuristic methods* are realistic approaches that may identify feasible solutions to the problem. They essentially use simple priority rules, such as shortest task first, to determine which task should receive resources and which task must wait.

  — *Optimizing methods,* such as linear programming, find the best allocation of resources to tasks but are limited in the size of problems they can efficiently solve.

- For multiproject scheduling, three important measures of effectiveness are schedule slippage, resource utilization, and level of in-process inventory.

- When a new project is added to a multiproject system, the amount of slippage is directly related to the average resource load.

- Mathematical programming models for multiproject scheduling aim either to minimize total throughput time for all projects, minimize the completion time for all projects, or minimize the total lateness (or lateness penalty) for all projects. These models are limited to small problems. There are a number of heuristic methods, such as the resource scheduling method, available for the multiproject scheduling problem.

In the next chapter, we move to the ongoing implementation of the project and consider the project information systems used for monitoring progress, costs, performance, and so on. The chapter also describes some available computer packages for this function.

GLOSSARY

Cost/Time Slope   The ratio of the increased cost for expediting to the decreased amount of time for the activity.

Followers   The tasks that logically follow a particular task in time.

Heuristic   A formal process for solving a problem, like a rule of thumb, that results in an acceptable solution.

Mathematical Programming   A general term for certain mathematical approaches to solving constrained optimization problems, including linear programming, integer programming, and so on.

Predecessors   The tasks that logically precede a particular task in time.

Priority Rules   Formal methods, such as ratios, that rank items to determine which one should be next.

Resource Leveling Approaches to even out the peaks and valleys of resource requirements so that a fixed amount of resources can be employed over time.

Resource Loading The amount of resources of each kind that are to be devoted to a specific activity in a certain time period.

Successors See followers.

Tree Search The evaluation of a number of alternatives that logically branch from each other like a tree with limbs.

QUESTIONS

Material Review Questions

1. Identify several resources that may need to be considered when scheduling projects.

2. What is resource loading? How does it differ from resource leveling?

3. What is an activity slope and what does it indicate?

4. Name four priority rules. What priority rule is best overall? How would a firm decide which priority rule to use?

5. Name three efficiency criteria that might be considered when choosing a multiproject scheduling system.

6. What is the average resource load factor? How is it used to determine project completion times?

7. What are two methods for addressing the constrained resources allocation problem?

8. How does the task life cycle type affect our attempts to level the resource loads?

9. What is a "system constrained" task?

10. How does the resource scheduling method heuristic work?

Class Discussion Questions

11. Why are large fluctuations in the demands for particular resources undesirable? What are the costs of resource leveling? How would a PM determine the "best" amount of leveling?

12. When might a firm choose to crash a project? What factors must be considered in making this decision?

13. Why is the impact of scheduling and resource allocation more significant in multiproject organizations?

14. How much should a manager know about a scheduling or resource allocation computer program to be able to use the output intelligently?

15. With the significantly increased power of today's computers, do you think the mathematical programming optimization approaches will become more popular?

16. What are some of the limitations of CPM?

17. Why is leveling of resources needed?

18. What are some implications of resource allocation when an organization is involved in several projects at once?

19. What are some of the indirect costs of crashing?

20. How might CPM be used for strategic planning purposes?

Questions for Project Management in Practice

Expediting Los Angeles Freeway Repairs
after the Earthquake

21. Of the six constraints, which were cost tradeoffs and which were performance trade-offs?

22. In what way were the performance trade-offs made? That is, how did they affect performance?

23. What kinds of resource allocation approaches discussed in the chapter were used in this situation?

Benefits of Resource Constraining
at Pennsylvania Electric

24. Why would the planning group use 40% more mechanics than necessary?

25. What does the availability in the chart represent? Why do the monthly values move up and down?

26. What does the scheduled amount represent? Why does it drop off in 1991? How can it exceed the availability?

Minnesota DOT Ties Projects to Resources
and Constraints

27. Why are the three areas of scheduling, funding, and human resource planning needed in such a system? Why aren't equipment planning and materials requirements included?

28. How would the system facilitate planning? Coordination? Control?

29. What other big-picture issues might this system be useful for besides identifying when projects might overly congest an area?

▨ PROBLEMS

1. Given the following network, determine the first activity to be crashed by the following priority rules:
   (a) Shortest task first
   (b) Minimum slack first
   (c) Most critical followers
   (d) Most successors

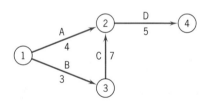

2. Using the network above and the additional information below, find:
   (a) The crash cost per day
   (b) Which activities should be crashed to meet a project deadline of 13 days at minimum cost. Assume partial crashing is allowed.

Activity	Crash Time (days)	Crashed Cost (total)	Normal Time (days)	Normal Cost
A	3	$500	4	$300
B	1	325	3	250
C	4	550	7	400
D	3	250	5	150

3. Consider the following network for conducting a two-week (10 working days) computer training class:

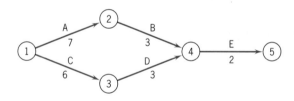

   (a) Construct a schedule showing:
      ESs for all activities
      LSs for all activities
      Slacks for all activities
      Critical path
   (b) Given the following.

Activity	Crash Time (days)	Crashed Cost (total)	Normal Time (days)	Normal Cost
A	4	$800	7	$500
B	2	350	3	200
C	4	900	6	500
D	1	500	3	200
E	1	550	2	300
		$3100		

1. Find the crash cost per day.
2. Which activities should be crashed to meet a project deadline of 10 days with a minimum cost? Assume partial crashing.
3. Find the new cost.
4. Is partial crashing an appropriate assumption in this kind of project?

4. Given the following highway rerouting project,

Activity	Immediate Predecessor	Activity Time (months)
A	—	4
B	—	6
C	A	2
D	B	6
E	C,B	3
F	C,B	3
G	D,E	5

(a) Draw the network.
(b) Find the ESs, LSs, and slacks.
(c) Find the critical path.
(d) If the project has a 1 1/2-year deadline for reopening, should we consider crashing some activities? Explain.

5. Given the following network for a stock repurchase project with outside consulting resource demands, construct a modified Gantt AOA chart with resources and a resource load diagram. Suggest how to level the outside consulting load if you can split operations.

Code: activity, time
      resource units

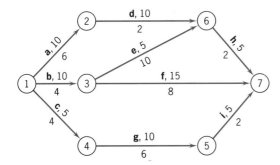

6. Reconsider Problem 18 in Chapter 8 under the constraint that the project must be completed in 16 weeks. This time, however, activities **c, f, h,** and **i** may be crashed as follows. Assume partial crashing.

Activity	Crash Time (weeks)	Additional Cost per Week
c	7	$40
f	6	20
h	2	10
i	3	30

Find the best schedule and its cost.

7. The following data were obtained from a study of the times required to conduct a consumer test panel study:

Activity	Crash Schedule Time	Crash Schedule Cost	Normal Schedule Time	Normal Schedule Cost
1–2	3	$6	5	$4
1–3	1	5	5	3
2–4	5	7	10	4
3–4	2	6	7	4
2–6	2	5	6	3
4–6	5	9	11	6
4–5	4	6	6	3
6–7	1	4	5	2
5–7	1	5	4	2

Note: Costs are given in thousands of dollars, time in weeks.
(a) Find the all-normal schedule and cost.
(b) Find the all-crash schedule and cost.
(c) Find the total cost required to expedite all activities from all-normal (case a) to all-crash (case b).
(d) Find the *least-cost* plan for the all-crash time schedule. Start from the all-crash problem (b). Assume partial crashing.

8. Given the data in Problem 7, determine the first activities to be crashed by the following priority rules:
(a) Shortest task first.
(b) Most resources first (use normal cost as the basis).
(c) Minimum slack first.
(d) Most critical followers.
(e) Most successors.

9. Consider Problem 14 in Chapter 8 again. Suppose the duration of both activities **A** and **D** can be reduced to one day, at a cost of $15 per day of reduction. Also, activities **E, G,** and **H** can be reduced in duration by one day at a cost of $25 per day of reduction. What is the least-cost approach to crash the project two days? What is the shortest "crashed" duration, the new critical path, and the cost of crashing?

10. Given a network for an HR training project with normal times and crash times (in parentheses), find the cost-duration history. Assume indirect costs for facilities and equipment are $100 per day. The data are:

Activity	Time Reduction, Direct Cost per Day
1–2	$30 first, $50 second
2–3	$80
3–4	$25 first, $60 second
2–4	$30 first, $70 second, $90 third

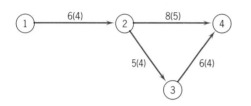

11. Reconsider Problem 2, assuming a fixed overhead cost of $30 per day but no project deadline. What is the least-cost crash program? If the overhead cost was $40? If it was $60?

12. The network for shooting a TV commercial as shown in the table has a fixed cost of $90 per day, but money can be saved by shortening the project duration. Find the least-cost schedule.

Activity	Normal Time	Crash Time	Cost Increase (1st, 2nd, 3rd day)
1–2	7	4	$30, 50, 70
2–3	9	6	40, 45, 65
1–3	12	10	60, 60
2–4	11	9	35, 60
3–4	3	3	—

13. Given the following project to landscape a new building site,

Activity	Immediate Predecessor	Activity Duration (days)	Resource Used
A	—	2	X , Y
B	A	2	X
C	A	3	X
D	B,C	4	X, Y
E	D	3	W, X
F	D	1	W, X, Y
G	E,F	2	X, Y

(a) Draw a Gantt chart using MSP.
(b) Find the critical path and project duration in days.
(c) Given that each resource is assigned 100% to each task, identify the resource constraints.
(d) Level the resources and determine the new project duration and critical path.
(e) Identify what alternative solutions can be used to shorten the project duration and not over-allocate the resources.

INCIDENTS FOR DISCUSSION

Bryce Power Tool Company

Kevin Ertle is the director of information technology (IT) for the Bryce Power Tool Company. A decision was made recently to upgrade Bryce's legacy systems to a comprehensive ERP system. The president of Bryce has indicated that he expects the modernization program to result in a significant improvement in new product time to market. Ertle is concerned with the possibility that his department will not have adequate resources to support the upgrade. Kevin believes he has enough staff to handle the aggregate IT requirements, but he is not too sure he will be able to supply the proper IT personnel at the times and quantities requested by the company's project managers.

To complicate matters further, the upgrade will be under the control of four different business unit project managers. Each major market segment has been recognized as a separate business unit with the authority to select IT subsystems for their segment based on a schedule that makes sense for it.

Kevin knows a little bit about resource allocation techniques. He remembers that one of the most effective allocation techniques is to work first on the activity with the minimum slack, so he has instructed his staff to approach any tasks they are assigned as members of a project team on that basis.

Questions: Is this technique a reasonable way to schedule the IT resources of Bryce? Why or why not? What complication is added by making this four separate projects?

Critical Care Hospital

Critical Care Hospital will be purchasing a CATSCAN (computerized axial tomography scanner) in the next

six months. The CATSCAN equipment will be installed in the radiology department and will require a significant renovation for the area. The scanner will arrive in about five months, but the construction project cannot be started until the unit is set in place. This will result in a project length of approximately 12 months. The hospital estimates the equipment will generate an income of $25,000 per month and is therefore in a hurry to complete the project. The project manager feels she may be able to cut the time on some aspects of the project, but at an increased cost. She has decided, in an effort to make the best decision, to use a resource allocation version of CPM.

Questions: What information must the project manager gather to use this method properly? How should she use this version of CPM to reduce the project time?

BIBLIOGRAPHY

ADLER, P. S., A. MANDELBAUM, V. NGUYEN, and E. SCHWERER. "Getting the Most out of Your Product Development Process." *Harvard Business Review,* March–April 1996.

ANDERSON, D. R., D. J. SWEENEY, and T. A. WILLIAMS. *An Introduction to Management Science,* 6th ed. Minneapolis, MN: West Publishing, 1991.

BADIRU, A. B. "Critical Resource Diagram: A New Tool for Resource Management." *Industrial Engineering,* October 1992.

BADIRU, A. B. "Incorporating Learning Curve Effects Into Critical Resource Diagramming." *Project Management Journal,* June 1995.

CORWIN, B. D. "Multiple R and D Project Scheduling with Limited Resources." *Technical Memorandum No. 122,* Department of Operations Research, Cleveland: Case Western Reserve University, 1968.

DAVIS, E. W. *Project Management: Techniques, Applications, and Managerial Issues,* 2nd ed. Norcross, GA: Institute of Industrial Engineers, 1983.

DAVIS, E. W., and J. H. PATTERSON. "A Comparison of Heuristic and Optimum Solutions in Resource-Con-

strained Project Scheduling." *Management Science,* April 1975.

FARID, F., and S. MANOHARAN. "Comparative Analysis of Resource-Allocation Capabilities of Project Management Software Packages." *Project Management Journal,* June 1996.

FENDLEY, L. G. "Towards the Development of a Complete Multiproject Scheduling System." *Journal of Industrial Engineering,* October 1968.

GEMMILL, D. D., and Y. W. TSAI. "Using a Simulated Annealing Algorithm to Schedule Activities of Resource-Constrained Projects." *Project Management Journal,* December 1997.

GILYUTIN, I. "Using Project Management in a Nonlinear Environment." *Project Management Journal,* December 1993.

GLAUBER, L. W. "Project Planning With Scitor's PS5000." *Project Management Journal,* June 1985.

GOLDRATT, E. M., and J. COX. *The Goal.* Great Barrington, MA: North River, 1992.

GOLDRATT, E. M. *Critical Chain.* Great Barrington, MA: North River, 1997.

HARRISON, F. L. *Advanced Project Management.* Hants, GB: Gower, 1983.

IBBS, C. W., S. A. LEE, and M. I. LI. "Fast-Tracking's Impact on Project Change." *Project Management Journal,* December 1998.

JOHNSON, R. V. "Resource Constrained Scheduling Capabilities of Commercial Project Management Software." *Project Management Journal,* December 1992.

KUMAR, V. K., and L. S. GANESH. "Use of Petri Nets for Resource Allocation in Projects." *IEEE Transactions on Engineering Management,* February 1998.

KURTULUS, I., and E. W. DAVIS. "Multi-Project Scheduling: Categorization of Heuristic Rules Performance." *Management Science,* February 1982.

KURTULUS, I., and S. C. NARULA. "Multi-Project Scheduling: Analysis of Project Performance." *IEEE Transactions on Engineering Management,* March 1985.

LEVY, N. S., and S. GLOBERSON. "Improving Multiproject Management by Using a Queuing Theory Approach." *Project Management Journal,* December 1997.

MILLS, N. L. "The Development of a University Sports Complex: A Project Management Application." *Computers and Industrial Engineering,* 1989.

MODER, J. J., C. R. PHILLIPS, and E. W. DAVIS. *Project Management With CPM, PERT and Precedence Diagramming,* 3rd ed. New York: Van Nostrand Reinhold, 1983.

MORSE, L. C., J. O. MCINTOSH, and G. E. WHITEHOUSE. "Using Combinations of Heuristics to Schedule Activities of Constrained Multiple Resource Projects." *Project Management Journal,* March 1996.

MOSHMAN, J., J. R. JOHNSON, and M. LARSEN. "RAMPS-A Technique for Resource Allocation and Multiproject Scheduling." *Proceedings,* Spring Joint Computer Conference, 1963.

NAVARRE, C., and J. SCHAAN. "Design of Project Management Systems from Top Management's Perspective," *Project Management Journal,* June 1990.

NICHOLAS, J. M. *Managing Business & Engineering Projects.* Englewood Cliffs, NJ: Prentice Hall, 1990.

PATTERSON, J. H., and W. D. HUBER. "A Horizon-Varying, Zero-One Approach to Project Scheduling." *Management Science,* February 1974.

STINSON, J. P., E. W. DAVIS, and B. KHUMAWALA. "Multiple Resource-Constrained Scheduling Using Branch and Bound." *AIIE Transactions,* September 1978.

TALBOT, F. B. "Project Scheduling with Resource-Duration Interactions: The Nonpreemptive Case." *Working paper No. 200,* Graduate School of Business Administration, Ann Arbor, MI: University of Michigan, January 1980.

TALBOT, F. B., and J. H. PATTERSON. "Optimal Methods for Scheduling Under Resource Constraints." *Project Management Quarterly,* December 1979.

TUKEL, O. I. "Scheduling Resource-Constrained Projects When Non-conformities Exist." *Project Management Journal,* September 1996.

TURBAN, E., and J. R. MEREDITH. *Fundamentals of Management Science,* 6th ed. Homewood, IL: Irwin, 1994.

WEAVER, J. "Mainframe ARTEMIS: More Than a Project Management Tool." *Project Management Journal,* April 1988.

WEIST, J. D. "A Heuristic Model for Scheduling Large Projects with Limited Resources." *Management Science,* February 1967.

WEIST, J. D. "Heuristic Programs for Decision Making." *Harvard Business Review,* September–October 1965.

WOODWORTH, B. M., and C. T. WILLIE. "A Heuristic Algorithm for Resource Levelling in Multi-Project, Multi-Resource Scheduling." *Decision Sciences,* 1975.

The following case describes the evolution of a new product and the project devised to take it to market. As well as discussing the issues of developing a work breakdown structure, network diagram, schedule, and resource loading diagrams for each of the involved departments, the case also brings up the issues of time–cost trade-offs, cash flows, and resource leveling.

C A S E

D. U. SINGER HOSPITAL PRODUCTS CORP.
Herbert F. Spirer

D. U. Singer Hospital Products Corp. has done suffi-cient new product development at the research and development level to estimate a high likelihood of technical success for a product of assured commer-cial success: A long-term antiseptic. Management has instructed Singer's Antiseptic Division to make a market entry at the earliest possible time; they have requested a complete plan up to the startup of production. Marketing and other plans following startup of production are to be prepared separately after this plan has been completed.

Project responsibility is assigned to the division's Research and Development Group; Mike Richards, the project scientist who developed the product, is assigned responsibility for project management. As-sistance will be required from other parts of the company: Packaging Task Force, R & D Group; Corporate Engineering; Corporate Purchasing; Hos-pital Products Manufacturing Group; Packaged Products Manufacturing Group.

Mike was concerned about the scope of the proj-ect. He knew from his own experience that a final formula had yet to be developed, although such de-velopment was really a "routine" function. The re-maining questions had to do with color, odor, and consistency additives rather than any performance-related modification. Fortunately, the major regula-tory issues had been resolved and he believed that submission of regulatory documentation would be followed by rapid approval as they already had a let-ter of approval contingent on final documentation.

But there were also issues in packaging that had to be resolved; development of the packaging design was one of his primary concerns at this time. Ulti-mately, there will have to be manufacturing proce-dures in accordance with corporate policies and

standards: capital equipment selection and procure-ment, installation of this equipment and startup.

Mike was concerned about defining the project unambiguously. To that end, he obtained an inter-view with S. L. Mander, the group vice-president.

When he asked Mander where his responsibility should end, the executive turned the question back to him. Mike had been prepared for this and said that he would like to regard his part of the project as done when the production process could be turned over to manufacturing. They agreed that according to Singer practice, this would be when the manufac-turing operation could produce a 95 percent yield of product (fully packaged) at a level of 80 percent of the full production goal of 10 million liters per year.

"But I want you to remember," said Mander, "that you must meet all current FDA, EPA, and OSHA regulations and you must be in compliance with our internal specification—the one I've got is dated September and is RD78/965. And you know that manufacturing now—quite rightly, I feel—in-sists on full written manufacturing procedures."

After this discussion, Mike felt that he had enough information about this aspect to start to pin down what had to be done to achieve these results. His first step in this effort was to meet with P. H. Docent, the director of research.

"You are naive if you think that you can just start right in finalizing the formula," said Docent. "You must first develop a product rationale (**a**).* This is a formally defined process according to company pol-icy. Marketing expects inputs at this stage, manufac-turing expects their voice to be heard, and you will have to have approvals from every unit of the com-

---

*Tasks which must be accounted for in a network plan are identified by lower-case alphabetic symbols in parentheses. Refer to Exhibit 1.

pany that is involved; all of this is reviewed by the Executive Committee. You should have no trouble if you do your homework, but expect to spend a good eight weeks to get this done."

"That certainly stretches things out," said Mike. "I expected to take 12 weeks to develop the ingredient formula (**b**) and you know that I can't start to establish product specifications (**c**) until the formula is complete. That's another three weeks."

"Yes, but while you are working on the product specifications you can get going on the regulatory documentation (**d**). Full internal specifications are not required for that work, but you can't start those documents until the formula is complete."

"Yes, and I find it hard to believe that we can push through both preparation of documents and getting approval in three weeks, but Environmental swears it can be done."

"Oh, it can be done in this case because of the preparatory work. Of course, I won't say that this estimate of three weeks is as certain as our other time estimates. All we need is a change of staff at the Agency and we are in trouble. But once you have both the specifications and the approval, you can immediately start on developing the production processing system (**g**)."

"Yes, and how I wish we could get a lead on that, but the designers say that there is too much uncertainty and they won't move until they have both specifications and regulatory documentation and approval. They are offering pretty fast response; six weeks from start to finish for the processing system."

"They are a good crew, Mike. And of course, you know that you don't have to delay on starting the packaging segment of this project. You can start developing the packaging concept (**e**) just as soon as the product rationale has been developed. If my experience is any judge, it will take a full eight weeks; you'll have to work to keep the process from running forever."

"But as soon as that is finished we can start on the design of the package and its materials (**f**) which usually takes about six weeks. Once that is done we can start developing the packaging system (**h**) which shouldn't take longer than eight weeks," concluded

Mike. At this point he realized that although Docent would have general knowledge, he needed to talk directly to the Director of Manufacturing.

"The first step, which follows the completion of the development of processing and packaging systems," said the Director of Manufacturing, "is to do a complete study of the facilities and equipment requirements (**i**). You won't be able to get that done in less than four weeks. And that must precede the preparation of the capital equipment list (**j**) which should take about three-quarters as long. Of course, as soon as the development of both the process system and packaging system are completed, you could start on preparing the written manufacturing facilities procedures (**q**)."

"But," said Mike, "Can I really finish the procedures before I have installed the manufacturing facilities (**p**)?"

"No, quite right. What you can do is get the first phase done, but the last three of the ten weeks it will take to do that will have to wait for the installation of the manufacturing facilities."

"Then this means that I really have two phases for the writing, that which can be completed without the manufacturing facilities installation (**q**), and that which has to wait for them (**q'**)."

"True. Now you realize that the last thing you have to do after completing the procedures and installing the equipment and facilities is to run a pilot test (**r**) which will show that you have reached a satisfactory level?"

"Yes. Since that must include debugging, I've estimated a six-week period as adequate." The director of manufacturing assented. Mike continued, "What I'm not sure of is whether we can run all the installation tasks in parallel."

"You can let the purchase orders and carry out the procurement of process equipment (**k**), packaging equipment (**l**), and facilities (**m**) as soon as the capital equipment list is complete. The installation of each of these types of equipment and facilities can start as soon as the goods are on hand (**n,o,p**)."

"What do you estimate for the times to do these tasks?" asked Mike. The director of manufacturing estimated 18, 8, and 4 weeks for the purchasing phases for each of the subsystems in that order and four weeks for each of the installations. "Then I can regard my job as done with the delivery of the procedures and when I show my 95 percent yield," said Mike, and the director of manufacturing agreed, but reminded Mike that none of the purchasing cycles could start until the capital equipment list had been prepared and approved (**j**) which he saw as a three-week task.

The executive committee of D. U. Singer Hospital Products Corporation set a starting date for the project of March 10 and asked Mike to project a completion date with his submission of the plan. The committee's request implied that whatever date Mike came up with was acceptable, but Mike knew that he would be expected to show how to shorten the time to complete the project. However, his task in making the schedule was clear; he had to establish the resource requirements and deal with calendar constraints as best as he could.

To this end, Mike had to get an estimate of resources which he decided to do by making a list of the activities and asking each group involved what was their level of employee input. The results of this survey are shown in Exhibit 1. For example, activity

a takes 8 weeks and requires 12 worker-weeks from R&D, or an average of 1.5 workers for the entire 8 week duration of activity **a**.

For the purposes of overall planning, the accounting department told Mike that he could estimate a cost of $600 per week per employee. This would enable him to provide a cash flow forecast along with his plan, which the chief accountant said would be expected, something that Mike had not realized.

Mike knew that it was customary at D. U. Singer to provide the following as parts of a plan to be submitted to the executive committee:

A. Statement of Objectives.

B. Work Breakdown Structure.

C. An activity-on-node (PERT) network.

D. A determination of the critical path(s) and the duration along the path.

E. An activity list, early-start schedule, slack list, and master schedule. Assume that every activity begins at its early start, regardless of resource constraints.

Exhibit 1   Labor Requirements (Worker-weeks)

Activity	Packaging Task Force	R & D Group	Corp. Eng.	H-P Manuf.	Pack. Prod. Manuf.	Maint.	Purchasing	Material & Other Direct Charges
a—prod. rationale	1	12	1	1	2	0	0	$ 0
b—dev. formula	0	16	4	2	0	0	0	500
c—prod. spec.	1	6	3	1	1	0	1	0
d—reg. document	0	12	4	2	0	0	0	0
e—dev. pkg. concept	12	8	4	2	8	0	2	4000
f—design pkg.	12	2	3	0	3	0	3	2000
g—dev. proces. sys.	0	18	12	12	0	0	0	0
h—dev. pkg. sys.	24	8	8	0	8	0	2	0
i—study facil./eqpt. req.	0	4	16	2	2	0	0	0
j—capital equip. list	0	1	3	0	0	0	1	0
k—procure proces. eqpt.	0	1	1	1	0	0	7	40,000
l—procure pkg. eqpt.	1	0	1	0	1	0	9	160,000
m—procure facil.	0	0	1	1	1	1	6	30,000
n—install proces. eqpt.	0	2	4	8	0	4	1	4000
o—install pkg. eqpt.	2	0	4	0	8	4	1	8000
p—install mfg. facil.	0	0	5	5	5	10	1	6000
q,q'—written procedures	5	5	5	10	15	10	0	5000
r—pilot test	3	6	6	6	6	6	0	0

F. A period labor requirements table for each group and the project as a whole. Include bar graphs to illustrate the labor loads.

G. A cumulative labor requirements table for each group and the project as a whole. Include line graphs to illustrate the cumulative loads.

H. A schedule based on the best leveling of labor requirements that could be achieved without lengthening project duration by more than 14 percent in calendar days.

I. A cash flow requirements graph for the project when leveled, assuming that charges are uniformly distributed throughout the activity.

Questions

1. Construct the nine elements of the plan identified above.

2. Analyze the plan for potential problems.

3. Analyze the plan for opportunities.

4. Should the executive committee approve the plan? Why or why not?

5. What alternatives might the executive committee suggest for analysis?

10

Monitoring and Information Systems

In this chapter, perhaps more than in any other, it would be helpful if we could consider everything at once. How is it possible to discuss monitoring without specifying what is to be controlled? On the other hand, how is it possible to specify a control system without understanding what aspects of a project are subject to measurement and how the measurement is to be accomplished? As a matter of fact, one could just as easily argue that evaluation, the primary subject of Chapter 12, should precede both monitoring and control. The placement of these chapters is arbitrary, and readers may feel free to read them in any order. Irrespective of the order in which one considers these subjects, however, their interdependence is clear.

Our fundamental approach to evaluation and control of projects is that these activities are, at base, the opposite sides of project selection and planning. The logic of selection, such as by the Project Portfolio Process described in Chapter 2, dictates the components to be evaluated, and the details of planning expose the elements to be controlled. The ability to measure is prerequisite to either.

For a continuously operating Project Portfolio Process, monitoring the critical project measures, such as by the Project Management Office described in Chapter 4, is required so projects can be terminated, if necessary, and new projects initiated. The same is true, of course, for the maintenance of a risk management system. Not only must the project performance be monitored, but the environment within which the project exists must also be observed and recorded. *Monitoring* is collecting, recording, and reporting information concerning any and all aspects of project performance that the project manager or others in the organization wish to know. In our discussion it is important to remember that monitoring, as an activity, should be kept distinct from controlling (which uses the data supplied by monitoring to bring actual performance into approximate congruence with planned performance), as well as from evaluation (through which judgments are made about the quality and effectiveness of project performance).

First we expand on the nature of this link between planning and control, including a brief discussion of the various aspects of project performance that need to be monitored. We also examine some of the problems associated with monitoring a project. Finally, we report on several computer software packages that can greatly increase the speed and effectiveness of project monitoring.

This book is addressed to practicing PMs as well as students of project management. Students resist the idea that PMs do not have immediate access to accurate information on every aspect of the project. But PMs know it is not always easy to find out what's going on when working on a project. Records are frequently out of date, incomplete, in error, or "somewhere else" when needed. A hospital executive of our acquaintance carried out a project that was designed to generate a major improvement in profitability by altering the patient mix. The hospital's accounting system could not report on the results of the project until six months later.

Throughout the chapter, our primary concern is to ensure that all parties interested in the project have available, *on a timely basis,* the information needed to exercise effective control over the project and the uncertainties that impact on it. The other uses for monitoring (e.g., auditing, learning from past mistakes, or keeping senior management informed), important as they are, must be considered secondary to the control function when constructing the monitoring system. The key issue, then, is to create an information system that gives project managers the information they need to make informed, timely decisions that will keep project performance as close as possible to the project plan.

One final note: In this chapter, we frequently refer to a "project monitor," a "project controller," or even to the "group" or "office" responsible for monitoring. These individuals and groups do in fact exist on most large projects. On a small project, it is likely that the person in charge of monitoring is the same person as the project controller—and the same person as the PM. That is, when we refer to the project monitor and controller, we are referring to roles needed in project management, not necessarily to different individuals.

Project Management in Practice
Using Project Management Software to Schedule the Olympic Games

The XV Olympiad in Calgary involved nearly 2000 athletes from 57 countries in 129 competitive events, attracted over 1,500,000 spectators, was covered by over 5000 journalists, and was run by a staff of 600 professionals complemented by 10,000 volunteers. For those 600 responsible for organizing, planning, scheduling, coordinating, and handling the information requirements for the 16-day extravaganza, the task was over-whelming. The top managers of the organizing committee thus turned to a Computer Based Project Planning and Scheduling (CBPPS) system for scheduling and managing the 30,000 tasks organized into 50 projects.

The goal for the Calgary Games was to provide the best games ever, but within the budget. The philosophy employed was to let each project manager plan his/her own project but meet firm

completion dates and budget limits. This made a lot of additional work for the upper managers since each project's reports and needs were different from every other project's. However, two major features of the project helped make this a success: (1) Knowing that the Games would happen on the scheduled date regardless of whether they were ready or not, and (2) Being such a high-visibility, challenging project that demands exceptional focus on the task.

To schedule the entire Winter Games, the 129-event, 16-day Olympics was broken down into 15-minute periods, except for short-track speed skating which was segmented into 1-minute intervals. There was a printout for every day by venue, minute by minute, and a complete set of drawings of every site, building, and room. Meticulous scheduling was necessary to ensure that the 2500 or so competitors, members of royalty, and government officials were at the right place at the right time. Support staff, including medical and security personnel, were also carefully scheduled for each event as crowds shifted from competition to competition. Transportation—600 buses—also had to be scheduled, oftentimes on short notice. The biggest concern was the weather, and sure enough, the Chinook winds forced the rescheduling of over 20 events, some of them twice!

Yet, the Calgary Games were the best yet, and organized better than ever before. Moreover, as compared to the budget overruns of many other cities, this Olympiad was completed under budget!

Source: R. G. Holland, "The XV Olympic Winter Games: A Case Study in Project Management," *PM Network,* November 1989.

10.1   THE PLANNING-MONITORING-CONTROLLING CYCLE

Throughout this book we have stressed the need to plan, check on progress, compare progress to the plan, and take corrective action if progress does not match the plan. The key things to be planned, monitored, and controlled are time (schedule), cost (budget), and performance (specifications). These, after all, encompass the fundamental objectives of the project.

There is no doubt that some organizations do not spend sufficient time and effort on planning and controlling projects. It is far easier to focus on doing, especially because it appears to be more effective to "stop all the talk and get on with the work." We could cite firm after firm that incurred great expense (and major losses) because the planning process was inadequate for the tasks undertaken.

- A major construction project ran over budget by 63 percent and over schedule by 48 percent because the PM decided that, since "he had managed similar projects several times before, he knew what to do without going into all that detail that no one looks at anyway."
- A large industrial equipment supplier "took a bath" on a project designed to develop a new area of business because they applied the same planning and control procedures to the new area that they had used (successfully) on previous, smaller, less complex jobs.
- A computer store won a competitive bid to supply a computer, five terminals, and associated software to the Kansas City office of a national firm. Admittedly insufficient planning made the installation significantly late. Performance of the software was not close to specified levels. This botched job prevented the firm from being invited to bid on more than 20 similar installations planned by the client.

The planning (budgeting and scheduling) methods we propose "put the hassles up front." They require a significantly greater investment of time and energy early in the life of the project, but they significantly reduce the extent and cost of poor performance and time/cost overruns. Note that this is no guarantee of a trouble-free project, merely a decline in the risk of failure.

It is useful to perceive the control process as a *closed-loop* system, with revised plans and schedules (if warranted) following corrective actions. We delay a detailed discussion on control until the next chapter, but the planning-monitoring-controlling cycle is continuously in process until the project is completed. The information flows for such a cycle are illustrated in Figure 10-1. Note the direction of the flows, information flowing from the bottom toward the top and authority flowing from the top down.

It is also useful to construct this process as an internal part of the organizational structure of the project, not something external to and imposed on it or, worse, in conflict with it. Finally, experience tells us that it is also desirable, though not mandatory, that the planning-monitoring-controlling cycle be the normal way of life in the parent organization. What is good for the project is equally good for the parent firm. In any case, unless the PM has a smoothly operating monitoring/control system, it will be difficult to manage the project effectively.

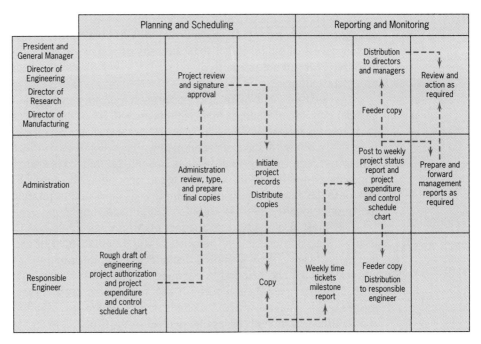

Figure 10-1   Project authorization and expenditure control system information flow. *Source: Dean (1968).*

Designing the Monitoring System

The first step in setting up any monitoring system is to identify the key factors to be controlled. Clearly, the PM wants to monitor performance, cost, and time but must define precisely which specific characteristics of performance, cost, and time should be controlled and then establish exact boundaries within which control should be maintained. There may also be other factors of importance worth noting, at least at milestones or review points in the life of the project. For example, the number of labor hours used, the number or extent of process or output changes, the level of customer satisfaction, and similar items may be worthy of note on individual projects.

But the best source of items to be monitored is the project action plan—actually, the set of action plans that describe what is being done, when, and the planned level of resource usage for each task, work package, and work element in the project. The monitoring system is a direct connection between planning and control. If it does not collect and report information on some significant element of the plan, control can be faulty or missing. The action plan furnishes the key items that must be measured and reported to the control system, but it is not sufficient. For example, the PM might want to know about changes in the client's attitudes toward the project. Information on the morale of the project team might be useful in preparing for organizational or personnel changes on the project. These two latter items may be quite important, but are not reflected in the project's action plans.

Unfortunately, it is common to focus monitoring activities on data that are easily gathered—rather than important—or to concentrate on "objective" measures that are easily defended at the expense of softer, more subjective data that may be more valuable for control. Above all, monitoring should concentrate primarily on measuring various facets of output rather than intensity of activity. It is crucial to remember that effective PMs are not primarily interested in how hard their project teams work. They are interested in achieving results.

The measurement of project performance usually poses the most difficult data gathering problem. There is a strong tendency to let project inputs serve as surrogate measures for output. If we have spent 50 percent of the budget (or of the scheduled time), we assume we have also completed 50 percent of the project or reached 50 percent of our performance goal. If the item being referenced is a small work unit, it does not make a significant difference if we are wrong. If, however, the reference is to a task or to the entire project, the assumption of input/output proportionality (hereafter, the "proportionality rule") is apt to be badly misleading.

One must also be aware of the fact that it is common to specify performance to a level of precision that is both unnecessary and unrealistic. For example, a communications software project specified that a telephone "information" system had to locate a phone number and respond to the querier in 5 seconds or less. Is 5.1 seconds a failure? Does the specification mean 5 seconds or less every time, or merely that response times should average 5 seconds or less? Is the specification satisfied if the response time is 5 seconds or less 90 percent of the time?

The monitoring systems we describe in this chapter, however, focus mainly on time and cost as measures of performance, not specifications. While we are most certainly concerned with keeping the project "on spec," and do consider some of the problems of monitoring output, the subject is not fully developed here because the software designed to monitor projects is not constructed to deal with the subject adequately. The matter will get more attention in Chapter 12 when auditing is discussed.

Given all this, performance criteria, standards, and data collection procedures must be established for each of the factors to be measured. The criteria and data collection procedures are usually set up for the life of the project. The standards themselves, however, may not be constant over the project's life. They may change as a result of altered capabilities within the parent organization or a technological breakthrough made by the project team; but, perhaps more often than not, standards and criteria change because of factors that are not under the control of the PM. For example, they may be changed by the client. One client who had ordered a special piece of audio equipment altered performance specifications significantly when electronic parts became available that could filter out random noises.

Standards may also be changed by the community as a response to some shift in public policy—witness the changes in the performance standards imposed on nuclear power installations or automotive exhaust systems. Shifts in the prime rate of interest or in unemployment levels often alter the standards that the PM must use for making project related decisions. The monitoring process is based on the criteria and standards because they dictate, or at least constrain, the set of relevant measures.

Next, the information to be collected must be identified. This may consist of accounting data, operating data, engineering test data, customer reactions, specification changes, and the like. The fundamental problem is to determine precisely which of all the available data should be collected. It is worth repeating that the typical determinant for collecting data too often seems to be simply the ease with which they can be gathered. Of course the nature of the required data is dictated by the project plan, as well as by the goals of the parent organization, the needs of the client, and by the fact that it is desirable to improve the process of managing projects.

Closely monitoring project work is often justified with the argument that keeping close track of progress will reduce the amount of crashing required near the end of the project. Partovi and Burton (1993) tested this argument and found that it was not strictly true. They examined five monitoring policies: no monitoring, monitoring at random times, equal interval monitoring, monitoring more frequently at the start of the project, and monitoring more frequently late in the project's life. They found that there was no significant difference in the amount of crashing effort expended whatever monitoring protocol was used, but that high frequency monitoring late in the project life was the best policy to prevent project lateness.

Perhaps the most common error made when monitoring data is to gather information that is clearly related to project performance but has little or no probability of changing significantly from one collection period to the next. Prior to its breakup, the American Telephone and Telegraph Company used to collect monthly statistics on a very large number of indicators of operating efficiency. The extent of the collection was such that it filled a telephone-book-sized volume known as "Ma Bell's Green Book." For a great many of the indicators, the likelihood of a significant change from one month to the next was extremely small. When asked about the matter, one official remarked that the mere collection of the data kept the operating companies "on their toes." We feel that there are other, more positive and less expensive ways of motivating project personnel. Certainly, "collect everything" is inappropriate as a monitoring policy.

Therefore, the first task is to examine the project plans in order to extract performance, time, and cost goals. These goals should relate in some fashion to each of the different levels of detail; that is, some should relate to the project, some to its tasks, some to the work packages, and so on. Data must be identified that measure achievement against these goals, and mechanisms designed that gather and store such data. If at least some of the data do not relate to the work unit level, no useful action is apt to be taken. In the end, it is the detailed work of the project that must be altered if any aspect of project performance is to be changed.

Similarly, the process of developing and managing projects should be considered and steps taken to ensure that information relevant to the diagnosis and treatment of the project's organizational infirmities and procedural problems are gathered and collected. A reading of the fascinating book *The Soul of a New Machine* (Kidder, 1981) reveals the crucial roles that organizational factors, interpersonal relationships, and managerial style play in determining project success.

How to Collect Data

Given that we know *what type* of data we want to collect, the next question is *how* to collect this information. At this point in the construction of a monitoring system, it is necessary to define precisely what pieces of information should be gathered and when. In most cases, the PM has options. Questions arise. Should cost data be gathered before or after some specific event? Is it always mandatory to collect time and cost information at exactly the same point in the process? What do we do if a specific item is difficult to collect because the data source (human) fears reporting any information that might contribute to a negative performance evaluation? What do we do about the fact that some use of time is reported as "hours charged" to our project, and we are quite aware that our project has been charged for work done on another project (but for the same customer) that is over budget? Are special forms needed for data collection? Should we set up quality control procedures to ensure the integrity of data transference from its source to the project information system? Such questions merely indicate the broad range of knotty issues that must be handled.

A large proportion of all data collected takes one of the following forms, each of which is suitable for some types of measures.

1. *Frequency counts* A simple tally of the occurrence of an event. This type of measure is often used for "complaints," "number of times a project report is late," "days without an accident," "bugs in a computer program," and similar items. The data are usually easy to collect and are often reported as events per unit time or events as a percent of a standard number. Even with such simple counts, data may be difficult to collect. Items such as "errors" or "complaints" often go unreported by individuals or groups not particularly eager to advertise malperformance.

2. *Raw numbers* Dates, dollars, hours, physical amounts of resources used, and specifications are usually reported in this way. These numbers are reported in a wide variety of ways, but often as direct comparisons with an expected or standard number. Also, "variances" are commonly reported either as the difference between actual and standard or as the ratio of actual to standard. Differences or ratios can also be plotted as a time series to show changes in system performance. When collecting raw project data, it is important to make sure that all data are collected from sources that operate on the same time intervals and with the same rules for data collection.

3. *Subjective numeric ratings* These numbers are subjective estimates, usually of a quality, made by knowledgeable individuals or groups. They can be reported in most of the same ways that objective raw numbers are, but care should be taken to make sure that the numbers are not manipulated in ways only suitable for quantitative measures. (See Chapter 2 for comments on measurements.) Ordinal rankings of performance are included in this category.

4. *Indicators* When the PM cannot measure some aspect of system performance directly, it may be possible to find an indirect measure or indicator. The speed with which change orders are processed and changes are incorporated into the project is often a good measure of team efficiency. Response to change may also be an indicator of the quality of communications on the project team. When using indicators to measure performance, the PM must make sure that the link between the indicator and the desired performance measure is as direct as possible.

5. *Verbal measures* Measures for such performance characteristics as "quality of team member cooperation," "morale of team members," or "quality of interaction with the client" frequently take the form of verbal characterizations. As long as the set of characterizations is limited and the meanings of the individual terms consistently understood by all, these data serve their purposes reasonably well.

Drug Counseling Program

A social service agency applied for and received funding for a special project to counsel male drug addicts between 18 and 24 years of age, and to secure full-time employment for each client (or part-time employment for clients who were still in school). To qualify for the program, the addicts must have been arrested for a crime, but not be classed as "repeat offenders." Further, the addict must be living with at least one member of his family who is a parent or guardian. Among other conditions placed on the grant, the agency was asked to develop a measure of effectiveness for the counseling program that was acceptable to the funding agency.

The primary measure of effectiveness adopted by most drug programs was "rate of recidivism." A recidivistic incident is defined as any re-arrest for a drug-related crime, or any behavior that resulted in the individual reentering the social service system after completing the program and being discharged.

While a "re-arrest" is most surely recidivistic, there were several cases in which former clients contacted the agency and asked to be re-admitted to the program. These voluntary re-admissions resulted when a former client either began to use drugs again or was fearful that he would begin again. It seemed to the agency professionals that voluntary re-admissions were successes, not failures.

A new measure of effectiveness was developed to replace "rate of recidivism." It was composed of scores on three different measures, combined with equal weighting.

1. Number of successive weeks of "clean urines."

2. Number of successive months of satisfactory employment (or schooling) experience.

3. Number of successive months of satisfactory behavior at home.

Scores on the second and third measures were based on interviews with employers, teachers, and parent(s).

After data collection has been completed, reports on project progress should be generated. These include project status reports, time/cost reports, and variance reports, among others. Causes and effects should be identified and trends noted. Plans, charts, and tables should be updated on a timely basis. Where known, "comparables" should be reported, as should statistical distributions of previous data if available. Both help the PM (and others) to interpret the data being monitored. Figures 10-2 and 10-3 illustrate the use of such data. Figure 10-2 shows the results of a count of "bugs" found during a series of tests run on a new piece of computer software. (Bugs found were fixed prior to subsequent tests.) Figure 10-3 shows the percent of the time a computer program retrieved data within a specified time limit. Each point represents a series of trials.

The PM can fit a statistical function to the data shown in Figure 10-2 and make a rough estimate of the number of tests that will have to be run to find some predetermined number of additional bugs in the program. By fitting a curve (formally or "by eyeball") to the data in Figure 10-3, the PM can estimate the cost and time (the number of additional trials and adjustments) required to get system performance up to the

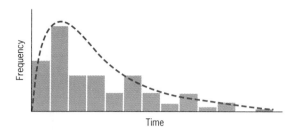

Figure 10-2   Number of bugs found during test of Datamix program.

specified level. (Curve and distribution fitting is easily done by use of Crystal Ball 2000®.)

The nature of *timeliness* will be amplified next, but it is important that the PM make sure that the PERT/CPM and Gantt charts in the project war room (office) are frequently updated. Monitoring can serve to maintain high morale on the project team as well as to alert team members to problems that will have to be solved.

The purpose of the monitoring system is to gather and report data. The purpose of the control system is to act on the data. To aid the *project controller,* it is helpful for the *monitor* to carry out some data analysis. Significant differences from plan should be highlighted or "flagged" so that they cannot be overlooked by the controller. The methods of statistical quality control are very useful for determining what size variances are "significant" and sometimes even help in determining the probable cause(s) of variances. Where causation is known, it should be noted. Where it is not known, an investigation may be in order. (It is also useful to remember that some things are more easily fixed than understood, in which case investigations may not be cost-effective.) The decisions about when an investigation should be conducted, by whom, and by what methods are the prerogative of the project controller, although the actual investigation may be conducted by the group responsible for monitoring.

The Emanon Aircraft Company example presented in Chapter 7 is a case in point. While the study team collected and analyzed a great deal of cost information during the process of finding the problem, the method used for the analysis was actually quite simple. The team compared forecast or estimated cost, F(t), with actual cost, A(t), for each batch of output from the manufacturing system. This analysis was done for each cost center. The ratio of actual cost to estimated cost was calculated and plot-

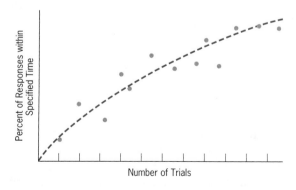

Figure 10-3   Percent of specified performance met during repeated trials.

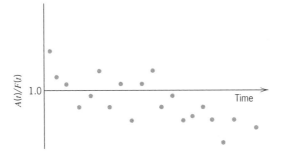

Figure 10-4   Ratio of actual material cost to estimated material cost. Emanon Aircraft Company.

ted as a time series, as in Figure 10-4.* Note that $A(t)/F(t) < 1$ when the cost forecast for a cost center is greater than actual. In this case, the cost involved was "material cost." Though careful statistical analysis was not necessary in this specific case, standard quality control techniques have wide application to project management (see any book on statistical quality control—Evans and Lindsay, 1993, for example). Time series analysis can often give the PM an early warning of problems.

At base, this provides a *management by exception* reporting system for the PM. But management by exception has its flaws as well as its strengths. It is essentially an "after-the-fact" approach to control. Variances occur, are investigated, and only then is action taken. The astute PM is far more interested in preventing problems than curing them. Therefore, the monitoring system should develop data streams that indicate variances yet to come. Obviously, such indicators are apt to be statistical in nature, hinting at the likelihood of a future problem rather than predicting it with certainty. An example would be a trend in the data showing a system heading out of control. Interested readers are referred to the "2-5-7 Rule" (see Shafer and Meredith, 1998, quality chapters). The PM may waste time and effort trying to deal with trouble that will not actually occur. This may be frustrating, but the costs of dealing with some nonproblems is usually minor when compared to the costs of dealing with real problems too late.

In creating the monitoring system, some care should be devoted to the issues of honesty and bias. The former is dealt with by setting in place an internal audit. The audit serves the purpose of ensuring that the information gathered is honest. No audit, however, can prevent bias. All data are biased by those who report them, advertently or inadvertently. The controller must understand this fact of life. The first issue is to determine whether the possibility of bias in the data matters significantly. If not, nothing need be done. Bias finding and correcting activities (cf. Chapter 7) are worthwhile only if data with less or no bias are required.

The issue of creating an atmosphere that fosters honesty on a project is widely ignored, but it is of major importance. A set of instructions to the PM on how to do this is not beyond the scope of this book, but if such instructions exist, we do not know of them. We do, however, have some advice to offer. The PM can tolerate almost any kind of behavior except dishonesty. Projects are vulnerable to dishonesty, far more

* Actual data were not used in constructing Figure 10-4, but the figure reflects the consultants' findings.

vulnerable than the ongoing operations of the parent organization. Standard operations are characterized by considerable knowledge about expected system performance. When the monitoring system reports information that deviates from expectations, it is visible, noteworthy, and tends to get attention. In the case of many projects, expectations are not so well known. Deviations are not recognized for what they are. The PM is often dependent on team members to call attention to problems. To get this cooperation, the PM must make sure that the bearer of bad news is not punished; nor is the admitter-to-error executed. On the other hand, the hider-of-mistakes may be shot with impunity—and then sent to Siberia.

There is some tendency for project monitoring systems to include an analysis directed at the assignment of blame. This practice has doubtful value. While the managerial dictum "rewards and punishments should be closely associated with performance" has the ring of good common sense, it is actually not good advice. Instead of motivating people to better performance, the practice is more apt to result in lower expectations. If achievement of goals is directly measured and directly rewarded, tremendous pressure will be put on people to understate goals and to generate plans that can be met or exceeded with minimal risk and effort.

Project Management in Practice
Tracking Scope Creep: A Project Manager Responds

Dear Editor:

The two-part *Scope Creep* article in the Winter and Spring issues of *Today's Engineer* presented an interesting case study. The engineering-only solution, however, misses the bigger issue—lack of a formal project management process. It is unfortunate that the need for formal project management is omitted from the article. A formal project management process is the cornerstone of on-time and on-schedule projects. Such a process includes:

- A formal project plan development process
- A tracking system capable of providing variance analysis data
- Managing project scope, schedule, and resource changes throughout the project life cycle.

This case study depicts an all-too-familiar scenario:

1. An engineer is selected as project manager—usually with no formal project management training.

2. The project team is composed of primarily engineers—marketing and other functional organizations are viewed as project outsiders, rather than team members, and do not participate in the planning process.

3. Project objectives and deliverables are poorly defined—usually by engineering—including only engineering deliverables.

4. A comprehensive work breakdown structure, task completion criteria, and network diagram are nonexistent—progress measurement is therefore somewhat arbitrary and difficult to ascertain.

5. Task duration estimates are probably determined by someone other than the task owner—making estimates invalid.

6. The project schedule is pasted together to look good and match target dates—missing the opportunity to use critical path method (CPM) to develop a credible schedule.

7. Resource requirements, including people and budget, are guesses—usually without the benefit of using a comprehensive CPM-developed preliminary schedule.

8. A risk management plan does not exist—most project risks are treated as surprises.

9. The project plan is not validated and baselined by the project sponsor—missing the opportunity to obtain team and sponsor commitment prior to implementation.

10. A formal project tracking and change management system does not exist—impossible to track a project without a plan to measure progress against and to manage changes.

Project management, like engineering, is a discipline that must be learned. Project management is not for everyone. It requires a different skill set than, say, engineering or marketing.

Source: J. Sivak, "Scope Creep: A Project Manager Responds," ©1998 IEEE. Reprinted with permission from *Today's Engineer*, Vol. 1, No. 3 (Summer), p. 8, 1998.

10.2 INFORMATION NEEDS AND THE REPORTING PROCESS

Everyone concerned with the project should be appropriately tied into the project reporting system. The monitoring system ought to be constructed so that it addresses every level of management, but reports need not be of the same depth or at the same frequency for each level. Lower-level personnel have a need for detailed information about individual tasks and the factors affecting such tasks. Report frequency is usually high. For the senior management levels, overview reports describe progress in more aggregated terms with less individual task detail unless senior management has a special interest in a specific activity or task. Reports are issued less often. In both cases, the structure of the reports should reflect the WBS, with each managerial level receiving reports that allow the exercise of control at the relevant level. At times it may be necessary to move information between organizations, as illustrated in Figure 10-5, as well as between managerial levels.

The proliferation of electronic mechanisms along with a wide array of software have made the process of collecting and disseminating information much faster and less arduous than seemed possible when the first edition of this book was written (Reingold, 1996). (And, of course, it follows that a great deal more information is being collected, and sometimes used.) The globalization of industry has lead to a sharp increase in the number of projects that are carried out in places far from some of the project workers and even from management. These *virtual* projects can be managed from remote locations only because the virtual meetings involved in planning and controlling the projects are conducted through electronic media. Use of the Internet and Web sites for projects allows communication of (and response to) the most complex information. Even tracking and control of multiple projects through electronic systems are quite feasible.

In addition to its use for conducting the routines of project management, the

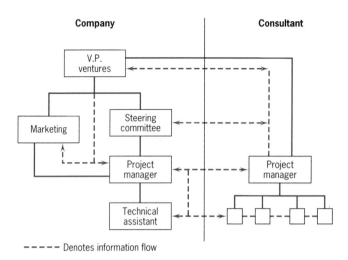

Figure 10-5   Reporting and information flows between organizations working on a common project.

Internet is a rich source of information, including building codes, databases on almost anything, the Yellow Pages for practically anywhere, patent information, and technical aid for managing projects, to mention only a small fraction of readily available information (Jensen, 1996). Many current project management software packages allow easy connection to the Internet and e-mail to transmit information, action plans, charts, networks, and reports practically anywhere. The material can be altered or updated and returned to the sender with minimal effort beyond that needed to move the information to the next cubicle.

> "E-mail is not to be used to pass on information or data. It should be used only for company business."

The relationship of project reports to the project action plan or WBS is the key to the determination of both report content and frequency. Reports must contain data relevant to the control of specific tasks that are being carried out according to a specific schedule. The frequency of reporting should be great enough to allow control to be exerted during or before the period in which the task is scheduled for completion. For example, efficacy tests of drugs do not produce rapid results in most cases. Thus, there is no reason for weekly (and perhaps not even monthly) reports on such tests. When test results begin to occur, more frequent reports and updates may be required.

In addition to the criterion that reports should be available in time to be used for project control, the timing of reports should generally correspond to the timing of project milestones. This means that project reports may not be issued periodically—excepting progress reports for senior management. There seems to be no logical reason, except for tradition, to issue weekly, monthly, quarterly, etc. reports. Few projects require attention so neatly consistent with the calendar. This must not be taken as advice to issue reports "every once in a while." Reports should be scheduled in the project plan. They should be issued on time. The report schedule, however, need not call for *periodic* reports.

Identification of project milestones depends on who is interested. For senior management, there may be only a few milestones, even in large projects. For the PM there may be many critical points in the project schedule at which major decisions must be made, large changes in the resource base must be initiated, or key technical results achieved. The milestones relevant to lower levels relate to finer detail and occur with higher frequency. Individual senior managers have widely varying preferences in the frequency and content of reports they wish to see. The PM is well advised to supply them. But irrespective of the senior manager's wishes, the PM must make sure that relevant information about progress is always included—and reported in a way it cannot be overlooked. It is also counterproductive to delay reporting on a current or immediately potential crisis until the next routine report is due.

The nature of the monitoring reports should be consistent with the logic of the planning, budgeting, and scheduling systems. The primary purpose is, of course, to ensure achievement of the project plan through control. There is little reason to burden operating members of the project team with extensive reports on matters that are not subject to control—at least not by them. For example, overhead costs or the in-house rental cost of the project war room are simply not appropriate considerations for a team member who is supervising a research experiment in polymer chemistry or designing the advertising campaign for a new brand of coffee. The scheduling and resource usage columns of the project action plan will serve as the key to the design of project reports.

There are many benefits of detailed, timely reports delivered to the proper people. Among them are:

- Mutual understanding of the goals of the project
- Awareness of the progress of parallel activities and of the problems associated with coordination among activities
- More realistic planning for the needs of all groups and individuals working on the project
- Understanding the relationships of individual tasks to one another and to the overall project
- Early warning signals of potential problems and delays in the project
- Minimizing the confusion associated with change by reducing delays in communicating the change
- Faster management action in response to unacceptable or inappropriate work
- Higher visibility to top management, including attention directed to the immediate needs of the project
- Keeping the client and other interested outside parties up to date on project status, particularly regarding project costs, milestones, and deliverables.

Report Types

> "One day my boss asked me to submit a status report to him concerning a project I was working on. I asked him if tomorrow would be soon enough. He said, 'If I wanted it tomorrow, I would have waited until tomorrow to ask for it!' "

For the purposes of project management, we can consider three distinct types of reports: routine, exception, and special analysis. The routine reports are those issued on a regular basis; but, as we noted above, *regular* does not necessarily refer to the calendar. For senior management, the reports will usually be periodic, but for the PM and lower-level project personnel, milestones may be used to trigger routine reports. At times, it may be useful to issue routine reports on resource usage periodically, occasionally on a weekly or even daily basis.

Exception reports are useful in two cases. First, they are directly oriented to project management decision making and should be distributed to the team members who will have prime responsibility for decisions or who have a clear "need to know." Second, they may be issued when a decision is made on an exception basis and it is desirable to inform other managers as well as to document the decision—in other words, as part of a sensible procedure for protecting oneself. (PMs should be aware that overuse of exception reporting will be perceived by top management as sheeplike, overly cautious behavior.)

Special analysis reports are used to disseminate the results of special studies conducted as part of the project or as a response to special problems that arise during the project. Usually they cover matters that may be of interest to other PMs, or make use of analytic methods that might be helpful on other projects. Studies on the use of substitute materials, evaluation of alternative manufacturing processes, availability of external consultants, capabilities of new software, and descriptions of new governmental regulations are all typical of the kinds of subjects covered in special analysis reports. Distribution of these reports is usually made to anyone who might be interested.

Meetings

To celebrate his 50th birthday, columnist Dave Barry listed "25 things you will learn in 50 years of living." The sixteenth was "If you had to identify, in one word, the reason why the human race has not and never will achieve its full potential, that word would be 'meetings.' " For a large majority of project managers and workers, meetings are as welcome as bad checks or unmentionable diseases. Widespread rumors that meetings were invented by Torquemada to the contrary, there is no doubt that meetings of project teams are necessary and often helpful. The main complaints are that they are interminably long, come to no conclusions, and waste everyone's time. Indeed, a short commentary on how not to run a meeting is entitled, "Creative Time Wasting" (Nevison, 1995).

Thus far, we have implicitly assumed that "reports" were written and disseminated by hard-copy, e-mail or by Internet. Far more often, however, all three types of reports are delivered in face-to-face meetings, and in telephone conference calls. Indeed, senior managers usually insist on face-to-face meetings for staying informed about project progress, and these meetings may touch on almost any subject relevant to the project. Project review meetings can be either highly structured (see Knutson, 1996, for instance) or deceptively casual, but they are always important.

A large majority of project meetings do not concern senior management. They are project team meetings, occasionally including the client, and concern the day-to-day problems met on all projects. There is no particular reason that these meetings need to be conducted in a manner that is so dreaded by attendees. A few simple rules can remove most of the onus associated with project meetings.

- Use meetings for making group decisions or getting input for important problems. Avoid "show-and-tell" meetings, sometimes called "status and review meetings." If the latter type of meeting has been used to keep project team members informed about what others are doing on the project, insist that such information be communicated personally or electronically by the relevant individuals to the relevant individuals. Only when there is a clear need, such as informing senior management of the project's status, and it is difficult for team members to "get together" on their own, are status and review meetings appropriate.

- Have preset starting and stopping times as well as a written agenda. Stick with both, and above all, do not penalize those who show up on time by making them wait for those who are tardy.

- Make sure that you (and others) do your homework prior to the meeting. Be prepared!

- If you chair the meeting, take your own minutes. Reality (and the minutes become reality as soon as the meeting is over) is too important to be left to the most junior person present. Distribute the minutes as soon as possible after the meeting, no later than the next work day.

- Avoid attributing remarks or viewpoints to individuals in the minutes. Attribution makes people quite wary about what they say in meetings and damps creativity as well as controversy. Also, do not report votes on controversial matters. It is, for example, inappropriate to report in the minutes that the project team voted to send a "Get Well" card to the boss; 4 yea and 3 nay.

- Avoid overly formal rules of procedure. A project meeting is not a parliament and is not the place for Robert's Rules of Order, though courtesy is always in order.

- If a serious problem or crisis arises, call a meeting for the purpose of dealing with that issue only. The stopping time for such meetings may be "When the problem has been solved."

Some types of meetings should never be held at all. A large, diversified manufacturing firm holds monthly "status and review" meetings in each of its divisions at which the managers of all projects report to a Project Review Committee (PRC). The divisional PRCs are made up of senior managers. At least one, and we are told more than one, of the PRCs apparently models its meetings on "Hell Week" at a nearby university fraternity. Hazing and humiliating the project managers who must report to the committee is standard practice. The results are to be expected. Projects are managed defensively. Creativity is avoided. Project managers spend time printing and distributing resumés. The best PMs do not stay long.

In 1976, Antony Jay (1995) wrote a classic article on how to conduct a meeting. We recommend it; it is still a classic.

Common Reporting Problems

There are three common difficulties in the design of project reports. First, there is usually too much detail, both in the reports themselves and in the input being solicited from workers. Unnecessary detail (or too frequent reporting) usually results in the reports not being read. Also, it prevents project team members from finding the information they need. Furthermore, the demand for large quantities of highly detailed input information often results in careless preparation of the data, thereby casting doubt on the validity of reports based on such data. Finally, the preparation and inclusion of unnecessary detail are costly, at the very least.

A second major problem is the poor interface between the project information system and the parent firm's information system. Data are rarely comparable, and interaction between the PM and the organization's accountants is often strained. In our experience, the PM may try to force a connection. It rarely works well. The parent organization's information system must serve as the definitional prototype for the project's information system. In effect, this means that the parent's accounting, engineering, marketing, finance, personnel, and production information systems should be used as the base on which the project's information system is built. Obviously, different types of reports must be constructed for managing the project, but they can be built by using standard data for the most part. The PM can feel free to add new kinds of data to the information base but cannot insist that costs, resource usage, and the like be reported in the project differently from how they are reported in the parent organization. (Clearly, this rule does not apply to information generated or requested by the PM for the purpose of project management.)

The project-oriented firm or the organization that simultaneously conducts a large number of projects can justify a customized project database and report system specifically tailored to its special needs. In such cases, the interface between the project information system and the organization's overall information system must be carefully designed to ensure that data are not lost or distorted when moving from one system to the other. It is also important to make sure that when cost/performance data are reported, the data represent appropriate time periods.

The third problem concerns a poor correspondence between the planning and the monitoring systems. If the monitoring system is not tracking information directly related to the project's plans, control is meaningless. This often happens when the firm's existing information system is used for monitoring without modifications specifically designed for project management. For example, an existing cost tracking system oriented to shop operations would be inappropriate for a project with major activities in the area of research and development. But as we just noted, the option of running the project from a different database is generally not viable. The PM's problem is to fit standard information into a reporting and tracking system that is appropriate for the project.

The real message carried by project reports is in the comparison of actual activity to plan and of actual output to desired output. Variances are reported by the monitoring system, and responsibility for action rests with the controller. Because the project plan is described in terms of performance, time, and cost, variances are reported for those same variables. Project variance reports usually follow the same format used by the accounting department, but at times they may be presented differently.

10.3 EARNED VALUE ANALYSIS

Thus far, our examples have covered monitoring for parts of projects. The monitoring of performance for the entire project is also crucial because performance is the *raison d'être* of the project. *Individual* task performance must be monitored carefully because the timing and coordination between individual tasks is important. But overall project performance is the crux of the matter and must not be overlooked. One way of measuring overall performance is by using an aggregate performance measure called *earned value.*

To see how the concept of earned value arose, consider Figure 10-6. In Figure 10-6a, acutual progress is plotted alongside planned ("scheduled") progress, and the "effective" progress time (TE) is noted on the time axis. Because progress is less than planned (in this example), TE is less than the actual time (TA). On the cost chart (Figure 10-6b) we see that the apparent variance between the scheduled and actual cost at this time (SC – AC) is quite small, despite the lack of progress (earned value, EV).

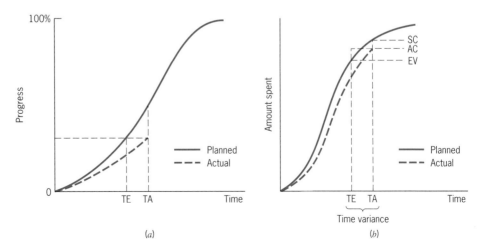

Figure 10-6   Cost-schedule reconciliation charts.

But this is misleading; the variance should be much more given the lack of progress. As we illustrate a bit later, the earned value chart is a combination of these two graphs to more accurately show schedule, cost, and "performance" (measured as value completed in earned dollars of progress).

There is a considerable body of literature devoted to earned value. To note only a few of the available items, see Barr (1996), Brandon (1998), the Flemming references, Garrehy (1999), Hatfield (1996), Project Management Institute (2000), and Singletary (1996). One must, however, exercise some care when reading any article on the subject. Various ratio index numbers have almost as many names (and hence, acronyms) as there are writers. Some authors take further license, see Brandon (1998) for instance, and also see the subsequent *Project Management Journal's* Correspondence column (September 1998, p. 53) for readers' reactions. We will adopt and stick to the PMBOK version of things, but will also note the names and acronyms used by Microsoft's Project®.* Any other names/acronyms will be identified with the author(s). A history of earned value from its origin in PERT/Cost to its culmination in C/SCSC (Cost/Schedule Control System Criteria) together with its techniques, advantages, and disadvantages is reported in a series in *PM Network* starting with Flemming and Koppelman (1994).

The Earned Value Chart and Calculations

As noted above, a serious difficulty with comparing actual expenditures against budgeted or *baseline* expenditures for any given time period is that the comparison fails to take into account the amount of work accomplished relative to the cost incurred. The earned value of work performed (*value completed*) for those tasks in progress is found by multiplying the estimated percent physical completion of work for each task by the planned cost for those tasks. The result is the amount that should have been spent on the task thus far. This can then be compared with the actual amount spent.

Making an overall estimate of the percent completion of a project, without careful study of each of its tasks and work units, is not sensible—though some people make such estimates nonetheless. Instead, it is apparent that at any date during the life of a project the following general condition exists: Some work units have been finished, and they are 100 percent complete; some work units have not yet been started, and they are 0 percent complete; other units have been started but are not yet finished, and for this latter group we may estimate a percent completion.

As we said, estimating the "percent completion" of each task (or work package) is nontrivial. If the task is to write a piece of software, percent completion can be estimated as the number of lines of code written divided by the total number of lines to be written—given that the latter has been estimated. But what if the task is to test the software? We have run a known number of tests, but how many remain to be run?

There are several conventions used to aid in estimating percent completion:

- The 50–50 estimate. Fifty percent completion is assumed when the task is begun, and the remaining 50 percent when the work is complete. This seems to

---

*Earlier versions of Microsoft Project used a slightly different way to calculate earned value variances. MSP 2002 shows alternative acronyms in the Help menu.

be the most popular rule, probably because it is relatively fair and doesn't require the effort of attempting to estimate task progress.

- The 0–100 percent rule. This rule allows no credit for work until the task is complete. With this highly conservative rule, the project always seems to be running late, until the very end of the project when it appears to suddenly catch up.
- Critical input use. This rule assigns progress according to the amount of a critical input that has been used. Obviously, the rule is more accurate if the task uses this input as true progress is being made (such as skilled labor on a skill-dependent task). If a task requires a machine as its critical input to achieve any progress and the machine needs to be purchased up front, then this rule would give full credit for task completion when virtually no progress had been made at all.
- The proportionality rule. This rule divides planned (or actual) time-to-date by total scheduled time [or budgeted (or actual) cost-to-date by total budgeted cost] to calculate percent complete. This is also a commonly used rule.

These rough guides to "percent completion" are not meant to be applied to the project as a whole, though sometimes they are, but rather to individual activities. For projects with few activities, rough measures can be misleading. For projects with a fairly large number of activities, however, the error caused by percent completion rules is such a small part of the total project time/cost that the errors are insignificant. More serious is the tendency to speak of an entire project as being "73 percent complete." In most cases this has no real meaning—certainly not what is implied by the overly exact number. Some authors assume that making estimates of percent completion is simple (Brandon, 1998, p. 12, col. 2, for instance). The estimation task is difficult and arbitrary at best, which is why the 50–50 and other rules have been adopted.

A graph illustrating the concept of earned value such as that shown in Figure 10-7 can be constructed using the above rules and provides a basis for evaluating cost and performance to date. If the total value of the work accomplished is in balance with the planned (baseline) cost (i.e., minimal scheduling variance), as well as its actual cost (minimal cost variance),then top management has no particular need for a detailed analysis of individual tasks. Thus the concept of earned value combines cost reporting and aggregate performance reporting into one comprehensive chart. The baseline cost to completion is indicated on the chart and referred to as the budget at completion (BAC). The actual cost to date can also be projected to completion, as will be shown further on, and is referred to as the estimated cost at completion (EAC).

We identify several variances on the earned value chart following two primary guidelines: (1) A negative variance is "bad," and (2) the cost and schedule variances are calculated as the earned value minus some other measure. Specifically, the *cost* (or *spending*) *variance* (CV) is the difference between the amount of money we budgeted for the work that has been performed to date (the budgeted cost of work performed or *earned value,* BCWP) and the actual cost of that work (ACWP). The *schedule variance* (SV) is the difference between the BCWP and the cost of the work we scheduled to be performed to date (BCWS). The *time variance* is the difference in

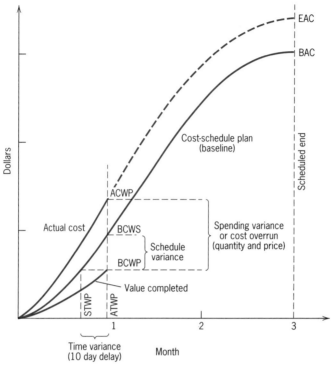

Figure 10-7 Earned value chart.

the time scheduled for the work that has been performed (STWP) and the actual time used to perform it (ATWP).* In compact form,

BCWP – ACWP = cost variance (CV, overrun is negative)
BCWP – BCWS = schedule variance (SV, behind is negative)
STWP – ATWP = time variance (TV, delay is negative)

Typically, variances are defined in such a way that they will be negative when the project is behind schedule and/or over cost. As we have noted, however, this practice is not universal either in the literature or in practice.

The variances are also often formulated as ratios rather than differences so that the cost variance becomes the Cost Performance Index (CPI) = BCWP/ACWP, the schedule variance becomes the Schedule Performance Index (SPI) = BCWP/BCWS, and the time variance becomes the Time Performance Index (TPI) = STWP/ATWP. Use of ratios is particularly helpful when an organization wishes to compare the performance of several projects—or project managers. As we just noted, however, the accuracy and usefulness of all these performance measures depend on the degree in which estimates of percent completion reflect reality.

---

*A fourth variance can be found. It is the difference between the cost that the project budget says should have been expended to date (BCWS) and the actual cost incurred to date by the project (ACWP). BCWS–ACWP is what we call the *resource flow variance*. (Note that the resource flow variance is not a "cash flow" variance.)

Cost and schedule variances (or CPI and SPI) are very commonly used. A short example illustrates their application. Assume that operations on a work package were expected to cost $1,500 to complete the package. They were originally scheduled to have been finished today. At this point, however, we have actually expended $1,350, and we estimate that we have completed two-thirds of the work. What are the cost and schedule variances?

$$\text{cost variance} = BCWP - ACWP$$
$$= \$1,500(2/3) - 1350$$
$$= -\$350$$
$$\text{schedule variance} = BCWP - BCWS$$
$$= \$1,500(2/3) - 1500$$
$$= -\$500$$
$$CPI = BCWP / ACWP$$
$$= \$(1,500\ (2/3)) / 1350$$
$$= .74$$
$$SPI = BCWP / BCWS$$
$$= \$(1,500\ (2/3)) / 1500$$
$$= .67$$

In other words, we are spending at a higher level than our budget plan indicates, and given what we have spent, we are not as far along as we should be (i.e., we have not completed as much work as we should have).

It is, of course, quite possible for one of the indicators to be favorable while the other is unfavorable. We might be ahead of schedule and behind in cost, or vice versa. There are six possibilities in total, all illustrated in Figure 10-8. The scenario shown in Figure 10-7, where both SV and CV are negative, is captured in arrangement *d* of Figure 10-8. The example immediately above, which also results in negative values of SV and CV, is arrangement *c* of Figure 10-8. Barr (and others) combines the two indexes, CPI and SPI, to make a type of "critical ratio" (described further in Chapter 11) called the Cost–Schedule Index (Barr, 1996, p. 32).

$$CSI = (CPI)(SPI)$$
$$= (BCWP/ACWP)\ (BCWP/BCWS$$
$$= BCWP^2 / (ACWP)(BCWS)$$

In our case,

$$= \$(1,500\ (2/3))^2 / (1,350)\ (1,500)$$
$$= \$1,000,000 / 2,025,000$$
$$= 0.49$$

As Barr writes, CSI < 1 is indicative of a problem.

One can continue the analysis to forecast the future of this work unit under the condition when no measures are taken to correct matters. The cost to complete the work unit can be estimated as the budgeted cost of the entire unit, less the earned value to date, adjusted by the CPI to reflect the actual level of performance. The budget at completion (BAC) in our example is $1,500. The budgeted cost of the work

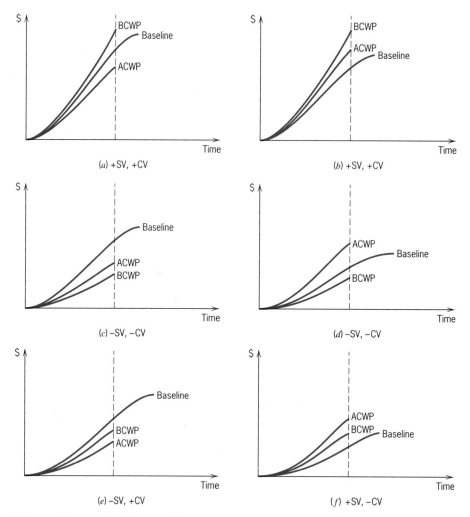

Figure 10-8 Six possible arrangements of ACWP, BCWP, and Baseline resulting in four combinations of positive and negative schedule variance (SV) and cost variance (CV). (Figure 10-7 is arrangement *d*.)

performed to date (BCWP) is $1,500 \times 2/3 = $1,000$. The estimated cost to complete (ETC) is defined as

$$ETC = (BAC - BCWP) / CPI$$
$$= \$(1,500 - 1,000) / 0.74$$
$$= \$676$$

The estimated cost at completion (EAC)—and we use Barr's term (1996) rather than Microsoft's FAC or any of the many other names in the literature—is the amount expended to date (ACWP) plus the estimated cost to complete (ETC):

$$EAC = ETC + ACWP$$
$$= \$676 + 1350$$
$$= \$2026$$

rather than the original estimate of $1,500. For a complete description of this approach to estimating the total cost of a work unit, or a set of work units, see Barr (1996). For similar approaches with different notation, see Flemming and Koppelman (1995) and elsewhere.

Thus far, the focus has been on measuring performance on a work unit rather than on the project as a whole. Where dealing with a specific work unit, the estimates of costs and time can be fairly precise. Even the estimate of percent completion can be made without introducing too much error when using, as we did above, the proportionality rule. Given the relatively short time frame and relatively small cost compared to the whole project, errors are not apt to be significant. Random errors in estimating will tend to cancel out and we can aggregate the work unit data into larger elements, e.g., tasks or even the whole project. (Bias in estimating is, of course, a different matter.) Although the measurement error may be minimal, for most projects there is still no sound basis for estimating percent completion of the project as a whole.

Even if this aggregation is feasible, the use of earned value analysis for forecasting project schedules and costs does not mean that the forecasts will make it possible to correct malperformance. The case for remediation is not hopeful. In a study of more than 700 projects carried out under Department of Defense contracts, the chances of correcting a poorly performing project more than 15 percent complete were effectively nil (Flemming and Koppelman, 1996). The study concludes that if the beginning of the project was underestimated and took longer and cost more than the plan indicated, there was little or no chance that the rest of the project would be estimated more accurately (p. 13ff). For relatively small deviations from plan, the PM may be able to do a lot a catching up.

If the earned value chart shows a cost overrun or performance underrun, the PM must figure out what to do to get the system back on target. Options include such things as borrowing resources from activities performing better than expected, or holding a meeting of project team members to see if anyone can suggest solutions to the problems, or perhaps notifying the client that the project may be late or over budget. Of course, careful risk analysis at the beginning of the project can do a great deal to avoid the embarrassment of notifying the client and senior management of the bad news.

Example: Updating a Project's Earned Value

We use a simple example to illustrate the process of determining the baseline budget and interim earned value and actual costs for a project. Table 10-1 presents the basic project information, and updated information as of day 7 in the project. The planned PERT/CPM AON diagram is shown in Figure 10-9, where path **a-c-e** is the critical path, with project completion expected at day 10. What has actually happened in the project is that the first activity, **a**, took 4 days instead of the planned 3 days to complete, delaying the start of both activities **b** and **c**. Activities **b** and **d** are proceeding as

Table 10-1. Earned Value Example (today is day 7)

Activity	Precedessor	Days Duration	Budget, $	Actual Cost, $	% Complete
a	—	3	600	680	100
b	a	2	300	270	100
c	a	5	800		80
d	b	4	400		25
e	c	2	400		0

expected, except of course for their one-day delay in initiation, but anyway, path **a-b-d** was not the critical path for the project.

Activities **a** and **b** are both completed and activity **d** is 25 percent finished, as appropriate for the end of day 7. However, due to its delay, activity **a** cost $80 more than budgeted. Hence, the project manager is trying to cut the costs of the remaining activities, and we see that activity **b** came in $30 under budget, which helps but does not fully offset the previous overrun. Currently, we see that activity **c** has been expedited and, although only having been underway for 3 days, is 80 percent complete. Thus, it might be back on schedule for expected completion by day 8, which would get the entire project back on schedule.

The baseline budget (BCWS) using the 50–50 rule is calculated in Figure 10-10 and graphed in Figure 10-12 where the BAC is listed as $2,500. The project's status and earned value (BCWP) as of day 7 are shown in Figure 10-11. Included in the figure is the actual cost (ACWP), but for only the completed activities, of course. These two running values are also plotted on Figure 10-12 where it can be seen that the schedule variance is currently 0 and the cost variance is $1,500 – 950 = +550.

But notice how these figures do not give a very accurate picture of project progress. The earned value up to now has been trailing the baseline and has only caught up because the 50–50 rule doesn't have any activity beginning or ending at day 6; however, with expediting activity **c**, we may in fact be back on schedule by day 8. The cost variance, however, is highly affected by the fact that actual costs are not recorded until the activity is 100 percent complete, combined with the impact of the 50–50 rule. The result is that the baseline and earned value cost figures will start to aggregate when activities begin but the actual costs will lag them considerably. Even

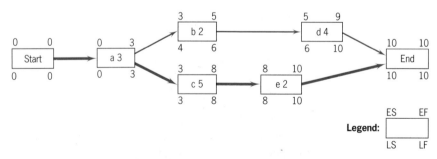

Figure 10-9   Example PERT AON diagram.

Activity \ Day	0–1	1–2	2–3	3–4	4–5	5–6	6–7	7–8	8–9	9–10
a	300		300							
b				150	150					
c				400				400		
d						200			200	
e									200	200
Total	300		300	550	150	200		400	400	200
Cum. Total	300	300	600	1150	1300	1500	1500	1900	2300	2500

Figure 10-10 Example baseline budget using the 50–50 rule.

though the proportionality rule would more accurately delay the aggregation of earned value costs, there would still be a positive bias if the actual costs were not calculated until the activities were completed. It would be more accurate, but considerably more complex, to apportion actual costs according to percentage activity completion. These effects are illustrated further in some of the problems at the end of the chapter.

Activity \ Day	0–1	1–2	2–3	3–4	4–5	5–6	6–7	7–8	8–9	9–10
a	300			300						
b					150	150				
c					400					
d							200			
e										
EV	300			300	550	150	200			
Cum. EV (BCWP)	300	300	300	600	1150	1300	1500			
Actual Cost				680		270				
Cum. Cost (ACWP)	0	0	0	680	680	950	950			

Figure 10-11 Example status at day 7.

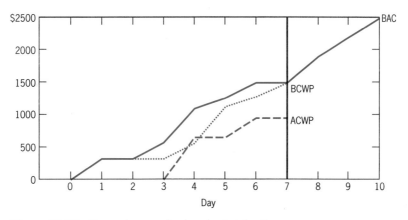

Figure 10-12   Example earned value chart at day 7.

MSP Variance and Earned Value Reports

Figure 10-13 shows an earned value budget for the Career Day project described in Chapter 5, Section 5.3. It includes all the budget, actual, and earned value figures for each work package in the project, as well as projections at completion. The budget was generated as a standard report from MSP. (Similar reports are available through most other PC project management software packages.) Note that the project is reported on at the work package level. The first two tasks, *Contact Organizations* and *Banquet and Refreshments* have been completed, and the third task, *Publicity and Promotion* is currently underway. The first four work packages under *Publicity and Promotion* have been completed, but the fifth and seventh are only partially finished. The sixth has not been started, nor has the fourth task, *Facilities,* been started. A compressed Gantt chart is shown on the right side.

The three columns of data on the right, BAC, FAC, and Variance, are "Budget at Completion," "Forecast at Completion," and the Variance or difference between BAC and FAC. For all activities that have been completed, BAC = BCWP and FAC = ACWP. Note that no variances are calculated for tasks that are incomplete. See the lines "Advertise in college paper" and "Organize posters," for example. The work packages that have not been completed, however, tell a different story. *Advertise in college paper* is 50 percent complete, and *Organize posters* is 45 percent complete. (The percent complete data are from another report.) *Class announcements* has not yet been started. Note that for *Advertise in the college paper,* the BCWP is 50 percent of the BCWS, which is to say that $82.50 is 50 percent of the BAC and FAC. Similarly for *Organize posters,* with $335.25 being 45 percent of BAC and FAC ($335.25/.45 = $745.00). When the two work packages are completed, however, and if there is still a cost variance, then BAC and FAC will no longer be equal. For a completed work package, the cost variance BCWP – ACWP = BAC – FAC.

Name	BCWS	BCWP	ACWP	Sch. Variance	Cost Variance	BAC	FAC	Variance	QTR 1, 1999			QTR 2, 1999		
									Jan	Feb	Mar	Jan	Feb	Mar
Contact Organizations	$3,797.30	$3,980.00	$3,920.00	$182.00	$60.00	$3,980.00	$3,920.00	$60.00						
Print forms	$645.00	$645.00	$645.00	$0.00	$0.00	$645.00	$645.00	$0.00						
Contact organizations	$840.00	$840.00	$728.00	$0.00	$112.00	$840.00	$728.00	$112.00						
Collect display information	$660.00	$660.00	$660.00	$0.00	$0.00	$660.00	$660.00	$0.00						
Gather college particulars	$520.00	$520.00	$520.00	$0.00	$0.00	$520.00	$520.00	$0.00						
Print programs	$687.00	$870.00	$922.00	$182.70	($52.00)	$870.00	$922.00	($52.00)						
Print participants' certificates	$445.00	$445.00	$445.00	$0.00	$0.00	$445.00	$445.00	$0.00						
Banquet and Refreshments	$1,220.00	$1,220.00	$1,200.00	$0.00	$20.00	$1,220.00	$1,200.00	$20.00						
Select guest speaker	$500.00	$500.00	$500.00	$0.00	$0.00	$500.00	$500.00	$0.00						
Organize food	$325.00	$325.00	$325.00	$0.00	$0.00	$325.00	$325.00	$0.00						
Organize liquor	$100.00	$100.00	$100.00	$0.00	$0.00	$100.00	$100.00	$0.00						
Organize refreshments	$295.00	$295.00	$275.00	$0.00	$20.00	$295.00	$275.00	$20.00						
Publicity and Promotion	$2,732.55	$2,797.75	$2,039.00	($434.80)	$258.75	$3,010.00	$2,870.00	$140.00						
Send invitations	$700.00	$700.00	$560.00	$0.00	$140.00	$700.00	$560.00	$140.00						
Organize gift certificates	$330.00	$330.00	$330.00	$0.00	$0.00	$330.00	$330.00	$0.00						
Arrange banner	$570.00	$570.00	$570.00	$0.00	$0.00	$570.00	$570.00	$0.00						
Contact faculty	$280.00	$280.00	$280.00	$0.00	$0.00	$280.00	$280.00	$0.00						
Advertise in college paper	$165.00	$82.50	$65.00	($82.50)	$17.50	$165.00	$165.00	$0.00						
Class announcements	$99.00	$0.00	$0.00	($99.00)	$0.00	$220.00	$220.00	$0.00						
Organize posters	$588.00	$325.25	$234.00	($253.30)	$101.25	$745.00	$745.00	$0.00						
Facilities	$200.00	$0.00	$0.00	($200.00)	$0.00	$200.00	$200.00	$0.00						
Arrange facility for event	$52.00	$0.00	$0.00	($52.00)	$0.00	$52.00	$52.00	$0.00						
Transport materials	$148.00	$0.00	$0.00	($148.00)	$0.00	$148.00	$148.00	$0.00						

Project: Career Day
Date: 3/24/99

Critical   Progress   ◇ Milestone
Noncritical   Summary   ◇ Rolled up

Figure 10-13   MSP budget sheet for career day project (cf. Chapter 5).

Project Management in Practice
Success through Earned Value at Texas Instruments

When Texas Instruments, Inc. wanted an imaging system designed for their Accounts Receivable department that would interface with their mainframe accounts receivable system, they turned to ViewStar Corporation to design it. Several leading edge technologies were desired so ViewStar compiled the work breakdown structure from which to plan the budget and track actual spending. However, the planned budget exceeded the contract funds available so the budget for se-

lected early-on tasks was arbitrarily reduced so the overall budget would match the contract funds because top management wanted to win this contract.

As the contract progressed, the underbudgeted items showed up quickly in the earned value chart, as illustrated below. Although funds were being expended at the planned rate, progress wasn't keeping up with the plan. However, with special attention to meeting *only* key require-

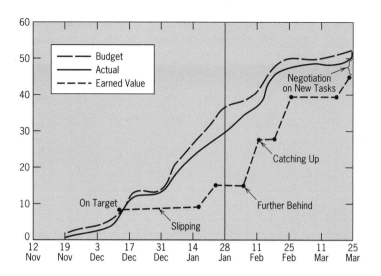

ments for later project tasks, earned value began to climb back toward plan. Near the very end of the project, the client asked for additional technology, which Viewstar easily provided in trade for Texas Instruments completing some of the high-earned-value production tasks themselves, thereby bringing the project in only one percent over budget.

Source: T. Ingram, "Client/Server, Imaging and Earned Value: A Success Story," *PM Network,* December 1995, pp. 21–25.

Cost/Schedule Control System Criteria (C/SCSC)

C/SCSC was developed by the U.S. Department of Defense in the late 1960s and for many years was required for defense projects. While it is no longer a requirement for DOD projects, it is still requested by some project funders and used by some project vendors. It is an extension of earned value analysis. C/SCSC, as its name implies, spelled out a number of standards of organization, accounting, budgeting, etc. that firms must meet if they are to be considered acceptable for government contracts. For an excellent extended discussion of C/SCSC together with the process for accomplishing it, see Lambert (1993). Also, an extensive bibliography is given in Christensen (1994).

The need to keep project performance, cost, and schedule related when monitoring projects has been emphasized in this chapter. This emphasis will be reinforced in Chapter 11. For purposes of control, it is just as important to emphasize the need to relate the realities of time, cost, and performance with the project's master plan. C/SCSC takes just such an approach, but there is a major caveat that must be heeded: *The set of project action plans (the project master plan) must be kept up to date.* These plans contain descriptions of each task together with estimates of the time and resources required by each. The plans are therefore the primary source of the STWPs, BCWSs, and BCWPs and the framework within which the ATWPs and ACWPs are collected.

Differences between work scheduled and work planned can develop from several different causes—for example, official change orders in the work elements required to accomplish a task, informal alterations in the methods used to accomplish specific tasks, or official or unofficial changes in the tasks to be accomplished. Similarly, cost variances can result from any of the above as well as from changes in input factor prices, changes in the accounting methods used by the project, or changes in the mix of input factors needed to accomplish a given task. If the plan is not altered to reflect such changes, comparisons between plan and actual are not meaningful.

Milestone Reporting

We referred earlier to milestone reports. A typical example of such a report is shown in Figure 10-14a, b, and Figure 10-15. In this illustration, a sample network with milestones is shown, followed by a routine milestone report form. A model top management project status report is illustrated in the next chapter. When filled out, these reports show project status at a specific time. They serve to keep all parties up to date

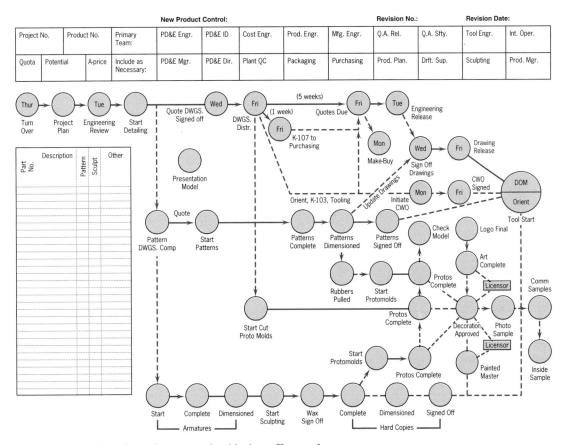

Figure 10-14a   Sample project network with sign-off control.

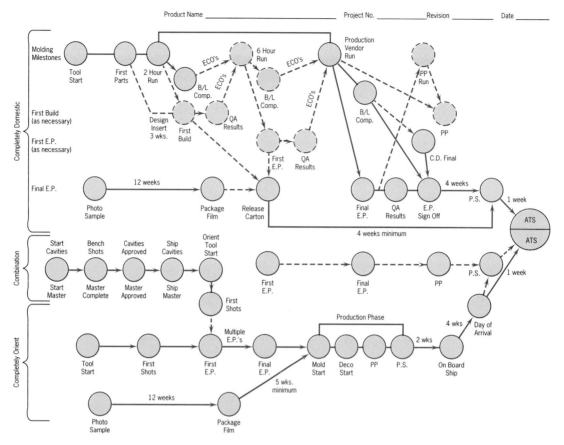

Figure 10-14b   Continuation of Figure 10-14a.

NAME						PROJECT PLAN	ENGR. REVIEW	DESIGN REVIEW	QUOTE QUES.	PAT SCULP COMPL.	PAT SCULP COMPL	QUOTES DUE	MAKE BUY
PROJECT NO.	PRODUCT NO.	MFG SOURCE	TURNOVER	ORIGINAL									
A = PRICE	QUOTA	POTENTIAL		CURRENT									
				ACTUAL									

ENGR. RELEASE	PROJECT REVIEW	RELEASE DWGS.	TOOL START	PHOTO SAMPLES	INSIDE SAMPLES	PKG. FILM	INSTR. LAYOUT	INSTR. FILM ART	FINAL PARTS	FIRST EP	FINAL EP	EP SIGN-OFF	ORIENT PS	OBS	PROD. PILOT	PT SIGN-OFF	PROD. START	ATS

Figure 10-15   Milestone monitoring chart for Figures 10-14 a and b.

on what has been accomplished. If accomplishments are inadequate or late, these reports serve as starting points for remedial planning.

Figures 10-14a and b show the network for a new product development project for a manufacturer. A steady flow of new products is an essential feature of this firm's business, and each new product is organized as a project as soon as its basic concept is approved by a project selection group. If we examine Figures 10-14a and b closely, we see that the sign-off control boxes at the top of the page correspond with sequences of events in the network. For example, look at the bottom line of the network in Figure 10-14a. The design of this product requires a sculpture that is formed on an armature. The armature must be constructed, and the sculpture of the product completed and signed off. Note that the sculpture is used as a form for making models that are, in turn, used to make the prototype product. The completion of the sculpture is signed off in the next-to-last box in the lower line of boxes at the top of the page.

A careful examination of Figure 10-14b reveals that it is a continuation of the previous page. Figure 10-14a is primarily concerned with product design and Figure 10-14b with production. The expected times for various activities are noted on the network, along with the various operations that must be performed. Figure 10-15 is a summary milestone report. Each project has a series of steps that must be completed. Each has an original schedule that may be amended for use as a current schedule. Steps are completed in actual times. This form helps program managers coordinate several projects by trying to schedule the various steps to minimize the degree to which the projects interfere with one another by being scheduled for the same facilities at the same time.

The next section of this chapter, which considers computerized project management information systems, contains several other examples of project reports.

10.4 COMPUTERIZED PMIS (PROJECT MANAGEMENT INFORMATION SYSTEMS)

The project examples used in Chapters 8 and 9 were small, so that the concepts could be demonstrated. But real projects are often extremely large, with hundreds of tasks and thousands of work units. Diagramming, scheduling, and tracking all these tasks is clearly a job for the computer, and computerized PMISs were one of the earlier business applications for computers. Initially, the focus was on simple scheduling packages, but this quickly extended to include costs, earned values, variances, management reports, and so on.

The earlier packages ran on large, expensive mainframe computers; thus, only the larger firms had access to them. Still, the use of these packages for managing projects on a day-to-day basis was not particularly successful. This was because of the inability of project managers to update plans in real time, mainframe computers typically being run in a batch rather than online mode. With the development and proliferation of microcomputers, and the corresponding availability of a wide variety of project management software, project managers use at least one PMIS.

These new microcomputer-based PMISs are considerably more sophisticated than earlier systems and use the microcomputer's graphics, color, and other features more

DILBERT reprinted by permission of United Features Syndicate, Inc.

extensively. Many systems can handle almost any size project, being limited only by the memory available in the computer. Many will handle multiple projects and link them together to detect resource over-allocation; e.g., Microsoft Project can consolidate more than 1000 projects. The PMIS trend of the early 1990s has been to integrate the project management software with spreadsheets, databases, word processors, communication, graphics, and the other capabilities of Windows-based software packages. The current trend is to facilitate the global sharing of project information, including complete status reporting, through local networks as well as the Internet.

Throughout this text we have illustrated software output from one project management software package, Microsoft's Project 2002® (MSP). A survey of project management tools recently published in *Project Management Journal* (Fox and Spence, 1998) polled 1000 members of the Project Management Institute and listed MSP as being used by 48.4 percent of respondents. Primavera Project Planner®, a system designed for very large projects, used by 13.8 percent was second. The development of these and other powerful software systems was accompanied by the development of desktop computers with memory, power, and speed undreamed of a few years ago. With project files stored in large memory banks on anything from a mainframe machine, to a minicomputer, and more frequently to workstations, servers, and PC's the software and project files became available on LAN and WAN systems, as well as through the Internet.

This area is developing so rapidly that any information given must be considered dated by the time it reaches print. The reader interested in current capabilities would be wise to refer to recent annual or monthly software reviews such as those in the Project Management Institute's annual Software Survey (2001), *PCMagazine* (1998), and *Federal Computer News* (1997). Of additional interest are the comments frequently appearing in *PMNetwork,* especially Harvey Levine's "Software Forum" column. Reviews of software are also widely available on the Internet at such magazine-sponsored Web sites as "qualitymag.com" and "zdnet.com" or sites sponsored by the software producers.

Current Software

The explosive growth of project management software during the early 1990s saw the creation of more than 500 packages. This software came in a wide variety of capabilities and prices. Some packages cost less than $50, and a few cost more than $100,000. A large majority, however, fall in the $400–$5,000 bracket and many of these sell for around $500. The mainstream products have roughly similar capabilities, with each having its individual strengths and weaknesses. The simple fact that the lower cost programs generally do not have the ability to do everything an experienced project manager might want has led to the rapid growth of a different type of software, the "add-on." Add-on software is specially crafted to accomplish specific tasks and to be fully compatible, sometimes almost seamlessly so, with specific general project management packages. Microsoft's market dominance means that a lion's share of the add-on software is compatible with MSP.

Until recently, most project management software was unable to handle three-time PERT input, and even now the ability to deal with cost and shedule risk management problems is quite limited. The result is that there are risk management add-on programs available. (We noted several in our discussion of simulation in Chapter 8.) These add-ons can handle quite sophisticated stochastic problems and transport information easily between the add-on and the host program. With the ability to perform simulations on project schedules or resource usage, the PM can observe the probable results of many different assumptions about resource availability and schedule uncertainties.

The prevalence of multiple project firms as well as the increasing number of firms that are project-oriented have led to the demand for software that will combine the data records for all projects into a single database. This ability is a central design feature of the newly released Microsoft Project 2002®. The purpose is to allow the PM to aggregate resource requirements, more easily spot resource and schedule conflicts, and to report on resource usage, personnel time charges, and the like to the firm's accounting system. These add-ons are often referred to as "consolidators" or "repositories" and "time capture" programs. (For an interesting description of such systems and the requirements they meet, see Levine, 1998). Additional add-ons deal with extensions to the earned value calculations, conformity with C/SCSC accounting and reporting rules, specialized cost management programs, responsibility charts, preparation of files for Internet use, e-mail systems, a variety of templates for project reports, LAN and WAN communication systems and workgroup capability, and so on. All this, of course, is useful if the basic project management software does not already have sufficient abilities—and if the PM needs them. While no single tool is a panacea, MSP is a competent, easy-to-use software package and its popularity means that a large number of "add-ons" are available.

Finally, it is worth noting that these systems can very easily be misused or inappropriately applied—as can any tools. The most common error of this type is managing the PMIS rather than the project itself. This and other such errors are described by Thamhain (1987):

- *Computer paralysis.* Excessive computer involvement with computer activity replacing project management; loss of touch with the project and its realities.
- *PMIS verification.* PMIS reports may mask real project problems, be massaged to look good, or simply verify that real problems exist, yet are not acted upon.

- *Information overload.* Too many reports, too detailed, or the distribution of reports, charts, tables, data, and general information from the PMIS to too many people overwhelms managers and effectively hides problems.

- *Project isolation.* The PMIS reports replace useful and frequent communication between the project manager and top management, or even between the PM and the project team.

- *Computer dependence.* PM or top management wait for the computer reports/results to react to problems rather than being proactive and avoiding problems in the first place.

- *PMIS misdirection.* Due to the unequal coverage of the PMIS, certain project subareas are overmanaged and other areas receive inadequate attention; symptoms of problems are monitored and managed (budget overruns, schedule slippages), rather than the problems themselves.

We have also found that problems can result when someone other than the PM attempts to update projects without involving the PM in the changes.

Choosing Software

When choosing project management software, the potential user should read several software surveys conducted with project managers. We have included several in the bibliography to this chapter (for example, Avots, 1987; Fox and Spence, 1998; Levine, 1998; and Project Management—Editor's Choice, 1998). All of these are now last year's news and thus, obsolete, but they clearly indicate the sorts of capabilities that are important to most users. Avots (1987)] warns against reviews in computer magazines because software specialists who know little or nothing about project management often write them. We suspect that this warning is not as relevant today as it was a few years ago. We would, however, strongly warn against allowing the organization's software technicians from making the choice, unaided. Software that appeals to software specialists is not necessarily the optimal choice for the project manager.

The following characteristics of generally desirable attributes in project management software are based on a number of user surveys and the comments of experienced PMs.

- *Friendliness.* For the novice user, this includes clear and logical manuals, help screens, tutorials, a menu-driven structure, easy editing, and so on. For firms implementing project management, this means the existence of an organized training program on the use of the software conducted by trainers who have some understanding of project management.

- *Schedules.* Gantt charts are mandatory, as well as automatic recalculation with updates of times, costs, and resources. Plots of earliest start, scheduled start, slack/float, latest finish, planned finish, and actual finish times are desirable. The software should also be able to display PERT/CPM networks. The time units for schedule display (and resource usage) should vary from minutes to months. The ability to handle three-time schedule inputs is desirable.

- *Calendars.* Either a job shop and/or calendar dates are necessary, plus the ability to indicate working days, nonworking days, and holidays for each resource used.
- *Budgets.* The ability to include a budget for planning, monitoring, and control. Especially desirable is the ability to interface this with a spreadsheet program.
- *Reports.* Individualizing report formats is most desirable. Again, having the ability to interface the reports with a word processing package is highly desirable.
- *Graphics.* The ability to see the schedule and interactions is especially important. For Gantt charts, the software should be able to show the technical dependencies between work units or tasks.
- *Charts.* Charts for responsibility and histograms for resources were deemed particularly useful.
- *Migration.* The ability to transfer data to and from spreadsheets, word processors, database programs, graphics programs, and desired add-on programs. The ability to interface with telecommunication systems and the Internet is required for most applications.
- *Consolidation.* The ability to aggregate multiple projects into a single database for determination of total resource usage and detection of resource conflicts. The software must have the ability to recalculate all schedules and resource records when updated information is added.

It is heartening to note that many of the current project management software packages have available almost all of the characteristics noted above. It is important, however, to remember that no one package will meet all needs. Numerous trade-offs exist not only between price and capability but also between functional capability, ease of use, complexity, and speed. In general, there are six areas of PMIS internal capabilities, separate from the ability to migrate data and communicate externally, that should be considered. These are project planning, resource management, risk management, tracking/monitoring, report generation, and decision aiding.

The potential purchaser of a PMIS should consider the intended use of the package, the background and needs of all the potential users, and the organizational setting where the package is to be employed, including the needs and orientation of those who will be receiving the reports and graphics.

A general PMIS selection process roughly based on Levine's excellent work (1987) is as follows:

1. Establish a comprehensive set of selection criteria, considering capabilities in project planning, resource management, tracking/monitoring, report generation, earned value/variance analysis, risk management.

2. Set priorities for the criteria, separating "must have" items from "nice to have" items and "not needed" items.

3. Conduct a preliminary evaluation of the software packages relative to the criteria using vendor-supplied data, product reviews, and software surveys.

4. Limit the candidate packages to three and obtain demos of each, evaluating the vendors at the same time in terms of interest, software maintenance, and support.

5. Evaluate each package with a standard project typical of your current and projected future needs. Make note of any weaknesses or strengths that are particularly relevant to your situation.

6. Negotiate on price, particularly if you are making a volume purchase or contemplating a site license. Include descriptions of vendor support, training, and product maintenance in the contract.

 # SUMMARY

In this chapter, we reviewed the monitoring function, relating it to project planning and control, and described its role in the project implementation process. The requirements for monitoring were discussed, in addition to data needs and reporting considerations. Last, some techniques for monitoring progress were illustrated and some computerized PMISs were described.

Specific points made in the chapter were:

- It is important that the planning-monitoring-controlling cycle be a closed loop cycle based on the same structure as the parent system.

- The first task in designing the monitoring system is to identify the key factors in the project action plan to be monitored and to devise standards for them. The factors should concern results, rather than activities.

- The data collected are usually either frequency counts, numbers, subjective numeric ratings, indicators, or verbal measures.

- Project reports are of three types: routine, exception, and special analysis.

- Project reports should include an amount of detail appropriate to the target level of management with a frequency appropriate to the

need for control (i.e., probably not weekly or other such regular basis). More commonly, reports occur near milestone dates.

- Three common project reporting problems are too much detail, poor correspondence to the parent firm's reporting system, and a poor correspondence between the planning and monitoring systems.

- The earned value chart depicts scheduled progress, actual cost, and actual progress (earned value) to allow the determination of spending, schedule, and time variances.

- There exist a great number of computerized PMISs that are available for PMs, with software evaluations occurring regularly in various magazines.

- Project managers' preferred PMIS features were friendliness, schedules, calendars, budgets, reports, graphics, networks, charts, migration, and consolidation.

In the next chapter, we move into the final phase of project implementation, project control. We discuss the different types of control and describe some techniques useful to the PM in controlling the project.

 # GLOSSARY

Computer Paralysis Excessive fascination or activity with the computer rather than the project itself such that the project suffers.

Cost (or spending) Variance The budgeted cost of the work performed less the actual cost of the work performed.

Earned Value An approach for monitoring project progress that relies on the budgeted cost of activities completed to ascribe value.

Friendliness When applied to computer use, this term refers to how easy it is to learn and/or use a computer or software package.

Hard Copy Printed information output, as opposed to screen output.

Information Overload Having an excess of information so that the information desired is difficult to locate.

Migration The ability to move files and data between software packages.

Monitor To keep watch in order to take action when progress fails to match plans.

Schedule Variance The budgeted cost of work completed less the budgeted cost of work scheduled at this time.

Software The instructions for running a computer.

Spreadsheet A matrix of data used with a computer. As the data in particular cells are changed, the results of other cells change also to keep in accordance.

Time Variance The scheduled time for the work completed less the actual time.

Variance A deviation from plan or expectation.

Windowing A computer software feature that allows different functions to be conducted in a separate section of the screen, called a window.

 QUESTIONS

Material Review Questions

1. Define *monitoring*. Are there any additional activities that should be part of the monitoring function?

2. Identify the key factors that need to be considered when setting up a monitoring system.

3. List some factors that would be difficult to monitor.

4. Describe routine reports and some problems with them.

5. What are the primary difficulties experienced in the design of project reports?

6. Describe the three variances of an earned value chart and explain their significance.

7. Can you identify other symptoms of computer misuse besides those in Section 10.3?

8. What types of measures do data come in?

9. What is "earned value"?

Class Discussion Questions

10. Discuss the benefits of timely, appropriate, detailed information. How can a value be assigned to these characteristics?

11. What are the advantages for a PM of having a computerized system over a manual one? The disadvantages?

12. A project is usually a one-time activity with a well-defined purpose. What is the justification of setting up a PMIS for such a project?

13. A more intensive, and extensive, monitoring system is needed in project management than in a functional organization. Why?

14. The earned value chart is an attempt to put the three-dimensional concept of Figure 1-1 (see

Chapter 1) into a two-dimensional format. Is it successful? What is missing?

15. How might a variance be traced back to its source?

16. How would a Project Management Information System differ from an ordinary Management Information System?

17. What type of general purpose software might project managers find useful?

18. How should a PMIS be chosen?

19. Discuss the uses of a PMIS in the different stages of the project life cycle.

20. Is it unethical, in an attempt to avoid a "shoot-the-messenger" response, to simply not mention bad news?

Questions for Project Management in Practice

Using Project Management Software to Schedule Olympic Games

21. Why did they need drawings of every site, building, and room?

22. How do you think they did planning for the bad weather?

23. Was scheduling the difficult aspect of planning the games or the logistics?

Tracking Scope Creep: A Project Manager Responds

24. Is the point of the letter to the editor about scope creep, or tracking? What is it about?

25. The author criticizes the selection of engineers for projects. Is the author saying engineers don't make good project managers?

26. In terms of monitoring and tracking, which of the ten oversights is probably most critical?

Success through Earned Value at Texas Instruments

27. Isn't arbitrarily reducing the available budget for tasks dangerous? What was ViewStar's probable strategic thinking here?

28. What would be the motivation of a project team that immediately falls behind schedule?

29. How did the trade late in the project between View-Star and Texas Instruments probably operate?

 PROBLEMS

1. Find the schedule and cost variances for a project that has an actual cost at month 22 of $540,000, a scheduled cost of $523,000, and an earned value of $535,000.

2. A sales project at month 5 had an actual cost of $34,000, a planned cost of $42,000, and a value completed of $39,000. Find the cost and schedule variances and the CPI and SPI.

3. A software development project at day 70 exhibits an actual cost of $78,000 and a scheduled cost of $84,000. The foreman estimates a value completed of $81,000. What are the cost and schedule variances and CSI? Estimate the time variance.

4. A project to develop a county park has an actual cost in month 17 of $350,000, a planned cost of $475,000, and a value completed of $300,000. Find the cost and schedule variances and the three indexes.

5. A consulting project has an actual cost in month 10 of $23,000, a scheduled cost of $17,000, and a value completed of $20,000. Find the schedule and cost variances and the three indexes.

6. A project to develop technology training seminars is 5 days behind schedule at day 65. It had a planned cost of $735,000 for this point in time, but the actual cost is only $550,000. Estimate the schedule and cost variances. Re-estimate the variances if the actual cost had been $750,000.

7. Given an activity in an advertising project whose planned cost was $12,000 but actual cost to date is $10,000 so far and the value completed is only 70 percent, calculate the cost and schedule variances. Will the client be pleased or angry?

8. For the following test marketing project at week 6, calculate the cost, schedule, and time variances. Also calculate the CPI, SPI, CSI, and the ETC and EAC.

Activity	Predecessors	Duration (weeks)	Budget, $	Actual Cost, $	% Complete
a	—	2	300	400	100
b	—	3	200	180	100
c	a	2	250	300	100
d	a	5	600	400	20
e	b,c	4	400	200	20

9. At week 24 of a project to shoot a television commercial, what should the expenditures be? If the earned value is right on schedule but the actual expenses are $9,000, what are the cost and schedule variances? What are the three indexes, the ETC, and the EAC?

Activity	Predecessors	Duration (Weeks)	Budget, $
a	—	6	900
b	—	6	1200
c	a	6	1200
d	a	12	1800
e	b,c	14	1400
f	b,c,d	10	1500
g	d,e	16	800

10. Resolve Problem 8 using MSP. Omit the calculations for CPI, SPI, and CSI.

11. Resolve the earned value example of Table 10-1 by recomputing Figures 10-10 and 10-11 using proportional budget figures. Replot Figure 10-12 using the new values.

12. Repeat Problem 11 using the 0–100 percent rule.

13. Draw an earned value chart for the end of the first week assuming the proportionality rule for Problem 14 in Chapter 8 given the following costs and percentage completions:

Activity	Budget, $	Actual, $	% Complete
A	600	400	100
B	300	450	100
C	150	100	100
D	750	60	
E	400	10	
F	100	50	
G	200	0	
H	400	0	
I	100	50	
J	100	0	

 INCIDENTS FOR DISCUSSION

Jackson Insurance and Title Company

Mark Suturana joined the Jackson Company six months ago. He is an experienced management information systems executive who has been given the task of improving the responsiveness of Jackson's data processing group to the end user. After several months of investigation, Mark felt certain he understood the current situation clearly enough to proceed. First, approximately 90 percent of all end user requests came to data processing (DP) in the form of a project, with the DP output either the final product of the project, or, more commonly, one step of a project. Accordingly, Mark felt he should initially direct his efforts toward integrating DP's approach to projects with the company's formal project management system.

It has been Mark's experience that most problems associated with DP projects revolve around poor project definition and inadequate participation by the end user during the system design phase. Typically, the end user does not become heavily involved in the project until the new system is ready to install. At that point, a great deal of work is required to adapt the system to meet end-user requirements. Mark decided to institute a procedure that put end-user cooperation and participation on the front end of the project. The idea was to define the objective and design of the system so thoroughly that implementation would become almost mechanical in nature rather than an introduction to the end user of "his or her new system."

Mark also recognized that something had to be done to control the programming quality of DP's out put. A more effective front-end approach to DP projects would subject DPmanagers to more intense pressure to produce results within user's needs, including time constraints. Mark was concerned that the quality of the DP output would deteriorate under those conditions, especially given the lack of technical expertise on the part of end users and outside project managers. To solve this problem, Mark recommended the creation of a DP quality assurance (QA) manager who would approve the initial steps of the projects and review each additional step. The QA manager would have the authority to declare any step or portion of the output inadequate and to send it back to be reworked.

Questions: Is this a good control system for DP? Why or why not? Does it also represent a good control point for company projects using DP to accomplish one portion of the project objective? What would be your answer if you were a non-DP project manager?

The U.S. Army Corps of Engineers

The U.S. Army Corps of Engineers has contracted with a medium-size excavation firm to construct a small series of three earthen dams as part of a flood control project in North Carolina. For economic reasons, dams #1 and #2 have to be constructed at the same time and dam #3 can only be built after #1 and #2 are completed. There is also a very important scheduled completion date that has to be met (relating to next year's flood season). The project is being handled by Bryan Johnson, who has been with the company for about a year.

This is a new job for Bryan in that he had never before headed more than one project at a time. About three months into the building of dams #1 and #2, he began to notice an information problem. He had supervisors from dams #1 and #2 reporting to him, but he never knew how far along they were in relation to each other. Since dam #3 cannot be built until both dams are fully complete, he cannot tell if it will be started on time and therefore completed on time. Realizing the situation was becoming serious, he began to wonder about how he could coordinate the projects. How could he tell where the projects were in relation to each other? How far were they *jointly* behind? Bryan's major problem was his inability to monitor and record the dual projects effectively.

Questions: What would you recommend to Bryan?

BIBLIOGRAPHY

Avots, I. "How Useful Are the Mass Market Project Management Systems?" *Project Management Journal,* August 1987.

Barr, Z. "Earned Value Analysis: A Case Study." *PM Network,* December 1996.

Bobrowski, P. M. "Project Management Control Problems: An Information Systems Focus." *Project Management Journal,* June 1989.

Brackett, S. W., and A. M. Isbell. "PMIS-An Integrated Approach for the Management and Distribution of Project Information." *Project Management Journal,* September 1989.

Brandon, D. M., Jr. "Implementing Earned Value Easily and Effectively." *Project Management Journal,* June 1998.

Christensen, D. S. "A Review of Cost/Schedule Control Systems Criterion Literature." *Project Management Journal,* September 1994.

Cleland, D. I., and W. R. King. *Systems Analysis and Project Management,* 3rd ed. New York: McGraw-Hill, 1983.

Dean, B. V. *Evaluating, Selecting, and Controlling R & D Projects.* New York: American Management Association Research Study 89, 1968.

Evans, J. R., and W. M. Lindsay. *The Management and Control of Quality,* 2nd ed. Minneapolis: West, 1993.

Farid, F., and Kangari, R. "A Knowledge-Based System for Selecting Project Management Microsoftware Packages." *Project Management Journal,* September 1991.

Fersko-Weiss, H. "Project Management Software Gets A Grip on Usability." *PC Magazine,* July 1992.

Flemming, Q. W., and J. M. Koppelman. *Earned Value Project Management.* Upper Darby, PA: Project Management Institute, 1996.

Flemming, Q. W., and J. M. Koppelman. "The Earned Value Body of Knowledge." *PM Network,* May 1996.

Flemming, Q. W., and J. M. Koppelman. "Forecasting the Final Cost and Schedule Results." *PM Network,* January 1996.

Flemming, Q. W., and J. M. Koppelman. "Taking Step Four With Earned Value: Establish the Project Baseline. *PM Network,* May 1995.

Flemming, Q. W., and J. M. Koppelman. "Taking Step Three With Earned Value: Estimate and Budget Resources." *PM Network,* January 1995.

Flemming, Q. W., and J. M. Koppelman "The 'Earned

Value'" Concept: Back to The Basics." *PM Network,* January 1994.

FORD, R. C., and F. S. McLAUGHLIN. "Ten Questions and Answers on Managing MIS Projects." *Project Management Journal,* September 1992.

FOX, T. L., and J. W. SPENCE. "Tools of the Trade: A Survey of Project Management Tools." *Project Management Journal,* September 1998.

GARREHY, P. J. "Project Managers Need Real-Time Data—and a Couple of ERP Modules of Their Own." *PM Network,* February 1999.

HATFIELD, M. A. "The Case for Earned Value." *PM Network,* December 1996.

JAY, A. "How to Run a Meeting." *IEEE Engineering Management Review,* Winter 1995 reprinted from the *Harvard Business Review,* March–April 1976.

JENSEN, C. A. "A Project Manager's On-Ramp to the Information Superhighway." *PM Network,* October 1996.

JOHNSON, R. V. "Resource Constrained Scheduling Capabilities of Commercial Project Management Software." *Project Management Journal,* December 1992.

KIDDER, T. *The Soul of a New Machine.* Boston: Little, Brown, 1981.

KNUTSON, J. "How to Prepare and Conduct a Project Review." *PM Network,* October 1996.

LAMBERT, L. R. "Cost/Schedule Control System Criteria (C/SCSC): An Integrated Project Management Approach Using Earned Value Techniques." In P. C. Dinsmore, ed., *The AMA Handbook of Project Management.* New York: AMACOM, 1993.

LEE, T. "Project Management for the Rest of Us." *Datamation,* January 1, 1993.

LEVINE, H. A. "PMI '97: A Report on the Exhibits." *PM Network,* January 1998.

LEVINE, H. A. "The Usability Factor: A Follow-Up." *PM Network,* January 1994.

LEVINE, H. A. "PM Software Forum." *Project Management Journal,* 1987 in (all issues). See "Hints for Software Selection," June and December 1987.

LEVINE, H. A. *Project Management Using Microcomputers.* Berkeley, CA: Osborne/McGraw-Hill, 1986.

LIBRATORE, M. J. "A Decision Support System Linking

Research and Development." *Project Management Journal,* November 1988.

MANDAKOVIC, T., and L. A. SMITH. "Defining Project Management Software." *Proceedings,* Decision Sciences Institute, November 1986.

MATTHEWS, M. D. "A Conceptual Framework for Project Management Software." *Project Management Journal,* August 1987.

MCFARLAN, W. "Portfolio Approach to Information Systems." *Journal of Systems Management,* January 1982.

National Software Testing Laboratories, Inc. "Ratings Report." *Software Digest,* October 1991.

NEVISON, J. M. "Creative Time Wasting." *PM Network,* November 1995.

PALLA, R. W. "Introduction to Microcomputer Software Tools for Project Information Management." *Project Management Journal,* August 1987.

PARTOVI, F. Y., and J. BURTON. "Timing of Monitoring and Control of CPM Projects." *IEEE Transactions on Engineering Management,* February 1993.

POSPISIL, C. J. "A PC-Based Scheduling System for a Transmission and Distribution Construction Department." *Project Management Journal,* September 1990.

Project Management Institute Standards Committee. *A Guide to the Project Management Body of Knowledge.* Upper Darby, PA: Project Management Institute, 1996.

"Project Management—Editor's Choice." *PC Magazine,* June 30, 1998.

"Project Management Software." *Federal Computer Week,* October 6, 1997. (Refer to http://www.few.com/pubs/gbb/1997/1006/gbbprojman-10-06-1997.html)

RAKOS, J. J. *Software Project Management.* Englewood Cliffs, NJ: Prentice Hall, 1990.

RANDALL, P. *Lotus Guide to One-Two-Three: Release 2.2.* New York: Lotus Books, 1990.

REINGOLD, J. "Project Management in the Information Age." *PM Network,* May 1996.

SHAFER, S. M., and J. R. MEREDITH. *Operations Management: A Process Approach with Spreadsheets.* New York: Wiley, 1998.

SINGLETARY, N. "What's the Value of Earned Value?" *PM Network,* December 1996.

Software Survey, *Project Management Institute,* 2001.

SPINNER, M. *Elements of Project Management: Plan, Schedule, and Control.* Englewood Cliffs, NJ: Prentice Hall, 1981.

THAMHAIN, H. J. "The New Product Management Software and Its Impact on Management Style." *Project Management Journal,* August 1987.

YAHDAV, D. "Project Spotlight: Project Management Gets Easier." *Computerworld,* October 19, 1992.

 The following case illustrates how easily a project can get into massive trouble when the customer changes policies, responsibilities, or managers on a project and the contractor fails to monitor these events. Because the terminology is rather specialized, it tends to mislead the reader into focusing on the technology instead of the crucial events happening on the project. There are also a great number of players in the project, and keeping them straight takes careful documentation. Finally, the case raises legitimate questions about how formally to manage a project when the customer is disposed to be rather informal and casual about activities.

C A S E

THE PROJECT MANAGER/CUSTOMER INTERFACE*
E. Filliben and J. L. Colley, Jr.

Reggie Brown, B&W Nuclear Service Company's (BWNS) project manager for Nita Light and Power's Green Meadow plant, reflected on the dilemma that had plagued him for over a year. His team had completed an outage for Green Meadow in October 1989. The project was originally designed as a fixed-price contract. Delays and an expanded scope, however, forced the outage to be changed to a time-and-materials job with a final price that was significantly higher than the original contract price. Now it was December 1990, well over a year after the completion of the outage, and the bill had still not been paid in full. Insisting that it was not responsible for the enormous overrun, the utility refused to pay what BWNS's Special Products and Integrated Services Division was charging. Brown knew that maintaining a good relationship with the customer had to take priority over getting the bill paid.

Background

The Special Products and Integrated Services Division (SPIS) had been working with Nita Light and Power (NLP) since 1983. Relations with the utility remained favorable throughout the 1980s as SPIS performed a wide variety of services for NLP. In the summer of 1989, NLP sought a fixed-price contract for work to be performed by SPIS. The focus of the work was the imminent Fall refueling outage and steam-generator inspection. SPIS representatives worked with the utility to develop the fixed-price contract, which totaled approximately $500,000. The contract assumed that SPIS crews would work on all three of the utility's generators concurrently.

There were, however, several early signs of potential problems. Reggie Brown had concerns about delays even before arriving on site in late August 1989. He expected the badging process to take longer than the time allotted. Moreover, the SPIS team knew that it would need to relieve stress in the tight-radius U-bends (rows 1 and 2) and perform additional roll inspection, none of which was contemplated at the time of the original request. Representatives approached Stan Goodsen, NLP's site manager, at the end of summer and explained that the outage could not be completed under the original terms in light of anticipated delays and increased work scope. Goodsen asked for a budget and a schedule and gave the go-ahead for a time-and-materials billing.

Brown's fear of delay was realized. First, over Labor Day weekend, badging was completed and the equipment was staged as far as possible. The process of badging involved a series of tests, including site-security and health-physics qualification, psychological assessment, background check, fingerprinting, and drug screening. The utility did not want to accept SPIS's badging; it wanted to have its own separate process, which was quite time-consuming. Second, because of a delay in the chemical-channelhead decontamination, the three generators were not turned over to SPIS personnel on time. The first generator was turned over ten days after the date promised. The second one was turned over twelve days later; the third, nine days after that.

Recognizing that the cost of the work was going to exceed the contracted amount because of the utility's delay in turning over the generators, Brown, as project manager, made numerous attempts to clarify the situation early on and avert any problems down the road. First, he requested that some of the SPIS personnel be sent home while they were waiting for the other generators to become available. NLP officials refused, however, saying that the other two steam generators would be available shortly and that the field crew needed to be ready to go as soon as they were available. Second, Brown sent letters detailing the situation to the people identified on NLP's original purchase order as the utility's representatives. The only response was from on-site personnel like Goodsen, who gave repeated assurances that the SPIS contract had been switched to time-and-materials.

Initially, BWNS sent 40 engineers and technicians to start the work. When the project was in full swing, close to 100 BWNS personnel were on site. Although the original contract was for approximately $500,000 worth of work, the actual bill came to over $1,500,000. Some of the overrun was attributable to U-bend stress relief and added plug inspec-

tion, all part of the expanded scope. Much of the overrun, however, was caused by underutilization of the personnel who were on site waiting for initial access to the generators. The outage was completed 44 days after it began, 22 days longer than originally anticipated (see Exhibit 1).

Green Meadow Purchasing Procedures

Complicating the overrun situation was the fact that the utility was in the process of converting its purchasing procedures from a centralized to a decentralized program. The Contract Administrative Group, located at NLP's corporate headquarters, was originally responsible for all initial contract negotiations; all added–scope issues such as delays had formerly been handled by the on-site technical people. Over the years the entire purchasing process had been quite informal, however, especially given SPIS's long-term relationship with NLP. In 1986, SPIS had, for example, completed a multimillion-dollar project at Green Meadow without any purchase order whatsoever. Now, under the new procedures, the individual generating plants would be responsible for handling the entire purchasing process. Unfortunately, SPIS was never adequately informed of the changes.

Under the new procedures, Lou Mayhew was assigned to the on-site Contract Administration Group.

Exhibit 1

The Project Manager Customer Interface

Timeline

August 31:	Verbal okay from Goodsen to go with a time-and-materials arrangement.
September 1:	Utilily shut down. All three generators scheduled to be delivered. None ready.
September 11:	First generator to SPIS.
September 23:	Memo from Goodsen confirming 8/31 authorization.
September 23:	Second generator to SPIS.
October 2:	Third generator to SPIS.
October 14:	Outage complete.

He was to be SPIS's main contact for contract negotiations. Because the SPIS team had worked at Green Meadow on two previous outages and was not aware of the purchasing reorganization, it followed the same procedures it had used before. Although SPIS personnel knew that Mayhew existed because he had participated in the technical presentations for both previous outages, both of those purchase orders had been signed downtown at the central office. As there was no indication that the procedures had changed, the original purchase order was sent to the central office.

The Invoice

After the outage was completed, a price estimate was compiled in November 1989. It totaled $1,600,000; additional services, worth an estimated $350,000, were provided at no cost. The estimate was sent to Bill Jones, a technical specialist who was Stan Goodsen's boss, with a carbon copy to Mel Carter in Purchasing. NLP personnel's initial reaction was that the estimate looked fine; because the utility had caused the considerable delay, SPIS was entitled to full reimbursement.

The release of the invoice estimate was followed by a meeting on site in February. Several representatives from SPIS sat down with Stan Goodsen and some technicians from the utility and presented them with an initial invoice for the outage. Throughout the process, SPIS's on-site personnel dealt extensively with Goodsen. Mayhew had been invited to the meeting but did not attend. Green Meadow's technical personnel agreed to accept the invoice "as is." With NLP's input, the actual bill was sent in February 1990 to Carter in the central office.

The utility usually paid its bills within 60 days. After 90 days, Reggie Brown still had not heard anything and was starting to get nervous. He recognized, however, that the bill had been sent with volumes of paper work, including the site sheets that had been signed daily by Goodsen, and he was sure that the utility's billing department was simply bogged down with paper work. Nevertheless, Brown decided to call the utility and inquire about the delay; he was assured that there was "no problem."

The utility eventually did send some money. By October 1990, SPIS had received a total of $1.2 million. Then, on October 17, 1990, Roger Roberts, regional sales manager for SPIS, received a letter from utility Vice President Rus Clemons requesting a meeting. On October 26, Roberts and Jacqueline Doyle, manager of Contract Management, traveled to the Green Meadow plant for a meeting. Reggie Brown, on a field assignment, was unable to attend. Neither Roberts nor Doyle knew quite what to expect.

The Negotiations

On the 26th, Roberts and Doyle met with three NLP officials, Sly Simmons, Lou Mayhew, and Mayhew's boss, Rick James. The committee from the utility informed the SPIS team that, because the original agreement had been a fixed-price contract, not only would the utility not pay any more money toward the $1.6 million SPIS said it owed, but also that BWNS owed Nita Light and Power $300,000 plus interest for the amount NLP had overpaid to date. Shocked, Roberts and Doyle responded with the memo from Stan Goodsen that converted the fixed-price contract to one for time and materials. Mayhew simply kept repeating one sentence, "The price is too high." From 9:00 A.M. to 2:00 P.M., in an extremely frustrating exchange, all that was accomplished was that the group finally agreed that the contract was on a time-and-materials basis. Once that agreement was reached, however, Mayhew alleged that SPIS had loaded the project with people.

The same group met again on November 9, 1990. At that meeting, Doyle and Roberts laid out the staffing proposal that was originally accepted by Green Meadow. Then they compared it with the job's actual staffing numbers, which were within two people of the projections. Doyle then pointed out that the promised production rate, 20 tubes per hour, was also met, as corroborated by the site sheets. The problem leading to the large overrun was the delay in the utility's relinquishment of the generators. During this meeting, Doyle and Roberts also presented NLP officials with an invoice for $250,000 to cover some of the $350,000 in expenses that were never charged on the first invoice, bringing the total cost of the outage to roughly $1,850,000.

Because they believed that much of the impasse thus far was due to the lack of technical understanding of the commercial representatives NLP sent to negotiate, Doyle, Roberts, and Brown requested that Green Meadow's technical people be included in a third meeting. The technical people had agreed to accept the initial invoice "as is." All subsequent negotiations were conducted with commercial representatives, i.e., the Contract Administration Group. These meetings were frustrating because the business group did not have a solid understanding of the technical aspects of the project and was, therefore, unsympathetic to SPIS's reasoning. During the third meeting, the utility's business representatives purportedly made a phone call to the technical people. SPIS later found out from on-site personnel, however, that the call was merely for show and that no attempt was made to include the technical group. Very little was resolved during the third meeting. The utility's technical and commercial people never met together to discuss the invoice.

In December 1990, $650,000 was outstanding on the bill ($1,850,000 in total charges – $1,200,000 previously paid). NLP officials offered $400,000, bringing SPIS's total received to $1.6 million. In deciding how to handle the shortfall, Doyle knew she had to balance the competing interests of maximizing profit and nurturing this long-term customer relationship.

Long-Term Ramifications

The overrun had other serious ramifications for SPIS's relationship with Green Meadow. NLP's next project was a five-outage package worth approximately $8 million. For this package, Green Meadow proposed all new terms and conditions that strongly favored the utility. Following its proposal of other terms and conditions, SPIS received no response for almost 18 months. Doyle and Brown started pushing Mayhew and James, who essentially responded, "Take it or leave it."

In February 1991, SPIS went all out with its proposal for the five-outage package. Its proposal won the technical staff's recommendation and also offered the best price. Green Meadow decided not to award a contract for all five at once, however, but rather to award the contract for the first (April) outage only. Despite the SPIS proposal's technical and price advantages, NLP awarded the outage to Westinghouse because the latter agreed to the utility's terms and conditions.

Word in the industry was that Westinghouse had performed well on the April outage, coming in eight hours ahead of schedule. Westinghouse did, however, contest $1 million after completing the outage.

Given the events of the past year, Doyle and Brown knew that SPIS faced an uphill battle for the remaining four outages. They reflected on the lessons they had learned and wondered how they could apply them in order to put the relationship with Nita Light and Power back on track.

Advice for Project Managers

In reflecting on SPIS's experience with NLP, Jacqueline Doyle provided some advice for project managers.

> It is crucial to know who is the authorized agent on site for the utility. I thought Goodsen was authorized. He obviously was not. Always find out who needs to know about progress and deviations from plans. Keep that person informed.
>
> Given the long-standing practice in the industry, it would not have been feasible to stop work in the middle. Building a relationship with the utility over the years means that you agree to work things out as partners. Invoices on a daily or at least weekly basis would have been a good idea in this case.
>
> The biggest lesson, though, was to send documentation to, and to communicate with, the commercial personnel on a regular basis. This communication can be complicated by the tension that often exists between technical people and commercial people. So even though day-to-day communication with the on-site technical group appears congenial, one person should be appointed to communicate with the business managers.

Doyle also cited the following responsibilities of project management:

- Know who the decision makers are
- Ask the right questions of the right people
- Control the customer
- Get money for work performed
- Persevere

QUESTIONS

1. What did Brown and BWNS do well in this situation? What could have been done better?

2. What factors outside Brown's control interfered with his efforts to work with the utility?

3. What skills does it take to be an effective interface with the customer?

4. Is the customer always right? Should BWNS try to win back NLP's business at this time?

5. How could Brown win back NLP's business? What should he do?

The following reading reports the results of a survey of PMI members concerning the computer tools they employ. The results identify the tools they use, their level of use, what they are used for, satisfaction with the tools, training received on the tools, and the adequacy of the tools. Software beyond project management packages are included in the survey.

R E A D I N G

SURVEY OF PROJECT MANAGEMENT TOOLS*
T. L. Fox and J. W. Spence

For carpenters, it is a hammer. For pilots, it is an instrument panel. For surgeons, it is a scalpel. These devices represent a primary tool of the trade for their users. Tools of the trade are those vital instruments without which completion of the tasks required for the job would be very difficult. In attempts to better serve the users of the tool, new features or enhancements are introducted periodically. However, sometimes these "improvements" can have unanticipated consequences, either negative or positive. For example, several versions of ergonomically improved hammers have been produced, but without successful adoption. When digital capabilities with specific, numeric displays were introduced into the cockpit of airplanes, pilots, who were accustomed to simply being able to scan their analog instruments, had to rethink the way in which they assessed their environment and physically "lock on" to the digital information. On the other hand, the introduction of lasers as surgical instruments has revolutionized the surgeons' job.

Virtually every profession has what would generally be regarded as special "tools of the trade," and project management is certainly no exception. A number of individuals have stated that the key to effective project management is the ability to track and control the progress of system projects (Rook, 1986; Zmud, 1980). Considering that many, if not most, projects are composed of hundreds of interrelated tasks, trying to track and control all those tasks effectively turns into a management nightmare. Therefore, using a computerized project management tool has become essential to achieving the requirements of effective project management (Moder, 1994; Shenhar & Laufer, 1995; Weil, 1986). Yet, we must be ever mindful that "improve-

---

*Tools of the Trade: A Survey of Project Management Tools. *Project Management Journal,* September 1998. ©1998 by the Project Management Institute. Reprinted by permission.

ments" in these tools should yield positive consequences for project managers, and therefore such "improvements" should be reevaluated periodically.

This paper presents the results of a nationwide survey of project managers who provided insight into their "tools of the trade," along with assessments of satisfaction, training, and use made of these tools. A discussion of each element is presented, followed by a conclusion regarding the current state of project managers' tools of the trade.

The Survey

A nationwide survey was sent to almost 1,000 project managers. These individuals were randomly selected from the membership of the Project Management Institute (PMI) and represented a cross-section of the entire United States, many different industries and varying company sizes. The accompanying cover letter asked the participants to complete the survey only if their primary job responsibilities included project management. A total of 159 responses were received, representing a response rate of 16.3%.

The participants were first asked to provide various demographic information. The respondents averaged 10.4 years of project management experience and 12.4 years of experience in the field of information systems. The vast majority of participants worked for companies described as focusing either on engineering or software development, while a much smaller percentage worked for companies that focused on hardware, or were either retailers or wholesalers. The types of projects these participants either participated in or managed within the past three years were primarily for in-house use, commercially contracted, or directly

marketed to external customers. The participants also indicated that a larger number of projects were worked on in the past three years with a calendar duration of six months or less, but considerably more time was expended managing those projects having a duration of greater than six months.

Next, the respondents were asked to identify as many as three computerized project management tools that they were currently using or had used within the past three years. For each of these tools the respondents were asked to list the primary use made of these tools and their level of satisfaction with the tools. The respondents were also asked to indicate (1) how much training, if any, they had received on the use of the tools, and (2) the perceived adequacy of this training. Lastly, the respondents were asked to indicate how much use they actually make of the tools, both with respect to the number of months the tools had been used and the number of hours per week each of the tools was used. The respondents also provided an indication of the perceived adequacy of this amount of use.

The Tools

A quick review of both the literature and the market indicates that there are many computerized project management tools available and the survey conducted confirmed those findings. The respondents generated a listing of 70 unique computerized project management tools that they were currently using or had used within the past three years. Ten of these tools were identified by almost 75% of the respondents, and therefore, subsequent analysis was limited to these top 10 choices. The top 10 most frequently listed tools and their relative percentage of respondents using those tools are shown in Table 1.

Table 1. Top 10 Project Management Tools

PM Tool (developer)	Percentage of Respondents Listing Tool
Microsoft Project (*Microsoft Corporation*)	48.4%
Primavera Project Planner (*Primavera Systems*)	13.8%
Microsoft Excel (*Microsoft Corporation*)	8.5%
Project Workbench (*Applied Business Technology*)	8.1%
Time Line (*Time Line Solutions*)	6.1%
SureTrak (*Primavera Systems*)	5.3%
CA-SuperProject (*Computer Associates, Int'l.*)	2.8%
Project Scheduler (*Scitor*)	2.8%
Artemis Prestige (*Lucas Management Systems*)	2.0%
FasTracs (Applied Microsystems)	2.0%

Table 2. Project Management Software by Type of Company

Type of Company		Artemis Prestige	CA-Super Project	FasTracs	MS Excel	MS Project	Primavera Project Planner	Project Workbench	Project Scheduler	SureTrak	Time Line	Total
Software	#	2	3	1	4	36	4	11	1	2	2	66
	%	3.0	4.5	1.5	6.1	**54.5**	6.1	*16.7*	1.5	3.0	3.0	100%
Hardware	#		1		2	11		3		1	1	19
	%		5.3		10.5	**57.9**		*15.8*		5.3	5.3	100%
Engineering	#	2	3	4	16	52	22	1	5	11	11	127
	%	1.6	2.4	3.1	12.6	**40.9**	*17.3*	0.8	3.9	8.7	8.7	100%
Retail	#				2	9	2	6		2	3	24
	%				8.3	**37.5**	8.3	*25.0*		8.3	12.5	100%
Wholesale	#		1		1	8	1	2			1	14
	%		7.1		7.1	**57.1**	7.1	*14.3*			7.1	100%
Legend	1st											
	2nd											

Clearly, Microsoft Project is by far the most frequently used computerized project management tool on the market today. This is consistent with previous surveys of project management tools (Levine, 1995). Levine contributed this leap to the top of the project management software sales to Microsoft Corporation's marketing and leveraging skills rather than the superb nature of the product, and comments that Microsoft Project is "far from being the perfect project management software package." Regardless, it remains the most widely used tool.

The second most widely used project management tool, as indicated by the survey, is Primavera Project Planning (also known as "P3") from Primavera Systems. This is considered to be a high-end tool, retailing for several thousand dollars and providing significantly more capability than a low-end tool such as Microsoft Project.

It is interesting to note that the next most widely used tool marketed specifically as a project management tool, ABT Project Workbench, was actually listed by fewer respondents than Microsoft Excel. Evidently, project managers do not rely solely on software packages

specifically designated as project management tools, but consider a variety of other general-purpose software tools such as spreadsheets as part of their menagerie. Other nontraditional project management tools that were mentioned by the respondents include word processing packages such as Microsoft Word and WordPerfect, presentation packages such as Microsoft PowerPoint, and database packages such as Microsoft Access.

A cross-tabulation of these top 10 project management tools in relation to the types of companies for which the participants work is shown in Table 2.

Table 2 shows both the number of users and relative percentage by tool and company type and indicates that Microsoft Project consistently is the tool of choice across company types. The second most frequently selected tool is Project Workbench for all types of companies except engineering. Engineering firms prefer Primavera Project Planner considerably more often than Project Workbench, and actually rank Project Workbench as the least used tool.

A further analysis compared which project management tools were used with respect to both the number of projects worked on having a calendar duration of either

Table 3. Project Management Tools by Project Duration

Type of Company		Artemis Prestige	CA-Super Project	FasTracs	MS Excel	MS Project	Primavera Project Planner	Project Workbench	Project Scheduler	SureTrak	Time Line	Total
< 6 mos.	#	1	4.9	2.4	6.9	8.5	5.1	4.2	5.7	7.4	7.4	6.85
	%	12.4	51.7	13.0	31.7	21.7	27.2	28.3	16.3	40.8	40.8	25.9%
> 6 mos.	#	3.4	2.3	2.0	5.8	5.4	6.3	3.1	22.5	5.0	5	5.65
	%	87.6	48.3	87.0	68.3	78.3	72.8	71.7	83.7	59.2	59.2	74.1%

Note: Average number of projects and average percentage of time worked on projects.

Table 4. *Exclusivity of Project Management Tool Use*

PMTool	Exclusivity
Project Workbench	72.3%
Microsoft Project	58.6%
Project Scheduler	50.1%
Microsoft Excel	47.5%
Artemis Prestige	45.0%
Primavera Project Planner	37.4%
SureTrak	32.7%
Time Line	29.9%
CA-SuperProject	28.7%
FasTracs	11.0%

less than six months or greater than six months, and the relative percentage of time spent working on the projects. This cross-tabulation is depicted in Table 3.

As indicated in Table 3, it is interesting to note that three tools—Artemis Prestige, Primavera Project Planner, and Project Scheduler—are used more often for long-term projects (greater than six calendar months duration) than short-term projects. The other seven tools are chosen more often for smaller-scale projects.

The respondents also were asked to indicate the percentage of time they used each tool compared to all tools listed. This is essentially a measure of exclusivity of use. This measure is listed in Table 4, in descending order of exclusivity. These results show that project managers who listed that they used Project Workbench, for example, use that particular tool 72.3 percent of the time, and use other project management tools 27.7 percent of the time.

In an open-ended question, the respondents were asked to indicate the primary use(s) for which they used each project management tool they had listed. A variety of responses were provided, which are summarized in Table 5.

It appears that project managers use all of the project management tools for essentially the same basic functions: planning, scheduling, tracking, and controlling their projects. Project managers also use the tools to varying degrees for budgeting and analysis.

Satisfaction with the Tools

The respondents were asked to rate, on a 5-point Likert scale, their satisfaction with each of the project management tools listed (a rating of "1" indicates a lack of satisfaction and a rating of "5" indicates excellent satisfaction). Satisfaction was measured using Doll and Torkzadeh's (1988) 12-item User Satisfaction Instrument. This instrument provides a measure of overall satisfaction, as well as a measure of satis-

Table 5. Primary Use(s) Made of Project Management Tools

PMTool	Primary Use(s)
Artemis Prestige	Multiproject planning and tracking; scheduling resources; cost analysis
CA-SuperProject	Small and large projects; scheduling; tracking and planning; training
FasTracs	Small projects; presentations; quick Gantt charts; scheduling analysis
Microsoft Excel	Budgeting; cost analysis; variance analysis; tracking and reporting; work breakdown structures (WBS)
Microsoft Project	Small, medium, and large projects; control and tracking; detailed scheduling; early project planning; communication; high-level planning; Gantt, CPM and PERT; planning, analyzing, tracking, reporting; total project management; "everything"
Primavera Project Planner	Large, complex multiproject environments; planning, scheduling, resource allocation, control; build overall detailed project plan; critical path analysis; client requested, corporate standard
Primavera SureTrak	Single and multiple projects—small, medium, and large; project scheduling, resource allocation, control
Project Scheduler	Multiproject; scheduling, resource management, budgeting, tracking
Project Workbench	Small, medium, and large projects; planning, estimating, scheduling, analyzing, tracking, reporting; WBS, Gantt, resource utilization
Time Line	Small-to medium-sized projects; planning, tracking, and scheduling

Table 6.   Satisfaction with Project Management Tools

PM Tool	Overall	Content	Accuracy	Format	Ease of Use	Timeliness
Project Scheduler	3.93	3.9	4.3	3.9	3.2	4.4
Primavera Project Planner	3.91	4.1	4.3	4.0	3.2	3.9
Project Workbench	3.90	3.9	4.3	3.8	3.5	4.1
Microsoft Excel	3.88	3.8	4.3	4.0	3.8	3.6
Primavera SureTrak	3.79	3.7	4.1	3.8	3.2	4.1
CA-SuperProject	3.75	3.8	4.3	3.8	3.0	3.8
Microsoft Project	3.64	3.5	3.9	3.6	3.6	3.8
Artemis Prestige	3.33	3.6	4.0	3.3	2.0	3.5
FasTracs	3.33	3.3	3.5	3.6	3.4	3.0
Time Line	3.24	3.0	3.5	3.2	3.2	3.6
Total	3.70	3.6	4.0	3.7	3.4	3.8

faction pertaining to each of five specific elements: content, accuracy, format, ease of use, and timeliness. The average satisfaction scores for each of the top 10 most frequently listed project management tools are shown in Table 6, in descending order of overall satisfaction.

Clearly, the most widely used project management tools are rated above average (an average rating is 3.0) both in overall satisfaction and for each of the five elements (the one exception being the ease-of-use rating for Artemis Prestige). Therefore, it appears that project managers are reasonably satisfied with the currently available selection of project management tools.

Training on the Tools

The respondents also provided in indication of how much training they received on the tools that they listed, as well as a measure of the perceived adequacy of this training. The measure of perceived adequacy of training on the project management tools was based on a 5-point Likert scale, with a "1" indicating totally inadequate and a "5" indicating totally adequate. Table 7 shows, in descending order, the average number of hours of training received on the 10 most frequently listed project management tools and the respective measure of perceived adequacy of this training.

Table 7.   Training on Project Management Tools

	Hours Reported		
	Excluded		Included
PM Tool	Average # of Hrs	Average Adequacy	Average Adequacy
Primavera Project Planner	31.00	3.53	3.60
Project Workbench	28.92	4.08	3.82
Project Scheduler	24.00	4.33	3.50
CA-SuperProject	16.00	3.00	2.50
Microsoft Project	13.61	3.41	3.13
Artemis Prestige	12.80	2.80	2.80
Microsoft Excel	11.43	3.29	3.20
Primavera SureTrak	9.71	3.29	2.82
Time Line	4.00	3.75	3.13
FasTracs	0.00	NA	3.00
Total	18.02	3.48	3.21

Several respondents reported that they had received no training on the use of a particular tool and subsequently did not report a measure of perceived adequacy of that training. Other respondents reported that they had received no training on the use of a particular tool, but subsequently did provide a measure of adequacy on the training, or lack thereof, on the tool. For example, every respondent who listed FasTracs reported that they had received no training on the use of the tool. However, several of these respondents rated the adequacy of the training, or lack thereof, which resulted in a mean score of 3.0. Overall, both measures of the perceived adequacy of training were above an average rating of 3.0, and thus it appears that project managers consider the training they receive on the use of the project management tools to be reasonably adequate.

Considering that several project managers reported a measure of perceived adequacy of training even if they had not received any training, a further analysis was conducted comparing the adequacy of training scores on those participants receiving training, regardless of how little, to those participants who did not receive training. Levene's (1960) test for equality of variance indicated that the variances were significantly different ($s_{training} = 3.48$, $s_{no\ training} = 2.67$, $F = 25.09$, $p = .000$). A t-test assuming unequal variances resulted in a significant t value of -3.65 (df = 86.42, $p = .000$), which confirmed this finding. Thus, obtaining even minimal training on the use of project management tools has a significant impact on perceived adequacy of training. Not surprisingly, the number of hours of training received and the perceived adequacy of this training were found to be significantly related and positively correlated. In other words, the more training, the better.

Additionally, the relationship between the measure of satisfaction with the project management tools and both the number of hours of training received and the perceived adequacy of this training was examined. Strong relationships were found in each case, and thus it appears that by obtaining training on the use of a project management tool, the project manager's overall satisfaction with that tool is increased.

Use of the Tools

As a final measure of the perceived adequacy of the project management tools, the project managers were asked to provide an indication of how much use is made of the tools and the perceived adequacy of this use. The respondents provided both a measure of duration (how many months the tool had been used) and intensity (how many hours each week the tool is used). This information, along with the measure of perceived adequacy of use, is summarized in Table 8. The project management tools are listed in descending order of the measure of perceived adequacy of use.

As Table 8 indicates, the project managers provided an above-average rating of the adequacy of use made of the tools. Additionally, a significant and positive correlation was found between the number of hours per week the tools were used and the perceived adequacy of this use. In other words, the more time spent using a project management tool, the higher the perceived adequacy of this use. Thus, it appears that project managers are indeed quite comfortable with the perceived

Table 8. Amount and Adequacy of the Use of Project Management Tools

PM Tool	# of Mos.	# of Hrs/Wek	Adequacy
FasTracs	39.80	1.25	5.00
Artemis Prestige	45.40	6.50	4.40
Microsoft Excel	43.78	13.00	4.39
Project Workbench	38.05	9.35	4.35
Primavera Project Planner	42.62	11.63	4.14
CA-SuperProject	31.29	5.80	4.00
Project Scheduler	24.14	11.83	4.00
Primavera SureTrak	13.23	4.15	3.85
Microsoft Project	24.49	6.06	3.83
Time Line	43.54	5.10	2.90
Total	30.81	7.51	3.96

adequacy of the use being made of the currently available project management tools. Generally, project managers had used the tools for at least one year, and often for several years. On average, project managers use the tools for the equivalent of almost an entire eight-hour workday each week.

Conclusion

This survey of project managers provides important insight into the project management tools currently being used by the profession. The survey confirms that there are literally dozens of project management tools on the market. However, the majority of project managers surveyed tend to use only a small subset of these tools, the most widely used being Microsoft Project. It is also interesting to note that project managers rely on nontraditional project management tools, such as Microsoft Excel, as readily as they do more project-focused tools. Although each project management tool is marketed and advertised as providing various features that other tools may not have, the uses made of all the tools are quite similar and focus on the basic project management tasks of planning, scheduling, tracking, and controlling. With respect to the perceived adequacy of this collection of project management tools, over-all the survey respondents indicated above-average ratings of satisfaction, adequacy of training, and adequacy of the use of the tools. It was confirmed that not only does receiving training on the use of a project management tool influence the perceived adequacy of the tool but also the overall satisfaction that a project manager has with respect to the tool.

Thus, it appears that project managers have quite a collection of project management tools at their disposal, and that they are relatively pleased with the adequacy of these tools. Considering that a computerized project management tool is an invaluable resource—the primary "tool of the trade"—for project managers, it is useful to periodically confirm that the tools are, in fact, meeting the needs of the professional.

References

DOLL, WILLIAM J., & TORKZADEH, GHOLAMREZA (1988, June). The measurement of end-user computing satisfaction. *MIS Quarterly,* 259–274.

LEVENE, H. (1960). Robust tests for equality of variances. *Contributions to Probability and Statistics.* Palo Alto, CA: Stanford University Press.

LEVINE, HARVEY A. (1995, July). Innovators? Or tripping over their egos? Winners and losers in the PM software industry. *PM Network,* 22–25.

MODER, JOSEPH J. (1994). Conjecture on the future direction of MPM. *Project Management Journal, 25* (3), 6–7.

ROOK, PAUL. (1986, January). Controlling software projects. *Software Engineering Journal,* 7–16.

SHENHAR, AARON J., & LAUFER, ALEXANDER. (1995, September). Integrating product and project management—A new synergistic approach. *Engineering Management Journal, 7* (3), 11–15.

WEIL, DAVID E. (1986). Retrospective application of project management software as a planning tool: A case study examining the preparation of a U.S. Environmental Protection Agency air quality criteria document. *Project Management Journal, 17* (2), 65–69.

ZMUD, ROBERT W. (1980, June). Management of large software development efforts. *MISQuarterly,* 45–55.

Questions

1. According to Tables 6 and 8, Microsoft Project is below the average of all the packages surveyed in overall satisfaction and adequacy, yet is number one in terms of use in Table 1. How can this be?

2. Of the factors listed in Table 6, which would be most important to you in selecting a project management package to use in planning a project? Which PM package rated tops on this category?

3. Based on the number of projects in Table 3 for which various software packages were used, what package was used the most for short projects? For long projects? What might you conclude from this?

4. For project managers trying to manage several projects at once, which package would probably be best, based on Table 5 and the other tables?

5. Based on these survey results, what would you predict will be the future of project management software packages?

CHAPTER

11

Project Control

In the previous chapter, we described the monitoring and information gathering process that would help the PM control the project. Control is the last element in the implementation cycle of planning–monitoring–controlling. Information is collected about system performance, compared with the desired (or planned) level, and action taken if actual and desired performance differ enough that the controller (manager) wishes to decrease the difference. Note that reporting performance, comparing the differences between desired and actual performance levels, and accounting for why such differences exist are all parts of the control process. In essence, control is the *act* of reducing the difference between plan and reality.

Although this chapter is primarily directed to the exercise of control by the project manager, we must note that the Project Management Office, or other project overseer reporting to upper management, also has a project control function. The aim of the project is to help achieve some strategic objective of the organization, and the regular deliberations of the PMO, council, or group charged with implementing the Project Portfolio Process must include an appraisal of the continuing value of the project in achieving those objectives. Using the information gained from monitoring the project, as well as information concerning changes in the organizational goals, resources, and strategy, this group may need to take some form of action (control) regarding the project, such as redirecting it, getting it back on track, or perhaps even terminating it. (We discuss the various forms and conditions of termination in Chapter 13.)

A special kind of control is exercised through risk management. The group responsible for risk management, be it the PMO or a specific group devoted to the subject, may exert its actions on the project but also may act on the environment, the major source of risk for the project. As you will see next, almost everything that can go wrong with project performance, cost, or schedule is the result of uncertainty. And the lion's share of the uncertainty has its source in systems that lie outside the project, its environment. When feasible, the group may act on these outside systems to decrease or remove threats to the project, but most often they are beyond the group's influence. All that can be done is to act on the project in order to mitigate or counteract the actions of these external systems.

As has been emphasized throughout this book, control is focused on three elements of a project—performance, cost, and time. The PM is constantly concerned with these three aspects of the project. Is the project delivering what it promised to deliver or more? Is it making delivery at or below the promised cost? Is it making delivery at or before the promised time? It is strangely easy to lose sight of these fundamental targets, especially in large projects with a wealth of detail and a great number of subprojects. Large projects develop their own momentum and tend to get out of hand, going their own way independent of the wishes of the PM and the intent of the proposal.

Think, for a moment, of a few of the things that can cause a project to require the control of performance, costs, or time.

Performance
Unexpected technical problems arise.
Insufficient resources are available when needed.
Insurmountable technical difficulties are present.
Quality or reliability problems occur.
Client requires changes in system specifications.
Interfunctional complications arise.
Technological breakthroughs affect the project.

Cost
Technical difficulties require more resources.
The scope of the work increases.
Initial bids or estimates were too low.
Reporting was poor or untimely.
Budgeting was inadequate.
Corrective control was not exercised in time.
Input price changes occurred.

Time
Technical difficulties took longer than planned to solve.
Initial time estimates were optimistic.
Task sequencing was incorrect.
Required inputs of material, personnel, or equipment were unavailable when needed.
Necessary preceding tasks were incomplete.
Customer-generated change orders required rework.
Governmental regulations were altered.

And these are only a few of the relatively "mechanistic" problems that can occur. Actually, there are no purely mechanistic problems on projects. All problems have a human element, too. For example, humans, by action or inaction, set in motion a chain of events that leads to a failure to budget adequately, creates a quality problem, leads the project down a technically difficult path, or fails to note a change in government regulations. If, by chance, some of these or other things happen (as a result of human action or not), humans are affected by them. Frustration, pleasure, determination, hopelessness, anger, and many other emotions arise during the course of a project. They affect the work of the individuals who feel them—for better or worse. It is over this welter of confusion, emotion, fallibility, and general cussedness that the PM tries to exert control.

All of these problems, always combinations of the human and mechanistic, call for intervention and control by the project manager. There are infinite "slips 'twixt cup and lip," especially in projects where the technology or the deliverables are new and unfamiliar, and PMs, like most managers, find control is a difficult function to perform. There are several reasons why this is so. One of the main reasons is that PMs, again like most managers, do not discover problems. Managers discover what Russell Ackoff (1974) once described as a "mess." A "mess" is a general condition of a system that, when viewed by a manager, leads to a statement that begins, "%#^@*&+#!" and goes downhill from there. It is the discovery of a mess that leads the PM to the conclusion that there is a problem(s) lurking somewhere around. In systems as complex as projects, the task of defining the problem(s) is formidable, and thus knowing what to control is not a simple task. Another reason control is difficult is because, in spite of an almost universal need to blame some person for any trouble, it is often almost impossible to know if a problem resulted from human error or from the random application of Murphy's Law.

PMs also find it tough to exercise control because the project team, even on large projects, is an "in-group." It is "we," while outsiders are "they." It is usually hard to criticize friends, to subject them to control. Further, many PMs see control as an ad hoc process. Each need to exercise control is seen as a unique event, rather than as one instance of an ongoing and recurring process. Whitten (1995) offers the observation that projects are drifting out of control if the achievement of milestones is being threatened. He also offers some guidelines on how to resolve this problem and bring the project back in control.

Because control of projects is such a mixture of feeling and fact, of human and mechanism, of causation and random chance, we must approach the subject in an extremely orderly way. In this chapter, we start by examining the general purposes of control. Then we consider the basic structure of the process of control. We do this by describing control theory in the form of a cybernetic control loop. While most projects offer little opportunity for the actual application of automatic feedback loops, this system provides us with a comprehensive but reasonably simple illustration of all the elements necessary to control any system. From this model, we then turn to the types of control that are most often applied to projects. The design of control systems is discussed as are the impacts that various types of controls tend to have on the humans being controlled. The specific requirement of "balance" in a control system is also covered, as are two special control problems: control of creative activities, and control of change.

All in all, it is our opinion that of all the major tasks of project management, control is the least understood. Most PMs are ill-at-ease while in the role of exercising control. Many seem to associate the notion of disciplinarian with control. A few simple suggestions might help. Avoid heavily criticizing people for actions they know (now) are wrong. A simple reminder will do. Avoid criticizing people in public under any circumstances. Recall, from time to time, that the people working for you are reasonably bright and almost never act out of malice—unless you have just violated the immediately preceding rule. Above all, fix first, blame later if you still have the energy and "simply must."

11.1 THE FUNDAMENTAL PURPOSES OF CONTROL

The two fundamental objectives of control are:

1. The regulation of results through the alteration of activities.
2. The stewardship of organizational assets.

Most discussions of the control function are focused on regulation. The PM needs to be equally attentive to both regulation and conservation. Because the main body of this chapter (and much of the next) concerns the PM as regulator, let us emphasize the conservationist role here. The PM must guard the physical assets of the organization, its human resources, and its financial resources. The processes for conserving these three different kinds of assets are different.

Physical Asset Control

Physical asset control requires control of the *use* of physical assets. It is concerned with asset maintenance, whether preventive or corrective. At issue also is the timing of maintenance or replacement as well as the quality of maintenance. Some years ago, a New England brewery purchased the abandoned and obsolete brewing plant of a newly defunct competitor. A PM was put in charge of this old facility with the instruction that the plant should be completely "worn out" over the next five-year period, but that it should be fully operational in the meantime. This presented an interesting problem: the controlled deterioration of a plant while at the same time maintaining as much of its productive capability as possible. Clearly, both objectives could not be achieved simultaneously, but the PM met the spirit of the project quite well.

If the project uses considerable amounts of physical equipment, the PM also has the problem of setting up maintenance schedules in such a way as to keep the equipment in operating condition while minimizing interference with ongoing work. It is critical to accomplish preventive maintenance prior to the start of that final section of the project life cycle known as the Last Minute Panic (LMP). (Admittedly, the timing of the LMP is not known, which makes the planning of pre-LMP preventive maintenance somewhat difficult.)

Physical inventory, whether equipment or material, must also be controlled. It must be received, inspected (or certified), and possibly stored prior to use. Records of all incoming shipments must be carefully validated so that payment to suppliers can be authorized. The same precautions applied to goods from external suppliers must also be applied to suppliers from inside the organization. Even such details as the project library, project coffee maker, project office furniture, and all the other minor bits and pieces must be counted, maintained, and conserved.

Human Resource Control

Stewardship of human resources requires controlling and maintaining the growth and development of people. Projects provide particularly fertile ground for cultivating people. Because projects are unique, differing one from another in many ways, it is possible for people working on projects to gain a wide range of experience in a reasonably short time.

Measurement of physical resource conservation is accomplished through the familiar audit procedures. The measurement of human resource conservation is far more difficult. Such devices as employee appraisals, personnel performance indices, and screening methods for appointment, promotion, and retention are not particularly satisfactory devices for ensuring that the conservation function is being properly handled. The accounting profession has worked for some years on the development of *human resource accounting,* and while the effort has produced some interesting ideas, human resource accounting is not well accepted by the accounting profession.

Financial Resource Control

Though accountants have not succeeded in developing acceptable methods for human resource accounting, their work on techniques for the conservation (and regulation) of financial resources has most certainly resulted in excellent tools for financial control.

It is difficult to separate the control mechanisms aimed at conservation of financial resources from those focused on regulating resource use. Most financial controls do both. Capital investment controls work to conserve the organization's assets by insisting that certain conditions be met before capital can be expended, and those same conditions usually regulate the use of capital to achieve the organization goal of a high return on investments.

The techniques of financial control, both conservation and regulation, are well known. They include current asset controls, and project budgets as well as capital investment controls. These controls are exercised through a series of analyses and audits conducted by the accounting/controller function for the most part. Representation of this function on the project team is mandatory. The structure of the techniques applied to projects does not differ appreciably from those applied to the general operation of the firm, but the context within which they are applied is quite different. One reason for the differences is that the project is accountable to an outsider—an external client, or another division of the parent firm, or both at the same time.

The importance of proper conformance to both organizational and client control standards in financial practice and recordkeeping cannot be overemphasized. The parent organization, through its agent, the project manager, is responsible for the conservation and proper *use of* resources owned by the client or owned by the parent and charged to the client. Clients will insist on, and the courts will require the practice of, *due diligence* in the exercise of such responsibility. While some clients may not be aware of this responsibility on the part of firms with whom they contract, the government is most certainly aware of it. In essence, due diligence requires that the organization proposing a project conduct a reasonable investigation, verification, and disclosure, in language that is understandable, of every material fact relevant to the firm's ability to conduct the project, and to omit nothing where such omission might ethically mislead the client. It is not possible to define, in some general way, precisely what might be required for any given project. The firm should, however, make sure that it has legal counsel competent to aid it in meeting this responsibility.

One final note on the conservationist role of the controller. The attitude or mind-set of the conservationist is often antithetical to the mind-set of the PM, whose attention is naturally on the use of resources rather than their conservation. The conservationist reminds one of the fabled librarian who is happiest when all the books are ordered neatly on the library shelves. The PM, often the manager and controller at one and the same time, is subject to this conflict and has no choice but to live with it. The warring attitudes must be merged and compromised as best they can. For an excellent work on the role of the manager as steward, see Block (1993).

Project Management in Practice
Extensive Controls for San Francisco's Metro Turnback Project

By the late 1980s, transportation in San Francisco's financial district, an area built over loose fill which had once been part of the bay, had become a serious problem. The recent addition of the Bay Area Rapid Transit (BART), plus the usual busses, metro, cabs, and commuting traffic made for severe congestion in the district. To provide relief, the city launched the MUNI Metro Turnback Project to increase capacity and provide for future expansion. The 11-year planned project consisted of building a pair of twin tunnels 18 feet in diameter and a sixth of a mile long under the busiest street in San Francisco, connected to a concrete box 23 feet high by 55 feet wide by a fifth of a mile long under the second busiest street, opening onto a 386 foot retaining wall and emerging surface track (see exhibit).

In addition to the inherent difficulties implied in the scope of the project as just described, the project was fraught with multiple challenges beyond just the disruption of traffic, business, events, and tourism:

1. The tunnels would pass directly over the BART tunnels, in places only 4.5 feet away, in loose fill and mud below the Bay water table.

2. Wooden pilings that had supported wharves and piers in bygone years would be encountered and would require major force to cut, further endangering the BART tunnels.

3. The excavation work would pass near many high valued buildings, some of historic designation.

4. The below-water table tunnels would run very close to the actual waters of San Francisco Bay, with the potential of a breakthrough.

5. Seismic activity was likely and there had been a recent major earthquake in the area which elevated the safety requirements.

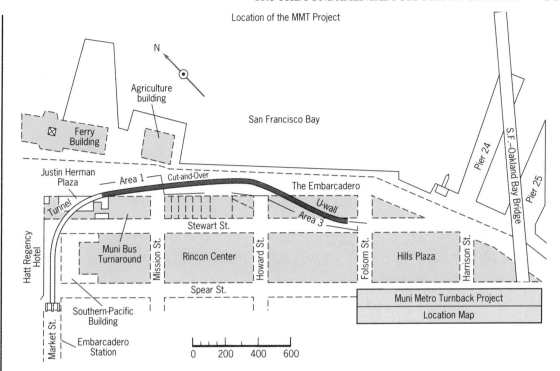

Location of the MMT Project

Clearly, very careful controls were needed to manage the project in terms of not only the above risks but also in terms of schedule and costs. This was achieved by the overarching Management Plan and Control system and its multiple subsidiary control systems based on the detailed work breakdown structure.

- The Project Code of Accounts included the work breakdown structure and Cost Code of Accounts which gave the appropriate schedule and cost codes for reporting and monitoring.
- The Control Budget included the quantities, costs, and job-hour allocations for the Project Code of Accounts plus any approved scope changes.
- The Trend Program tracked scope changes and identified any potential cost impact due to new changes, ideas, directions, or requirements. Project managers used this tool to make cost/benefit decisions to keep costs under control.

- The Scope Change Log listed any changes identified from the Trend Program which then had to either be approved or deleted.
- A Monthly Contract Cash Flow Schedule reflected expenditures so contractor invoices could be compared with the expenditure schedule.
- The Contractual Milestone Summary Schedule (CMSS) was the overall plan for the total construction scope. The schedule was issued monthly for comparison of actual with planned progress. Analyses were made of critical and near-critical paths, areas of high risk, opportunities for schedule improvement, and so on.
- The Construction Schedule was derived from the CMSS above and was for coordination with the general contractor.
- The Three-Week Rolling Construction Schedule showed completed activities the previous week and those planned for the

current and coming weeks. It was used to monitor progress against the baseline Construction Schedule.

- Quality Control and Quality Assurance responsibilities were segregated and partitioned between the contractor and construction management.

- A system of Contractor's Nonconformance Reports and Corrective Action Reports was established. By the end of the project, only 30 of these reports had been issued over the 11-year duration.

Opening ceremonies for the project were held in December 1996. Over the 11-year period, the project came in only two month's late (due to 17 new fire code requirements late in the project) and $22 million under budget.

Source: C. Wu and G. Harwell, "The MUNI Metro Turnback Project," *PM Network,* May 1998, pp. 49–55.

11.2 THREE TYPES OF CONTROL PROCESSES

The process of controlling a project (or any system) is far more complex than simply waiting for something to go wrong and then, if possible, fixing it. We must decide at what points in the project we will try to exert control, what is to be controlled, how it will be measured, how much deviation from plan will be tolerated before we act, what kinds of interventions should be used, and how to spot and correct potential deviations before they occur. In order to keep these and other such issues sorted out, it is helpful to begin a consideration of control with a brief exposition on the theory of control.

No matter what our purpose in controlling a project, there are three basic types of control mechanisms we can use: cybernetic control, go/no-go control, and postcontrol. In this section we will describe these three types and briefly discuss the information requirements of each. While few cybernetic control systems are used for project control, we will describe them here because they clearly delineate the elements that must be present in any control system, as well as the information requirements of control systems.

Cybernetic Control

Cybernetic, or steering, control is by far the most common type of control system. (*Cyber* is the Greek word for "helmsman.") The key feature of cybernetic control is its automatic operation. Consider the diagrammatic model of a cybernetic control system shown in Figure 11-1.

As Figure 11-1 shows, a system is operating with inputs being subjected to a process that transforms them into outputs. It is this system that we wish to control. In order to do so, we must monitor the system output. This function is performed by sensors that measure one or more aspects of the output, presumably those aspects one wishes to control. Measurements taken by a sensor are transmitted to the comparator, which compares them with a set of predetermined standards. The difference between actual and standard is sent to the decision maker, which determines whether or not the difference is of sufficient size to deserve correction. If the difference is large enough

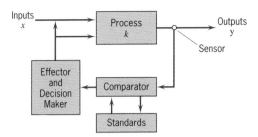

Figure 11-1 A cybernetic control system.

to warrant action, a signal is sent to the effector, which acts on the process or on the inputs to produce outputs that conform more closely to the standard.

A cybernetic control system that acts to reduce deviations from standard is called a *negative feedback loop.* If the system output moves away from standard in one direction, the control mechanism acts to move it in the opposite direction. The speed or force with which the control operates is, in general, proportional to the size of the deviation from standard. (Mathematical descriptions of the action of negative feedback loops are widely available. (See, for example, van Gigch, 1978.) The precise way in which the deviation is corrected depends on the nature of the operating system and the design of the controller. Figure 11-2 illustrates three different response patterns. Response path A is direct and rapid, while path B is more gradual. Path C shows oscillations of decreasing amplitude. An aircraft suddenly deflected from a stable flight path would tend to recover by following pattern C.

Types of Cybernetic Control Systems   Cybernetic controls come in three varieties, or *orders,* differing in the sophistication with which standards are set. Figure 11-1 shows a simple *first-order* control system, a goal-seeking device. The standard is set and there is no provision made for altering it except by intervention from the outside. The common thermostat is a time-worn example of a *first-order* controller. One sets the standard temperature, and the heating and air-conditioning systems operate to maintain it.

Figure 11-3 shows a *second-order* control system. This device can alter the system standards according to some predetermined set of rules or program. The complexity of second-order systems can vary widely. The addition of a clock to the thermostat to allow it to maintain different standards during day and night makes the thermostat a second-order controller. An interactive computer program may alter its

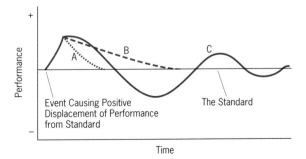

Figure 11-2 Typical paths for correction of deviation of performance from standard.

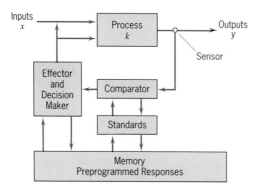

Figure 11-3 A second-order feedback system—preprogrammed goal changer.

responses according to a complex set of preprogrammed rules, but it is still only a second-order system. Many industrial projects involve second-order controllers—for example, robot installations, flexible manufacturing systems, and automated record-keeping or inventory systems.

A *third-order* control system (Figure 11-4) can change its goals without specific preprogramming. It can reflect on system performance and decide to act in ways that are not contained in its instructions. Third-order systems have reflective conscious-ness and, thus, must contain humans. Note that a second-order controller can be programmed to recognize patterns, and to react to patterns in specific ways. Such sys-tems are said to "learn." Third-order systems can learn without explicit preprogram-ming, and therefore can alter their actions on the basis of thought or whim. An ad-vantage of third-order controllers is that they can deal with the unforeseen and unexpected. A disadvantage is that, because they contain human elements, they may lack predictability and reliability. Third-order systems are of great interest to the PM, for reasons we now discuss.

Information Requirements for Cybernetic Controllers   In order to establish total control over a system, the controller must be able to take a counteraction for every action the system can take. This statement is a rough paraphrase of Ashby's Law of Requisite Variety (Schoderbek, Schoderbek, and Kefalas, 1989). This implies that the PM/controller is aware of the system's full capabilities. For complex systems, particularly those containing a human element, this is simply not possible. Thus, we

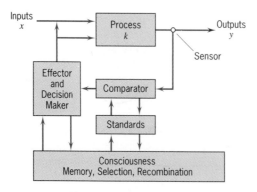

Figure 11-4 A third-order feedback system—reflective goal changer.

need a strategy to aid the PM in developing a control system. One such strategy is to use a cost/benefit approach to control—to control those aspects of the system for which the expected benefits of control are greater than the expected costs. We are reminded of a firm that manufactured saw blades. It set up a project to reduce scrap losses for the high-cost steel from which the blades were made. At the end of the one-year project, the firm had completed the project—cost $9,700, savings $4,240. (Of course, if the savings were to be repeated for several years, the rate of return on the project would be acceptable. The president of the firm, however, thought that the savings would decline and disappear when the project ended.)

Relatively few elements of a project (as opposed to the elements of a system that operates more or less continuously) are subject to automatic control. An examination of the WBS or the details of an action plan will reveal which of the project's tasks are largely mechanistic and represent continuous types of systems. If such systems exist, and if they operate across a sufficient time period to justify the initial expense of creating an automatic control, then a cybernetic controller is useful.

Given the decisions about what to control, the information requirements of a cybernetic controller are easy to describe, if not to meet. First, the PM must define precisely what characteristics of an output (interim output or final output) are to be controlled. Second, standards must be set for each characteristic. Third, sensors must be acquired that will measure those characteristics at the desired level of precision. Fourth, these measurements must be transformed into a signal that can be compared to a "standard" signal. Fifth, the difference between the two is sent to the decision maker, which detects it, if it is sufficiently large, and sixth, transmits a signal to the effector that causes the operating system to react in a way that will counteract the deviation from standard. If the control system is designed to allow the effector to take one or more of several actions, an additional piece of information is needed. There must be built-in criteria that instruct the effector on which action(s) to take.

Knowledge of cybernetic control is important because all control systems are merely variants, extensions, or nonautomatic modifications of such controls. Because most projects have relatively few mechanistic elements that can be subjected to classic cybernetic controls, this concept of control is best applied to tracking the system and automatically notifying the PM when things threaten to get out of control.

Go/No-go Controls

Go/no-go controls take the form of testing to see if some specific precondition has been met. Most of the control in project management falls into this category. This type of control can be used on almost every aspect of a project. For many facets of performance, it is sufficient to know that the predetermined specifications for project output have been met. The same is often true of the cost and time elements of the project plan.

It is, of course, necessary to exercise judgment in the use of go/no-go controls. Certain characteristics of output may be required to fall within precisely determined limits if the output is to be accepted by the client. Other characteristics may be less precisely defined. In regard to time and cost, there may be penalties associated with nonconformance with the approved plans. Penalty clauses that make late delivery costly for the producer are often included in the project contract. At times, early delivery can also carry a penalty (e.g., when a just-in-time supply system is involved). Cost overruns may be shared with the client or borne by the project. Some contracts arrange for the first $X of cost overrun to be shared by client and producer, with any further overrun being the producer's responsibility. The number and type of go/no-go controls on a project are limited only by the imagination and desire of the contracting parties.

The project plan, budget, and schedule are all control documents, so the PM has a predesigned control system complete with prespecified milestones as control checkpoints. Control can be exercised at any level of detail that is supported by detail in the plans, budgets, and schedules. The parts of a new jet engine, for instance, are individually checked for quality conformance. These are go/no-go controls. The part passes or it does not, and every part must pass its own go/no-go test before being used in an engine. Similarly, computer programs are tested for bugs. The program passes its tests or it does not.

Go/no-go controls operate only when and if the controller uses them. In many cases, go/no-go controls function periodically, at regular, preset intervals. The intervals are usually determined by clock, calendar, or the operating cycles of some machine system. Such periodicity makes it easy to administer a control system, but it often allows errors to be compounded before they are detected. Things begin to go awry just after a quarterly progress check, for instance, and by the time the next quarterly check is made, some items may be seriously out of control.

Project milestones do not occur at neat, periodic intervals; thus, *controls should be linked to the actual plans and to the occurrence of real events, not simply to the calendar.* Senior management should review all projects at reasonably frequent intervals. We will discuss such reports shortly, but the PM cannot control the project properly with a strictly periodic reporting system.

The PM must keep abreast of all aspects of the project, directly or through deputies. Competent functional managers understand the importance of *follow-up,* and the project manager's work provides no exception. Control is best exerted while there is still time for corrective action. To this end, the PM should establish an *early warning system* so that potential problems can be exposed and dealt with before they turn into full-fledged disasters. One way to construct such an early warning system is to set up a project forecast data sheet. On this sheet, outputs or progress are forecast by period. Actual output or progress is then checked against the forecast, period by period.

For an early warning system to work, it must be clear that the messenger who brings bad news will not be shot, and that anyone caught sweeping problems and mistakes under the rug will be. As we have said before, the most important rule for any subordinate is the Prime Law of Life on a project: Never let the boss be surprised!

Controls have a tendency to terrorize the insecure and to induce high anxiety in everyone else. The result is avoidance, and avoidance is exactly what the PM cannot tolerate. Unless deviation from plan is discovered, it cannot be corrected. Therefore, a spirit of trust between superior and subordinate at all levels of the project is a prime requisite for the effective application of control.

One form of go/no-go control that has gained popularity (Cooper, 1988) is that of phase-gated processes (also mentioned in Chapter 5). Rather than waiting until the project is completed, and then finding out that it doesn't achieve the objectives of the organization, the phase-gate process controls the project at various points throughout its life cycle to make sure it remains on course and of value to the organization. This process is most commonly used for new product/service development projects where it is important to constantly evaluate the match between the changing, dynamic market and the changing nature of the new product/service under development. At the launch of the new development project, a series of "gates" are planned, whereby the project cannot continue with funding until each gate has been successfully passed. The initial gates tend to be conceptual- and performance based while the latter are more market oriented, such as whether we should commit to producing this prototype for the mass market.

The criteria for passing each gate are developed in the project planning stage. There is a wide range of reasons for terminating a project midstream; for example, most of the benefits have already been achieved and further expenditures aren't warrented, or the market potential of the project has changed substantially. Other possible reasons easily come to mind: critical personnel have left the organization, the project costs have gotten out of hand, a competitor has already come out with a better product at a cheaper price, and so on.

Information Requirements for Go/No-Go Controls   Most of the input information needed to operate go/no-go project control has already been referenced directly or implied by the previous discussion. The project proposal, plans, specifications, schedules, and budgets (complete with approved change orders) contain all the information needed to apply go/no-go controls to the project. Milestones are the key events that serve as a focus for ongoing control activity. These milestones are the project's deliverables in the form of in-process output or final output. If the milestones occur on time, on budget, and at the planned level of quality, the PM can take comfort from the fact that things are proceeding properly. Perhaps just as important to the PM, senior management can be equally comfortable with the project—and with the project manager as well.

Except for a few important projects, senior managers usually cannot keep up with the day-to-day or week-to-week progress of work; nor should they try. Senior management does, however, need a monthly or quarterly status review for all projects. The project status report contains a list of the important milestones for each project together with the status of each. If many of the projects are similar—such as construction projects or marketing projects, for example—the milestones will be of similar type, and one table can show the status of several projects in spite of the fact that each milestone may not be applicable to each and every project. The Elanco Animal Health Company, a division of Eli Lilly and Company, uses such a report. A generalized version of Elanco's Project Status Report is shown in Figure 11-5. The Gantt chart (see Chapter 8) is also a convenient way to present senior managers with information on project status.

Either of these report forms can be altered to contain almost any additional information that might be requested. For example, the Gantt chart can be annotated with footnotes indicating such matters of interest as the resources required to get a late

Task	Project #1	Project #2	Project #3
Priorities set	C	C	C
PM selected	C	C	C
Key members briefed on RFP	C	C	C
Proposal sent	C	C	C
Proposal accepted as negotiated	C	C	C
Preliminary design developed	C	W/10	C
Design accepted	C	W/12	C
Software developed	C	NS/NR	N/A
Product test design	C	W/30	W/15
Manufacturing scheduled	C	NS/HR	W/8
Tools, jigs, fixtures designed	W/1	NS/HR	W/2
Tools, jigs, fixtures delivered	W/2	NS/HR	W/8
Production complete	NS/HR	NS/HR	NS/HR
Product test complete	NS/HR	NS/HR	NS/HR
Marketing sign-off on product	NS/HR	NS/HR	NS/HR

Notes:

N/A—Not applicable
C—Completed
W—Work in progress (number refers to month required)
NS—Not started
NR—Need resources
HR—Have resources

Figure 11-5   Sample project status report.

milestone back on schedule, or a statement of how an activity must be changed if it is to be approved by a regulatory agency. The information requirements for such extensions of standard reports must be set on an ad hoc basis. For the most part, such information will be readily available within the project, but occasionally, external sources must be utilized. If the PM ensures that the status reports given to senior management contain information that is current enough to be actionable (and always as accurate as required for control), little else can be done to furnish the decision makers with the proper data for them to exercise control. Some firms are now putting such control information on the Internet to make it instantly available to all parties on a worldwide basis. Some guidelines for this approach are given in Seesing (1996).

The PM is well advised to insist that status reports make clear the implications of specific conditions where those implications might be overlooked—or not understood—by senior managers. If meetings between senior management and project managers are used to report project status and progress, it is critical to remember that the process employed in such meetings should not be punitive or intimidating. As we pointed out in Chapter 10, punitive meetings do far more damage than good.

Postcontrol

Postcontrols (also known as postperformance controls or reviews, or postproject controls or reviews) are applied after the fact. One might draw parallels between postcontrol and "locking the barn after the horse has been stolen," but postcontrol is not a vain attempt to alter what has already occurred. Instead, it is a full recognition of George Santayana's observation that "Those who cannot remember the past are condemned to repeat it." Cybernetic and go/no-go controls are directed toward accomplishing the goals of an ongoing project. Postcontrol is directed toward improving the chances for future projects to meet their goals.

Postcontrol is applied through a relatively formal document that is usually constructed with four distinct sections.

The Project Objectives   The postcontrol report will contain a description of the objectives of the project. Usually, this description is taken from the project proposal, and the entire proposal often appears as an appendix to the postcontrol report. As reported here, project objectives include the effects of all change orders issued and approved during the project.

Because actual project performance depends in part on uncontrollable events (strikes, weather, failure of trusted suppliers, sudden loss of key employees, and other acts of God), the key initial assumptions made during preparation of the project budget and schedule should be noted in this section. A certain amount of care must be taken in reporting these assumptions. They should not be written with a tone that makes them appear to be excuses for poor performance. While it is clearly the prerogative, if not the duty, of every PM to protect himself politically, he or she should do so in moderation to be effective.

Milestones, Checkpoints, and Budgets   This section of the postcontrol document starts with a full report of project performance against the planned schedule and budget. This can be prepared by combining and editing the various project status reports made during the project's life. Significant deviations of actual schedule and budget from planned schedule and budget should be highlighted. Explanations of why these deviations occurred will be offered in the next section of the postcontrol report. Each deviation can be identified with a letter or number to index it to the explanations. Where the same explanation is associated with both a schedule and budget deviation, as will often be the case, the same identifier can be used.

The Final Report on Project Results   When significant variations of actual from planned project performance are indicated, no distinction is made between favorable and unfavorable variations. Like the tongue that invariably goes to the sore tooth, project managers focus their attention on trouble. While this is quite natural, it leads to complete documentation on why some things went wrong and little or no documentation on why some things went particularly well. Both sides, the good and the bad, should be chronicled here.

Not only do most projects result in outputs that are more or less acceptable, most projects operate with a process that is more or less acceptable. The concern here is not on what the project did but rather on how it did it. Basically descriptive, this part of the final report should cover project organization, an explanation of the methods used to plan and direct the project, and a review of the communication networks, monitoring systems, and control methods, as well as a discussion of intraproject interactions between the various working groups.

Recommendations for Performance and Process Improvement   The culmination of the postcontrol report is a set of recommendations covering the ways that future projects can be improved. Many of the explanations appearing in the previous section are related to one-time happenings—sickness, weather, strikes, or the appearance of a new technology—that of themselves are not apt to affect future projects, although other, different one-time events may affect them. But some of the deviations from plan were caused by happenings that are very likely to recur. Examples of recurring problems might be a chronically late supplier, a generally noncooperative functional department, a habitually optimistic cost estimator, or a highly negative project team member. Provision for such things can be factored into future project plans, thereby adding to predictability and control.

Just as important, the process of organizing and conducting projects can be improved by recommending the continuation of managerial methods and organizational systems that appear to be effective, together with the alteration of practices and procedures that do not. In this way, the conduct of projects will become smoother, just as the likelihood of achieving good results, on time and on cost, is increased.

Postcontrol can have a considerable impact on the way projects are run. A large, market-driven company in consumer household products developed new products through projects that were organized in matrix form, but had a functional tie to the marketing division. PMs were almost always chosen from the marketing area. Members of the project team who represented R & D had argued that they should be given a leadership role, particularly early in the project's life. Marketing resisted this suggestion on the grounds that R & D people were not market oriented, did not know what would sell, and were mainly interested in pursuing their own "academic" interests. After reading the perennial R & D request in a postcontrol report, the program manager of one product line decided to reorganize a project as requested by R & D. The result was not merely a successful project, but was the first in a series of related projects based on extensions of ideas generated by an R & D group not restricted to work on the specific product sought by marketing. Following this successful experiment, project organization was modified to include more input from R & D at an earlier stage of the project.

There is no need to repeat the information requirements for postcontrol here. It should be noted, however, that we have not discussed the postcontrol audit, a full review and audit of all aspects of the project. This is covered in Chapter 12.

11.3 COMMENTS ON THE DESIGN OF CONTROL SYSTEMS

Irrespective of the type of control used, there are some important questions to be answered when designing any control system: Who sets the standards? How realistic are the standards? How clear are they? Will they achieve the project's goals? What output, activities, behaviors should be monitored? Should we monitor people? What kinds of sensors should be used? Where should they be placed? How timely must the monitoring be? How rapidly must it be reported? How accurate must the sensors be? How great must a difference between standard and actual be before it becomes actionable? What corrective actions are available? Are they ethical? What are the most appropriate actions for each situation? What rewards and penalties can be used? Who should take what action?

If the control system is to be acceptable to those who will use it and those who will be controlled by it, the system must be designed so that it appears to be sensible.

Standards must be achievable by the mechanical systems used. Control limits must be appropriate to the needs of the client—that is, not merely set to show "how good we are." Like punishment, rewards and penalties should "fit the crime."

In addition to being sensible, a good control system should also possess some other characteristics.

- The system should be flexible. Where possible, it should be able to react to and report unforeseen changes in system performance.
- The system should be cost effective. The cost of control should never exceed the value of control. As we noted above, control is not always less expensive than scrap. One study (Heywood and Allen, 1996) has found that the cost of control in projects ranges from as much as 5 percent of total project costs for small projects to less than one percent for very large projects.
- The control system must be truly useful. It must satisfy the real needs of the project, not the whims of the PM.
- The system must operate in an ethical manner.
- The system must operate in a timely manner. Problems must be reported while there is still time to do something about them, and before they become large enough to destroy the project.
- Sensors and monitors should be sufficiently accurate and precise to control the project within limits that are truly functional for the client and the parent organization.
- The system should be as simple as possible to operate.
- The control system should be easy to maintain. Further, the control system should signal the overall controller if it goes out of order.
- The system should be capable of being extended or otherwise altered.
- Control systems should be fully documented when installed, and the documentation should include a complete training program in system operation.

No matter how designed, all control systems we have described use feedback as a control process. Let us now consider some more specific aspects of control. To a large extent, the PM is trying to anticipate problems or catch them just as they begin to occur. The PM wants to keep the project out of trouble because upper management often bases an incremental funding decision on a review of the project. This review typically follows some particular milestone and, if acceptable, leads to a follow-on authorization to proceed to the next review point. If all is not going well, other technological alternatives may be recommended; or if things are going badly, the project may be terminated. Thus, the PM must monitor and control the project quite closely.

The control of performance, cost, and time usually requires different input data. To control performance, the PM may need such specific documentation as engineering change notices, test results, quality checks, rework tickets, scrap rates, and maintenance activities. Of particular importance here is carefully controlling any changes, usually increases, in performance due to "scope creep," the natural inclination of the customer to change the deliverables as they obtain better information about their needs over time. Scope creep is not always the fault of the customer, however; sometimes the team members themselves, in an effort to do their best work, unwittingly increase the scope of the project. The PM must be constantly on guard to identify such changes. We will have more to say about this shortly.

For cost control, the manager compares budgets to actual cash flows, purchase orders, labor hour charges, amount of overtime worked, absenteeism, accounting variance reports, accounting projections, income reports, cost exception reports, and the like. To control the schedule, the PM examines benchmark reports, periodic activity and status reports, exception reports, PERT/CPM networks, Gantt charts, the master project schedule, earned value graphs, and probably reviews the WBS and action plans.

Auditing will be discussed in Chapter 12, but it needs a brief mention here. It is basically an investigation and count to identify and locate all elements of a project. The PM may find a particular activity perplexing or not understand why it is taking longer than it should or costing more than expected. An audit would provide the data to explain the unusual nature of the discrepancy. The PM may choose to do the audit or have the organization's accountant perform the work.

A large variety of new tools have recently become available for the control of projects such as benchmarking (discussed briefly in Chapter 8 and again later in this chapter in more detail), quality function deployment, stage-gate processing, self-directed teams, the design-build approach, and so on. Thamhein (1996) describes these tools and offers suggestions for selecting and implementing them according to individual circumstances of the project.

Some of the most important analytic tools available for the project manager to use in controlling the project are variance analysis and trend projection, both of which have been discussed earlier in this book. The essence of these tools is shown in Figure 11-6. A budget, plan, or expected growth curve of time or cost for some task is plotted. Then actual values are plotted as a dashed line as the work is actually finished. At each point in time a new projection from the actual data is used to forecast what will occur in the future if the PM does not intervene. Based on this projection, the manager can decide if there is a problem, what action alternatives exist, what they will cost and require, and what they will achieve. Based on this analysis, the PM will decide what to do. Trend projection charts can even be used for combined performance/cost/time charts, as illustrated in Figure 11-7. Earned value analysis was also described earlier.

Critical Ratio Control Charts

On occasion it may be worthwhile, particularly on large projects, for the PM to calculate a set of critical ratios for all project activities. The critical ratio is

(actual progress/scheduled progress) X (budgeted cost/actual cost)

The critical ratio is made up of two parts—the ratio of actual progress to scheduled progress, and the ratio of budgeted cost to actual cost. (In the language of earned value, the budgeted cost is the BCWP and the actual cost is the ACWP. Hence, the

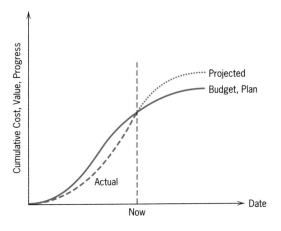

Figure 11-6   Trend projection.

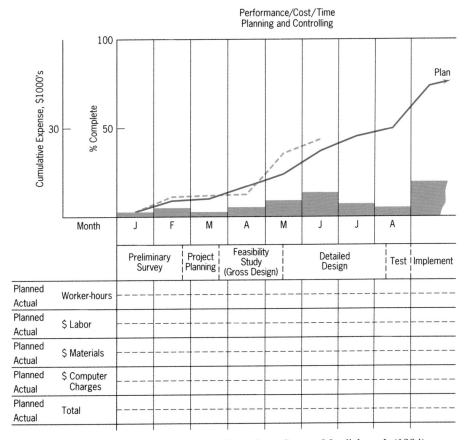

Figure 11-7   Integrated performance cost/time chart. *Source*: Murdick et al. (1984).

Table 11.1.   (Actual Progress/Scheduled Progress) × (Budgeted Cost/Actual Cost)

Task Number	Actual Progress		Scheduled Progress		Budgeted Cost		Actual Cost		Critical Ratio
1	(2	/	3)	×	(6	/	4)	=	1.00
2	(2	/	3)	×	(6	/	6)	=	0.67
3	(3	/	3)	×	(4	/	6)	=	0.67
4	(3	/	2)	×	(6	/	6)	=	1.50
5	(3	/	3)	×	(6	/	4)	=	1.50

cost term of the critical ratio is the CPI. And if the schedule term were expressed in monetary units, it would be the SPI, making the critical ratio simply the CSI.) *Cæteris paribus,* to quote any economist who ever lived,* a ratio of actual to scheduled progress greater than one is "good." If the ratio is less than one, it is "bad." Similarly with the ratio of budgeted to actual cost—never forgetting *cæteris paribus.* Assuming moderately accurate measures for each element of each ratio (an assumption that rivals *cæteris paribus* for its *chutzpa*), the critical ratio is a good measure of the general health of the project. Note that the critical ratio is the product of the two separate ratios. This way of combining the two underlying ratios weights them equally, allowing a "bad" ratio for one part to be offset by an equally "good" ratio in the other. The PM may or may not agree that this results in a valid measure of project "health."

Consider Table 11-1. We can see that the first task is behind schedule but also below budget. If lateness is no problem for this activity, the PM need take no action. The second task is on budget but its physical progress is lagging. Even if there is slack in the activity, the budget will probably be overrun. The third task is on schedule, but cost is running higher than budget, creating another probable cost overrun. The fourth task is on budget but ahead of schedule. A cost saving may result. Finally, the fifth task is on schedule and is running under budget, another probable cost saving.

Tasks 4 and 5 have critical ratios greater than 1 and might not concern some PMs, but the thoughtful manager wants to know why they are doing so well (and the PM may also want to check the information system to validate the unexpectedly favorable findings). The second and third activities need attention, and the first task may need attention also. The PM may set some critical-ratio control limits intuitively. The PM may also wish to set different control limits on different activities, controlling progress in the critical path more closely than on paths with high slack.

Charts can be used to monitor and control the project through the use of these ratios. Figure 11-8 shows an example. Note that the PM will ignore critical ratios in some ranges, and that the ranges are not necessarily symmetric around 1.0. Different types of tasks may have different control limits. Control charts can also be used to aid in controlling costs (Figure 11-9), work force levels, and other project parameters.

---

*For those who have never been blessed with a course in economics, this Latin phrase means "other things being equal." The phrase is the economist's equivalent of the physicist's frictionless plane. It does not and cannot exist in fact.

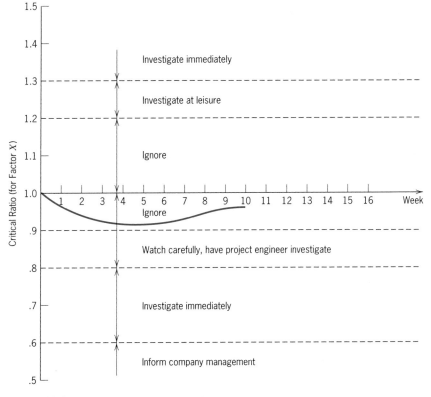

Figure 11-8　Critical ratio control limits.

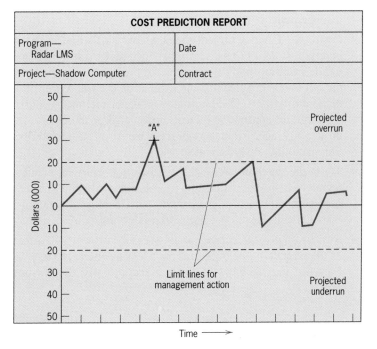

Figure 11-9　Cost control chart. *Source:* Hajek (1977).

Benchmarking

Another recent addition to the arsenal of project control tools is *benchmarking,* or making comparisons to "best in class" practices across organizations. This concept is explained and demonstrated in many recent publications (see, e.g., Byrne, 1999; Gupta and Graham, 1997; Ibbs and Kwak, 1998; Thamhaim, 1996; Toney, 1997). One case study (Gupta and Graham, 1997) points out the importance of including the customer's perceptions in the benchmarking study or else the data may be accurate but not give the firm any insight into why customers don't recognize their top-level quality. A recent benchmarking study (Ibbs and Kwak, 1998) to generate input for the Project Management Maturity Model measured project processes, tools, techniques, and practices across a range of industries, the six life-cycle phases, and the eight knowledge areas of the PMBOK. Graphs were then generated to show the distribution of scores in these industries across the various factors.

Another recent study (Toney, 1997) benchmarked Fortune 500 firms in terms of best practices and key success factors for projects being conducted in functional organizations. The conclusions of the study were reported in four major areas, as described next. These areas are typically the responsibility of the Project Management Office.

- *Promoting the benefits of project management* Have the project manager report to a senior executive with multifunctional authority. Identify and nurture senior officers who champion project management. Conduct training in project management. Participate in project management benchmarking forums. Partner with educational and professional project management organizations. Use a variety of sources to communicate the benefits of project management to senior management.

- *Personnel* Pay for project management skills and high-risk projects through bonuses, stock options, and other incentives. Employ team-based pay. Create job descriptions and career paths for project managers. Develop a checklist for project manager selection and evaluation criteria. Offer project manager development programs. Design project manager retention programs. Offer advanced training and continuing education for project managers. Design a broadbased project manager evaluation process based on project skills, customer satisfaction, negotiation skills, and so on.

- *Methodology* Standardize the organization's project management methods. Integrate the project management processes. Develop project management into a core competence of the organization. Develop a standard process for change management. Develop a standard process for conflict management.

- *Results of project management* Measure project performance and the impact of the project on the organization. Measure the value received from the project. Measure the riskiness of the project. Identify the lessons learned from the project.

Project Management in Practice
Schedule and Cost Control for Australia's New Parliament House

Over seven years in the making, Australia's new Parliament House at Canberra is actually a suite of buildings costing about $982 million! Meant to be an enduring symbol of the values and expectations of Australia and a source of pride for its citizens, the complex will consist of 5000 rooms, 40,000 items of furniture, 50,000 square meters of stonework, 7350 doors, and 170,000 square meters of drywall. To excavate the site, over one million cubic meters of rock was moved, and 170,000 cubic meters of concrete was poured to form the foundation. At its busiest

point, the complex was costing $1.2 million per working day.

Given the immensity of the project, the information systems to control its design, construction, and furnishing were equally extensive. Procedures were devised for planning, cost control, tendering, contract commencement, drawing and samples, purchasing, stores control, contracts administration, accounts, general administration, and accident prevention. In the area of contracts alone, 540 separate contracts were awarded. And 20,000 drawings were prepared, with 750,000

Project Control Process

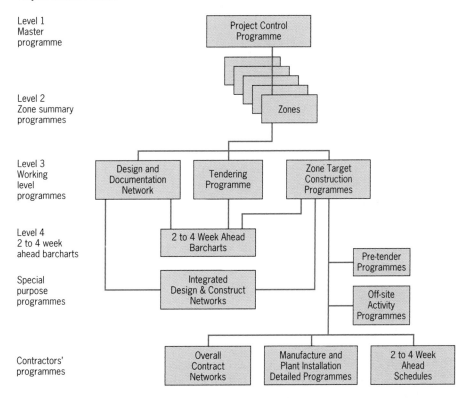

The old parliament house (foreground) and the complex of buildings that comprise the new parliament house (background) in Canberra, Australia.

prints issued. Thus, computerized systems were developed for the data associated with contracts and bids, drawings, information requests, site instructions, change proposals, shop drawings, asset registers, time reporting, cost reporting, budgetary control, contracts payments, consultants' fees, and reimbursables.

Time control is based on monitoring at four levels of detail giving progressively more programming detail on aspects of the project. Special purpose programs are included for specific problems or requirements. In addition to exception reports, progress review and coordination meetings help management focus attention on the areas of concern. The overall control system is illustrated in the previous figure.

Cost control is based on the philosophy that 80 percent of the cost is designed in and only 20 percent is due to construction variations. Thus, attention was focused on three points during the design process: early on, to identify allocations and deviations; halfway through to check costs again; and at the completion. Still, ongoing cost control is necessary and performance against budget is measured monthly. Forecasts are also revised every six months to check for any problems ahead.

With such attention to control, the citizens of Australia are looking forward to the completion of their new "house."

Source: T. R. Nixon, "Project Management at the New Parliament House, Canberra," *Project Management Journal,* September 1987.

11.4 CONTROL AS A FUNCTION OF MANAGEMENT

With a few rare exceptions, control of projects is always exercised through people. Senior managers in the organization are governed by the CEO who is directed by such groups as the executive committee and/or board of directors/trustees. Senior managers, in turn, try to exercise governance of project managers, and project managers try to exert control over the project team and others representing functions that are involved with the project. The purpose is always the same—to bring the actual schedule, budget, and deliverables of the project into reasonably close congruence with the planned schedule, budget, and deliverables. In this and the following sections of this chapter, we discuss the design and use of control systems with some emphasis on the ways in which people respond to various types of control. A number of the points we cover in these sections are discussed at greater length in William Newman's (1975) excellent classic, *Constructive Control*. Its insights are as fresh today as they were when the book was written.

Finally, it should be noted that much of the literature on total quality management (TQM), ISO 9000 standards, employee involvement (EI), and the functioning of teams is devoted to techniques for developing creativity and synergistic problem solving through effective teamwork. What is almost never discussed is the implicit assumption that teams have a sense of direction, and are attempting to achieve some specified objectives. All of this implies control. Even the most chaotic brainstorming session is aimed at the solution of specific problems. Control is a necessary and inherent part of life in any organization. It is not helpful to think of control as coercive, though, at times, it may be. We prefer to think of control as the maintenance of ethical goal-directed behavior.

The PM is always subject to such eternal verities as the law of gravity, the laws of thermodynamics, and the brute fact that the exercise of managerial control will result in distorting the behavior of subordinates. The job of the PM/controller is to set controls that will encourage those behaviors/results that are deemed desirable and discourage those that are not. The unspoken assumption here is that control systems motivate individuals to behave in certain ways. While this may seem obvious, it is not the bland assertion it appears to be. The entire subject of motivation is a complex and rich field for research, and there are several theories about the nature of motivation. Each has its supporters and critics. We adopt no particular theory here; we do, however, argue that the control mechanisms described in this chapter provide a context within which motivation takes place. Thus, while control does not provide a good explanation for the presence or absence of motivation, control does indicate the direction toward which the motivated person will move (Livingston and Ronen, 1975).

Though control does not ensure motivated behavior, individual reactions to the various types of control systems do affect levels of motivation. By and large, people respond to the goal-directedness of control systems in one of three general ways: (1) by active and positive participation and goal seeking; (2) by passive participation in order to avoid loss; and (3) by active but negative participation and resistance—usually not active resistance to the goal, but failure to undertake those activities that will result in goal achievement. Which of the three resemble a given individual's reaction to control depends on several variables, including such things as the specific control mechanism used, the nature of the goal being sought, the individual's self-image, assessment of the value of the goal, expectation of being able to achieve the goal, and basic tolerance for being controlled.

While human response to specific types of control is typified by its variety, some generalizations are possible.

Cybernetic Controls   Human response to steering controls tends to be positive. Steering controls are usually viewed as helpful rather than as a source of unwelcome pressure if the controllees perceive themselves as able to perform inside the prescribed limits. Contrary to the popular song, it is not the "impossible dream" that motivates goal-seeking behavior, but rather a moderately good chance of success.

Of course, response to steering control is dependent on the individual's acceptance of the goal as appropriate. Indeed, no control system is acceptable if the objective of control is not acceptable. Further, the source of control must be seen as legitimate for the control mechanism to be accepted.

While it appears to be true that humans respond positively to steering controls, they may not be so positive about the monitoring systems that drive the control mechanisms. Grant, Higgins, and Irving (1988) have shown that computerized performance monitoring and control systems are viewed as mixed blessings and have both functional and dysfunctional effects. These monitoring systems, though not used for true cybernetic controls, are fairly common in software projects.

Go/No-go Controls   Response to go/no-go controls tends to be neutral or negative. The reason appears to be related to the inherent nature of this type of control system. With go/no-go control systems, "barely good enough" results are just as acceptable as "perfect" results. The control system itself makes it difficult for the worker to take pride in high-quality work because the system does not recognize gradations of quality. In addition, it is all too common to be rather casual about setting the control limits for a go/no-go control; the limits should be very carefully set. The fact that this kind of control emphasizes "good enough" performance is no excuse for the nonchalant application of careless standards.

While go/no-go control is the most frequent type of control exercised on projects, the impact of such control on the project team seems, to us, to be less negative than Newman (1975, pp. 41–42) suggests. Perhaps this is because *project team performance* is the primary focus of control rather than specific items of work performed by individuals. The quality of the project taken as a whole serves as the source of satisfaction to the group, not the quality of bits and pieces. It also appears clear that the quality of the project also serves as a source of satisfaction with the process of doing projects. The entire subject of human response to control in a project environment is a prime area for additional research.

Postcontrols   Postcontrols are seen as much the same as a report card. They may serve as a basis for reward or punishment, but they are received too late to change current performance. Whether reaction to postcontrol is positive, neutral, or negative seems to depend on the "grade" received. In cases where a series of similar projects must be undertaken, postcontrols are regarded as helpful in planning for future work, but considerable care must be devoted to ensuring that controls are consistent with changing environmental conditions. To be effective, management must provide an incentive for project managers to study postcontrol reports, and to determine corrective procedures for problems exposed by the reports, as well as procedures that will replicate the techniques and systems that appear particularly helpful.

Because postcontrols are placed on the process of conducting a project, as well as on the usual time, cost, and performance standards, they may be applied to such areas as interproject communications, cooperation between the groups working on related task elements, the quality of project management, and the nature of interaction with the client. Application of control to such matters presents severe measurement problems. Often it is difficult to detect gross differences in the quality of intergroup communications, for example, or to relate these differences, if detected, to aspects of the project that can be controlled. To say that these matters are difficult to measure and control is not, of course, to obviate the need for control. The soft side of project performance is no less important in the longer run than the easier-to-measure hard side.

11.5 BALANCE IN A CONTROL SYSTEM

When developing a control system, it is important that the system be *well balanced*. Unfortunately, the concept of balance is fuzzy—difficult to explain, difficult to achieve, and difficult to recognize. Though precise definition is impossible, we can describe some general features of a balanced control system, and also indicate some of the things a controller can do to achieve good balance in a system.

- A balanced control system is built with cognizance of the fact that investment in control is subject to sharply diminishing returns. Costs increase exponentially as the degree of control increases linearly and the optimal level of control varies with project size (Heywood and Allen, 1996).

- A balanced control system recognizes that as control increases past some point, innovative activity is more and more damped, and then finally shut off completely.

- A balanced control system is directed toward the correction of error rather than toward punishment. This requires a clear understanding of the fact that the past cannot be changed, no matter how loudly the manager yells.

- A balanced system exerts control only to the degree required to achieve its objectives. It rarely pays to spend dollars to find lost pennies, nor is it sensible to machine a part to the ten-thousandth if the client's requirements are to the tenth.

- A balanced system utilizes the lowest degree of hassle consistent with accomplishing its goals. The controller should avoid annoying those people whose cooperation is required to reach system objectives.

> My sister passed away, and her funeral was scheduled for Monday. When I told my boss, he said she died so that I would have to miss work on the busiest day of the year. He then asked if we could change her burial to Friday. He said, "That would be better for me."

To sum up, a balanced control system is cost effective, well geared for the end results sought, and not overdone. The causes of imbalance are legion. For example, the application of across-the-board controls is usually not a good idea. Treating everyone alike appeals to a naive sense of equity, but better results are usually achieved by treating everyone individually.

Across-the-board freezes on expenditures or on hiring tend to reward those who have already overspent or overhired and to penalize the frugal and efficient. The side-effects of this are often quite odd. Some years ago, Procter & Gamble put a freeze on hiring into effect for an engineering development laboratory. Project managers who were shorthanded hired temporary labor, including highly skilled technicians from Manpower and similar firms. P & G's accounting system allowed temporary labor to be charged to material accounts rather than to the salary account. The lesson to be learned is that results-oriented, creative project managers tend to see across-the-board controls as a challenge and a barrier to be circumvented.

Other common causes of imbalance are these:

1. Placing too much weight on easy-to-measure factors and too little weight on difficult-to-measure, soft factors (the so-called intangibles).

2. Emphasizing short-run results at the expense of longer-run objectives—possibly one of the most serious problems facing industry today.

3. Ignoring the changes in the structure of organizational goals that result from the passage of time or changes in the firm's circumstances. For example, high quality and strict adherence to delivery schedules might be extremely important to a new firm. Later, perhaps, expense control might be more important.

4. Overcontrol by an aggressive executive often causes trouble. In an attempt to create a reputation for on-time delivery, one overly zealous PM put so much pressure on the project team that on-time shipments took precedence over proper test procedures. The result was serious malfunctions of the product and its subsequent recall.

5. Monitoring and controlling items may lead some people to ignore anything that is not measured. "If it isn't counted, it doesn't count," is the attitude. This factor was responsible for the failure of many attempts at Management-by-Objectives.

Achieving balance in a control system is rather easy to discuss but quite difficult to accomplish. Several principles must be simultaneously upheld. Perhaps most important is the need to tie controls directly to project objectives. Occasionally, firms establish tortuous, indirect linkages between control and objective, apparently on the theory that people should not be aware of or understand the controls under which they must operate. It is as if the firm were trying to trap employees unethically. Such control systems rarely work because they rest on two fallacious assumptions: (1) that people are generally perverse and will avoid trying to accomplish a known objective, and (2) that people are too stupid to see through the misdirection.

In addition to linking controls to objectives, controls should be closely and directly related to specific performance outcomes. Start by defining the desired results as precisely as possible. System actions that can cause deviation from the desired results are then examined and controls are designed for these actions, beginning with those that can be the source of serious deviation, particularly those that cause trouble with high frequency or without advance notice, such as scope creep.

The PM should also examine all controls in terms of the probable reactions of individuals to the proposed controls. One asks, "How will the various members of the project team react to this control?" If negative reaction is likely, the control should be redesigned.

The problem of developing a good balance between long-run and short-run control objectives is delicate, not because the blending is inherently difficult, but because the PM is often preoccupied with urgent short-run problems rather than longer-run problems that can always be "temporarily" set aside no matter how important the results may be at some later date. Even the timing and sequences of monitoring and controlling can affect the likelihood of time and cost overruns (Partovi and Burton, 1993).

A good rule for the controller is to place the control as close as possible to the work being controlled and to design the simplest possible mechanism to achieve control. Giving the worker direct control over quality has had impressive results in Japanese production processes as well as at the Lincoln Electric Company in the United States. Similar results were achieved by a major producer of housing units. Carpenters, masons, electricians, and other workers were given considerable discretion over specific production methods. Projects on which this approach was employed showed significantly improved quality when compared to projects built by standard methods.

The most important step in constructing a balanced control system must be taken far in advance of the time when control systems are usually designed. Every step of project planning must be undertaken with the understanding that *whatever work is planned will also have to be controlled.* As we have emphasized, planning and control are opposite sides of the same coin. No amount of planning can solve the current crisis, but planning combined with the design and installation of appropriate control mechanisms can go a long way toward crisis prevention.

An excellent example of integrating the planning and control functions is provided by Mead Data Central, a producer of large-scale database systems and a subsidiary of Mead Corporation. In its *Project Management Development Guide,* Mead describes six stages of the project life cycle as seen from its point of view. For each stage, the purpose is carefully explained and the deliverables for that stage are listed. For example, the list of deliverables for the feasibility stage contains these items: project description, project number, preliminary business case, project requirements document, and so forth. For each deliverable, the individual(s) and/or groups responsible are noted. This was among the earliest examples of what later came to be known as a "phase-gate" system.

An extensive glossary of terms is included in the document so that inexperienced project workers can understand what is meant by such diverse terms as "escalation document," "functional audit," "milestone," "not-to-do list," "project cost tracking," and "release readiness statement." In addition, the *Development Guide* summarizes the tasks that must be performed by each of the functional areas or individuals during each stage of the life cycle. The work of the Idea Champion, the Market Managers, the Business Management Process Director, the Project Review Committee, and so on is well defined. The result is an effective integration of planning and control that is available to anyone working on the organization's projects.

A senior executive at a large industrial firm that carries out many projects each year sees control in a slightly different light. Noting that differences between plan and reality usually represent problems for project managers, he remarked: "If you are solving problems faster than they are arriving to be solved, you have the project under control. If not, you haven't."

11.6   CONTROL OF CREATIVE ACTIVITIES

Some brief attention should be paid to the special case of controlling research and development projects, design projects, and similar processes that depend intimately on the creativity of individuals and teams. First, the more creativity involved, the greater the degree of uncertainty surrounding outcomes. Second, too much control tends to inhibit creativity. But neither of these dicta can be taken without reservation. Control is not necessarily the enemy of creativity; nor, popular myth to the contrary, does creative activity imply complete uncertainty. While the exact outcomes of creative activity may be more or less uncertain, the process of getting the outcome is usually not uncertain.

In order to control creative projects, the PM must adopt one or some combination of three general approaches to the problem: (1) progress review, (2) personnel reassignment, and (3) control of input resources.

Progress Review

The progress review focuses on the process of reaching outcomes rather than on the outcomes per se. Because the outcomes are partially dependent on the process used to achieve them, uncertain though they may be, the process is subjected to control. For example, in research projects the researcher cannot be held responsible for the outcome of the research, but can most certainly be held responsible for adherence to the research proposal, the budget, and the schedule. The process is controllable even if the precise results are not.

Control should be instituted at each project milestone. If research results are not as expected or desired, milestones provide a convenient opportunity to assess the state of progress, the value of accomplishment to date, the probability of valuable results in the future, and the desirability of changes in the research design. Again, the object of control is to ensure that the research design is sound and is being carried out as planned or amended. The review process should be participative. Unilateral judgments from the superior are not apt to be accepted or effective. Care must be taken not to overstress method as opposed to result. Method is controllable, and should be controlled, but results are still what count.

Personnel Reassignment

This type of control is straightforward—individuals who are productive are kept; those who are not are moved to other jobs or to other organizations. Problems with this technique can arise because it is easy to create an elite group. While the favored few are highly motivated to further achievement, everyone else tends to be demotivated. It is also important not to apply control with too fine an edge. While it is not particularly difficult to identify those who fall in the top and bottom quartiles of productivity, it is usually quite hard to make clear distinctions between people in the middle quartiles.

Control of Input Resources

In this case, the focus is on efficiency. The ability to manipulate input resources carries with it considerable control over output. Obviously, efficiency is not synonymous with creativity, but the converse is equally untrue. Creativity is not synonomous with extravagant use of resources.

The results flowing from creative activity tend to arrive in batches. Considerable resource expenditure may occur with no visible results, but then, seemingly all of a sudden, many outcomes may be delivered. The milestones for application of resource control must therefore be chosen with great care. The controller who decides to withhold resources just before the fruition of a research project is apt to become an ex-controller.

Sound judgment argues for some blend of these three approaches when controlling creative projects. The first and third approaches concentrate on process because process is observable and can be affected. But process is not the matter of moment; results are. The second approach requires us to measure (or at least to recognize) output when it occurs. This is often quite difficult. Thus, the wise PM will use all three approaches: checking process and method, manipulating resources, and culling those who cannot or do not produce.

11.7   CONTROL OF CHANGE AND SCOPE CREEP

In Chapter 6, we discussed the fact that the original plans for projects are almost certain to be changed before the projects are completed. The changes, we noted, result from three basic causes: (1) uncertainty about the technology on which the work of the project or its output is based; (2) an increase in the knowledge base or sophistication of the client/user leading to scope creep; and (3) a modification of the rules applying to the process of carrying out the project or to its output. All three of these causes are especially common in software projects, where scope creep is legendary. When either the process or output of a project is changed, there is almost always a concomitant change in the budget and/or schedule.

Conversations in recent years with more than 500 project managers have convinced us that coping with changes and changing priorities is perceived as the most important single problem facing the PM—or if not the most important, certainly the most irritating. When a senior financial officer of a toy manufacturing firm makes an offhand, negative comment about the color of a toy, and triggers a "total redesign" of the toy, thereby invalidating an already approved design, schedule, and budget, the project manager and the design artist may consider murder. (It is probable that a knowledgeable jury would find such action justifiable.)

The most common changes, however, are due to the natural tendency of the client and project team members to try to improve the product or service. New demands and performance requirements become apparent to the client which were not realized at the time of project initiation. New technologies become available or better ideas occur to the team as work progresses. As noted earlier, the later these changes are made in the project, the more difficult and costly they are to complete. Without control, a continuing accumulation of little changes can have a major negative impact on the project's schedule and cost.

Leffingwell (1997) suggests that interaction between the project team and the customer should be regularized by partnering. The customer may then take some official responsibility for helping to manage project scope. When the client is a part of the parent organization, the problem is often more difficult. Jealousy, mistrust, and conflict between departments (e.g., the traditional battle between marketing and engineering) leads to uncontrolled scope creep and to inevitable delays and budget overruns (Gibson, 1998).

There is, however, no insurance against the risks associated with project changes. Total quality management and employee involvement will help if both the deliverable and the process by which it is to be produced are carefully studied by thoughtful teams that represent the interests of the major stakeholders in any project, the client, senior management, the project team, and the community. Also, a thorough knowledge of production processes will help avoid some manufacturability-related engineering changes (Saeed, Bowen, and Sohoni, 1993). Since prevention of change is not possible, the PM's best hope seems to lie in controlling the process by which change is introduced and accomplished. Control of change is, therefore, one of the primary concerns of risk management.

This is accomplished with a formal *change control system* which, in some industries, is a part of their *configuration management system* responsible for integrating and coordinating changes throughout the systems development cycle. The purpose of the formal change control system is to:

- review all requested changes to the project (both content and procedures)
- identify all task impacts
- translate these impacts into project performance, cost, and schedule
- evaluate the benefits and costs of the requested changes
- identify alternative changes that might accomplish the same ends
- accept or reject the requested changes
- communicate the changes to all concerned parties
- ensure that the changes are implemented properly
- prepare monthly reports that summarize all changes to date and their project impacts

The following simple guidelines, applied with reasonable rigor, can be used to establish an effective change control procedure. The guidelines can also be integrated into the risk management system as a way to manage the risks imposed by scope creep.

1. All project contracts or agreements must include a description of how requests for a change in the project's plan, budget, schedule, and/or deliverables will be introduced and processed.

2. Once a project is approved, any change in the project will be in the form of a *change order* that will include a description of the agreed-upon change together with any changes in the plan, budget, schedule, and/or deliverables that result from the change.

3. Changes must be approved, in writing, by the client's agent as well as by an appropriate representative of senior management of the firm responsible for carrying out the project.

4. The project manager must be consulted on all desired changes prior to the preparation and approval of the change order. The project manager's approval, however, is not required.

5. Once the change order has been completed and approved, the project master plan should be amended to reflect the change, and the change order becomes a part of the master plan.

The process of controlling change is not complicated. If the project is large, Roman (1986, p. 274) suggests a change control board, a group representing all interested parties that processes all requests for change. For the typical small- or medium-sized project, however, the problem of handling change need not be complex. The main source of trouble is that too many project managers, in an attempt to avoid anything that smacks of bureaucracy, adopt an informal process of handling requests for change. Misunderstanding often arises from this informality, and the PM finds that the project becomes committed to deliver a changed output of extended scope, but will have to swallow the additional cost involved, and will have to scramble to meet the old, unchanged schedule.

The problems associated with dealing with change orders informally are particularly severe in the case of software and information system projects. We resist the notion that computer-oriented projects are significantly different from other types of projects in this regard. (For a diametric view, see Roetzheim, 1993.) Nonetheless, the precise techniques of managing projects are not independent of the technology applied on the project. Service sector projects often require different planning and control methods than do construction projects or R & D projects.

The severity of the problem of dealing with change in software projects, it seems to us, is caused by two, interrelated factors. First, software and information systems experts too often fail to explain adequately to the client the real nature of the systems they develop. Second, clients too often fail to make an adequate effort to understand the systems that become the lifeblood for their organizations. All too often, the systems developer is preoccupied by the technical demands of the systems and is ignorant of the user's needs. And all too often, the user views the systems developer as a practitioner of some arcane art that cannot be penetrated by normal minds. "What we have here is a failure to communicate." The client has no real idea of what is involved in changing a software project in order to provide another useful feature not specified in the original project requirements. The software technician, eager to please the customer, agrees to provide the utility, but does not make clear to the client the level of effort and time that will be required. The project is late, over budget, and the customer is angry. This scenario is played out again and again with neither side profiting from the experience. The formal process for change suggested above tends to reduce the degree of misunderstanding and disappointment.

Difficult as it may be, control is an important part of the PM's job on every project. Perhaps the most helpful advice we can give the PM is, in the language of the 1970s, to "hang loose." One effective project manager of our acquaintance tells his project team, "I will not accept crises after 4:30 P.M. You are limited to one crisis per day. Crises are not cumulative. If you don't get yours in today, you do not get two tomorrow." All this is said, of course, with good humor. Team members understand that the PM is not serious, but his projects seem to progress with exceptional smoothness. Crises do occur from time to time, but everyone on the team works to prevent them by applying control in an effective and timely manner.

Project Management in Practice
Better Control of Development Projects at Johnson Controls

The Automotive Systems Group of Johnson Controls was having trouble controlling their product development programs with each project being managed differently, disagreements about who was responsible for what, projects failing because of rapid company growth, and new employees having trouble fitting into the culture. For a solution, they went to their most experienced and successful project managers and condensed their knowledge into four detailed procedures for managing projects. Because these procedures are now common to all projects, they can be used to train new employees, standardize practices, create a common language, tie together different company functions, create common experiences, act as implicit job descriptions, and create a positive overall project management culture.

The first procedure is project approval for authorizing the expenditure of funds and use of resources. The sales department must first provide a set of product/market information, including financial data, project scope, critical dates, and engineering resource requirements before management will approve the project. Thus, projects are now scrutinized much more closely before work is started and money spent—when more questions are asked and more people are involved, better decisions tend to be made.

The second procedure is the statement-of-work, identifying agreements and assumptions for the project. Here, both the customer and top management must sign off before product design work begins, thereby reducing misunderstandings regarding not only product specifications, prices, and milestones but also intangible product requirements, explicit exclusions, and generic performance targets. Maintaining this documentation over the life of the project has helped avoid problems caused by late product changes from the customer, particularly for 3–5 year projects where the personnel rotate off the project. Customers have, however, been slow to agree to this level of documentation because it limits their ability to change timing, prices, and specifications late in the program when they are more knowledgeable about their needs.

The third procedure is the work breakdown structure, consisting of nine critical life-cycle phases running from definition through production. Included in each of these nine phases are four key elements: the tasks, the timing of each task, the responsible individuals, and the meeting dates for simultaneous engineering (a formalized procedure at Johnson Controls).

The fourth procedure is a set of management reviews, crucial to successful project completion. Both the content and timing of these reviews are specified in advance and progression to the next phase of a project cannot occur until senior management has approved the prespecified requirements, objectives, and quality criteria for that phase. The procedure also specifies questions that must be answered and work that must be reviewed by senior management.

Through the use of these procedures, which are updated and improved with each new project experience, the learning that occurs in the organization is captured and made useful for future projects.

Source: W. D. Reith and D. B. Kandt, "Project Management at a Major Automotive Seating Supplier," *Project Management Journal,* September 1991.

 ## SUMMARY

As the final subject in the project implementation part of the text, this chapter described the project control process in the planning-monitoring-controling cycle. The need for control was discussed and the three types available were described. Then the design of control systems was addressed, including management's role, achieving the proper balance, and attaining control of creative activity as well as handling changes.

- Control is directed to performance, cost, and time.
- The two fundamental purposes of control are to regulate results through altering activity and to conserve the organization's physical, human, and financial assets.
- The three main types of control processes are cybernetic (either first-, second-, or third-order), go/no-go, and postcontrol.
- The postcontrol report contains four sections:
  –Project objectives

  –Milestones and budgets

  –Final project results

  –Recommendations for improvement
- The trend projection curve, critical ratios, and the control chart are useful control tools.
- Control systems have a close relationship to motivation and should be well-balanced; that is, cost-effective, appropriate to the desired end results, and not overdone.
- Three approaches to the control of creativity are progress review, personnel reassignment, and control of inputs.
- The most irritating problem facing a PM is the control of change.

In the next chapter, we initiate the project termination part of the text, beginning with evaluation and auditing. This topic is closely related to the postcontrol topics in this chapter.

 ## GLOSSARY

Champion A person with organizational clout who takes on personal responsibility (though not usually day-to-day management) for the successful completion of a project for the organization.

Control Assuring that reality meets expectations or plans. Usually involves the process of keeping actions within limits to assure that certain outcomes will in fact happen.

Control Chart A chart of a measure of performance—commonly a quality characteristic—over time, showing how it changes compared to a desired mean and upper and lower limits.

Critical Ratio A ratio of progress (actual/scheduled) times a cost ratio (budgeted/actual).

Cybernetic An automatic control system containing a negative feedback loop.

Early Warning System A monitoring system that forewarns the project manager if trouble arises.

Go/No-Go Initially, a type of gauge that quickly tells an inspector if an object's dimension is within certain limits. In the case of project management, this can be any measure that allows a manager to decide whether to continue, change, or terminate an activity or a project.

 QUESTIONS

Material Review Questions

1. What is the purpose of control? To what is it directed?

2. What are the three main types of control system? What questions should a control system answer?

3. What tools are available to the project manager to use in controlling a project? Identify some characteristics of a good control system.

4. What is the mathematical expression for the critical ratio? What does it tell a manager?

Class Discussion Questions

12. How might the project manager integrate the various control tools into a project control system?

13. How could a negative feedback control system be implemented in project management to anticipate client problems?

14. How does the earned value approach achieve the objective of the trend projection curve in Figure 11–6?

15. What other project parameters might a control chart be used for? How would their limits be set?

16. Control systems are sometimes classified into two categories, preventive and feedback. How do the three types of systems described in the chapter relate to these two categories?

Questions for Project Management in Practice

Extensive Controls for San Francisco's Metro Turnback Project

24. Draw a hierarchy/organization chart illustrating your interpretation of the various control systems/programs described in the writeup.

25. How do you think Quality Control and Quality As-

5. Describe the relationship between motivation and control.

6. How is creativity controlled?

7. What are go/no-go gauges?

8. What is a champion?

9. Describe a cybernetic control system.

10. What should the postcontrol report include?

11. How should change be controlled?

17. How do internal and external controls differ?

18. What are some difficulties encountered when attempting project control?

19. How might the information required for control systems be collected?

20. How might the information collected through the control system be used on subsequent projects?

21. How does the control of creative projects differ from the control of ordinary projects?

22. Where might ethical issues arise for a PM in the stewardship of the company's resources?

23. Why is the control of change such a difficult problem for a PM?

surance were divided? Who was responsible for each and what did the responsibilities of each entail?

26. This project was critically aware of the possibility of "scope creep" over the 11-year duration of the project. How did they propose to control this danger?

Schedule and Cost Control for Australia's New Parliament House

27. Compare the construction look-ahead schedules for this project and the SF Metro Turnback project.

28. How did they control costs in this project?

29. Where in the contracting process was "scope creep" controlled?

Better Control of Development Projects at Johnson Controls

30. Summarize the unique way Johnson achieved control over their projects.

31. How did "scope creep" enter the projects in the past? Which procedure is now directed at controlling this effect?

32. Which of the four procedures is probably most critical to successful projects?

33. What is the term used in the chapter for the senior management review described in the fourth procedure?

PROBLEMS

1. Given the following information, calculate the critical ratios and indicate which activities are on target and which need to be investigated. Comment on the situation for each of the activities.

Activity	Actual Progress	Scheduled Progress	Budgeted Cost	Actual Cost
A	2 days	2 days	$40	$35
B	4 days	6 days	$30	$40
C	1 day	3 days	$50	$70
D	3 days	2 days	$25	$25

2. Calculate the critical ratios for the following activities and indicate which activities are probably on target and which need to be investigated. Comment on each activity.

Activity	Actual Progress	Scheduled Progress	Budgeted Cost	Actual Cost
A	4 days	4 days	$60	$40
B	3 days	2 days	$50	$50
C	2 days	3 days	$30	$20
D	1 day	1 day	$20	$30
E	2 days	4 days	$25	$25

3. Given the following information about a showroom renovation, which activities are on time, which are early, and which are behind schedule?

Activity	Budgeted Cost	Actual Cost	Critical Ratio
A	$60	$40	1.0
B	$25	$50	0.5
C	$45	$30	1.5
D	$20	$20	1.5
E	$50	$50	0.67

4. Design and plot a critical ratio for a computer installation project that had planned constant, linear progress from 0 to an earned value of 200 over a 100 day duration. In fact, progress for the first 20 days has been: 2, 3, 4, 6, 7, 9, 12, 14, 15, 17, 20, 21, 21, 22, 24, 26, 27, 29, 31, 33. What can you conclude about this project?

5. Design and plot a critical ratio for a Web site project that has planned constant, linear spending from 0 to a total of 1000 over a 100 day duration. In fact, daily spending for the first 15 days has been: 11, 10, 9, 10, 11, 12, 11, 9, 8, 9, 10, 12, 14, 11, 7. What can you conclude about this project?

6. Industrial Building, Inc., has two project teams installing virtually identical, 4-story commercial buildings for a customer in two separate cities. Both projects have a planned daily cost of 100 and a planned daily earned value of 100. The first six days for each team have progressed as follows:

Day	Team A: Earned Value	Team B: Earned Value	A: Cost	B: Cost
1	90	90	95	95
2	92	88	98	94
3	94	95	101	102
4	98	101	106	109
5	104	89	116	99
6	112	105	126	118

Compare the two projects in terms of general progress and according to critical ratios.

7. Samson Building, Ltd., is also constructing an identical building for the same customer as in Problem 6 and has the following earned values and costs for the first six days: EV: 90, 88, 95, 101, 89, 105; Cost: 92, 88, 93, 98, 85, 100. Compare this project to the two in Problem 6.

8. The following information concerns progress at day 40 of an Internet marketing project. Determine if the project is in control based on time and cost to date. If not, what is the cost overage or underage?

Activity	Duration	Budget	Actual Cost	% Completed
1-2	10	300	250	100
2-3	8	400	450	100
2-4	12	350	380	100
4-3	0	0	0	
3-5	18	405	400	70
5-6	16	450	—	0

INCIDENTS FOR DISCUSSION

Speciality Service, Inc.

Speciality Service, Inc., is a field computer repair operation serving the small commercial industry in seven states. Speciality Service has one operation in each state, and they vary in size from 50 to 240 employees. A disturbing trend has been developing for the last couple of years that Speciality Service management wishes to stop. The incidence of tardiness and absenteeism is on the increase. Both are extremely disruptive in a custom packing operation. Speciality Service is nonunion in all seven locations, and since management wants to keep this situation, it wants a careful, low-key approach to the problem. Jason Horn, assistant personnel manager, has been appointed project manager to recommend a solution. All seven operations managers have been assigned to work with him on this problem.

Jason has had no problem interfacing with the operations managers. They have very quickly agreed that three steps must be taken to solve the problem:

1. Institute a uniform daily attendance report that is summarized weekly and forwarded to the main office. (Current practice varies from location to location, but comments on attendance are normally included in monthly operations reports.)

2. Institute a uniform disciplinary policy, enforced in a uniform manner.

3. Initiate an intensive employee education program to emphasize the importance of good attendance.

The team has further decided that the three-point program should be tested before a final recommendation is presented. They have decided to test the program at one location for two months. Jason wishes to control and evaluate the test by having the daily attendance report transmitted to him directly at headquarters, from which he will make the final decision on whether to present the program in its current format or not.

Questions: Does this monitoring and control method appear adequate? What are the potential problems?

Night Tran Construction Company

Night Tran Construction Company specializes in building small power plants, mostly for utility companies. The company was awarded a contract approximately two years ago to build such a power plant. The contract stated a project duration of three years, after which a 1 percent penalty would be invoked for each additional month of construction. Project records indicate the utility plan is only 50 percent completed and is encountering continuing problems. The owner of Night Tran Company, concerned over the potential losses, investigated the project and found the following: There was an excessive number of engineering design changes; there was a high work rejection rate; and the project was generally understaffed. As a result, she directed the project manager to develop a better system of project control and present this method to the board members in one week.

Questions: If you were the project manager, what characteristics would you be looking for in the new control system? Will a new control system be adequate for the problem? Explain.

BIBLIOGRAPHY

ACKOFF, R. L. "Beyond Problem Solving." *Decision Sciences,* April 1974.

AMRINE, H. T., J. A. RITCHEY, and O. S. HULLEY. *Manufacturing Organization and Management,* 5th ed. Englewood Cliffs, NJ: Prentice Hall, 1987.

ARCHIBALD, R. D. *Managing High Technology Programs and Projects.* New York: Wiley, 1992.

BLOCK, P. *Stewardship.* San Francisco: Berrett-Koehler, 1993.

BOBROWSKI, P. M. "Project Management Control Problems: An Information Systems Focus." *Project Management Journal,* June 1989.

BRAZ, E. F. "Project Management Oversight: A Control Tool of Owners of Engineering and Construction Projects." *Project Management Journal*, March 1989.

BYRNE, J. "Project Management: How Much is Enough?" *PM Network,* February 1999.

CAMMANN, C., and D. A. NADLER. "Fit Control Systems to Your Management Style." *Harvard Business Review,* January–February 1976.

CESTIN, A. A. "What Makes Large Projects Go Wrong." *Project Management Quarterly,* March 1980.

COOPER, R. G. "The New Product Process: A Decision Guide for Management." *Journal of Marketing Management*, Vol. 3, No. 3 (Winter), 1994.

GIBSON, L. "Project Scope Creep." *Today's Engineer,* Spring 1998.

GRANT, R. A., C. A. HIGGINS, and R. H. IRVING. "Computerized Performance Monitors: Are They Costing You Customers?" *Sloan Management Review,* Spring 1988.

GUPTA, V. K., and D. J. GRAHAM. "A Customer-Driven Quality Improvement and Management Project at Diamond Offshore Drilling." *Project Management Journal,* September 1997.

HAJEK, V. G. *Management of Engineering Projects.* New York: McGraw Hill, 1977.

HEYWOOD, G. E., and T. J. ALLEN. "Project Controls: How Much is Enough." *PM Network,* November, 1996.

HOWARD, D. C. "Cost Schedule Control Systems." *Management Accounting,* October 1976.

IBBS, C. W., and Y. -H. KWAK. "Benchmarking Project Management Organizations." *PM Network,* February 1998.

KARAA, F. A., and B. ABDALLAH. "Coordination Mechanisms During the Construction Project Life Cycle." *Project Management Journal,* September 1991.

KERZNER, H. "Evaluation Techniques in Project Management." *Journal of Systems Management,* February 1980.

LEFFINGWELL, D. "Engage! Involve the Customer to Manage Scope." *PM Network*, August 1997.

LIKIERMAN, A. "Avoiding Cost Escalation on Major Projects." *Management Accounting,* February 1980.

LIVINGSTON, J. L., and R. RONEN. "Motivation and Management Control Systems." *Decision Sciences,* April 1975.

MURDICK, R. G. et al. *Information Systems for Modern Management,* 3rd ed. Englewood Cliffs, NJ: Prentice Hall, 1984.

NEWMAN, W. H. *Constructive Control.* Englewood Cliffs, NJ: Prentice Hall, 1975.

PARTOVI, F. Y., and J. BURTON. "Timing of Monitoring and Control of CPM Projects." *IEEE Transactions on Engineering Management,* February 1993.

ROETZHEIM, W. H. "Managing Software Projects: Unique Problems and Requirements." In P. C. Dinsmore, ed., *The AMA Handbook of Project Management.* New York: AMACOM, 1993.

ROMAN, D. D. *Managing Projects: A Systems Approach.* New York: Elsevier, 1986.

SAEED, B. I., D. M. BOWEN, and V. S. SOHONI. "Avoiding Engineering Changes through Focused Manufacturing Knowledge." *IEEE Transactions on Engineering Management,* February 1993.

SAITOW, A. R. "CSPC: Reporting Project Progress to the Top." In E. W. Davis, ed., *Project Management: Techniques, Applications and Managerial Issues.* Norcross, GA: American Institute of Industrial Engineers, 1976.

SANDERS, J. "Effective Estimating Process Outlined." *Computer World,* April 7, 14, and 21, 1980.

SCHODERBEK, C. G., P. P. SCHODERBEK, and A. G. KEFALAS. *Management Systems,* 4th ed. Homewood, IL: Irwin, 1989.

SEESING, P. R. "Distributing Project Control Database Information on the World Wide Web." *PM Network,* October 1996.

SETHI, N. K. "Project Management." *Industrial Management,* January–February. 1980.

SNOWDON, M. "Measuring Performance in Capital Project Management." *Long Range Planning,* August 1980.

THAMHAIN, H. J. "Best Practices for Controlling Technology-Based Projects." *Project Management Journal,* December 1996.

TIONG, R. L. K. "Effective Controls for Large Scale Construction Projects." *Project Management Journal,* March 1990.

TONEY, F. "What the Fortune 500 Know about PM Best Practices." *PM Network*, February 1997.

VAN GIGCH, J. P. *Applied General Systems Theory, 2nd ed.* New York: Harper & Row, 1978.

WEBER, F. M. "Ways to Improve Performance on Projects." *Project Management Quarterly,* September 1981.

WHITTEN, N. "Managing Priorities Effectively." *PM Network,* July 1995.

YUNUS, N. B., D. L. BABCOCK, and C. BENJAMIN. "Development of a Knowledge-Based Schedule Planning System." *Project Management Journal,* December 1990.

The following case illustrates the control actions a small firm's president used to implement a successful project that saved his firm, and launched it into a new area of business. The project had many points of crisis, and control was required to keep it on track. Although the project involved the implementation of a new technology, many of the critical issues requiring careful control were human and behavioral. The case includes important data for economic analysis of the project, its justification, and the justification of a potential follow-on project.

C A S E

PEERLESS LASER PROCESSORS
Jack R. Meredith, Marianne M. Hill, and James M. Comer

Owner and President Ted Montague was sitting at his desk on the second floor of the small Groveport, Ohio plant that housed Peerless Saw Company and its new subsidiary, peerless Laser Processors, Inc. As he scanned over the eight-page contract to purchase their third laser system, a 1200-watt computerized carbon dioxide (CO2) laser cutter, he couldn't help but reflect back to a similar situation he faced three years ago in this same office. Conditions were significantly different then. It was amazing, Ted reflected, how fast things had changed in the saw blade market, especially for Peerless, which had

Sales		$5,028,067
Costs:		
Materials	1,860,385	
Labor	905,052	
Variable overhead	1,106,175	
G&A	553,087	
Contribution to profit		603,368

Exhibit 1: Peerlees Financial Data, 1983

jumped from an underdog to the technology leader. Market data and financial statements describing the firm and its market environment are given in Exhibits 1 and 2.

History of Peerless Saw Company

Peerless Saw Company was formed in 1931, during the Great Depression, in Columbus, Ohio, to provide bandsaw blades to Ford Motor Company. It survived the Depression and by 1971, with its nonunionized labor force, it was known for its quality bandsaw and circular saw blades.

But conditions inside the firm warranted less optimism. The original machines and processes were now very old and breaking down frequently, extending order backlogs to 20 weeks. However, the owners were nearing retirement and didn't want to invest in new machinery, much less add capacity for the growing order backlog which had been building for years.

By 1974 the situation had reached the crisis point. The OPEC oil embargo provided the last straw, creating havoc in the saw blade market as in many other markets at the time as firms rushed to stockpile scare resources and critical materials, creating artificial shortages for everyone. At that point Ted Montague had appeared and, with the help of external funding, bought the firm from the original owners. Ted's previous business experience was in

Year	Sales (M)	Market Share (%)
1983	$5.028	29
1982	3.081	27
1981	2.545	25
1980	2.773	25

Exhibit 2: Sales and Market Data, 1983

food processing, and he had some concern about taking charge of a metal products company. But Ted found the 40 employees, 13 in the offices and 27 (divided among two shifts) on the shop floor, to be very helpful, particularly since they now had an owner who was interested in building the business back up.

Peerless survived the embargo, and the 1974 recession as well, so that by early 1976 Ted felt comfortable with his knowledge of the business. At that point he had a feel for what he believed were the more serious problems of the business and hired both a manufacturing manager and a manufacturing engineer, Con Wittkopp, to help him solve the problems. The most shopworn machines at Peerless were the over 30-year-old grinding machines and vertical milling machines. Committed to staying in business, Ted arranged for capital financing to design and build a new facility and replace some of the aging equipment. In 1977 the firm moved into new quarters in Groveport, not far from Columbus, with 7000 additional square feet of floor space. He also ordered seven new grinders from Germany and five new vertical mills. In order to determine what bottlenecks and inefficiencies existed on the shop floor, Ted also devised and installed a cost tracking system.

Laser Cutting Technology

By 1978, the competition had grown quite strong. In addition to the growing number of direct domestic competitors, foreign firms were mounting a devastating attack on the more common saw blade models, offering equivalent quality off the shelf for lower prices. Furthermore, many users were now tipping their own blades, or even cutting them themselves, further reducing the salable market. Sales were down while costs continued to increase and the remaining equipment continued to age and fail. Ted and Con looked into new technologies for saw blade cutting. They felt that Computer Numerical Control (CNC) machining couldn't be adapted to their needs, and laser cutting had high setup times, was underpowered, and exhibited a poor cut texture. (Ted remarked that "It looked as though an alligator had chewed on it.")

By early 1981, advances in laser cutting technology had received a considerable amount of publicity so Ted and Con signed up to attend a seminar on the subject sponsored by Coherent, one of the leaders in industrial laser technology. Unfortunately, at the last minute they were unable to attend the seminar and had to cancel their reservations.

Ted was under pressure from all sides to replace their worn out punch presses. No longer able to delay, he had contracts made up to purchase three state-of-the-art, quick-change, Minster punch presses. As he sat at his desk on the second floor of the Groveport building, scanning the Minster, Inc. contracts one last time before signing, Con came in with a small piece of sheet steel that had thin, smooth cuts through it.

It seems that a salesperson had been given Ted and Con's names from the seminar registration list and decided to pay them a call. He brought a small piece of metal with him that had been cut with a laser and showed it to Con. This was what Con brought into Ted's office. Impressed with the sample, Ted put the contracts aside and talked to the salesperson. Following their talk, Ted made arrangements to fly out to Coherent's headquarters in Palo Alto, California, for a demonstration.

In July 1981, Ted and con made the trip to Palo Alto and were impressed with the significant improvements made in laser cutting technology since 1978. Setups were faster, the power was higher, and the cuts were much cleaner. Following this trip, they arranged to attend the Hanover Fair in Germany in September to see the latest European technology. There they were guaranteed that the newer, higher powered lasers could even cut one-quarter-inch steel sheets.

In November, Ted and con returned to Palo Alto, making their own tests with the equipment. Satisfied, Ted signed a contract for a 700-watt laser cutter,* one of the largest then available, at a price close to $400,000 although the cutter couldn't be delivered until September 1982.

In addition to the risk of the laser technology, another serious problem now faced Ted and Con—

obtaining adequate software for the laser cutter. Ted and Con wanted a package that would allow off-line programming of the machine. Furthermore, they wanted it to be menu driven, operable by their current high school educated workers (rather than by engineers, as most lasers required), and to have pattern search capability.

Coherent, Inc. was simply not in the off-line software business. Since Ted and Con did not want to learn to write their own software for the cutter, Coherent suggested a seminar for them to attend where they might find the contact they needed.

Con attended the session but was shocked at the "horror stories" the other attendees were telling. Nevertheless, someone suggested that he contact Battelle Laboratories in Columbus for help. Fearing their high class price tag but with no other alternative, Ted and Con made arrangements to talk with the Battelle people.

The meeting, in March 1982, gave Ted and Con tremendous hope. Ted laid out the specifications for the software and, surprisingly, it appeared that what they wanted could possibly be done. The price would be expensive, however—around $100,000— and would require seven months to complete. The timing was perfect. Ted arranged for a September completion, to coincide with the delivery of the laser cutter. In the next seven months Con worked closely with Battelle, constantly redesigning and respecifying the software to improve its capabilities and avoid unsolvable problems and snags.

Finally, in September 1982, a 2-inch-high printout of Fortran code, programmed into a DEC PDP-ll computer, was delivered and matched via an RS-232 interface with the recently delivered laser cutter. But when the system was turned on, nothing happened. As Ted remarked, "Disaster City!" The software problem was solved within a day but the laser cutter had to be completely rebuilt on site. For almost 100 days the bugs had to be worked out of the system. "It was just awful."

The months of debugging finally resulted in a working system by December 1982. Meanwhile, Ted and the machine operator, Steve, spent four hours every Friday morning in training at Battelle to learn how to use the system. Con and another opera-

---

*The contract included extensive ancillary equipment and hardware.

tor did the same on Friday afternoons. Con and Ted later remarked that the "hardest" part of the training was learning to find the keys on the keyboard.

Initially, Ted and Con thought that they might have enough business to keep the laser busy during one shift per day. As it turned out, running the system was considerably more operator dependent than they had expected for a computerized system. Though anyone in the shop could learn to use the system, the operator had to learn how to work with the system, finessing and overriding it (skipping routines, "tricking" it into doing certain routines) when necessary to get a job done. Ted described this as "a painful learning curve." Thus, only an experienced operator could get the volume of work through the system that was "theoretically" possible. Nevertheless, once thoroughly familiar with the system, one operator could easily handle two cutters at the same time, and probably even three.

Within the next 17 months, Peerless put 4000 saw patterns on the system and started running the cutter for two full shifts. Due to increased demand they added another laser cutter, using the same computer system, and by November 1983 were running both cutters throughout two full shifts.

Marketplace and Competitive Effects

As of 1984, Peerless saw a number of improvements in their operations, and some significant changes in their market as well. In 1979 they had a 14-week delivery lead time. Part of the reason for this was that 25 percent of their orders had to be renegotiated with the customer because the old tooling couldn't handle the job. This slowed down the work tremendously. With the laser cutter this has been reduced to just three weeks, heat treating being the bottleneck (two full weeks).

Though they weren't making any blades that could not be made in 1979, their product mix changed considerably. In 1979 they made primarily 8-, 10-, 12-, and 14-inch saw blades. With the new capabilities of the laser cutter they were now making a much wider variety of blades, and more complex blades as well. As a matter of fact, they were producing the more difficult blades now, and at less cost.

For example, with the laser cutter, it took one-seventh the amount of time to cut a blade as it did previously, and one-eighth the number of machine operators. The resulting average cost saving was 5 to 10 percent per blade, reaching a maximum of 45 percent savings (on labor, material, and variable overhead) on some individual blades. Although cost savings allowed Peerless to cut prices on their blades, more significantly, they had an improved product, faster lead times, and more production capability.

Production capability was of particular importance. Peerless found that the ability to do things for customers that simply couldn't be done before changed the way customers ordered their blades. Because of their new capability, they were now seeing fewer repeat orders (although the batch size remained about the same) and considerably more "creativity" on the part of their customers. Orders now came to them as "The same pattern as last time except . . ." Customers were using Peerless' new capability to incrementally improve their saw blades, trying to increase capacity, or productivity, or quality by even 1 or 2 percent, based on their previous experimentation. Peerless had discovered, almost by accident, a significant competitive advantage.

Ted was intrigued with the way the laser cutter had revived Peerless. He stated that, based on payback or return on investment (ROI) criteria, he could not have justified the investment in the laser cutter beforehand. But more significantly, if he were to go through the figures now, after the tremendous success of the laser cutter, he still would not be able to justify the cutter on payback or ROI grounds. The point was, the new technology had changed the market Peerless was selling to, although the customers remained largely the same. The laser cutter in fact "created" its own market, one that simply could not exist prior to this technology. It filled a need that even the customers did not know existed.

Despite the increased speed of the laser cutter, it was not necessary to lay anyone off, though some employees' jobs changed significantly. The laser system was purposely packaged so that the existing employees could work with it and contribute to its success, even though they may have had only high school educations.

Ted continued to push the concept of a small, high-quality, technologically advanced business staying ahead of the same foreign competition that was wrecking havoc on the major corporations in America.

Ted summarized the benefits the new technology brought as:

- Decreased product cost
- Increased product quality
- Ability to use a sophisticated technology
- Ability to do what couldn't be done before, more responsive to the market
- An inspiration to visiting customers
- A positive image for the firm
- Adds "pizzazz" and "mystique" to the firm
- Allows entry into new fields

Peerless in 1984

In September 1984 Ted created a new division, Peerless Laser Processors, Inc. to handle general laser cutting of other types of parts besides saw blades. By then, Peerless had logged 10,000 hours on the laser cutters and had placed 6000 patterns on the system, adding new ones at the rate of 300 a month. Due to continuing customer requests that had never originally been considered, or even dreamed of, the software has been under constant revision and improvement by Battelle. Ted noted that, even though the need for revisions is expected to continue, it would neither pay to hire a software programmer nor would the job be interesting enough to keep one for long.

Ted and Con felt that generic-computer-assisted design/computer-aided manufacturing (CAD/CAM) systems available today would not help their situation. The unneeded capabilities tend to slow down the system, and in their new business the main com-

petitive factor, given other constants such as quality, is: "How fast can you do the job?"

Peerless also hired two additional sales representatives, with one now in the field and two in the office at all times. They also hired an engineer to develop new applications on a full-time basis for Peerless Laser Processing. As Con noted, "The problem is recognizing new applications while still doing your own work." They discovered, for example, that they could now make their own shuttles for their double disk grinders instead of purchasing them.

Peerless now has five U.S. competitors in the laser cutting business. Of course, Germany and Japan, among others, are still major competitors using the older technology. For the future, Ted sees the lasers becoming more powerful and having better control. He sees applications growing exponentially, and lasers doing welding and general fabrication of parts as well. He sees other technologies becoming competitive also, such as water jet and electrodischarge machining (EDM).

For Peerless, Ted's immediate goal is to attain a two-week lead time for sawblades and even better customer service, possibly including an inventory function in their service offerings. For the long run, Ted's goal is to become a "showcase" operation, offering the best in technology and quality in the world. As Ted put it: A company is like a tree. It only succeeds if it continues to grow, and you've got to grow wherever there's an opportunity. There are a maximum number of sawblades needed in the world, but no cap on what else the technology can do. We're only limited by our own imagination and creativeness and desire to make technology do things. That's our only restriction. What it fundamentally comes down to is this: Is a railroad a railroad or a transportation company? Are we a sawblade company or are we a company that fabricates metals into what anyone wants?

▉ QUESTIONS

1. How did the laser cutter "save" Peerless Saw Company when it could not be justified on payback or ROI grounds? Does this mean that the economics of automation is not important, or at least were not for Peerless?

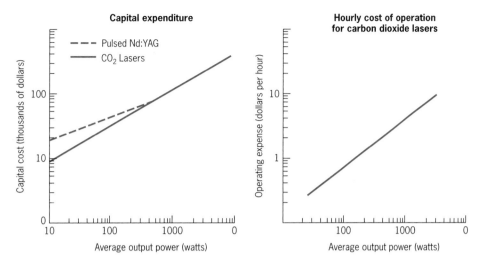

Exhibit 3: Laser Characteristics. *Source*: S. S. Charschan, and R. Webb "Considerations for Lasers in Manufacturing," in M. Bass, ed. *Laser Materials Processing*, North Holland, 1983.

2. Compare the decision Ted faces now—the 1200-watt laser purchase—with the decision he faced in 1981 when he was considering the three punch presses. Structure the investment decision for each of these cases. (Assume a computer costs about $20,000 and software about $80,000. Training costs are included in this charge.) Consider costs, benefits, and risks. How has the decision environment changed? Is Ted more or less comfortable with this decision? How is this decision easier? How is it harder?

3. What do you think the potential problems might be in purchasing the 1200-watt laser? What about the potential benefits? Will this laser have the same impact on the business as the first laser? What are the strategic variables involved in these decisions?

4. Estimate costs and revenues for this new system to perform a payback analysis. Use the variable cost data in Exhibit 3; assume the laser cuts at the rate of 40 inches per minute, that a typical blade of 14 inches sells for $25 (33% discount for volumes near

100 units), and the same computer and software will be used as currently. Material load time for a 10-blade sheet of steel is one minute. Use a 3-inch arbor hole size and assume that a cut tooth doubles the cut distance. How would you address the quantification of the intangible benefits the new system might provide? Is the new system justified on an economic basis? How might this system be more or less justifiable on an economic basis than the first laser system?

5. What are the organizational/behavioral considerations involved in this purchase? Are they the same as the first laser? How might this system be more or less justifiable on a noneconomic basis than the first laser system?

6. Ted is thinking about offering 25 of his largest customers the opportunity to tie into his system directly from their offices. What benefits would this offer to the customers and Peerless? What problems might it pose?

7. Advise Ted on the purchase of the new laser system.

The following article reports on a study of hundreds of project managers and the challenges and barriers they perceived in successfully controlling projects. The potential problems leading to schedule slips and budget overruns are identified and compared to the directly observed reasons. Also, the general managers' reasons for the slips and overruns are compared to the project managers' reasons and significant differences are noted. Last, the criteria that seem to be important to control are listed and discussed.

The value of this article for managers is the insight it gives concerning what needs to be controlled to bring about successful projects. The major factors are defining a detailed project plan that includes all key project personnel, reaching agreement on the plan among the project team members and the customer, obtaining the commitment of management, defining measurable milestones, and detecting problems early.

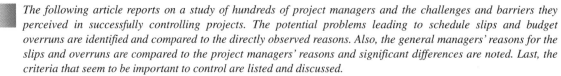

R E A D I N G

CONTROLLING PROJECTS ACCORDING TO PLAN*
H. J. Thamhain and D. L. Wilemon

Few project managers would argue the need for controlling their projects according to established plans. The challenge is to apply the available tools and techniques effectively. That is, to manage the effort by leading the multifunctional personnel toward the agreed-on objectives within the given time and resource constraints. Even the most experienced practitioners often find it difficult to control programs in spite of apparent detail in the plan, personnel involvement, and even commitment. As summarized in Table 1, effective program management is a function of properly defining the work, budgets, and schedules and then monitoring progress. Equally important, it is related to the ability to keep personnel involved and interested in the work, to obtain and refuel commitment from the team as well as from upper management, and to resolve some of the enormous complexities on the technical, human, and organizational side.

Responding to this interest, a field study was initiated to investigate the practices of project managers regarding their project control experiences. Specifically, the study investigates:

1. Type of project control problems experienced by project managers.
2. Project management practices and performance.
3. Criteria for effective project control.

*Criteria for Controlling Projects According to Plan. *Project Management Journal,* June 1986. ©1986 by the Project Management Institute. Reprinted by permission.

Table 1. Challenges of Managing Projects According to Plan

Rank	Challenge	Frequency (mentioned by % of PMs)
1	Coping with End-Date Driven Schedules	85%
2	Coping with Resource Limitations	83%
3	Communicating Effectively among Task Groups	80%
4	Gaining Commitment from Team Members	74%
5	Establishing Measurable Milestones	70%
6	Coping with Changes	60%
7	Working Out Project Plan Agreement with Team	57%
8	Gaining Commitment from Management	45%
9	Dealing with Conflict	42%
10	Managing Vendors and Subcontractors	38%
11	Other Challenges	35%

Method of Investigation

Data were collected over a period of three years from a sample of over 400 project leaders in predominantly technical undertakings, such as electronics, petrochemical, construction, and pharmaceutical projects. The data were collected mostly by questionnaires from attendees of project management workshops and seminars, as well as during in-plant consulting work conducted by the authors. Selectively, questionnaires were followed up by personal interviews. All data were checked for relevant sourcing to assure that the people who filled in the questionnaire had the minimum project leadership qualifications we established. These included: two years of experience in managing multidisciplinary projects, leading a minimum of three other project professionals, and being formally accountable for final results.

Sample Characteristics

The final qualifying sample included 304 project leaders from 183 technical projects. The leaders had an average of 5.2 years of project management experience. As shown by the sigma/standard deviation,* the sample data are distributed widely:

Number of Project Leaders in Sample	304
Number of Projects in Sample	183
Number of Project Leaders per Project	1.66 ($\sigma = 1$)
Project Size (Average)	\$850K ($\sigma = 310$K)
Project Duration (Average)	12 Months ($\sigma = 4$)
Multidisciplinary Nature (Average)	8 Team Members ($\sigma = 5$)
Project Management Experience/PM	5.2 Years ($\sigma = 2.5$)
Number of Previous Projects/PM	6 ($\sigma = 4.5$)

Data were collected in three specific modes: (1) Open-ended questions leading to a broad set of data, such as condensed in Table 2, and used for broad classifications and further, more detailed investigations; (2) Specific questions, requested to be answered on a tested five-point scale, such as shown in Figure 1. The scores enabled subsequent data ranking and correlation analysis; and (3) Interviews leading to a discussion of the previous findings and further qualitative investigations into the practices and experiences of project managers and their superiors.

All associations were measured by utilizing Kendall's Tau rank-order correlation. The agreement between proj-

Table 2. Potential Problems* (subtle reasons) Leading to Schedule Slips and Budget Overruns

01	Difficulty of Defining Work in Sufficient Detail
02	Little Involvement of Project Personnel During Planning
03	Problems with Organizing and Building Project Team
04	No Firm Agreement to Project Plan by Functional Management
05	No Clear Charter for Key Project Personnel
06	Insufficiently Defined Project Team Organization
07	No Clear Role/Responsibility Definition for Project Personnel
08	Rush into Project Kick-off
09	Project Perceived as Not Important or Exciting
10	No Contingency Provisions
11	Inability to Measure True Project Performance
12	Poor Communications with Upper Management
13	Poor Communications with Customer or Sponsor
14	Poor Understanding of Organizational Interfaces
15	Difficulty in Working across Functional Lines
16	No Ties between Project Performance and Reward System
17	Poor Project Leadership
18	Weak Assistance and Help from Upper Management
19	Project Leader Not Involved with Team
20	Ignorance of Early Warning Signals and Feedback
21	Poor Ability to Manage Conflict
22	Credibility Problems with Task Leaders
23	Difficulties in Assessing Risks
24	Insensitivity or Organizational Culture/Value System
25	Insufficient Formal Procedural Project Guidelines
26	Apathy or Indifference by Project Team or Management
27	No Mutual Trust among Team Members
28	Too Much Unresolved/Dysfunctional Conflict
29	Power Struggles
30	Too Much Reliance on Established Cost Accounting System

*The tabulated potential problems represent summaries of data compiled during interviews with project personnel and management.

---

*The distribution of the sample data is skewed. The sigma/standard deviation listed in parentheses corresponds to the positive side only.

Rank by		Reason or Problem	Rarely Sometimes Often Most Likely Always	Agreement between GM & PM
General Managers	Project Managers		1 2 3 4 5	
1	10	Insufficient Front-End Planning		Disagree
2	3	Unrealistic Project Plan		Strongly Agree
3	8	Project Scope Underestimated		Disagree
4	1	Customer/Management Changes		Disagree
5	14	Insufficient Contingency Planning		Disagree
6	13	Inability to Track Progress		Disagree
7	5	Inability to Detect Problems Early		Agree
8	9	Insufficient Number of Checkpoints		Agree
9	4	Staffing Problems		Disagree
10	2	Technical Complexities		Disagree
11	6	Priority Shifts		Disagree
12	10	No Commitment by Personnel to Plan		Agree
13	12	Uncooperative Support Groups		Agree
14	7	Sinking Team Spirit		Disagree
15	15	Unqualified Project Personnel		Agree

Figure 1   Directly observed reasons for schedule slips and budget overruns.

ect managers and their superiors on the reason for project control problems was tested by using the nonparametric Kruskal-Wallis one-way analysis of variance by ranks, setting the null-hypothesis for agreement at various confidence levels depending on the strength of the agreement or disagreement as specified in the write-up.

Discussion of Results

The results of this study are being presented in four parts. First, the reasons for poor project control are analyzed as they relate to budget overruns and schedule slips. Second, the less tangible criteria for these control problems are discussed. This part shows that many of the reasons blamed for poor project performance, such as insufficient front-end planning and underestimating the complexities and scope, are really rooted in some less obvious organizational, managerial, and interpersonal problems. Third, the relationship between project performance and project management problems is discussed, and fourth, the criteria for effective project controls are summarized.

The Reasons for Poor Project Control.   Figure 1 summarizes an investigation into 15 problem areas re-

garding their effects on poor project performance. Specifically, project managers and their superiors (such as senior functional managers and general managers) indicate on a five-point scale their perception of how frequently certain problems are responsible for schedule slips and budget overruns. The data indicate that project leaders perceive these problem areas in a somewhat different order than their superiors.

While *project leaders* most frequently blame the following reasons as being responsible for poor project performance:

1. Customer and Management Changes
2. Technical Complexities
3. Unrealistic Project Plans
4. Staffing Problems
5. Inability to Detect Problems Early

Senior management ranks these reasons somewhat differently:

1. Insufficient Front-End Planning
2. Unrealistic Project Plans

3. Underestimated Project Scope

4. Customer and Management Changes

5. Insufficient Contingency Planning

On balance, the data support the findings of subsequent interviews that project leaders are more concerned with external influences such as changes, complexities, staffing, and priorities while senior managers focus more on what should and can be done to avoid problems. In fact, the differences between project leaders' and senior/superior management's perceptions were measured statistically by using a Kruskal-Wallis analysis of variance by ranks, based on the following test statistics:

Strong Agreement: If acceptable at > 99% confidence

Agreement: If acceptable at > 90% confidence

Weak Agreement: If acceptable at > 80% confidence

Disagreement: If rejected at 80% confidence

Project leaders disagree with their superiors on the ranking of importance for all but six reasons. What this means is that while both groups of management actually agree on the basic reasons behind schedule slips and budget overruns, they attach different weights. The practical implication of this finding is that senior management expects proper project planning, organizing, and tracking from project leaders. They further believe that the "external" criteria, such as customer changes and project complexities, impact project performance only if the project had not been defined properly and sound management practices were ignored. On the other side, management's view that some of the subtle problems, such as sinking team spirit, priority shifts, and staffing, are of lesser importance might point to a potential problem area. Management might be less sensitive to these struggles, get less involved, and provide less assistance in solving these problems.

Less Obvious and Less Visible Reasons for Poor Performance. Managers at all levels have long lists of "real" reasons why the problems identified in Figure 1 occur. They point out, for instance, that while insufficient front-end planning eventually got the project into trouble, the real culprits are much less obvious and visible. These subtle reasons, summarized in Table 2, strike a common theme. They relate strongly to organizational, managerial, and human aspects. In fact, the most frequently mentioned reasons for poor project performance can be classified in five categories:

1. Problems with organizing project team

2. Weak project leadership

3. Communication problems

4. Conflict and confusion

5. Insufficient upper management involvement

Most of the problems in Table 2 relate to the manager's ability to foster a work environment conducive to multidisciplinary teamwork, rich in professionally stimulating and interesting activities, involvement, and mutual trust. The ability to foster such a high-performance project environment requires sophisticated skills in leadership, technical, interpersonal, and administrative areas. To be effective, project managers must consider all facets of the job. They must consider the task, the people, the tools, and the organization. The days of the manager who gets by with technical expertise or pure administrative skills alone, are gone. Today the project manager must relate socially as well as technically. He or she must understand the culture and value system of the organization. Research* and experience show that effective project management is directly related to the level of proficiency at which these skills are mastered. This is also reflected in the 30 potential problems of our study (see Table 2) and the rank-order correlations summarized in Table 3. As indicated by the correlation figure of $\tau = -.45$, the stronger managers felt about the reasons in Figure 1, the stronger they also felt about the problems in Table 2 as reasons for poor project performance. This correlation is statistically significant at a confidence level of 99 percent and supports the conclusion that both sets of problem areas are related and require similar skills for effective management.

Management Practice and Project Performance. Managers appear very confident in citing actual and potential problems. These managers are sure in their own mind that these problems, summarized in Figure 1 and Table 2, are indeed related to poor project performance. However, no such conclusion could be drawn without additional data and the specific statistical test shown in Table 3. As indicated by the strongly negative correlations between project performance and (1) potential problems ($\tau = -.55$) and (2) actual problems ($\tau = -.40$), the presence of either problem will indeed result in lower performance. Specifically, the stronger and more fre-

---

*For a detailed discussion of skill requirements of project managers and their impact on project performance see H. J. Thamhain & D. L. Wilemon, "Skill Requirements of Project Managers," *Convention Record, IEEE Joint Engineering Management Conference,* October 1978 and H. J. Thamhain, "Developing Engineering Management Skills" in *Management of R &D and Engineering,* North Holland Publishing Company, 1986.

quently project managers experience these problems, the lower was the manager judged by superior managers regarding overall on-time and on-budget performance.

Furthermore, it is interesting to note that the more subtle potential problems correlate most strongly to poor performance ($\tau = -.55$). In fact, special insight has been gained by analyzing the association of each problem to project performance separately. Taken together, it shows that the following problems seem to be some of the most crucial *barriers* to high project performance:

- Team organization and staffing problems
- Work perceived as not important, challenging, having growth potential
- Little team and management involvement during planning
- Conflict, confusion, power struggle
- Lacking commitment by team and management
- Poor project definition
- Difficulty in understanding and working across organizational interfaces

Table 3. Correlation of Project Management Practices to Performance

Potential Problems vs. Actual	Correlation of (1) Potential Problems (Table 2) and (2) Directly Observed Reasons for Budget and Schedule Slips (Figure 1)	$\tau = -.45^*$
Potential Problems vs. Performance	Correlation of (1) Potential Problems Leading for Budget and Schedule Slips (Table 2) and (2) Project Performance (Top Management Judgment)	$\tau = -.55^*$
Actual Problems vs. Performance	Correlation of (1) Directly Observed Reasons for Budget and Schedule Slips (Figure 1) and (2) Project Performance	$\tau = -.40^*$

*99% Confidence Level (p = .01)

All Tau values are Kendall Tau Rank-Order Correlation.

- Weak project leadership
- Measurability problems
- Changes, contingencies, and priority problems
- Poor communications, management involvement and support

To be effective, project leaders must not only recognize the potential barriers to performance, but also know where in the life cycle of the project they most likely occur. The effective project leader takes preventive actions early in the project life cycle and fosters a work environment that is conducive to active participation, interesting work, good communications, management involvement, and low conflict.

Criteria for Effective Project Control

The results presented so far focused on the reasons for poor project performance. That is, what went wrong and why were analyzed. This section concentrates on the lessons learned from the study and extensive interviews investigating the forces driving high project performance. Accordingly, this section summarizes the criteria which seem to be important for controlling projects according to plan. The write-up follows a recommendations format and flows with the project through its life cycle wherever possible.

1. ***Detailed Project Planning.*** Develop a detailed project plan, involving all key personnel, defining the specific work to be performed, the timing, the resources, and the responsibilities.

2. ***Break the Overall Program into Phases and Subsystems.*** Use Work Breakdown Structure (WBS) as a planning tool.

3. ***Results and Deliverables.*** Define the program objectives and requirements in terms of specifications, schedule, resources and deliverable items for the total program and its subsystems.

4. ***Measurable Milestones.*** Define measurable milestones and checkpoints throughout the program. Measurability can be enhanced by defining specific results, deliverables, technical performance measures against schedule and budget.

5. ***Commitment.*** Obtain commitment from all key personnel regarding the problem plan, its measures and results. This commitment can be enhanced and maintained by involving the team members early in the project planning, including the definition of results, measurable milestones, schedules, and budgets. It is through this involvement that the team members gain a detailed understanding of the work

to be performed, develop professional interests in the project and desires to succeed, and eventually make a firm commitment toward the specific task and the overall project objectives.

6. ***Intra-Program Involvement.*** Assure that the interfacing project teams, such as engineering and manufacturing, work together, not only during the task transfer, but during the total life of the project. Such interphase involvement is necessary to assure effective implementation of the developments and to simply assure "doability" and responsiveness to the realities of the various functions supporting the project. It is enhanced by clearly defining the results/deliverables for each interphase point, agreed upon by both parties. In addition, a simple sign-off procedure, which defines who has to sign off on what items, is useful in establishing clear checkpoints for completion and to enhance involvement and cooperation of the interphasing team members.

7. ***Project Tracking.*** Define and implement a proper project tracking system which captures and processes project performance data conveniently summarized for reviews and management actions.

8. ***Measurability.*** Assure accurate measurements of project performance data, especially technical progress against schedule and budget.

9. ***Regular Reviews.*** Project should be reviewed regularly, both on a work package (subsystem) level and total project level.

10. ***Signing-On.*** The process of "signing-on" project personnel during the initial phases of the project or each task seems to be very important to a proper understanding of the project objectives, the specific tasks, and personal commitment. The sign-on process that is so well described in Tracy Kidder's book, *The Soul of a New Machine,* is greatly facilitated by sitting down with each team member and discussing the specific assignments, overall project objectives, as well as professional interests and support needs.

11. ***Interesting Work.*** The project leader should try to accommodate the professional interests and desires of supporting personnel when negotiating their tasks. Project effectiveness depends on the manager's ability to provide professionally stimulating and interesting work. This leads to increased project involvement, better communications, lower conflict, and stronger commitment. This is an environment where people work toward established objectives in a self-enforcing mode requiring a minimum of managerial controls. Although the scope of a project may be fixed, the project manager usually has a degree of flexibility in allocating task assignments among various contributors.

12. ***Communication.*** Good communication is essential for effective project work. It is the responsibility of the task leaders and ultimately the project manager to provide the appropriate communication tools, techniques, and systems. These tools are not only the status meetings, reviews, schedules, and reporting systems, but also the objective statements, specifications, list of deliverables, the sign-off procedure and critical path analysis. It is up to the project leaders to orchestrate the various tools and systems, and to use them effectively.

13. ***Leadership.*** Assure proper program direction and leadership throughout the project life cycle. This includes project definition, team organization, task coordination, problem identification and a search for solutions.

14. ***Minimize Threats.*** Project managers must foster a work environment that is low on personal conflict, power struggles, surprises, and unrealistic demands. An atmosphere of mutual trust is necessary for project personnel to communicate problems and concerns candidly and at an early point in time.

15. ***Design a Personnel Appraisal and Reward System.*** This should be consistent with the responsibilities of the people.

16. ***Assure Continuous Senior Management Involvement, Endorsement, and Support of the Project.*** This will surround the project with a priority image, enhance its visibility, and refuel over all commitment to the project and its objectives.

17. ***Personal Drive.*** Project managers can influence the climate of the work environment by their own actions. Concern for project team members, ability to integrate personal goals and needs of project personnel with project goals, and ability to create personal enthusiasm for the project itself can foster a climate of high motivation, work involvement, open communication, and ultimately high project performance.

A Final Note

Managing engineering programs toward established performance, schedule, and cost targets requires more than just another plan. It requires the total commitment of the performing organization plus the involvement and help of the sponsor/customer community. Successful program managers stress the importance of carefully designing the project planning and control system as well as the structural and authority relationships. All are critical to the implementation of an effective project control system. Other organizational issues, such as management style, personnel appraisals and compensation, and intraproject communication, must be carefully considered to make the system self-forcing; that is, project personnel throughout the organization must feel that participation in the project is desirable regarding the fulfillment of their professional needs and wants. Furthermore, project personnel must be convinced that management involvement is helpful in their work. Personnel must be convinced that identifying the true project status and communicating potential problems early will provide them with more assistance to problem solving, more cross-functional support, and in the end will lead to project success and the desired recognition for their accomplishments.

In summary, effective control of engineering programs or projects involves the ability to:

- Work out a detailed project plan, involving all key personnel
- Reach agreement on the plan among the project team members and the customer/sponsor
- Obtain commitment from the project team members
- Obtain commitment from management
- Define measurable milestones
- Attract and hold quality people
- Establish a controlling authority for each work package
- Detect problems early

Questions

1. Why do project managers and senior general managers see the reasons for project difficulty differently?

2. Why do the potential problems correlate more strongly with poor performance than the actual problems?

3. Overall, what do you conclude are the reasons for poor project performance?

4. Relate the findings in this article to the PM in Practice SF Turnback project control process and the PM in Practice Johnson Controls project management procedures.

5. Of the types of control discussed in the chapter, which type(s) is this article referring to?

CHAPTER

12

Project Auditing

In the previous chapter, we discussed postcontrol. Postcontrol is not meant to change what has already happened. Quite the opposite, postcontrol tries to capture the essence of project successes and failures so that future projects can benefit from past experiences. To benefit from past experiences implies that one understands them, and understanding requires evaluation. But project evaluation is not limited to after-the-fact analysis. While the project as a whole is evaluated when it has been completed, project evaluation should be conducted at a number of points during the life cycle.

A major vehicle for evaluation (but by no means the only one) is the *project audit,* a more or less formal inquiry into any aspect of the project. We associate the word *audit* with a detailed examination of financial matters, but a project audit is highly flexible and may focus on whatever matters senior management desires. Note that there are also other types of audits such as *ethics audits* which can be helpful when employing project management in an organization. For example, as Schaefer and Zaller (1998, p. 40) note, "Ethics is not a matter of right or wrong; it is a process by which an organization evaluates decisions," a process that is most certainly relevant to project management! And in addition to project audits, there are also other kinds of project evaluations, such as project *reviews;* see Sangameswaran (1995) for more details.

The term *evaluate* means to set the value of or appraise. Project evaluation appraises the progress and performance of a project compared to that project's planned progress and performance, or compared to the progress and performance of other, similar projects. The evaluation also supports any management decisions required for the project. Therefore, the evaluation must be conducted and presented in a manner and format that assures management that all pertinent data have been considered. The evaluation of a project must have credibility in the eyes of the management group for whom it is performed and also in the eyes of the project team on whom it is performed. Accordingly, the project evaluation must be just as carefully constructed and controlled as the project itself.

In this chapter, we describe the project audit/review/evaluation, its various forms and purposes, and some typical problems encountered in conducting an audit/ evaluation. For an excellent general work on evaluation, see Meyers (1981).

12.1 PURPOSES OF EVALUATION—GOALS OF THE SYSTEM

Certainly the major element in the evaluation of a project is its "success." In a study of a variety of different kinds and sizes of industrial projects (Shenhar, Levy, and Dvir, 1997), 127 project managers identified 13 factors constituting four independent dimensions of project success, from their perspective as project managers. The first and most straightforward dimension is the project's *efficiency* in meeting both the budget and the schedule. The second and most complex dimension is that of *customer impact/satisfaction.* This dimension includes the obvious factors of meeting the project's technical and operational specifications but also includes factors relating to loyalty and repurchase: fulfilling the customer's needs, actual use by the customer, solving a major operational problem of the customer, and the perennial challenge of customer satisfaction.

The third dimension, again somewhat straightforward and expected, is *business/ direct success,* measured here primarily in terms of level of commercial success and market share. For internal projects, however, the factors might include such measures as yields, cycle times, processing steps, quality, and so on. The last dimension, somewhat more difficult and nebulous to ascertain, is *future potential.* This includes factors relating to opening a new market, developing a new line of products or services, or if an internal project, developing a new technology, skills, or competences.

Beyond the straightforward considerations of project success, another primary purpose of evaluation is to help translate the achievement of the project's goals into a contribution to the parent organization's goals. To do this, all facets of the project are studied in order to identify and understand the project's strengths and weaknesses. It is the equivalent of an application of TQM to project management. The result is a set of recommendations that can help both ongoing and future projects to:

- Identify problems earlier
- Clarify performance, cost, and time relationships
- Improve project performance
- Locate opportunities for future technological advances
- Evaluate the quality of project management
- Reduce costs
- Speed up the achievement of results
- Identify mistakes, remedy them, and avoid them in the future
- Provide information to the client
- Reconfirm the organization's interest in and commitment to the project

These purposes—and there are many others—relate quite directly to how well the project team is meeting the stated project objectives. (For brevity, we will refer to them as "direct goals.") They ignore, however, many costs and benefits to the project, to its team members, and to the parent organization that are not overtly established as objectives. Evaluation often makes recommendations that relate to these ancillary, unplanned but important contributions to the project and its parent. Some examples of recommendations concerning these "ancillary goals" include attempts to:

- Improve understanding of the ways in which projects may be of value to the organization
- Improve the processes for organizing and managing projects
- Provide a congenial environment in which project team members can work creatively together
- Identify organizational strengths and weaknesses in project-related personnel, management, and decision-making techniques and systems
- Identify and improve the response to risk factors in the firm's use of projects
- Improve the way projects contribute to the professional growth of project team members
- Identify project personnel who have high potential for managerial leadership

Identification of the direct goals of a project is *relatively* easy. It requires only a careful reading of the project proposal and a close examination of any documentation that indicates why the project was selected or undertaken. If such a document exists, it is a statement of the project's direct goals. If no such document exists, and all too often it will not, a few interviews with the individuals in charge of making decisions about projects will help to expose the direct goals that the firm is seeking by supporting the project. On the other hand, identification of ancillary goals is a difficult and politically delicate task.

The adjective "ancillary" is not a sufficient descriptor, though it is the best single word we could find. Synonyms are "helpful," "subsidiary," "accessory," and the like, and we have all these things in mind. In addition, the ancillary goals are usually not overtly identified. For the most part, they are "hidden" by accident, not by purpose. Finding them requires deductive reasoning. Organizational decisions and behaviors imply goals, often very specific goals, that are simply not spelled out anywhere in the organizational manuals. For example, most executives desire to operate their organizations in such a way that people enjoy the work they do and working together, but only occasionally do firms publish such statements. Few firms would disavow this objective, they simply do not *overtly* subscribe to it. Even so, this particular objective affects the decisions made in almost every firm we know.

There are tough problems associated with finding the ancillary goals of a project. First, and probably the most important, is the obvious fact that one cannot measure performance against an unknown goal. Therefore, if a goal is not openly acknowledged, project team members need not fear that their performance can be weighed and found wanting. The result is that goals appearing in the project proposal must be recognized and are a source of some anxiety in members of the project team. But "unwritten" goals can often be ignored. Again, ancillary goals are rarely disclaimed; they are merely not mentioned.

Whether or not anxiety about meeting ancillary goals is deserved is not relevant. Particularly in this era of corporate "restructuring," anxiety is present. It is heightened by the fear that an evaluation may not be conducted "fairly," with proper emphasis on what is being accomplished rather than stressing shortcomings. If the self-image of the project team is very strong, this barrier to finding ancillary goals of the project may be weak, but it is never absent.

A second problem arises during attempts to find the ancillary goals of a project. Individuals pursue their own individual ends while working for organizations. At times, however, people may be unwilling to admit to personal goals—goals they may see as not entirely consistent with organizational objectives. For example, a person may seek to join a project in order to learn a new skill, one that increases that person's employment mobility. At times, the scientific direction taken by R & D projects is as much a function of the current interest areas of the scientists working on the project as it is the scientific needs of the project. While such purposes are not illegitimate or unethical, they are rarely admitted.

A third problem arises through lack of trust. Members of a project team are never quite comfortable in the presence of an auditor/evaluator. If the auditor/evaluator is an "outsider"—anyone who cannot be identified as a project team member—there is fear that "we won't be understood." While such fears are rarely specific, they are nonetheless real. If the auditor/evaluator is an "insider," fear focuses on the possibility that the insider has some hidden agenda, is seeking some personal advantage at the expense of the "rest of us." The motives of insider and outside alike are distrusted. As a result, project team members have little or no incentive to be forthcoming about their individual or project ancillary goals.

Finally, a fourth problem exists. Projects, like all organizations that serve human ends, are multipurposed. The diverse set of direct and ancillary, project and individual goals do not bear clear, organizationally determined (or accepted) priorities. Various members of the project team may have quite different ideas about which purposes are most important, which come next in line, and which are least important. In the absence of direct questions about the matter, no one has to confront the issue of who is right and who is wrong. As long as the goals and priorities are not made explicit, project team members can agree on *what* things should be done without necessarily agreeing (or even discussing) *why* those things should be done. Thus, if some of the project's objectives are not openly debated, each member can tolerate the different emphases of fellow team members. No one is forced to pick and choose, or even to discuss such matters with co-workers.

All in all, the task of finding the ancillary goals of a project is difficult. Most evaluations simply ignore them, but the PM is well advised to take a keen interest in this area, and to request that evaluations include ancillary goals, the project's and the parent organization's, if not those of individuals. Even though one must usually be satisfied with rough, qualitative measures of ancillary-goal achievement, the information can be valuable. It may provide insight into such questions as: What sorts of things motivate people to join and work on projects? What sorts of rewards are most effective in eliciting maximum effort from project personnel? What are the major concerns of specific individuals working on the project?

In Chapter 4, we alluded to the importance of the project "war room" (office) as a meeting place for the project team, as a display area for the charts that show the project's progress, as a central repository for project files and reports, and as an office for the PM and other project administrators. The war room is also the "clubhouse" for the project team members and serves an important ancillary goal. It is to the project what the local pub was to "that old gang of mine." The camaraderie associated with a successful, well-run project provides great satisfaction to team members. The project office, therefore, fills an emotional need as well as meeting its more mundane, direct administrative goals.

Project Management in Practice
Lessons from Auditing 110 Client/Server and Open Systems Projects

In an 11-year audit of 110 client/server and open systems projects, one auditor boiled the differences between success and failure down to four foundational concepts.

1. *Objectivity regarding scope, budget, deadlines, and solution design.* Lack of objectivity in these areas is one of the basic causes of project failure. Decisions concerning the business case for initiating the project and establishing all of its parameters need to be scrutinized for bias and inadequate diligence.

2. *Experienced people at all levels in the project.* Having experienced people on both the client side and the contractor side helps in a number of areas: maintaining a cooperative, problem-solving attitude; enforcing milestones and deliverables, using professional project management techniques, and maintaining continuous user involvement.

3. *Authority matched with responsibility.* Since a project is usually established with a certain scope but limited budget and schedule, the project manager needs to have the authority to make tradeoffs between these objectives. This level of authority needs to be present on both the client side as well as the contractor side.

4. *Accountability sufficient to ensure that all parties perform as promised or are definitely held responsible.* Accountability needs to be thoroughly detailed in the original contracts and purchase orders. It should include details concerning the project champion, the original estimator, suppliers, the client team and users, and the contractor team. Keeping projects short, such as under six months, keeps from diluting accountability through personnel turnover.

Source: T. Ingram, "Client/Server and Imaging: On Time, On Budget, As Promised," *PM Network,* December 1995, pp. 13–18.

12.2   THE PROJECT AUDIT

The project audit is a thorough examination of the management of a project, its methodology and procedures, its records, its properties, its budgets and expenditures, and its degree of completion. It may deal with the project as a whole, or only with a part of the project. The formal report may be presented in various formats, but should, at a minimum, contain comments on the following points:

1. *Current status of the project.* Does the work actually completed match the planned level of completion?
2. *Future status.* Are significant schedule changes likely? If so, indicate the nature of the changes.
3. *Status of crucial tasks.* What progress has been made on tasks that could decide the success or failure of the project?
4. *Risk assessment.* What is the potential for project failure or monetary loss?
5. *Information pertinent to other projects.* What lessons learned from the project being audited can be applied to other projects being undertaken by the organization?
6. *Limitations of the audit.* What assumptions or limitations affect the data in the audit?

These six parts of the audit report will be discussed in more detail in the next section of this chapter.

Note that the project audit is not a financial audit. The audit processes are similar in that each represents a careful investigation of the subject of the audit, but the outputs of these processes are quite different. The principal distinction between the two is that the financial audit has a limited scope. It concentrates on the use and preservation of the organization's assets. The project audit is far broader in scope and may deal with the project as a whole or any component or set of components of the project. It may be concerned with any aspect of project management. Table 12-1 lists the primary differences between financial and project audits.

While the project audit may be concerned with any aspect of project management, it is not a traditional management audit. Management audits are primarily aimed at ensuring that the organization's management systems are in place and operative. The project audit goes beyond this. Among other things, it is meant to ensure that the project is being *appropriately* managed. Some managerial systems apply fairly well to all projects; for example, the techniques of planning, scheduling, budgeting, and so forth. On the other hand, some management practices should differ with different types of projects. See Ruskin and Estes (1985) for an interesting discussion of the project management audit and Sangameswaran (1995) and Corbin et al. (2001) for some guidance on auditing do's and don'ts.

In the previous chapter, we argued that software projects were not *significantly* different from other types of projects. We stand on that position, but we also note that they possess some unique characteristics worthy of recognition and response. For ex-

Table 12-1.   Comparison of Financial Audits with Project Audits

	Financial Audits	*Project Audits*
Status	Confirms status of business in relation to accepted standard	Must create basis for, and confirm, status on each project
Predictions	Company's state of economic well-being	Future status of project
Measurement	Mostly in financial terms	Financial terms plus schedule, progress, resource usage, status of ancillary goals
Record-keeping system	Format dictated by legal regulations and professional standards	No standard system, uses any system desired by individual organization or dictated by contract
Existence of information system	Minimal records needed to start audit	No records exist, data bank must be designed and used to start audit
Recommendations	Usually few or none, often restricted to management of accounting system	Often required, and may cover any aspect of the project or its management
Qualifications	Customary to qualify statements if conditions dictate, but strong managerial pressure not to do so	Qualifications focus on shortcomings of audit process (e.g., lack of technical expertise, lack of funds or time)

ample, computer-based projects are ordinarily very labor-intensive while many manufacturing projects, for instance, are highly capital intensive. A thoughtful manager will simply not adopt the same managerial approach to each. The need for and value of a participative style (TQM, EI, etc.) is well established in the case of labor-intensive projects where problems are often ill-structured. If the project is capital intensive and characterized by well-structured problems, the need for and value of a participative style is *relatively* diminished. (The reader must not read these statements as degrading the value of participative management. It is simply more valuable and relevant in some cases than others.)

To sum up, the management audit looks at managerial systems and their use. The project audit studies the financial, managerial, and technical aspects of the project as an integrated set applied to a specific project in a specific organizational environment.

Depth of the Audit

There are several practical constraints that may limit the depth of the project auditor's investigation. Time and money are two of the most common (and obvious) limits on the depth of investigation and level of detail presented in the audit report. Of course, there are costs associated with the audit/evaluation process over and above the usual costs of the professional and clerical time used in conducting the audit. Accumulation, storage, and maintenance of auditable data are important cost elements. Remember that such storage may be critically important in meeting the test of "due diligence" noted in Chapter 11. (Remember, too, that destruction of business data may be illegal under certain circumstances.)

Also serious, but less quantifiable, are two often overlooked costs. First, no matter how skilled the evaluator, an audit/evaluation process is always distracting to those working on the project. No project is completely populated with individuals whose self-esteem [defined by Ambrose Bierce (1991) as "an erroneous appraisement"] is so high that evaluation is greeted without anxiety. Worry about the outcome of the audit tends to produce an excessive level of self-protective activity, which, in turn, lowers the level of activity devoted to the project. Second, if the evaluation report is not written with a "constructive" tone, project morale will suffer.* Depending on the severity of the drop in morale, work on the project may receive a serious setback. The more difficult the technical problems of the project, the more project workers are apt to react strongly to negative criticism. Because the whole process is threatening to the auditees, the auditor should exercise care and discretion in writing the report.

It is logical to vary the depth of the investigation depending on circumstances and needs unique to each project. While an audit can be performed at any level the organization wishes, three distinct levels are easily recognized and widely used: the general audit, the detailed audit, and the technical audit. The general audit is normally most constrained by time and resources and is usually a brief review of the project, touching lightly on the six concerns noted earlier. A typical detailed audit is conducted when a follow-up to the general audit is required. This tends to occur when the general audit has disclosed an unacceptable level of risk or malperformance in some part(s) of the project. The depth of the detailed audit depends on the importance of the questionable issues and their relationship to the objectives of the project—the more serious, or potentially serious, the greater the depth.

At times, the detailed audit cannot investigate problems at a satisfactory technical level because the auditor does not possess the technical knowledge needed. In such cases, a technical audit is required. Technical audits are normally carried out by a qualified technician under the direct guidance of the project auditor. In the case of very advanced or secret technology, it may be difficult to find qualified technical auditors inside the organization. In such cases, it is not uncommon for the firm to use academic consultants who have signed the appropriate nondisclosure documents. Although not a hard and fast rule, the technical audit is usually the most detailed.

Timing of the Audit

Like audit depth, the timing of a project audit will depend on the circumstances of a particular project. Given that all projects of significant size or importance should be audited, the first audits are usually done early in the project's life. The sooner a problem is discovered, the easier it is to deal with. Early audits are often focused on the technical issues in order to make sure that key technical problems have been solved or are under competent attack. Ordinarily, audits done later in the life cycle of a project

---

*The evaluator is well advised to remember two fundamental principles: (1) Constructive criticism does not feel all that constructive to the criticizee; and (2) Fix first, then blame—if you have any energy left.

are of less immediate value to the project, but are of more value to the parent organization. As the project develops, technical issues are less likely to be matters of concern. Conformity to the schedule and budget becomes the primary interest. Management issues are major matters of interest for audits made late in the project's life (e.g., disposal of equipment or reallocation of project personnel).

Postproject audits are conducted with several basic objectives in mind. First, a postproject audit is often a legal necessity because the client specified such an audit in the contract. Second, the postproject audit is a major part of the Postproject Report, which is, in turn, the main source of managerial feedback to the parent firm. Third, the postproject audit is needed to account for all project property and expenditures.

Additional observations on the timing and value of audits are shown in Table 12–2.

12.3 CONSTRUCTION AND USE OF THE AUDIT REPORT

The type of project being audited and the uses for which the audit is intended dictate some specifics of the audit report format. Within any particular organization, however, it is useful to establish a general format to which all audit reports must conform. This makes it possible for project managers, auditors, and organizational management all to have the same understanding of, and expectations for, the audit report as a communication device. If the audit report is to serve as a communication device, there must also be a predetermined distribution list for such documents. When distribution is highly restricted, the report is almost certain to become the focus for interpersonal and intergroup conflict and tension.

While a few PMs insist on a complicated format for evaluation reports tailored to their individual projects, the simpler and more straightforward the format, the better. The information should be arranged so as to facilitate the comparison of predicted versus actual results. Significant deviations of actual from predicted results should be

Table 12–2. Timing and Value of Project Audits/Evaluations

Project Stage	Value
Initiation	Significant value if audit takes place early—prior to 25 percent completion of initial planning stage
Feasibility study	Very useful, particularly the technical audit
Preliminary plan/schedule budget	Very useful, particularly for setting measurement standards to ensure conformance with standards
Master schedule	Less useful, plan frozen, flexibility of team limited
Evaluation of data by project team	Marginally useful, team defensive about findings
Implementation	More or less useful depending on importance of project methodology to successful implementation
Postproject	More or less useful depending on applicability of findings to future projects

highlighted and explained in a set of footnotes or comments. This eases the reader's work and tends to keep questions focused on important issues rather than trivia. This arrangement also reduces the likelihood that senior managers will engage in "fishing expeditions," searching for something "wrong" in every piece of data and sentence of the report. Once again, we would remind PMs of the dictum "Never let the boss be surprised."

Negative comments about individuals or groups associated with the project should be avoided. Write the report in a clear, professional, unemotional style and restrict its content to information and issues that are relevant to the project. The following items cover the *minimum* information that should be contained in the audit report.

1. *Introduction*   This section contains a description of the project to provide a framework of understanding for the reader. Project objectives (direct goals) must be clearly delineated. If the objectives are complex, it may be useful to include explanatory parts of the project proposal as an addendum to the report.

2. *Current Status*   Status should be reported as of the time of the audit and, among other things, should include the following measures of performance:

   Cost: This section compares actual costs to budgeted costs. The time periods for which the comparisons are made should be clearly defined. As noted in Chapter 7, the report should focus on the *direct* charges made to the project. If it is also necessary to show project *total* costs, complete with all overheads, this cost data should be presented in an *additional* set of tables.

   Schedule: Performance in terms of planned events or milestones should be reported (see Figures 10-15 and 11-5 as examples). Completed portions of the project should be clearly identified, and the percent completion should be reported on all unfinished tasks for which estimates are possible.

   Progress: This section compares work completed with resources expended. Earned value charts or tables (see Figures 10-7 and 10-13) may be used for this purpose if desired, but they may lack the appropriate level of detail. The requirement here is for information that will help to pinpoint problems with specific tasks or sets of tasks. Based on this information, projections regarding the timing and amounts of remaining planned expenditures are made.

   Quality: Whether or not this is a critical issue depends on the type of project being audited. Quality is a measure of the degree to which the output of a system conforms to prespecified characteristics. For some projects, the prespecified characteristics are so loosely stated that conformity is not much of an issue. At times, a project may produce outputs that far exceed original specifications. For instance, a project might require a subsystem that meets certain minimum standards. The firm may already have produced such a subsystem—one that meets standards well in excess of the current requirements. It may be efficient, with no less effectiveness, to use the previously designed system with its excess performance. If there is a detailed quality specification associated with the project, this section of the report may have to include a full review of the quality control procedures, along with full disclosure of the results of quality tests conducted to date.

3. *Future Project Status*   This section contains the auditor's conclusions regarding progress together with recommendations for any changes in technical approach, schedule, or budget that should be made in the remaining tasks. Except in unusual circumstances, for example when results to date distinctly indicate the undersirability of some preplanned task, the auditor's report should consider only work that has already been completed or is well under way. No assumptions should be made about technical problems that are still under investigation at the time of the audit. Project audit/evaluation reports are not appropriate documents in which to rewrite the project proposal.

4. *Critical Management Issues*   All issues that the auditor feels require close monitoring by senior management should be included in this section, along with a brief explanation of the relationships between these issues and the objectives of the project. A brief discussion of time/cost/performance trade-offs will give senior management useful input information for decisions about the future of the project.

5. *Risk Management*   This section should contain a review of major risks associated with the project and their projected impact on project time/cost/performance. If alternative decisions exist that may significantly alter future risks, they can be noted at this point in the report. Once again, we note that the audit report is not the proper place to second-guess those who wrote the project proposal. The Postproject Report, on the other hand, will often contain sections on the general subject of "If only we knew then what we know now."

6. *Caveats, Limitations, and Assumptions*   This section of the report may be placed at the end or may be included as a part of the introduction. The auditor is responsible for the accuracy and timeliness of the report, but senior management still retains full responsibility for the interpretation of the report and for any action(s) based on the findings. For that reason, the auditor should specifically include a statement covering any limitations on the accuracy or validity of the report.

Responsibilities of the Project Auditor/Evaluator

First and foremost, the auditor should "tell the truth." This statement is not so simplistic as it might appear. It is a recognition of the fact that there are various levels of truth associated with any project. The auditor must approach the audit in an objective and ethical manner and assume responsibility for what is included and excluded from consideration in the report. Awareness of the biases of the several parties interested in the project—including the auditor's own biases—is essential, but extreme care is required if the auditor wishes to compensate for such biases. (A note that certain information *may* be biased is usually sufficient.) Areas of investigation outside the auditor's area of technical expertise should be acknowledged and assistance sought when necessary. The auditor/evaluator must maintain political and technical independence during the audit and treat all materials gathered as confidential until the audit is formally released.

Walker and Bracey (1980) develop an even stronger case for the "independence" of the auditor. They argue that independence is essential for management's ability to assemble information that is both timely and accurate. They also list the following steps for carrying out an audit:

- Assemble a small team of experienced experts
- Familiarize the team with the requirements of the project
- Audit the project on site
- After completion, debrief the project's management
- Produce a written report according to a prespecified format
- Distribute the report to the PM and project team for their response
- Follow up to see if the recommendations have been implemented

If senior management and the project team are to take the audit/evaluation seriously, all information must be presented in a credible manner. The accuracy of data should be carefully checked, as should all calculations. The determination of what information to include and exclude is one that cannot be taken lightly. Finally, the auditor should engage in a continuing evaluation of the auditing process in a search for ways to improve the effectiveness, efficiency, and value of the process.

Project Management in Practice
Auditing a Troubled Project at Atlantic States Chemical Laboratories

In the late 1990s, Atlantic States Chemical Laboratories (ASCL) received a contract from an entrepreneurial firm, Oretec, to conduct a unique type of chemical analysis on special alloys they had created in their own laboratories in the interest of identifying potentially successful commercial alloys. The contract emphasized quality of the effort and speed of continuing laboratory analyses. The contract duration would be open-ended with payment at the monthly rate of $100,000. The liaison officer from Oretec would have access to ASCLs laboratory work for observation.

As work progressed, the liaison officer became more involved in the project, pressuring the team to alter their approach and skip the usual repeat-verification procedures in the interest of time. On two occasions, the ASCL team devised an analysis indicating that a commercially successful product could be produced. The liaison officer was gratified with the effort and asked for

suggestions on how to produce the product commercially. However, tests at Oretec indicated that these approaches would not work. As the project mid-point passed, the pressure for more and faster analyses increased even more, with the liaison officer becoming more belligerent and difficult to please. Soon thereafter, the president of ASCL received a letter from Oretec voicing a number of complaints and terminating the contract effective immediately. Puzzled by the unexpected displeasure of their client with no indication of trouble on the project from internal sources, the president requested a comprehensive audit of the project.

The audit reported the following:

1. *Overview Points:*
   - The original approach to the project was sound but was altered by the client's liaison officer; nevertheless, significant findings were still made.

- The analyses themselves were conducted properly.
- There were several analytical successes during the project (each identified).
- Commercialization was not ASCL's responsibility but the client's, even if ASCL suggested some possible processes.
- There was excessive involvement of the liaison officer in the management of the project, including frequent changes of direction.
- Ongoing project management decisions and changes were not documented by ASCL, nor communicated to the client.

2. *Analysis of Client's Criticism* (about half of the criticisms were valid, details described)

3. *Further Points of Note:*

- The commercialization processes proposed by ASCL have, in fact, been successfully used in similar instances. The client's tests indicating their unacceptability are incorrect.

- The reports provided by ASCL and criticized by the client as incomplete were redirected by the liaison officer to be prepared quickly and informally. The reports of project analysis success would not have been understandable to the client's management, only to technical personnel or the liaison officer.
- Management gave insufficient guidance/support to the project leader in his relations with the client.

4. *Recommendation:* Establish a formal procedure for identifying high-risk projects at the contract stage and monitoring them carefully for deviations from plan. The factors contributing to making this a high-risk project were inadequate funding, insufficient time, low chance of success, an unsophisticated client, and excessive access to ongoing project activities by the client.

Source: J. Meredith, consulting project.

12.4   THE PROJECT AUDIT LIFE CYCLE

Thus far, we have considered the project audit and project evaluation as if they were one and the same. In most ways they are. The audit contains an evaluation, and an evaluator must conduct some sort of audit. Let us now consider the audit as a formal document required by contract with the client. If the client is the federal government, the nature of the project audit is more or less precisely defined, as is the audit process.

Like the project itself, the audit has a *life cycle* composed of an orderly progression of well-defined events. There are six of these events.

1. *Project Audit Initiation*   This step involves starting the audit process, defining the purpose and scope of the audit, and gathering sufficient information to determine the proper audit methodology.

2. *Project Baseline Definition*   The purpose of this phase is to establish performance standards against which the project's performance and accomplishments can be evaluated. This phase of the cycle normally consists of identifying the performance areas to be evaluated, determining standards for each area through bench-

marking or some other process, ascertaining management performance expectations for each area, and developing a program to measure and assemble the requisite information.

Occasionally, no convenient standards exist or can be determined through benchmarking. For example, a commodity pricing model was developed as part of a large marketing project. No baseline data existed that could serve to help evaluate the model. Because the commodity was sold by open bid, the firm used its standard bidding procedures. The results formed baseline data against which the pricing model could be tested on an "as if" basis. Table 12-3 shows the results of one such test. CCC is the firm and the contracts on which it bid *and won,* together with the associated revenues (mine net price × tonnage), are shown. Similar information is displayed for Model C, which was used on an "as if" basis so the Model C Revenue column shows those bids the model *would have won,* had it actually been used.

3. *Establishing an Audit Database* Once the baseline standards are established, execution of the audit begins. The next step is to create a database for use by the audit team. Depending on the purpose and scope of the audit, the database might include information needed for assessment of project organization, management and

Table 12–3.   Performance against Baseline Data

				19xx Bid Performance for Model "C"—State of _____		
		Award				
Destination	Tonnage	CCC Bid	Model "C" Bid	Mine Net Price	CCC Revenue	Model "C" Revenue
D1-2	3800		X	$4.11		$15,618
D1-7	1600		X	3.92		6,272
D2-7	1300		X	4.11		5,343
D3-2	700	X		5.13		3,591
D3-3	500	X		5.22	$2610	
D3-4	600		X	5.72		3,432
D3-5	1200		X	5.12		6,144
D3-6	1000		X	5.83		5,830
D4-6	700		X	4.88		3,416
D4-8	600		X	5.34		3,204
D5-1	500	X		3.54	1770	
D6-1	1000	X	X	4.02–3.92	4020	3,920
D6-2	900	X		4.35	3915	
D6-5	200	X		3.75	750	
D6-6	800		X	3.17		2,536
D7-5	1600		X	5.12		8,192
D7-8	2600		X	5.29		13,754
D8-2	1600	X	X	4.83	7728	7,728
D8-3	2400		X	4.32		10,368
				Total revenue	$20,793	$99,348
				Total tonnage	4700	21,500
				Average mine net	$4.42	$4.62

control, past and current project status, schedule performance, cost performance, and output quality, as well as plans for the future of the project. The information may vary from a highly technical description of performance to a behaviorally based description of the interaction of project team members.

Because the purpose and scope of audits vary widely from one project to another and for different times on any given project, the audit database is frequently quite extensive. The required database for project audits should be specified in the project master plan. If this is done, the necessary information will be available when needed. Nonetheless, it is important to avoid collecting "anything that might be useful," since this can place extraordinary information collection and storage requirements on the project.

4. *Preliminary Analysis of the Project*   After standards are set and data collected, judgments are made. Some auditors eschew judgment on the grounds that such a delicate but weighty responsibility must be reserved to senior management. But judgment often requires a fairly sophisticated understanding of the technical aspects of the project, and/or of statistics and probability, subjects that may elude some managers. In such an event, the auditor must analyze the data and then present the analysis to managers in ways that communicate the real meaning of the audit's findings. It is the auditor's duty to brief the PM on all findings and judgments *before* releasing the audit report. The purpose of the audit is to improve the project being audited as well as to improve the entire process of managing projects. It is not intended as a device to embarrass the PM.

5. *Audit Report Preparation*   This part of the audit life cycle includes the preparation of the audit report, organized by whatever format has been selected for use. A set of recommendations, together with a plan for implementing them, is also a part of the audit report. If the recommendations go beyond normal practices of the organization, they will need support from the policy-making level of management. This support should be sought and verified *before* the recommendations are published. If support is not forthcoming, the recommendations should be modified until satisfactory. Figure 12-1 is one page of an extensive and detailed set of recommendations that resulted from an evaluation project conducted by a private social service agency.

6. *Project Audit Termination*   As with the project itself, after the audit has accomplished its designated task, the audit process should be terminated. When the final report and recommendations are released, there will be a review of the audit process. This is done in order to improve the methods for conducting the audit. When the review is finished, the audit is truly complete and the audit team should be formally disbanded.

12.5   SOME ESSENTIALS OF AN AUDIT/EVALUATION

For an audit/evaluation (hereinafter, simply a/e) to be conducted with skill and precision, for it to be credible and generally acceptable to senior management, to the project team, and to the client, several essential conditions must be met. The a/e team

Final Report, Agency Evaluation, Sub-Committee II
Physical Plant, Management of Office, Personnel Practices

Summary of Recommendations

Recommendations which require Board action.

1. The Board of _____ should continue its efforts to obtain additional funds for our salary item.

2. The cost of Blue Cross and Blue Shield insurance coverage on individual employees should be borne by _____.

Recommendations which can be put into effect by *Presidential Order* to committees, staff, or others.

3. The House Committee should activate, with first priority, the replacement of the heating/air conditioning system. Further, this committee should give assistance and support to the Secretary to the Executive Director in maintenance and repair procedures.

4. A professional library should be established even if part time workers must share space to accomplish this.

5. Our insurance needs should be re-evaluated.

6. All activities related to food at meetings should be delegated to someone other than the Secretary to the Executive Director.

7. Majority opinion—position of Administrative Assistant and Bookkeeper will need more time in the future.
   Minority opinion—positions of Administrative Assistant, Bookkeeper, and Statistical Assistant should be combined.

8. The Personnel Practices Committee should review job descriptions of Bookkeeper and Statistical Assistant and establish salary ranges for those two positions and that of the Administrative Assistant.

9. Dialogue between the Executive Director, his secretary, and the Administrative Assistant should continue in an effort to streamline office procedures and expedite handling of paperwork.

10. The written description of the Personnel Practices Committee should include membership of a representative of the nonprofessional staff.

11. The Personnel Practices Committee should study, with a view toward action, the practice of part-time vs. full-time casework staff.

Figure 12–1   Sample recommendations for a social service agency.

must be properly selected, all records and files must be accessible, and free contact with project members must be preserved.

The A/E Team

The choice of the a/e team is critical to the success of the entire process. It may seem unnecessary to note that team members should be selected because of their ability to contribute to the a/e procedure, but sometimes members are selected merely because they are available. The size of the team will generally be a function of the size and complexity of the project. For a small project, one person can often handle all the tasks of an a/e audit, but for a large project, the team may require representatives from several different constituencies. Typical areas that might furnish a/e team members are:

- The project itself
- The accounting/controller department
- Technical specialty areas
- The customer
- The marketing department
- Senior management
- Purchasing/asset management
- The personnel department
- The legal/contract administration department

The main role of the a/e team is to conduct a thorough and complete examination of the project or some prespecified aspect of the project. The team must determine which items should be brought to management's attention. It should report information and make recommendations in such a way as to maximize the utility of its work. The team is responsible for constructive observations and advice based on the training and experience of its members. Members must be aloof from personal involvement with conflicts among project team staff and from rivalries between projects. The a/e is a highly disciplined process, and all team members must willingly and sincerely subject themselves to that discipline.

Access to Records

In order for the a/e team to be effective, it must have free access to all information relevant to the project. This may present some problems on government projects that may be classified for reasons of national security. In such cases, a subgroup of the a/e team may be formed from qualified ("cleared") individuals.

Most of the information needed for an a/e will come from the project team's records and those of the Project Office, and/or from various departments such as accounting, personnel, and purchasing. Obviously, gathering the data is the responsibility of the a/e team, and this burden should not be passed on to the project management team, though the project team is responsible for collecting the usual data on the project and keeping project records up to date during the project's life.

In addition to the formal records of the project, some of the most valuable information comes from documents that predate the project—for example, correspondence with the customer that led to the RFP, minutes of the Project Selection Committee, and minutes of senior management committees that decided to pursue a specific area of technical interest. Clearly, project status reports, relevant technical memoranda, change orders, information about project organization and management methods, and financial and resource usage information are also important. The a/e team may have to extract much of these data from other documents because the required information is often not in the form needed. Data collection is time-consuming, but careful work is absolutely necessary for an effective, credible a/e.

As information is collected, it must be organized and filed in a systematic way. Systematic methods need to be developed for separating out useful information. Most important, stopping rules are needed to prevent data collection and processing from continuing far past the point of diminishing returns. Priorities must be set to ensure that important analyses are undertaken before those of lesser import. Also, safeguards are needed against duplication of efforts. The careful development of forms and procedures will help to standardize the process as much as possible.

Access to Project Personnel and Others

Contact between a/e team members and project team members, or between the a/e team and other members of the organization who have knowledge of the project, should be free. One exception is contact between the a/e team and the customer; such contacts are *not made without clearance* from senior management. This restriction would hold even when the customer is represented on the audit team, and should also hold for in-house clients.

In any case, there are several rules that should be followed when contacting project personnel. Care must be taken to avoid misunderstandings between a/e team members and project team members. Project personnel should always be made aware of the in-progress a/e. Critical comments should be avoided. Particularly serious is the practice of delivering on-the-spot, off-the-cuff opinions and remarks that may not be appropriate or represent the consensus opinion of the a/e team.

The a/e team will undoubtedly encounter political opposition during its work. If the project is a subject of political tension, attempts will most certainly be made by the opposing sides to co-opt (or repudiate) the a/e team. As much as possible, they should avoid becoming involved. At times, information may be given to a/e team members in confidence. Discreet attempts should be made to confirm such information through nonconfidential sources. If it cannot be confirmed, it should not be used. The auditor/evaluator must protect the sources of confidential information and must not become a conduit for unverifiable criticism of the project.

12.6   MEASUREMENT

Measurement is an integral part of the a/e process. Many issues of what and how to measure have been discussed in earlier chapters, particularly in Chapter 2. Several aspects of a project that should be measured are obvious and, fortunately, rather easy to measure. For the most part, it is not difficult to know if and when a milestone has been completed. We can directly observe the fact that a building foundation has been poured, that all required materials for a corporate annual report have been collected and delivered to the printer, that all contracts have been let for the rehabilitation of an apartment complex, that the navigation instruments for a new fighter aircraft have been tested, or that all case workers have been trained in the new case management techniques. At times, of course, milestone completion may not be quite so evident. It may be difficult to tell when a chemical experiment is finished, and it is almost impossible to tell when a complex computer program is finally "bug free." Largely, however, milestone completion can be measured adequately.

Similarly, performance against planned budget and schedule usually poses no major measurement problems. We may be a bit uncertain whether or not a "nine-day" scheduled completion time should include weekend days, but most organizations adopt conventions to ease these minor counting problems. Measuring the actual expenditures against the planned budget is a bit trickier and depends on an in-depth understanding of the procedures used by the accounting department. It is common to imbue cost data with higher levels of reality and precision than is warranted. Still, while there may be some unique difficulties raised when we attempt to measure the time/cost/performance dimensions of a project, these problems are usually tractable.

When the objectives of a project have been stated in terms of profits, rates of return, or discounted cash flows, as in the financial selection models discussed in Chapter 2, measurement problems may be more obstinate. The problem does not often revolve around the accounting conventions used, though if those conventions have not been clearly established in advance there may be bitter arguments about what costs are appropriately assigned to the individual project being evaluated. A far more difficult task is the determination of what revenues should be assigned to the project.

Assume, for example, that a drug firm creates a project for the development of a new drug and simultaneously sets up a project to develop and implement a marketing strategy for the potential new drug and two existing allied drugs. Assume further that the entire program is successful and large amounts of revenue are generated. How much revenue should be assigned to the credit of the drug research project? How much to the marketing project? Within the marketing project, how much should go to each of the subprojects for the individual drugs? If the entire program is treated as one project, the problem is less serious; but R & D and marketing are in different functional areas of the parent organization, and each may be evaluated on the basis of its contribution to the parent firm's profitability. The year-end bonuses of divisional managers are determined in part (often in large part) by the profitability of the units they manage. Figure 12-2 illustrates project baseline data established for a new product. This figure shows the use of multiple measures including price, unit sales, market share, development costs, capital expenditures, and other measures of performance.

There is no theoretically acceptable solution to such measurement problems, but there are politically acceptable solutions. All the cost/revenue allocation decisions must be made when the various projects are initiated. If this is done, the battles are fought "up front," and the equity of cost/revenue allocations ceases to be so serious an issue. As long as allocations are made by a formula, major conflict is avoided—or, at least, mitigated.

If multiobjective scoring models rather than financial models are being used for project selection, measurement problems are somewhat exacerbated. There are more elements to measure, some of which are objective and measured with relative ease. But some elements are subjective and require reasonably standard measurement techniques if the measures are to be reliable. Interview and questionnaire methods for gathering data must be carefully constructed and carried out if the project scores are

PRODUCT _____   DATE _____

MARKET _____

DATE OF FIRST SALE: U.S. _____

O.U.S. _____

	1ST YEAR			2ND YEAR			3RD YEAR			4TH YEAR			5TH YEAR			TOTAL		
	MIN	B.E.*	MAX	MIN	B.E.	MAX	MIN	B.E.	MAX	MIN	B.E.	MAX	MIN	B.E.	MAX	MIN	B.E.	MAX
1. Total Market Size:																		
2. Expected Market Share:																		
3. Kg. or Units:																		
4. Est. Selling Price:																		
5. Gross Sales:																		
6. Est. COPS %:																		
7. Gross Margin %:																		
8. Est. Marketing Expense %:																		
9. Marketing Margin %:																		
10. Loss on Profit from other Products List:																		
11. Est. Profit:																		
12. Development Expenses:																		
13. Capital Expenditures:																		

*Best estimate.

Figure 12–2   Baseline marketing data for a new product.

to be taken seriously. Criteria weights and scoring procedures should be decided at the start of the project.

A Note to the Auditor/Evaluator

A kindly critic and colleague uses what he calls the "rules of engagement" to explain to his students how to schedule interviews, conduct interviews, get copies, limit the scope of activities, and handle the many mundane tasks included in auditing/evaluating projects. While the phrase "rules of engagement" seems a bit warlike to us, we do have some similar advice for the auditor/evaluator.

Above all else, the a/e needs "permission to enter the system." It is difficult to describe precisely what is meant by that phrase, but every experienced auditor or evaluator will know. Senior management can assign an individual to the job of heading an audit/evaluation team, but this does not automatically imply that project personnel will accept that person as a legitimate a/e. There will be several indicators if the a/e is not accepted. Phone calls from the a/e will be returned only at times when the a/e is not available. Requests for information will be politely accepted, but little or no information will be forthcoming—though copious, sincere apologies and semi-believable excuses will be. Interviews with project team members will be strangely contentless. Attempts to determine the project's ancillary goals will be unavailing, as will attempts to get team members to discuss intrateam conflict. Everyone will be quite pleasant, but somehow promises of cooperation do not turn into fact. Always, there are good excuses and looks of wide-eyed innocence.

If the a/e is reasonably likable and maintains a calm, relaxed attitude, the project team generally begins to extend limited trust. The usual first step is to allow the a/e qualified access to information about the project. Missing information from the official project files is suddenly found. The a/e has then been given tentative permission to enter the system. If the a/e deals gently with this information, neither ignoring nor stressing the project's shortcomings while recognizing and appreciating the project's strengths, trust will be extended, and the permission to enter the system will no longer be tentative.

Trust-building is a slow and delicate process that is easily thwarted. The a/e needs to understand the politics of the project team and the interpersonal relationships among its members, and must deal with this confidential knowledge respectfully. On this base is trust built and meaningful audit/evaluation constructed. There is an almost universal propensity for the a/e to mimic Jack Webb's Sgt. Friday on the old Dragnet TV show—"Just give me the facts, ma'am." It is not that simple, nor are any processes involving human beings that simple.

SUMMARY

This chapter initiated our discussion of the final part of the text, project termination. A major concluding step in the termination process is the evaluation of the project process and results, otherwise known as an audit. Here we looked at the purposes of evaluation and what it should encompass: the audit process and measurement considerations, the demands placed on the auditor, and the construction and design of the final report.

Specific points made in the chapter were these:

- The purposes of the evaluation are both goal-directed, aiding the project in achieving its objectives, and also aimed at achieving unspecified, sometimes hidden, yet firmly held, ancillary objectives.

- The audit report should contain at least the current status of the project, the expected future status, the status of crucial tasks, a risk assessment, information pertinent to other projects, and any caveats and limitations.

- Audit depth and timing are critical elements of the audit because, for example, it is much more difficult to alter the project based on a late audit than an early audit.

- The difficult responsibility of the auditor is to be honest in fairly presenting the audit results. This may even require data interpretation on occasion.

- The audit life cycle includes audit initiation, project baseline definition, establishing a database, preliminary project analysis, report preparation, and termination.

- Several essential conditions must be met for a credible audit: a credible a/e team, sufficient access to records, and sufficient access to personnel.

- Measurement, particularly of revenues, is a special problem.

In the next chapter, we move into the final state of the project management process, termination. There we will look at when to terminate a project and the various ways to conduct the termination.

GLOSSARY

Audit   A formal inquiry into some issue or aspect of a system.
Baseline   A standard for performance, commonly established early on for later comparisons.

Evaluate   To set a value for or appraise.
Risk Analysis   An evaluation of the likely outcomes of a policy and their probability of occurrence, usually conducted to compare two or more scenarios or policies.

QUESTIONS

Material Review Questions

1. Give some examples of ancillary project objectives.

2. When should an audit be conducted during a project? Is there a "best" time?

3. What occurs in each stage of the audit life cycle?

4. What items should be included in the audit status report?

5. What access is required for an accurate audit?

6. Why is measurement a particular problem in auditing?

7. What is a "baseline"?

8. What is the purpose of a risk analysis?

9. What are the essential conditions of a credible audit?

Class Discussion Questions

10. In a typical project, do you feel frequent brief evaluations or periodic major evaluations are better in establishing control? Why?

11. Do you think that project evaluations cost-justify themselves?

12. What steps can be taken to ease the perceived threat to team members of an external evaluation?

13. What feedback, if any, should the project team get from the evaluation?

14. During the project audit, a tremendous amount of time can be wasted if a systematic method of information handling is not adopted. Briefly explain how this systematic method may be developed.

15. "Evaluation of a project is another means of project control." Comment.

16. Why is it better to rely on several sources of information than just a few?

17. What could be some advantages and disadvantages of the following sources of information: (a) charts, (b) written reports, and (c) firsthand observation?

18. Why is it important to use outside auditors rather than inside auditors who would be more familiar with the company and the project?

19. What kinds of reports might be sent to customers?

20. What would you identify as the ethical responsibilities of an auditor?

Questions for Project Management in Practice

Lessons from Auditing 110 Client/Server and Open Systems Projects

21. Which of the four concepts is the most important, in your opinion?

22. Elaborate on item 3.

23. What lessons might you have expected that aren't included?

Auditing a Troubled Project at Atlantic States Chemical Laboratories

24. Was this a good use of the audit concept?

25. What was the major problem in this project?

26. In spite of the recommendation, ASCL had already had a "problem project" list and system in place. Why do you think it may not have caught this particular project? Will the new procedure do any better?

 INCIDENTS FOR DISCUSSION

Gerkin Pension Services

Dana Lasket was the project manager of a project with the objective of determining the feasibility of moving a significant portion of Gerkin's computing capacity to another geographical location. Project completion was scheduled for 28 weeks. Dana had the project team motivated, and at the end of the twentieth week the project was on schedule.

The next week, during a casual lunch conversation, Dana discovered that the vice-president of finance had serious doubts about the validity of the assumptions the team was using to decide which computers should be relocated.

Dana tried to convince him that he was wrong during two follow-up meetings, with no success. In fact, the more they talked, the more convinced the vice-president became that Dana was wrong. The project was too far along to change any assumptions without causing significant delays. In addition, the vice-president was likely to inherit the responsibility for implementing any approved plans for the new location. For those reasons, Dana felt it was essential to resolve the disagreement before the scheduled completion of the project. Dana requested a project auditor be assigned to audit the project, paying special attention to the as-sumptions made to identify the computers to be moved.

Questions: Is this a good use of the audit technique? Will it be helpful here? Why or why not?

General Ship Building Company

General Ship Building has a contract with the Department of the Navy to build three new aircraft carriers over the next five years. During the construction of the first ship, the project manager formed an auditing team to audit the construction process for the three ships. After picking the audit team members, he requested that they develop a set of minimum requirements for the projects and use this as a baseline in the audit. While reviewing the contract documents, an auditing team member discovered a discrepancy between the contract minimum requirements and the Navy's minimum requirements. Based on his findings, he has told the project manager that he has decided to contact the local Navy contract office and inform them of the problem.

Questions: If you were the project manager, how would you handle this situation? How can a customer be assured of satisfactory contract completion?

 BIBLIOGRAPHY

BALACHANDRA, R., and J. A. RAELIN. "How to Decide When to Abandon A Project." *Research Management*, July 1980.

BIERCE, A. *The Devil's Dictionary.* New York: Dell Publishing, 1991.

CORBIN, D., R. COX, R. HAMERLY, AND K. KNIGHT. "Project Management of Project Reviews," *PM Network*, March 2001.

DEVAUX, S. A. "When the DIPP Dips: A P&L Index for Project Decisions." *Project Management Journal,* September 1992.

FREEMAN, M., and P. BEALE. "Measuring Project Success." *Project Management Journal,* March 1992.

JACKSON, B. "Decision Methods for Evaluating R& D Projects." *Research Management,* June–August 1983.

KERZNER, H. "Evaluation Techniques in Project Management." *Journal of Systems Management,* February 1980.

MEYERS, W. R. T*he Evaluation Enterprise.* San Francisco: Jossey-Bass, 1981.

NEWTON, J. K. "Computer Modeling for Project Evaluation." *Omega,* May 1981.

RUSKIN, A. M., and W. E. ESTES. "The Project Management Audit: Its Role and Conduct." *Project Management Journal,* August 1985.

SANGAMESWARAN, A. "A Key to Effective Independent Project Reviews." *PM Network,* April 1995.

SCHAEFER, A. G., and A. J. ZALLER. "The Ethics Audit for Nonprofit Organizations." *PM Network,* April 1998.

SHENHAR, A. J., O. LEVY, and D. DVIR. "Mapping the Dimensions of Project Success." *Project Management Journal,* June 1997.

STUCKENBRUCK, L. C., and C. L. MYERS. "Project Evaluation." *A Special Summer Issue of the Project Management Journal,* August 1985.

TURNER, W. S., III. *Project Auditing Methodology.* Amsterdam: North Holland, 1980.

WALKER, M. G., and R. BRACEY. "Independent Auditing As Project Control." *Datamation,* March 1980.

The following reading shows that project audits and evaluations help further knowledge concerning good project practice and improving the understanding of those in the organization about neighboring functions. However, most current audits/evaluations appear to be shallow, based on naive assumptions, and remedies for project difficulties tend to be superficial. Yet audits and evaluations were important learning experiences and are undervalued in organizations in terms of the insights they can provide about good project management.

R E A D I N G

AN ASSESSMENT OF POSTPROJECT REVIEWS*
J. S. Busby

Potential Benefits.   Many organizations set out to do postproject reviews, and for some compelling reasons:

- People do not automatically learn from their own experience, even as isolated individuals. They have to test new experiences against their existing knowledge and revise that knowledge in order to learn. A good example is learning about

people. You can encounter a person on several occasions, but you do not learn from these occasions in any profound sense until you make a decision about the person (Eraut, 1994). It is at this point that you assemble the different experiences you have had and draw some coherent conclusions. The upshot is that, if you want to learn from experience, you consciously have to reflect on it.

- The knowledge of what occurred is usually dispersed among several people. We do many things, especially in organizations, where outcomes are not directly observable. (We might not know, for instance, how readily users of our new product design adapt to the demands made on them.) Therefore, we need to consult other people to know the outcomes of our performance.

- The knowledge needed to diagnose outcomes is similarly dispersed among several people. For instance, people commonly make wrong assumptions about why others fail in their duties, and these misconceptions need to be corrected if reasonable remedies are to be identified for such failings. So, again, if we want to learn from experience, we must do so collectively.

- Dissemination matters, often critically. Organizations are rarely so specialized that every task of type *X* always goes to individual *A*. Some organizations seem to arrange things in such a way that tasks always go to the people least qualified to do them. Therefore, what one person learns from doing a project needs to be disseminated to others who might fill similar roles in the future. And, of course, this dissemination does not happen as a matter of course. Repeated errors are a characteristic of organizational life. Learning from experience within an organization has to be a public, recorded activity.

In some organizations, retrospective reviews are a natural and integral part of their operations; these include organizations that are highly regarded, such as military air forces (Lipshitz, Popper, & Oz, 1996).

Potential Drawbacks. The reality is, however, that postproject reviews are often curtailed and sometimes fall into complete disuse. Even when they are enthusiastically conducted, their outcomes are poorly disseminated. The reasons for this neglect include:

- They take time. This is especially a problem in project-oriented firms since project managers want to minimize costs allocated to their projects (particularly toward the end), and the beneficiaries of postproject reviews are future projects, not current ones.

- Reviews involve looking back over events that project participants are likely to feel cynical or embarrassed about. Looking forward to new work is more appealing.

- Maintaining social relationships typically matters more to most people than accurate diagnoses of isolated events. People can be reluctant to engage in activity that might lead to blame, criticism or recrimination (Argyris, 1977).

- Many people think that experience is a necessary and sufficient teacher in its own right. According to this point of view, if you have an experience you will necessarily learn from it, and if you have not had the experience you will not learn from someone else who has. We tried to suggest above this is not so, but many people believe it is and are predisposed against postproject reviews.

So the question is, given cogent reasons on both sides, should we conduct postproject reviews? And how should we conduct them?

The Study

Four postproject review meetings were studied in three companies. All the projects involved in the study had values of several hundred thousand to a few million dollars, and all involved extensive engineering design and development activity. All three companies supplied capital equipment to industrial users, although they came from different sectors: one in electrical equipment, one in a coating plant, and one in precision product machinery. One of the companies had a policy of always running postproject reviews, but the other two did so only intermittently.

Discourse analyses of the postproject review meetings were performed (Stubbs, 1983). This kind of analysis involves a detailed inspection of what took place in the meetings. It means dividing up the transcripts into small speech units—typically sentences—and working out the structure of the conversation that these sentences comprise in general rather than particular terms. The advantage of discourse analysis is that it gives a detailed and comprehensive picture of what actually takes place, and generates fairly clear evidence for any conclusions you draw. The drawback is that it is very time-consuming and one cannot cover very many situations. Therefore, the observations we discuss later in the paper are based on clear evidence, but we cannot claim you would see the same thing in postproject reviews in other organizations.

How Did People Learn?

The first thing of interest was how people, collectively, went about learning from project reviews.

Dialectic Argument. First, the participants commonly resorted to a dialectic form of argument. One person would voice an explanation of something, another would come back with a contradictory explanation, and someone would find a third explanation that incorporated both the previous ones, i.e., a case of thesis, antithesis, and synthesis. For instance, in one case the participants were trying to explain why a handover meeting had been missed. One person thought another party had simply ignored a request to participate, the other party argued that it had received inadequate notice of the meeting, and the synthesis was simply that the two parties had insufficient knowledge of the others' time constraints. This kind of argument reflects the common fact that there are several sides to an event, and no one person alone has enough information to consider all sides of the argument. One person can argue one case, another can argue the opposite, and the meeting can reach a conclusion about where the best explanation lies.

Event Rehearsal. Second, a lot of mental rehearsal, or replay, of event sequences occurred. For example, a common case involved participants recalling their interactions with clients about successive changes to design requirements. This kind of replay is a natural process because one of the tests of whether A caused B is whether it preceded it, and building up a picture of event sequences therefore helps us infer why things happened the way they did. That said, there are two caveats. The first is that, despite the importance of time and deadlines during the projects, the review participants verbally rehearsed event sequences but did not put times against those events. (There were a couple of exceptions to this.) And second, precedence is only a partial indication of causality and people are susceptible to inferring causality when none exists (Tversky & Kahneman, 1982).

Mental Simulation. The third thing that was observed was that a kind of mental simulation was very common. This simulation almost always took the form of working out what would have happened had people's practices been different. For instance, in one case, the review participants reasoned about how the outcome would have been different had they used a different supplier. This kind of simulation used the informal, mental models that the participants had about how one event caused another. So, in the case of reasoning about the use of a different supplier, one participant would make a statement about how using the alternative supplier would have meant a greater need for coor-

dinating effort. And another participant then argued that this would have led to a missed deadline since there were no available staff to provide this effort.

Simulation is somewhat similar to replay, except that it involved hypothetical events rather than actual ones. The extent of this simulation is significant in several ways. For a start, working forward from doing something to its result, called *causal reasoning,* is something we know that people instinctively prefer to the opposite, *diagnostic reasoning* (Tversky & Kahneman, 1982). Diagnostic reasoning involves working back from some result to the action that caused it. People generally have less facility with diagnostic reasoning than with causal reasoning. Causal reasoning can also be more acceptable socially because it avoids the question of who did what, concentrating instead on what would happen if someone did something else. The result of this, unfortunately, is a lack of deep diagnosis. Instead of tracing back the chain, or network, of causes and effects, people jump to possible remedies and work forward to simulate their results.

It would be wrong to paint simulation as a wholly misguided strategy, however. In particular, there is a side-benefit, in that it can help you learn from very few examples. If you have very small numbers of experiences from which to reason, maybe just one, it is hard to draw dependable conclusions. By simulating what would have happened had things been a little different you can effectively broaden the sample of experiences from which to draw conclusions (March, Sproull, & Tamuz, 1991).

Review Structure. The reviews that were observed differed in their general structure. In the two firms for which reviews were new, the structure of the review matched the structure of the project. The chairmen divided up the project into roughly chronological stages, asked people to say how successful the outcomes were, and encouraged them to work out why the less successful ones turned out so. In the firm that had had experience with running reviews, the chairman asked people to compile individual lists of good and bad things they had observed about the project, and then encouraged the participants to group these under a set of common headings. This structure had been adopted because the organization had found with the chronological approach that the reviews lasted too long. In our observations, the discussion processes that took place, and the effectiveness of the reviews, seemed to be unrelated to the overall structure. The successes and failings seemed to be common to the different structures. It was also observed that the intended structure of the reviews was easily sidetracked. Events are so densely interconnected that participants often had to move from one topic to another to reconstruct what happened because they realized in examining the first topic that another was more important.

The one characteristic that differentiated the reviews, in a way that seemed to matter, was the presence of outsiders. The chairman of one review had invited managers of new projects to attend the review, which was an important way of disseminating the results. There was no apparent evidence that the presence of outsiders inhibited the working of the review, but it did mean that the outsiders obtained quite a profound understanding of what had succeeded and failed on the project under review. They not only saw the headlines but also saw the reasoning that led up to the review's conclusions and got a sense of the context in which the project had taken place. Such a sense of context is usually vital in gaining a meaningful understanding of how things succeed or fail.

Historical References.   Our next observation is concerned with how review participants referred to history. In principle, historical references should be central to the diagnostic process. You cannot know whether an event on a single project (like an earthquake or a bankruptcy) is unique, frequent or systemic unless you examine other completed projects. In fact, there were few historical references; only six were made in 12 hours of review meetings. Those that there were had three different functions:

1. Using historical events as evidence for some explanation of events.
2. Demonstrating that there had been some change in the firm by contrasting recent events with historical ones.
3. Explaining people's behavior. (For example, people historically had become used to working in a particular way and carried on working in that way even when it became less appropriate.)

There were *no* historical references that simply helped people understand whether events on the project being reviewed were systemic. You could therefore argue that, as a means of learning from a specific experience, the postproject reviews failed to draw effectively on broader experience.

What Did People Learn?

As might be expected, some of the learning that took place involved disseminating knowledge of both successful and unsuccessful practices. For example, in one review, the project managers of new projects were able to hear about the consequences of having a single individual exercising both technical and managerial roles. It was evidently a poor practice. It is impossible to know, of course, if these managers of new projects would actually reproduce those practices in similar circumstances. So we can only say that there has been dissemination of what is called "propositional" knowledge, knowledge that, essentially, you can articulate but not necessarily practice.

Some of the knowledge that was learned was not so much task knowledge as knowledge that helped social relationships. For example, people would find out how hard others' jobs were, understand how severe were the constraints others operated under, and how hard it could be for others to be helpful. Knowing other people's points of view is an important kind of knowledge for effective members of organizations, and evidently it is not always learned during normal working activity.

Another important kind of knowledge was complexity. For example, there were several instances where individual participants had thought they had known why some event had happened, but in the reviews found out the explanation was far more clouded. The case of a late handover meeting illustrated this: everyone had had different ideas about why it had been late, but all turned out to be oversimplified. Individuals had each attributed the delay to a single cause, whereas the reality turned out to be a complex combination of several causes. Although this kind of learning, or really *unlearning,* is as good as any other, people feel less happy about it. It makes their models of their world less definite and more complicated. And it usually means that, contrary to what they might have thought, many problems do not have straightforward remedies.

How Well Did People Learn?

The next question addressed in the analysis was how well the learning process went in the reviews. Although it might seem unfair to do so, our approach was to look for flaws and limitations in the reasoning process that took place. It is unfair in that it might wrongly give the impression that the general level of learning was poor. We did it because it is easier to identify problems than successes. It also gives clues to how the reviews can be improved.

Attribution Problems. First, the reviews demonstrated *attribution bias.* One manifestation of attribution bias is that the participants in a process tend to overemphasize the role of the environment and underemphasize their own involvement when explaining results. You could expect review meetings to tend to blame factors beyond the participants' control and parties not represented at the reviews for problems during the project. Our observations indicated a strong tendency to explain problems by referring to other parties. On only two occasions did an individual admit an error or a need to change a way of working. This said, occasionally a participant would say something like "Okay, the customer was the problem, but was there anything *we* could have done?" It is characteristic of most successful individuals and firms to have an "internal locus of control"; that is, to believe that events are within their control, for then they devote effort to exerting control. It is therefore important to ask what could have been done to remedy a problem, even if you believe it had external causes.

Excessive Concreteness. It is hard to provide objective evidence but the analysis at least suggested that review participants were too narrowly specific in their diagnoses. For instance, locating a piece of equipment in a place where it was hard to install and maintain was diagnosed as a slip. No attempt was made to determine whether it reflected a more general difficulty with visualizing installation and maintenance problems during equipment design. Too much specificity means missing bigger problems, tackling intermediate rather than basic causes, and implementing remedies that are too elaborate. There were very few examples of generalization during the review—very few occasions when participants asked something like "Is this a case of a bigger problem?" or "Are we missing something bigger?"

Overall, review participants were therefore too concrete in their diagnoses. The inevitable result is strictly *incremental learning:* learning by small revisions to current knowledge rather than wholesale replacements of it. The result of persistently incremental learning is an inability to react to large changes in the environment. We had no indication that any of the firms currently faced such large changes, but most organizations face them at some time and becoming habituated to in-

cremental learning means they will be ill-placed to cope with large changes.

Shallow Diagnosis. Another characteristic of the reviews was an absence of deep diagnosis. It was mentioned in the previous section that the participants preferred causal reasoning (reasoning forward from cause to effect) to diagnostic reasoning (effect to cause). They were also very reluctant to ask others for diagnoses. No one, during the course of the reviews, asked a diagnostic "why"; they only asked clarifying "whys," as in "why was it poor?" meaning "in what way was it poor?" rather than "what were the causes of it being poor?" The explanation in the last section for the absence of diagnosis was cognitive, involving the preferred styles with which individuals reason. One could probably add social convention. Participants could well have been reluctant to ask others why they had done something because they were reluctant to sour their relationships with them. Sacrificing the truth about a single event that is now beyond correction may be necessary in order to maintain good relationships with a person you might have to work with in the future.

Organizations like the ones studied here also strongly promote the norm of being constructive: managers prefer people who "come to them with solutions, not problems," and it is virtually an automatic response when asked about the value of criticism to say it is important "provided it is constructive." This norm means that people will draw back from exploring the causation behind a problem unless they know they can provide a solution; not so much because they are intrinsically reluctant to criticize but because they know it does not look good to others in the organization to criticize gratuitously.

Lack of Data. A further issue that emerged from the analysis was the lack of reference to objective outcome data, especially costs and time scales that would not have been hard to collect from the firms' records. In some cases participants spent much time trying to recall when things in fact happened. In other cases, there was obvious uncertainty about how well the project had performed financially. Both conditions could have been answered easily by a little research into the record. Given that these outcomes are so central to most people's ideas about project success, it could be argued that such outcomes should be central to the review process. There *was* one occasion in which costs were available and were an important part of the review. This involved remediation costs: that is, the costs needed to put right errors or problems in preceding parts of the project. Even there, though, the figures were not clear-cut because the accounting basis that underlay them was unknown to the participants. In one sense, accounting conventions are irrelevant to diagnoses of project problems, but, when one does not know what they are, it is hard to know how big were the problems one actually encountered.

In fact, far more references were made during the reviews to practices than to outcomes. Instead of examining how far, say, costs deviated from budget and working out why, most of the time people examined how they worked and whether they could have done better. This seems to be putting the cart before the horse, and one could put this down to the mainly technical participants showing too little concern with business matters. But there are reasons to be concerned more with practices than outcomes. First, outcomes such as financial performance are determined jointly by project members' activities and the environment they work in. This means that poor financial performance does not necessarily indicate poor practices. It also means that the thing project members have most direct control over is their practices, not project outcomes. Thus, they have a natural incentive to examine practices rather than outcomes. Second, global outcomes of complex undertakings like projects generally provide poor feedback when they are composed of many different kinds of activities. It is like trying to learn a complex skill such as driving by being told only how long your complete journey took. For the review participants, project costs and timings were not especially helpful indicators of how well they performed their tasks (even if they are obviously informative to senior project managers).

Interpretation Errors. Even when outcomes were referred to, people sometimes appeared to make interpretation errors. For instance, in one case it turned out that the siting of a piece of equipment was poor because it made maintenance of the equipment difficult. The equipment was small, of low value, and needed relatively little maintenance, so the problem was dismissed as being very minor and led to no further discussion. We would say, however, that this easy dismissal makes the error of assuming that minor outcomes reflect minor causes. The question of maintainability is important for customers in industrial plant industries, sometimes critical. This interpretative error suggested that the organiza-

tion's engineers had too little awareness of the issue, perhaps through a lack of training, a lack of formal process, or a lack of knowledge transfer among different engineers. None of this was explored. Naturally, organizations with limited time and resources pay most attention to big outcomes, not small ones. The danger of doing so in an unthinking way is that one misses big issues simply because, on isolated occasions, they happen not to have big outcomes. However, later the outcome might be major and adverse; good learning stimulated by a minor adverse outcome could pay big dividends in the future.

How Worthwhile Was It?

After the reviews had taken place, participants were interviewed, for about 10 minutes each, and the researcher spoke informally to members of the other reviews immediately after they had finished. None of the participants dismissed them as worthless, but none gave the reviews unqualified support. There was skepticism in particular about any prospect that the reviews would actually make a difference. Part of this skepticism undoubtedly lay in people's cynicism about organizations, conditioned by long experience of managerial activities that led to no obvious improvement. But part of it lay in the unconvincing nature of the remedies that were explored in the reviews. Two of the reviews were distinctly hurried toward the end, so remedies received only superficial treatment. Yet, even in the others, remedies were not analyzed, only proposed and briefly contested. Side-effects were not explored and implementation was not planned. At best, there was only an acknowledgment in one of the reviews that someone would have to go away and plan the remedies in more detail. Given that organizational interventions invariably have unfavorable side-effects, and that their implementation is generally protracted and messy, people will naturally be skeptical about remedies that receive only glancing attention.

In all then, a number of limitations in the learning process existed during the course of the reviews. In previous sections the neglect of history, the lack of generalization, and the lack of any profound diagnosis was mentioned. The superficial treatment given to remedies has just been mentioned. However, it was also evident from the analyses that these reviews had a number of important functions:

- They gave people a chance to demonstrate their concern with the organization's objectives.

- They helped people correct misconceptions they had learned in the course of normal project activity.

- They gave people the chance to explain and justify their actions in a way that was not always open to them during the project.

- They suggested available practices that had not been realized by those who might have used them.

- They promoted collective remedies and engendered feelings of commitment to them. Remedies were sometimes dismissed for their superficiality, as explained, but at least they were voiced collectively.

- The reviews had an important disseminating function, although this requires sharing the review results with outsiders. Most review participants who have worked on the project under the microscope say things like "I already knew X." But typically it does not occur to them to go around other projects telling people about X—maybe because they do not realize X matters to others, did not know they knew X until it was pointed out, or were just too busy to think about anything to do with X. Whatever the case, postproject reviews (provided you invite along outsiders) helped X get out. We found, however, that people generally underestimated the dissemination function of postproject reviews.

What Should You Do?

The Shortfalls. The three greatest shortfalls in the reviews that were studied were that people were overspecific, ahistorical and undiagnostic. Being too specific in your learning actually refers to two different things. One way to be too specific is to have too narrow a view of the process you are learning about. If you think of an engineering project just in terms of what the project manager can affect, for instance, you will not question whether there is something to be learned about, say, the process of assigning project managers. The other way to be too specific is to view what you are learning about too literally. If it turns out that a product fails because a wall thickness of a designed part was insufficient you could diagnose this as a failure to specify adequate wall thickness. You could go on to add something to your codes of practice that says all wall thickness should be checked with the chief engineer. But you could go to a more general level and diagnose this as a failure among designers to

understand the extremes of operating duty that their products have to meet. You might then think of remedies to do with giving designers greater exposure to customers using their products. Both types of overspecificity cause learning to be less effective than it should be. Therefore, the messages are try to learn about the bigger system, not just day-to-day activities, and try to think of particular failings as examples of more general types of failing.

How much do people think about history? The answer seems to be "not much," since only six references of any kind to historical experience occurred throughout the reviews. The big problem of *not* referring to history is that you will not learn what types of problems are unique and what types are characteristic or systemic. Also, you will have an excessive confidence in any remedies you plan. But, having said this, the way you use history is not clear cut. There are two common aphorisms about learning from history that seem to contradict each other: one is "There is nothing new under the sun" and the other is "History never repeats itself." The first suggests that knowing history is essential because the future will resemble it. The second suggests that knowing history is dangerous because you can be trapped into believing that the future will be the same as the past. The important point is to look at history at the right level of generality. Your next product development will be unique because in all its detail it will differ in many respects from previous developments. At the same time, you simply would not be able to do it if it were wholly unique. You still have to go through very similar processes, deal with very similar *kinds* of objects, and so on.

Finally, true diagnosis was mostly absent. Why, given the extent to which people are encouraged to adopt cause-effect analysis, fishbone diagrams, problem-solving devices, and so on, do they not practice causal diagnosis? As with other matters, you can take your explanation either from individual psychology or from organizational behavior. The psychological explanation has to do with the distinction between causal reasoning and diagnostic reasoning that was mentioned earlier. Individuals simply seem to find it easier to reason from cause to effect than vice versa. The organizational explanation is that most people regard it as a social requirement to avoid direct criticism of one another, especially if they have to maintain some kind of long-term relationship. Most people are not going to sacrifice good long-term relationships for the sake of one or two accurate diagnoses of events that cannot be undone. And they have probably reached their own, private diagnosis of events anyway, and do not see a need for a collective diagnosis. The fact that the collective diagnosis could be better than their private one may not even occur to them. Moreover, it is a social norm to be constructive—emphasizing the search for better ways rather than the diagnosis of a bad way. Unfortunately, the consequence of all this very reasonable avoidance of deep diagnosis is shallow understanding and, most likely, wrong remedies that treat symptoms rather than causes. Ineffective post mortems, like ineffectual people, avoid conflict in the name of long-term ends, but ultimately sacrifice long-term ends for short-term comfort. Getting an organization to do the opposite (pursue long-term ends and endure a lack of short-term comfort) is ultimately a test of leadership, of moral courage, persuasiveness, and will.

Recommendations. We would recommend the following "watchwords" for review chairpersons:

1. Encourage deep diagnosis. Use cause-effect diagrams if they are likely to help.

2. Encourage attention to history. Ask whether similar things have occurred historically.

3. Encourage the examination of the bigger system beyond the immediate confines of the project.

4. Discourage glib categorization. There is little that cannot be put down to "communications problems" in complex projects, but categorizing something this way is only a starting point to the diagnosis, not a finishing point. It is easy to put down as a communications problem, for example, two people making different assumptions about who has responsibility for a particular action. A proper diagnosis would examine how different assumptions arise and why they persist even when they lead to errors.

5. Plan remedies properly by examining side-effects and thinking through the implementation. If this has to be the subject of a second meeting, then so be it. Chairpeople need to have the maturity to realize that suggested but unplanned remedies will simply deepen review participants' cynicism.

6. Invite key outsiders to postproject reviews to assist in dissemination. In one of the reviews we studied, managers of new projects were invited, and this was probably far more effective at dissemination

than written summaries would have been. Written summaries tend to be written from one person's standpoint, so one often does not know how contentious certain issues were. And these summaries often lack the detail that adopting a new practice depends on.

Most people would probably count such practices as common sense. It is therefore important to be aware that such practices often failed to materialize—even among the highly intelligent, knowledgeable, and thoughtful people who ran the reviews we studied.

Summary

Overall, in the light of this study, we would come out strongly in favor of postproject reviews (provided you do not call them "post mortems"). We could spot flaws in the ones we saw, but they were still valuable. And most of the organizations we worked with had not run them before, so judging them by the first-of-kind would not be reasonable. This study, while limited, points the direction for additional research in this important area of project management.

References

ARGYRIS, C. (1977, September–October). Double loop learning in organizations. *Harvard Business Review,* 115–125.

ERAUT, M. (1994). *Developing Professional Knowledge and Competence* (p. 51). London: Falmer Press.

LIPSHITZ, R., POPPER, M., & OZ, S. (1996). Building learning organizations: The design and implementation of organizational learning mechanisms. *Journal of Applied Behavioral Science, 32* (3), 292–305.

MARCH, J. G., SPROULL, L. S. & TAMUZ, M. (1991). Learning from samples or one of fewer. *Organization Science, 2* (1), 1–13.

STUBBS, M. (1983). *Discourse Analysis.* Oxford: Basil Blackwell.

TVERSKY, A., & KAHNEMAN, D. (1982). Causal schemas in judgments under uncertainty. In D. Kahneman, P. Slovic, & A. Tversky (Eds.), *Judgment under Uncertainty: Heuristics and Biases* (pp. 117–128). Cambridge University Press.

Questions

1. Why do you think organizations tend to ignore post-project evaluations?

2. How could the concept of making such evaluations mandatory be implemented?

3. Evaluate their advice for conducting postproject evaluations.

4. How does an understanding of how people learn affect project audits and evaluations?

5. How can an auditor/evaluator avoid the shortfalls described in the article?

6. Summarize the author's recommendations.

Project Termination

As it must to all things, termination comes to every project. At times, project death is quick and clean, but more often it is a long process; and there are times when it is practically impossible to establish that death has occurred. The skill with which termination, or a condition we might call "near termination," is managed has a great deal to do with the quality of life after the project. The termination stage of the project rarely has much impact on technical success or failure, but it has a great deal to do with residual attitudes toward the project—the "taste left in the mouth" of the client, senior management, and the project team. It also has a great deal to do with learning about the things that lead to success—or failure.

At this point, the joy of discovery is past. Problems have been solved, bypassed, lived with, or ignored. Implementation plans have been carried out. The client is delighted, angry, or reasonably satisfied. In construction-type projects where the project cadre remains intact, the termination issue is eased because the team moves on to another challenge. For nonrecurring projects, the issue is far more akin to the breakup of a family. While the members of the family may be on the best of terms, they must now separate, go their individual ways, divide or dispose of the family property, and make plans for individual survival. Unless the project life was only a few weeks or a few months, the change is stressful. For projects organized as weak matrices, there will be only a few individuals, perhaps only the project manager, who "belong" to the project. This may represent an even more stressful situation than the breakup of a large project family because there is less peer group support and few or no sympathetic colleagues with whom to share the anxieties associated with transfer to a new project or back to a functional group.

The process of termination is never easy, always complicated, and, as much as we might wish to avoid it, almost always inevitable. The problem is how to accomplish one of the several levels of what is meant by project termination with a minimum of trouble and administrative dislocation.

In this chapter, we examine the variety of conditions that may be generally referred to as *project termination*. As indicated above, some projects are not actually terminated, but rather are severely slowed down. We then view some decision-aiding models that can assist an organization in making the termination decision. This requires us to return to the subject of evaluation and discuss indicators of success and failure in projects. We also discuss some procedures that decrease the pain of termination, and others that reduce the administrative problems that often arise after projects have been terminated. We look into the typical causes of termination, and finally note that the preparation of a project history is an integral part of the termination process.

13.1   THE VARIETIES OF PROJECT TERMINATION

For our purposes, a project can be said to be terminated when work on the substance of the project has ceased or slowed to the point that further progress on the project is no longer possible, when the project has been indefinitely delayed, when its resources have been deployed to other projects, or when project personnel (especially the PM) become personae non gratae with senior management and in the company lunchroom. There may seem to be a spark of life left, but resuscitation to a healthy state is most unlikely. On rare occasions, projects are reborn to a new, glorious existence (Baker, 1997). But such rebirth is not expected, and project team members who "hang on to the bitter end" have allowed optimism to overcome wisdom. The PM must understand that the ancient naval tradition that the captain should go down with the ship does not serve the best interests of the Navy, the crew, the ship, and most certainly not the captain.

On the other hand, the captain must not, ratlike, flee the "ship" at the first sign of trouble. In the next section of this chapter, we note many of the signs and signals that indicate that the project may be in real trouble. At this point, it is appropriate to consider the ways in which a project can be terminated. There are four fundamentally different ways to close out a project: extinction, addition, integration, and starvation.

Termination by Extinction

The project is stopped. It may end because it has been successful and achieved its goals: The new product has been developed and handed over to the client; the building has been completed and accepted by the purchaser; or the software has been installed and is running.

The project may also be stopped because it is unsuccessful or has been superseded: The new drug failed its efficacy tests; the yield of the chemical reaction was too low; there are better/faster/cheaper/prettier alternatives available; or it will cost too much and take too long to get the desired performance. Changes in the external environment can kill projects, too. The explosion of the Challenger stopped a number of space shuttle projects overnight. More recently, extraordinary cost escalation in the technology and materials associated with automotive racing caused the ruling bodies of both Formula 1 and Indy-car racing to stop (and even repeal) technological change in their respective venues.

A special case of termination by extinction is "termination by murder."* There are all sorts of murders. They range from political assassination to accidental projecticide. When senior executives vie for promotion, projects for which the loser is champion are apt to suffer. Corporate mergers often make certain projects redundant or irrelevant. NCR was forced to cancel several projects following its merger into AT&T, and probably several more when NCR was more recently unmerged.

Two important characteristics of termination by murder, premeditated or not, are the suddenness of project demise and the lack of obvious signals that death is imminent.

When a decision is made to terminate a project by extinction, the most noticeable event is that all activity on the *substance* of the project ceases. A great deal of organizational activity, however, remains to be done. Arrangements must be made for the orderly release of project team members and their reassignment to other activities if they are to remain in the parent organization. The property, equipment, and materials belonging to the project must be disbursed according to the dictates of the project contract or in accord with the established procedures of the parent organization. Finally, the Project Final Report, also known as the *project history,* must be prepared. These subjects will be covered in greater detail later in this chapter.

Termination by Addition

Most projects are "in-house," that is, carried out by the project team for use in the parent organization. If a project is a major success, it may be terminated by institutionalizing it as a formal part of the parent organization. NCR Corporation (prior to its merger and demerger with AT&T), for example, used this method of transforming a project into a division of the firm and then, if real economic stability seems assured, into an independent subsidiary. Essentially the same process occurs when a university creates an academic department out of what originally was a few courses in an existing department. For example, most software engineering and/or information systems departments began by reorganizing an engineering or business school "subspecialty" into a full-fledged department.

When the project is made a more or less full-fledged member of the parent, it lives its first years in a protected status—much as any child is protected by the adults in the family. As the years pass, however, the child is expected gradually to assume the economic responsibilities of full adulthood.

When project success results in termination by addition, the transition is strikingly different from termination by extinction. In both cases the project ceases to exist, but there the similarity stops. Project personnel, property, and equipment are often simply transferred from the dying project to the newly born division. The metamorphosis from project to department, to division, and even to subsidiary is accompanied by budgets and administrative practices that conform to standard procedure in

---

*The authors thank Professor Samuel G. Taylor (University of Wyoming) for noting this special case of termination by extinction.

the parent firm, by demands for contribution profits, by the probable decline of political protection from the project's corporate "champion," indeed by a greater exposure to all the usual stresses and strains of regular, routine, day-to-day operations.

It is not uncommon, however, for some of the more adventurous members of the project team to request transfers to other projects or to seek the chance to start new projects. Project life is exciting, and some team members are uncomfortable with what they perceive to be the staid, regulated existence of the parent organization. The change from project to division brings with it a sharply diminished sense of freedom.

This transition poses a difficult time for the PM, who must see to it that the shift is made smoothly. In Part I of this book, and especially in Chapter 3, we referred repeatedly to the indispensable requirement of political sensitivity in the PM. The transition from project to division demands a superior level of political sensitivity for successful accomplishment. Projects lead a sheltered life, for all the risks they run. The regular operating divisions of a firm are subjected to the daily infighting that seems, in most firms, to be a normal result of competition between executives.

Project Management in Practice
Nucor's Approach to Termination by Addition

Nucor, one of the early steel "minimills," is a highly entrepreneural firm with a compound growth rate of 23 percent per year. In 1987, its sales were $851 million with an executive staff of only 19 monitoring the operations of 23 plants and 4600 employees. As part of its strategy, Nucor in 1983 decided to move into the flat rolled steel market, the largest market for steel products. They thus initiated the construction of a major plant in Crawfordsville, Indiana, which would comprise over 20 percent of their total assets.

As another part of its strategy, Nucor does its own construction management, with most of the construction team then transitioning into permanent positions in the newly constructed plant. In this case, four managers started the conceptual team for the new facility and then brought in 19 other people from outside the company to form the rest of the construction team, none of them ever having built a steel mill before. The manager on the conceptual team for the new plant was the lead person on the site determination team and became the general manager of the facility. The field shift superintendents on the construction project will have permanent managerial responsibility for the melt shop, the hot mill, and the cold mill. The engineers will become supervisors in the mill. Even the secretary/clerk will have a position in the new facility.

Nucor also relies heavily on the services and capabilities of its suppliers in the construction process, since they are such a small firm. But it also reflects Nucor's "lean and mean" philosophy. In this case, the only error the construction team made was underestimating the engineering time required from suppliers, the time coming in at about double the estimate. Even so, the engineering costs (and probably most other labor costs, too) apparently only ran about 20 percent of what it historically costs to build this type of steel facility!

Source: R. Kimball, "Nucor's Strategic Project," *Project Management Journal*, September 1988.

Termination by Integration

This method of terminating a project is the most common way of dealing with successful projects, and the most complex. The property, equipment, material, personnel, and functions of the project are distributed among the existing elements of the parent organization. The output of the project becomes a standard part of the operating systems of the parent, or client.

In some cases, the problems of integration are relatively minor. The project team that installed a new piece of software, instructed the client in its operation and maintenance, and then departed, probably left only minor problems behind it, problems familiar to experienced managers. If the installation was an entire flexible manufacturing system, however, or a minicomputer complete with multiple terminals and many different pieces of software, then the complexities of integration are apt to be much more severe. In general, the problems of integration are inversely related to the level of experience that the parent organization (or client) has had with: (1) the technology being integrated and (2) the successful integration of other projects, regardless of technology.

Most of the problems of termination by addition are also present when the project is integrated. In the case of integration, the project may not be viewed as a competitive interloper, but the project personnel being moved into established units of the parent organization will be so viewed. Also, the project, which flourished so well in its protected existence as a project, may not be quite so healthy in the chill atmosphere of the "real world." The individuals who nurtured the project may have returned to their respective organizational divisions, and may have new responsibilities. They tend to lose their fervid interest in the "old" project.

Following is a list of a few of the more important aspects of the transition from project to integrated operation that must be considered when the project functions are distributed.

1. *Personnel*   Where will the project team go? Will it remain a team? If the functions that the team performed are still needed, who will do them? If ex-team members are assigned to a new project, under what conditions or circumstances might they be temporarily available for help on the old project?

2. *Manufacturing*   Is training complete? Are input materials and the required facilities available? Does the production system layout have to be replanned? Did the change create new bottlenecks or line-of-balance problems? Are new operating or control procedures needed? Is the new operation integrated into the firm's computer systems?

3. *Accounting/Finance*   Have the project accounts been closed and audited? Do the new department budgets include the additional work needed by the project? Have the new accounts been created and account numbers been distributed? Has all project property and equipment been distributed according to the contract or established agreements?

4. *Engineering*   Are all drawings complete and on file? Are operating manuals and change procedures understood? Have training programs been altered appropriately for new employees? Have maintenance schedules been adjusted for the change? Do we have a proper level of "spares" in stock?

5. *Information Systems/Software*   Has the new system been thoroughly tested? Is the software properly documented and are "comments" complete? Is the new system fully integrated with current systems? Have the potential users been properly trained to use the new system?

6. *Marketing*   Is the sales department aware of the change? Is marketing in agreement about lead times? Is marketing comfortable with the new line? Is the marketing strategy ready for implementation?

7. *Purchasing, Distribution, Legal, etc.*   Are all these and other functional areas aware of the change? Has each made sure that the transition from project to standard operation has been accomplished within standard organizational guidelines and that standard administrative procedures have been installed?

Termination by Starvation

There is a fourth type of project termination, although strictly speaking, it is not a "termination" at all. It is "slow starvation by budget decrement." Almost anyone who has been involved with projects over a sufficient period of time to have covered a business recession has had to cope with budget cuts. Budget cuts, or decrements, are not rare. Because they are common, they are sometimes used to mask a project termination.

There may be a number of reasons why senior management does not wish to terminate an unsuccessful or obsolete project. In some firms, for example, it is politically dangerous to admit that one has championed a failure, and terminating a project that has not accomplished its goals is an admission of failure. In such a case, the project budget might receive a deep cut—or a series of small cuts—large enough to prevent further progress on the project and to force the reassignment of many project team members. In effect, the project is terminated, but the project still exists as a legal entity complete with sufficient staff to maintain some sort of presence such as a secretary who issues a project "no-progress" report each year. In general, it is considered bad manners to inquire into such projects or to ask why they are still "on the books."

13.2   WHEN TO TERMINATE A PROJECT

The decision to terminate a project early, by whatever method, is difficult. As we emphasized in Chapter 4, projects tend to develop a life of their own—a life seemingly independent of whether or not the project is successful. In an early article on the subject of terminating R & D projects, Buell (1967) suspected that the main reason so little information was available on the subject was that it was hard to spell out specific guidelines and standards for the decision. He expressed strong doubts about the ability to "wrap everything up in a neat set of quantitative mathematical expressions," and then went on to develop an extensive set of questions that, if answered, should lead management to a decision. While these questions were aimed at R & D projects, they have wide, general applicability. Paraphrased and slightly modified to broaden and extend them beyond R&D projects, they are:

- Is the project still consistent with organizational goals?
- Is it practical? Useful?
- Is management sufficiently enthusiastic about the project to support its implementation?
- Is the scope of the project consistent with the organization's financial strength?
- Is the project consistent with the notion of a "balanced" program in all areas of the organization's technical interests? In "age"? In cost?
- Does the project have the support of all the departments (e.g., finance, manufacturing, marketing, IT, legal, etc.) needed to implement it?
- Is organizational project support being spread too thin?
- Is support of this individual project sufficient for success?
- Does this project represent too great an advance over current technology? Too small an advance?
- Is the project team still innovative, or has it gone stale?
- Can the new knowledge be protected by patent, copyright, or trade secret?
- Could the project be farmed out without loss of quality?
- Is the current project team properly qualified to continue the project?
- Does the organization have the required skills to achieve full implementation or exploitation of the project?
- Has the subject area of the project already been "thoroughly plowed"?
- Has the project lost its key person or champion?
- Is the project team enthusiastic about success?
- Can the potential results be purchased or subcontracted more efficiently than developed in-house?
- Does it seem likely that the project will achieve the minimum goals set for it? Is it still profitable? timely?

We could add many other such questions to Buell's list. For instance:

- Has the project been obviated by technical advances or new products/services developed elsewhere?
- Is the output of the product still cost effective?
- Is it time to integrate or add the project as a part of the regular, ongoing operation of the parent organization?
- Would we support the project if it were proposed today at the time and cost required to complete it?
- Are there better alternative uses for the funds, time, and personnel devoted to the project?
- Has a change in the environment altered the need for the project's output?

Such questions clearly overlap, and the list could easily be extended further. Dean (1968) reports that the probabilities of technical and/or commerical failure are the two most important reasons for terminating projects (see Table 13-1), according to the executives he surveyed. Balachandra and Raelin (1980) and Raelin and Balachandra (1985) performed a discriminant analysis on 23 factors involved in terminating projects, not as a decision model, but as a way of highlighting the various factors involved and their relevance to the termination problem, as related to projects in general.

Compared to the great level of research and thought concerning the project selection decision before the 1980s (see also Chapter 2), there was relatively little research published on the termination decision. But even this bit was more than the work devoted to defining project success. As interest in project termination increased in the mid-1980s, interest in understanding project success also rose. Baker, et al. (1983) looked at factors associated with R & D project success and failure. Pinto and Slevin (1987, 1988) surveyed experienced PMs and found ten factors that the managers felt to be critical to successful project implementation (see Table 13-2). Jiang, et al. (1996) surveyed information system "business professionals" on the relative importance of the Pinto and Slevin critical success factors and came to roughly similar conclusions.

Ingram (1994, p. 33) studied 62 client/server and open systems projects and found, among several other conclusions, that "effective project management is directly linked to positive project outcomes while technical elegance shows only a minor correlation." Shenhar, et al. (1997) surveyed project managers and found four "dimensions of project success": the efficiency with which the project is carried out,

Table 13-1.   Rank Order of Important Factors Considered in Terminating R&D Projects (36 companies)

Factors	*No. of Companies Reporting the Factor as Being Important*
Technical	
Low probability of achieving technical objectives or commercializing results	34
Technical or manufacturing problems cannot be solved with available R&D skills	11
Higher priority of other projects requiring R&D labor or funds	10
Economic	
Low profitability or return on investment	23
Too costly to develop as individual product	18
Market	
Low market potential	16
Change in competitive factors or market needs	10
Others	
Too long a time required to achieve commerical results	6
Negative effects on other projects or products	3
Patent problems	1

Source: Dean (1968).

Table 13-2   Critical Success Factors in Order of Importance

1. *Project Mission*—Initial clearly defined goals and general directions.
2. *Top-Management Support*—Willingness of top management to provide the necessary resources and authority/power for project success.
3. *Project Schedule/Plan*—A detailed specification of the individual action steps for project implementation.
4. *Client Consultation*—Communication, consultation, and active listening to all impacted parties.
5. *Personnel*—Recruitment, selection, and training of the necessary personnel for the project team.
6. *Technical Tasks*—Availability of the required technology and expertise to accomplish the specific technical action steps.
7. *Client Acceptance*—The act of "selling" the final project to its ultimate intended users.
8. *Monitoring and Feedback*—Timely provision of comprehensive control information at each stage in the implementation process.
9. *Communication*—The provision of an appropriate network and necessary data to all key actors in the project implementation.
10. *Trouble-shooting*—Ability to handle unexpected crises and deviations from plan.

Source: Pinto and Slevin (1987).

the customer's satisfaction and willingness to use (and repurchase) the product, the impact of the project on the organization carrying it out, and the degree to which the project contributes to the firm's future. Many other researchers also attacked the problem of defining project success or delineating the path to it (see, e.g., Freeman and Beale, 1992; Matzler and Hinterhuber, 1998; Might and Fischer, 1985). Balachandra and Friar (1997) have done an extensive review of the relevant literature and concluded that market, technological, and organizational factors are associated with success in R&D and new product development projects depending on whether the innovation is incremental or radical, the technology is low or high, and the market is new or existing.

A particularly important finding of Baker, et al. (1983) is that the *factors associated with project success are different for different industries.* Baker's work was restricted to R&D projects, but the Pinto and Slevin study covered many different types of projects. They found that the success-related factors differed between fundamentally different types of projects—between R&D and construction projects, for example. At the very least, the factors and their relative importance are idiosyncratic to the industry, to the project type, and, we suggest, possibly to the firm.

Out of this work came some models that could be used to predict project success or failure, based on certain project characteristics or practices. Pinto and Mantel (1990), using Pinto's work cited above, reported on factors that were associated with project failure. The factors differed for the type of project involved (R&D vs. construction), for the project's position in the life cycle, as well as for the precise way in which "failure" was defined. Green, Welsh, and Dehler (1993) found that a poor fit with the firm's existing technological expertise and/or with its existing marketing area and channels was a good early predictor of project termination. Kloppenborg and Plath (1991) described precursors to success and failure for projects intended to implement expert systems, and Beale and Freeman (1991) modeled project success, differentiating between factors exogenous and endogenous to the project and the project team.

In the face of this diversity of success factors, it is interesting to note that there are relatively few fundamental reasons why some projects fail to produce satisfactory answers to Buell's questions.

1. *A Project Organization Is Not Required*   The use of the project form of organization was inappropriate for this particular task or in this particular environment. The parent organization must understand the conditions that require instituting a project.

2. *Insufficient Support from Senior Management*   Projects invariably develop needs for resources that were not originally allocated. Arguments between functional departments over the command of such resources are very common. Without the direct support of a champion in senior management, the project is almost certain to lose the resource battle.

3. *Naming the Wrong Person as Project Manager*   This book is testimony to the importance of the PM. A common mistake is to appoint as PM an individual with excellent technical skills but weak managerial skills or training.

4. *Poor Planning*   This is a very common cause of project failure. In the rush to get the substance of the project under way, competent planning is neglected. In such cases, crisis management becomes a way of life, difficulties and errors are compounded, and the project slowly gets farther behind schedule and over budget. Indeed, careful planning is associated with success in almost all empirical research on project success—Tom Peter's "Ready, Fire, Aim" to the contrary notwithstanding. Not only is proper planning often cited as a *success factor*, lack of planning is cited as a *cause of failure* (Black, 1996).

These, and a few other reasons, are the base causes of most project failures. The specific causes of failure, for the most part, derive from these fundamental items. For example,

- No use was made of earlier project Final Reports that contained a number of recommendations for operating projects in the future.
- Time/cost estimates were not prepared by those who had responsibility for doing the work.
- Starting late, the PM jumped into the tasks without adequate planning.
- Project personnel were moved without adjusting the schedule, or were reassigned during slow periods and then were unavailable when needed.
- Project auditors/evaluators were reluctant to conduct careful, detailed meaningful evaluations.
- The project was allowed to continue in existence long after it had ceased to make cost-effective progress.

- Evaluations failed to determine why problems were arising during the early phases of the project life cycle due to inadequate, or no, risk assessment and management.

All these causes of failure underline the need for careful evaluation at all stages of the project. But at the same time, it is most important for the reader to note that the lion's share of the attention given to the termination issue is focused on the failing project. It is equally or more important to terminate successful projects at the right time and by proper methods. One rarely mentioned problem affecting many organizations is the inability or unwillingness of successful project managers working on successful projects to "let their projects go." This is a particularly difficult problem for in-house projects. The PM (and team) simply will not release the project to the tender care of the client department. An outstanding technical specialist and manager conducting communications projects was released from employment simply because she insisted on maintaining semipermanent control of projects that had essentially been completed, but which were not released to the users because they "needed further testing" or "fine-tuning."

Also, little consideration has been given to *how* the termination decision is made and *who* makes it. We feel that a broadly based committee of reasonably senior executives is probably best. The broad organizational base of the committee is needed to diffuse and withstand the political pressure that accompanies all terminations—successes and failures alike. To the extent possible, the criteria used by the termination committee should be written and explained in some detail. It is, however, important to write the criteria in such a way that the committee is not frozen into a mechanistic approach to a decision. There are times when hunches should be followed (or rejected) and blind faith should be respected (or ignored). It depends on whose hunches and faith are under consideration (Baker, 1997).

Project Management in Practice
Terminating the Superconducting Super Collider Project

On October 19, 1993, Congress pulled the plug on the Superconducting Super Collider (SSC) project, ending 11 years of work costing over $2 billion dollars and throwing 2000 people out of work. The objective of the planned $11 billion SSC was to accelerate subatomic particles within a 54-mile underground circular chamber to almost the speed of light and smash them together at energies of 40 trillion electronic volts. The benefits to society of these experiments were unclear, some maintaining they could have been enormous, but others including congressmen were less sure.

The project also suffered from an identity crisis. It was not clear if this was to be a U.S. "first" in basic science or a "world" science project, funded in its early stages by a $1 billion commitment from other nations. Although the costs of the SSC had ballooned, the main reason it was terminated was that it lost its political support. Although the SSC scientists and backers had rallied good will among universities, schools, and scientific meetings, the potential benefits of the project never reached the Clinton administration, where it only enjoyed lukewarm support at best.

When a $4 trillion budget deficit appeared likely, the SSC project was sacrificed.

Source: B. Baker and R. Menon, "Politics and Project Performance: The Fourth Dimension of Project Management," *PM Network,* November 1995, pp. 16–21.

The gigantic tunnels for the supercollider are prepared first.

13.3 THE TERMINATION PROCESS

The termination process has two distinct parts. First is the decision whether or not to terminate. Second, if the decision is to terminate the project, the decision must be carried out.

The Decision Process

Decision-aiding models for the termination decision fall into two generic categories. First, there are models that base the decision on the degree to which the project qualifies against a set of factors generally held to be associated with successful (or failed) projects. Second, there are models that base the decision on the degree to which the project meets the goals and objectives set for it.

Most of the research on factors associated with success and failure can be used to "predict" project success. Pinto's work with Slevin (1987, 1988) and Mantel (1990) can be used in that way. Tadisina (1986), working with a set of factors associated with project success found by Baker, et al. (1983), suggested a variety of termination-decision models that could be used if the success-related factors were monitored and used as input data in the models. Freeman and Beale (1992) focused their decision model on the net present value of the project, which is determined by transforming a number of success-related factors (from the sponsor's and the project manager's points of view) into NPV equivalents. Riggs, et al. (1992) determined a set of success-related factors pertaining to government (NASA) projects by polling experienced managers using the Delphi method. From this, they developed statistically generated "success predictor models" for manned and unmanned space projects. Finally, Chi and his colleagues (1997) developed a model for the termination decision on the projects that have an uncertain completion time and have some salvage value.

The use of models that measure project success or failure based on its achievement of present goals is subject to debate.

Balachandra and Raelin (1980; see also Raelin and Balachandra, 1985) state that project selection models are not appropriate for the project termination decision. Kumar, et al. (1996, p. 277) agree. The argument is that the data requirements for selection models are too large and costly. They also argue that the evaluation of factors in project selection models may change as projects are evaluated at different stages in their life cycles. They note that the probability of technical success of a project is usually estimated to be close to 1.0 early in the life cycle, but lower during later stages when the technical problems are known. This, they say, would bias decisions in favor of new projects and against ongoing ones.

Lee and Mantel (1986) think that the first argument is generally untrue of those selection models actually being used, which are typically of modest size. As we have remarked elsewhere in this book, the uncertainty associated with most projects is not concerned with whether or not the project objective is technically achievable, but rather with the time and cost required to achieve it. The fact that selection criteria may change between the time that the project is started and the time it is judged for possible termination is not a relevant criticism of the use of a selection model. Indeed, whatever the source of the criteria for termination, they should be determined by the organization's policy at the time the decision is made—not judged by the policy of some prior time.

Adopting the position that sunk costs are not relevant to current investment decisions, we hold that the primary criterion for project continuance or termination is *whether or not the organization is willing to invest the estimated time and cost required to complete the project, given the project's current status and current expected outcome.* We emphasize that this criterion can be applied to any project. While we maintain the position that sunk costs are irrelevant, not everyone agrees (Keil, et al., 1995).

Shafer and Mantel (1989) developed a project termination decision support system (DSS) based on a constrained weighted factor scoring model (see Chapter 2). The capabilities of most popular spreadsheets allow direct modeling of the scoring model, allow customized menus, and allow decision makers to adapt and enhance the model as they gain experience in the use of the DSS. The database requirements include data on the project, on the parent organization, and on the environment. The criteria on which projects are rated, the specifics of the scores, and the relative weights of the criteria are often developed by organizational executives using the Delphi method. For a description of the use of the Delphi method to develop criteria weights, see the Web site for this book. If it seems desirable, the weights may be determined through discriminant analysis, as in (Balachandra and Raelin, 1980; Raelin and Balachandra, 1985; Tadisina, 1986).

Just as decision criteria, constraints, weights, and environmental data are unique to each organization, so are the specifics of using this (or any) decision model. A detailed discussion of various potential decision rules that might be useful with such a model can be found in Shafer and Mantel (1989). Figure 13-1 illustrates the structure of this model.

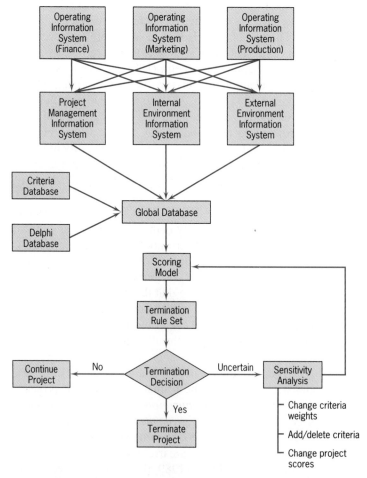

Figure 13-1 DSS structure for a project termination decision. *Source:* Shafer and Mantel (1989).

The Implementation Process

Once it has been decided to terminate a project, the process by which it will be terminated must be implemented. The actual termination can be planned and orderly, or a simple hatchet job. The former is apt to have significantly better results, and so we suggest that the termination process be planned, budgeted, and scheduled just as is done for any other phase of the project life cycle. Such a project is illustrated in Figure 13-2. Archibald (1992) has prepared an extensive checklist of items covering the closeout of both the administrative and substantive parts of the project (see Figures 13-3a and b).

In some organizations, the processing of the project closeout is conducted under the direct supervision of the PM, but this often raises dilemmas. For many PMs, termination signals the end of their reign as project leader. If the PM has another project to lead, the issue may not be serious; but if there is no other project and if the PM faces a return to a staid life in a functional division, there may be a great temptation to stretch out the termination process.

An examination of Figures 13-2 and 13-3a and 13-3b shows that implementing termination is a complex process. Note that in Figure 13-3b such items as A-4, B-4, C-3, and G-2, among many others, are actually small projects. It is all too easy, at this final stage of the game, to give this mountain of paperwork a "lick and a promise"—easy, but foolish. Someone must handle all the bureaucratic tasks, and if the PM leaves many loose ends, he or she will rapidly get a reputation for being slipshod, a characterization not associated with career success.

The PM also has another option, to ignore the termination process entirely. The evaluation has already been conducted and praise or censure has been delivered. Rather than deal with termination, the PM may let the project administrator handle things. Project team members may well have similar feelings and reactions, and may seek new jobs or affiliations before the project actually ends, thereby dragging out some final tasks interminably.

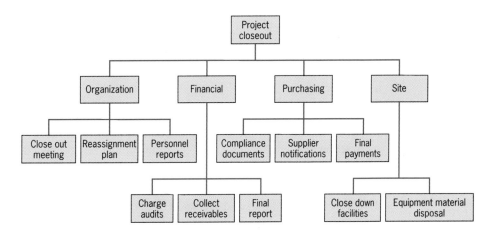

Figure 13-2 Design for project termination.

PROJECT TITLE _____   COMPLETION DATE _____

CONTRACT NO. _____   COST TYPE _____

CUSTOMER _____   PROJECT MGR. _____

The project close-out check lists are designed for use in the following manner:
Column I—Item No.: Each task listed is identified by a specific number and grouped into categories. Categories are based on functions, not on organizations or equipment.
Column II—Task Description: Task descriptions are brief tasks that could apply to more than one category but are listed only in the most appropriate category.
Column III—Required, Yes or No: Check whether the item listed applies to the project.
Column IV—Date Required: Insert the required date for accomplishment of the task.
Column V—Assigned Responsibility: Insert the name of the person responsible to see that the task is accomplished on schedule. This may be a member of the Project Office or an individual within a functional department.
Column VI—Priority (PR): A priority system established by the Project Manager may be used here; e.g., Priority #1 may be all tasks that must be accomplished before the contractual completion date, Priority #2 within 2 weeks after the completion date, etc.
Column VII—Notes, Reference: Refer in this column to any applicable Procedures, a government specification that may apply to that task, etc.

Figure 13-3a   Instructions for project termination checklist. *Source:* Archibald (1992).

Special *termination managers* are sometimes useful in completing the long and involved process of shutting down a project. In such cases, the PM is transferred to another project or reassigned to a functional "home." The termination manager does not have to deal with substantive project tasks and therefore may be a person familiar with the administrative requirements of termination and the environment within which the project will be operating (if it continues to live). If personnel performance evaluations are required, and they usually are, they must be prepared by the PM or whoever supervised the work of each individual team member, not by a specially appointed termination manager.

If technical knowledge is required during the termination process, a member of the project team may be upgraded and assigned responsibility for the termination. This "promotion" is often a motivator and will provide development experience for the team member.

The primary duties of the termination manager are encompassed in the following nine general tasks:

1. Ensure completion of the work, including tasks performed by subcontractors.
2. Notify the client of project completion and ensure that delivery (and installation) is accomplished. Acceptance of the project must be acknowledged by the client.
3. Ensure that documentation is complete, including a terminal evaluation of the project deliverables and preparation of the project's Final Report.
4. Clear for final billings and oversee preparation of the final invoices sent to the client.
5. Redistribute personnel, materials, equipment, and any other resources to the appropriate places.

Item No.	Task Description	Required Yes	Required No	Required Date	Assigned Responsibility	PR.	Notes Reference
A.	*Project office (PO) and Project Team (PT) Organization*						
1.	Conduct project close-out meeting						
2.	Establish PO and PT release and reassignment plan						
3.	Carry out necessary personnel actions						
4.	Prepare personal performance evaluation on each PO and PT member						
B.	*Instructions and Procedures* issue instructions for:						
1.	Termination of PO and PT						
2.	Close-out of all work orders and contracts						
3.	Termination of reporting procedures						
4.	Preparation of final report(s)						
5.	Completion and disposition of project file						
C.	*Financial*						
1.	Close out financial documents and records						
2.	Audit final charges and costs						
3.	Prepare final project financial report(s)						
4.	Collect receivables						
D.	*Project Definition*						
1.	Document final approved project scope						
2.	Prepare final project breakdown structure and enter into project file						
E.	*Plans, Budgets, and Schedules*						
1.	Document actual delivery dates of all contractual deliverable end items						
2.	Document actual completion dates of all other contractual obligations						
3.	Prepare final project and task status reports						
F.	*Work Authorization and Control*						
1.	Close out all work orders and contracts						
G.	*Project Evaluation and Control*						
1.	Assure completion of all action assignments						
2.	Prepare final evaluation report(s)						
3.	Conduct final review meeting						
4.	Terminate financial, manpower, and progress reporting procedures						
H.	*Management and Customer Reporting*						
1.	Submit final report to customer						
2.	Submit final report to management						
I.	*Marketing and Contract Administration*						
1.	Compile all final contract documents with revision, waivers, and related correspondence						
2.	Verify and document compliance with all contractual terms						
3.	Compile required proof of shipment and customer acceptance documents						
4.	Officially notify customer of contract completion						
5.	Initiate and pursue any claims against customer						
6.	Prepare and conduct defense against claims by customer						
7.	Initiate public relations announcements re. contract completion						
8.	Prepare final contract status report						
J.	*Extension-New Business*						
1.	Document possibilities for project or contract extensions, or other related new business						
2.	Obtain commitment for extension						
K.	*Project Records Control*						
1.	Complete project file and transmit to designated manager						
2.	Dispose of other project records as required by established procedures						
L.	*Purchasing and Subcontracting*						
	For each Purchase Order and Subcontract:						
1.	Document compliance and completion						
2.	Verify final payment and proper accounting to project						
3.	Notify vendor/contractor of final completion						
M.	*Engineering Documentation*						
1.	Compile and store all engineering documentation						
2.	Prepare final technical report						
N.	*Site Operations*						
1.	Close down site operations						
2.	Dispose of equipment and material						

Figure 13-3b Checklist for project termination. *Source*: Archibald (1992).

6. Clear project with legal counsel or consultant. File for patents if appropriate. Record and archive all "nondisclosure" documents.

7. Determine what records (manuals, reports, and other paperwork) to keep. Ensure that such documents are stored in the proper places and that responsibility for document retention is turned over to the parent organization's archivist.

8. Ascertain any product support requirements (e.g., spares, service), decide how such support will be delivered, and assign responsibility.

9. Oversee the closing of the project's books.

It is likely that tasks 1 to 3 will be handled by the regular PM immediately before the project termination process is started. If the termination manager must handle these tasks, technical support will almost certainly be needed. Of course, many of the tasks on this list will be quite simple if the project is not large, but even with small- or medium-sized projects, the PM should make sure all items are covered.

Item 5 on this list deserves some amplification. The PM can do a great deal to reduce the problems of termination by dealing with these issues well before the actual termination process begins. As we noted in Chapter 2, arrangements for the distribution and disposal of property and equipment belonging to the project should be included in the proposal and/or in the contract with the client. Obviously, this does not stop all arguments, but it does soften the conflicts. Dealing with project personnel is more difficult.

Most PMs delay the personnel reassignment/release issue as long as possible for three main reasons: a strong reluctance to face the interpersonal conflicts that might arise when new assignments and layoffs are announced; worry that people will lose interest and stop work on the project as soon as it becomes known that termination is being considered; or concern—particularly in the case of a pure project organization—that team members will try to avoid death by stretching out the work as far as possible.

As long as the PM has access to the functional managers' ears, any team member who "quits work" before the project is completed or stalls by stretching out tasks or creating task extensions would be subject to the usual sanctions of the workplace. The PM should make it quite clear that on-the-job resignations and tenure-for-life are equally unacceptable.

The first problem results when project leadership is held by a managerially weak PM. The height of weakness is demonstrated when the PM posts a written list of reassignments and layoffs on the project's bulletin board late Friday afternoon and then leaves for a long weekend. A more useful course of action is to speak with project members individually or in small groups, let them know about plans for termination, and offer to consult with each in order to aid in the reassignment process or to assist in finding new work. (A preliminary announcement to the entire project team is in order because the interviews may cover several weeks or months.) It is almost impossible to keep termination plans a secret, and to confront the matter immediately tends to minimize rumors.

In a large project, of course, the PM will not be able to conduct personal interviews except with a few senior assistants. The project's personnel officer, or a representative from the parent firm's personnel department, can serve instead. This may seem like an unnecessary service to the team members, but a reputation of "taking care of one's people" is an invaluable aid to the PM when recruiting for the next project.

Termination by murder makes it very difficult to follow these suggestions about dealing with project personnel. The project's death often occurs with so little warning that the PM learns of the fact at the same time as the project team—or, as sometimes happens, learns about it from a member of the project team.

There is little the PM can do in such a case except to try to minimize the damage. The team should be assembled as rapidly as possible and informed, to the best of the PM's ability, about what has happened. At this point the PM should start the reassignment/release process.

13.4   THE FINAL REPORT—A PROJECT HISTORY

Good project management systems have a memory. The embodiment of this memory is the Project Final Report. The final report is not another evaluation; rather, it is the history of the project. It is a chronicle of the life and times of the project, a compendium of what went right and what went wrong, of who served the project in what capacity, of what was done to create the substance of the project, of how it was managed. We learn from experience only if the experience is preserved and studied (Whitten, 1999).

The elements that should be covered in the final report are listed below. When considering these elements it is also beneficial to consider where the source materials can be found. For the most part, the required information is contained in the project master plan, a document that includes the proposal, all action plans, budgets, schedules, change orders, and updates of the above. In addition to the master plan, all project audits and evaluations also contain required input data. Almost everything else required by the final report is reflective, based on the thoughts of the PM and others involved in the project. There is little problem in knowing where the needed documents should be kept—in the project's files. Making sure that they are, in fact, there and that they are, in fact, up to date is a serious concern.

The precise organization of the final report is not a matter of great concern; the content is. Some are organized chronologically, while others feature sections on the technical and administrative aspects of the project. Some are written in a narrative style and some contain copies of all project reports strung together with short commentaries. What matters is that several subjects should be addressed, one way or another, in the final report.

1. *Project Performance* A key element of the report is a comparison of what the project achieved (the terminal evaluation) with what the project tried to achieve (the project proposal). This comparison may be quite extensive and should include explanations of all significant deviations of actual from plan. A final earned value discussion can also be helpful. Because the final report is not a formal evaluation, it can reflect the best judgment of the PM on why the triumphs and failures oc-

curred. This comparison should be followed with a set of recommendations for future projects dealing with like or similar technical matters.

2. *Administrative Performance*   The substantive side of the project usually gets a great deal of attention, while the administrative side is often ignored until administrative problems occur. There is also a strong tendency on the part of almost everyone to treat the "pencil pushers" with grudging tolerance, at best. The administration of a project cannot solve technical problems, but it can enable good technology to be implemented (or prevent it). Administrative practices should be reviewed, and those that worked particularly well or poorly should be highlighted. It is important, when possible, to report the reasons why some specific practice was effective or ineffective. If poor administration is to be avoided and good practices adopted, it is necessary to understand why some things work well and others do not in the environment of a particular organization. This becomes the basis for the recommendations that accompany the discussion.

3. *Organizational Structure*   Each of the organizational forms used for projects has its own, unique set of advantages and disadvantages. The final report should include comments on the ways the structure aided or impeded the progress of the project. If it appears that a modification to the accepted form of project organization—or a change to a different basic organizational form—might be helpful for project management, such a recommendation should be made. Obviously, recommendations should be accompanied by detailed explanations and rationales.

4. *Project and Administrative Teams*   On occasion, individuals who are competent and likable as individuals do not perform well as members of a team when a high level of interpersonal communication and cooperation is required. A confidential section of the final report may be directed to a senior personnel officer of the parent organization, recommending that such individuals not be assigned to future projects. Similarly, the PM may recommend that individuals or groups who are particularly effective when operating as a team be kept together on future projects or when reassigned to the firm's regular operations.

5. *Techniques of Project Management*   The outcome of the project is so dependent on the skill with which the forecasting, planning, budgeting, scheduling, resource allocation, risk management, and control are handled that attention must be given to checking on the way these tasks were accomplished. If the forecasts, budgets, and schedules were not reasonably accurate, recommendations for improved methods should be made. The techniques used for planning, control, and risk management should also be subject to scrutiny.

For each element covered in the final report, recommendations for changing current practice should be made and defended. Insofar as is possible, the implications of each potential change should be noted. Commonly ignored, but equally important, are comments and recommendations about those aspects of the project that worked unusually well. Most projects, project teams, and PMs develop informal procedures that speed budget preparation, ease the tasks of scheduling, improve forecasts, and the like. The final report is an appropriate repository for such knowledge. Once reported, they can be tested and, if generally useful, can be added to the parent organization's list of approved project management methods.

The fundamental purpose of the final report is to improve future projects. It is ultimately focused on the project itself and on the process by which the project was conducted. Data on the project and its outcomes are available in the many interim reports, audits, and evaluations conducted during the project's life. But data on the process come largely from the PM's recollections. To ensure that significant issues are included, the PM should keep a diary. The PM's diary is not an official project document, but rather an informal collection of thoughts, reflections, and commentaries on project happenings. Such a diary tends to be a rich source of unconventional wisdom when written by a thoughtful PM. It may also be a great source of learning for a young, aspiring PM. Above all, it keeps ideas from "getting lost" amid the welter of activity on the project.

Occasionally, the project diary serves a purpose not originally intended. A PM working for a Minnesota highway construction company made a habit of keeping a project diary, mostly for his own interest and amusement. The firm was sued as the result of an accident on a road under construction. The plaintiff alleged that the highway shoulder was not complete nor was it marked "Under Construction" at the time of the accident. The PM's diary noted daily progress on the road, and it showed that the relevant piece of the road had been completed several days prior to the accident. The company successfully defended its position. All company PMs keep diaries now. A vice president of the firm mentioned that they are the same type of diary his high-school-aged daughter uses.

SUMMARY

At last, we come to the completion of our project—termination. In this chapter we looked at the ways in which projects can be terminated, how to decide if a project should be terminated, the termination process, and the preparation of the Project Final Report.

Specific points made in the chapter were these:

- A project can be terminated in one of four ways: by extinction, addition, integration, or starvation.

- Making a decision to terminate a project before its completion is difficult, but a number of factors can be of help in reaching a conclusion.

- Most projects fail because of one or more of the following reasons:

  Inappropriate use of the project form of organization

  Insufficient top-management support

  Naming the wrong project manager

  Poor planning

- Studies have shown that the factors associated with project success are different for different industries and the various types of projects.

- Success-related factors, or any factors management wishes, can be used in termination decision models.

- Special termination managers are often used, and needed, for closing out projects. This task, consisting of eight major duties, is a project in itself.

- The Project Final Report incorporates the process knowledge gained from the project. In addition to preservation of project records, the Final Report embodies the experience from which we learn. It should include:

  Project performance comments

  Administrative performance comments

  Organizational structure comments

  Personnel suggestions, possibly a confidential section

GLOSSARY

Termination by Addition   Bringing the project into the organization as a separate, ongoing entity.

Budget Decrement   A reduction in the amount of funds for an activity.

Termination by Extinction   The end of all activity on a project without extending it in some form, such as by inclusion or integration.

Termination by Integration   Bringing the project activities into the organization and distributing them among existing functions.

Termination by Murder   Terminating a project suddenly and without warning, usually for a cause not related to the project's purpose.

Termination by Starvation   Cutting a project's budget sufficiently to stop progress without actually killing the project.

Termination Manager   An administrator responsible for wrapping-up the administrative details of a project.

 QUESTIONS

Material Review Questions

1. List and briefly describe the ways projects may be terminated.

2. What problems may occur if the project manager does not have a follow-on project when the current project nears termination?

3. What are the primary duties of a termination manager?

4. On termination of a project, what happens to the information gathered throughout the course of the project?

5. What is a budget decrement?

6. Identify the four reasons for project termination.

7. What does the Project Final Report include?

8. What factors are considered most important in the decision to terminate a project?

9. What issues should be considered when using the termination-by-integration method?

Class Discussion Questions

10. Discuss the impact, both positive and negative, of termination on the project team members. How might the negative impact be lessened?

11. If the actual termination of a project becomes a project in itself, what are the characteristics of this project? How is it different from other projects?

12. Discuss some reasons why a Project Final Report, when completed, should be permanently retained by the firm.

13. What elements of the termination process may be responsible for making a project unsuccessful?

14. How is discriminant analysis used in project management?

15. What are some characteristics of a good termination manager?

16. How might one choose which termination method to use?

17. Why might a failing project not be terminated?

18. How can termination for reasons other than achievement of project goals be avoided?

19. What must the project manager do in planning, scheduling, monitoring, and closing out the project?

Questions for Project Management in Practice

Nucor's Approach to Termination by Addition

20. Why would Nucor have thought they could build a new steel mill with one-tenth the engineering resources it normally requires?

21. What characteristics of this project termination made it a termination by addition?

22. What other ways could Nucor have terminated this project? What terms would you give these approaches?

Terminating the Superconducting Super Collider Project

23. Which of the various forms of termination was this?

24. How does the reading at the back of this chapter relate to this termination decision?

25. The authors of this article maintain that politics is an important element of project implementation. Do you agree? Was this project terminated through "political" means?

■ INCIDENTS FOR DISCUSSION

Electrical Broom and Supply Co.

IMSCO began manufacturing and distributing electrical brooms to industrial customers 43 years ago. Mr. Bretting, president of IMSCO, has been toying with the idea of using IMSCO's manufacturing and distribution expertise to begin making and selling consumer products. He has already decided that he cannot sell any of his current products to consumers. Also, if IMSCO is going to go to the trouble of developing consumer markets, Mr. Bretting feels very strongly that their first product should be something new and innovative that will help establish their reputation.

He thinks that the expertise required to develop a new product exists within the company, but no one has any real experience in organizing or managing such a project. Fortunately, Mr. Bretting is familiar with a local consulting firm that has a good reputation and track record of leading companies through projects such as this, so he contacted them.

Three months into the project, Mr. Bretting contacted the program manager/consultant and mentioned that he was worried about the amount of risk involved in trying to introduce such an innovative consumer product with his current organization. He was worried that the project was oriented too strongly toward R&D and did not consider related business problems in enough depth. (This was a complete about-face from his feelings three months earlier, when he had approved the first plan submitted with no changes.)

Mr. Bretting suggested that the consultant modify the existing project to include the introduction of a "me-too" consumer product before IMSCO's new product was defined and tested. Mr. Bretting thought that some experience with a "me-too" product would provide IMSCO management with valuable experience and would improve later performance with the new product. He allowed the R&D portion of the project to continue concurrently, but the "me-too" phase would have top priority as far as resources were concerned. The consultant said she would think about it and contact him next week.

Questions: If you were the consultant, what would you recommend to Mr. Bretting? Would you continue the relationship?

Excel Electronics

Excel Electronics is nearing completion of a three-year project to develop and produce a new pocket Phone-Fax-Internet device (PFI). The PFI is no larger than a cigarette pack but has all the power and features of full sized devices. The assembly line and all the production facilities will be completed in six months and the first units will begin production in seven months. The plant manager believes it is time to begin winding the project down. He has three methods in mind for terminating the project: extinction, addition, and integration, but he is not sure which method would be best.

Question: Which of the three methods would you recommend, and why?

BIBLIOGRAPHY

ARCHIBALD, R. D. *Managing High Technology Programs and Projects,* 4th ed. New York: Wiley, 1992.

BAKER, B. "Great Expectations." *PM Network,* May 1997.

BAKER, N. R., S. G. GREEN, A. S. BEAN, W. BLANK, and S. K. TADISINA. "Sources of First Suggestion and Project Success/Failure in Industrial Research." *Proceedings, Conference on the Management of Technological Innovation,* Washington, D.C., 1983.

BALACHANDRA, R., and J. H. FRIAR. "Factors for Success in R&D and New Product Innovation: A Contextual Framework." *IEEE Transactions on Engineering Management,* August 1997.

BALACHANDRA, R., and A. J. RAELIN. "How to Decide When to Abandon a Project." *Research Management,* July 1980.

BEALE, P., and M. FREEMAN. "Successful Project Execution: A Model." *Project Management Journal,* December 1991.

BLACK, K. "Causes of Project Failure: A Survey of Professional Engineers." *PM Network,* November 1996.

BUELL, C. K. When to Terminate a Research and Development Project. *Research Management,* July 1967.

CHI, T., J. LIU, and H. CHEN. "Optimal Stopping Rule for a Project with Uncertain Completion Time and Partial Salvageability." *IEEE Transactions on Engineering Management,* February 1997.

DEAN, B. V. *Evaluating, Selecting, & Controlling R & D Projects.* New York: American Management Association, 1968.

FREEMAN, M., and P. BEALE. "Measuring *Project Success." Project Management Journal,* March 1992.

GREEN, S. G., M. A. WELSH, and G. E. DEHLER. "Red Flags at Dawn or Predicting Project Terminations at Start Up." *Research-Technology Management,* May–June 1993.

HOCKNEY, J. W., and K. HUMPHREYS. *Control and Management of Capital Projects,* 2nd ed. New York: McGraw-Hill, 1991.

INGRAM, T. "Managing Client/Server and Open Systems Projects: A 10-Year Study of 62 Mission-Critical Projects." *Project Management Journal,* June 1994.

JIANG, J. J., G. KLEIN, and J. BALLOUN. "Ranking of System Implementation Success Factors." *Project Management Journal,* December 1996.

KEIL, M., D. P. TRUEX, III, and R. MIXON. "The Effects of Sunk Cost and Project Completion on Information Technology Project Escalation." *IEEE Transactions on Engineering Management,* November 1995.

KLOPPENBORG, T. J., and D. A. PLATH. "Effective Project Management Practices during Expert Systems Implementation." *Project Management Journal,* December 1991.

KUMAR, V., A. N. S. PERSAUD, and U. KUMAR. "To Terminate or Not an Ongoing R&D Project: A Managerial Dilemma." *IEEE Transactions on Engineering Management,* August 1996.

LEE, W., and S. J. MANTEL, JR. "An Expert System for Project Termination." *Proceedings, First International Conference on Engineering Management,* Arlington, VA, September 1986.

MATZLER, K., and H. H. HINTERHUBER. "How to make product development projects more successful by integrating Kano's model of customer satisfaction into quality function deployment." *Technovation,* January 1998.

MIGHT, R., and W. A. FISCHER. "The Role of Structural Factors in Determining Project Management Success." *IEEE Transactions on Engineering Management,* May, 1985.

NORTHCRAFT, G. B., and M. A. NEALE. "Opportunity Costs and the Framing of Resource Allocation Decisions." *Organizational Behavior and Human Decision Processes,* 1986, pp. 348–356.

NORTHCRAFT, G. B., and G. WOLF. "Dollars, Sense, and Sunk Costs: A Life Cycle Model of Resource Allocation Decisions." *Academy of Management Review,* Vol. 9, No. 2, 1984.

PINTO, J. K., and S. J. MANTEL, JR. "The Causes of Project Failure." *IEEE Transactions on Engineering Management,* November 1990.

PINTO, J. K., and D. P. SLEVIN. "Critical Factors in Successful Project Implementation." *IEEE Transactions on Engineering Management,* February 1987.

PINTO, J. K., and D. P. SlEVIN. "Project Success: Definitions and Measurement Techniques." *Project Management Journal,* February 1988.

"Project Management Tasks: Wrap Up." *Design News,* April 19, 1982.

RAELIN, J. A., and R. BALACHANDRA. "R&D Project Termination in High-Tech Industries." *IEEE Transactions on Engineering Management,* February 1985.

RAMAMURTHY, K. "The Influence of Planning on Implementation Success of Advanced Manufacturing Technologies." *IEEE Transactions on Engineering Management,* February 1995.

RIGGS, J. L., M. GOODMAN, R. FINLEY, and T. MILLER. "A Decision Support System for Predicting Project Success." *Project Management Journal,* September 1992.

SHAFER, S. M., and S. J. MANTEL, JR. "A Decision Support System for the Project Termination Decision." *Project Management Journal,* June 1989.

SHENHAR, A. J., O. LEVY, and D. DVIR. "Mapping the Dimensions of Project Success." *Project Management Journal,* June 1997.

STAW, B. M., and J. ROSS. "Knowing When to Pull the Plug." *Harvard Business Review*, March–April, 1987.

TADISINA, S. K. "Support System for the Termination Decision in R&D Management." *Project Management Journal,* November 1986.

WHITTEN, N. "Are You Learning From Project to Project?" *PM Network*, March 1999.

WOLFF, M. F. "Knowing When the Horse Is Dead." *Research Management*, November 1981.

Epilogue

We wrote this epilogue eight years ago. It briefly notes our thoughts on the state of the field as well as on three problems that need some solution for the field to continue to prosper and grow. While we detect some optimistic signs, we see no reason to change our minds about the need to solve these three problems. On a happier note, we view the state of the profession with optimism. The number of books and articles about the theory and practice of project management and its many aspects has grown rapidly, giving all of us access to new insights and ideas.

The practice of project management continues its rapid expansion. It is now unusual to find medium-sized or large firms that do not conduct real projects more or less professionally managed. Some large firms work on projects that number in the thousands. The field of project management is a maturing body of knowledge. While it is not yet "full grown," in our opinion it is, at worst, in late adolescence or early adulthood.

On a positive note, the emergence of the project-oriented organization is clear evidence of the value and power of project management as a way to get things done. It is common for one project manager to manage several projects at the same time, not because there is a severe shortage of project managers but because the tools of the trade are good enough to produce multiproject managerial competence. Perhaps the field's greatest impact has been the speed with which it can implement organizational change. Project management—together with concurrent engineering—have shortened the path from an innovative idea through product development to product distribution and sale to a degree not dreamed of a decade ago. It is not too strong to argue that these two related disciplines, PM and CE, are among the primary forces behind a major change in the way the global economy operates. This is a true paradigm shift, a phrase all too often misapplied, in the conduct of global competition.

In the epilogue to the fourth edition of this book, we took the fact that Microsoft Project® software failed to calculate earned value in the Project Management Institute's recommended way as evidence of the profession's lack of ability to adopt and promulgate industry standards. If this was true—and we suspect it may not have been—Microsoft and the profession have both matured. Microsoft Project 2002® now does earned value right. We also suspect that this says something good about both Microsoft and the project management profession.

On balance, the future of project management is bright. The field is thriving and has developed far beyond classification as "another management fad." Growth is still accelerating, yet problems still remain. Can we, as a group of practitioners, develop a set of standards that guide and stabilize, but do not rigidify? Can we forge an identity that is professional—but not pompous? and not apologetic?

Finally, five years ago we identified three major, unsolved problems that we feel must be solved, or dissolved, if project management is going to move to a significantly higher level of sophistication. One problem concerns the ability of project managers to learn from the experiences of others. The second problem has to do with our ability to manage conflict. The third is raised when we consider project management as a career.

ON THE NEED FOR A UNIVERSAL INFORMATION SYSTEM

Almost 30 years ago, Greiner* published a classic article on the fundamental problems that arise as organizations grow, and on the stages of organizational development through which they pass during growth. The fifth and most highly developed stage, he called "growth through collaboration." It is characterized by a managerial focus on problem solving and innovation. The organizational structure is a "matrix of teams," and its managerial style is participative. It is controlled by "mutual goal setting," and the reward system is the "team bonus." We can identify a great many firms that represent, for the most part, the fifth stage of growth: Procter & Gamble, General Electric, Cisco, Bank One, Microsoft, AOL Time Warner, 3M, Merck, Merrill Lynch, and Chrysler, among a great many others.

According to Greiner, every stage of growth is followed by a specific type of "crisis" that moves the organization into its next stage of evolution. He was unable to identify the type of crisis that follows growth through collaboration, but we think it is a Crisis of Communication.

In Chapter 11, we discussed the need for postproject control, and in a later chapter the need for a project history. Both were required so that project managers could learn from the successes and failures of their peers, as well as from their own experiences. At this writing, no one has developed an information system that would allow storage and retrieval of the requisite data. Such a system would have to be loaded with all that we learn through experience on our projects. Retrieval is the problem. Information would be stored in the language of the project that generated it, but it

---

*L. E. Greiner. "Evolution and Revolution as Organizations Grow." *Harvard Business Review*, July–August 1972.

would have to be retrieved in the language of the searcher. While "keywords" enable cross-disciplinary communication between a limited few areas of knowledge, we have not yet solved the general problem of n-language information storage and retrieval. To sound a mildly optimistic note, however, we see an increasing emphasis on Postproject Reports in the project management literature.

ON THE NEED FOR CONFLICT RESOLUTION
IN MATRIX MANAGEMENT

There is little doubt that the use of project organization will continue to grow rapidly in the foreseeable future. There is also little doubt that the lion's share of such projects will be transdisciplinary and will be organized internally as matrices. The unfocused nature of functional project organization and the expense of pure project organization make it obvious that when both effectiveness and efficiency are required, the matrix organization will be utilized. Multidisciplinary projects operating in a matrix setting, however, are typified by significantly high levels of conflict.

Matrix managers describe themselves as having large responsibilities and no authority. In essence, this complaint has its source in the unwillingness of functional managers to make acceptable (to the project manager) commitments, or to meet their commitments (once made) in a timely manner. One such incident can cause a matrix project to fail. This is the primary source of conflict in matrix projects. It represents a power struggle between the project manager and the rest of the organization. It is inherent in any system that segments the tasks of managers, giving some task responsibilities to one manager and other task responsibilities to others. In a matrix system, the project manager has control over what is done and when, while functional managers control how things are done and who will do them. Once this division of power is made, conflict must result.

The inevitability of conflict as well as the need for resolving it is clearly recognized in the project manager's demands for "support from top management," and for a "clear mission statement, with clear priorities." Almost never are these demands met at a level that would neatly resolve all conflict. Kalu* has suggested a framework for managing projects in complex organizations that would develop a distribution of work and responsibility in such a way that conflict would be reduced or avoided. Unfortunately, the data and analytic requirements of Kalu's model are such that only a few very large organizations could experiment with his method.

The level of conflict existing on large numbers of matrix projects is not, in our judgment, insupportable. It is, however, so great that it preoccupies a great many project managers, and diverts their minds and their energies from the work of the project. We need a quantum jump in our knowledge of conflict resolution.

---

*T. C. U. Kalu. "A Framework for the Management of Projects in Complex Organizations." *IEEE Transactions on Engineering Management,* May 1993.

ON THE NEED FOR NEW METHODS
OF REWARDING EXCELLENCE

In all the history of this and other developed nations, we have never learned how to reward the people who work in our enterprises without promoting them. If an individual excels at a task, we promptly reward that person by taking away that work. This practice gave birth to such interesting axioms as the Peter Principle. The more productive an individual is, the more likely it is that we will reduce the organization's productivity by moving that individual to another job. We continue in this way until the individual ceases to be productive. Our society needs to develop a reward system that does not require such a sacrifice.

This is a serious problem for all industry, but it has a special application to project management. In Chapter 1, we wrote of the professionalization of project management. We now call into question the degree to which professionalization can progress unless a new method of rewarding excellence is found. Project management is, at best, a middle-management function. It is not, in general, seen as the culmination of a career, but rather as a challenging and interesting stepping stone to senior management. Project-oriented organizations are, however, growing in importance to our economy, and the role of the project manager is becoming evermore significant. The job is extraordinarily complex and is demanding beyond belief. Excellent project managers are rare and their worth exceeds that of rubies. To retain such managerial paragons in positions of managerial value, we must find a way to reward them without removing them from the very work that is so valuable.

Photo Credits

Chapter 1: *Page 18:* AP/Wide World Photos. **Chapter 2:** *Page 89:* Corbis Sygma. **Chapter 3:** *Pages 138, 155, & 156:* AP/Wide World Photos. **Chapter 4:** *Page 222:* Courtesy Sasol Limited, photo by William Majafe. **Chapter 5:** *Page 248:* Courtesy of Kodak. *Page 260:* Owen Franken/Corbis Images. **Chapter 7:** *Page 335:* Courtesy NASA. **Chapter 8:** *Pages 381 & 382:* AP/Wide World Photos. *Page 421:* Corbis Digital Stock. **Chapter 9:** *Page 444:* SABA. **Chapter 10:** *Page 507:* Steve Powell/Getty Images News and Sport Services. **Chapter 11:** *Page 582:* Courtesy Australian Consulate. **Chapter 13:** *Page 654:* John Bird Photography.

Name Index

Subject Index

■ *Red entry numbers (W . . .) indicate those names that are located in the appendix section, which can be found on this book's Web site at http://www.wiley.com/college/project@MGT.y*